TimeOut
Budapest

Penguin Books

PENGUIN BOOKS

Published by the Penguin Group
Penguin Books Ltd, 27 Wrights Lane, London W8 5TZ, England
Penguin Putnam Inc., 375 Hudson Street, New York, New York 10014, USA
Penguin Books Australia Ltd, Ringwood, Victoria, Australia
Penguin Books Canada Ltd, 10 Alcorn Avenue, Toronto, Ontario, Canada M4V 3B2
Penguin Books (NZ) Ltd, 182-190 Wairau Road, Auckland, New Zealand

Penguin Books Ltd, Registered offices: Harmondsworth, Middlesex, England

First published 1996
Second edition 1998
Third edition 1999
10 9 8 7 6 5 4 3 2 1

Copyright © Time Out Group Ltd, 1995, 1998, 1999
All rights reserved

Colour reprographics by Precise Litho, 34–35 Great Sutton Street, London EC1
Printed and bound by William Clowes Ltd, Beccles, Suffolk NR34 9QE

Edited and designed by
Time Out Guides Limited
Universal House
251 Tottenham Court Road
London W1P 0AB
Tel + 44 (0)171 813 3000
Fax + 44 (0)171 813 6001
Email guides@timeout.com
www.timeout.com

Editorial
Editorial Director Peter Fiennes
Editor Dave Rimmer
Deputy Editor Lily Dunn
Contributing Editor Peterjon Cresswell
Proofreader Rhonda Carrier
Indexer Kathy Grocott-Ward

Design
Art Director John Oakey
Art Editor Mandy Martin
Senior Designer Scott Moore
Designers Benjamin de Lotz, Lucy Grant,
Paul Mansfield, Thomas Ludewig
Picture Editor Kerri Miles
Picture Researchers Olivia Duncan-Jones, Kit Burnet
Scanning & Imaging Chris Quinn

Advertising
Group Advertisement Director Lesley Gill
Sales Director Mark Phillips
International Sales Manager Mary L Rega
Advertisement Sales (Budapest) Ujházy Média
Advertising Assistant Ingrid Sigerson

Administration
Publisher Tony Elliott
Managing Director Mike Hardwick
Financial Director Kevin Ellis
Marketing Director Gillian Auld
General Manager Nichola Coulthard
Production Manager Mark Lamond
Accountant Bridget Carter

Features in this guide were written and researched by:
Introduction Dave Rimmer. **History** Bob Cohen. **Budapest Today** Bob Cohen. **Language** Bob Cohen **Folk & Folklore** Bob Cohen. **Architecture** Carolyn Smith. **Budapest by Season** Peterjon Cresswell. **Sightseeing** Peterjon Cresswell, Bob Cohen, Reuben Fowkes, Dave Rimmer, Carolyn Smith. **Museums** Ildikó Lázár. **Art Galleries** Gabriella Bartha, Carolyn Smith. **Accommodation** Esther Holbrook. **Cafés & Coffeehouses** Peterjon Cresswell, Dave Rimmer. **Pubs & Bars** Peterjon Cresswell, Dave Rimmer. **Restaurants** Martin Iain, Bob Cohen, Dave Rimmer. **Shopping & Services** Christina Crowder, Dave Rimmer. **Baths** Adam Lebor, Dave Rimmer. **Children** Ildikó Lázár. **Film** Os Davis. **Gay & Lesbian** Jean-Jacques Soukoup. **Media** Bob Cohen. **Music: Classical & Opera** Nicholas Jenkins. **Music: Rock, Roots & Jazz** Michael J. Kovrig. **Nightlife** Reuben Fowkes. **Sport & Fitness** Peterjon Cresswell. **Theatre & Dance** Kim Willcox. **Danube Bend** Peterjon Cresswell, Tom Popper. **Balaton** Dave Rimmer. **Overnighters** Peterjon Cresswell, Dave Rimmer, Tom Popper. **Bratislava** Dave Rimmer, Tom Popper. **Vienna** Dave Rimmer. **Zagreb** Reuben Fowkes. **Further Abroad** Peterjon Cresswell, Dave Rimmer. **Directory** Christopher Condon, Reuben Fowkes, Ildikó Lázár, Dave Rimmer.

The Editor must express gratitude to the following:
Above and beyond: Chris Condon, Peterjon Cresswell, Hadley Kincade, Michael J. Kovrig, Ildikó Lázár, Tom Popper. *Technical assistance*: Steve Carlson, Malcolm Carruthers, Adam Lebor. *Casual labour*: Sharon Lougher. *Crisis management*: Eszther Budai, Adrienne Haspel, László Horváth, Krisztina Schuller. *Extra-curricular*: Camille Defourny, Kevin Ebbutt, Oran MacCuirc, Martin Rimmer, Hans van Vliet. *Love and pálinka*: the Sixtus family. *Paradise and lunch*: the Ottoman Society.

Maps by Mapworld, 71, Blandy road, Henley-on Thames, Oxon RG9 1QB.

Photography by Hadley Kincade except: p26 EPA/PA; pages 241, 246, 248, 252 Panos Pictures.
Black and white printing by Adam Eastland.

Contents

About the Guide

This is the third edition of the *Time Out Budapest Guide*, one of our ever-expanding series on the world's most crucial cities. We've dusted it down, smartened it up, and taken it out for a good, hot meal. We've reassessed the city's attractions, searched out the new and the vital, and mapped the changing shape of this ancient but volatile city.

Though any visit to the Hungarian capital will be enhanced by a copy of this guide, this is more than a book for casual visitors and tourists. While detailing the main sights and major monuments, we also direct you to Budapest's coolest cafés, darkest dives, most crucial scenes, sharpest shopping opportunities and finest new places to lunch and dine – all rated and reviewed with an objective eye. We highlight not only the traditional must-sees, but also the obscure and the eccentric, the most curious backwaters of this most curious capital – places that tourists rarely see.

We've also worked to upgrade the guide's user-friendliness. Addresses, phone numbers, transport details, opening times, admission prices and credit card details have all been checked and re-checked. We've added map references to our listings, linked to the maps in the back of this book. We've also tried to note those places where some English is spoken.

Checked & correct

All information was checked and correct at the time of writing, but please bear in mind that in a city such as Budapest, still in transition to a free market economy, things are liable to sudden and unpredictable change. Clubs and bars wink in and out of existence with particular regularity.

Addresses

Budapest is divided into 23 districts, *kerületek*, indicated by a Roman numeral before the street name. Postcodes are written in four figures, the middle two indicating the district: 1051 is District V. The postman will recognise both forms but deliver a four digit-coded letter quicker. In listings we've used the Roman numeral form because it's easier for finding your way around town.

Although we've spelled out the words for road (*út*) and street (*utca*), on street signs and in other publications you may see utca abbreviated to *u.*. As some streets in different districts may have the same name, it's always best to pay attention to which one you're heading for on the map. Other terms and abbreviations include: *híd* bridge; *rakpart* embankment; *tér* square; *körút* ring road; *piac* market; *pályaudvar* (abbreviated as *pu.*) station.

Prices

Listed prices should be treated as guideline rather than gospel. Inflation and fluctuating exchange rates mean prices change rapidly, particularly in shops or restaurants. Most are quoted in forints, but some services which cater to foreigners – particularly hotels – give rates in Deutschmarks, and occasionally US dollars or Austrian Schillings. If you find prices and services differing wildly from our assessments, ask if there's a reason. If there's not, take your custom elsewhere and then please let us know. We endeavour to give the best and most up-to-date advice, so we always want to hear if someone has been ripped off or given the runaround.

Credit cards

Credit cards are still not widely used in Budapest, although this is slowly changing. The following abbreviations have been used: **AmEx**: American Express; **DC**: Diners' Club; **JCB**: Japanese credit cards; **MC**: Mastercard/Access; **V**: Visa.

To boldly go

In chapters without listings, such as History or Architecture, places **highlighted in bold** are also listed elsewhere in the guide and can be found in the index.

Right to reply

It should be stressed that the information we offer is impartial. No institution or enterprise has been included because it has advertised in any of our publications. Rigorous impartiality and cosmopolitan critical assessment are the reasons our guides are so successful. But if you disagree with our opinions, please let us know; your comments are always welcome. You'll find a reader's reply card at the back of this book.

> There is an online version of this guide, as well as weekly events listings for several international cities, at http://www.timeout.com

Introduction

Most weekdays when I'm in Budapest, I slip over the Danube to go swimming in Buda. Whatever my mood, whatever the weather, I always look up as the tram rattles over Szabadság Bridge. The riverscape spreads out beyond the window – the cliffs of Gellért Hill looming gauntly, the Castle District caught in a shaft of sunlight, wooded hills a distant backdrop as bridges span the swift, strong waters. And something inside me sighs.

Saturday mornings, I take the waters at the Rudas. It's a decade since my first visit to these magnificent Ottoman baths, but lolling in the central pool, looking up at the domed roof and watching shafts of sunlight stab through the steam and gloom, its beauty always strikes me afresh.

There's something about the Hungarian capital that gets its claws into you, something that runs even deeper than a magnificent cityscape which constantly surprises, every twist and turn revealing some architectural curiosity or sudden view. For the first-time visitor it can be an intriguingly bewildering place. The language is indecipherable. The locals put their first name last, their last name first and say 'helló' when they mean good-bye. Dig a little deeper and Hungarians seem to inhabit a dream of historical grandeur, reflected in the imperial proportions of this essentially nineteenth-century city. Despite all the new malls and multiplexes, brand-name burgers and mobile phones, Budapest has an inner life quite different from anywhere else in Europe.

Divided by the Danube into hilly Buda and flat Pest, the city is likewise tugged culturally in different directions. Is it a passionate southern city or a hard-working northern one? Still part of eastern Europe or attached to the west? The last outpost of

Germanic Europe or the beginning of the Balkans? The answer in every case is both and neither. It's Budapest, caught in the middle, alone and unique.

Then factor in a sharp social divide. On one side are the young and ambitious, making the most of new freedoms and opportunities. On the other side are the old and those otherwise unable to adapt, still subsisting courtesy of the old state institutions and drowning their economic sorrows in pálinka and cheap wine.

As a visitor, you'll find yourself among the better off. Even on a relatively modest holiday budget you can afford to do pretty much whatever you want – check out an opera or a football match, ride around everywhere in cabs, dine in the best restaurants, party all night and still have change for more. Budapest is the last cheap, civilised city in Europe. (Unless you count Prague, of course, but those of us who love the Hungarian capital know that it is superior to the Czech Disneyland in almost every respect.)

I first visited Budapest on 1 May 1989 – the very cusp of the 'change of systems' – and was captivated by its idiosyncrasies. Over a decade of further visits, I've watched it change, acquiring a glitzy new surface that only partially obscures the doggedly eccentric city underneath. Right now it offers the best of both worlds – reasonable efficiency with charmingly ragged edges, an affordable level of creature comfort coupled with enough curiosities to keep anyone entertained for a while. Millennial Budapest might be slowly getting hammered into the postmodern shapelessness of most western cities, but it's never going to take the process lying down. *Dave Rimmer*

In Context

Key Events

Early History
c1000 BC Celtic and Illyrian tribes inhabit the Danube Basin.
c500 BC Proto-Hungarians begin southwest migration from Siberia.
35 BC Romans come, see and conquer Danube Basin, now known as Pannonia.
6 AD Pannonians rebel against Romans.
430-452 Huns make Hungary base for European excursion.

The Hungarians Enter Europe
700-850 Hungarians serve as vassals of the Khazar Empire in southern Russia.
895 King Árpád leads Hungarians across Carpathians into the Danube Basin.
955 King Otto of Bavaria defeats Hungarians at Augsburg, ending period of Hungarian raids.
972 King Géza and son Vajk convert to Christianity.
1000 Vajk enthroned as King István (Stephen) with a crown donated by Pope in Rome.
1006 Revolt of pagan Hungarian leaders.
1066 First written example of Hungarian.
1222 'Golden Bull' signed by nobles at Rákos meadow, defining the Hungarian nation.
1241 Mongol Invasion.
1243 King Béla IV decrees the building of fortified towns. Buda gains in importance.
1301 House of Árpád ends with King Otto.
1396 Hungarians defeated by Ottoman Turks at Nicopolis.
1456 János Hunyadi defeats Turks at Belgrade.
1458 Hunyadi's son Mátyás crowned King of Hungary. Buda's first 'golden age'.
1490 King Mátyás dies, leading to chaos between nobles and peasants.
1514 Peasants revolt, unsuccessfully. Tripartum law enacted, reducing peasantry to serfdom.

The Turkish Era
1526 Turks led by Suliman the Magnificent defeat Hungarians at battle of Mohács, then burn Buda.
1541 Buda occupied by Turks.
1683 Turks defeated at Siege of Vienna
1686 Habsburgs defeat Turks at Siege of Buda. Buda burned. Again.
1699 Turks relinquish claims to Hungary.

The Habsburg Era
1703 Hungarians led by Ferenc Rákóczi rebel unsuccessfully against Austrians.
1723 Habsburgs claim right to rule under the Hungarian crown.
1808 The Embellishment Act sets guidelines for the urban development of Buda and Pest.
1839-49 Construction of the Chain Bridge.

1848 Hungarians rebel unsuccessfully against the Austrians. Again.
1867 *Ausgleich* signed, uniting Austria and Hungary as imperial equals.
1873 Pest, Buda and Óbuda united as Budapest.
1896 Budapest hosts Millennial Exhibition.
1914 Austria-Hungary enters World War I.
1918 Austria-Hungary loses World War I. Hungary declares independence from Austria.
1919 Shortlived Soviet under Béla Kun. Romanian army occupies Budapest. Return of Admiral Horthy.
1920 Treaty of Trianon signed. Hungary loses two thirds of its territory to neighbouring states.
1938 Hungary, allied with Nazi Germany, receives a part of Slovakia under the Second Vienna Awards.
1940 Hungary awarded most of Transylvania. Hungarian troops assist Nazi invasion of Yugoslavia.
1943 Hungarian Army defeated by Russians.
1944 Horthy kidnapped by Nazis, Arrow Cross Party begins murders and mass deportations of Jews to concentration camps.
1945 Red Army captures Budapest.

Communist Hungary
1946 Hungarian monarchy abolished and a Hungarian People's Republic declared.
1948 Land ownership collectivised.
1949 Mátyás Rákosi, Communist chief, executes traditional Hungarian Communist Party leaders.
1953 Stalin dies. Rákosi replaced by Imre Nagy, then by Ernő Gerő. Hungary beat England 6-3.
1956 Hungarians revolt against Russian occupation. Hungarian Socialist State proclaimed by Imre Nagy, but Russian tanks soon move in. Budapest in ruins. János Kádár placed in power by Russians.

The Kádár Era
1963 Kádár declares a partial amnesty for those jailed for their role in the 1956 revolt.
1968 Hungary aids Russia in crushing the Prague Spring. Kádár institutes his 'New Economic Mechanism' allowing restricted private enterprise.
1978 Crown of St Stephen returned to Hungary.

The Change of Systems
1989 Kádár dies. Mass protest. Reform Communists promise free elections. East Germans flee via Hungary. Communist Party defunct.
1990 Hungarian elections elect conservative government headed by Hungarian Democratic Forum (MDF). Hungary declared a Republic.
1994 Socialist Party trounces MDF in second democratic election. Gyula Horn named prime minister.
1998 Elections replace Socialists with a FIDESZ-led coalition. Vicktor Orbán is new prime minister.
1999 Hungary joins Nato.

History

Nobody knows quite where they came from, but the Hungarians have had an eventful time of it over the last thousand years.

Early History

Budapest's strategic and majestic geographical location has long made it the key to the major events and trends in the history of the Danube basin. Perched on limestone hills which rise abruptly above the Danube, some 20 kilometres below the dramatic bend which sends the river flowing southward to the Black Sea, Buda's location offers a virtually impregnable defensive position and potential control of Central Europe's main waterway to all those who occupy it.

The earliest history of the region, like that of so much of Europe at the time, was a decidedly low-brow affair. Archaeologists have turned up evidence of human habitation as early as 500,000 BC. Agricultural communities sprang up around the River Tisza, where large neolithic sites have been discovered. During the first millennium BC, Illyrian populations shared the plains with groups of Celtic peoples, known as the Eravi. The recent excavation of a large Celtic site on Gellért Hill is the first Eravi settlement found in Budapest itself.

It isn't until the expansion of the Roman Empire under Julius Caesar that the Danube basin enters written history. The region was conquered without resistance in 35 BC, officially incorporated into the Roman Empire in 14 BC under the name Pannonia, then promptly revolted against Rome in 6 AD. This encouraged the Romans to build up their defences through military settlements. Several Hungarian towns begin their modern existence at this point, including Pécs, Szombathely and Buda.

Known to the Romans as Aquincum for the copious mineral waters that flow from the limestone rocks of the Buda hills, Roman Buda was a modest trading town on the very edge of the Roman Empire. Today, one can visit the ruins of classical Aquincum in the Óbuda district (*see chapters* **Sightseeing** *and* **Museums**), which boasts the remains of an ancient amphitheatre. More Roman ruins (the aptly named 'Minor Aquincum') can be seen along the Danube in Pest, at Március 15 tér just north of Erzsébet Bridge.

Shields up – Roman memorial at Március 15 tér.

THE ASIANS ARE COMING!

As the Roman Empire withered, political and cyclical climatic changes in Central Asia forced the first of a series of migrations of various Altaic peoples westward in what becomes known, depending on to whom you are speaking, as either the 'Age of Barbarians' or the 'Age of Migrations'. The Romans, no longer able to maintain their over-extended Empire against repeated waves of Goths, Gepids, Alans and Vandals, began to withdraw from Pannonia.

In 430, the Huns, a central Asian confederacy of Turkic-speaking nomads, burst into Europe. Under the leadership of Attila they defeated the armies of Romans and vassals alike until finally, in 453, the Pope came in person to beg mercy. Attila returned to Pannonia without sacking Rome, but died mysteriously on the very night of his wedding to the princess Ildikó.

With the death of their leader, the Huns returned to their central Asian homelands. Next out of Asia were the Avars in the seventh century. They, in turn, came under pressure from the Bulgar Empire, another Turkic-speaking confederacy from the Volga steppes. Meanwhile, Transdanubia in the west was being populated by more sedentary, agricultural Slavs, most closely related to today's Slovenians. Many place names bear witness to early Slav settlement, such as Pécs, Debrecen, Balaton and Visegrád.

The Hungarians enter Europe

The origins of the Hungarian people is a topic debated to this day, most loudly by Hungarians themselves (*see page 7* **Where on earth are they from?**). The Magyars are a branch of the Finno-Ugric language grouping, a subgroup of the Altaic language family which includes the Finns, Turks, Mongolians and a host of Siberian peoples. (*See also chapter* **Language**.) The earliest Hungarian homeland was in the dense forests between the Volga river and the Ural mountains. Hungarian's closest linguistic relatives today are Vogul (Mansi) and Ostyak (Hanti) spoken by 35,000 fur trappers and fishermen on the left bank of the Ob river in the northern Ural region of Siberia. You can still buy 'three fish' using Hungarian if you ever find yourself on the Ob in need of lunch.

These proto-Hungarians broke off from their northern relatives around 500 BC and moved south into the central Volga region. In the first centuries AD, the Hungarians came into contact with Turkic cultures pushing west; one group became known as the Huns. It is possible that some Magyars rode with Attila, but historically speaking, the Magyars first became known in the seventh and eighth centuries as vassals of the Turkic-speaking Khazar Empire between the Black and Caspian seas. The

Széchenyi – 'the greatest Hungarian'.

Khazars engaged nomadic tribes, such as the early Hungarians, to act as border guards.

In the ninth century, the Hungarians left their base in 'Levedia' (today's Ukraine) and settled in the land of 'Etelköz', meaning 'between the rivers', in today's Moldavia. From here they raided deep into Frankish Europe. St Cyril described the horde of Magyars he met in 860 as *luporum more ululantes*, 'howling in the manner of wolves'. Faced with a howling gang from Asia pillaging the Holy Roman Empire, western Christendom reacted by amending the Catholic mass with the words 'Lord save us from sin and the Hungarians'.

While the main Magyar armies spent the spring of 895 raiding Europe, their villages in Etelköz were devastated by Bulgars and Petchenegs. The surviving tribes of Magyars, led by their king, Árpád, fled across the Verecke pass in the northern Carpathians and on to the Hungarian plain in 895. Meeting little resistance from the local Slavs, Goths and Avars, the Hungarians pushed their competitors, the Bulgars, south of the Danube, and began raiding as far west as France, Germany and northern Spain. The Hungarians were defeated by King Otto I at the Battle of Augsburg in 955. Retiring to Pannonia, the Hungarians realised that alliance with a major power might be a good idea. This meant dealing with the Christian Church.

Hungary was sandwiched between the Holy Roman and Byzantine empires and King Géza, Árpád's grandson, requested missionaries be sent from Rome to convert the Magyars to the western Church, a fact still trumpeted by Hungarians as a decision to be 'linked with the west'. King Géza was baptised along with his son, Vajk, who took the name István (Stephen) upon his accession to the Hungarian throne on Christmas Day 1000.

King István didn't have an easy time convincing his countrymen. Tribes loyal to the older, shamanic religion led a revolt against István in 1006. One consequence was the death of Venetian missionary Saint Gellért (Gerard), who was put into a spiked barrel and rolled down Gellért Hill into the Danube by miffed Magyar traditionalists. King István crushed the revolt and set about destroying the power of the chieftains by appropriating their land and setting up a new class of nobles. He also began minting coins, forging alliances, building castles and all the other things that early medieval rulers did on the road to feudalism.

Medieval Hungary

With St Stephen's conversion to Christianity, Hungary had made a religious and political commitment to the Holy Roman Empire. But the country was still in a state of cultural flux between east and west, as symbolised by the mixed Byzantine/Roman manufacture of St Stephen's crown (*see page 20* **Tales of a crown**). Budapest itself was, at this time, of little importance. The main centres of power were the King's palace in Székesfehérvár, the Queen's residence in Veszprém and the seat of ecclesiastical power in Esztergom.

Stephen's son, Imre, died young, and the next 200 years saw a succession of weak kings and struggles for the throne of the House of Árpád. Turning mounted central Asian nomads into medieval European serfs did not prove an easy task and revolts among the tribal Magyar nobility were common until the late twelfth century.

The tensions between the landowning nobility and the office of the King were eventually settled by the signing of the 'Golden Bull' under King András in 1222. This document granted the landed nobility exemption from taxation (among other privileges), it recognised the 'Nation' as such and it laid the framework for an annual assembly of nobles, the Diet. This was to be held in Rákos meadow in Pest; the annual gathering of the nation's high

Where on earth are they from?

Ever since the Hungarians arrived in Europe, conjecture as to their origins has been rife. The Byzantines mislabelled them 'Turks' or 'Ungeri' after the 'Ten Arrows' confederation of Central Asian tribes. Medieval Hungarian chroniclers recorded that the Hungarians came from 'Magna Hungaria' somewhere in the east, and ever since King Béla IV sent the monk Julianus to the Volga to search for those lost Magyars, Hungarians have been diligently researching their origins.

For a long time, Hungarians were fascinated by the myth of Hun origins. Poet János Arany's epic poem about the Huns, written in the nineteenth century, influenced several generations of Hungarians into believing a literary device to be the explanation of their national origins. (Attila is still a common first name here).

In the 1840s, explorer Sándor Körösi Csoma travelled to Tibet and China in search of lost Hungarians. He didn't find any, but he did remain convinced that the Uighur Turks were the ancient progenitors of modern Hungarians. This idea found eager adherents during the pre-

World War II epoch among right-wing 'Turanian' parties, who envisioned a Turko-Uralic master race including both the Hungarians and the Japanese. Strangely enough, the idea has recently been revived, and Hungarian archaeologists are again digging around in Uighur cemeteries.

Political prejudice has led some Hungarians to the idea that descent from the Uralic Voguls and Ostyaks, who live in what used to be the Soviet Union, was a commie plot to tie the Magyars to Mother Russia. A favourite alternative theory is that Hungarians are descendants of the Sumerians, and thus, by extension, are the founders of modern civilisation. This is supported by the fact that half a dozen Sumerian vocabulary items sound vaguely Hungarian.

Given the way the political wind blows, there is always room for another theory. Assorted Hungarian 'linguists' have published studies 'proving' that the Hungarians are related to the Incas, the Australian Aboriginals, the California Miwok Indians and the Tibetans.

and mighty provided a push that helped Pest grow into a central market town.

All was going well, in a medieval kind of way, when the next big gang from central Asia gate-crashed central Europe. The Mongol invasion of 1241 devastated Hungary as towns were sacked, crops were burned, and entire regions depopulated. The Mongols retreated a year later after the death of Genghis Khan, but the experience was sobering for King Béla IV, who ordered a series of defensive castles to be built. Buda became the site of one such castle, and once built, it soon came to dominate the Hungarian realm.

In order to repopulate the devasted countryside, Béla IV invited foreign craftsmen, traders, clergy and peasants from the west, especially Germans, Czechs and Italians. Central Asian Cumans and Jász who had fled the Mongol onslaught were granted land east of Pest as border guards.

Béla's son, King András III, died without leaving an heir, thus ending the House of Árpád. Robert Charles of Anjou was crowned King of Hungary in 1310. Under his son, Louis the Great, Hungary's frontiers were extended by alliance to include Dalmatia, the Banat of Serbia and part of Poland.

In 1396, Hungary's King Sigismund led an ill-fated attack on the Turks at Nicopolis, ending in a defeat that marked the beginning of the Turkish advance into Europe. Things went from bad to worse until a Transylvanian prince, János Hunyadi, stemmed the Turkish advance in Serbia and finally regained control of Belgrade in 1456. Church bells rang all over Europe. Hunyadi's death soon after led to the usual bloody struggle for the throne, and in 1458 one of Hunyadi's sons, Mátyás Corvinus, found himself king by default at the age of 16.

With Mátyás, Buda became the true focus of Hungarian life, a position it has never surrendered since. Revered as Hungary's 'Renaissance King', Mátyás undertook extensive building within Buda Castle. Among his achievements was the Royal library, one of the world's largest, intended to attract wandering scholars to Buda.

Mátyás also created one of the first standing armies in European history. Comprising professional soldiers, foreign and domestic, the 'Black Army' was able to keep both Turks and rebellious nobles at bay. Meanwhile, his second wife, Queen Beatrice, introduced courtly customs and fashions from her native Italy to the relatively backwoods court of Hungary.

Hungarian historians refer to these years as the 'Hungarian Renaissance' a term which should be taken with a few grains of salt. Still, as medieval courts go, Mátyás' showed a distinctly humanistic streak. Mátyás spent a lot of his time galloping around the countryside, disguised as a lowly peasant and seeking out injustices in the feudal system, which, given the nature of medieval soci-ety, must have been quite an easy job. Even to this day, his name still symbolises justice and good governance. 'Mátyás is dead' goes the oft-spoken Hungarian saying, 'and justice died with him.'

Certainly, when Mátyás died heirless in 1490, the legacy of culture and order he had built more or less collapsed. It soon became business as usual for the unruly nobility, who chose a Bohemian, Ulászló, as king. Under Ulászló the nobles began appropriating common land and taxes, they sold off the Buda library and dismissed the standing army. In 1496 a pogrom against the Jews broke out in Buda, and the survivors then fled en masse to Bulgaria.

In 1514 the Pope ordered a new crusade against the Turks. Hungary's peasantry, under the leadership of György Dózsa, a Transylvanian Captain, rallied near Pest and turned against the nobles. As is usual with peasant revolts, the peasants were quickly and soundly defeated. Dózsa was executed in particularly artful fashion: he was enthroned as 'king of the peasants' on a red-hot iron dais.

With Dózsa's defeat the nobility voted in a new law which superseded the Golden Bull of 1222. The Tripartum law, which was effectively in force right up to 1848, reduced the peasantry to serfdom and forbade them to bear arms. The timing could not have been worse.

Turkish rule

When the young Hungarian King Lajos II, with 10,000 armoured knights, met the Turkish cavalry on the swampy plains of Mohács on 29 August 1526, 80,000 Ottoman spahis routed the Hungarians in under two hours. King Lajos, thrown from his horse, drowned in a muddy stream, trapped in heavy armour. After Mohács, the Turks turned north, sacking and burning Buda. They retreated briefly, but returned in 1541 to occupy the castle. Thus Buda became the seat of power in Ottoman Hungary, rebuilt as a Turkish provincial capital.

Hungary was divided in three. A rump Hungary ruled by the Habsburgs existed in the west and north. The Turks controlled the heartland with Transylvania nominally independent as a principality under Turkish control. While the countryside became a theatre of border warfare on the marches of Ottoman Europe, Buda developed into a provincial Ottoman town. The **Mátyás templom** (Matthias Church) was converted into a mosque, and the thermal springs inspired the construction of Turkish baths (*see chapter* **Baths**). An Ottoman chronicler recorded that Buda boasted four major mosques, 34 smaller mosques, three dervish monasteries, and ten schools.

Sephardic Jews, refugees from the Spanish Inquisition, settled along today's Táncsics Mihály utca. Muslim Gypsies, known as 'Copts' (that is Egyptians) settled around the Vienna Gate working as armourers. The bulk of Buda's Turkish residents lived below the Castle in today's Víziváros, behind Batthyány tér and around today's Bem tér. Bosnians and Serbs worked in the Ottoman gunpowder factories and conducted trade along the Danube. This neighbourhood, between the Castle and Gellért Hill became known as Tabán (from the Turkish tabahane, or armoury). The neighbourhood continued to be a centre for southern Slavs, and it was here that the modern Serbo-Croatian literary language was created during the nineteenth century (Tabán became a night-life centre for artists and peasants until the quarter was torn down on the orders of Admiral Horthy in the 1930s: he felt it spoiled his view from the palace.)

Pest was a city mostly populated by Magyars. Few Hungarians resided in Buda, since there were no churches there. The upheaval of the Protestant Reformation made itself felt throughout the Hungarian region during the Turkish occupation. The rulers didn't care about the theological squabbles of their Christian subjects. Still, anti-clericalism

and wariness of the Catholic Habsburgs among the petty nobles made an attractive recruiting ground for Protestant reform in Hungary, while the austere tenets of Calvinism found eager adherents in the Great Plain.

The Turkish defeat at the siege of Vienna in 1683 signalled the end of the Turkish threat to Christian Europe. In 1686 the Habsburgs turned the tables on the Ottomans, attacking their stronghold at **Buda Castle** and defeating the Turks after a six-week siege. The victors looted and pillaged Buda and Pest, so that Buda was again reduced to a pile of post-war rubble, while Pest was virtually depopulated. After a further decade of war the Turks lost the rest of their Hungarian realm and relinquished their claims at the Peace of Karlowitz in 1699.

Habsburg Budapest

At the beginning of the eighteenth century, both Buda and Pest were ruins. As an Austrian principality, Hungary was ruled by Vienna, but governed as a province from Pozsony (today's Bratislava). The Habsburgs suspended the constitution and placed the country under military occupation. Counter-Reformation measures were then undertaken to ensure nobles' loyalty to their Catholic Habsburg rulers, including the sale of 42 Protestant pastors as galley slaves in Naples. In the meantime, claims for land redistribution after 150 years of Turkish rule was proving fertile ground for corruption.

In 1703 the Hungarians rebelled, led by the Transylvanian magnate Ferenc Rákóczi. Once again Hungary was shattered by a War of Independence. This one lasted eight years and ended with the signing of the Treaty of Szatmár. Rákóczi died in Turkish exile. To prevent further rebellion by the feisty Hungarians, the Austrians blew up every castle in the country and ordered that the walls be dismantled from each fortified town or church. Today, the visitor to Hungary can view the ruins of many such castles, but if you want to see the intact versions you will have to go north to Slovakia.

Buda's strategic and economic value was not lost on the industrious Austrians. Rebuilding would take some time, but it is during this period that Buda and Pest began to acquire the central European character that makes this city at times seem even more *mitteleuropäisch* than its sister, Vienna.

The reign of the Empress Maria Theresa (1740-80) marks the beginnings of the real integration of Austria and Hungary. Hungary's nobility began to look more and more towards Vienna as the centre of power. While the upper crust built baroque palaces and commissioned ornate churches, the majority of the peasantry lived as impoverished serfs using medieval agricultural technology.

Rakoczi – rebel leader.

Plaques around town note the high-water mark of the 1838 flood.

One of the Austrians' ambitious programmes was to repopulate Hungary with immigrants from throughout the Habsburg realms. Lands left fallow by centuries of war and rebellion were laid open for settlement. In the west and south, German settlers from Swabia, known as Svábs, were given land, while Slovaks, fleeing overpopulation in the Carpathian highlands, settled on the great plains. Buda was reborn as the German town of Ofen, while Pest developed into a commercial centre for the grain and livestock produced on the Hungarian plains and shipped along the Danube.

Evidence of this immigration policy is still very much present to this day in the makeup of Budapest's suburban villages. In the Buda hills, villages such as Budakeszi and Zsámbék can boast bilingual Sváb communities. In the Pilis Hill villages to the north of Budapest you can find Svábs mixed with Slovaks, Gypsies, and Serbian communities, all refugees who fled here during Turkish times.

Meanwhile, Jews began moving back to the city from Bohemia and Galicia, settling in Pest, just beyond the the now dismantled city walls in what is today District VII. This neighbourhood became the centre of Hungarian Jewry, and is still the most complete Jewish quarter remaining in eastern Europe, known, since World War II, as the Ghetto. (See chapters Budapest By Area and Sightseeing.)

Apart from a few revolts (such as the Transylvanian Székely Rebellion in 1764), the eighteenth

was a relatively quiet century, in which Hungary was seen as an agricultural backwater feeding an ever more industrialised Austria. Maria Theresa's successor, Joseph II (1780-90) began a reform programme of taxing noble estates, granting rights to serfs and constructing hospitals and schools. Ever the pragmatist, Joseph retracted these reforms on his deathbed, allowing his more conservative-minded successor, Leopold II (1790-92) to reinstate the wonderful world of feudalism.

Repercussions of the French Revolution were felt all across Europe; Hungary was no exception. A conspiracy of Hungarian Jacobins was nipped in the bud, although their ideas gained an audience through the Hungarian-language writings of Ferenc Kazinczy. As the nineteenth century dawned, Hungarians eagerly embraced the Magyar tongue as a revolutionary and literary language. After centuries of war, immigration, and official neglect, the Hungarian language was now spoken only by peasants, and only in the Calvinist east of the country did any of the nobles continue to speak Magyar.

Loath to use German, the language of the occupying Austrians, many people continued to use the Latin language between themselves, using Hungarian, or any of the other local languages, only when speaking to peasants. Hungarian now began to revive as a literary language, uniting people as 'Hungarian' instead of 'Habsburg'.

Ferenc Deák – architect of the 1867 Ausgleich.

REFORM

The period of national revival in the early nineteenth century is known in Hungary as the Reform. Buda and Pest perked up under the Embellishment Act, an 1808 law which began to plan the city on more modern development ideas. After a particularly nasty year of Danube floods in 1838, first Vienna and then Pest were redesigned along a pattern of concentric ringed boulevards.

The personality who embodies the Hungarian national emergence in the early nineteenth century was Count István Széchenyi (1791-1860). A figure of amazing energy, Széchenyi – as a writer, entrepreneur, ardent capitalist and patron of the arts – set the trend among the nascent urban nobility by being an ardent Anglophile. Having visited England several times, he introduced such British inventions as flush toilets, steam shipping on the Danube and horse racing, as well as founding the Hungarian Academy of Sciences.

Among Széchenyi's English inspirations was the first bridge across the Danube. Hitherto traffic between Buda and Pest had been conducted by ferry or by a rather clumsy removeable pontoon bridge. Széchenyi imported the English designer William Tierney Clark and Scotsman Adam Clark as supervising engineer and the Széchenyi lánchíd (Chain Bridge) was constructed between 1839-49 (*see chapter* **Sightseeing**).

While Széchenyi championed the ideal of economic development within the Habsburg Empire, other members of the Hungarian Diet were less accommodating to the Austrians. Lajos Kossuth, one of the now landless gentry who were flocking to Pest, became an eloquent voice of nationalist and liberal sentiment against Austrian rule.

Pressure on Habsburg internal affairs elsewhere led to a lessening of repression in 1839, and a reform-orientated liberal Diet was convened, led by Ferenc Deák. Lajos Kossuth became the editor of the leading Hungarian newspaper, the Pesti Hírlap, and his editorials lambasted the Austrian administration. Kossuth stressed increased political independence from Vienna, and his uncompromising stand led to his becoming the bitter opponent of Count Széchenyi.

Against this background the Parisians rose and overthrew the French monarchy for the second time. Civil nationalist uprisings spread across Europe like wildfire, threatening the old monarchical order. On 3 March 1848, Kossuth delivered a parliamentary speech demanding an end to the feudal sysytem – tax privileges, serfdom, the whole lot. On 13 March, the revolutionary spirit reached the streets of Vienna.

THE REVOLT OF 1848

Two days later, on 15 March 1848, Kossuth met with the cream of Hungarian dissident liberals in the Pilvax coffeehouse in Pest to develop a revolutionary strategy. Among them was the poet Sándor Petőfi who, later that day, famously read his newly penned poem *Nemzeti dal* ('National Song') on the steps of the **National Museum** –

an event still commemorated annually. A proposal for a liberalised constitution with Hungary given far-reaching autonomy was dispatched to Vienna that day and consented to by the Hungarian Diet and the frightened Imperial government. On 7 April the Emperor sanctioned a Hungarian Ministry headed by Lajos Batthyány, and including Kossuth, Széchenyi and Deák. Hungarian was made the language of state; freedom of the press, assembly and religion were granted; noble privileges were curtailed; and peasants were emancipated from serfdom.

This might have satisfied less demanding nationalist sentiments, but Kossuth, as Finance Minister, wanted a financial and military structure separate from the Imperial Austrians. The new Hungarian Diet went against the Emperor and voted in funding for the creation of a 200,000-man army. Kossuth's intentions were noble, but his tactic was shortsighted. Hungary's minorities comprised over 50 per cent of the population, and they essentially lost all rights under the new constitution. Vienna, occupied with its own security problems, organised a Croatian invasion of Hungary to induce a compromise and soon the entire region was at war. The Hungarians could not expect much aid from the ethnic minorities within the scope of Kossuth's rather narrow nationalism.

During the early, heady days of the rebellion, Pest was the scene of fervent pro-independence sentiment. But Buda and Pest fell early to the Austrian Army and the Hungarian government moved to Debrecen while fighting continued. By the spring of 1849, the Hungarian troops had the upper hand.

A newly enthroned Habsburg Emperor, Franz Joseph, appealed to the Tsar of Russia for help in defending the endangered European institution of absolute, incompetent and unresponsive monarchy. The Tsar, of course, agreed. With the help of Russian troops the rebellion was quickly, and brutally, crushed, and Kossuth, like his predecessor Rákóczi, fled to Turkey.

Petőfi was killed on a battlefield in Transylvania and Count Széchenyi suffered a nervous breakdown and spent the rest of his days in a sanatorium. The Hungarian generals who surrendered to the Russians at Arad were shamefully executed, and the anniversary of that day is still a national day of mourning.

TURNING DEFEAT INTO GOLDEN AGE

With the crushing of the 1849 rebellion, Hungary fell into one of its periodic post-defeat depressions. Thousands went into exile. Hungarian prisoners were made to construct a huge Austrian military blockhouse, the **Citadella**, atop Gellért Hill. Its guns were intended as a deterrent to any future Hungarian attempts to dislodge Habsburg power.

The Austrians' military defeat in Italy in 1859, however, made accommodation with the Magyars a political necessity. In Pest, the remnants of the Liberal Party coalesced around Ferenc Deák, who published a basis for reconciliation with the Austrians in 1865.

The Ausgleich, or Compromise, of 1867 made Hungary more of an equal partner in the Habsburg Empire. Austria-Hungary was to be a single nation with two governments and two parliaments, although ruled by Habsburg Royalty who would recognise the legitimacy of the unclaimed crown of St István. New tariff agreements made Hungarian products more competitive than before, and the agreement allowed for the establishment of a Hungarian army. In 1868, Transylvania, in violation of previous agreements, was incorporated into Hungary proper, while Croatia was unhappily subordinated to the Hungarian Crown.

THE RISE OF PEST

The 50 years between the signing of the Compromise and World War I are rightly remembered as the Golden Years of Budapest. The city boomed with new industry and building, and the population exploded from 280,000 in 1867 to almost a million on the eve of war. In 1867 Buda and Pest together were the seventeenth largest city in Europe; by 1900 Budapest was the sixth.

Part of the prosperity was due to the better trade position won by Hungary in the 1867 agreement. With trade tariffs reduced, Hungarian products quickly flooded the rest of the Austrian Empire and came into demand abroad. The Danube provided the main route for grain sold north to Germany and for manufactured goods shipped south towards the Balkans. An extensive rail system was introduced with Pest as its hub. In 1870 Pest appointed a Council of Public Works, modelled on the London Metropolitan Board of Works, to supervise the reconstruction of the city.

Buda, Óbuda and Pest were officially united as a single city, Budapest, in 1873. There were monumental urban development projects, including the construction of boulevards such as Andrássy út and the Nagykörút (*see chapter* **Sightseeing**). Gentry and noble families competed to have palaces constructed in the garden suburbs that sprung up around the old city centre.

Hungarian culture was focused on the Pest side. Buda was primarily a German-speaking town of dour burghers and irrelevant nobility, but arts and politics were increasingly being conducted in Hungarian on the Pest side. The booming growth of the Hungarian language went hand in hand with the Magyarisation policies of Prime Minister Kálmán Tisza (1875-90). Tisza suspected that the Austrians could endanger Hungary's newly strengthened position by leverage among the non-

Vajdahunyad Castle in City Park – built for the 1896 Magyar Millennium.

Flawed treaties never die

The Hungarian obsession with the Trianon Treaty reminds even the most casual visitor that in this part of the world the wounds of history have still to heal.

When the Treaty Conference in Versailles dealt with Hungarian territorial claims after World War I, Hungary sent its best diplomats but was in a terrible bargaining position – on the losing side and surrounded by states that had gained military control of Hungarian regions inhabited by disgruntled minorities. The Serbs, Czechoslovaks and Romanians who, aligned with France, were known as the Little Entente, all pressed claims for regions previously part of Hungary.

The Treaty did contain some glaring injustices. Romania was granted not only Transylvania, but also the mostly Hungarian towns of Szatmár, Nagyvárad (Oradea), Arad and Temesvár (Timişoara) simply because the rail line that linked them seemed a strategic prize. Southern Slovakia ended up containing large regions with a dense Hungarian minority simply because the Danube formed a neat frontier.

Throughout the 1920s and 1930s it seemed that there was no other political goal besides the regaining of lands lost in the Treaty. The slogan 'Nem! Nem! Soha!' ('No! No! Never!') was chanted as speech after speech was made condemning the treaty. Ire about Trianon and an attempt to reclaim former territories was a direct factor in Hungary's decision to align with Nazi Germany.

In most cases, the treatment of the newly created Hungarian minorities in the lost Trianon regions was remarkably bad. Language rights were lost, schools were closed, and most of the talented Hungarians left for 'Small Hungary'.

Today, Hungarians remain outraged over Trianon and politicians regularly invoke the treaty. In 1990, when Hungary's then prime minister József Antall claimed that he was the 'prime minister of 15 million Hungarians', neighbouring countries rounded on him to accuse him of 'Trianon revisionism'.

Today, Hungarian minorities in former Yugoslavia, Romania and Slovakia feel that their rights to self-determination in simple things such as schooling and choice of names are under attack. The thousands of Transylvanian Hungarians who live and work illegally in Budapest are a reminder that flawed treaties never die – they just age gracelessly.

Hungarian minorities of the Empire just as it had in 1848. His response was a programme designed to assimiliate the assorted Croats, Slovaks and Romanians of the Hungarian realm.

Tisza declared that all schools would have to teach in Magyar, and attempts were made to have Magyar become the language of churches. The assimilation policy laid the groundwork for the minority unrest and resentment that festers to this day among Hungary's neighbours.

The corollary to the minority issue, however, was that adoption of Hungarian became the linguistic ticket to success in Budapest. A lively literary life began to grow in Hungarian, as artists, students, politicians and other society figures met to congregate, socialise and exchange ideas in Pest's many coffeehouses.

THE 1896 EXHIBITION

By the 1890s, Budapest was the fastest-growing metropolis in Europe. The Emperor Franz Joseph, on the twenty-fifth anniversary of the 1867 agreement, issued a decree that Budapest was to be a capital equal to that of Austria. Budapest became the focus of a new sense of Hungarian national confidence. In anticipation of the millennial anniversary of the Honfoglalás, the Hungarian invasion of the Danube Basin, a huge exposition was planned for 1895. The untimely death of the exhibition's designer caused a minor delay, but with typical Hungarian aplomb this was duly taken care of by an official declaration that the invasion had occurred in 896, and since then the history books have been amended to include the new date.

The Millennium celebration in the **Városliget** (City Park) became an overt expression of this new national confidence. Continental Europe's first underground railway whisked visitors beneath Andrássy út to the fairground at today's **Hősök tere** (Heroes' Square), where they were met by the gargantuan memorial to King Árpád and his tribal Magyar chieftains. A miniature of Transylvania's Vajdahunyad Castle was constructed to house exhibits and today still houses the Agriculture Museum. Across the way, the Wampetics Gardens, the home to celebrity chef Károly Gundel (now the Gundel restaurant), served up traditional Hungarian cuisine prepared with a touch of French flair making Hungarian food the culinary fad of the new century.

TOWARDS THE TWILIGHT

In the wake of the Millennium celebration, Hungarian confidence in the bright future was at an all-time high. The turn of the century was the golden age of Hungarian literature and arts. Mór Jókai was one of the most widely translated novelists in the world. Endre Ady's volume of new poetry, *Új versek*, sparked a veritable literary explosion. Béla

Bartók and Zoltán Kodály were creating the study of ethnomusicology and composing masterpieces of modern music based on Hungarian folk traditions. Budapest became the in-spot for the vacationing upper crust of Europe.

Amid the heady confidence in culture, politics began to take an ominous turn. The city had largely been developed on credit, and the apparent opulence of Pest façades to this day contrasts with the poverty of the courtyards within. Working class unrest had first asserted itself on the first great May Day demonstration in 1890 and its influence grew over the next decade.

The new Hungarian **Parliament** building, opened in 1902, was the largest in the world, naively anticipating a long and prosperous rule. It was never a site for decorous politics, however, as representatives were not allowed to read speeches, leading to a tendency for rambling outbursts, nationalist *braggadacio* and occasional riots among the representatives, as in 1904. The ageing Deák wing Liberals were challenged by newer right-wing elements who introduced Austrian-influenced anti-Semitism, previously alien to Hungarian political and social life, into political dialogue.

THE LIGHTS GO OUT

National tensions within the Habsburg Empire came to a head in the years just before World War I. Hungary's Magyarcentric and high-handed administration of the majority of peoples within the realm had helped fuel resentment and nationalism.

When Gavrilo Princip, the leader of a minor Serb radical student group in Habsburg-occupied Sarajevo shot dead the Archduke Franz Ferdinand, war was declared against Serbia. What should have been a minor provincial police action rapidly turned into World War I.

Although Hungary could count itself lucky that the war was not fought on Hungarian land, by 1918 the Habsburgs, with Hungary beside them, faced defeat along with their German allies.

The Horthy era

With the signing of the Armistice on 11 November 1918, World War I came to an end, and with it the Austro-Hungarian Empire. Hungary declared its independence as a republic on 16 November, with Mihály Károlyi as president. The country was faced by serious shortages, unresolved minority problems, and a ring of unsympathetic neighbours aligned with France. No clear demarcation line existed in the border regions, and Serbian troops occupied Pécs while the French camped in Szeged.

Hungarian diplomatic efforts at the Peace Conferences in Versailles went badly, and when the allies showed their determination to hand over two-thirds of Hungary's territory to the neighbouring states of the Little Entente, the Károlyi government resigned and handed power to the Social Democrats. They in turn made a coalition with the new Hungarian Communist Party.

On 21 March the Hungarian Soviet Republic was declared by Béla Kun, who went about forming a Red Army, nationalising banks and sending emissaries to the new Soviet Union. Kun hoped, as much as any Hungarian nationalist, to regain the territories lost in the war, but the Soviets did not heed his calls for aid. In response to the threat of expanding Bolshevism, Czech and Romanian armed forces entered Hungary. The Hungarians fought doggedly, but nevertheless the Romanian Army reached Budapest on 3 August 1919. Kun and his ministers quickly fled to Vienna, most of them never to return (among them László Moholy-Nagy, the Bauhaus genius, and Béla Lugosi, under-Minister of Culture and future Dracula). The Romanian Army did little to endear themselves to the citizens of Budapest. The soldiers bivouacked in the middle of the posh Oktogon intersection and plundered the city at will, finally clearing out of Budapest in November 1919.

Hungary entered a new phase of history when Admiral Miklós Horthy, hero of the Battle of Rijeka, entered Budapest from Szeged mounted on a white horse at the head of 25,000 Hungarian troops. The weeks that followed were known as the 'White Terror', as Communists, Social Democrats and Jews were hunted down and killed for collaboration with the Kun regime. On 25 January 1920, elections brought in a Christian-right coalition Parliament, with Admiral Horthy acting as regent in place of a claimant to the crown. Hungary was now a political incongruity – a monarchy without a king, led by an admiral without a navy.

On 4 June 1920, the Treaty of Trianon was signed in Versailles, France (*see page 14* **Flawed treaties never die**). Traffic in Budapest came to a halt, shops closed, black flags flew from buildings. Overnight, Hungary lost two thirds of its territory and a third of its Hungarian population. Budapest was now the only major city in Hungary, a city of one million in a country of seven million. Refugees clogged the city, unemployment raged and the economy virtually came to a standstill.

THE 'SILVER AGE'

A new political coalition, led by the Christian National Party and the peasant-orientated Smallholders' Party, came to power under the leadership of Count Gábor Bethlen, a hard-nosed conservative. He kept left and right in check and worked abroad to gain international credit and sympathy.

In October 1921, Habsburg pretender Charles IV flew in from Switzerland to head a monarchist coup with the help of loyalist troops. Horthy

Raoul Wallenberg memorial.

crushed the coup at the airfield in Budaörs, assisted by a paramilitary militia led by radical right-wing leader Gyula Gömbös. Their relationship would have serious consequences, as Gömbös's increasingly anti-Semitic appeals to nationalism became more and more the accepted political tone.

The Horthy governments advocated economic growth of rural areas and referred to Budapest as a somehow 'un-Hungarian' den of iniquity. Yet Budapest continued to be the economic and social focus of the nation's growth. Financial stability returned in the late 1920s, but when world stock prices collapsed in 1929, labour discontent rose sharply. Count Bethlen resigned and Horthy appointed Gyula Gömbös as Prime Minister.

Budapest in the 1920s and 1930s was not quite as dark as politics would suggest. Whereas the turn of the century was referred to as Budapest's Golden Age the inter-war period is remembered as the Silver Age, at least in art and society.

During the 1920s, Hungary's spas and casinos were the playgrounds of European high society. The Prince of Wales, the King of Italy, Evelyn Waugh and countless millionaires flocked to Budapest for the good life it promised, including the legalised brothels that offered both discretion and the *filles hongroises* who were well known for their beauty. When HL Mencken visited in 1930 he wrote to his wife: 'This town is really astounding. It is far the most beautiful that I have ever seen. I came expecting to find a dingy copy of Vienna but it makes Vienna look like a village.'

Culturally, Budapest was experiencing a renaissance. The coffeehouses still provided a home for an active literary output that was gobbled up by an adoring public. Avant-gardists grouped around Lajos Kassák and his Bauhaus-influenced journal *Ma* (*Today*), while liberal nationalists such as Gyula Illyés created a distinctly Hungarian genre of literature known as the *népi írók* ('folky writers'), focusing on peasant themes and village histories.

THINGS GO ASTRAY

Nevertheless, the organic make-up of Budapest society was coming apart. The Jews of Hungary were the first to feel the changing winds when access to higher education and certain professions were curtailed under the Numerus Clausus law in 1928. Prime Minister Gömbös was attracted by dreams of a Fascist Hungarian-Italian-German 'axis' (Gömbös coined the term), and worked to bring Hungary closer to Nazi Germany. German investment gained the Fascists influential friends and Oktogon was even renamed Mussolini tér.

When Germany annexed Austria and invaded the Sudetenland in 1938, Hungarian hopes for regaining the lands lost in the Trianon treaty soared. The second Vienna Award in November 1938 returned a part of Slovakia to Hungary, and in 1940 Hungary was awarded most of Transylvania. When Germany declared war on the United States after Pearl Harbor in 1941, Hungary immediately followed suit.

Still, all was not entirely fine between the Hungarians and the Germans. Gömbös had died and the new Prime Minister, Count Pál Teleki, who mistrusted the Nazis, worked to keep Hungary out of combat and resisted German demands for increased deportations of Jews. Teleki, an anglophile noble of the old school, would not stand for Germany infringing on Hungarian sovereignty *vis-à-vis* its own citizens, even Jews. Hungary, however, invaded Yugoslavia alongside the Germans in 1941, and when Vojvodina was returned, Hungarian troops took part in massacres of Jews and Serbs. When Hungary joined Germany in the invasion of Russia, Count Teleki did the noble thing and committed suicide.

Hungary's participation in the Russian invasion was disastrous. At Stalingrad in January 1943 the Russians captured the entire Hungarian second army. As the Soviets closed in on Budapest, American and British bombing sorties against Hungarian arms factories began to level parts of Angyalföld and Zugló in Pest. The Nazis tightened

Former defence Ministry on Disz tér – bullet-pocked since 1945.

their internal control of Hungary with the arrival of German troops in March 1944. Hungarian officials continued to resist German demands for more Jewish deportations, but it became harder when Adolf Eichmann moved his SS headquarters to the Buda Hills. Jews were herded into the Ghetto in District VII, while the Astoria Hotel across the street served as Wehrmacht Headquarters.

In October 1944, Admiral Horthy saw that there was no hope in continuing the war and made a speech calling for an armistice. The SS responded by kidnapping Horthy and on the morning of 15 October 1944 German troops occupied the **Buda Castle Palace**. The Nazi puppet Ferenc Szálasi and his Fascist Arrow Cross Party took control of Hungary. Extra trains were put on to take Budapest's Jews to the gas chambers at Auschwitz. Arrow Cross thugs raided the ghettos, marched Jews to the Danube bank and shot them. With Russian tanks at the outskirts of Pest, Jews were marched to concentration camps in Austria.

Many of the Jews who survived owed their lives to Raoul Wallenberg, a Swedish diplomat posted in Budapest. Wallenberg had safe houses set up for Jews around Budapest, and issued many with fake Swedish passports. One moment he would be charmingly negotiating with German officers, the next personally pulling Jews off trains bound for Auschwitz. When the Russians surrounded Pest, Wallenberg drove to meet them. He was never seen again. Soviet authorities claimed he died in 1947, but survivors of the Siberian prison camps reported that he may have been alive as recently as the 1970s. Two memorials now stand to him in Buda and Pest (*see page 83* **Back on the block**).

Just as Marshal Malinovski's tanks were about to enter Budapest in November 1944, Stalin gave a personal order for the Red Army to split and pursue German divisions in south Hungary. The Germans made a last-ditch stand in Budapest. The result was that Budapest and its citizens were caught in the crossfire of an artillery battle that lasted months, killing many more civilians than combatants. The Russians advanced west through Pest's neighbourhoods in bloody door-to-door fighting. By the time the Red Army took control of Pest, the Germans had entrenched themselves in Buda around Castle Hill. While Russian tanks could easily control Pest's boulevards, the fighting in Buda's twisting, medieval streets was hellish. By the time the Germans finally surrendered on 4 April 1945, the castle was in complete ruins, and not one bridge was left standing over the Danube.

Communism

When Budapest residents finally climbed out of their basements and shelters, it was as if they had been transported to some desolate planet. One of Europe's most beautiful cities had been reduced to a heap of smoking rubble. Rebuilding Budapest would occupy its citizens for the next 30 years.

The task of restoring order fell to the Soviet military government, who placed loyal Hungarian Communists in all positions of power. Nevertheless, an election held in November 1945 was won by the Smallholders' Party, the only legitimate pre-war party still in existence. Even with vote rigging, the Communists only garnered 17 per cent, but Soviet authorities insisted they remain in power, and nobody was in a position to argue.

In February 1946, the Monarchy was abolished and a Hungarian Republic proclaimed. Two weeks later the Paris Peace treaty was signed, compounding the loss of land under Trianon by granting a slice of east Hungary to the USSR. Communist authorities controlling the Interior Ministry set up a secret police force, known as the ÁVO and run by László Rajk, to root out dissent. Thousands were picked up off the streets and sent to the Soviet Union for *malenkaya robota* ('a little work'). Many were never heard from again.

Changes in the social fabric of Budapest were also part of post-war city planning. Budapest neighbourhoods lost some of their unique social identity as the Communists attempted to homogenise areas in support of a classless society. Apartments went to whomever the local *tanács* (council – a new term translated from the Russian 'soviet') decided. The empty flats left by the annihilation of the Jews in Budapest's Districts VII and VIII were given to migrant workers, many of them Gypsies. Other neighbourhoods, now anonymous block jungles such as Lágymányos or Angyalföld were envisaged as 'Workers' Utopias'.

The Communists went forward with the nationalisation of industry and education. In 1948 a plan was introduced to collectivise landholdings, effectively neutralising the Smallholders' Party. The Communist hold on Hungary was complete.

Tensions arose between those Hungarian Communists who had spent the war in the Soviet Union and those who had lived underground in Budapest. In 1949, the scales of power tipped in favour of the Moscow loyalists, led by Mátyás Rákosi. Using the spectre of pro-Yugoslav 'Titoism' as a weapon, old-time party members – among them secret police chief László Rajk – were tried as foreign spies and executed.

By the early 1950s, Hungary was one of the dimmest lights trimming the Iron Curtain. Informers were everywhere, classic Hungarian books were banned, church leaders imprisoned and middle class families persecuted as class enemies.

During his years in power Mátyás Rákosi pursued a cult of personality that even Stalin found embarrassing. Rákosi's face was on huge street murals, his picture hung in every office. Children

General Bem points the way forward for the 1956 Uprising.

Tales of a crown

The greatest treasure of the Hungarian nation is, indisputably, the crown of St Stephen. Much more than a mere relic of a bygone king, to Hungarians it symbolises their independence and alone confers legitimacy on the governments of the nation.

Born Vajk, son of Grand Duke Géza who converted to Catholicism and great-great grandson of Árpád, St Stephen (Szent István in Hungarian) assumed the throne in 1000 AD. The upper part of the crown was a gift from Pope Sylvester II in Rome, and is decorated with gems and small images of eight of the apostles, while the lower part of the crown is of Byzantine manufacture and was added later by King Géza I. It is thought that the two crowns were probably joined together during the reign of King Béla III (1172-96).

Stephen's acceptance of the crown acknowledged fealty to the Holy Roman Empire. It is just the sort of bauble a medieval Pope might give to a recently converted pagan chieftain he wasn't too sure about, but the crown is nevertheless an impressive bit of Byzantine-Gothic

finery and, under constant armed guard, is exhibited in the National Museum along with St Stephen's golden orb and embroidered coronation cape.

The crown has had some interesting adventures. During the Mongol invasion in 1242 it was smuggled to safety in the back of a hay cart. Somewhere along the way it got dropped and the crown acquired a sportingly bent look.

As the symbol of the legitimacy of Hungarian governments, the Habsburgs carried the thing off to Vienna for a while. Under the Dual Monarchy it was understood that the Habsburg emperors would rule Hungary in the name of St Stephen's crown, and would travel to Budapest for a special coronation ceremony.

At the end of World War II, the crown was again smuggled out of Hungary, this time by forces wishing to deny legitimacy to the Communists. It languished in Fort Knox until 1978 when President Jimmy Carter decided to return it to Hungary. Emigrant Hungarians in the US were outraged that Carter would thus legitimise a Communist government.

---

wrote poems about him while peasant women embroidered his ugly mug on pillows of red silk.

A brief respite came with Stalin's death in 1953. Rákosi was removed from office and replaced with Imre Nagy, a more humanistic Communist with a sense of sympathy for Hungarian national ideals. It didn't last long. Rákosi, backed by Moscow, accused Nagy of 'deviationism' and came back into power in 1955.

HUNGARIAN REVOLUTION OF 1956

By June 1956, well known Hungarian intellectuals and writers began openly to criticise the Rákosi regime, using the forum of the Petőfi Writers' Circle for unprecedented free debate. The Kremlin, now led by Krushchev, poured oil on the flames of discontent by replacing Rákosi with the equally despicable Stalinist, Ernő Gerő.

On 23 October 1956, Budapest students marched to the statue of the 1848 Polish hero General Bem (*see above*) to express solidarity with reform policies taking place in Poland. The demonstration continued across the river to Parliament, its ranks swelled by thousands of workers, then moved to the Hungarian Radio Headquarters on Bródy Sándor utca behind the National Museum. During the demonstration, sharpshooters from the ÁVH (as the ÁVO were now known) on the roof of the Radio building shot into the crowd. Police and

members of the Hungarian Army who were in the area responded by attacking the ÁVH men, and street fighting broke out. When Russian tanks showed up, they were met by determined fire from partisan freedom fighters who had been armed by rebel workers from the arms factories in 'Red Csepel', one of the staunchest Communist districts in Budapest.

By 23 October, all of Hungary was in revolt. The statue of Stalin which stood near Heroes' Square was sawn off at the ankles, pulled down and spat on by angry crowds. ÁVH men were pulled out of the Interior Ministry and executed on the street. Imre Nagy was reinstated as Prime Minister and General Pál Maléter pledged the loyalty of the Hungarian Army to the new government. Many political prisoners were freed.

After the first few days of fighting, Russian troops began a hasty retreat from Hungary on 29 October. For the next few days a dazed euphoria swept the nation. Hungarians believed that the West would come to their aid, as promised daily by Radio Free Europe. It was an unfortunate miscalculation, compounded by the Suez Canal Crisis, which distracted Western attention.

On 1 November, claiming Hungary had illegally seceded from the Warsaw Pact, Russian tanks re-invaded and on 4 November once again entered Budapest. As tanks rolled down the boulevards,

Hungarians put up a dogged defence. Battles took place at the Kilián Army Barracks (corner of Üllői út and József körút) and the fortress-like **Corvin cinema** nearby. In Buda, armed workers fought to prevent the approaching tanks from entering Pest through Széna tér. At Móricz Zsigmond körtér students stopped tanks by spreading oil on the cobbled streets and pulling grenades on strings underneath the stalled vehicles.

Soon, however, Hungarian resistance was brutally crushed. Imre Nagy took refuge in the Yugoslav embassy, but was captured when he accepted an armistice agreement. He and most of the other members of the Hungarian revolutionary council were executed in secret. Thousands of Hungarians were sent to prison and 200,000 fled the country.

THE KÁDÁR YEARS

The stranglehold lasted until the 1960s, when amnesties were granted and János Kádár began a policy of reconciliation. His was a balancing act between hard-line Communism and appeasing the population. While Hungary maintained a strong Cold War stance and toed the Moscow line, Hungarians enjoyed a higher standard of living than most of Soviet eastern Europe. Hungary was known as 'the happiest barracks in the bloc'.

Life under Kádár meant more food in the shops, but it also meant banned books and 'psychological hospital' prisons for dissenters. Unlike his predecessors, Kádár allowed limited celebration of certain national traditions. Petőfi and Kossuth were extolled as precursors of the proletarian revolution. During the 1960s, Hungary finally began to resemble its old self. The rubble from World War II and the 1956 revolution was cleared away, historic buildings were restored. Tourism began to grow, although Western visitors were still followed around by government spies after dinner.

Kádár's balancing act was well proven in 1968. When Czechoslovakia irked the Soviets with the reform atmosphere of the Prague Spring, Hungarian troops loyally participated in the invasion. At the same time Kádár introduced his 'New Economic Mechanism', an economic reform that broke with hard-line Communist theory and laid the ground for entrepreneurship. Kádár came to represent 'Communism with a human face'.

During the 1980s, however, it became obvious that the 'New Economic Mechanism' was flawed. Hungary became ever more dependent on foreign trade, and inflation rose. The black market in Western goods belied the ability of a command economy to provide basic goods and services, and Hungary's relations with its Warsaw Pact neighbours began to show signs of strain.

A growing number of writers and other public figures started to test the limits of open criticism, and by the 1980s Hungary was the centre of eastern Europe's boom in underground *samizdat* literature. Typically, the Hungarian government was not pleased, but instead of jailing dissidents outright, authorities played a cat-and-mouse game with *samizdat* publishers, prosecuting them not for what they had written but for distributing their literature without using the national postal service, an economic crime. Western support for open debate came in odd ways. Billionaire Hungarian financier George Soros made deals to supply basic materials for hospitals and educational institutions. Soros also provided scholarships for Hungary's dissidents to study democratic practice at universities in the West, and made the production of *samizdat* literature commonplace by flooding the country with free photocopy machines. (*See page 275* **Speculating for democracy**).

As it became obvious that the aged Kádár was no longer fit to rule, younger party members began to take positions of power. Known as the 'Miskolc Mafia', after the city where they had begun their political careers, many, such as Prime Minister Károly Grósz and his successor Miklós Németh, openly tolerated debate, while opening more doors for 'market socialism' and freer expression.

GOODBYE, IRON CURTAIN

In 1989 the bubble burst. In June, people took to the streets to rebury the remains of Imre Nagy. It was a hero's funeral attended by thousands. Soon after, a huge demonstration was held at Heroes' Square to protest against Romania's treatment of its Hungarian minority. Allowing public protest was a major shift in government policy.

Two events in the late spring of 1989 signalled the end of Communism. One was the government declaration that political parties could form to discuss the possibility of free elections. The second was the mass exodus of East Germans to the West through Hungary. When Hungary ceremonially cut the barbed wire fence on its Austrian border, thousands of East Germans poured into Hungary on 'vacation'. Those wishing to go to the West were housed and fed by the Hungarian government. East Germany's faltering Communist government was incensed when trainloads of refugees were taken by the Hungarian government on 'tours' that dropped them conveniently by the Austrian border.

Hardline Communists in Hungary were alarmed and some factions called out the old Communist Workers guard in August 1989. An armed militia of geriatric hardliners, the Workers' Guard, shot several East Germans before the more moderate Hungarian Army protested and put an end to the vigilantism. The failure of the Workers' Guard marked the end of Communist hegemony.

Soon the 'reform Communists' led by Imre Pozsgay announced that free elections would take place in 1990. The Communist party threw in the hat, changed its name to the Hungarian Socialist Party and declared that it was running in the elections.

Hungary had tipped over the first domino. The collapse of Communism followed throughout eastern Europe. Hungarians breathed a sigh of collective relief, and then got down to the very Hungarian business of politics.

The post-Communist decade

Early 1990 was a period of intoxicating possibilities for Hungarians. All talk was focused on new-found freedoms, democracy and market capitalism. A new era had dawned and many Hungarians were quick to position themselves in the emerging social and economic picture. Just as many, however, found themselves bystanders, watching the changes from afar, confused and frustrated by yet another upheaval in history. With elections set for March 1990, Hungarians set about forming political parties – lots of them. Eventually, of 150 or so parties, about six became contenders. The old dissidents coalesced around the Free Democrats (SZDSZ) while a national student activist group formed the Young Democrats (FIDESZ, which has now added NPP – 'National Middle Class Party' – to the name). The Communists split into the Socialist Party (MSZP) and the hardcore Workers' Party (Munkáspárt). Christian Democrats and the reformed Smallholders' Party held broad appeal. The Hungarian Democratic Forum (MDF) represented a mixed bag of nationalist and conservative views.

The SZDSZ and the MDF ran neck and neck during the first democratic elections since World War II, with the MDF winning the first round of elections. During the run-offs, however, the MDF began to use nationalist, sometimes anti-Semitic rhetoric, which many interpreted as an attempt by the MDF to present themselves as *népi-nemzeti* ('folkish-national') conservatives. It was rhetoric that would pigeonhole the MDF for the next five years, eventually weakening their voter base and causing splits in the party.

With a conservative, MDF-led coalition in Parliament, medical historian József Antall became prime minister, while dissident writer Árpád Göncz assumed the largely ceremonial position of president. The 'change of systems' (*rendszerváltás*) brought more than just democratic government. The face of Budapest changed as new businesses opened and the bright windows of western fast-food restaurants and brand-name clothing shops began replacing the city's classy old neon. Business centres sprouted all over town. Street names were changed, so that Lenin Boulevard and Marx Square were no longer, and their respective statues and monuments were removed to the **Statue Park** (*see chapter* **Museums**). Red stars were taken down, and a law was signed that made any public use of 'symbols of tyranny' (such as red stars or swastikas) a criminal offence.

DISTURBING SIGNS

As economic changes took place, a new class arose in Budapest, the entrepreneur or *menedzser*. Many young Hungarians found opportunities working in western businesses. Many others, however, found the changes confusing, and Hungarians have been overwhelmed by new regulations. Unemployment rose as state industries were privatised or shut down. The standard of living for many dropped below Communist-era levels, when prices were fixed and services subsidised by the state. Crime rose as the divide between rich and poor grew sharper, although rates remain laughably low compared to virtually any other world capital, and violent crime is rare.

Prime minister Antall, whose illness had been an increasingly public secret, died in December 1993. Stiff and paternalistic, he had appealed to Hungarians who found his aristocratic bearing attractively old fashioned. Others were surprised by Antall's inability or unwillingness to condemn right-wing radicals within his governing coalition. The MDF likewise became embroiled in a protracted war between the government and the media over the control of state TV.

Hungary's economic problems, including foreign debt, an unwieldy privatisation process, and a small internal market, made the expected post-Communist boom appear to fizzle. The ruling MDF coalition paid the price by losing the 1994 election to the Socialist Party, led by Gyula Horn, the man who, as Communist foreign minister, had given the order to open the borders in 1989. But whatever nostalgia voters may have had for the 'good old 1980s' was dashed when the Socialists, along with their coalition partners the SZDSZ, prescribed a no-nonsense policy of austerity and belt tightening. This meant forint devaluations, slashes in social funding, rocketing energy prices and shock-therapy privatisation measures to get Hungary on track for eventual EU membership.

Predictably, this course proved internationally effective but meant domestic disaster during the 1998 elections. FIDESZ, realising that it was a mere junior partner in a left coalition government, abruptly shed its liberal feathers and began goose-stepping to a conservative nationalist beat, simultaneously comparing itself to both Tony Blair and Margaret Thatcher. It worked with the voters, and by careful politicking FIDESZ now leads a strong right-conservative majority in parliament.

Built for the Magyar Millennium – continental Europe's first underground railway.

Governance continues to maintain a strong partisan flavour. Conservative rhetoric in Hungary invariably means nostalgia for Horthy-era values, and Budapest is once again viewed as being somehow 'un-Hungarian' and sinful. When the SZDSZ city government attempted to construct a new National Theatre, the FIDESZ feds nixed the funding – lest those sneaky liberals complete a project with 'national' overtones – leaving Budapest with a very large and ugly hole in the middle of downtown Deák tér. FIDESZ also nixed plans for a fourth metro line, although city officials have now found alternative international funding. Prime Minister Orbán refuses to even speak with old ally and Budapest mayor Gábor Demszky – a petulant and childish state of affairs. Meanwhile, the FIDESZ-led coalition has focused its energies on tax cheats – creating three new secret police agencies (ahh nostalgia!) to track down the culprits, and then named a new tax minister who just happened to be under investigation for multi-million-forint tax fraud himself. Meanwhile, pork barrel appointments have become commonplace, and Smallholders' Party populist leader and agriculture minister József Torgyán was named president of Ferencváros Football Club (yes, they are the ones whose supporters give a Nazi salute when they score a goal).

Meanwhile, Hungary was admitted (along with Poland and the Czech Republic) into Nato in March 1999. Within three days Nato forces began bombing Serbia. Hungary immediately felt itself forced to backpedal from any military commitment that might endanger the large Hungarian minority in the Serbian Vojvodina region. True to history, Hungary once again finds itself faced with difficult choices in a turbulent region.

Domestically, however, there have been improvements in Budapest life. The mafia wars of the mid-1990s have ceased, not least because the Slovak secret services stopped supplying mob goons with grenades after one 1998 street attack nearly blew up a Váci utca burger outlet. Taxi drivers are no longer quite so daring at rip-offs, and most Hungarian restaurants now realise that Italian food is not based on ketchup. Sleaze is being replaced by middle-class respectability. Budapest life is again peaceful and – as Hungarians almost prefer it – boring.

While the tenor of political debate is pretty tense, politics remains in the realm of the abstract. Hungarians view politics the way they view their football – they're passionately partisan but choose to watch it from a safe seat in the stadium. Yet regardless of the changes that sweep through Hungary every few decades, Budapest remains one of the world's most wondrous cities, managing to maintain its beauty and dignity without hiding the wrinkles and warts that provide it with such a deep sense of character. Budapest wears its age and scars of its history for all to see.

Budapest Today

The youth live in a jeans ad, the élite head for the hills – but money isn't everything in the new Budapest.

'*Nem úgy van most mint volt régen...*' Back in the late 1980s this Transylvanian village song, performed by Márta Sebestyén and Muzsikás, could be heard blasting from almost every corner of Budapest – the past blaring back as prologue, the country as the voice of the city. The song became the anthem of the SZDSZ liberal dissident party, and college kids sang it with factory workers in bars. Today you probably won't hear it at all. Why? As the song says '*Things ain't like they used to be...*'

Budapest is always changing. For the tourist, it doesn't quite know how to present itself, and in fact, it doesn't really care. For Hungarians, Budapest is Goddess and Whore combined, a necessary urban evil to provincials, a beloved icon to those who grew up here. It's easy to see both sides of the argument. Western franchises take over the downtown, fast food is everywhere, the ancient cobbler's shop is now an aerobics salon, and the beat of commercial techno blares from every taxi. But the flower seller will still remember your wife's birthday, the flat you live in is a bullet-pocked rebel headquarters from 1956, and you can still sit for hours pouring over newspapers and sipping coffee at a table that was poet Endre Ady's favourite at the coffeehouse just down the road.

Sure, things are a lot different than they were under communism, as the lead line of any English-language newspaper article in town will proclaim – endlessly. A lot of the niceties have vanished. Coffeehouses have been replaced by pizza bars and brand-name burger joints. People work more, and less time is spent sipping idle *fröccs* after idle *fröccs* in garden wine taverns, wondering what life after communism might be like. For one thing, daily life has become far more expensive. Much of what is sold in stores is imported, and thus heavily taxed, and wages are still only a fraction of western norms. Class distinctions, one of the most tenacious features of Hungarian language and society, and the one directly attacked by communist urban society, is back with a mobile-bleeping vengeance.

The élite, of course, have always been around in some form – noble, communist or yuppie. There really isn't any such thing as 'old money' here. Today's élite continue to isolate themselves up in Buda's wooded hills, send their children to private schools, summer in the Caribbean, and speak near flawless English learned at Oxford or Harvard. A notch down, quite well down, is the *menedzser*

class, resplendent in electric-purple business suits with cellular phones glued to their ears. A menedzser doesn't necessarily *menedzs* anything. A menedzser knows somebody who knows somebody and has a wad of business cards to prove it. If you prised open his leather briefcase you'll probably find his lunch and a jazz mag or two. It's a sense of style, a life of hopping from one bankruptcy to another with a smile and a tax dodge, all in search of the one big kill.

And then there is the youth class – the young office staffers and computer proles. These were the target of the post-1990 western advertising offensive – the *Drang nach Youth Market* – and they show it. They party hard, they spend every last forint on clothes and cars and hair mousse, they can quote Beavis and Butthead – and they still live with Mum and Dad. Their English is usually rudimentary but with a perfect pop music accent – with MTV, who needs travel? – and in summer they migrate to the

Western franchises take over the downtown.

Another mall shoots up in central Pest.

breeding grounds at Lake Balaton. It was for them that the annual rock festival 'Student Island' was set up, and it was for them that the sponsors encouraged the organisers to change its name to 'Pepsi Island'. Pepsi instead of Traubi Szoda, Marlboro instead of Sopianae, Johnnie Walker instead of *pálinka*. Life is one long Replay Jeans ad.

And of course, there is the *kis ember*, the 'little guy', that semi-fictional statistic of the pollsters, the head of the family with two working parents paying 45 per cent income tax and just about managing to make ends meet so they can take the kids on holiday to Lake Velence and maybe replace an item of furniture every year.

But money isn't everything, especially in Hungary. There is the still the 'intellectual', living from translating advertorials in fly-by-night lifestyle magazines while feverishly reciting Hungarian poetry to the hard-of-hearing in noisy bars. Without a Great Enemy, Hungarian literature and arts have suffered a crisis of identity, often slipping into derivative and plagiaristic shadows of western trends. The public ignores Hungarian writers in favour of Stephen King in translation, and hardbacks cost 500 per cent more than they did six years ago. Hungarian film-makers must contend with Hollywood-hungry filmgoers, while the local film industry survives by attracting western film productions to Budapest locations.

Budapest is still the Mecca for Hungary's students, many realising that a major in Law may serve them better than a degree in sixteenth-century Hungarian poetry. And – since Hungary's birth and death rates are chronically locked in minus population growth – there is an ever-growing class of pensioners, who toiled under the socialist system for decades and now eke out a living on ever-shrinking pensions in what was once promised to them as Workers' Heaven. The luckier ones have children in the higher echelons. Most don't. And there are other groups that didn't exist before 1990. Rural migrants who have fled from crushing underdevel-opment in eastern Hungary. Transylvanian Hungarians who have left Romania. Refugees from the Balkan wars. The homeless.

And of course, there are the westerners. Most of the English-speaking ones call themselves 'expats', a term loaded with class conceit. Before 1989 foreign residents were rare and valued, and most were on first-name basis with each other. No longer. Budapest, luckily, never reached the stature of Prague as a magnet for western youth in search of that unwriteable novel. Budapest was too incomprehensible, too far from Disneyland. Budapest meant business. The city did attract thousands of westerners in the early 1990s, as well as Asians, North Africans, even Canadians, but today their number is far smaller. Hungary no longer needs foreign managers and business consultants as they did in 1990 – the new middle class have been trained in the west and can mismanage a bank just fine on their own, thank you. The foreign community tends to divide into two classes – those who can't speak Hungarian (mostly business appointments from foreign multinationals) and those who can. These range from English teachers to retirees to rap singers, Americans, Irish, Serbs, Dutch and French all speaking their amusingly accented Magyar with bemused locals. A night out with this crowd can seem like partying in the revolving bar atop the tower of Babel.

Budapest is again learning how to come into its own as a world-class city, a distinction it lost after World War I. As Hungary strives to become a member of the EU, the city strains between Euro-conformity and remaining a loose and wine-fuelled *mitteleuropäisches Schlamperei*. Nothing made this clearer than Hungary's uncomfortable position in the Kosovo conflict in 1999. Newly inducted into Nato, Hungary had to balance ingrained pacifism and the interests of its large Hungarian minority in Serbia with Nato's sudden demands, including using Ferihegy Airport for warplanes. Thousands of Yugo families took shelter in Budapest, clogging cafés

No longer the young ones

In 1989, when the world press focused on Hungary leading the breakup of Communism, the cameras were aimed at dynamic FIDESZ, 'the Young Democrats'. While other parties humped about nationalist myths, FIDESZ was on the front line. Viktor Orbán gave speeches about Transylvanian rights. Tamás Deutsch was arrested in Prague supporting Czech dissidents. Gábor Fodor debated legal circles around the communists. Today FIDESZ is the ruling party of the government, and my, how they have changed!

Originally, FIDESZ's credibility was its youth. When political parties formed in the late 1980s, no member of FIDESZ had served in the communist party. As the student council of the Bibó Law College, a residential dormitory for out-of-town students, FIDESZ served as a legitimate forum for discussions of democratic institutions. The student government soon registered as a media-savvy political party, galvanising youthful support. It worked. When democratic elections were held in 1990, FIDESZ won a healthy bloc of seats in parliament as a partner in the liberal oppsition to the increasingly right-wing nationalist MDF coalition, and maintained a high profile as protectors of minority rights, free press and educational reform.

Today, it is hard to reconcile the paunchy right-wing politicos of FIDESZ-MPP with the dynamic young earring-wearing liberal activists who were approached in 1990 to pose for Levi's advertisements and whose anthem was the catchy rock number *Listen to Your Heart*. Three factors can explain this. One is age. The second is money. And most important is number three: power.

With power, cracks began to appear. Within the opposition FIDESZ bridled against their forced alliance with the Socialist party, whom they labelled as ex-communist opportunists. Soon, however, FIDESZ were involved in a number of scandals related to the party's ownership of private companies, including a shady limosine rental service, and the sale of their party headquarters in cooperation with erstwhile political

enemies, the ruling Magyar Democratic Forum. With their popularity at an all-time low FIDESZ decided to change track and become a 'conservative' party. The FIDESZ which used to restrict membership to under-30s started hitting 30, so they appended the term MPP ('Hungarian Middle-Class Party') to their name. The face of the party switched from Fodor's amiable intellectuality to Orbán's provincial arrogance. With messy ideological issues behind them, FIDESZ went on to cash in on popular discontent with the socialist government's economic measures, and glided into a neat victory in the 1998 elections, leading a right-wing governing coalition with an absolute majority.

The new FIDESZ reflects an anglophile fascination with Thatcherism. They revel in 'governing without an opposition', much to the fury of the opposition, and their old business manager now runs the finance ministry. In summer 1998, the press revealed that FIDESZ companies had been involved in a flurry of shady dealings involving the stolen passports of several foreigners. Allegations of financial wrongdoing, influence peddling, and administrative manipulation, however, are viewed by the average Hungarian as a normal part of the democratic process. Stuffy, provincial, and combative, FIDESZ's popularity seems to continue untarnished. Just watch your passport around them.

Victor Orbán (left) – provincial arrogance.

with anxious faces. Tourists cancelled bookings, and Hungary again came to know what it feels like to be a front-line state in a volatile region. This was not what everyone expected back in 1989. Ten years will do a lot to preconceptions, though. Yours as well.

Hungarians seem to take it all in their stride. They've seen it all before. Doggedly pessimistic, charmingly romantic, occasionally didactic about

their own culture, the Magyar proudly maintains a sense of 'Us' and 'Them' (in this case, 'You') – a well-defined line between the proper way things should be (as they are done in Hungary) and the baffling and incomprehensible universe clamouring just beyond Hegyeshalom (or worse, Záhony). Don't expect fawning admiration for the west. A smile and a shot of Unicum will suffice to show appreciation.

Language

Fancy learning a few words of the most difficult language in the known universe? Nincs semmi gond!

Easy, simple, clear Hungarian.

Perhaps nowhere else in Europe will the traveller be confronted by as great a linguistic barrier as in Hungary. The Hungarian language is renowned the world over for its difficulty, which for most foreigners boils down to the fact that Hungarian bears absolutely no resemblance to any language they may have previously encountered. In other countries, picking up a bit of the local lingo can be an enjoyable pastime. A few words of French? *Pas de problème.* A bit of Plattdeutsch? *Kein Problem.* A smattering of any Slavic tongue? *Nema problema.* Hungarian? *Nincs semmi gond!*

Hungarian is a Finno-Ugric language, part of the greater family of Altaic-Uralic languages that includes Turkish, Finnish and Mongolian. Much is made of Hungarian's relationship to Finnish, but that kinship is distant indeed and the two languages are mutually unintelligible. As the main language of the Ugric stock, Hungarian is related most closely to two spoken languages by a few people in the Ural mountains of north-west Siberia, Vogul and Ostyak. When the Hungarians moved southward and adopted the equestrian and agricultural cultures of the southern steppes they adopted many terms from Turkic and Iranian languages, such as names for livestock and farm implements – the words for 'customs official' (*vám*) and 'bridge' (*híd*) are borrowed from the Alan language, spoken today in Ossetia.

After the Magyars established themselves in Europe, their language became infused with many Slavic, Latin and, later, German terms. The first written document containing any Hungarian – a few score place names in a mostly Latin document – was the 1055 deed of foundation for Tihany Abbey, these days preserved at Pannonhalma Abbey near Győr. Hungarian has shown itself to be an extremely conservative language and medieval Hungarian is easily understood by a modern Magyar. There are various regional accents but relatively few dialects, although Budapest boasts a slangy style of rapid-fire speech peppered with foreign vocabulary, especially borrowings from Yiddish, Gypsy and German.

There are so few terms in Hungarian that are cognate with words from the Indo-European language family that every new word requires prodigious feats of learning. Then comes grammar. Beginners memorise a whole series of conjugations simply to begin mangling the idea of 'I have' (*nekem van* 'it is for/of/to me'). Prepositions come after the noun as suffixes and their use is usually quite different from English, so that you have to know that 'to go to' may be different if you're going to a place that is enclosed, geographical, or personal (*házba*, to the house; *Pestre*, to Pest; *hozzánk*, to our house). Furthermore, each Hungarian town has its own

A rough guide to Hungarian

Maddeningly difficult though Hungarian may be, learning a few words and phrases will make life easier – both for you, and for any Hungarians you may encounter. *Igen* (yes), *nem* (no) and *jó reggelt* (good morning), *jó napot* (good day) and *jó estét* (good evening) are all fairly easy, but you'll probably find *viszontlátásra* (goodbye) a mouthful. In shops and among friends you can use the informal short version, *viszlát*.

Meanwhile, *szervusz* is an all-purpose, informal greeting meaning either hello or goodbye, as is the even more informal *szia*. Older women still like to be greeted with *kezét csókolom* (literally, 'I kiss your hand'). Confusingly, Hungarians usually use the English 'hello' to mean 'goodbye'.

The word *kérem* serves a lot of purposes. Its first meaning is 'please', but it also means 'excuse me' when trying to attract a waiter's attention; it can be the answer to *köszönöm* (thank you), and if you pronounce it as a question it means 'pardon?'. If you don't understand what you are being told, you can also say *Bocsánat, nem értem* (Sorry, I don't understand). And then *Nem beszélek magyarul* (I don't speak Hungarian), although that will probably have become obvious by this point.

Hol van? (where is it?) is useful. The answer will probably include a lot of *itt* (here), *ott* (there), *innen* (from here), *onnan* (from there), *jobbra* (to the right), *balra* (to the left) and *egyenesen* (straight ahead).

Hungarian makes a noun plural by adding a '-k' sometimes with a link vowel. *Busz* (bus) becomes *buszok*; *csirke* (chicken) becomes *csirkék*. You don't form the plural, though, when stating a number of things, such as *négy alma* (four apples) or *száz forint* (one hundred forints).

Shop assistants hardly ever speak anything other than Hungarian. *Mennyibe kerül?* (how much is it?), *ez* (this), *az* (that) and some adjectives such as *kicsi* (small), *nagy* (large), *régi* (old), *új* (new), *piros* (red), *fehér* (white) and *fekete* (black) should help.

When asking for something say *Kérek egy/kettő/három jegyet/kávét* (I want a/two/three tickets/coffees). Finally, if you are completely lost, try *Beszél itt valaki angolul?* (does anyone speak English here?).

Pronunciation

Accents denote a longer vowel, except for é (ay) and á (as in father). The stress is always on the first syllable. Double consonants are pronounced longer (*kettő, szebb*).

Add 't' to nouns when they are the object of the sentence: 'I would like a beer' is *Kérek egy sört* (*sör* + t).

a – like 'o' in hot
á – like 'a' in father
é – like 'a' in day
i – like 'ee' in feet
ö – like 'ur' in pleasure
ü – like 'u' in French tu
ő, ű – similar to ö and ü but longer
sz – like 's' in sat
cs – like 'ch' in such
zs – like the 's' in casual
gy – like the 'd' in dew
ly – like the 'y' in yellow
ny – like the 'n' in new
ty – like the 't' in tube
c – like 'ts' in roots
s – like 'sh' in wash

Useful words & phrases

Yes *Igen*
No *Nem*
Maybe *Talán*
(I wish you) good day *Jó napot (kívánok)* (formal)
Hello *Szervusz* (informal); *szia* (familiar)
Goodbye *Viszontlátásra* (formal)
'Bye *Viszlát*
How are you? *Hogy van?* (formal); *hogy vagy?* (familiar)
I'm fine *Jól vagyok*
Please *Kérem*
Thank you *Köszönöm*
Excuse me *Bocsánat*
I would like *Kérek...* (an object)

post-preposition to indicate that you are in that town. You can be 'in London' (*Londonban*) but you are *Budapesten, Pécsett, Debrecenben*. Easy, simple, clear Hungarian.

Luckily, Hungarian has a few features that make things easier. There is no gender, not even a different pronoun for 'he' and 'she'. Past and future tenses are relatively easy and regular. And Hungarians are delighted to hear foreigners attempt their language. If you intend to stay for more than a few weeks, the best book to learn Hungarian is probably *Colloquial Hungarian* by Jerry Payne (Routledge). *See also chapter* **Further Reading**.

A good rule of thumb is that the younger the Hungarian, the more likely they will be to speak English. Today Hungarians are becoming more aware of the need to learn foreign languages. Private language schools these days do a boom-

I would like (to do something) *Szeretnék...* (add infinitive)

Where is...? *Hol van...?*

Where is the toilet? *Hol van a wc?* (**wc** *vay tzay*)

Where is a good/cheap/not too expensive restaurant?*Hol van egy jó/olcsó/nem túl drága étterem?*

When? *Mikor?* Who? *Ki?*

Why? *Miért?* How? *Hogyan?*

Is there...? *Van...?*

There is none *Nincs*

How much is it? *Mennyibe kerül?*

Open *Nyitva;* closed *zárva*

Entrance *Bejárat;* exit *kijárat*

Push *Tolni;* pull *húzni*

Men's *Férfi;* women's *női*

Good *Jó;* bad *rossz*

I like it *Ez tetszik*

I don't like it *Ez nem tetszik*

I don't speak Hungarian *Nem beszélek Magyarul*

Do you speak English? *Beszél angolul?*

What is your name? *Mi a neve?*

My name is... *A nevem...*

I am (English/American) *(angol/amerikai) vagyok*

Railway station *Pályaudvar;* airport *repülőtér*

Ticket office or cash desk *Pénztár*

I would like to go to Pécs *Pécsre szeretnék menni*

I would like two tickets *Két jegyet kérek*

When is the train to Vienna? *Mikor indul a bécsi vonat?*

(At) three o' clock *Három óra (kor)*

I feel ill *Rosszul vagyok*

Doctor *Orvos*

Pharmacy *Patika/gyógyszertár*

Hospital *Kórház*

Ambulance *Mentőautó;* police *rendőrség*

Days of the week

Monday *Hétfő*

Tuesday *Kedd*

Wednesday *Szerda*

Thursday *Csütörtök*

Friday *Péntek*

Saturday *Szombat*

Sunday *Vasárnap*

Numbers

zero *nulla*

one *egy*

two *kettő* (note the form *két,* used with an object: *két kávét two coffees*)

three *három*

four *négy*

five *öt*

six *hat*

seven *hét*

eight *nyolc*

nine *kilenc*

ten *tíz*

eleven *tizenegy*

twelve *tizenkettő*

thirteen *tizenhárom*

twenty *húsz;* twenty-five *huszonöt*

thirty *harminc*

thirty-four *harmincnégy*

forty *negyven*

forty-one *negyvenegy*

fifty *ötven*

sixty *hatvan*

seventy *hetven*

eighty *nyolcvan*

ninety *kilencven*

one hundred *száz*

one hundred and fifty *százötven*

two hundred *kettőszáz*

three hundred *háromszáz*

one thousand *ezer*

ten thousand *tízezer*

one million *millió*

one billion *milliárd*

Crucial phrases

Where is a good bar? *Hol van egy jó kocsma?*

What are you having? *Mit tetszik inni?*

Cheers! *Egészségedre* (Egg-aysh-ayg-ed-reh)

God! You drink like a brushmaker! *Istenem! Úgy iszol, mint egy kefekötő!*

Which football team do you support? *Melyik foci csapatnak drukkolsz?*

I love you *Szeretlek*

It is hopeless *Reménytelen*

Could you call a cab for me? *Tudna nekem egy taxit hívni?*

It's all the same to me! *Nekem nyolc!*

---

ing business teaching English and German, but under Communism, Hungarians were forced to study Russian in school, and it became a badge of pride to fail the eight-year course – not the best experience of foreign-language acquisition. Standards for foreign-language ability have stayed rather low, as the 'Welcome In Hungary' sign on the way into town from Ferihegy airport or a glance at any English-language menu will confirm. Common errors include such appetising terms as 'paste covered with greaves' for noodles with bacon bits, and 'fried innard glands' for sweetbreads.

Much of the blame for such merry mistranslations must lie with one László Országh, who edited the standard postwar Hungarian-English dictionary. Országh was a less than spectacular linguist who was known to confiscate his students' copies of other English dictionaries and tear them up in front of his classes. His main experience with native English-speakers came during his term as a prisoner-of-war in 1945. The only available native anglophone was an errant bachelor from Nottingham who was paid for his assistance in beer. Not surprisingly, some of the entries in Országh's dictionary are quite bizarre.

Many of these Országhisms are stubbornly defended by Hungarians, including translating *vadspenót* (wild spinach) as 'English/false mercury, good King Henry', and *fesztelnit* (to unscrew) as 'to uncock the cock'. The dictionary also includes strange idiomatic explanations, such as 'to sit down under an insult' and 'in consequence of the lucky concurrence of circumstance' (we'll meet again).

Another infuriating feature of Hungarian English is that translations attempt to use the most convoluted English constructions possible – a hangover from the dense Hungarian literary style and a mistrust of colloquialism in print. Hungarian uses the article before each noun, so translations abound in 'the' constructions, such as 'The Students of the School of the Agriculture study the biology and the animals'.

All these linguistic hurdles are well worth the effort, however, since every Hungarian knows that Hungarian is the perfect language. This is a qualitative judgement that any Hungarian will be happy to explain to you. Shakespeare, you will be informed, sounds much better in Hungarian than in the original English. The same holds true for Woody Allen films, Winnie the Pooh and *Flintstones* cartoons (which are dubbed in squeaky voices, in rhyme). The verb for 'to explain' is *magyarázni*, 'to Hungarianise'. This may sound absurd, but Hungarians are very proud of their unique ability to understand Hungarian.

What makes a Magyar laugh?

Why do police cars have stripes? So the policeman can find the doors!

This, ladies and gents, is Hungarian humour. Or what functions as such in Magyar. When not fatalistically bemoaning the hopelessness of it all or pursuing yet another romantic dead-end, Hungarians spend a large amount of their day doubled over in crippling fits of laughter. Yet it is hard to define a particularly Hungarian type of joke, or even what the national sense of humour consists of. Police jokes?

At the core, Hungarian humour, like Magyar poetry, is untranslatable. Irony plays a big part. *What's the difference between a Hungarian pessimist and a Hungarian optimist? The pessimist says things can't possibly get worse. The optimist, however, says no, things can get worse.* Puns, word play, and slight deviations in the language's complex grammar can cause howling, knee-slapping, beer-spitting gales of explosive laughter. And yet, after midnight, five pálinkas into the evening, one can eavesdrop on a group of factory workers telling jokes about a little fox meeting a bear in the woods and stealing his bicycle. Even these jokes are imported from Russian tradition, albeit with a slight linguistic spin that makes 'bicycle' rhyme with – well, you get the idea.

For an east European people, one would expect at least some ethnic jokes. Hungarians do without, preferring jokes about the stupidity of policemen or poking fun at the priapic Székelys of Transylvania. Of course, there are a few objectionable dialect jokes concerning gypsies and soap, and everyone knows a few jokes concerning Kohn and Grun, the archetypal old Jewish guys living on Dohány utca in District VII.

Kohn is walking on Dohány utca and sees that Grun has opened a pastry shop. Kohn goes to the door, and sees a sign: 'We do not serve Jews'. On entering, he asks: 'Grun, you open a confectioner's on Dohány utca and you don't serve Jews! Are you crazy?' Grun says: 'Calm down. Have you tasted my pastries yet?'

During the years of Communist rule a sly and cynical humour was the common person's weapon against the Communists and Russian occupiers.

The teacher in a Communist school asks the students 'If Capitalism is the act of Man exploiting Man, how can we define Marxism?' Moriczka raises his hand: 'Marxism is exactly the opposite!'

Alas, since 1990 a lack of a common enemy has meant a lack of common laughs. But political humour is topical and since the ascendancy of the right-wing FIDESZ-led government, Budapest has at least come up with one new political joke:

What's the difference between God and Prime Minister Viktor Orbán? God doesn't want to be Viktor Orbán.

But for the most part, Magyar humour remains impenetrable to the outsider. Grab a copy of the weekly satire magazine *Hócipő* ('Snowshoes') if you want to watch incomprehensible humour in action. Take it to a pub, leave it on a table, and watch as the locals erupt in hopeless fits of hilarity. Then ask them to explain the jokes. They can't. You'll never understand. Welcome to Hungary.

Folk & Folklore

Urban Hungary is still not far removed from its rural roots – packed dance houses are just one facet of a thriving folk culture.

When Béla Bartók and Zoltán Kodály roamed the Hungarian countryside collecting folk songs at the turn of the century, they were not just creating the science of modern ethnomusicology out of thin air. They were also helping to cement the identity of the modern Hungarian nation to its rural folk traditions. Twentieth-century Hungarian culture still flexes between its classical and folk traditions in art, literature and music. Many urban Hungarians are not far removed from their rural roots, and often all it takes is a fiddler and a shot of home brew to make an urban modern office worker jump into an ancient village boot-slapping dance.

Of course, with tourist dollars in view, Hungarians can turn on the kitsch with a vengeance. Since Communist times there has been a tendency to pack bus-loads of tourists out to the Puszta for 'genuine folkloric shows' that include a bit of costumed dancing, a gypsy orchestra, a horse show with traditionally costumed *csikós* cowboys, and dinner at a country *csárda*. Avoid such excursions.

If you really want to see a thatched village full of peasants in embroidered vests and odd hats dancing to discordant fiddles, you will have to do what Hungarians do – go to Transylvania, the multi-ethnic northern region of Romania that has managed to avoid much of the twentieth century. Modern villages in Hungary tend to be much of a muchness since the Communists provided cheap loans to replace traditional thatched homes with boring, box-like housing. Traditions do survive, but tend only to be passed on when there is nothing good on cable TV. Nevertheless, within an hour of Budapest there are several villages that come close to being living museums.

VENERABLE VILLAGES

Hollókő, in the Nógrád hill country, is a well-preserved Palóc village with old-style wooden houses, a ruined castle and a magnificent wooden church to which the older women still wear folk costumes on Sunday. Peasants sell embroideries and beadwork in front of their houses, and visitors can stay in peasant homes renovated in traditional style. Hollókő is on the UNESCO list of world treasures and there are bus tours to the region. Check with local travel agents for information. Other villages in the Galga valley and Nógrád region are less spectacular, but just as authentic.

Other village regions worth seeing include the Őrség, near Szentgotthárd on the Austrian border, or the Szatmár and Nyírség region near the Soviet

Modern office workers jump into an ancient village boot-slapping dance.

Buda's acoustic oasis

Tucked away in south Buda, the Fonó Budai Zeneház is one of the few places one can go to hear live music that doesn't fit the 'boom-boom' commercial beat of the late twentieth century. The Fonó ('Spinning Room') marches to its own rhythm, and that means jazz, folk and experiments in-between. Amplifiers are not forbidden in the house, but nobody here seems to like or need them. The Fonó is an acoustic oasis in a desert of digital remixes.

The Fonó is a rare success in the complex world of presenting live music in Budapest. In the early 1990s, live music was popping up everywhere as people realised that there were no more commissars to prevent 'unchaperoned' social events. It didn't last, and by 1998 most of the decent music clubs had been closed by the city, taken over by the mafia or given way to discos. Meanwhile, a talented bunch of folk and jazz musicians, desperate for something they could call a full-time job, managed to turn the canteen of a former aluminium factory into a concert hall. They added a recording studio, shaped up the bar, invited artists to decorate the walls, and hoped that quality would offset their out of the way location in a sea of Buda council blocks.

Today the Fonó is just about the only place where a dedicated music head can drop in and hear something new and non-commercial. The Fonó is also the only place where one can count on hearing live traditional folk in a concert setting. At least twice a week there is a casual dance or concert, with wild, whining fiddles, groaning basses, and tables full of illegal workers from Transylvania screaming out their folk songs after too many drinks. From 1997 until

Fonó – *wall of sound.*

1999 the Fonó sponsored a series called 'The Last Hour'. Each week they brought in a different village band representing disappearing traditions of Transylvania or Slovakia, fed and housed them for a week, recorded their repertoire, and gave them a concert and dance party. The best of the programme is being released on a series of CDs on the Fonó's own label.

Jumping from strength to strength, the Fonó expanded to include one of the best jazz and world music CD shops in town, fixed up the garden stage area in the back for summer concerts, and took over the old factory hangar behind the club for larger concerts and rave events. There's also a bar with that most un-Hungarian of facilities: a non-smoking section.

Fonó Budai Zeneház
XI. Sztregova utca 12 (206 5300). Tram 47.
Open *CD shop & café* 10am-midnight Tue-Sat.
Concerts *from* Ft500. **No credit cards.** Some English spoken.

---

border. Closer to home, villages to the north of Buda in the Pilis hills, particularly Csobánka and Pomáz (on the HÉV line near Szentendre), are pleasant for an afternoon walk. Both are home to multi-ethnic populations with Serbian, Slovak, Sváb German, Gypsy and Hungarian backgrounds.

West of Budapest is a series of pleasant villages that are easy to reach by local bus from Moszkva tér. Budakeszi (bus 22) was originally a Sváb-German village known as Wudigeiss, but today is more or less a suburb of Buda, with restaurants and beer gardens for the yuppies who are snatching up peasant homes. You can see ornately carved wooden gates at the entrances to homes built by the Székelys who were settled here from Romanian Bukovina in the 1940s.

But the easiest way to see old ladies wearing strange embroidered things on their heads is to go to any of the vegetable markets that ring the downtown area. At Bosnyák tér (bus 7), the peasant women who sell in the rear of the market continue to wear folk costumes, as do those at the Skála Open Market in Buda (end of the tram line 4).

Gypsies

One group of Hungarians that does preserve a visible sense of folkloric identity are the gypsies, or Roma. Stereotypes of Hungary always include the romanticised gypsy musician, serenading noblewomen beneath moonlit castle windows. The truth is, Hungary is home to at least half a million gypsies and their life is anything but romantic.

The Roma are essentially a European nationality without a nation. Their language, Romanes, is related to northern Indian languages such as Hindi and Punjabi, and it is conjectured that they left India due to war or famine around the eighth century. The majority of Roma in Hungary are referred to as Oláh, or Vlach gypsies (*vlashiko roma* in their own language) who came into Hungary after the abolition of slavery in Romania in 1855. They guard their traditions closely, and the women continue to wear the traditional voluminous skirts. Many came to Budapest in the postwar period to find work on construction sites.

The Hungarian 'musician gypsies' form a separate group among Roma, with their own dialect of Romanes and a hereditary tradition of professional musicianship. Few still speak Romanes, and most work in agriculture and industry since the market for violin bands has shrunk.

As all over Europe, Hungary's gypsies face massive discrimination. Most live at or below the poverty level, finding only menial or unskilled employment. Many Hungarians see gypsies as nothing but thieves and beggars. But although the most visible gypsies may be the women begging coins downtown, the vast majority are working in regular, if low-paid, jobs.

Today gypsies are organising to demand basic rights. There are Roma political parties and schools for gypsy children, taught in Romanes. A gypsy cultural revival has blossomed and bands such as Kalyi Jag, Ando Drom and Romanyi Rota have produced tapes and CDs of traditional Roma music, predominantly vocal backed with guitars, mandolins and milk-churn percussion. There is also Fekete Vonat, a gypsy rap group. *See page 204* **Goulash gangstas**.

Folk arts

Collections

Museum of Ethnography
Néprajzi Múzeum
V. Kossuth Lajos tér 12 (332 6340). M2 Kossuth tér/Tram 2. **Open** 10am-5.30pm Tue-Sun.
Admission Ft300; Ft150 students, children.
Housed in a beautiful nineteenth-century palace, the permanent exhibition includes costumes, household objects and tools from all of Hungary's historical regions, but most of the accompanying information is only in Hungarian. *See also chapter* **Museums**.

The Open Air Village Museum
Szabadságforrás út, Szentendre (06 26 312 304). HÉV to Szentendre then bus 8. **Open** *1 Apr-31 Oct* 9am-5pm Tue-Sun. **Admission** Ft350; Ft150 children.
Designed in the 1950s to make 'ethnographic' research easier by transporting village homes to Szentendre, this Skansen-like village exhibits peasant homes with original furnishings, wooden churches and farm implements. *See also chapter* **Museums**.

Purchasing folk arts

The state-owned folklore shops (*Népművészeti bolt*) are full of folk-costumed dolls, factory-produced weaving and machine-carved woodwork. Some stuff is worthwhile: plates painted in floral patterns or the dull-finished black ceramics of the Great Plains are good buys, but a visit to a flea market will produce finer quality for half the price.

Markets such as the Bolhapiac (*see chapter* **Shopping & Services**), the Nagy Vásárcsarnok (*see chapter* **Sightseeing**) and the various district produce stalls are also places to buy folk textiles. These make convenient gifts: easy to pack, light and hard to break in transit. Since most items are for local use, prices are affordable if you avoid buying them in obvious tourist spots like Váci utca.

You'll recognise the peasant ladies selling them by their dress. White kerchiefs and red skirts signal those from Transylvanian Szék, and yellow-kerchiefed ones in green wool are from Kalotaszeg. *See also chapter* **Shopping & Services**.

Folk music & dance

Budapest is one of the few capitals where you can still find an active traditional music and folk dance scene. A visit to a 'Dance House' (*Táncház*) is one of the best ways to meet locals and learn directly what it is that makes them so, well, Hungarian.

The Dance House Movement began in the 1970s among young Hungarians sick of dictated versions of folklore and the syrupy style of restaurant music favoured by programmers. Fiddler Béla Halmos and singer Ferenc Sebő pioneered the revival by going to elder village musicians to encourage a link with traditions still strong in the country. The search for pure sources led to Transylvania, where isolation had preserved the context of old music.

By the 1970s, folk music was becoming rare in Hungary. Old women still sang, but their grandchildren preferred the Beatles to ancient ballads. Collectivisation put shepherds and their music out of business and recorded music was killing off village gypsy bands. Younger musicians revived the context of traditional music at the right time, and soon it was a mark of rebellion to have a fiddle band at your wedding or to know a few old dances.

Back in Budapest, urban bands opened up Dance Houses on the Transylvanian model – rented rooms where young people made their own entertainment with fiddles, dancing and lots of illicit plum brandy. The most famous of the Dance House bands, Muzsikás, used the raw, traditional sounds of the Transylvanian string bands, the shepherds' goatskin bagpipes, and the directness of folk texts sung by Márta Sebestyén to protest against the government's strongarm cultural policies, providing a musical voice to the dissident movement in a way that local rock never did.

Today the Dance Houses are still going, but the level of attendance is a dim echo of pre-capitalist days, when thousands would crowd the dance-floors in a show of national pride and defiance. Faced with competition from discos and TV, and lamed by the fact that folk music is now required in schools, musicians now sometimes outnumber the dancers.

Bands that play the capital weekly include Téka, the Ökrös Band, Kalamajka and Méta. Basic instrumentation includes lead violin, gut-strung bass and the kontra, a three-string viola with a flat bridge that enables it to play full, rich chords in the skewed rhythms of Transylvania. Extra fiddles, cimbalom (hammered dulcimer), duda (double chanter bagpipes), hurdy gurdy or reeds may round out the ensemble. Traditional gypsy string bands from Transylvanian villages also make regular appearances in Budapest's Dance Houses and bands such as Kalyi Jag, Ando Drom and Ternipe perform the music of Hungary's contemporary gypsy communities. Keep an eye on **Almássy tér Recreation Centre** for these events.

Dance Houses tend to be open from October to the end of May. There is usually a weekend summer Dance House on somewhere but venues change, and few tourist services keep info on the folk scene. Check the English-language website of the Folk Dancers' Professional Association for info on Dance House times and locations: www.datanet.hu/tanchaz/thmain.htm. Admission is usually around Ft250-Ft450. In addition to those listed below, there are also Dance House nights at Fonó, especially on Wednesdays when traditional village bands are featured. *See page 32* **Buda's acoustic oasis**.

Csángó Dance House

Marczibányi téri Művelődési Ház, XII Marczibányi tér 5A, (212 5789). M2 Moszkva tér. **Open** *Sept-June* 8pm-midnight Wed.

The Csángós are two pockets of Hungarians, one in the Gyimes region of Transylvania and one in the Szeret valley of Moldavia, who play a rough, energetic music reflecting the oldest Magyar traditions. Using instruments such as the gardon (a cello-shaped string instrument hit with a stick), the koboz (similar to the Arabic oud but smaller and louder), fiddles and Moldavian flutes, Csángó music, as played by house band Tatros, has injected the Budapest folk scene with a loud rocking rhythm.

Kalamajka Dance House

Belvárosi Ifjúsági Művelődési Ház, V. Molnár utca 9, (317 5928). M3 Ferenciek tere. **Open** *Sept-June* 8pm-1am Sat.

The biggest weekend dance, with dancing and instruction on the second floor and jam sessions and serious pálinka abuse on the fourth. The Kalamajka band is led by Béla Halmos, who started the Dance House movement in the 1970s, and usually there are guest performances by traditional villagers or visiting renowned folk bands.

Méta Dance House

Józsefvárosi Club, VIII. Somogyi Béla utca 13 (318 7930). M3 Blaha Lujza tér/tram 4, 6. **Open** *Sept-May* 7pm-midnight Sun.

A small weekend get-together in the basement of a local school. Excellent band with a woman lead fiddler plays music from Szatmár.

Muzsikás Club

Marczibányi téri Művelődési Ház, XII. Marczibányi tér 5/a (212 5789). M2 Moszkva tér. **Open** *Sept-May* 8pm-midnight Thur.

Hosted by Muzsikás. Little dancing, but a chance to hear them jam in a relaxed atmosphere.

Almássy tér Sunday Dances

Almássy téri Szabadidőközpont, VII. Almássy tér 6 (352 1572). M2 Blaha Lujza tér/tram 4, 6. **Open** 6pm-midnight Sun.

From 6pm to 10pm folkies dance to electric Greeks Sirtos in the main hall, while upstairs a small fanatic band of Magyar dancers twirl to the Kalotaszeg sounds of the Berkó Band until midnight.

Festivals

Best are the Kaláka festivals in Miskolc and Sopron, which also showcase foreign acts. The National Folk Festival (Országos Táncháztalálkozó) is held at the Sportcsarnok in March – information from the Association of Folk Dancers (Szakmai Ház; 201 3766) or the Dance House Union's website: www.datanet.hu/tanchaz/thmain.htm.

Performances by folk dance troupes such as the State Folk Ensemble or the Bartók Dance Ensemble most often take place at the Budai Vigadó, I. Corvin tér 8 (201 5928, M2 Batthyány tér) or the Fővárosi Culture Centre, XI. Fehérvári út 47 (203 3868). **Almássy tér Recreation Centre** also hosts special folk music events.

Almássy tér Recreation Centre

Almássy téri Szabadidőközpont
VII. Almássy tér 6 (352 1572). M2 Blaha Lujza tér.

Specialist shops

The best folk and world music CD selection in town can be found in the shop at Fonó. *See page 32* **Buda's acoustic oasis**.

Pro Folk

VII. Dohány utca 74 (351 3341). M2 Blaha Lujza tér/tram 4, 6/bus 7. **Open** 10am-5pm Mon-Thur; 10am-2pm Fri. Some English spoken. **No credit cards.**

Sells Magyar musical necessities as hurdy gurdies, zithers and bagpipes, plus music books and CDs.

Kodály Zoltán Music Store

V. Múzeum körút 21 (317 3347). M2 Astoria/tram 47, 49/bus 7. **Open** 10am-6pm Mon-Fri; 10am-2pm Sat. **Credit** AmEx, EC, V.

Widest selection of Hungarian folk, plus world music, classical and lots of old vinyl.

Architecture

Reinventions, reconstructions and houses that speak Hungarian – there's more to Budapest's architecture than meets the eye.

Frigyes Feszl's ornamentation on the Vigadó.

In 1904, leading architect Béla Lajta complained about the eclecticism that dominated Budapest: 'The visitor from abroad should find houses here that speak Hungarian, and those houses should teach him to speak Hungarian himself.' The sentiment has been echoed by critics as diverse as Stalinist-era minister of culture József Révai (who ordered 'Socialist content with national form') and organicist Imre Makovecz, Hungary's only practising architect of international renown and the profession's leading dissident of the Kádár era.

National self-image is paralleled by a *bricolage* urbanism. The reconstruction of the Castle District and churches that survived Ottoman rule juxtapose fragments of contrasting eras with cubist simultaneity. More subtle is the montage of space. Examine the turn-of-the-century capital and you'll find Vienna and Paris. After World War I Berlin, Rome and Moscow sneak into view, though often where you'd least expect it. Today, despite its builders' nationalist intentions, Budapest stands in for other cities as a film location. Its relationship to Vienna is the most curious. Textbooks tell of a his-

toric antipathy to the Habsburg's imperial capital, but a careful viewing of certain scenes from film noir classic *The Third Man* (1949) shot amid the ruins of postwar Vienna reveals a mirror image of this one – elements of Budapest apparently in reverse.

1686-1867

This fusion of detail had an early precedent. Shards of Gothic, Renaissance and Turkish architecture were integrated in the rebuilding of Buda after the Habsburg reconquest in 1686. Reconstruction of the Castle District after World War II uncovered many more remains, which were then combined with the restoration. Baroque façades, particularly on I. Úri utca, often include Gothic windows and door frames. Reconstructed merchants' houses can be found at I. Tárnok utca 14 and 16 and distinctive *sedilias* (seats for servants inside the gateway) at I. Országház utca 9, I. Szentháromság tér 5 and 7. Traces of Turkish rule are the most elusive. Many churches were converted into mosques during the century-and-a-half occupation, yet turned back when the Habsburgs recaptured the city, and their minarets were destroyed. Jesuits even consecrated the tiny domed **Tomb of Gül Baba**. The **Inner City Parish Church** still contains a *mihrab* (prayer niche) and the Alsó Víziváros Parish Church on I. Fő utca 32 displays distinctive ogee-shaped windows on its south wall. The most enduring Turkish contribution to the city are the bathhouses. The **Rudas, Rác** and **Király** baths are still all in use under their original copper domes.

Habsburg reconquest found Budapest with a largely Protestant population. The Baroque was critical to the counter reformation. Its curving sensuality and rich iconography of churches such as the **Church of St Anne** were a seductive contrast to Protestant austerity. Catholic authorities revived the medieval cult of the Holy Kings to legitimise Habsburg rule. Frescoes and altar statues of István, László and Imre can be seen in the Krisztinaváros parish church (I. Krisztina tér), while Szent István's Holy Right Hand is on show in the **Basilica of St Stephen**. Rich terracottas, pinks and ochres, greens and blues complement the elegant carving and ironwork of the aristocratic mansions. The **Museum of Music History**, once the home of the Erdődy family, is a particularly fine example. Houses in the *copfstil*, a Hungarian rococo, can be found at I. Fő utca 20 and I. Batthyány tér 3. Their undulating roofs with tiny oval windows were mimicked in the vernacular architecture of the Puszta. The largest secular baroque buildings were military. The former City Hall at V. Városház utca 9-11 began life as a hospital for veterans of the war against the Turks, while the **Citadella** on Gellérthegy was constructed to assert Habsburg control after the Hungarian defeat in 1849. The grid street layout of the Lipótváros bears witness to the Új épület, a massive Habsburg barracks that stood on the site of today's **Szabadság tér**.

Lipótváros was the first area of Pest subjected to the rationalism of Enlightenment planning. The Embellishment Committee, set up in 1808, dignified the emerging polis with the neo-classical style. The identification of the city with Athena followed – a virgin goddess in sympathy with the city's autonomy and a divine patron of the craft of building. Statues of Athena can be found in the courtyards of the City Hall and in the covered arcade on V. József Attila utca. The austerity of neo-classicism implies a subtle dissidence, an aesthetic affront to the baroque of aristocratic Buda. The desire for independence and prosperity is clear in the surviving neo-classical monuments. Pannónia, with the Hungarian coat of arms on her shield, sits in the tympanum of the **National Museum**. Mihály Pollack's Grecian design followed the idiom set by the British Museum and the Altes Museum in Berlin and was the fourth museum of its kind in the world. The 1830s also saw the construction of the Chain Bridge, Hungary's first permanent crossing over the Danube. The Habsburg court branded Palatine Archduke Joseph, the Emperor's Regent, a rebel for his support in improving the city's infrastructure. It's no accident that the first neo-classical buildings in Pest were Protestant churches. The Lutheran church on Deák tér dates from 1809.

1867-1918

In the decades of the Dual Monarchy after 1867, Budapest expanded with astonishing speed. Preparation for the 1896 Millennial celebrations spurred the building of the capital's most important monuments. Though he died in 1891, architect Miklós Ybl emerged as the leading light of the city's transformation. His funeral procession, which paid respects at his major monuments, was literally *in memoriam* of his impact on the city. The **Opera**, Basilica of St Stephen, Ybl Kiosk (now the **Várkert Casino**) and the Várkertbazár opposite, all draw heavily on Renaissance symbolism and allegory in their detailing. The **Parliament** and the reconstruction of the **Mátyás templom** also date from this time.

Monumental planning was designed to legitimise the city's new status as an imperial capital. Boulevards such as Andrássy út, Bajcsy-Zsilinszky út and the Nagykörút carved through the poorer areas of the city and facilitated the policing of growing unrest. A selective reinvention of Hungarian history pervades these new monuments. Styles deployed in the neo-Gothic Mátyás templom and neo-Romanesque **Fisherman's Bastion** romanticised medieval Christian values. The **Turul Statue** by the Castle and the intricate ironwork of the Parliament gates allude to the mythical pagan-divine ancestry of Árpád, legendary founder of the Hungarian nation. The spirit of experimentation that characterised the 1896 exhibition pavilions exerted a profound impact on architecture in the years that followed, though the Vajdahunyad Castle (now housing the **Agriculture Museum**) is all that remains of the exhibition structures that filled the park.

Buildings were designed from pattern books. Gothic and Renaissance-style entrance halls contrast neo-baroque ornamentation, but the luxury of the now crumbling courtyard blocks of Districts V, VI and VII is superficial. Façades decked with cherubs, devils and voluptuous caryatids hide courtyards with the sparsest of detail, where entire families often lived in only one room. Allusions to

Miksa Róth's Hungária mosaic shimmers above the former Turkish Banking house on V. Szervita tér.

alchemy and freemasonry abound – iconography of the national movement. The entrance to V. Báthory utca 24, where sphinxes sit on Hermes' winged helmet, is particularly intriguing. Colossal debts incurred in the city's expansion are reflected in the opulence of financial institutions. The proportions of the former Stock and Commodity Exchange on the west side of Szabadság tér (now the headquarters of Magyar Televízió) were deliberately distorted to overawe with the power of money. The former headquarters of the Domestic Savings Bank (now the **British Embassy**) is one of the few accessible to the visitor. The magnificent undulating glass ceiling of the former cashiers' hall was restored during a 1993 refurbishment.

New construction techniques were deployed to the full. The **Great Market Hall** and the Eiffel company's Nyugati station (1877) both revel in a palatial use of iron and glass. Experimentation was also a driving force behind art nouveau. Emil Vidor's apartment blocks at VI. Városligeti fasor 24 and V. Honvéd utca 3 are close to Belgian contemporaries, while the influence of the Viennese secession is marked in the simplicity and elegance of the American Embassy (V. Szabadság tér 10-12) and Luxus department store at V. Vörösmarty tér 3. The geometric brick detailing of XIV. Cházár András utca 5 draws on Czech Cubism. Decorative arts and fine craftsmanship were integral to the turn-of-the-century oeuvre. Zsolnay tiles, manufactured in Pécs, were important in creating a distinctive sense of place and frost-resistant glazes ensured that their rich colours survived. The rich interior of the **Zeneakadémia** exploits the potential of the material. Curvaceous iron doorways with flower and bird motifs can be spotted all over the city centre, notably at **Gresham Palace**, and organic forms underly the interior of the Philanthia flower shop (V. Váci utca 9). Stained glass by pre-Raphaelite József Rippl-Rónai can be seen in the **Ernst Múzeum**, while Miksa Róth's Hungária mosaic shimmers above the former Turkish Banking House at V. Szervita tér 3.

Questions of national identity preoccupied intellectuals throughout the nineteenth century and parallel attempts to develop a national style of architecture. Disillusionment after the 1848 defeat led to the belief that Hungary's salvation lay in its eastern origins and folk culture. Frigyes Feszl's ornamentation for the **Vigadó** included frog fastenings from Hussar's uniforms, the faces of Hungarian peasants and Tibetan heads. The **Central Synagogue** is in a Moorish-inspired Romantic style. Orientalism resonated later in the designs of the **Párizsi Udvar** and the **Museum of Applied Arts**. Ancient Middle Eastern symbolism is evident in Béla Lajta's mausoleums in the Jewish part of Újköztemető and **Kerepesi** cemeteries and in his motifs on the Parisiana nightclub, now the **Új Színház**.

Ödön Lechner made it his life's cause to develop a distinctive Hungarian architecture. He believed that the new idiom should emerge with the use of modern materials and structural applications, yet also made a serious study of Hungarian folk art, which he brought to life in three dimensions. The gracious curves of the **Museum of Applied Arts** and the magnificent **Former Royal Post Office Savings Bank** are enhanced by soft colours and light that give them a magical aura. The playful surreality of his decoration is comparable to that of Antoni Gaudí. A group of architects called A Fiatalok ('The Young Ones'), students of Lechner, looked to medieval folk architecture as the basis for an authentic national style and conducted detail-collecting expeditions much like the musical odysseys of Bartók and Kodály. Their style has become known as the 'National Romantic' and can be seen in the **Werkerle Housing Estate** in Kispest, built between 1909-14. Béla Lajta pursued an urban version of the Hungarian idiom. His Rózsavölgyi House at V. Szervita tér 5 prefigures the internationalist avant garde. Here, and on the magnificent doors of his Trade School (VIII. Vas utca 11), the use of folk art is purely decorative, while the dynamic corner curves of VIII. Népszínház utca 19 presage Expressionist form. The tension between these two trends – urban modernist versus rural romantic – continued to dominate the architecture of the interwar period.

1918-45

Conservative tastes dominated building in the 1920s. Garden suburbs sprang up under the Horthy regime for refugees fleeing territories lost after Trianon. The residents of Szent Imre Kertváros in Pestszentlőrinc (District XVIII), which was intended to reflect the traditional communities they had left behind, paid for its construction themselves. Though now in a sad state of disrepair, many of the tiny houses mimic the neo-baroque mansions of the aristocracy. Public buildings of the Horthy era, such as Szent Imre Church (XI. Villányi út 23-25), as well as many of the larger mansions on Gellérthegy, were also designed in a neo-baroque style. In contrast to its original anti-puritan allure, the style was deployed here in reaction to the liberalism and 'immorality' of the city.

The Hungarian avant garde of the 1920s was centred around the journal *Ma* (*Today*), edited by Lajos Kassák, whose Futurist poems and Constructivist paintings reside at the **Kassák**

Decorative use of folk art on the doors of Béla Lajta's Trade School.

Múzeum. The Horthy dictatorship forced Kassák and other leading lights into exile. László Moholy-Nagy and Marcel Breuer found fame at the Bauhaus, as did Ernst Kállai in the Der Stijl group. But Lajos Kozma, a colleague of Lajta and founder of the Hungarian Werkbund, stayed behind. His career was stifled for over a decade because of political involvement in 1919. Farkas Molnár later returned and with József Fischer led the Hungarian branch of the CIAM. Molnár's villa at XII. Lejtő utca 2a won a prize in the Milan Triennial of 1933, while Fischer's villas at II. Baba utca 14 (now a children's hospital) and II. Szépvölgyi út 88b are key examples of Expressionist modernism. Kozma's **Átrium** cinema and apartment block can be found at II. Margit körút 55. All three architects were among those who designed the 1931 **Napraforgó utca experimental housing estate**. Margit körút boasts several other gems from the 1930s. The former Manfred Weiss Pension Fund apartment at No. 17 displays a futuristic elegance, with lifts in glass tubes centred in the elliptical stairwell, while the angry red Jellinek building (No. 67) points to the influence of Russian Constructivism. Újlipótváros, particularly the area around Szent István Park, became a showcase for 1930s modernity. Strict supervision over scale and adherence to building regulations engendered a cultivated rationality despite the speculative nature of development. Popular modernism is at its most refined at XIII. Pozsonyi út 51-53.

The Modern movement also reflected the political complexity of the interwar period and hints at totalitarianism. A fierce art deco style characterises the former transformer station and apartments of the Electricity Board built in 1931 (V. Markó utca 9/Honvéd utca 22-24), and defines the façade of the **Hungarian Museum of Electrotechnics**. VII. Madách tér was built on the scale of dictators and Zarathustra looks down with disdain from the apartment block at VI. Bajcsy-Zsilinszky út 19. The monumental classicism of Mussolini creeps into the design of the **Palatinus Strand**, Gyula Rimanóczy's church and bus station on II. Pasaréti tér as well as the **Budapest Sportcsarnok**. Classicism enabled Rimanóczy to gain major commissions well into the 1950s.

1945-53

Shock at war devastation was intensified by subsequent social upheaval. Rebuilding Budapest became a priority of psychological and political importance. The policy of reconstruction, which took decades, was to restore monuments to their pre-war state. Restoration of the Mátyás templom, for instance, adhered to Schulek's original design. The need for a sense of historical continuity was exploited by the Rákosi regime and turned into a strategy for the maintenance of power. Radical replanning of Budapest didn't get very far, but the regime did attack the 'the visual landscape of everyday life'. Streets were renamed rather than obliterated and the names of Communist leaders were used alongside those of Hungarian national heroes. The occasional corner still displays the old street signs,

József Finta's Bank Center – high-tech construction that refuses to engage with the city.

crossed through since the demise of Communism. Shopfronts were another battleground. The campaign to end competition between individual shops led to the destruction of many art nouveau interiors. Soviet war memorials turned Budapest into a necropolis. Tombs were built in public places such as the park on XII. Csörsz utca and Ludovika Gardens in Csepel (District XXI). Statues of Stalin and Lenin once standing in the **City Park** were infused with an almost religious significance. Stalin was pulled down in 1956, but other statues, including the Soviet soldier from the **Liberty Statue**, can now be found in the **Statue Park**. **Népstadion**, the major monument of the Rákosi regime, was designed to express the ideology of the Ready to Work and Fight movement – 50,000 people gave their labour 'voluntarily' to build it.

Modernist architecture, initially favoured for new building, was denounced as 'incomprehensible' by the Rákosi regime. The Le Corbusier-inspired trade union headquarters (VII. Dózsa György út 84a) and the parliamentary offices at V. Széchenyi rakpart 19 were the most vehemently condemned. Erzsébet tér bus station was also lambasted but became the first post-1945 building to be protected as a national monument. Adapting to the leftward lurch, architects tempered party dictats of socialist realism with Italian modernism and the Scandinavian classicism of Asplund. The College of Fine Arts (II. Zugligeti út 9-25) and the Dubbing Film Studio (II. Hűvösvölgyi út 68) have both been recommended for national protection. Large-scale housing development was begun as late as 1955. Flats on estates such as XIV. Kerepesi út and IX. Üllői út were comfortable but small, the absence of privacy compounded by thin walls. Social activity was meant to take place in the workplace and in 'culture houses' such as the **Almássy tér Recreation Centre** which are still important in city life.

1953-99

The Kádár government was quick to eradicate signs of the 1956 uprising, although bulletholes can be seen down many sidestreets and the **New York Kávéház**, its façade smashed into by a tank, is still unrepaired today. The thaw after Stalin's death in 1953 had already begun to work its way into the architecture of the city. Oszkár Kauffman's Madách Színház at VII. Erzsébet körút 31 blends socialist realism with art deco traits. The angular asymmetry of Constructivism and Expressionism returned. Gábor Bachman's deconstructivist designs of the 1980s fragment the style to expose the banality of the Kádár-era 'good life' epitomised by eszpresszó bars and the new-style apartment blocks, such as VIII. Üllői út 60-62, IX. Üllői út 81, and the Lottóház at 37-39. The typographic exuberance of the last surviving neon on

the Nagykörút is cosmetic, announcing simply 'Shoe shop' or 'Food'. Yet architects of the time seized the opportunity to catch up. The Therapeutic Equipment Factory (1963) at XIII. Dózsa György út 144 displays many of the fashionable forms of contemporary western modernism, while the ribbed concrete vaults of Moszkva tér metro station trumpet the achievement of completion.

By the late-1960s architecture had been relegated to a subsection of the building industry. Prefabricated concrete housing estates such as József Attila Housing Estate on IX. Üllői út were the result. Antal Csikvári's 1974 industrial complex at III. Bécsi út 186, a sculptural mass of raw concrete, is a welcome articulation of individuality, while the work of Imre Makovecz, at that time excommunicated from the profession, has since brought contemporary Hungarian architecture to international attention. Makovecz claims to invoke the magic latent in peasant folk culture. His houses on Sashegy in District XII and on II. Törökvész lejtő draw on the symbolic form of Siberian nomad shelters. His approach is best suited to metaphysical exploration, as in his interior for the Mortuary Chapel in **Farkasréti Cemetery**.

These days the spotlight has returned to Budapest's shopfronts and interiors. Western retail logos and brash fast-food chains dominate the Nagykörút. Old-style shopfronts and signs are again symbolising resistance, this time to rampant commercialism. Eszpresszó bars from the 1950s, such as the **Bambi**, hold out against change, while the brass-and-mirror tack in newer bars feigns membership of the affluent west. **Café Mozart**, the ultimate in postmodern indelicacy, reduces coffeehouse culture to a mythologised 'central European experience'. But a sense of irony prevails in the pastiche. **Marxim** pizzeria serves up Stalinist kitsch with tomato ketchup. The **Statue Park** attempts to construct a critique of Stalinism while treating the statues with dignity in their obsolescence.

The city has been reduced to a theatrical backdrop. Confronted by commercialisation, crumbling nineteenth-century architecture achieves a dignity it lacked in its prime. The 1994 collapse of an apartment building on VI. Ó utca highlighted the poor state of the city's infrastructure. Historic landmarks of the poorer areas, such as the **Gozsdu udvar** (*see page 62* **Enigma of the udvar**), are literally rotting away. While George Morriose's **Institut Français** enhances the Buda waterfront, postmodern Hungarian architecture has little to recommend it. The scale of high-tech constructions such as József Finta's **Grand Hotel Korvinus Kempinski**, his police HQ at XIII. Teve utca or his Bank Center on V. Bank utca, boosts the dramatic tension of the city but refuses to engage with it. Shut out, the city turns its back.

Budapest by Season

Slaughter a pig, spray someone with perfume, deify a mummified right hand – Budapest has rituals for all seasons.

Like other central European cities, Budapest is bitter in winter and blazing hot in high summer, with a mood that changes accordingly. Spring and autumn offer the gentlest, most palatable weather. In August many locals leave town.

Meanwhile Hungarian traditions have survived two World Wars and 40 years of Communism. Although western greeting cards conglomerates try and push new traditions such as Valentine's Day, Hungarians aren't really interested, preferring to honour Saint Stephen's Day. Whitsun has only recently come back into the calendar. Christmas is a stay-at-home-with-the-family affair, New Year more a street party. Every day at the workplace is an excuse for celebrating some colleague's Name Day, as important a social event as birthdays.

Information & tickets

For information on events, try the English-language weekly *Budapest Sun*, or the Hungarian *Pesti Est* or *Open*, pocket-sized listings weeklies available free at bars and venues around town.

Central Theater Booking Office

VI. Andrássy út 18 (312 0000). M1 Operaház. **Open** 9am-1pm, 2pm-6pm, Mon-Thur; 9am-5pm Fri. Some English spoken.
Branch: II. Moszkva tér 3 (212 5678).

Tourinform

V. Sütő utca 2 (317 9800). M1, M2, M3 Deák tér. **Open** 9am-7pm Mon-Fri; 9am-4pm Sat, Sun. English spoken.

Vigadó Ticket Service

Vörösmarty tér 1 (327 4322). M1 Vörösmarty tér. **Open** 9am-7pm Mon-Fri; 10am-3pm Sat, Sun. English spoken.
Tickets for virtually everything.

Public holidays

New Year's Day (1 Jan); **Revolution Day** (15 Mar); **Easter Monday**; **International Labour Day** (1 May); **Whit Monday**; **Saint Stephen's Day** (20 Aug); **Remembrance Day** (23 Oct); **Christmas Day, Boxing Day** (25, 26 Dec).

Spring

The biggest cultural event in the calendar, the Budapest Spring Festival, ushers in more modest counterparts nationwide, and signals the patter of little feet – the first bus-loads of Japanese tourists.

March 15 Public Holiday

Revolution Day commemorates poet Sándor Petőfi reciting his *Nemzeti Dal* (national song) on the steps of the National Museum in 1848, the event commonly held to have launched the national revolution, although according to some histories, he actually only read the poem at the Pilvax coffeehouse. Gatherings at Petőfi's statue were illegal until 1990, current mayor Gábor Demszky receiving a serious biffing by police in his dissident days. Now he stands with an ironic smile on his face in the official ceremony with prominent politicians outside the National Museum. The city gets decked out in red, white and green, big time.

Budapest Spring Festival

Tickets & information from the Budapesti Fesztiválközpont, VIII. Rákóczi út 65 VI/66 (333 2337/fax 210 5906). M2 Blaha Lujza tér/tram 4/6. **Box office** *Feb-Mar* 10am-6pm Mon-Fri.
The most prestigious event in the arts calendar. Once a bonanza of internationally renowned talent from the world of classical music, more a fortnight's showcase for domestic artists from the world of music, painting, sculpture and drama in these days of budget-tightening. Some dance and folk acts are also featured at venues around the city. *See chapters* **Theatre & Dance** *and* **Music: Classical & Opera**.
Website: www.bmc.hu

Easter Monday

Public holiday
The most drunken occasion in a calendar soaked with them, Easter Monday is when the menfolk go door-to-door indulging in the pagan rite of *locsolkodás* – they spray women with cheap perfume, the women present them with large doses of *pálinka* in return. The fun traditionally starts as early as 6am, and by 9am every male is past caring. By 10am the streets get ugly. Don't leave the house after 1pm if you can possibly help it.

Labour Day

Public holiday. **Date** 1 May.
No longer a forced wave at medal-festooned leaders along Dózsa György út, May Day still brings a lot of people to various entertainments in the city parks. Open-air May Day (Majális) events from pre-Communist days are organised in village squares, a more recent tradition being the rock festival at the Tabani Szabadtéri szinpad in the afternoon (bus 5, tram 18).

Summer

Summer is the season of no shame. Budapesters strip to the bare essentials as the temperature climbs into the '40s. At weekends and for most of August, they leave the heat and the traffic fumes for the tourists, to spend time at the family weekend home, or to be medievally promiscuous down at the Balaton. There are open-air festivals at Szeged, Diósgyőr Castle in Miskolc, Győr and Pécs. Don't think about getting any business done in town after 10am on a Friday.

Budapesti Bucsú

Information *Budapesti Fesztivalközpont, VIII. Rákóczi út 65 IV/66 (333 2337).* **Date** last weekend in June.
It might seem a little churlish, but Budapest still celebrates the 1991 withdrawal of Soviet troops from Hungary. Music, dance and theatre events are organised in city squares and parks.

Bastille Day

Institut Français, I. Fő utca 17 (202 1133). M2 Batthyány tér/bus 86. **Date** July 14, from 8pm.
Free open-air ball between the Danube and the French Institute, who celebrate Bastille Day by inviting leading accordion players from France, laying out a decent spread of French wines and snacks (though don't expect to get anywhere near it), and setting off loads of fireworks. Attracts a big crowd.

Budafest

Information *VIP-Arts Management, VI. Hajós utca 13-15 (302 4290/opera 353 0170).* **Date** mid-Aug.
Budafest is a week of top-flight performances at a time of year when a lot of lesser classical talent is wasted on second-rate cash-ins for bus-loads of Austrian tourists. Prices for the Opera House events are high, but the quality of what's on offer is undeniable. One main composer is featured, although not exclusively, each year, generally because of an anniversary of some kind. *See chapter* **Music: Classical & Opera**.

Hungaroring

Information *Ostermann Formula-1, V. Apáczai Csere János utca 11 (317 2811).* **Date** second weekend in August.
The biggest event in the Hungarian sporting calendar, the loss-making Hungarian Grand Prix nearly went under in the mid-1990s, but Government intervention saved the day. It is, after all, a good week-

Spray perfume or paint eggs at Easter.

end's trade for the city's hoteliers and restaurateurs (not to mention strip club bosses). The course itself is at Mogyorod, 20km from Budapest on the M3 motorway. *See chapter* **Sport & Fitness**.

Sziget Fesztival

Information *Sziget Csoport Kulturális Egyesület, XI. Lónyay utca 18b (218 8693).* **Date** Aug.
Now attracting thousands of young music-loving campers from across Europe, the Sziget ('Island') Fesztival is a week-long open-air party on an otherwise deserted island in the Danube, with dozens of music stages, rave marquees and other attractions and audiences staggering from beer tent to beer tent. Big name acts headline the main stage every evening, and literally everyone from the domestic scene is featured at least once. *See chapter* **Music: Rock, Roots & Folk**.

St Stephen's Day

Public holiday. **Date** 20 Aug.
Hungarians celebrate their founding father in style. Every town and village gets decked out in the national colours, while in Budapest cruise boats and river-view restaurants are booked up weeks in advance for the huge fireworks display set off from Gellért Hill at 9pm. Stake your place among the crowds by the Danube from early evening.

World Music Day

Information *Malacka BT, VIII. Mikszáth Kálmán tér 2 (318 0684).* **Date** nearest weekend to 21 June.

Although a French invention, Hungary takes World Music Day to heart. Nearly every town of any size has some kind of concert, usually in the main hall or square. In Budapest, while leading venues open their doors to jazz, folk and rock musicians, stages are set up for the eclectic international talent in open spaces such as Városliget, Népliget and Klauzal tér.

World Music Festival

Budai Parkszinpad, XI. Kosztolányi Dezső tér. Tram 6, bus 1, 7, 27, 40, 127, 153 to Móricz Zsigmond körtér. **Information** *Mandel Productions, 2040 Budaörs, PO Box 180 (06 30 9423 590).* **Date** June/early July.

Thanks to sponsorship, Budapest's annual World Music Festival has enjoyed a higher profile of late. Organiser Robert Mandel, a leading exponent of the crank-lute, had to try various venues before settling on the Budai Parkszinpad, between Móricz

Zsigmond körtér and Kosztolányi Dezső tér. A two-day event, it's pretty much a lucky bag of whoever happens to be touring eastern Europe at the time. *Website: www.womufe.matav.hu*

Autumn

The Indian summer of early autumn sees the city at its best, slowly emptying of tourists, its cultural life starting up again. Bars, clubs and concert halls re-open their doors to local audiences still bronzed and guilty from summer weekends at the Balaton.

Budapest International Wine Festival

Information *Bacchus Arts Studio, V. Vörösmarty tér 1 (317 7031). M1 Vörösmarty tér.* **Date** Sept.

The most gregarious of the city's annual trade fairs, the country's leading wine producers descending on

Hungary's right-hand man

Every year, on the afternoon of 20 August, the dried and grisly right hand of St Stephen (Szent István) – the holiest relic in Christian Hungary – is taken from its chapel in Pest's **St Stephen's Basilica** and, with much ecclesiastical pomp and splendour, paraded around the parking lot before a crowd of adoring Magyars. It could be a scene from the Middle Ages: mitred bishops and dour priests behind ancient church banners, the crowd in embroidered Habsburg jackets, folk costumes, feathered hats. And this is one of the few really 'happy' holidays in the morose Hungarian calendar. You would at least expect the hand to wave hello.

Given the medieval growth market in holy relics, there is speculation that the hand actually belongs to some twelfth-century peasant. But in any case, it is probably the oldest hand you are likely to see in Hungary and as such is quite impressive. One prefers to imagine it alive and attached to the arm of the glorious first king of Hungary. Clasping the mitt of some Anjou pretender. Slapping the face of an upstart Petcheneg vassal. Dipping into a trencher of roasted hind at a banquet with the Byzantine ambassador. And who knows what this hand was doing when it was only 14 years old?

The hand isn't the only dodgy manifestation of Magyar Stephanophilia. Staring deeply at you from the Hungarian 10,000-forint note, looking

for all the world like Kenneth Branagh playing Richard III, is Stephen. Or at least, somebody closely related to him. It's actually a portrait of his grandfather Árpád. When the photogravure for the bill was made the artist came up against a small problem: only one image of István exists from his lifetime, and as all the early chroniclers agreed, István had a face that could scare an orangutan. A great guy, but not much to look at.

Why the adulation? St Stephen was born Vajk, the grandson and scion of Árpád, the chieftain who had crossed the Carpathians and established a Magyar fiefdom in Pannonia. István's decision to convert to Christianity in AD 998 is hailed by modern Hungarians as a conscious and progressive choice to ally himself with the west, which at the time consisted of a bunch of murderous Teutons and Celts painting themselves blue. In fact, he was wise enough to realise that alliance with the Byzantines would probably swamp the ship of his newly independent state. Nevertheless, Hungarian intellectuals are united in the belief that István somehow had a premonition that Hungary would want to be a member of the EC and NATO and get Eurosport on cable, and they never let you forget it.

Istvan's coronation in AD 1000 also ties in neatly with the second millennium, and the Hungarian government has made István the official sponsor of the celebrations – after pulling out of a Disney-sponsored 2000 celebration that would have given Mickey centre stage. Expect to see a lot of Stevie on everything from T-shirts to beer mugs in the new millennium. And don't miss the festival in the castle and the firework display over the Danube at night – a pyromaniac's delight!

St Stephen's Basilica – *for 364 days of the year, home of the Holy Right Hand.*

Budapest to woo international buyers with chamber concerts in the Castle District, and wine-tasting and folk-dancing in Vörösmarty tér. For a less commercial appreciation of a real *szuret* – grape harvest – head out of town to Székszard or Eger (*see chapter* **Overnighters**), but remember to pack the aspirins.

Budapest Autumn Festival

Information (*see* **Spring Festival**). **Date** late Sept/early Oct.

The leading annual contemporary arts festival, focusing on cinema, fine arts, dance and theatre.
Venues: *Nemzeti Színház, V11. Hevesi Sándor tér 4 (322 0014). Trolleybus 73, 76.*
Petőfi Csarnok, Városliget, XIV. Zichy M. utca 14 (343 4327). M1 Széchenyi fürdő.
Várszínház, I. Színház utca 1-3 (375 8649). Bus 16 or castle minibus.
Ernst Museum, V1. Nagymező utca 8 (341 4355). M1 Operaház.

Budapest Music Weeks

Information *Budapest Filharmónia, VI. Jókai utca 6 (318 0314). M1 Oktogon/tram 4, 6.* **Date** late Sept/Oct.

The traditional opening of the classical music season, often with a major concert as near the anniversary of Bartók's death (Sept 25) as possible. Two weeks of performances, usually at the Vigadó or Zeneakadémia. *See chapter* **Music: Classical & Opera.**

Music of Our Time

Information (*see* **Music Weeks**). **Date** late Sept/Oct.

When top-notch classical musicians can let their hair down and enjoy the less stringent demands of Hungary's leading contemporary composers, many of whom compose pieces especially for this ten-day event.

Remembrance Day

Public holiday. **Date** 23 Oct.

The anniversary of the 1956 Hungarian Uprising is a national day of mourning. Wreath-laying ceremonies take place at plot 301 of Újköz Cemetery, where rebellious 1956 leader Imre Nagy was secretly buried after his execution. There is also a flag-raising ceremony in Kossuth tér, an excuse for right-wing groups to gain media attention. Black-edged flags are flown around town.

Winter

Hungarian winters seem to go on forever, with temperatures dropping below zero, and snow piled up on Budapest's slushy pavements. Shops slowly fill in town, but without the hard-sell of the west. Villagers gather for the annual *disznóvágás*, or pig-killing, a bloody, drunken ritual.

Mikulás

St Nicholas' Day. **Date** 6 Dec.

On the eve of 6th December, children put out their shoes on Budapest's window sills for Santa to fill

Magyars buy flowers for any occasion.

with chocolates, fruit and little pressies. He is assisted by *krampusz*, the bogey-man, with whom naughty children are threatened. In most places, the bogey-man's appearance is token: small krampusz puppets, hung on a gilded tree-branch, *virgács*, are also left by Santa.

Karácsony

Public holiday. **Date** 25, 26 Dec.

Trees and tacky presents line the Nagykörút from mid-December. The traditional Christmas meal is carp, happy to be out of the Danube mud and cavorting in the clear water of a Hungarian family's bathtub – until the evening of 24 December when the festive meal and present-giving take place. Christmas is a family affair, and apart from special events in major hotels, the city shuts up shop for two days from lunchtime on 24 December. Those staying in Budapest would be advised to accept any invitation going or stock up the kitchen and curl up with several hefty novels. Life doesn't get back to normal until after the New Year.

Magyar Film Szemle

Hungarian Film Festival. **Date** early Feb.

Information *c/o Filmunio Hungary, VI. Városligeti fasor 38 (351 7760/fax 351 7766).*

A reasonably modest screening of the year's best Magyar films, although the occasional Hollywood star with Hungarian connections can be seen passing through town for the long weekend in early February. Translations are provided for the main features and screenings are held at various cinemas around town.

Szilveszter

New Year's Eve. **Date** 31 Dec.

Szilveszter is when everyone takes to the streets in style, down the Nagykörút and around Blaha Lujza tér in particular. Most major places of entertainment will put on some kind of special event. Buses and trams in Budapest run all night long. The national anthem solemnly booms out of everyone's radios at midnight. Afterwards it's champers, kisses, handshakes and fireworks. Merriment continues into the next day, a public holiday, when *korcsonya*, a dish made from pork fat, is liable to wobble its way into your hangover.

Sightseeing

Sightseeing

From the UNESCO-designated Castle District to the gritty backstreets of downtown Pest – Budapest teems with things to see.

Chain Bridge and Castle Hill – one of the world's most magical urban landscapes.

At I. Clark Ádám tér, near the **Funicular** that leads up to the Castle District, stands a thing resembling a giant, elongated doughnut. This is the Zero Kilometre Stone, the point from which all distances to Budapest are measured and thus the official centre of town. And centre it is, between the Danube, central Europe's main waterway, and the Castle District, the rocky promontory that throughout history offered a controlling vantage over the river – together the main reason why there was ever a settlement here in the first place.

From this intersection, the Chain Bridge stretches over the Danube into Pest. Completed in 1849, it was the first permanent crossing over the river (before that were only rickety pontoon bridges in summer, occasional ferries or perilous treks across thin ice in winter). It was this bridge – designed by Englishman William Tierney Clark (who also did London's Hammersmith Bridge) but built by Scotsman Adam Clark (no relation, but the one who had the square and tunnel named after him) – that allowed the subsequent incorporation of Buda, Pest and Óbuda into one single city in 1872. Other routes

from here prod north and south along the Danube, while the Clark Ádám alagút (tunnel) conveys traffic beneath Castle Hill and into Buda beyond.

The Danube sweeps by strong and wide, though here it is at its narrowest and currents are relatively weak. The river is a vital part of Budapest – the only city on the river's long course between Black Forest and Black Sea where the Danube flows straight through the middle. There are quiet parks on its Margaret and Óbuda islands. Spectacular views from its bridges – upstream from Szabadság híd or downstream from Margit híd – form part of the urban landscape, even though the waterfront is sadly underused away from the stretch with all the major hotels.

Always present in the panorama from the Buda Hills, the Danube asserts itself even when out of sight. Come down one of the Pest streets leading to the embankment and the light changes as you approach the river, the result of refraction and sudden space. The Danube is rarely blue, however. More usually it's a dull and muddy brown, sometimes a murky green. After heavy rainfall to the

north, it can swell to twice its volume, flooding over the lower embankment, and asserting the fact that most of the water which falls on central Europe ends up draining right through the dead centre of the Hungarian capital.

RUINS & REINVENTIONS

The area covered by modern Budapest has been settled since pre-Roman times. Wars, invasions, revolutions and occupations, from the Mongol horde who gatecrashed in 1241 through to the aerial bombardments of 1945 and street battles of 1956, have wiped out much of what was here before the latter half of the nineteenth century. Even the Castle District is largely a reconstruction of a reconstruction.

Nevertheless, from the Ottoman period until the Communist days, each phase in Budapest's history has left its mark, and there are even some extant Roman ruins, though these are poorly cared for. In particular, the expansion of Pest and the invention of Hungarian national identity in the late nineteenth century have left both a series of grandiose monuments and some extraordinary architecture. Much of this costs nothing to see. Such admission prices as there are will usually be negligible, although guided tours can be costly. Even the farthest flung sights – such as the ruins and museums of Óbuda, assorted cemeteries and architectural experiments on the outskirts – are easily accessible by public transport. Apart from in the most-visited places, however, English-language documentation will be thin on the ground.

In this chapter we take you around Budapest by area, single out the most important sights, and round up an assortment of other things to see and do. Places marked **in bold**, if not listed in this chapter, will be found with full listings information in the appropriate chapters elsewhere in the book.

Budapest Card

If trying to do a lot of sightseeing in a hurry, consider the Budapest Card, available from main Metro stations, information offices, travel agencies and some hotels. This allows two or three days' unlimited travel on public transport, free entry to 55 museums and some other sights, plus a range of discounts around town. A card is valid for one adult plus one under-14-year-old and costs Ft2,450 for two days, Ft2,950 for three. Of course, it's even cheaper to follow our customised Budapest by public transport tour – *see page 68* **The sights, sorted**.

Buda

Older than Pest, more conservative and residential, and notably devoid of decent bars, Buda is sort of disjointed. The Castle and Gellért Hills carve up the central area into a patchwork of separate parts. The continuation of the Nagykörút runs round the back of these two urban hummocks, losing definition

View from **Basilica of St Stephen**. *Page 66.*

between Moszkva tér and Móricz Zsigmond körtér, the north and south hubs of public transport on this side of the river. To the north and west of the central area, smart residential districts amble up into still higher hills – green and spotted with villas in a way that, from a distance, can remind of Los Angeles. *See page 74* **A tale of two cities**.

Castle District

Wandering around the streets at the north end of the Vár – the Castle District – you'll see surnames against the doorbells of small baroque houses. This is perhaps the most surprising thing about this whole historic area: people still live here.

Without that reminder, the Vár appears to be nothing but one big tourist attraction – and certainly no visit to Budapest is complete without at least one afternoon up here. Apart from the obvious major landmarks – the former **Royal Palace** complex, the **Mátyás templom** and the **Fisherman's Bastion** – the narrow streets and open squares that top this 60-metre hill also contain no fewer than nine museums, from the dreary waxworks in the **Panoptikum** through appealing oddities such as the **Museum of Commerce & Catering** to national institutions such as the **Széchényi Library** and the **National Gallery**, as well as assorted other churches, mansions and statues. Practically every building, as the ubiquitous

stone plaques with their Hungarian-only inscriptions indicate, seems to have been declared a *Műemlék* – an historic monument.

The air of unreality is abetted by the quiet. You have to have a permit, or else be staying at the **Hilton Hotel**, to bring a car into the Castle District, and though there are plenty of parked vehicles, there is no through traffic. A few souped-up horses and carts with traditionally costumed coachmen (you can rent them at Szentháromság tér) clatter along backstreets bearing parties of sightseers. The small Várbusz comes up from Moszkva tér to circle the district every few minutes. But otherwise the only street noises are the prattle of tour groups and the whirr of Japanese video cameras. Most of the shops are tourist-orientated, selling lacy folk items, overpriced antiques, 35mm film, postcards and strings of dried paprika. Locals have to dive downhill to Moszkva tér or **Déli station** to buy their bread and *túró*.

But the feeling that nothing here is really real is an accurate one. Buda Castle has been destroyed and rebuilt so many times that virtually nothing historically authentic remains. Though it was inhabited in celtic times, the first major settlement on the hill was in the thirteenth century. That was promptly trashed by the Mongols.

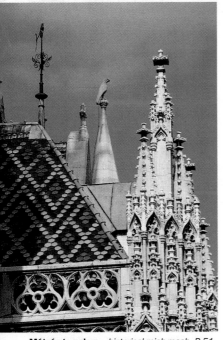

Mátyás templom – *historical mish-mash. P 51.*

King Mátyás built a renaissance palace, then the Turks showed up in 1541 and wrecked the place again. Everything they built was in turn destroyed when Habsburg-led armies chased them back out in 1686. Rebuilt once more, it was damaged during the 1848-49 War of Independence, rebuilt again in the latter half of the nineteenth century, somehow managed to get through World War I unscathed, and was pounded back into rubble in 1945.

Post-war reconstruction, which took decades, has both followed the way things were before the war, and incorporated earlier bits and pieces unearthed in wartime ruins. Many baroque houses were built on medieval foundations, and all this has been faithfully reproduced.

A lot of it was only simulated history anyway. Bits of the Mátyás templom date back to the thirteenth century, but the nineteenth-century reconstruction by Frigyes Schulek, who also designed the phony ramparts of the Fisherman's Bastion, romanticised the thing according to then current notions about Hungarian national identity. Add touches such as the **Sikló** – funicular – and the **Turul Statue**, and what you get is a sort of historical theme park: Dual Monarchyland.

The Royal Palace, which looks splendid from over the river, is pretty boring up close. Nothing here now but the musuems. Even the Habsburgs, for whom it was originally built, never stayed here much. The crenellated Fisherman's Bastion, guarded by a statue of St Stephen, offers fantastic views across the Danube and Pest, but isn't quite the same now one can't wander at will, and instead must pay an entrance fee to help save 'this internationally recognised value of Hungarian architecture'. Here one can sit and drink the worst and most overpriced beer in Budapest – we'd swear it must be watered down – and listen to competing musics from the violinist in one of the turrets, and cocktail piano drifting up from the terrace behind the mirror glass Hilton which has somehow managed to worm its way into this UNESCO-protected area.

Tóth Árpád sétány, the promenade on the other side, overlooks ugly Déli station, the houses of Krisztinaváros and a telecommunications centre that looks like something out of *Thunderbirds*. It's pleasant under the chestnut trees, especially at sunset. Relatively tourist-free, this is where the old folk of the Castle District come to stroll.

If you walk up to the north end of the hill, along the Anjou Bastion past the artillery pieces behind the **Museum of Military History**, you'll find the Memorial to the last Pasha of Buda. Vizir Abdurrahman Abdi Arnaut Pasha was killed and buried here in 1686. 'A valiant foe,' reads the inscription, 'may he rest in peace.' People still sometimes leave fresh flowers at his grave. The nearby Vienna Gate, which looks much older, was built in 1936 to commemorate the 250th anniversary of the victory over the Turks.

Fisherman's Bastion – *no one ever cast a line into the river from up here.*

In a way the only real piece of history in the whole Castle District is the wrecked stump of the former Ministry of Defence, down at the south end of Disz tér, unrestored and bullet-pocked from the last desperate battles between Nazis and Soviets.

The best time to look around here is early in the morning before the tourists all decant from their coaches. Little happens in the Castle District at night, although it can all be very atmospheric in the dark. The **Dominican Restaurant Hilton** is the only restaurant we'd recommend. If you want to pause for a coffee or beer in the middle of all this relentless sightseeing, both the Café Miró and Café Pierrot are refreshingly unhistorical.

Fisherman's Bastion

Halászbástya
I. Várhegy. Várbusz/bus 16. **Admission** Ft100.
Open 24 hours daily. **No credit cards. Map A3**
There are several stories explaining why this vantage point has a piscine name. Some claim that the Fisherman's Guild defended this part of the Castle; others that there was a medieval fisherman's quarter down below. Certainly no one ever cast a line into the river from way up here. Built between 1890 and 1905 by Frigyes Schulek and intended to harmonise with his romanticised reconstruction of the nearby **Mátyás templom**, it has seven turrets, one for each of the original Hungarian tribes. It's worth Ft100 for the view.

Funicular

Sikló
I. Clark Ádám tér (201 9128). Tram 19/bus 16, 86, 105. **Open** 7.30am-10pm daily. Closed every other Monday, 7.30am-3pm. **Tickets** Ft200; Ft100 children. **Map B4**
Budapest's funicular (*sikló*) crawls up the side of Castle Hill in a minute or two. The panorama of Pest unfolds as you ascend. Until it was hit by a shell in the Soviet bombardment of 1945, the sikló had functioned continually since it first climbed up the hill in 1870. Originally it was built to provide cheap transport for clerks working in the Castle District and in those days was powered by a steam engine. It was restored and electrified in 1986.

Mátyás templom

I. Szentháromság tér 2. Várbusz/bus 16. **Open** 7am-7pm daily. **Admission** *treasury* Ft150; Ft50 concs. **Map A3**
Mátyás templom, a neo-Gothic extravaganza, takes its name from the great Hungarian King Mátyás the Just (aka Good King Mátyás) who twice got married here. Parts of its structure date from the thirteenth century, but much of it was reconstructed in the nineteenth century and, like most of the Castle District, the church is a historical mish-mash. When Istanbul, rather than Vienna, ruled Buda, the church was converted into a mosque. The building suffered terribly during the 1686 siege of Buda and was

Turul Statue – *mythical protector of the Hungarian nation.*

mostly restored in the nineteenth century by Frigyes Schulek, who returned to the original thirteenth-century plan but also added his own decorative details, such as the gargoyle-bedecked stone spire. The interior is almost cloyingly detailed and includes the entrance to the Museum of Ecclesiastical Art in the crypt.

Royal Palace

I. Budavári palota. Várbusz/bus 16. **Open** times vary depending on museum. **Map B4**

The former Royal Palace has been destroyed and rebuilt many times. What you see today is a post-war reconstruction of an architectural hotch-potch from the eighteenth, nineteenth and twentieth centuries. The first royal residence here was constructed by King Béla IV after the 1241 Mongol invasion but it was under the reign of King Mátyás (1458-90) that the Royal Palace reached its apogee. Mátyás' Renaissance-style palace had hot and cold running water and fountains that sometimes spouted wine. This palace was badly damaged during the Turkish siege of 1541 and the area was completely laid waste when recaptured from the Turks in 1686. Empress Maria Theresa caused a new 203-room palace to be built in the late eighteenth century. This was badly damaged in the 1848-49 War of Independence, then reconstructed and expanded once more, only to be trashed yet again at the end of World War II. That battering revealed Gothic and Renaissance foundations, which have been included in the post-war reconstruction. Visitors are thus greeted by a melange of architectural styles, including baroque and Gothic elements. The Palace now houses a complex of museums, including the **Budapest History Museum**, the **Hungarian National Gallery** and the **National Széchényi Library**.

Turul Statue

I. Szent György tér. Várbusz/bus 16/Sikló. **Map B4**

Wings outstretched and with a sword grasped in fierce talons, Gyula Donáth's giant bronze eagle (1905), visible from across the Danube, shrieks at tourists getting off the nearby Sikló. The best view is from the steps leading down to the Palace where his pained expression smacks more of constipation than ferocity. This mythical protector of the Hungarian nation raped the grandmother of Árpád, legendary conqueror of the Carpathian Basin, and sired the first dynasty of Hungarian kings. Later he flew with the invading tribes, carrying the sword of Attila the Hun. In Siberian mythology the eagle is the creator of the world, lord of the sun. By claiming ancestry from this creature, ancient Magyars believed they were descended from gods. In the nineteenth century, romanticised eastern origins stressed a cultural and ethnic difference from the hated Austrians. Yet by 1896 Habsburg Emperor Franz Joseph was portrayed as the second Árpád, founder of the thousand-year Dual Monarchy. The Turul myth, co-opted to serve this new master, was positioned here by the Palace. The turul-eagle is a common motif on turn-of-the-century Budapest buildings. The main gates of the Parliament building have a row of fierce wrought-iron specimens and golden turuls guard the Szabadság híd.

The Tabán, Gellért Hill & surrounds

Krisztinaváros sits below the Castle District to the west. Apart from the enormous, and enormously ugly, Déli pályaudvar – the station for trains to the Balaton, Croatia and other points south-west – there isn't much noteworthy about the area.

South of here, between Castle Hill and **Gellért Hill**, is the Tabán. Now a public park, this was once an ancient and disreputable quarter inhabited by Serbs, Greeks and Gypsies, most of whom made their living on the river. The Horthy government levelled it in the 1930s and only a few bits and pieces remain. Appropriately enough for an area once renowned for its gambling dens, one of these is the **Várkert Casino**, housed in a Miklós Ybl-designed neo-Renaissance-style pump house (it used to furnish water for the Royal Palace) near the **Semmelweis Museum of Medical History**. Ybl also designed the nineteenth-century exterior of the **Rác baths**, over on the other side of the park below Gellért Hill. The original domed Turkish pool survives within, and on summer nights the garden next door, reinvented as the **Rác kert**, buzzes with outdoor nightlife.

On the other side of the roads that feed traffic on and off Erzsébet híd (Elizabeth Bridge), the only building between Gellért Hill and the Danube, stands the **Rudas**, most beautiful, atmospheric and (though men-only) least gay of all the Turkish bathhouses. It doesn't look much from outside, though. On the cliff behind it, over the road from the number 7 bus stop, plaques note several springs that emerge from the hill at this point, variously christened Rákóczi, Gül Baba, Beatrix, Kinizsi and Musztafa. This last is named after Sokoli Mustapha, pasha from 1566-78, who caused the Rudas to be constructed.

Gellért Hill rises steep at this point. Looking up you'll sometimes see rock climbers scaling the limestone cliffs. An easier route is to take the path that leads up to the **Gellért Statue**. The martyred bishop is enclosed by a colonnade and brandishes a crucifix at motorists crossing Elizabeth Bridge. Paths meander up and around the hill and it's easy to find your way to the top. Villas are dotted across the south and west slopes but here there are only trees, through which one catches steadily more spectacular views of the Danube and Pest rooftops beyond. Once this hill was covered in vines, but a nineteenth-century epidemic of phylloxera destroyed them all. In photographs of turn-of-the-century Budapest, the hill looks barren and forbidding. Some fig trees have survived, though, brought here by the Ottomans in the sixteenth century.

Gellért Statue – *blessing Elizabeth Bridge.*

The grim **Citadella** on the 230-metre summit was built by the Austrians to assert their authority after the 1848-49 War of Independence. It's now a quiet spot with extraordinary views and a variety of tourist amenities, although the Hungarian army still sets up camp here every August to supervise the **St Stephen's Day** fireworks. The **Liberty Statue**, a figure apparently doing some form of aerobics with a palm frond, towers above the ramparts, flanked below by sprightly statues of Progress and Destruction.

From here any number of paths lead down the other side of the hill. On the way you might pass the **Cave Church**, an odd and somewhat spooky place of worship run by monks of the Hungarian Paulite order. At the Buda foot of Szabadság híd (Freedom Bridge) stands the four-star **Gellért Hotel**, an imposing art nouveau edifice with a complex of thermal baths and swimming pools behind. This is Budapest's most famous hotel, built 1912-18. The **Gellért Eszpresszó** is a good spot for a conservative coffee-and-cake experience, although the terrace is rather noisy. And even if you don't want to swim or soak, it's worth poking your head round the **Gellért baths'** entrance in Kelenhegyi út just to clock the impressively ornate secessionist foyer. Refreshment in less ornate surroundings, including the best *meleg szendvics* in town, can be found at the nearby **Libella** café.

The **Technical University** stands to the south of the Gellért on what was once a marsh, and Bartók Béla út runs round the south side of the hill.

From about 200 metres down, the view of Szabadság híd's green metal girders sweeping across the line of the road is a unique piece of cityscape. This busy shopping street and some of the roads off it (Mészöly utca, Lágymányosi utca) also have an assortment of interesting turn-of-the-century buildings, notably Ödön Lechner's number 40, and József Fischer's numbers 15B and 49.

Roads off to the right lead up to the leafy residential district of Gellért Hill. A statue of Géza Gárdonyi, famous for authoring an adventure novel about the 1552 Siege of **Eger**, one of Hungary's few famous victories, occupies the triangle where Bercsényi utca meets the main road. Just beyond Móricz Zsigmond körtér, terminus for assorted trams and buses and very much the border between the city centre and the outlying industrial suburbs to the south, is a small park, whose theatre, the Budai Parkszinpad, is the venue for the annual **World Music Festival** each June. The park also contains an austere statue of Bartók and a supposedly bottomless lake (actually four metres deep). The Baroque façade of Szent Imre's church over the way on Villányi út lends some historical atmosphere, but like so much else in Budapest, it's a bit of a fake, built in 1938.

Cave Church
Sziklatemplom
XI. Gellérthegy (385 1529). Just up from Szent Gellért tér, opposite the side of the Gellért Hotel.
Tram 19, 47, 49/bus 7. **Open** 9-11am, noon-4.30pm, 6-8pm, daily. **Admission** free. **Map C5**
Although the caves were inhabited 4,000 years ago, the Cave Church was only dedicated in 1926. It feels much older. Popular enough to be expanded in 1931 by Count Gyula Zichy, archbishop of Kalocsa, who had helped re-establish the Hungarian Paulite order of monks. The monastery next door opened in 1934, and the monks resumed their work after an interval of 150 years – their order had been dissolved by Emperor Joseph II and sent into exile. The Communists jailed the monks in the 1950s and the cave was boarded up for decades, re-opening in August 1989.

Citadella
XI. Gellérthegy. Bus 27. **Map B5**
After the failed Hungarian revolution of 1848, the Habsburgs built the Citadella in 1851 as an artillery redoubt. Its commanding view put the city within easy range should the Magyars choose to get uppity again. The Ausgleich of 1867 that gave Hungary a measure of autonomy under the Dual Monarchy meant that its guns were never fired in anger against the city. In fact the new administration planned to destroy it as a symbol of reconciliation, but that proved too costly. The site now houses a youth hostel, restaurant and disco and an exhibition of the area's history since its settlement by the Celts. It's quiet up here and the views north and south along the Danube are splendid.

Gellért Statue

XI. Gellérthegy. Tram 18, 19/bus 7. **Map B5**

Built in 1904, this 11-metre sculpture of Bishop Gellért (Gerard) raising his cross dominates the Buda side of the Elizabeth Bridge. Below it is an artificial waterfall, which dates from the same time. Like so many Hungarian heroes, Bishop Gellért met a tragic end – originally an Italian missionary, he was the country's first Christian martyr and legend has it that in 1046 he was nailed into a barrel by pagans and rolled down Gellért Hill into the Danube.

Liberty Statue

Szabadság szobor
XI. Gellérthegy. Bus 27. **Map C5**

Perched above the Citadella and visible from all over the city is the 14-metre Liberty Statue, commemorating liberation from fascist rule. You will hear stories that the figure was originally commissioned from sculptor Zsigmond Kisfaludy-Stróbl as a memorial to the son of Admiral Horthy, the ultra right-wing leader of the interwar years, and that the palm branch was meant to be a propeller blade (Horthy junior was a pilot). But this is nonsense. It was built to celebrate the liberation of Budapest from the Horthyites and, visible from all over town, has become one of the symbols of the city. As such it's a rare example of surviving Soviet statuary, although the bronze figures of Soviet soldiers that once stood at its base have been moved, like most other public monuments of that period, to the **Statue Park**.

Liberty Statue – *symbol of the city.*

The Víziváros

From the north-east side of the Castle District, ancient streets cascade down towards the Danube. The Víziváros (Water Town) is one of Budapest's oldest districts. It's a quiet and conservative area where nothing very much happens, stretching about a mile north from Clark Ádám tér to the foot of Margaret Bridge, gradually widening west away from the river and towards Moszkva tér.

Main street is Fő utca (it means just that: 'main street') a thoroughfare of Roman origin that runs parallel to the Danube-hugging Bem rakpart. Down here are medieval houses, baroque churches, small squares and narrow roads leading up to the Castle. George Maurois' **Institut Français** at number 17 is one of the city's few decent postmodern buildings, enjoying a prominent waterfront location used for a flashy fireworks display every 14 July, Bastille Day. A nineteenth-century water meter a little further down towards the Chain Bridge, at the stop for tram 19, is the Folyamat Galéria, a tiny exhibition space that contains miniature art installations. *See page 98* **Street scene**.

Batthyány tér is the centrepiece of the Víziváros, opening from Fő utca out on to the Danube, where Parliament looms large on the opposite bank. It's a busy and interesting square, with a desultory flea market in the middle and an assortment of notable, mostly eighteenth-century architecture round the edges. The **Church of St Anne** on the southern side is one of Hungary's finest baroque buildings. The middle-class ladies of Buda gather for coffee and cakes in St Anne's former presbytery, now the **Angelika café**, where light seeps in through atmospheric stained glass windows. Number 4 was built in 1770 as the White Cross Inn and is these days called the Casanova House – he supposedly once stayed here – while number 3 next door is a rare example of a late baroque style called *copfstil*. The 1902 market hall now houses a modern supermarket with depressing piped Muzak. The floating **Hotel Dunapart** is moored nearby.

Batthyány tér is also a public transport hub: various buses leave from here, and underground there is both a station on the M2 line and the southern terminal of the HÉV line that runs north to **Szentendre**. The station boasts Budapest's first privately owned public convenience, which has clean towels and plastic flowers.

Further north along Fő utca at 70-72 is the forbidding Military Court of Justice, used as a prison and headquarters by both the Gestapo in the Nazi times, and the secret police in the Stalinist 1950s. Here Imre Nagy and associates were tried in secret and condemned to death after the 1956 revolution. A block away is the **Király Gyógyfürdő**, another leftover from the Turkish days and, unlike the other Ottoman bathhouses, interesting to view from outside as well as in.

Church of St Anne – *baroque façade crowned by the eye in the triangle.*

The street ends at Bem tér, where there's a statue of General Joseph Bem. A Pole, Bem led the Hungarian army in the War of Independence. On 23 October 1956, this small square was the site of a huge demonstration – partly because people wished to express their approval of political changes in Poland. It was the beginning of the revolution that was to end so starkly just three blocks back down the road.

Church of St Anne

Szent Anna templom
I. Batthyány tér 8 (201 3404). M2 Batthyány tér.
Open *services* 6.45-9am, 4-7pm, daily; 7am-1pm Sun and public hols. **Admission** free. **Map B3**
Visited at dusk, as weary shoppers pop in to say their prayers, St Anne's captivates the senses. The whispering of catechisms echoes around its emptiness and there's a faint smell of incense in the air. Earthquakes, floods, metro construction and Stalinism couldn't destroy one of Hungary's finest baroque monuments. If you only visit one church in Budapest, this should be it. Construction began in 1740, to the plans of the Jesuit Ignatius Pretelli. Máté Nepauer, one of the most prominent architects of the Hungarian baroque, oversaw its completion in 1805. The façade is crowned by the eye-in-the-triangle symbol of the Trinity, while Faith, Hope and Charity loiter around the front door. The theatricality of the interior is typical of the baroque. Larger-than-life statues are frozen in performance on the High Altar, framed by black marble columns representing the

Temple of Jerusalem. The Trinity above is held aloft by angels, cherubim strike poses around the supporting altars, and a heavenly orchestra perches atop the undulating line of the organ pipes. But despite all the melodrama St Anne's feels remarkably suburban. With the vases of flowers and framed oval paintings of saints and notables, it's easy to imagine that you're admiring the chintz in God's front room. Speckled turquoise-green walls and potted trees framing the altar of St Francis Xavier add to the cosy effect.

Moszkva tér & the Rózsadomb

Ugly and dilapidated, Moszkva tér, a major public transport hub connecting the Buda Hills to the rest of town, bustles with lowlife. From 5am it's an unofficial labour market: Romanians and Gypsies gather outside the station, waiting for someone to come along and hire them for a day's work. All day long, as trams going in several directions pull in and out and the *várbusz* nips up to the Castle District, police check the papers of anyone sitting around who looks like they might be an illegal immigrant. Hungarians from rural areas also cluster here, selling flowers, fruit and lace tablecloths to rush-hour crowds.

The **Mammut Center** mall on Lövőház utca has recently arrived to dominate commerce in the neighbourhood, but there are still small hold-outs against postmodernity. In nearby Retek utca, the

Szent Jupát restaurant serves cheap and hearty platefuls deep into the night. The **Auguszt Cukrászda** on Fény utca serves some of the city's finest cakes and pastries. And a short walk on to Kis Rókus utca, up one side of the enormous Ganz tram factory, leads to the **Marxim**, where pizzas are served up with Stalinist kitsch. But despite all the bustle, Moszkva tér remains principally a tawdry transition zone that most pass through without stopping.

And very different from the Rózsadomb, which it serves. Down near the Buda foot of Margaret Bridge, you can walk up the narrow, cobbled Gül Baba utca and come to the **Tomb of Gül Baba**, the northernmost Islamic holy place in Europe. This is also the foot of the Rózsadomb – Rose Hill – Budapest's poshest residential district. This villa-speckled hill has long been known as the 'millionaires' district'. Whereas in cities such as London, Paris and Berlin the rich settled in western areas while prevailing winds blew industrial effluents towards working-class east ends, in Budapest avoiding the smoke has always been a matter of altitude. It was said in Communist times that inhabitants of the airy Rózsadomb had the same life expectancy as in Austria, while the citizens of polluted Pest below had the life expectancy of Syria: two continents in one city. And it isn't much less of a contrast today.

Unless you're either staying here or visiting one of the area's many garden restaurants, such as the **Vadrózsa** or **Remiz**, there aren't many reasons to go to the Rózsadomb. The yurt houses designed by Imre Makovecz on Törökvész utca are one architectural attraction. The fascinating **Napraforgó utca experimental housing estate**, where each house has been built in a different style of the modern movement, is another. Near the picturesquely decayed concrete bus terminal at Pasaréti tér (the Origo eszpresszó here is worth a look for its tatty 1960s fittings) stands the **Bartók Memorial House**, the composer's former residence, now a concert venue as well as a museum. The **Szépvölgy** and **Pálvölgy caves** burrow beneath the outskirts of this area. But otherwise you'll see a lot of embassies, flash cars, tasteless new villas and a huge variety of Hungarian 'Beware of the Dog' signs.

Tomb of Gül Baba

Gül Baba Türbéje

II. Mecset utca 14 (no phone). Tram 4, 6. **Open** 10am-4pm Tue-Sun. **Admission** Ft100; Ft50 concs. **No credit cards. Map D1**

Perched at the top of Buda's last surviving Turkish street is the northernmost Islamic place of pilgrimage in Europe. Gül Baba was a Turkish Dervish and member of the Bektashi order. His name means 'father of roses' and according to local folklore, he introduced the flower to Budapest, thus giving the name Rózsadomb (Rose Hill) to the area. (Actually he died just after the capture of Budapest in 1541 and never had time to plant any roses.) Inside the mausoleum there are verses inscribed by Turkish traveller Evliya Tselebi in 1663 as well as antiquities and furnishings donated by Hungarian Muslims. It's a peaceful spot, recently renovated (with help from the Turkish government) and suffused with the air of tranquillity that always shrouds Islamic holy sites.

The Buda Hills

From opposite the unappealingly cylindrical Budapest Hotel on Szilágyi Erzsébet fasor, you can catch the cog railway up to the summit of Széchenyi Hill, a ride of about 20 minutes. There's no view to speak of, unless you count the large building festooned with radar dishes, but you immediately feel as if you're out of the city. It's quiet and in summer there's a cool breeze.

There are wooded hills all around the western fringes of Buda, most of them criss-crossed with hiking trails. At weekends these can get quite crowded. You can ramble all you like, but take a good map and a strong pair of hiking boots and keep a sharp eye out for rampaging wild boar.

Otherwise, you can walk across the park from the cog railway terminal and hop on the narrow-gauge **Children's Railway**. This was formerly the Pioneers' Railway, named after the Communist youth organisation whose membership supplied the conductors and ticket collectors. Its charming trains, open to the breeze and still manned by children, snake hourly through the Buda Hills. The line meanders through woodland and retains a vaguely socialist flavour: the kids wear uniform hats and neckerchiefs, salute guards at stations, punch all tickets conscientiously and insist you remain seated when trains are in motion. Some of the stations still sport murals of idealised socialist youth diligently enjoying their leisure time.

Near the end station of Hűvösvölgy you'll find a small amusement park and the popular **Náncsi Néni** restaurant. Or you can get off earlier at János-hegy, from where it's a brisk 15-minute walk up to the 527-metre summit of Budapest's highest hill. Here the view from the Erzsébet lookout tower puts the city in context: the Buda Hills roll around and behind; Castle Hill looks small and barely significant down below; the Danube bisects the entire landscape; and way over on the other side, the outskirts of Pest shade into a patchwork of fields that in turn disappear into a flat, dusty horizon – the beginning of the Great Hungarian Plain.

From a terminal by the buffet below, the **Libegő** – chair-lift – will convey you back down into urban Buda, the city spread grandly before you as you ride. Be warned, though: if you get the last Children's Railway train, you won't make it over the hill in time to catch the final chair-lift.

Station to station

Nyugati – Pest's oldest station.

First and last experience of Hungary for many travellers, Budapest's railway stations are its real frontiers. Keleti announces the east. Armies of students hustling for youth hostels assault your train; announcement jingles echo atonally to introduce tannoy voices incomprehensible to foreign ears; departure boards announce destinations both exotic and dangerous; money-changers hustle for hard currency; Chinese and Gypsy families decant to sell their wares.

This Beaux Arts palace, originally finished in 1884, has recently been renovated – this has removed some of the ragged edges but it's still a grand old place, and the café sports a pianist. Paintings in the international ticket hall are by Mór Than and Károly Lotz, decorators of the Opera House and Parliament. Oeil-de-boeuf windows line the curving roof and the lacy ironwork on the main gates contrasts with the heaviness of stone. Outside stands a statue of Gábor Baross, pioneer of the phenomenal Hungarian rail expansion that began in 1867 and was used by the Hungarians to keep its empire's minorities dependent: all railway lines had to go through Pest. To this day there is still no direct line from Vienna to Zagreb.

With St Stephen's crown perched on its apex, Nyugati is Budapest's oldest station. Constructed by the Eiffel Company (1877), the symmetry of its main shed and the weightlessness of the thin cast iron supports calm the pressure of departure. The ironworked arching is more reminiscent of Parisian greenhouses than a hectic railway terminus and the outside world seems remote as yellow trams blur through the glass façade. Postmodernity has cheapened its refinement. With boilers of occasional 'nostalgia' trains snorting steam, it's still possible to imagine Nyugati's heyday. But the Beaux Arts restaurant is now a McDonald's with synthetic plants and bulbous white lights.

Déli, ruining the view from Castle Hill, is the newest of Budapest's stations. While its pre-war terminus was the departing-point for newly-weds off to honeymoon in Venice, modern Déli brings you back down to earth. The stench of urine hits as soon as you leave the metro. Fly-posters peel and people sleep rough. This really is the last resort. Finished in 1977, György Kővári's design exemplifies Communist shoddiness and superficiality. Its metal cladding is buckling and the marble facing falling off in dirty great lumps.

Pest

Though situated in the south part of District V, the Belváros (Inner City), dates back to medieval times, the current shape of Pest – as resolutely flat as Buda is jaggedly hilly – is essentially nineteenth century. Its great boulevards were laid out in 1872, the same year that the three towns of Buda, Pest and Óbuda were merged to form one single city.

The main lines can be quickly drawn. District V lies at the heart of Pest, divided into the Belváros in the south and the Lipótváros – the financial and government quarter – to the north. Both lie inside the Kiskörút, first of a series of concentric semi-circular boulevards that are cut through by roads radiating from the centre. The spaces outlined by these major roads contain the various different districts. The two big circular roads – Kiskörút and Nagykörút (Small and Great Boulevards) – themselves have their own atmosphere and take on some of the character of the districts they traverse, but are here treated as if districts in their own right.

Raday utca – interesting shops and bars.

Belváros

Trace the line of the Kiskörút from Fővám tér to Deák tér. Now move your finger west along Harmincad utca, past the Erzsébet tér bus station and the **Kempinski Hotel**, past the British Embassy and the neighbouring **Sushi** bar. Dogleg into Vörösmarty tér, sweep by the **Gerbeaud** patisserie and the M1 terminus, and go down to the Danube at Vigadó tér. The area you have outlined, bounded by the river to the west, is the Belváros, or Inner City.

The area south of Kossuth Lajos utca is one of Pest's most appealing quarters. Though the Danube is mostly invisible (one or two streets that run out on to it offer sudden, startling views of Gellért Hill) its narrow, quiet streets make it feel like a waterfront district. Apart from the old Customs House (now the Economic University) on the Kiskörút, the dock for international Danube traffic (notably jetfoils to Bratislava and Vienna), complete with customs area, is on this stretch of riverfront, as are the **Govinda** and **Taverna Dionysos** restaurants and the **Capella** nightclub.

The south stretch of Váci utca, between Kossuth Lajos utca and Fővám tér, has recently been pedestrianised and new life has quickly seeped into the area as fashion shops and terrace cafés have opened up next to older antique and collectors' shops.

Though much of the commerce is tourist-orientated, this area is dotted with some decent restaurants and bars, such as the **Fregatt**, **Fatál** and **Club Verne**. The **Janis Pub**, **Old Amsterdam** and the **Irish Cat** are all also nearby, making this perhaps Budapest's premier district for pub-crawling – particularly as the streets are so atmospheric at night.

The **Serbian Orthodox Church** nestles in a garden up Szerb utca, near the **Rhythm 'n' Books** shop which offers world music and English-language reading. The former home of chanteuse and actress Katalin Karády – Hungary's answer to Marlene Dietrich – is around the corner at Nyári Pál utca 9, complete with plaque where flowers are still left to her memory. But this is a quarter for quiet strolling rather than serious sightseeing.

All this changes at Ferenciek tere (named after the Franciscan Church that stands near the University Library). The extraordinary 1913 **Párizsi udvar** on the other side of Kossuth Lajos utca heralds the beginning of Budapest's prestige shopping district, though around here there are also more notably ancient monuments, including the **Inner City Parish Church**, Pest's oldest building, down towards the bridge. From here on up to Vörösmarty tér, Váci and its environs are pedestrianised and bustle with street hustlers and expensive shops, both aiming their pitch at the equally numerous tourists.

Although the westerner will not find it very impressive (it's mostly souvenir shops and western retail chains), Hungarians are proud of Váci utca. It's what they think the tourists want. Budapesters will invariably bring visitors to Váci, although they rarely shop here (too expensive) and more or less visit as tourists themselves. Brash, tacky, full of life and, a decade after Communism, still remarkably bare of decent clothes shops, it remains interesting principally for anthropological reasons: grab a table outside **Gerbeaud**, **Cyrano** or **Anna Café**, prepare yourself for a heftier bill than you'd receive elsewhere in town, and settle back to study the holidaying habits of the lesser spotted Austrian package tourist.

The area west of Váci, between Petőfi Sándor utca and the Károly körút, is dominated by two huge bureaucratic complexes: the Budapest City Hall and the Pest County Hall. Narrow streets and small squares lead through to Deák tér. Szervita tér has the Hungaria mosaic topping number 5 and Béla Lajta's Rózsavölgyi House next door, occupied on the ground floor by the **Rózsavölgyi Zeneműbolt** – a music shop dating from the Communist era that still offers, among a stock of modern CDs and one of Budapest's best classical music departments, an assortment of bizarre vinyl bargains. The more mainstream Fotex is just a few doors away.

The Danube Korzó, Budapest's premier promenade, is almost as busy as Váci. It begins at the convergence of Március 15 tér, with its stubby

The Clothild Buildings flank Kossuth Lagos utca on the approach to Elizabeth Bridge.

Roman ruins, and Petőfi tér, with its statue of the national poet. From here to Vigadó tér is the city's main gay cruise, though you'd not notice if you weren't looking for it. At Vigadó tér are buskers, stalls selling folkloric souvenirs and the **Vigadó** itself, Budapest's second-best concert hall. The Korzó continues from here on up to Roosevelt tér, where statues of Deák and Széchenyi stand among the trees and the **Gresham Palace** faces off against the Chain Bridge.

On the river side of this main stretch is the track for the number 2 tram and various odd attractions – an Irish restaurant called, for some reason, Columbus, on one moored boat; a Renault car showroom on another – while above them tower many of Budapest's most prestigious hotels, including the **Marriott** and **Atrium Hyatt**, all of them architecturally quite uninspiring. But these need not spoil the view of the Chain Bridge ahead and Castle District opposite. Particularly when lit up at night and reflected in the river, whether under a clear, starry sky or softened by trails of autumn mist, these form one of the most magical urban landscapes in the world.

Inner City Parish Church

Belvárosi Plébiánatemplom
V. Március 15 tér (no phone). M3 Ferenciek tere.
Open 9am-12.30pm, 6-7pm, Mon-Sat; 6.30-7.30am, 6-7pm, Sun; **Latin mass** 10am Sun. **Map C4**

Founded in 1046 as the burial site of the martyred St Gellért, this is Pest's oldest building, although little of its original structure remains. It's an extraordinary mixture of styles – Gothic, Islamic, baroque and neo-classical – testifying to the city's turbulent history. The beauty of its interior is in the light and shadow of the Gothic vaulting and most of the older detail is in the sanctuary, around the altar. You will have to dodge unfriendly 'Stop tourists!' signs or visit on a Sunday after the Latin mass to see them. Behind the High Altar you'll find Gothic sedilias and a Turkish prayer alcove, surprisingly intact from when the church was used as a mosque. Outside, it's still possible to make out the Gothic stones. The remains of the Roman outpost Contra Aquincum lie north of the church.

Párizsi udvar

V. Ferenciek tere 10-11/Petőfi Sándor utca 2-8.
M3 Ferenciek tere/tram 2/bus 7. **Map C4**
Henrik Schmahl's Párizsi udvar was completed in 1913 and still functions as a shopping arcade today. Gold-leaf mosaics announce its presence to the street, neon signs glow enticingly from the cavernous oriental interior, and 50 nude ceramic figures solicit from portholes above the third storey. Outraged critics charged the arcade with 'lacking good taste and discretion' – not bad going considering the moral and aesthetic standards of the time. It began life as the Inner City Savings Bank, a function clear in its ornamentation. Bees, sym-

bols of thrift, can be found throughout the building, while heavenly banking is presided over by the archangel Gabriel on the white pyrogranite reliefs below the gable. Classical-style mosaics with gorgons' heads and theatrical masks smother the porch, juxtaposed with Islamic geometric motifs. This curious eclecticism continues inside the arcade with its intricate detailing and arched glass ceiling by Miksa Róth. The mock grandeur of the arcade tails off into Kígyó udvar, 1970s strip lighting starkly filtered through metal lattice. Gone are the days when they made tack with flair.

Serbian Orthodox Church

Szerb templom
V. Szerb utca 2-4 (137 4230). M3 Kálvin tér/tram 47, 49. **Open** for High Mass only 10.30am Sun.
Service 60-90 minutes. **Map C5**
Announced at the corner of Veres Pálné utca by painted tiles of St George spiking the dragon, this secluded church was begun in 1698 following the Turkish defeat, and subsequently modified in the mid-eighteenth century. Constructed to serve the Serbian craftsmen and merchants who lived in this waterside district, it still has a congregation of their descendants, plus refugees from the recent war. The church is only open for mass on Sundays. It's an overpowering experience. With clouds of incense and votive candles flickering, the service is sung throughout by priests. Acoustics are superb. As the litany reverberates around the glowing ochre interior, the light picks out the gold leaf of the neo-Renaissance iconostasis that hides the gleaming altar. The congregation stands during mass. Carved wooden pews with high

arms give you something to lean on as your head goes dizzy and the ethereal blue of the ceiling frescoes starts to spin. Visitors leave spellbound.

Lipótváros

The northern part of District V – the Lipótváros – is Budapest's quarter for business and bureaucracy. There are few shops in this area, though **Bestsellers** bookstore on Október 6 utca is an obvious rallying-point for Anglophones. Once almost totally devoid of decent bars and restaurants, these broad, blocky late-nineteenth century streets, almost Prussian in feel, have now begun to acquire a little life at night and in places postively buzz at lunchtime. **Lou Lou**, **Gandhi**, **Café Kör** and **Iguana** all offer more than acceptable eats, while the stretch of Nador utca between Vértanuk tér and Zoltéan utca has various 24-hour bars and presszós such as the **Tulipán**.

On Vértanuk tere, standing at the crest of a small bridge and looking both wistfully towards Parliament and determinedly away from the Soviet obelisk, is Tamás Varga's 1996 statue of Imre Nagy, tragic hero of the 1956 uprising.

The remarkably ugly Basilica of St Stephen points its façade down Zrínyi utca towards **Gresham Palace** and the river. Principal attraction within is the mummified right hand of St Stephen, which every 20 August is paraded around the car park outside – *see page 45* **Hungary's right-hand man**. József Finta's glossy new postmodern Bank Center, cousin to his **Grand Hotel**

Basilica of St Stephen – *did God want it built at all? See page 66.*

Enigma of the udvar

Built in 1904, the Gozsdu udvar was the heart of the Jewish quarter and once thrived with artisans' workshops. Now, rotting through guilt and loneliness, the empty blocks stare hollow-eyed.

Győző Czigler designed the seven interlocking courtyards and apartment buildings that link Király utca 15 with Dob utca 16 for the Gozsdu Elemér Alapítvány. This charitable foundation, set up by a wealthy Romanian merchant, aimed to ease the chronic housing shortage that greeted skilled craftsmen from the far reaches of the Austro-Hungarian Empire. Czigler's design is a premodern anomaly in his otherwise historicist CV. His 1886 neo-Renaissance Saxenhaler Palace (now housing the **Postal Museum**) bears no relation, nor his former National Casino at Semmelweiss utca 1-3, never mind the neo-baroque **Széchenyi Fürdő** (1913) that crowned his career. Even in its prime the Gozsdu udvar was no conventional architectural masterpiece. It exerts its fascination through enigma.

The udvar's animating principle is akin to a Venus Fly Trap. The curve of the ground plan draws in the curious passerby while its linearity entraps. The udvar progresses through what Greek mathematicians called 'gnomonic expansion'. Each of the square arches recapitulates the initial square at the threshold. When the passerby steps over the threshold and enters this first square, the structure of the udvar becomes an extension of their person. The microcosm beholds the macrocosm: an image of God. A similar principle of sacred geometry guides the design of Hindu temples.

Then there is the paradox thrown up by the confrontation of style. Czigler designed the udvar on the cusp of major shifts in the early modern movement. You'll find art nouveau detailing in the banisters and light holders of the stairwells, yet the brutality of the square of the passageway arches suggests a turn towards functionalism. An assertion of the Egyptian. An aesthetic argument with those who were paying him. And the udvar's form and orientation make it peculiarly receptive to the passage of the sun. There is a moment in the early morning when the balance of light and dark inverts. A fraction of a second when all that has been light becomes dark, and vice versa. A missed heartbeat.

In its decline, the udvar has been claimed by the film industry. Ralph Fiennes, Robin Williams and Terry Gilliam have all graced the square. Wander through on the right day and you might find yourself confronted with extras dressed as Arrow Cross fascists in a low-budget Holocaust film, or thrust into a magical Chinatown, fierce reds complementing the ochre and gold. Architecture as Golem: the further the past recedes the more the udvar is transformed by projection, taking on a life of its own.

Plans for a new boulevard linking the two körúts have thwarted several schemes for redevelopment since the 1970s, yet the udvar remains prime real estate. Postmodern territorial exchanges are touted in 1999 as Romanian businessmen backed by their government demand the return of its ownership to Bucharest. Yet how much longer the udvar's apartment blocks will actually stand is anyone's guess. The majority of tenants were paid to leave in 1994, pending supposed refurbishment, and today the structures are beyond repair.

Gozsdu udvar

VII. Dob utca 16/Király utca 15. M2 Astoria, M1, M2, M3 Deák tér/tram 47, 49. **Open** 6am-10pm daily. **Map D4**

Gozsdu udvar – *'gnomonic expansion'.*

Korvinus Kempinski a few blocks south, adds a forbidding blue glass and polished granite sheen to the south-east corner of Szabadság tér.

Constructed during Hungary's brief flirtation with imperialism and conceived as the hub of the fin-de-siècle economy, Szabadság tér (Liberty Square) was intended to be an image of power and prosperity. It's still dominated by the Dual Monarchy's central bank (now the National Bank at number 9) and the Stock and Commodity Exchange (now the headquarters of Magyar Televízió at number 17). Symbolism was paramount to planners of the square, built on the site of the Új Épület, the Habsburg barracks where leaders of the nascent

Ödön Lechner's **Former Royal Post Office Savings Bank**. *See page 64.*

Hungarian nation had been imprisoned and executed in 1849. Nationalism was to triumph at the expense of good design. The Stock and Commodity Exchange was completed in 1899. With a distorted perspective and exaggerated scale, the mammoth proportions of its entrance and central vaulted hall are terrifying. In the 1920s Szabadság tér became the site of the 'sacred flagstaff', a Hungarian flag flown at half-mast over a mound of soil from territories lost at Trianon.

After World War II, the Soviet Army erected an obelisk commemorating its dead right on top of the sacred mound. The obelisk still stands, with a star on top and reliefs of Soviet soldiers besieging Budapest at its base. One nationalist memorial remains. A diagonal block away down Auflich utca, on the corner of Báthory utca and Hold utca, the Eternal Flame commemorates Count Lajos Battyhány, prime minister of the 1848 provisional government, executed by firing squad at this stop on 6 October 1849.

The American Embassy stands at number 12 and note, nearby, the small statue of US General Harry Hill Bandholtz. An officer of the peace-keeping force in 1919, he saved the treasures of the National Museum from rampaging Romanian soldiers by 'sealing' the doors with the only official-looking seals he had to hand: censorship seals. The Romanians saw the American eagle and backed off down the steps.

Everything around here seems to have some kind of nationalist function. Even the brightest spot of this sombre, officious quarter – Ödön

Lechner's startlingly ornate and colourful **Former Royal Post Office Savings Bank** – was built around forms Lechner considered to be 'original' pre-Christian Hungarian patterns and thus the basis for a new nationalist architecture. Behind the US Embassy and a block south of the Eternal Flame, it's one of the city's most extraordinary buildings. The only pity is that there's nowhere to step back and take a good look at it.

The same can't be said of the **Parliament**, one of Budapest's most conspicuous structures. Built, like the rest of Lipótváros, at a time when Hungary, getting its first and only taste of empire, was in a position to boss around a few Slovaks, Romanians and Croats, it was the largest parliament in the world when it opened in 1902 – larger even than the British Parliament (whose neo-Gothic style and riverside location it aped) then still administering the biggest empire the world has ever seen. Its 691 rooms have never been fully utilised, even in the 16 years before Trianon dismembered Hungarian imperial pretensions. The business of governing Hungary today takes up only 12 per cent of the space. (Offices for the various parties are down the road in the Fehérház – 'White House' – at Széchenyi rakpart 19, formerly the Communist Party headquarters.)

The **Museum of Ethnography**'s position, opposite Parliament on Kossuth Lajos tér and looking pretty governmental itself, says much about how seriously Hungarians take their folk traditions. Along Balassi Bálint utca to the north, the venerable **Szalai cukrászda** and the recent-

ly opened **Markó Könyvszalon** serve coffees, pastries and snacks. Falk Miska utca, running parallel a block further away from the river, is a street of upmarket art galleries, such as the Yoko Ono-owned **Galéria 56**, and antique shops such as the **Pintér Antik Diszkont**.

Former Royal Post Office Savings Bank

Magyar Királyi Takarék Pénztár

V. Hold utca 4, entrance from Szabadság tér 8 (302 3000 ext 3072). M3 Arany János utca. **Open** 9am-2pm Thur, tours of building once a year only; phone for details of open day in Sept. **Map C3**

Ödön Lechner's recently restored masterpiece (1901) is Budapest's most innovative building, worthy of a Gaudí or Jujol. The buildings all around allow tantalising glimpses of its flashing white ceramic or writhing gold serpents crowning green tiles. Lechner's finesse lies in the restraint of his folk-motif detailing combined with a meticulous attention to form. The exuberant colours and sinuous shapes put eclectic Budapest to shame. The bank was founded for peasants and other working people. The folk-art sources and playfulness of the decoration are part of the bank's accessibility. The lights flanking its entrance writhe like sea horses and Zsolnay bees march up to hives perched on top of the verticals. Floral motifs pattern its upper reaches, like the embroidery on those white lace tablecloths sold around Váci utca. The cashiers' hall is the only part accessible to the visitor. Lechner's irreverent style was abhorred by the establishment and banned from public buildings in 1902. This, alas, was his last major commission. Other Lechner buildings worth seeing include the **Museum of Applied Arts** and the **Institute of Geology** at XIV. Stefánia út 14. (*See also chapter* **Architecture**.)

Gresham Palace

V. Roosevelt tér 6. Tram 2. **Map C3**

Designed by Zsigmond Quittner assisted by the Vágó brothers, responsible for much of Budapest's finest 1930s modern architecture, the 'Palace' was commissioned by the Gresham Insurance Society of London and completed in 1906. Today it's a film noir set waiting for its femme fatale. The harsh light of bare neon exposes the extent of ruin with stark contrast, glass and ceramic blackened and decaying. The eroticism of its curves and seediness of disrepair call to mind Walter Benjamin's Arcades Project – venture into the glass-roofed passage and you enter the repressed memory of the capital. Flashbacks of a grander era are still in evidence: the stained glass by Miksa Róth, the wrought-iron peacock gates blighted by late twentieth-century signage, the traces of mosaic detailing on the façade (a gold-haloed relief of Charles Gresham, the company's founder, crowns the gable) combined with the electric geometric detail of the interior, prefiguring art deco. But not for much longer. While residents' action has delayed redevelopment for several years, negotiations are now underway for their departure

Spanning the Danube

Budapest is the most Danubian of all the settlements on central Europe's main waterway. The river defines the city, separating the mentalities of Buda and Pest. On a national level the bridges join rural Hungary with cosmopolitan Europe – an economic necessity recognised by Count István Széchenyi, who organised construction of the Chain Bridge (Lánchíd), Budapest's first modern bridge.

But the Danube has been both a psychological and political frontier since it formed the *limes* of the Roman Empire, separating urban imperialism from the nomadic cultures of the unconquered plains beyond. The Romans built the first permanent crossing: a wooden construction that stood near today's Árpád híd.

Projections of national and civic self-image characterise the design of today's bridges. The Chain Bridge, guarded by stone lions and lit up at night, has a strength and grandeur despite its postcard picturesqueness. It opened in 1849 after the defeat of the Independence movement, yet crystallises the optimism of metropolitan expansion and national ambition. Conversely, the mythical turuls and the shields of 'Greater' Hungary on Szabadság Bridge (1896 – originally named Franz Joseph I Bridge) betray an ambivalence towards the future.

The views from the Elizabeth (Erzsébet) and Margaret (Margit) Bridges are more memorable than the structures themselves. But Margaret Bridge has a Parisian sophistication, mirroring the self-perception of Pest's emerging bourgeoisie.

While the bridges opened up new areas of Budapest for development, the older city suffered. Construction of Elizabeth Bridge (1903) destroyed Pest's medieval centre and the Tabán near Castle Hill. Hungary's first heritage campaign was formed to save the Inner City Parish Church and the road off the bridge obligingly swerves round it.

The Danube bridges have a strategic vulnerability, their destruction a blow to civic and national pride. The Austrians attempted to blow up the Lánchíd in 1849. The Nazis demolished them all in 1945. Memorials to a temporary bridge that carried public transport until 1956 can be found near the Parliament and on the opposite quay at Batthyány tér.

Szabadság Bridge sweeps across the line of Bartók Béla út.

Parliament – *beautifully sited establishment kitsch.*

following the sale of the building to a US hotel chain. Uncertainty shrouds both timescale and the degree to which original architectural features will be respected. Get there first.

Parliament

Országház
V. Kossuth Lajos tér (268 4904). M2 Kossuth Lajos tér/tram 2. Tours in English. *When Parliament is sitting* 10am Wed-Sun; *recess* 8am-4pm Mon, Wed, Thur, Sat, Sun; 8am-2pm Fri.
Tickets Ft900; Ft400 concs from Door 11 to right of main entrance. EB400. **No credit cards.** English spoken. **Map B2**

Centrepiece of the extraordinary invention of history that transformed Budapest at the turn of the century, Imre Steindl's Országház was completed in 1902, six years too late for the Millennium celebrations it was intended to crown. It's beautifully sited: the prominence of its position on the curve of the Danube defines the city and exploits the elegance of the Danube sweep. The building itself, however, is an exercise in establishment kitsch – gloriously so – and it's easy to mock its pretensions: the incongruous eclecticism, the gaudiness of the renovated interior, the iconographic intensity which threatens to overwhelm the assiduous observer. Yet while only five per cent of Budapest's adult population had the right to vote at the time of construction, the country had an electoral turn out of nearly 60 per cent in 1998. A country that enjoys its democracy celebrates it with bright lighting and 88lbs of gold leaf. Lighter moments cheer even the most cynical of anarchist hearts. The guided tour passes the numbered cigar

holders outside the Upper House, where members left their havanas during debates. Note also the shield of Transylvanian Prince János Hunyadi, vanquisher of the Turks, where a wolf bays at a crescent moon, beside a gold star.

Basilica of St Stephen

Szent István Bazilika
V. Szent István tér 33 (117 2859). M3 Arany János utca. **Open** *mass* 7-9am, 5.30-8pm, daily. *Treasury* 10am-5pm Mon-Sat, 1-5pm Sun. *Tower* 9.30am-6pm daily. **Admission** *Treasury* Ft120; Ft80 concs; *tower* Ft400; Ft300 concs. For evening concerts, tickets from VII. Erzsébet körút 29. **Map C3**

The Basilica of St Stephen was designed in 1845 by József Hild, but only consecrated in 1905, the Basilica is Budapest's largest church. Construction was so disrupted by wars and the deaths of its two major architects that one wonders if God actually wanted it built at all. The original dome collapsed in an 1868 storm. An exasperated Miklós Ybl, its new architect, had the entire building demolished and rebuilt the original neo-classical edifice in the heavy neo-Renaissance style favoured by the Viennese court. In World War II the Basilica was devastated by Allied bombing. Restoration only began in 1980 and has yet to be finished. Many prominent artists contributed to the interior, best appreciated during the evening choral and organ concerts. Gyula Benczúr's painting of Szent István offering the Hungarian crown to the Virgin Mary rises above one of the altars, and Miksa Róth's stained glass windows depicting the Holy Kings decorate the Chapel of the Sacred Right. Here lies the main reason to visit. The

mummified fist of Szent István lives in a Mátyás templom-shaped trinket box – a bit like Thing from the Addams Family. Ft20 in the slot lights up this gruesome relic. *See page 45* **Hungary's right-hand man**.

Kiskörút

The southern half of the Kiskörút follows the line of the old city walls – extant portions of which can be seen in Bástya utca behind Vámház körút and also a few yards down Ferenczy István utca off Múzeum körút. The Kiskörút begins at Fővám tér at the Pest foot of Szabadság Bridge, Gellért Hill standing craggily opposite. Marxist philosopher and literary critic George Lukács used to live just by here, in a fifth-floor flat at Belgrád rakpart 2. On the south side of the small square are two buildings: the **Budapest University of Economic Science**, facing the Technical University over the river; and the restored **Great Market Hall** (Nagy Vásárcsarnok), an indoor emporium of stalls selling every kind of meat, fish, vegetable and fruit. The former, designed by Miklós Ybl in neo-Renaissance style, was originally the Main Customs Office (hence Fővám – 'main customs'). The latter was in those days the city's main wholesale market. At one time an underground canal ran from the Danube, taking barges through the customs house and into the market.

Vámház körút leads up to Kálvin tér, named after the ugly Calvinist church on the square's south side. This was once the city's eastern gate and, with the pink, postmodern **Korona Hotel** bridging Kecskeméti utca, still feels somewhat gate-like. From here two roads stab out eastwards into the city: Baross utca, which runs through the heart of District VIII, and Üllői út, which forms the border of Districts VIII and IX and leads eventually to Ferihegy airport. Ráday utca, a narrow commercial street leading off to the south-west, has some interesting shops and bars, including the **Shiraz Persian Sandwich Club**, **El Greco** and **Paris, Texas**.

The next stretch is Múzeum körút, named for the **National Museum** on the east side. The fourth institution of its kind in the world when it was built between 1837-47, it was then so far out of town that cattle are said to have once wandered in. St Stephen's rather bent Crown is the main treasure here. Every 15 March the neo-Classical building gets decked out in red, white and green and crowds fill the forecourt to hear speeches from the steps. This is to commemorate the moment in 1848 when Sándor Petőfi launched the revolt against the Habsburgs by standing here and reading out his evidently inflammatory National Song. On the next corner is the century-old **Múzeum** restaurant, while over the road is the **Központi Antikvárium** and other antiquarian booksellers.

Múzeum körút ends at **Astoria**, where the grand but faded 1912 hotel dominates the intersection to which it has lent its name. Westwards, Kossuth Lajos utca leads towards the Danube and Elizabeth Bridge. East of here it continues as Rákóczi út past Blaha Lujza tér towards Keleti station which, on a clear day, you can spy in the distance. The **Népstadion**, Hungary's biggest sports arena, lies beyond it.

Károly körút continues on up to Deák tér, passing on the right the enormous **Central Synagogue** which guards the entrance to District VII, and a huge apartment block, bridging Madách út, that looks like 1950s Soviet architecture but was actually built in the late 1930s. It was intended as the start of a new avenue but never got further than a couple of blocks.

The 47 and 49 trams run this far up the Kiskörút and Deák tér is the central hub of Budapest's transport network: all three metro lines intersect in the station below, where there's also the cute little **Underground Railway Museum**. Sütő utca, off Deák tér to the south-west by the austerely neo-classical Lutheran Church, has the main office of **Tourinform** – the best place in town to pick up free maps and find details of cultural events.

The old city walls here curved west to meet the river at Vigadó tér. The Kiskörút, however, flattens out and continues on up north past the **Basilica of St Stephen** and down Bajcsy-Zsilinszky út, a drab boulevard named after a right-wing politician who turned anti-fascist.

Central Synagogue – *see page 68.*

The sights, sorted

It's Thursday so it must be Budapest. Given the velocity of modern travel, or the understandable tendency of some to party all night and neglect the cultural itinerary, here we present a lightning tour of the principal attractions. For the price of one Ft700 day ticket (*napijegy*), let the city's speedy transport system whisk you around it all in four hours flat.

Begin at Deák tér, hub of the city's public transport, and take tram 47 or 49 tram down the Kiskörút, quickly rattling past the **Central Synagogue** (1), the **Astoria Hotel** (2) and the **National Museum** (3) before hitting the Danube at Fővam tér by Szabadság Bridge. After a quick peek at the **Great Market Hall** (4), change on to tram 2 running north along the river. Sights whizz by in rapid succession: the Elizabeth and Chain Bridges, the **Inner City Parish Church** (5) the **Vigadó** (6), **Gresham Palace** (7) and **Parliament**. (8). At Vigadó tér you can stop off for a quick bit of shopping in nearby Váci utca, and all along this stretch the views of Gellért Hill and Castle Hill are unsurpassable.

From the tram 2 terminus at Jaszai Mári tér, by Margaret Bridge, change on to the two-a-minute tram 4 or 6 running back down the Nagykörút into central Pest, riding two stops past the **Vigszínház** (9) and **Nyugati Station** (10) to Oktogon. Here dive on to the M1 metro – a sight in itself – which will deliver you to **Heroes' Square** (11) in five minutes or Széchenyi fürdő in seven. Either quickly take in the square's statues and skateboards, **Műcsarnok** (12) and **Museum of Fine Arts** (13), or go for a more leisurely stroll around the Zoo (14), **Vidám Park** (15), **Széchenyi baths** (16), and Vajdahunyad Castle (housing the **Museum of Agriculture**) (17). Then it's back to the stop for the red bus 4 (not the ordinary bus 4) where Andrássy út meets Heroes' Square.

This whisks you on the overland route down the boulevard, back past Oktogon, the **Opera House** (18) and the **Basilica** (19), before crossing the Danube on the Chain Bridge. Allow 12 minutes to reach Clark Ádám tér on the Buda side. Ahead is the **Funicular** (20), which beams you up to the Castle District, with the **Royal Palace and National Gallery** (21), **Mátyás templom and Fisherman's Bastion** (22) and all the other smaller sights of the area. You'll only have to wait an average four minutes in either Disz tér or Szentháromság tér for a dinky Várbusz to escort you over the cobbled streets of Buda, through the Bécsi kapu and down to its terminus above Moszkva tér.

Across Moszkva tér, board tram 4 or 6. From here it's three stops to the Buda foot of Margaret Bridge, from where you can wander up to clock the **Tomb of Gül Baba** (23). From the north side of the road running under the bridge, catch bus 86 heading south. This passes the **Király** baths (24) on Fő utca before dumping you at Battyhány tér, where you can gawp at the **Church of St Anne** (25) and the view of Parliament over the river.

Climb onto a tram 19. This takes you south down the Buda embankment past the Institut Français, Chain Bridge and the Várkert Casino, with views of central Pest beyond. Rattle on under Elizabeth Bridge, pass the **Rudas** (26) baths (the **Rác** baths (27) are also nearby) and get off at Szent Gellért to clock the **Gellért Baths and the Cave Church** (28) (the **Citadella** (29) is a steep climb up from here, but you can always hail a taxi).

Here endeth the tour. You can take refreshment at the **Gellért Eszpresszó** or the nearby **Libella**, or hop on a tram 47 or 49, rattle across Szabadság Bridge and end up back at Deák tér where you started. Bingo. Budapest's principal sights, sorted.

His half-sitting, half-standing statue in Deák tér supposedly depicts the moment he was arrested in Parliament. With grasping hand outstretched, he looks like a man outraged because his pint has just been stolen.

Bajcsy-Zsilinszky út is boring and undistinguished, save the enormous figure who languishes on top of a building at the corner of Ó utca, and the startling glimpse of the **Former Royal Post Office Savings Bank** afforded by looking left down Nagysándor utca, a street that also contains the **Via Luna** restaurant. On the corner of

Alkotmány utca, just before the Kiskörút joins the Nagykörút at Nyugati tér, stands **Becketts** – the huge Irish pub and restaurant that provides expensive beer, bad music and 'rugger' on Sky Sports for Budapest's expatriate business community.

Central Synagogue

Nagy Zsinagóga
VII. Dohány utca 2 (342 8949). M2 Astoria. **Open** *synagogue* 10am-3pm Mon-Fri, Sun; *museum* 10am-4pm Mon-Fri; 10am-1pm Sun. **Admission** *synagogue* by donation; *museum* Ft600; Ft200 concs. Heroes' Temple prayer 6pm Fri, 9am Sat. **Map D4**

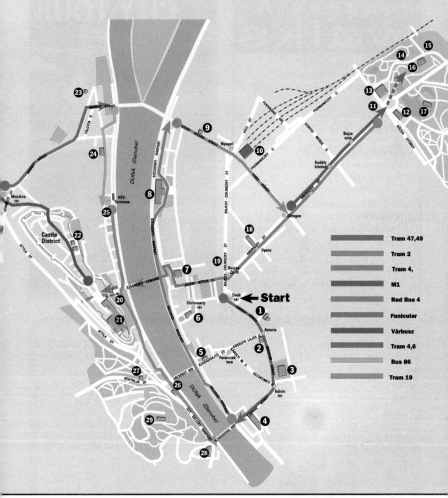

Map labels:

- Tram 47,49
- Tram 2
- Tram 4,
- M1
- Red Bus 4
- Funicular
- Várbusz
- Tram 4,6
- Bus 86
- Tram 19

Start

DUNA (Danube)

Castle District

Moszkva tér

HÉV-Terminus

Nyugati

Oktogon

Opera

Deák tér

Astoria

Vörösmarty tér

Ferenciek tere

Kálvin tér

Moszkva tér

MARGIT KÖRÜT

SZÉCHENYI RAKPART

SZÉCHENYI-LÁNCHÍD

ERZSÉBET HÍD

SZABADSÁG HÍD

PETŐFI HÍD

HEGYALJA UT

ATTILA UT

BAJCSY-ZSILINSZKY UT

ANDRÁSSY UT

VÁCI UT

PODMANICZKY U.

DÓZSA GYÖRGY

Bajza utca

Kodály körönd

Designed by Lajos Förster and completed in 1859, this is the second-largest synagogue in the world after New York's Temple Emmanuel. Seating 3,000 and too big to heat, it has never been used in winter. The synagogue is a monument to the patriotism of the Hungarian Jewish bourgeoisie. Newly cleaned brickwork glows in blue, yellow and red, the heraldic colours of Budapest. Fresh gold leaf gleams on Moorish domes, their orientalism a reaction against Austrian rule. Interlaced eight-pointed stars in the brick detailing, continued in the stained glass and mosaic flooring inside, are a symbol of regeneration – appropriate once again after the recently com-

pleted $10-million, ten-year facelift financed by the Hungarian government and Tony Curtis' Emmanuel Foundation. The divisions of its central space are based on the cabbalistic Tree of Life, giving it a similar floor plan to a Gothic cathedral. The dark wooden pews are numbered, some poignantly tagged with names of those long dead, and its freshly painted ceiling entwines Stars of David outlined in gold leaf. An inscription of Jaweh surrounded by a blaze of glory radiates above the Arc of the Covenant, lit from overhead by an opening in its covering dome.

The synagogue's annexe, the Heroes' Temple, designed by Ferenc Faragó and László Vágó in

1929-31, is a memorial to Hungarian Jews who died fighting in World War I. The simple concrete arching colonnade encloses the Garden of Remembrance, now a mass grave for Jews massacred by fellow Hungarians in 1945. Imre Varga's weeping willow memorial to those killed in concentration camps is visible from Wesselényi utca. Family names of the dead are inscribed on its leaves. Towards the end of World War II, 20,000 Jews were herded inside here, 7,000 of whom perished within.

Great Market Hall

Nagy Vásárcsarnok
IX. Fővám tér (218 5322). Trams 2, 47, 49. **Open** 7am-6pm Mon-Fri; 7am-1pm Sat. **Map D5**
The three-storey Great Market Hall was opened in 1897. It was a spectacular shopping mall in its day, featuring barges gliding down an indoor canal to deliver the stallholders' goods, with a railway line that went up to the market gates. Under Communism the building began to crumble and fall apart, but the city council decided to restore the site rather than demolish it and the market reopened in 1994 with a gleaming new Zsolnay tile roof. Even without the indoor canal, the Great Market Hall is still pretty grand. About 30,000 shoppers a day pass through the hall, trawling the 180 stalls for fresh vegetables, meat, fish, bread and cheeses. There's also a big supermarket in the basement, where the **Ázsia** also keeps foreigners supplied with exotic non-Hungarian ingredients. Liveliest on a Saturday morning.

Nagykörút

At exactly 4,114 metres, the Nagykörút is the longest thoroughfare in the city, running from Petőfi Bridge in the south to Margaret Bridge in the north and passing through Districts IX, VIII, VII, VI and XIII en route. Trams 4 and 6 run the whole distance, starting at Móricz Zsigmond körtér in Buda, and ending up back on that side of the river in Moszkva tér.

A busy commercial boulevard built, like much of nineteenth-century Pest, entirely in eclectic style, it is here, rather than on upmarket Váci utca, that the real day-to-day business of downtown Budapest takes place. American fast-food franchises thrive on every other corner, but new western logos haven't quite driven out all the beautifully dated neon signs.

On the Ferenc körút stretch you'll see people dressed in green and white – the colours of **Ferencváros**, the local football club, Hungary's most popular and known for its bone-headed rightwing following. The ugly concrete building on the south-west corner of the Üllői út intersection is known as the Lottóház – its apartments were given away as prizes in the 1950s. The contrast with Ödön Lechner's extraordinary and colourful **Museum of Applied Arts** round the corner couldn't be more complete. The building on the south-east side is a former army barracks. This and the **Corvin multiplex** tucked away in Corvin köz behind the intersection were the scenes of fierce fighting during the 1956 revolution.

Kerepesi Cemetery – *communists toe the line in death as in life. See page 84.*

Margaret Bridge – *crossing the river with Parisian sophistication.*

Continuing north as József körút, the boulevard acquires a disreputable air as it passes through District VIII. Sleazy bars advertise sex shows, the **Stex Alfréd** gambling complex does a brisk trade and downmarket whores ply their wares day and night in the streets behind Rákóczi tér. One shop on this stretch (it's on the west side, near the Baross utca tram stop) sells absolutely nothing but soda syphon chargers. Running off to the left at this point, Krúdy Gyula utca is fast becoming one of the city's most fashionable streets.

At Blaha Lujza tér, Népszínház utca runs away south-east towards **Kerepesi cemetery** and the vast and seedy **Józsefvárosi piac**, the place to buy Chinese tat. Rákóczi út runs back towards Astoria and on up to Keleti station, its façade quite distinct from this vantage. Frank Zappa fans will appreciate **Z Hangelemez** in the courtyard of Rákóczi út 47, one of Budapest's more curious record shops. 'Blaha', as it's universally known, has the **Centrum Corvin** department store and an M2 metro station.

As it passes into District VII and its name changes to Erzsébet, the körút gets noticeably glitzier. Cinemas and theatres, such as the **Hunnia** and **Horizont**, begin to appear, and a hotel complex has been converted into the **Hotel Royal Club & Café** and the **Royal 2000 Funky Club**. This is the best stretch for elegantly quaint neon. A block up from Blaha the venerable **New York Kávéház**, rammed by a tank in 1956, stands in dire need of renovation. The **Fészek** restaurant and artists' club, a block away down Dob utca, has managed to survive the

twentieth century intact, and offers peaceful summer dining in a picturesquely tatty inner courtyard, formerly a monks' cloister.

Crossing Király utca, a lively street worth delving into, Erzsébet changes into Teréz körút as it stumbles into District VI. The **Zeneakadémia**, Budapest's principal concert hall, is a block west down Király on the corner of Liszt Ferenc tér.

Oktogon, where the Nagykörút intersects broad Andrássy út, is the grandest intersection, once lined with coffeehouses but now sadly dominated by burger joints. In the Communist days this was November 7 Square; under Horthy it was named after Mussolini. The M1 metro stops here, on its way underneath Andrássy út to **Heroes' Square** and the **Városliget** (City Park) beyond.

Teréz körút is the flashiest segment of boulevard and brightest at night. Here there are more cinemas, such as the **Művész** and **Metro**, various restaurants and bars, and the respectable **Béke Radisson Hotel** in the run-up to the Nagykörút's most magnificent landmark: **Nyugati station**. Built by the Eiffel company in 1874-77 (in the low-rent shopping complex underneath, everything seems to be named after Eiffel: tacky shops, amusement arcades, dowdy coffee bars), it's a pale-blue palace of iron and glass. The panes in front allow you to see inside the station, making arriving and departing trains part of the city's street life. In the early 1970s this became literally so, when one engine crashed through the façade and came to rest at the tram stop. The **E-Play** disco occupies two floors of Nyugati's eastern tower.

Over the road, the mirror glass frontage of the Skála is by contrast oddly forbidding for a department store, despite attempts to enliven the square with summer lunchtime concerts. Its role as the retail hub of this end of town was, at the time of going to press, about to be upstaged by the enormous new West End City Center mall, behind Nyugati station along Váci út.

Views of Nyugati from Szent István körút are spoilt by the unsightly road bridge carrying traffic over Nyugati tér between Bajcsy-Zsilinszky út and Váci út, which leads on up to the busy Lehel tér produce market. The only stretch that isn't named after a Habsburg, Szent István körút is also the only part where there's very much of interest at night. **Okay Italia** does a roaring trade, while **Szieszta** purveys pizzas until 4am. The **Franklin Trocadero** is Budapest's only Latin dance club.

Built in the 1930s and originally a middle-class Jewish district, Újlipótváros and its main thoroughfare, Pozsonyi út, is also lively by day, with lots of small shops, a busy street life and the Szent István Park opening out on to the Danube. There's nothing in particular to see, but these are amiable streets for a stroll.

Centrepiece of this last stretch of körút is the stubbily baroque **Vígszínház** (Comedy Theatre). Built in 1896 and renovated in 1995, this has pretensions of grandeur, but in a certain light looks like nothing so much as a tawdry end-of-the-pier attraction. The **Művész Bohém Kávéház** behind it is a charming spot for dinner. Szent István körút ends at Jászai Mari tér, terminus of the number 2 tram. Here traffic sweeps on to Margit híd (Margaret Bridge), a Y-shaped construction that leads not only to Buda and the Rózsadomb, but also to the traffic-free and wooded park of **Margaret Island**.

Margaret Island

Neither Pest nor Buda, the Margaret Island (Margitsziget), which stretches from Margaret Bridge to Árpád Bridge, a walk of about 20 minutes, is named after the thirteenth-century King Béla IV's ultra-pious daughter, St Margaret. The ruins of her Dominican nunnery still stand on the island's east side not far from the remains of a Franciscan church. Margaret Island is also known as 'Rabbit Island', a reference to ancient times when this island was wooded, difficult for humans to get to, and filled (presumably) with rabbits.

In summer the island is jammed with people heading to either the Hajós Alfréd swimming pool or the Palatinus Strand to swim and splash about. The Hajós pool complex includes a diving pool, an open-air pool and a children's pool. At the **Palatinus Strand**, as well as at the **Thermal Hotel Margitsziget**, there are thermal baths fed from springs on the island. (*See also chapters* **Sport & Fitness** *and* **Baths**.)

Several relics survive from the island's time as a religious centre. On the east side are the ruins of the Dominican church and convent, where there is a shrine to St Margit herself. Further north is the Premonstratensian Chapel, orginally built in the twelfth century on an older site and reconstructed in 1930-31. North of the Dominican ruins is an array of busts and sculptures of Hungarian artists and writers, near the Open-Air Theatre and the UNESCO-protected water tower.

In the summer it's possible to hire bicycles (bring ID to leave as a deposit) or strange pedal-

A pleasant retreat from the city.

powered and canopied two-seater contraptions. Lazier visitors can ride in a horse-drawn buggy.

For all its central location, Margaret Island feels pleasantly distant from the city. Private cars are banned and the island is the ideal place for an afternoon spent strolling among the 10,000 trees.

New York Kávéház

VII. Erzsébet körút 9/11 (322 3849). M2 Blaha. Tram 4, 6. **Open** *café* 10am-midnight, *restaurant* noon-3.30pm, 6.30-11pm, daily. **Credit** AmEx, DC, EC, MC, V. **Map E4**

Don't visit for the overpriced cappuccino (*see also* chapter **Cafés & Coffeehouses**) but do go look at the architecture. Built in 1894 by Alajos Hauszmann (the architect also then responsible for renovations to the Royal Palace) the spectacular neo-baroque interior with twisting columns, cheeky cherubs, lush vel-

vets, and marble and gold leaf caused a sensation at its opening and still draws crowds of tourists to what was once the main hangout of literary and artistic Budapest. Nymphs and satyrs cavort on the ceilings, and 'New Yorkia' brandishes a miniature Statue of Liberty near the expresso bar. Peering through the plastic plants spot the caricatures of the journalists of the 1950s and '60s who made it their haunt, from the newspaper offices that used to occupy the upper floors. Rammed by a tank in 1956, its façade still hasn't been renovated. Visit before it all falls down.

A tale of two cities

For the tourist, a trip to Hungary's capital is dominated by the majestic sights of Buda. For the average Pest resident, Buda is a place you either live in because you are well off, or you go there for picnics. For a Buda resident, Pest is a place you go to work, and then hightail it out of before dark.

Buda is old, proud, quiet and a bit dotty, like an old aunt you only visit on weekends. It owns a poodle. It never puts its rubbish on the street. It goes to bed early. It glows with pride as it watches busloads of Belgian schoolkids gawp at its churches.

Pest is the anomoulous schizo in the flat next door. Beautiful, confusing, often loud and incomprehensible and quite likely to keep you awake far into the night if you aren't careful. It prefers a pit bull terrier. It's too old to be considered the 'new' side of town, and too new to worry about safe sex. For a tourist, it doesn't quite know how to present itself, and is mostly too busy to care.

The differences go back a long way. Buda, location of the Royal Palace, was the seat of power. Whether you wanted to cosy up to some corrupt king or just burn his playhouse down for the umpteenth time always led you to the western bank of the Danube. Of course, to get there you might have had to bribe, burn or pillage your way across Pest, a sleepy market town on the east bank. Things haven't changed a whole lot today, in fact.

When the Turks occupied Buda very few Hungarians resided on the western bank of the Danube, mainly because there were no churches in Turkish Buda. Bosnians, Serbs, Gypsies and Sephardic Jews made up the bulk of the working and trading classes. After the Habsburgs retook the castle in 1686, Buda was repopulated by German-speaking Swabians. Buda thus maintained a Catholic loyalist bent towards the Habsburg regime which persevered into this century. German was still widely

spoken in Buda in the early twentieth century, and pockets of Sváb Germans still maintain their disinct language and beery gemütlichkeit – complete with oom-pah brass bands – in Óbuda and Budaőrs, as well as in nearby villages such as Solymar and Budakeszi.

Pest, on the other hand, had always been a city speaking Hungarian. Economically and culturally locked in with the Hungarian plains, Pest became a melting pot where the different nationalities of the Carpathian basin forged themselves a new identity based on speaking Hungarian. It was in Pest that Magyars, Slovaks, Jews, Germans and others united in 1848 as Hungarians, and speaking Hungarian was the passport to acceptance in society, literature and business. Apart from late night partying in the Tabán district, Buda became quite socially irrelevant. When Admiral Horthy, the ultimate party pooper, ordered the Tabán destroyed in the 1930s, he basically nailed the coffin shut on having fun in Buda. It was like ploughing Montmartre into a parking lot.

The dichotomy of a dour, conservative Buda versus a lively, progressive Pest continues to this day. People tend to stick to their own side of the river when going out casually. Buda's hills provide a fresher atmosphere in the dusty hot summers, so the upper classes reside there – especially in posh Rózsadomb. Working-class families prefer shady but flat Zugló in Pest. Even though there is a large university complex in south Buda, students socialise in Pest, where almost all concert venues and late-night bars are located.

It doesn't stop there. Most art collections are in Buda. All of the football stadiums are in Pest. Buda's groceries stock olive oil and raddiccio, while Pest's are museums of starchy Hungarian staples. Bread is generally thought to be better in Buda than in Pest. Wine is cheaper in Pest. And everyone knows that the most beautiful girls all live in Újpest.

The archangel Gabriel at Heroes' Square lords it over Andrássy út.

Andrássy út & District VI

Andrássy út, built between 1872-85 with the continent's first electric underground railway running underneath, is the spine of District VI. Intended as Budapest's answer to the Champs-Elysées, it stretches for 2.5 kilometres and has had a variety of names: Sugárút (Radial Avenue), Andrássy út (after the nineteenth-century statesman), Sztalin út and the tongue-twisting Népköztársaság útja (Avenue of the People's Republic) before being renamed Andrássy once more in 1989.

After a decade of 'transition', Andrássy út is finally beginning to attract the kinds of shops and businesses that can do justice to its grand proportions – car showrooms, jewellery shops, grand cafés – especially on its liveliest stretch, between Bajcsy-Zsilinszky út and Oktogon. The venerable **Művész** coffeehouse and **Irók Boltja** (Writers' Bookshop) are down here, as are the **Belcanto** and **Bombay Palace** restaurants, and the **Goethe Institut** with its **Eckermann** café.

Few individual buildings stand out from the uniform eclectic style, with two notable exceptions: Miklós Ybl's **Opera House**, where the appeal of the architecture is perhaps greater than the quality of the productions, and Béla Lajta's extraordinary 1910 Parisiana nightclub (now **Új Színház**), a worthwhile 50-metre detour down Dalszínház utca.

Nagymező utca, with the main **MÁV** office on the corner (best place to get advance train tickets), is known as Budapest's Broadway. Here there are some recently renovated West End-style theatres (including the **Thália** and the **Operett**) and a couple of nightspots, notably the **Piaf**, after-hours hangout for an older arty set. Nagymező utca is on the up, and there is talk of pedestrianisation.

The area to the north and west of Andrássy – a triangle also bounded by Teréz körút and Bajcsy-Zsilinszky út – is by day a dull commercial district (although it does include **Wave** and **Trance**, two of the city's better specialist record shops) but by night offers a cluster of eccentric bars and restaurants. **Aloe Kávézó, Articsóka, Pizza Bella, Marquis de Salade, Noiret** and **Crazy Café** are all around here.

More nightlife can be found on Liszt Ferenc tér, which leads from Andrássy up to the Zeneakadémia, and the square bustles with people on a summer evening with tables outside **Incognito, Café Mediterran, Café Vian** and assorted other venues.

One curiosity on the first stretch of Andrássy út. In the courtyard of No. 27 there's the Esperanto centre. Hungary is the only country in the world with state exams in Esperanto, and where the 'universal tongue' (modelled on Romanian and invented by a Pole) is accepted as a second language for university entrance requirements. It's taught in about 30 schools and an estimated 50,000 Hungarians speak it – meaning, ironically, they have not one language nobody else in the world understands, but two.

The middle stretch of Andrássy út – between Oktogon and the Kodály körönd – is the most boring part, with mainly institutional and bureaucratic buildings. The unprepossessing number 60, though, was once feared enough to make people cross the road to avoid it. These days sporting a Chemokomplex sign, it was the secret police headquarters for both the Horthy and Communist regimes. The **Lukács** at number 70 is one of Budapest's more venerable coffeehouses, now forming part of a bank. Over the road at number

69 there's the neo-Renaissance Képzőművészeti Főiskola (Old Exhibition Hall), now the College of Fine Arts, which also contains the **Budapest Puppet Theatre**.

Kodály körönd is the Rond-Point of Andrássy út, and was clearly once very splendid. The four palatial townhouses that enclose it are dilapidated but still fascinating. The composer Zoltán Kodály used to live in the turreted number 87-89, and his old apartment now serves as the **Kodály Memorial Museum**. Off to the west at Sziv utca 16 there's a plaque marking the house where Arthur Koestler lived as a child.

The final stretch of Andrássy út is wider than the rest of it, mostly occupied by villas set back from the road. This is Budapest's main diplomatic quarter and many embassies are here and in the surrounding streets (Benczúr utca is shady and quiet and full of art nouveau mansions, one of which houses the **British Council**). The Yugoslav embassy where Imre Nagy holed up for a while in

1956 is the last building on the southern corner by Hősök tere. This stretch also features the **Made Inn Music Club**, a combination rock club and terrace restaurant, and the **Média Club Étterem**, a press club where the bar is open to the public.

Opera House

Magyar Állami Operaház
VI. Andrássy út 22 (353 01 70). M1 Opera. **Open** *box office* 10am-7pm Tue-Sat when there is a performance; 10am-1pm, 4-7pm, Sun when there is a performance. **Credit** AmEx. Some English spoken. **Map D3**

Miklós Ybl's neo-Renaissance Opera House was the most culturally significant of the monuments built to commemorate the Millennium celebrations. Completed in 1884, it was also one of the few actually finished in time. Financial constraints forced Ybl to scale down his proposals, but the interior is still lavish. Seven kilograms of gold were used to gild the intimate auditorium and 260 bulbs light up the enormous chandelier. The Opera House's cultural importance has always been linked to Hungarian national identi-

Heroes' Square – St Stephen brandishes his customised cross.

ty. Ybl, who personally supervised every detail, subverted the implied colonialism of the Viennese-favoured neo-Renaissance style by incorporating masonic allusions, such as the smiling sphinxes and the alchemical iconography on the wrought-iron lamp-posts. Ferenc Erkel, the Opera's first director, composed the doleful Hungarian national anthem. Operas by Erkel, Liszt, Kodály and Bartók are still prominent on the programme.

Új Színház

VI. Paulay Ede utca 35 (269 6021). M1 Opera. **Open** for performances. **Tickets** from box office or Andrássy út 18. Closed mid-June-Sept. **No credit cards. Map D3**

Originally built as the Parisiana nightclub (1910), Béla Lajta's striking symmetrical geometric design peeps out from behind the far grander Ballet School on Andrássy út. It's well worth the short detour. Nine ceramic angels with gold inlaid wings carry turquoise mosaic plaques with the letters of its name. The polished granite of its façade is punctuated by grey monkeys. Ziggurat motifs on the door, continued inside, hint at the possible Babylonian origins of his inspiration. Meticulously restored inside, it's worth the ticket price for a look around.

Heroes' Square & City Park

A symbol of confident nineteenth-century nationalism, Heroes' Square (Hősök tere) is a monumental celebration of mythic Magyardom. Completed for the 1896 Magyar Millennium that celebrated the anniversary of Hungarian tribes arriving in the Carpathian basin, it's flanked by the **Műcsarnok** and the **Museum of Fine Arts** and centred on the Archangel Gabriel, perched on top of a 36-metre column and staring boldly down Andrássy út. Gabriel gets pole position because, according to Hungarian legend, Pope Sylvester II sent a crown to King Stephen after his personal intervention. Perched in the two colonnades are statues of assorted Hungarian kings and national heroes, from St Stephen to Lajos Kossuth. Now often crowded with skateboarders, Heroes' Square has witnessed many key events of modern Hungarian history – most recently the ceremony to mark the reburial of Imre Nagy, leader of the 1956 revolution, the event that in June 1989 marked the rebirth of democracy in Hungary. Nagy's remains are at **Újköztemető Cemetery.**

Hősök tere is essentially the front gate to City Park (Városliget) – Pest's most interesting park. Laid out by the French designer Nebbion, it includes a boating lake, the **Széchenyi baths**, the **Zoo**, **Vidám** (Amusement) **Park**, the **Transport Museum** and **Petőfi Csarnok** concert hall (and its weekend **Bolhapiac** – flea market) among its amenities. Once the site of the 1896 Magyar Millennium exhibition, the theme-park feel of the place survives in the Disneyfied mock-Transylvanian design of Vadjahunyad castle, now

home to the **Agriculture Museum**, which embodies bits of every Hungarian architectural style up to the nineteenth century. In the courtyard nearby stands Miklós Ligeti's sculpture of well-known chronicler Anonymous. People take snaps of each other sitting in the hooded figure's lap. There's also a statue of George Washington in the park, erected in 1906 through subscriptions from Hungarian emigrants to the US. Just next to the Zoo, **Gundel** restaurant offers an expensively recreated taste of the old days.

Vidám Park

XIV. Állatkerti körút 14/16 (343 0996). M1 Széchenyi fürdő. **Open** *summer* 9.45am-8pm Tue-Sun; *winter* 9.45am-sunset Tue-Sun. **Admission** Ft100; Ft50 children. **No credit cards. Map F1**

The old-style rides in this vintage amusement park – a beautiful Victorian merry-go-round, an assortment of ancient test-your-strength machines, 'dodzsem' cars, laughably tame ghost trains, the world's slowest big wheel and a wooden roller coaster that appears to be held together by chewing-gum and string – are gradually being replaced by more modern western rides. Though it's recently been acquired by a western company, and further modernisations are clearly imminent, the Vidám ('Happy') Park still retains an appealingly ramshackle charm. The János Vitéz Barlangvasút – a 'cave railway' featuring cutesy dioramas from Sándor Petőfi's children's poem *Kukorica Jancsi*, recited over speakers as you ride through – is one defiantly Hungarian attraction. There's also an amusement park for toddlers right next door.

Zoo

Állatkert

XIV. Állatkerti út 6-12 (268 1970). M1 Széchenyi fürdő. **Open** *summer* 9am-7pm Tue-Sun; *winter* 9am-4pm Tue-Sun. **Admission** Ft500, Ft400 children. **No credit cards. Map E1**

Budapest's Zoo, completed in 1911, once had buildings that placed every animal in an architectural surrounding supposedly characteristic of its place of origin. Until recently all that remained of these were Neuschloss-Knüsli's extraordinary Elephant House and the Main Gate, though there's also a Palm House built by the Eiffel company. Renovations are now well under way, however, and the faux Moorish Africa House complex looks splendid after a Ft110 million overhaul. Conditions for the animals are also improving giving lions, panthers, leopards and elephants a bit more room to breathe and prowl. Children can pet tame animals in the Állatsimogató (stroking zoo), open in the summer.

District VII

Like so much else in Budapest that dates from the latter half of the last century, the **Central Synagogue** on Dohány utca is grandiose and simply enormous – so big it's impossible to heat and has never been used in winter. Though tucked dis-

Zoo – *faux Moorish Elephant House. P77.*

creetly behind the junction with Károly körút – you don't see the thing until you're almost upon it – the building stands like some twin-domed Moorish fortress, guarding the district behind.

District VII, or Erzsébetváros, between the Kiskörút and the Nagykörút, Andrássy út and Rákóczi út, is Budapest's Jewish quarter, established here in the eighteenth century when Jews were still forbidden to live within the city walls. These days people call it 'the Ghetto', although it never was one until 1944-45, when Arrow Cross fascists walled off this whole area and herded the Jewish community inside. The junction by the Central Synagogue was one of two entrances.

It's not as picturesque or as ancient as Prague's Jewish quarter, but although 700,000 Hungarian Jews were murdered in the Holocaust, enough survived to mean that District VII is still a living community. You can occasionally hear Yiddish spoken on Kazinczy utca, or eat a kosher pastry at the **Fröhlich Cukrászda** on Dob utca. Several synagogues in the area are still active – the small Heroes' Temple (named for Jewish soldiers killed in World War I) behind the Central Synagogue, the Orthodox synagogue on Kazinczy utca and a hidden Hasidic prayer house in the courtyard of Vasvári utca 5 – and a number of Jewish organisations have their headquarters at Síp utca 12.

The Orthodox complex, including the **Carmel Pince** restaurant, is centred around the corner of Dob utca and Kazinczy utca – dominated by the 1910 synagogue whose façade gracefully negotiates the curve of the street. The Rumbach Sebestyén utca synagogue – a Moorish structure by Otto Wagner –

can only be seen from the outside. Resoration is bogged down in ownership disputes.

The community has survived both an exodus of younger, wealthier Jews into less noisy and congested districts, and post-war attempts by the Communist government to homogenise the area. If you'd survived the Holocaust, you got to keep your flat. Workers brought into Budapest to work on the reconstruction of the city were housed in the empty properties.

Many of these were Gypsies and District VII is now also the Gypsy quarter – although the heart of Gypsy territory is beyond the Nagykörút, an area of broken phone boxes, repair shops and dingy borozós where people have wine for breakfast. In that area there's the drab **Nemzeti Színház**, which looks more like a National Car Park than a National Theatre, as well as the **Stamp Museum**, but otherwise it's pretty devoid of particular things to see. Ármin Hegedűs's 1906 Primary School at Dob utca 85 is definitely worth a detour, though.

The heart of the Jewish quarter is Klauzál tér, featuring assorted Jewish businesses and the District VII market hall. In summer, old men play cards and chess under the trees. The best taste of how it once was is afforded by the **Gozsdu udvar** – a linked series of courtyards running between Dob utca and Király utca. *See page 62* **Enigma of the udvar**.

Király utca was 70 per cent Jewish at the turn of the century. It's still full of character and commotion, with old Stalinist-style shop signs, curious courtyards and an informal market for dodgy goods on the corner of Kis Diófa utca. The backstreets are dark, narrow, tatty and full of odd detail. Síp utca has some fascinating buildings, including the secessionist Metro Klub on the corner of Dohány utca sporting one of Budapest's best old neon signs, and a number 11 with neo-Gothic doorways, gargoyles and the statue of a seventeenth-century halberdier. Kazinczy utca is intriguing too, with the stretch between Wesselényi utca and Király utca containing the 1930s **Hungarian Museum of Electrotechnics** in a sort of junior totalitarian style, the Orthodox synagogue, and a final stroll up to the **Wichmann** bar, a lonely but welcoming tavern that by night casts an almost medieval glow.

A fine mini-pub crawl can be had around here, taking in the Wichmann, **Sixtus**, and Incognito and Café Mediterran up on Liszt Ferenc tér, and then maybe moving over Andrássy to Piaf and beyond. If you're walking alone, though, be just a little bit wary at night.

District VIII

Outside of its central tip, District VIII is a crime-ridden, run-down area that is Budapest's red light district and heartland of the mafia, both Ukrainian and Chinese. (If Pest ever acquires a Chinatown, this is where it will be.) But it's not all lowlife.

Klauzál tér – open-air chess at the heart of District VII.

Bounded by Üllői út and Rákóczi út, the urban pie-slice of Józsefváros, as District VIII is also known, has its point at the National Museum. In Pollack Mihály tér behind, former mansions rub shoulders with the socialist-realist Magyar Rádió headquarters, scene of much bloodletting in 1956. Krudy Gyula utca beyond is now a hub of the fashionable 'alternative', with the **Darshan Udvar** and **Café**, the **Iguana** clothes shop, and **IndieGo** and **CD Bar** music shops beginning to create a kind of counter-cultural critical mass. Around the corner on Baross utca is the **Egyedi Ruha Galéria** and other clothing shops. The **Fél 10** can be found at No. 30. Hungry shoppers might seek out **Club 93 Pizzeria** on Vas utca, one of the city's few gay-owned venues.

The area beyond the Nagykörút is vast and unpredictable. On and around Népszinház utca there are many fine buildings, such as Béla Lajta's 1912 Harsányi House at No. 19 and the Trade School at Vas utca 11, designed by Lajos Kozma. To the north, Köztársaság tér boasts the Erkel Szinház and a highrise housing project of the mid-1930s pioneered by the Hungarian section of the CIAM. Continue east up Dologház utca and on the corner with Fiumei út you'll find the macabre reliefs of the former Budapest Labour Insurance building. Its central tower (1931) is all that is left of the city's first (and only) skyscraper.

But the area south of Népszinház utca, centred on Matyás tér, is the heart of Józsefváros. It's an area of friendly antagonisms, where grass often grows through cracks in the pavement and the stranger is just as likely to be entertained by a guitar-playing Roma transvestite as challenged to a game of billiards by a grandmother on her fourth pálinka of the afternoon. Prostitutes work the squares and street corners. Many of the shops are Chinese discount stores or sad old repair shops. Eclectic façades are shabby and crumbling while overgrown inner courtyards buzz with a ragged, almost medieval life.

Acute poverty bred generations of the Awkward Squad. A broken plaque on Leonardo da Vinci utca 32 notes the illegal offices of the 1930s Communist Party secretariat and the murder of its officials. You'll also find the experimental photography of the **Bolt Galéria** at No. 40. Bullet holes still riddle the streets behind key 1956 flashpoints. Scaffolding on the ELTE Sociology Department on Bródy Sándor utca dates from the fighting outside Magyar Rádió next door. Many of those executed following the uprising lived in District VIII. Photography in the Budapest Collection of the Ervin Szabó Library testifies to the devastation of the area caused by the Soviet intervention, tanks rolling down the tiniest of streets.

The spirit of resistance also infused Józsefváros Jewish life before World War II. **MTK**, the district's cup-winning football team, is still proud of its anti-Nazi history. Pelé and Sylvester Stallone played here during filming of the 1981 *Escape to Victory*. The Zsibárus Ház (Magdolna utca 40-46, Lujza utca 16 and Dobozi utca 19-21) was the only place in Budapest where the Arrow Cross were

District VIII – prostitutes and Chinese restaurants.

met with armed Jewish resistance. Grimmer is the knowledge that Józsefvárosi palyaudvar was selected by Adolf Eichmann for the Holocaust deportations. The Jewish section of **Kerepesi Cemetery** still lies desecrated. These days Gypsies and Chinese comprise the most significant communities. Several Roma civil rights organisations are based in District VIII, including the Roma Parliament.

Venture into a bar or two – perhaps the Falatozó Büfé at Magdolna utca 53 or the Kis Prater at Baross utca 82 – and you'll find a warm, though starkly impoverished, neighbourhood atmosphere. Just don't knock over anyone's drinks or wave your wallet around, and remain a little watchful on the streets.

Other hoods

Óbuda

The oldest part of the city (in archeological terms, at least), Óbuda was a separate village until 1873 and still has something of a different vibe from the rest of Budapest. This may not last for much longer, though. A new shopping complex, surrounded by offices and eateries, has begun to lend the regenerated centre of Óbuda the sanitised buzz of the metropolis rather than the quaint time-warp of a half-abandoned village.

The Romans established the town of Aquincum here, although no one knew it had been there until late in the nineteenth century. All that's left are remains of a military amphitheatre on the corner of III. Nagyszombat utca and Pacsirtamező utca, a few columns under Flórián tér and the disappointing contents of the **Aquincum Museum**. The road to Aquincum from central Óbuda is also littered with occasional Roman remains, caked in layers of traffic grime.

The Magyars arrived in the ninth century, christening the area Buda, which later got changed to Óbuda (Old Buda) when the first Royal Palace went up on Castle Hill.

Despite the clusters of tower blocks and the Flórián tér flyover, the area was pretty much forgotten about until the recent redevelopment. Low-roofed houses slowly crumble around the spankingly gaudy Kolosy tér shopping centre, whose car park gleams with the flash western motors belonging to the city's young business crowd gathered at the **Rolling Rock**.

Locals still consider themselves proudly independent of Budapest – the chant of Óbuda's football club (III. kerület TVE) is 'Come on you district!' – a hangover from the days when the area had an industry based on shipbuilding and viticulture. These days the old factories and boatyards at the southern end of Óbuda island (also known as Hajógyári sziget – 'boat factory island') are slowly being colonised by nightlife venues and offices for the culture industries.

Apart from Aquincum's Roman ruins, a few art museums (the **Kiscelli**, the **Vasarely** and the **Budapest Galéria**) and the **Supersonic Technicum** nightclub, the only reasons to come up here are the stretch of bars and stalls selling

Óbuda – littered with Roman remains.

Csepel Island – pockets of heavy industry.

cheap fish on the Danube by Római fürdő. For a week or so every August, the area buzzes with activity as Hungary's rocking youth crams out Óbuda Island for the **Sziget** festival (*see chapter* **Budapest By Season**).

Csepel

Budapest's industrial District XXI perches at the very tip of Csepel Island, to the south of the centre. Militant and independent-minded, it was known as 'Red Csepel' in the interwar years. In 1944 Csepel was the site of one of the few successful acts of mass resistance to the Nazis as locals refused to be evicted en masse, and in 1956 its local workers' council was one of the longest to hold out against the Soviets.

It's easily reached by the HÉV from Boráros tér, an interesting ride running down by the Danube. Szent Imre tér is the centre of the area. Down the end of Tanácsház utca is the main gate for the enormous Csepel Iron and Metal Works. Founded as the Manfred Weiss Works and for a while in the 1950s named after Mátyás Rákosi (the huge Lenin statue that once stood outside the gates is now a feature of the **Statue Park**). The Csepel Works are no longer one monolithic state enterprise, employing the population of a small town, with its own shops, nursery and sports club. But pockets of industry still operate within the complex, their owners encouraged by low rents.

Although it is not strictly speaking allowed, it's easy to get inside the works. Tell them you're visiting the Gyártörténi Múzeum (the 'Factory History' Museum which exists on Központi út inside, but is invariably closed) and they'll issue you with a pass resembling a raffle ticket. After that, feel free to browse and poke around among this cornucopia of ducts and chimneys, back lanes with corrugated tin roofing and ivy-covered brick, desolate workshops full of interesting and intriguing debris, and odd old Communist displays of nuts and bolts. And if that's not enough, with the handful of new businesses, you'll even find some street life in the complex, including a few cafés and a bicycle shop.

Around Béke tér, near the terminus of the HÉV, various run-down but friendly bars provide a dilapidated dose of local pride.

Farther-flung

Caves

Budapest's caves are unique because they were formed by hot thermal waters underground, rather than by cold rainwater from above. This created unusual rock formations rather than gigantic dripstone columns or cave chambers. Szemlő-hegy and Pálvölgy were only discovered this century. Both provide a cheap, refreshing afternoon's entertainment. For the Catacombs of Buda Castle, *see chapter* **Museums**.

Szemlő-hegy

II. Pusztaszeri út 35 (315 8849). Bus 29. **Open**
10am-3pm Wed-Sun. **Admission** Ft250; Ft150
concs. **No credit cards**. No English spoken.
Szemlőhegyi Cave is one of rare beauty, formed by
thermal waters. Its entrance was only discovered in
1930 and it was opened to the public 56 years later.
Although the tour is short, some 2km covered in 25
minutes, the weird and bulbous mineral formations
spark the imagination. The air is clear and clean;
Szemlő-hegy is an underground therapy centre for
those suffering from respiratory illnesses. Hourly
guided tours are in Hungarian or German. At the
entrance you'll find a café and a modest exhibition.

Pálvölgy

II. Szépvölgyi út 162 (388 9537). Bus 65, 65A.
Open 10am-4pm Tue-Sun. **Admission** Ft250; Ft150
concs. **No credit cards**. No English spoken.
Just a ten-minute walk from Szemlő-hegy, Pálvölgy
is the only Buda cave that evokes the sense of awe
and curiosity that drove explorers underground in
the early part of the twentieth century, when these
caverns were discovered. A sign warns three
groups against entering: children under four and
the physically and alcoholically challenged, so don't
visit the bar by the entrance until after you've nego-
tiated the 600-odd steps, steep climbs and low-hang-
ing rock formations. This is the longest, most
impressive cave in the Buda Hills and potholers
uncover new sections every year. Hourly guided
tours last 30 minutes.

Cemeteries

Farkasréti Cemetery

Farkasréti temető
*XI. Németvölgyi 99 (319 3092). Tram 59 from
Moszkva tér/bus 8, 8A, 53.* **Open** 7am-9pm Mon-Fri;
9am-5pm Sat, Sun. **Admission** free.
Tucked away in the hills of District XI, it's here you'll
find one of the most outstanding works of Imre
Makovecz – the mortuary chapel (1975). Giant wings
of the souls of the dead open to lead you inside the
wooden-ribbed oesophagus of a mythical beast. Be
discreet on entering as the chapel is in pretty much

Back on the block

On April 9th 1999 a ceremony was held to celebrate the return to Szent István Park of the
Raoul Wallenberg memorial. Pál Pátzáy's two-
metre high bronze statue, depicting a male nude
beating a snake to death with a truncheon, has
been recast and put back on its pedestal after a
50-year enforced absence. The monument was
erected in memory of the Swedish wartime
diplomat who managed to save at least 30,000
Hungarian Jews from Auschwitz. His unortho-
dox methods involved bullying, bribery and the
issuing of dodgy Swedish diplomatic papers
(known as 'Wallenberg passports') in a desperate race against Nazi efforts to liquidate the
Budapest ghetto in the last months of the war.

On 9 April 1949, council workmen managed to
pull down Pátzáy's allegory of Wallenberg the
anti-fascist hero and make off with it in a truck,
just hours before the monument was due to be officially inaugurated. The bizarre dawn raid was
almost certainly ordered by Soviet authorities,
who did not want attention drawn to the fate of
the courageous Swedish diplomat. In January
1945, as the Red Army marched into Budapest,
Wallenberg had set off confidently by car towards
Debrecen for a meeting with Soviet high command; neither he nor his driver were ever seen
again. It is still not known for sure whether he died
of a heart attack in a Moscow prison in 1947, perished in a Siberian gulag or ended his days in a
mental hospital during the Brezhnev era.

Wallenberg's statue languished for less than
a year in a city warehouse (in the company of
other politically disgraced monuments) before it
was wheeled out to be exhibited at the First
Hungarian Fine Arts Exhibition of 1950 as the
Antifasiszta ('Anti-Fascist'). It went on to be
erected a few years later in front of a pharmaceutical factory in Debrecen, with the new name
of *Kígyóölő* ('Snake-killer'). An identical copy
was procured by the Indonesian leader Sukarno
after an official state visit in 1962, and a half-
size version stands outside the radiological
department of Budapest's SOTE medical university. It clearly wasn't the statue that the
authorities objected to – they liked Pátzáy's easy
symbolism and classical figurative style – but
rather its identification with Wallenberg.

Although there have been many other
attempts over the years to honour Budapest's
Swedish hero – he has his own street, plaque,
memorial park and a sophisticated monument
by the sculptor Imre Varga on Szilágyi Erzsébet
fasor in Buda – none are as poetically satisfying
as the return of Pál Pátzáy's brash socialist-
realist sculpture to its original location.
Incidentally, Pátzáy's other famous statue was
also removed from its plinth not so long ago, and
can now be seen in the **Statue Park**; Vladimir
Ilych, however, has considerably less chance of
finding himself back on the streets of Budapest
than did Wallenberg.

constant use. In the cemetery itself you'll find the grave of Béla Bartók and lots of intriguing winged wooden grave markers. Look out for inscriptions in an ancient runic Székely alphabet. Detailed maps of the cemetery's 'residents' can be picked up from the information building to the left of the main gate.

Kerepesi Cemetery

Kerepesi temető
VIII. Fiumei út 14 (210 1500). M2 Keleti/tram 23, 24, 28. **Open** *7am-6pm daily.* **Admission** *free.*
Map F4
Declared a 'decorative' cemetery in 1885, Kerepesi is where you'll find the names behind the streets; politicians, poets, novelists, singers and industrialists, chosen by governments to represent the way they wanted their eras remembered. Street names might change, but corpses are not disinterred, giving you a comprehensive overview of the Hungarian establishment of the last 100 years. Monumentally planned, it's a popular place for a stroll. Wide leafy avenues direct you towards strategic mausoleums – romantic novelist Mór Jókai and arch-compromiser Ferenc Deák, bourgeois revolutionary Lajos Kossuth and that other nationalist favourite, Count Lajos Batthyány. Nearby, music-hall chanteuse Lujza Blaha is tucked up in a four-poster bed, serenaded by adoring cherubs. Toeing the party line in death as in life, the regimented black granite gravestones of Communist cadres carry identical gold stars, while the totalitarian-proportioned Worker's Pantheon has its own special gate on to Fiumei út. Anarchist poet Attila József, thrown out of the 1930s Communist party but rehabilitated during the 1950s, was buried here more than 20 years after his suicide. Styles of burial have changed. Thousands mourned the first prime minister of post-Communist democracy, József Antall, in a candle-lit vigil, yet his grave is marked by a simple cross.

Újköztemető Cemetery

X. Kozma utca 8-10 (260 5549). Tram 28, 37. **Open** *dawn-dusk, hours vary depending on season; always open Aug-Apr 7.30am-5pm, May-July 7am-8pm, daily.*
Surprisingly lively for a place of the dead. The main entrance bustles with old women selling flowers and the gravestones are packed in tight. People visit to see the final resting place of Imre Nagy, the prime minister who defied the Soviets in 1956. You'll find him in Plot 301, along with 260 others executed for their parts in the Uprising, in the farthest corner of the big map to the right of the entrance. Empty coach parks, a traffic barrier and a police guard let you know you've arrived. Transylvanian markers outline the mass grave behind a Székely gate proclaiming a 'National Pantheon'.

Housing estates

Napraforgó utca experimental housing estate

Napraforgó utcai Mintatelep
II. Napraforgó utca 1-22. Tram 56/bus 5.

Completed in 1931, the 22 houses on this fascinating street exemplify different styles of the interwar modern movement. Modelled on the Deutsche Werkbund's Weißenhofsiedlung in Stuttgart and commissioned by the City Council's Board of Public Works, it was intended to demonstrate the possibilities of combining industrial production methods with traditional craftsmanship and to convert the provincial taste of Horthyite Budapest to progressive international design. But whereas the Stuttgart project employed only the rising stars of the European rationalist avant garde, Napraforgó utca combines the founders of the Hungarian CIAM (Molnár, Fischer, Masirevich, Kertesz) with those who had been prominent architects of Budapest's art nouveau and were then at the end of their careers. No. 14 was designed by Heinrich Böhm and Ármin Hegedüs, architects of the Turkish Banking House on Szervita tér, while Nos. 1 and 11 were contributed by László Vágó, co-designer of the Metró Áruház and the Hungarian Printer's Union Apartments at VIII. Gutenberg tér 4. Lajos Kozma, a former interior designer (he worked with Béla Lajta on the Rozsavölgyi House) and founder of the Hungarian Werkbund, later became editor of *Új Épitészet* (New Architecture) and was the first Director of the Institute of Applied Arts. His art deco buildings on the estate (Nos. 6-8) are among the few accorded monument protection. Tempering the avant garde with a curious romanticism, Kertesz's brick house at No. 9 is the least rational, while dogmatically austere No. 15, designed by Bauhaus-trained Ferenc Molnár and Pál Ligeti is the most didactic, and exerted tremendous influence on the Hungarian avant garde. The other influential building here – expressionist architect József Fischer's orange house at No. 20 – has tragically been destroyed, mourned with a single white rose in its letter box.

Wekerle Housing Estate

Wekerle lakótelep
XIX. Kispest. M3 Határ út/bus 48, 99.
Like a rustic Transylvanian version of an English garden suburb, the Wekerle (1910-14) started life as the Kispest Worker and Clerk Settlement and is still mainly working class. The architects, Fiatal Csoport ('Young Ones'), strove to improve the national standard of proletarian housing. A sense of unreality pervades the estate. Bicycling old ladies career down ash-lined lanes. Snack bars are run from garages, but there are few shops. The estate has its own kindergartens, schools and police station. Kós Károly tér, surrounded by apartment blocks, is the centrepiece. Pitched roofs tower over long thin windows and wooden balconies. The wooden arch over the junction of Hungária út and the square has recently been restored. There's a cinema and a bar, but the Catholic church takes central place. The residents' association at number 10 has a noticeboard indicating the millions of forints you now need to buy a Wekerle flat. Architectural romanticism is fashionable again.

Museums

Bizarre exhibits, wonderful buildings, temporary gems – restoration continues as Budapest's collections find their feet.

The weird and the wonderful are the attraction of Budapest's museums, from sixteenth century winged-altarpieces in the **National Gallery** to giant tram wheels in the **Foundry Museum** or shiny black pumps in the completely eccentric **Sewerage Works Museum**. Magyar cuisine, Communist-era statues, Asian art or Roman ruins – it's all here. Many buildings have now been renovated and some even have alarm systems, after thefts from the **Jewish Museum** and the **Fine Arts Museum**.

Some museum buildings surpass their collections, such as the renovated **Geological Institute** or the magnificent **Museum of Applied Arts** – both designed by Ödön Lechner – or the Baroque monastery that houses the **Kiscelli Museum**. The National Gallery in the Royal Palace is worth a visit for its collection, its building and its location in the Castle District.

Although lack of resources is still a problem, recent restoration and expansion have produced excellent results. The new light fixtures at the **Museum of Fine Arts** or the highly interactive exhibitions in the **Museum of Natural History** are a pleasant surprise to Hungarians more used to the bland and badly lit. Today buildings look nicer, paintings seem more pleasantly presented, many feature English captions and most house a variety of tempting temporary exhibits. All this has its price. Ten years ago an average museum ticket was Ft20, but even then most visitors came on Tuesday when admission was free. Today the charge is Ft300 plus.

Most museums also offer a variety of cultural programmes. The **Museum of Ethnography** organises seasonal craft fairs, where you can learn how to make old-fashioned Christmas-tree ornaments or paint traditional Easter eggs. Folk music complements crafts at the **Open-Air Folklore Museum** near Szentendre. The otherwise bizarre **Agriculture Museum** (full of stuffed animals and odd tools) in the City Park offers summer garden classical music concerts and Saturday morning children's shows. Fashion shows and techno parties brighten the dark brick walls of Óbuda's Kiscelli Museum crypt.

Museum of Ethnography – *defiantly non-folky building. See page 86.*

Museums usually open Tuesday to Sunday, 10am to 6pm, some closing earlier in winter. Ticket offices close an hour before the museum does. Attendants know better than you that half an hour is not enough to take a look at the one crucial painting that brought you to Budapest. But then Hungarian museum attendants usually know everything better than anybody.

English-language booklets are available in most museums. Where indicated below, you can buy an English booklet (EB Ft200, for example), or call to arrange a guided tour in English. *Pesti Műsor* and the *Budapest Sun* list permanent and temporary exhibitions as well as any special events.

Budapest Card

If you're planning on doing a lot of museums in a hurry, get hold of a Budapest Card. On sale at main Metro stations, information offices, travel agencies and some hotels, this credit card-sized gizmo allows free entry to 55 museums, plus two or three days' unlimited travel on the public transport system. A card is valid for one adult and one minor up to the age of 14 and costs Ft2,490 for two days, Ft2,950 for three days.

National institutions

Museum of Applied Arts

Iparművészeti Múzeum
IX. Üllői út 33-37 (217 5222). M3 Ferenc körút/tram 4, 6. **Open** 10am-6pm Tue-Sun. **Admission** Ft200; Ft50 concs. **No credit cards**. Some English spoken. **Map D5**

Established in 1872 to showcase Hungarian art objects and furnishings which had already won international acclaim, the Museum of Applied Arts then found its permanent home in this magnificent Ödön Lechner building (*see chapter* **Architecture**), opened for the 1896 Millennium. Its permanent exhibition of furniture and objets d'art, 'Style Periods of the Applied Arts in Europe', is clearly explained in English with plenty of historical detail. A far-sighted purchasing policy at the 1900 Paris Expo meant that the museum was well furbished with secession, Jugenstil and art nouveau pieces from the very outset, but some important items are collecting dust in the back – few visitors find out about the Fabergé eggs, Tiffany glass and Lalique crystal in a back room near the staircase.

Museum of Ethnography

Néprajzi Múzeum
V. Kossuth Lajos tér 12 (332 6340). M2 Kossuth tér/tram 2. **Open** 10am-6pm Tue-Sun. **Admission** Ft300; Ft150 concs. Call to arrange guided tour in English, Ft4,000 for parties up to five. EB Ft700. **No credit cards**. Some English spoken. **Map C4**

Despite poor planning and an unwillingness to rotate an enormous collection (too much of which languishes in the basement), this worthwhile museum

offers a comprehensive illustration of Hungarian village and farm life, folk customs and folk art. Each display is accompanied by English text, rendering the rented cassette from the front desk unnecessary. Starting one flight up, the exhibition goes from folk costumes to a colour-coded regional ethnic breakdown in 1909 map form. There are usually a couple of temporary photo exhibitions – recent topics included contemporary Israel and Norwegian folklore. Every March the museum hosts the World Press Photo exhibition, and holds Christmas and Easter fairs inviting regional groups for dance displays and mystery plays, proving the folk tradition to be a living one. The building is anything but folky, though – a monumental, gilt-columned edifice with ceiling frescoes by Károly Lotz, built between 1893 and 1896 to serve as the Supreme Court, though it never did.

The Open Air Village Museum

Szentendre, Szabadságforrás út (06 26 312 304). HÉV to Szentendre then bus 8. **Open** 1 Apr-31 Oct 9am-5pm Tue-Sun. **Admission** Ft350; Ft150 children. **No credit cards**. Some English spoken.

You can happily spend the afternoon here, if traditional crafts, architecture and folklore grab you. The place is forever expanding, with new old peasant houses, mills and barns added each year. Most weekends between Easter and autumn harvest you'll find craft workshops and folk concerts where you can also learn how to make traditional instruments, baskets and pottery or bake cheese scones. Restaurant, café and lashings of ice-cream. Very child friendly.

Museum of Fine Arts

Szépművészeti Múzeum
XIV. Hősök tere (343 9759). M1 Hősök tere. **Open** 10am-5.30pm Tue-Sun. **Admission** Ft500; Ft200 concs; Ft700 family ticket; English tours (Ft4,000 for up to five people) can be arranged on the spot in summer, otherwise contact Zoltán Bartos on ext 137. Some English spoken. **Map E1**

While the National Gallery is Hungary's prime venue for Hungarian art, the country's major European display is here. The museum has invested in new light fixtures and reorganised its magnificent Spanish collection, the best outside Spain, putting all El Greco and his school into one place along with the Madrid and Andalusian Schools. The basics were acquired by the Esterházy family in 1818, who later added Goyas and Riberas. Other highlights include an excellent Venetian collection (particularly Titian and Giorgioni), a Dürer, several Breughels, a doubtful but beautiful Raphael and some Leonardos. The vast collection of drawings and graphics from the Renaissance to the present is generally rotated in small, temporary exhibits. The museum stages the most important temporary exhibitions in the grand halls leading from the entrance.

Hungarian National Gallery

Magyar Nemzeti Galéria
I. Buda Palace, Wings B, C, E (375 7533 ext 423). Várbusz from M2 Moszkva tér/bus 16. **Open**

Apr-Oct 10am-6pm Tue-Sun; *Nov-Mar* 10am-4pm Tue-Sun. **Admission** Ft300; Ft100 concs; guided tour Ft2,000 up to five people. EB Ft300. Some English spoken. **Map B4**

The purpose of this vast museum is to chronicle Hungarian art since the birth of the nation and it requires more than one visit to take in all the permanent exhibits of paintings, sculptures, ecclesiastical art, medallions and graphics. The two collections considered the most important are its fifteenth- and sixteenth-century winged altarpieces (so-called because of their ornately carved pinnacles which create a light, soaring effect); and its mid-nineteenth- to early twentieth-century art. Most of the work here is derivative of major European art movements such as Classicism, Impressionism, Fauvism, Art Nouveau. There are depictions of Hungarian history by Viktor Madarász and lively sculptures of Hungarian peasants by Miklós Izsó. Also noteworthy are the works of impressionist József Rippl-Rónai, Hungary's Whistler (he even painted his mother), and if you go to the upper galleries there are some great early twentieth-century painters such as the symbolists Lajos Gulácsy and János Vaszary, the mad, self-taught genius Tivadar Koszta Csontváry and the tragic figure of István Farkas, a Jew murdered at the end of the war. The Gallery, along with the Museum of Fine Arts (devoted to non-Hungarian works), also hosts important temporary exhibitions. For an extra Ft150 entrance fee, a guide will take you round the Palatine Crypt beneath the museum, built in 1715 as part of the Habsburg reconstruction of the palace.

National Museum

Nemzeti Múzeum

VIII. Múzeum körút 14-16 (338 2122). M3 Kálvin tér/tram 47, 49. **Open** *summer* 10am-6pm, *winter* 10am-5pm, Tue-Sun. **Admission** Ft400; Ft150 concs; guided tour in English, Ft600 per person. EB Ft1,600. Some English spoken. **Map D4**

The oldest museum in Budapest (and the fourth such museum to be built anywhere at all – Mihály Pollack's design followed the Grecian idiom of the British Museum) was also the site of the reading of Petőfi's 'National Song' on 15 March 1848, which heralded the start of the revolt against Habsburg domination. The two permanent exhibitions are the history of Hungary from its foundation to the nineteenth century, and the history of Hungary in the twentieth century. The former takes in the sainted King Stephen who was crowned Hungary's first king in 1000, (his crown and coronation robes are on display – *see page 20* **Tales of a crown**). It continues through the Ottoman occupation in the sixteenth century, the revolution of 1848 and the Magyar millennium in 1896, with jewels, armour, flags, documents, old photographs and paintings. The twentieth-century section begins with the collapse of the Monarchy, and continues through World War I, the 1919 revolution and the restora-

National Museum – *Grecian idiom, Magyar contents.*

tion of dictatorship in 1920, with contemporary propaganda, suites of furniture and shop window displays. Watch out for the wonderful posters of happy workers waving to a fat bald Rákosi, Hungary's Stalin, as he leads them forward to Socialism.

National Széchényi Library
Országos Széchényi Könyvtár
I. Buda Palace, Wing F (224 3848). Várbusz from M2 Moszkva tér/bus 16. **Admission** Ft100, Ft50 concs, for exhibits; passport required to enter library. **Open** 10am-4.30pm Mon, Tue; 10am-6pm Wed-Fri. **No credit cards.** Some English spoken. **Map B4**
Seven storeys housing over two million books and even more manuscripts (as well as collections on music, theatre, graphics, newspapers and journals), with the aim of gathering anything related to Hungary or in Hungarian published anywhere in the world. To browse or research, bring a passport and ask for English-speaking staff who will help you with the engaging (if noisy) retrieval system by which books are sent down on automated carts. The building is named after Count Ferenc Széchényi (father of nineteenth-century reformer, István) who donated his library to the state in 1802. The institution has volumes (codices, or corvina in Hungarian) which belonged to King Mátyás, who owned one of the largest collections in Renaissance Europe, sadly rarely displayed. The exhibits on the first floor usually feature Hungarian and German writers, with occasional displays of book illustrations. The library also has a secret passage, a lift (Ft20) that climbs from the bottom of Castle Hill (by the stops for the 78 or 5 bus and or 18 tram).

History

Agriculture Museum
Mezőgazdasági Múzeum
XIV. Vajdahunyad Castle in Városliget (343 8573). M1 Hősök tere. **Open** 10am-5pm Tue-Sat; 10am-6pm Sun. **Admission** Ft200; Ft100 concs. EB Ft200. **No credit cards.** No English spoken. **Map F1**
Antique ploughs and the history of cattle breeding sit oddly inside the mock-Baroque wing of a fake Transylvanian castle – built for the 1896 Magyar Millennium exhibition and the only structure to have survived. The dozen exhibits range from snoozers such as the History of Grain Production to one on the Hungarian rural ritual pig-killing (*see chapter* **By Season**), but the building is definitely worth a look and the hunting hall has rows of stuffed stags and shelved antlers beneath a magnificently vaulted and painted ceiling. Temporary exhibits have included 'Jews in the Hungarian Countryside', or 'Life in a Medieval Village'.

Aquincum Museum
Aquincumi Múzeum
III. Szentendrei út 139 (250 1650). HÉV Aquincum. **Open** *ruins* (Apr-Oct) 9am-6pm Tue-Sun; *museum* 9am-5pm Tue-Sun. **Admission** Ft300; Ft150 concs. EB Ft500. **No credit cards.** No English spoken.

Workers' housing estates and a motorway dwarf the numerous Roman ruins scattered throughout Óbuda. The largest concentration is at this site, where most of Aquincum's 4,000 or so residents lived. This was the capital of Pannonia Inferior, the Roman province that covered most of what is now western Hungary. The exhibit tells of a comfortable town keeping up with the Juliuses and the garrison stationed at what is now Árpád Bridge. Famed for its spas, sadly little remains except a remarkable water organ found in 1931 – the only one complete enough to be replicated. Within the vast Flórián tér underpass, the so-called Baths Museum – ruins of Roman baths – are closed indefinitely but the unexciting remnants can be viewed from outside the glass enclosure. There's also a small amphitheatre by the HÉV station across the road, normally open the same hours or by request at the museum. Likewise, the Hercules Villa is out of the way on a suburban street and comprises what little is left of a Roman official's villa, with a few faded pieces of mosaic depicting the legendary strongman.
Hercules Villa, III. Meggyfa utca 19-21 (250 1650).

Budapest History Museum
Budapesti Történeti Múzeum
I. Buda Palace, Wing E (375 7533 ext 243). Várbusz from M2 Moszkva tér/bus 16. **Open** 10am-6pm Mon, Wed-Sun. **Admission** Ft300; Ft150 concs. EB Ft200-Ft800. **No credit cards.** Some English spoken. **Map B4**
The main exhibit on Budapest starts from the earliest tribal settlements, featuring loads of fascinating artefacts and excavation photos, with descriptions in English. Recently renovated, the museum presents the city in an attractive historical light. 'Budapest in Modern Times', for example, tracks the city's identity as a large urban centre, a metropolis that prompted even the lethargic Habsburgs into making it the royal seat. The display focuses on certain key symbols: Charles of Lothringen's triumphal Arch to celebrate the defeat of the Ottomans; the Danube which both divides and unites Budapest; the May Day 1919 red drapes which represent the Socialist ideal; and contemporary urban sites including József Finta's hotels and bank centres contrasted with Imre Makovecz's organic villas and yurt houses (*see chapter* **Architecture**). A dark room is full of ghoulish Gothic statues unearthed at the Castle pre-dating King Mátyás. The lower levels are partially reconstructed remains of Mátyás' palace, with a vaulted chapel and music room. The upper floor houses temporary exhibits, generally of a historical nature.

Catacombs & Wax Museum
Panoptikum
I. Úri utca 9 (212 0207). Várbusz from M2 Moszkva tér/bus 16. **Open** 10am-7.30pm Tue-Sun; closed Dec, Jan. **Admission** Ft800; Ft650 concs, tour and EB included. **No credit cards.** English spoken. **Map B3**

Sadly the worst – and most expensive – exhibition in Budapest offers the only way into the Castle Hill's 10km network of caves and man-made passageways (*see chapter* **Sightseeing**). This sorry excuse for a museum, and its mandatory tours in appalling English every 15 minutes, offer mouldy, sloppy wax figures of medieval Magyars and a scattering of torture instruments.

Museum of Military History

Hadtörténeti Múzeum
I. Tóth Árpád sétány 40 (355 8849). Várbusz from M2 Moszkva tér. **Open** 10am-5pm Tue-Sat; 10am-6pm Sun. **Admission** Ft250; Ft80 concs; Ft1,000 guided tour. **No credit cards. Map A3**
Permanent displays in this former eighteenth-century Castle District barracks include 'The History of Hand Weapons from the Stone Axe to the Pistol' and 'Thirteen Days' – a look at the street fighting of the 1956 revolution. Recent exhibitions have featured Hussars, toy soldiers, eighteenth-century fighting techniques and other martial matters.

Óbuda Local History Exhibit

Óbudai Helytörténeti Gyűjtemény
Zichy Mansion, III. Fő tér 1 (250 1020). HÉV Árpád híd. **Open** 2-6pm Tue-Fri; 10am-6pm Sat, Sun. **Admission** Ft120; Ft60 concs; EB Ft100. **No credit cards.** No English.
A single corridor of this mansion displays old photos and artefacts on Óbuda, plus rooms set up in Secession and Sváb (ethnic German) styles, and a delightful room full of toys, including a Herend tea service for dolls.

Semmelweis Museum of Medical History

Semmelweis Orvostörténeti Múzeum
I. Apród utca 1-3 (201 1577). Tram 18. **Open** 10.30am-5.30pm Tue-Sun. **Admission** Ft100; Ft50 concs; Ft500 tour in English. **No credit cards.** Some English spoken. **Map B4**
'Mother's Saviour', Dr Ignác Semmelweis (1818-63), who discovered the cure for puerperal fever – blood poisoning contracted during childbirth – was born in this very building. His belongings on display are overshadowed by a general exhibit on the history of medicine. These items from all over the world include a medieval chastity belt, eighteenth-century beeswax anatomical models and a portrait of Hungary's first female doctor, Vilma Hugonai. Another room contains the 1786 Holy Ghost Pharmacy transported whole from Király utca.

Statue Park

Szobor Park
XXII. Balatoni út (227 7446). Yellow bus for Érd from Kosztolányi Dezső tér/tram 49. **Open** *May-Sept* 8am-8pm, *Oct-Feb* 10am-dusk, daily. **Admission** Ft200; Ft150 concs; EB Ft600. **No credit cards.** Some English spoken.
This unique outdoor museum on the south-west edge of the city is a dumping ground for the politically incorrect monuments of the Communist era. It was opened in 1993 after the 42 works were removed

from their prominent positions around the city. The latest acquisition is the statue of Lenin that once stood outside the gates of the Csepel Ironworks (*see chapter* **Sightseeing**) and joining comrades Marx, Engels and Béla Kun. Most of the statues are in blocky socialist-realist form, some quite massive, such as a terrifying sailor modelled on a call-to-arms poster by the 1919 Communist government, or the Soviet soldier that once guarded the Liberation Monument. With your ticket you're given a sheet outlining layout, date, artist and former location, but for further information you'll need the Ft600 catalogue. The ticket booth also sells Commie kitsch such as the Molotov cocktail drink.

Arts

Ferenc Hopp Museum of Eastern Asiatic Arts

Kelet-Ázsia Művészeti Múzeuma
VI. Andrássy út 103 (322 8476). M1 Bajza utca. **Open** 10am-6pm Tue-Sun. **Admission** Ft160; Ft50 concs; call to arrange guided tour, Ft2,500 for parties up to five. EB Ft450-Ft1,800. **No credit cards.** Some English spoken. **Map E2**
One of Budapest's two major Asian art collections (the other is at the nearby **György Ráth Museum**), the Ferenc Hopp's ancient works include Buddhist art in China, Lamaist scroll paintings and Gandhara sculpture, old Indian art influenced by ancient Greece. By the end of his life, after five trips round the world, this successful businessman turned collector (1833-1919) had amassed over 4,000 pieces.

György Ráth Museum

VI. Városligeti fasor 12 (342 3916). Trolleybus 70, 78. **Open** 10am-5.45pm Tue-Sun. **Admission** Ft160; Ft50 concs; EB Ft200-Ft800; call to arrange guided tour in English, Ft2,500 for parties up to five. **No credit cards.** Some English spoken. **Map E2**
Chinese and Japanese works make up this excellent collection in the former home of the artist and art historian who collected them. The displays, accompanied by English texts are more detailed than most Hungarian museums'. Note the wonderful snuff bottles, scroll paintings and tools in the Chinese collection, and the miniature shrines, Samurai armour and finely carved lobster on a lacquer comb in the Japanese rooms upstairs. There are also temporary exhibitions from other Far Eastern countries.

Kiscelli Museum

III. Kiscelli utca 108 (250 0304). Tram 17 then bus 165. **Open** 10am-6pm Tue-Sun. **Admission** Ft200; Ft100 concs. **No credit cards.** Some English spoken.
This Baroque Trinitarian monastery built in 1745 atop a wooded hill in Óbuda houses an important collection of Hungarian art from about 1880-1990. The works displayed upstairs include turn-of-the century masters and paintings influenced by the Impressionists, pre-Raphaelites, Cubists and Surrealists. Among them are Rippl-Rónai's *My Parents After 40 Years of Marriage*, János Kmetty's

Jewish Museum – *plenty of ritual objects, little pre-war history.*

cubist *City Park*, and works by Alajos Stróbl, Károly Ferenczy, Margit Anna and many others. There are also engravings of eighteenth- to nineteenth-century Budapest – you'll recognise the vantage point from what is now Petőfi bridgehead in Pest, in an 1866 engraving by Antal Ligeti, showing the newly built Chain Bridge, the church at Kálvin tér, Castle Hill and Citadella, and the twin domes of the new Dohány utca Synagogue. Downstairs are the Golden Lion Pharmacy (formerly at Kálvin tér), old printing presses (you can print out a takeaway copy of Petőfi's National Song), and classical statuary from early nineteenth-century Pest façades. The most atmospheric part of the complex is the ruined church, its bare brick walls left intact after World War II bombing and now transformed into a dim, ghostly gallery. These days it's often used to stage operas, fashion shows and other performances.

Zsigmond Kun Folk Art Collection
Kun Zsigmond Népművészeti Gyűjtemény
III. Fő tér 4 (368 1138). HÉV Árpád híd. **Open** 2-6pm Tue-Fri; 10am-6pm Sat, Sun. **Admission** Ft120; Ft60 concs. EB Ft100. **No credit cards.** No English spoken.
'Zsigi bácsi' (Uncle Sigi), as the attendants refer to him, is a 103-year-old ethnographer who lived in this eighteenth-century apartment. It now serves as a showcase for his collection of folk art, some 1,000 pieces from nineteenth- and early twentieth-century Hungary, including hand-painted furniture, textiles, pottery and carvings. Particularly notable are ceramics from his hometown Mezőtúr in northern Hungary and the replica of a peasant stucco oven.

Music

Béla Bartók Memorial House
Bartók Béla Emlékház
II. Csalán utca 29 (394 2100). Bus 5. **Open** 10am-5pm Tue-Sun. **Admission** Ft200; Ft100 concs. **No credit cards.** Some English spoken.
The composer lived here with his wife and two sons from 1932 until he left an increasingly fascist Hungary in 1940. The house has some of his original furnishings and an exhibit of Bartók memorabilia, such as the folk art collection that he amassed while travelling the region tune hunting. This includes photos, letters and notes, plus the composer's paintings, graphics and sculptures. Chamber concerts are often staged here on Fridays (*see chapter* **Music: Classical & Opera**), outdoors in summer, by Imre Varga's Bartók statue.

Kodály Memorial Museum & Archive
Kodály Emlékmúzeum és Archivum
VI. Andrássy út 87-89, in courtyard (352 7106). M1 Kodály körönd. **Open** 10am-4pm Wed; 10am-6pm Thur-Sat; 10am-2pm Sun. **Admission** Ft50; Ft30 concs; EB Ft80. **No credit cards.** Some English spoken. **Map E2**
Where Zoltán Kodály lived from 1924 until his death in 1967. His library, salon and dining room have been left in their original state, with an eclectic range of furnishings as well as folk art objects the composer bought while collecting songs. His bedroom displays manuscripts including sections of the *Psalmus Hungaricus* and *Buda Castle Te Deum*.

Franz Liszt Museum

Liszt Ferenc Múzeum
VI. Vörösmarty utca 35 (322 9804 ext 16).
M1 Vörösmarty utca. **Open** 10am-6pm Mon-Fri;
9am-5pm Sat. **Admission** Ft150; Ft80 concs;
EB Ft1,000. **No credit cards.** No English.
Map D3

Liszt lived here from 1881 until his death in 1886.
The three-room flat is preserved with his furniture
and other possessions, including a composing desk-
cum-keyboard. Text in English. Free concerts most
Saturday mornings.

Museum of Music History

Zenetörténeti Múzeum
I. Táncsics Mihály utca 7 (375 9011 ext 164).
Várbusz from M2 Moszkva tér. **Open** 4-8pm Mon;
10am-6pm Wed-Sun. **Admission** Ft300; Ft150
concs. EB Ft200. **No credit cards.** Some English
spoken. **Map A3**

Beethoven was a guest here in 1800, when it was
the the Erdődy family palace. Within are many
seventeenth- to nineteenth-century classical and
folk instruments. In the classical section these vary
from delicately ornamented lyres to a unique,
tongue-shaped violin, and from a gardon (a crude
cello) to bagpipes and cowhorns in the folk section.
The minimalist, orderly arrangement puts the
instruments' beauty in full focus. As well as temporary exhibits of musically themed contemporary
art, there is also a collection of Bartók manuscripts. Occasional summer concerts in the lovely
back garden.

Theatre

Gizi Bajor Theatre Museum

Bajor Gizi Színészmúzeum
XII. Stromfeld Aurél út 16 (356 4294). Bus 112.
Open noon-4pm Tue; 2-6pm Thur; 10am-6pm Sat,
Sun. **Admission** Ft100; Ft50 concs. **No credit
cards.** No English spoken.

Lovely, turn-of-the-century villa once home to theatre and film actress Gizi Bajor (1893-1951). The
exhibit is devoted to actors from the Hungarian
National Theatre and early cinema, with plenty of
old photographs and Bajor's original furnishings.

Religion

Bible Museum

Biblia Múzeum
IX. Ráday utca 28 (217 6321). M3 Kálvin tér. **Open**
10am-5pm Tue-Sun. **Admission** free. EB Ft160.
Some English spoken. **Map D5**

Facsimilies, pictures and texts at a dusty Calvinist
seminary illustrating '3,000 years of the Holy
Bible', – the sort of thing which reluctant Sunday
school students get dragged to. Rare interesting
items include a 1534 Hebrew Bible from Basle and
a 1599 12-language New Testament from
Nuremberg. Also missionary Bibles in Tamil,
Khmer and Cherokee.

Ecclesiastical Art

Egyházművészeti Gyűjtemény
I. Mátyás Templom, Szentháromság tér (355 5657).
M2 Moszkva tér then Várbusz/bus 16. **Open** 9am-
7pm daily. **Admission** Ft80; Ft30 concs. **No credit
cards.** Some English spoken. **Map A3**

Begins in a partially reconstructed medieval crypt
(head downstairs from the south-east aisle of the
church), with a red marble sarcophagus containing
bones from the Royal Tomb of Székesfehérvár. A
passageway leads back up to the St Stephen
Chapel, its walls showing scenes from the life of
Hungary's first king. The chapel and gallery contain ecclesiastical treasures, but little of note since
the best are at Esztergom. *See chapter* **The
Danube Bend**.

Jewish Museum

Zsidó Múzeum
VII. Dohány utca 2 (342 8949). M2 Astoria/tram
47, 49. **Open** Apr-Oct 10am-3pm Mon-Thur; 10am-
3pm Fri; 10am-2pm Sun. **Admission** Ft600; Ft200
concs. Guided tours in English, Ft1,200. **No credit
cards.** English spoken. **Map D4**

This small museum, with eighteenth- to nineteenth-
century ritual objects from the region, is in a wing of
the **Central Synagogue** (*see chapter* **Sightseeing**)
complex and on the site where Zionist leader
Theodore Herzl was born. The collection is arranged
in three rooms according to function: Sabbath, holidays and life-cycle ceremonies. The fourth room covers the Hungarian Holocaust – one photo shows
corpses piled up in front of this same building after a
massacre by Hungarian Arrow Cross fascists. What
is missing from the museum – in fact from nearly all
Hungarian museums – is any exhibit on pre-war
Hungarian Jewry, though there are plans to open an
archives section to create exhibits on the topic.
Though founded in 1931 when Hungarian Jews were
feeling fairly secure, many more objects were given
to the collection after their owners were murdered in
the Holocaust. Well documented in English, plus
English-speaking staff and tours.

The Lutheran Museum

Evangélikus Múzeum
V. Deák tér 4 (317 4173). M1, M2,
M3 Deák tér/tram 47, 49. **Open** 10am-6pm
Tue-Sun. **Admission** Ft200; Ft100 concs.
EB Ft200. **No credit cards.** Some English spoken.
Map C4

Adjoining Budapest's main Lutheran Church, this
museum traces the history of the Reformation in
Hungary. On display is a facsimile of Martin
Luther's last will and testament (the church archive
has the original); the first book printed in
Hungarian, a New Testament from 1541; and a pul-
pit cover from 1650 with an embroidered tableau of
the 12 apostles (for some reason all have red noses).
A small display commemorates Gábor Sztehló, a
pastor who rescued over 2,000 Jewish children during World War II. There's some English text but
also usually an English-speaking attendant can do
a better job.

Hungarian Museum of Electrotechnics.

Golden Eagle Pharmaceutical Museum

Arany Sas Patikamúzeum
*I. Tárnok utca 18 (375 9772). Várbusz from M2
Moszkva tér/bus 16.* **Open** 10.30am-5.30pm Tue-Sun.
Admission Ft100; Ft50 concs. EB Ft600. **No credit
cards.** Some English spoken. **Map A3**
The Golden Eagle was the first pharmacy in Buda
to be established after the expulsion of the Turks,
although it was in nearby Disz tér until the mid-eighteenth century. The current house dates from the fifteenth century, one of the oldest in the Castle
District. The museum is an eye-catching hodge-
podge of Hungarian and pharmaceutical history in
the Castle District – jugs and bottles from every era
and part of the world, and old, hand-painted
Hungarian pharmacy furnishings. Highlights are an
excellent reconstruction of an alchemist's laborato-
ry; mummy powder from Transylvania (believed to
cure epilepsy); and a large painting of a sweet-faced
nun performing, as they did in the Middle Ages, the
duties of a chemist. The staff speak English, German
or French and can show you around.

Industry

Foundry Museum

Öntödei Múzeum
II. Bem József utca 20 (201 4370). Tram 4, 6. **Open**
10am-5pm daily. **Admission** Ft150; Ft70 concs. EB
Ft100. **No credit cards.** No English spoken. **Map B2**
The original building of the Ganz Foundry (1845-
1964), one of the big players in Hungary's industrial revolution, displays exhibits on metalwork, and
cast-iron products from giant tram wheels and turn-
of-the-century street lamps to decorative architectural elements and a woman-shaped stove.

Capital Sewerage Works Museum

Fővárosi Csatornázási Művek Múzeuma
II. Zsigmond tér 1-4 (335 4984). Tram 17. **Open**
10am-3pm Mon-Fri. **Admission** free. EB free. Ring
bell at gate. No English spoken.
Yes, this place is for real, and even whiffs just a little bit (it's still in operation). The museum is located in a modest, rather pretty brick and stucco
building (1912) full of curvy, shiny, black pumps
which look like giant snails. There's also a
Secession-style Siemens switchboard.

Hungarian Museum of Electrotechnics

Magyar Elektrotechnikai Múzeum
*VII. Kazinczy utca 21 (322 0472). M2 Astoria/tram
47, 49.* **Open** 11am-5pm Tue-Sat. **Admission** free.
No credit cards. No English spoken. **Map D4**
Housed in a 1930s transformer station, the outside
of which looks like a set from Terry Gilliam's
Brazil. Men in white coats demonstrate things that
crackle and spark and present the world's first electric motor, designed by a Hungarian Benedictine
monk. There are also old household appliances and
an exhibit on the electrification of the Iron Curtain.
The collection of consumption meters is amusingly tedious, as are the switches throughout the ages.

Trades

Museum of Commerce & Catering

Kereskedelmi és Vendéglátói Múzeum
*I. Fortuna utca 4 (375 6249). Várbusz from
M2 Moszkva tér.* **Open** 10am-5pm Wed-Fri;
10am-6pm Sat, Sun. **Admission** Ft100;
Ft50 concs. **No credit cards.** No English spoken.
Map A3
The Museum of Commerce & Catering is a fascinating small museum. The Commerce section features advertisements from 1900 through to the
middle of the century, including Hungary's first
electric billboard (which the attendant will turn on
for you). It advertises Buck's Beer, with a goat
leaping toward a frothy mug. A bizarre highlight
is a stuffed dog atop a His Master's Voice phono-
graph – which raps its paws against the glass case.
The recently added permanent exhibition
'Hospitable Budapest: Tourism and Hospitality in
the City 1873-1930' includes objects from
Budapest's old hotels and coffee houses plus historical documentation on the city's transformation
from an imperial seat to a bustling modern metropolis. There are only a few captions in English, but
all the exhibits are colourful and visual.

Leisure

Sport & Training Museum

Testnevelési és Sportmúzeum
XIV. Dózsa György út 3 (252 1695, ask for Sport Museum). M2 Népstadion. **Open** 10am-4pm Sat-Thur. **Admission** Ft100; Ft50 concs. **No credit cards.** No English spoken.
Part of the huge **Népstadion** sports complex (*see chapter* **Sport & Fitness**). Temporary exhibits on current and past sports themes, in Hungarian only.

Stamp Museum

Bélyeg Múzeum
VII. Hársfa utca 47 (342 3757). M1 Vörösmarty utca. **Open** 10am-6pm Tue-Sun. **Admission** Ft50; Ft30 concs. **No credit cards.** No English spoken. **Map D3**
Thousands of stamps from every corner of the world. Kept in a large room above a post office, the collection resembles a well-organised card catalogue, with 3,000 pull-out boards of stamps organised by continent and country.

Natural History

Natural History Museum

Természettudományi Múzeum
VII Ludovika tér 2 (313 0842). M3 Klinikák or Nagyvárad tér/tram 24. **Open** 10am-6pm Mon, Wed-Sun. **Admission** Ft240; Ft120 concs. EB Ft500. **No credit cards.** English spoken. **Map F6**
The permanent 'Human Beings and Nature in Hungary' at the Natural History Museum looks at the geological changes in the region and the use of natural resources. The exhibition uses graphics, photos and interactive devices as well as displays to take you over the millennia. There are also minerals and fossils, a mammoth and an elephant skeleton, a discovery room where you can experiment with fossils, feathers and tools. Temporary exhibitions have recently included Mummies, expedition photos from Nepal, and an interactive exhibit on environment protection. Outside the museum is a park full of old fossils and stones.

The Geological Institute Museum

Magyar Állami Földtani Intézet Múzeuma
XIV. Stefánia út 14 (267 1427). Bus 7/trolleybus 75. **Open** 10am-4pm Thur, Sat, Sun. **Admission** Ft150, Ft50 concs. English brochures, free and guided tour in English, Ft500. **No credit cards.** Some English spoken.
The contents of the Geological Museum are small and of little interest to anyone who isn't really, really into rocks. The real attraction is its building, a fascinating example of Hungarian art nouveau designed by Ödön Lechner (*see chapter* **Architecture**). Inside, the first section deals with the history of Hungarian Geology, while the second section's displays include 20 million year-old rhino footprints. There is a two-hour guided tour plus English captions.

Public services

Museum of Firefighting

Tűzoltó Múzeum
X. Martinovics tér 12, inside fire station (261 3586). Tram 28. **Open** 9am-4pm Tue-Sat, 9am-1pm Sun. **Admission** free. **No credit cards.** No English spoken.
The Museum of Firefighting displays the history of firefighting in Hungary, with items and reproductions from Aquincum, statues of St Flórián (the patron saint of firemen), a horse-drawn engine from 1899, and the first motorised water-pump, brought to Hungary from England by Széchényi's son Ödön in 1870. There's also the original motorised dry extinguisher invented by Hungarian Kornél Szilvay in 1928. In a still-functioning fire station, next door to an art nouveau church.

Géza Kresz Emergency & Ambulance Service Museum

Kresz Géza Mentőmúzeum
V. Markó utca 22 (3111 666 ext. 4188). M3 Nyugati. **Open** 9am-2pm daily. **Admission** Ft60; Ft20 concs. **No credit cards.** No English spoken. **Map C2**
Dr Kresz (1846-1901) founded Hungary's first volunteer ambulance service in 1887. Medical rescue history is covered in excruciating Hungarian-only detail. Listed opening hours may prove unreliable.

Postal Museum

Posta Múzeum
VI. Andrássy út 3 (342 7938). M1, M2, M3 Deák tér/tram 47, 49. **Open** 10am-5.30pm Tue-Sun. **Admission** Ft50; Ft30 concs. **No credit cards.** No English. **Map C3**
The Postal Museum, the richly frescoed and wainscoted former apartment of the wealthy Saxlehaner family now displays everything related to the Hungarian postal service. The frescoes in the entrance and stairway are by Károly Lotz, whose work also adorns the Opera House. The second room both preserves the appearance of a bourgeois home and looks like an everyday post office. Further on are old delivery vehicles and wartime radio transmitters. Good English text at the front desk guides you through.

Telephone Museum

Telefónia Múzeum
I. Úri utca 49 (201 2243). Várbusz from M2 Moszkva tér. **Open** 10am-6pm Tue-Sun. **Admission** Ft50; Ft30 concs. **No credit cards.** Some English spoken. **Map A3**
Although touted as great for kids, they'll need a degree in engineering to understand the long, dry, techie text in Hunglish at the Telephone Museum. Possibly exciting when few Hungarians had a phone (ironically the switchboard was invented by a Hungarian, Tivadar Puskás), now kids can use old-fashioned exchanges, or dial up a bad Hungarian pop song on a c1970 phone. Lots of old equipment and photos.

Underground Railway Museum – *'Madam, is this seat taken?' 'Yes, you dummy!'*

Science

Palace of Wonders

Csodák Palotája
XIII. Váci út 19 (350 6131). M3 Lehel tér. **Open**
9am-5pm Tue-Fri; 10am-6pm Sat, Sun. **Admission**
Ft400; Ft350 concs. **No credit cards**. English
spoken. **Map D2**

Central Europe's first interactive science museum.
Although on nothing like the scale of London's
National Science Museum – it's on the top floor of
an old warehouse building – it does boast such wonders as a whispering mirror, a flying carpet and an
independent-minded shadow. Kids can push, pull
and press to their hearts' delight as there are a host
of devices that light up, make noises and react to
various commands, plus video telephones and
Fakir's beds. On top of all this, most attendants are
English-speaking teachers.

Transport

Transport Museum

Közlekedési Múzeum
*XIV. Városligeti körút 11 (343 0565). Trolleybus 72,
74.* **Open** 10am-5pm Tue-Fri; 10am-6pm Sat, Sun,
holidays. **Admission** Ft150; Ft60 concs. EB Ft300.
No credit cards. No English spoken. **Map F2**

Remains of the pre-war Budapest bridges are displayed in front of this large museum, covering every

aspect of transport in Hungary with English captions. Guided tours in English can also be arranged
in advance. Kids should enjoy the antique cars,
trams, steam train and model boats, and can try out
some of the engines in the big hall on the ground
floor, but that's it for hands-on stuff. The rail models include a realistic miniature Hungarian countryside, with Stalinist high-rises on the town outskirts
and A-frame weekend cottages, demonstrated on the
hour. The other part of the museum, 'Aviation', is a
short walk away, on the second floor of the Petőfi
Csarnok concert hall (open 10am-6pm Tue-Sun,
closed Nov-Mar, same admission). Small planes,
gliders and helicopters fill two halls – the oldest a
1921 Junkers F13 and a 1909 monoplane replica. The
aerospace section is dead boring.

Underground Railway Museum

Földalatti Múzeum
*Deák tér metro station, near Károly körút exit. M1,
M2, M3 Deák tér/tram 47, 49.* **Open** 10am-6pm
Tue-Sun. **Admission** Ft90 or one transport ticket;
free children. **No credit cards**. No English spoken.
Map C4

If you're passing through Budapest's main metro
intersection, pop in for a look at several original carriages from continental Europe's first underground,
built in 1896. There are plans, as yet vague, for the
museum to start running nostalgia tours with the
original train running from Hősök tere to Deák tér.

Art Galleries

No longer forbidden, art in Budapest is still in transition – from the three Ts to the three Cs and beyond.

The art scene in Budapest is becoming much the same as in any western city, but with a few unique twists of its own – entertainment value is less important to curators, and big shows are mounted more for a professional crowd than the general public. Small openings, on the other hand, can be very entertaining indeed, without any consumerist burden of expectation.

Once upon a time, though, art in Hungary was categorised by the three Ts: *tiltott, tűrt, támoga-tott* – forbidden, tolerated and supported, with constantly changing boundaries between them. These days the situation is more complex, with no overarching ideology for artists to define themselves within or against.

The *rendszerváltás* ('change of systems') finished off the category of forbidden artists, only to strip their art of its vital context. Many of these artists found themselves in deep trouble again as soon as there was no enemy to fight against. An important archive of forbidden art – particularly from the 1970s avant garde – is **Artpool** (*see below*), which also holds a vast amount of research material on Miklós Erdély. Even he, the main figure of underground resistance, started painting in a depoliticised manner in the 1980s. He is probably one of the few artists whose work goes beyond daily political resistance, and it remains amazingly universal.

Erdély's students, members of the Indigo (a contraction of the Hungarian for 'inter-disciplinary thinking') group such as János Sugár and András Böröcz, went on to make progressive art that did not compromise. The generation that followed in the mid-1980s was the first for decades that found itself free of the necessity to use encoded language. Artists such as the Hejettes Szomlyazók group could afford to be naive, emotional and anti-professional – their name means 'deputy thirsters', deliberately misspelled.

But art is elsewhere now, in an increasingly complex and expanding system that's still in transition. Art is at the three Cs – **c3** (*below*) – where progressive experimentation in media art is happening through collaboration between local artists and others of international renown. Art is everywhere, from state-run establishments to private galleries and international institutions catering to all tastes and budgets.

Current information on temporary exhibits (*kiállítások*) and performances can be found in *index*, a listing of all that's worthy in public and private spaces, recently started as an 'art project' by two artists. It also has a map of the city's exhibition spaces and can be picked up at the larger venues listed below. *Pesti Est* and *Open*, competing free weeklies available almost everywhere, also carry exhibition listings in Hungarian. The free monthly *Budapest Panorama*, in five languages including English and available at hotels and in tourist offices, lists the main exhibitions.

If you're in Budapest for a longer period, you can subscribe to c3's mailing list for information on local programmes and openings by sending a message with 'subscribe' in the subject field to program-request@c3.hu. To read about international projects and hear about invitations for submissions, follow the same procedure at artinfo-request@c3.hu.

Műcsarnok – *exhibition palace. Page 97.*

Ernst Múzeum – *art nouveau doors.*

Antique-hunters and those seeking cheaper early twentieth-century artworks should scout around the many galleries on V. Falk Miksa utca, although the stack 'em high, price 'em low atmosphere that prevails in several is offputting for the serious connoisseur. *Műértő* (*Art Connoisseur*, with an English supplement) compiling exhibitions, auctions and commercial galleries, can be picked up at the major hotels or bought at any newspaper stand.

Many galleries close during July and through to mid August. Do ring first.

Public galleries & spaces

Black-Black Galéria
IX. Balázs Béla utca 20 (221 8963). **M3 Klinikák.** **Open** 10am-8pm Sat and for one-off performances and events. **Admission** varies. **No credit cards.** Some English spoken. **Map E6**
Run by theatre leader Triceps from Novi Sad and connected to Neoists and other regular guests of international performance art festivals. Marginal, guerilla and provocative.

Budapest Galéria Kiállítóterem
Budapest Gallery Exhibition Space
V. Szabadsajtó út 5 (318 8097). **M3 Ferenciek tere/tram 2/bus 7.** **Open** 10am-6pm Tue-Sun. **Admission** Ft100; Ft50 children. **No credit cards.** Some English spoken. **Map C4**
Contemporary painting, sculpture, graphic art, installations and applied art from Hungary and abroad. Some of the shows use the street viewpoint strategically and large windows allow instant consumption. Budapest Galéria also runs the Kiállítóháza (*see below*), the **Imre Varga Exhibit**

(*see under* **Collections**) and is responsible for the caretaking and installation of public monuments in the city.

Budapest Galéria Kiállítóháza
Budapest Gallery Exhibition House
III. Lajos utca 158 (388 6771).Tram 1. **Open** 10am-6pm Tue-Sun. **Admission** Ft100; Ft50 children. **No credit cards.** No English spoken.
Exhibition space for mainly contemporary Hungarian art within medieval walls, also housing a collection of classicist sculptures by Imre Varga's tutor, Pál Pátzay. Worth a look if there is a group show on. Near the **Óbudai Társaskör Galéria** (*see below*) and on the way to the **Kiscelli Museum** (*see chapter* **Museums**).

Dorottya Galéria
V. Dorottya utca 8 (266 0223). **M1 Vörösmarty tér/tram 2.** **Open** 10am-6pm Mon-Fri; 10am-2pm Sat. **Admission** free. Some English spoken. **Map C4**
An airy gallery linked to the **Műcsarnok** (*see below*) and devoted to more marginal art forms, such as set design, installation, media art and architecture.

Ernst Múzeum
VI. Nagymező utca 8 (341 4355). **M1 Opera.** **Open** 10am-6pm Tue-Sun. **Admission** Ft100; Ft50 children. **No credit cards.** Some English spoken. **Map D3**
Recognisable at ground level by its beautiful brass art nouveau doors, this was designed as an exhibition space in a block of artists' studios commissioned by the private collector Lajos Ernst in 1912. These days it is run by the **Műcsarnok** (*see below*) and shows contemporary Hungarian avant-garde works as well as smaller international exhibits of quality. Always worth a visit.

Fészek Galéria
VII. Kertész utca 36 (342 6548). *Tram 4, 6.* **Open** 2-7pm Mon-Fri. **Admission** free. Some English spoken. **Map D3**
Gallery for more traditional genres. The club also hosts concerts and theatre performances for token fees. You may encounter some hostility if you are not willing to check your coat in – this is a club, Ladies and Gentlemen! *See also chapter* **Restaurants**.

Liget Galéria
XIV. Ajtósi Dürer sor 5 (351 4924). *Tram 74, 75/bus 7 Dózsa György út.* **Open** 2-6pm Mon, Wed-Sun. Openings on Fri. **Admission** free. Some English spoken. **Map F2**
Tiny gallery beside the Városliget showing mainly conceptual art, video and photography.

Ludwig Museum Budapest/Museum of Contemporary Art
Wing A, Buda Palace, I. Dísz tér 17(375 9175). *Várbusz from M2 Moszkva tér/bus 16.* **Open** 10am-6pm Tue-Sun. **Admission** Ft200; Ft100 children. **No credit cards.** Some English spoken. **Map B4**
Reliable member of the Ludwig network, with the predictable pieces by Warhol, Rauschenberg, Oldenburg, Lichtenstein, Jasper Johns, and trans-

avant-garde and contemporary Russian artists set against works by Hungarian artists from the past three decades, including Lakner, Keserü, Konkoly, Tót, Erdély, Molnár, Bak, Nádler, Jovánovics, Haraszty, Baranyay, Galántai, Maurer and Hencze. Of the 800 Picassos belonging to the Ludwig collection three late works are here. Several temporary exhibitions are usually being juggled at the same time, and the Ludwig has recently started a Project Room for site-specific collaborative or solo works. A must on the CV of any Hungarian artist seeking international recognition – the canon is made here. Openings usually on Thursday. Guided tours and workshops for children by appointment.

MAMÜ Galéria
VII. Damjanich utca 39, entrance on Murányi utca (306 1587). Tram 70. **Open** *3-7pm Wed, Fri, Sat. Openings on Fri.* **Admission** *free. English spoken.* **Map F2**
Small gallery in a cellar run by the association with the same dada-ist name. MAMÜ once meant 'Artists' Studio from Marosvásárhely' (Romania), but mutated in 1991 into *ma születő művek* – 'works born today' – after the majority of the (mainly Hungarian) artists were successfully 'shipped' to Hungary. Its most recent retrospective catalogue features the biggest number of beards and moustaches seen since the hippie era, and hardly any women at all. Openings are accompanied by performances, actions, concerts and the ubiquituous *pogácsa* and cheap wine.

Műcsarnok
Palace of Exhibitions
XIV. Dózsa György út 37 (343 7401). M1 Hősök tere. **Open** *museum 10am-6pm Tue-Sun; library and archive 10am-6pm Mon-Fri.* **Admission** *Ft300; Ft100 children.* **Credit** *shop AmEx, DC, MC, JCB, V. Some English spoken.* **Map E1**
Budapest's largest and most prestigious contemporary exhibition hall shows Hungarian and international artists. Also a lively lecture and film programme plus occasional performances by internationally renowned artists. It also hosts art workshops for kids on Sundays. There are no permanent exhibits. Check current programme for details.

Óbudai Pincegaléria
Zichy Mansion, III. Fő tér 1 (250 0288). HÉV Árpád híd/tram 1/bus 6, 60, 86. **Open** *May, Sept, Oct 2-6pm Tue-Fri; 10am-6pm Sat, Sun.* **Admission** *Ft30.* **No credit cards.** *No English spoken.*
Small gallery in the cellar of the mansion that also hosts the **Kassák** and **Vasarely Museums** and the shows of the Óbuda local history collection. The same profile as the Óbudai Társaskör Galéria, *below.*

Óbudai Társaskör Galéria
III. Kis Korona utca 7 (250 0288) Tram 1/bus 6, 60. **Open** *2-6pm Tue-Sun. Closed in Summer.* **Admission** *30Ft.* **No credit cards.** *No English spoken.*
For over 20 years this tiny vault in the cellar of the local community centre has displayed both 'forgot-

ten' *oeuvres* and first shows. Often features artists who did or will get international acknowledgement. To get here you might walk through an absorbed card-playing crowd or a classical concert.

Stúdió Galéria
V. Képíró utca 6 (267 2033/studio@visio.c3.hu). M3 Kálvin tér/tram 47, 49. **Open** *2-6pm Mon-Sat. Closed Aug.* **Admission** *free. English spoken.* **Map D5**
Shows and successfully promotes about 300 artists under the age of 35, members of the Studio of Young Artists Association. Exhibitions change every fortnight, with openings on Tuesdays. A climax is the Gallery by Night events at the **Budapest Spring Festival** (*see chapter* **Budapest by Season**), with a late opening each night for about a week. Check local listings press for details.
Website: www.c3.hu/fkse

Trafó Galéria
IX. Liliom utca 41 (215 1600/456 2040/ trafo@trafo.c3.hu). M3 Ferenc körút/tram 4, 6. **Open** *4-7pm Mon-Sat; 2-8pm Sun. Openings Fri.* **Admission** *Ft200; Ft100 concs.* **No credit cards.** *English spoken.* **Map E5**
The gallery in this hip arts centre shows newest works, collaborations and experiments by Hungarian and international artists. Some events are co-organised with the British Council, Goethe Institute or other national cultural foundations. Exhibitions are accompanied by public discussions

The tiny **Liget Galéria** *– see page 96.*

Street scene

In March 1999 Trafó hosted a show of 'Real Art', documenting and organising a bus tour of 'found sites', fragments of urban fabric that constantly inspire – piss-soaked corners, bullet holes and shrapnel lesions on the façades, scrapes and scratches on the walls, scaffoldings, lost gloves, Mondrianesque institutional flooring and glass bricks in the pavement, lit from cellars below.

The ready-mades were squatted and appropriated for the time of the show, just as a billboard at Lövölde tér (*right*) has been hijacked by artists from **Stúdió Galéria** (*see page 97*). Their conceptual project, provocatively subverting the function of an advertising space, often stirs trouble on the border between Districts VI and VII – or is simply an eye-opener for a Hungarian public corrupted by poor-quality advertising visuals.

An older and more subtle street site dear to many Budapestans in the know is the Folyamat Galéria, housed in a nineteenth-century water meter, still measuring the Danube's ebbs and flows beside the tram 19 stop on Bem rakpart north of the Chain Bridge. Probably the tiniest gallery in the world of any international renown,

it holds its 'openings' every Monday at 7pm, when an official from the Mid-Danube Waterworks comes to pick up the graph drawn by the analogue device, and replaces last week's artwork with a new one. Sometimes sinister sounds might emanate from the box or scandalous images can be viewed through the small porthole in the housing. The Waterworks grins and bears the trouble this occasionally causes them, and proudly keeps an archive of a decade of installations by artists from all over the world. (You can see it at their headquarters at VIII. Rákóczi út 41, by appointment with Miklós Egri, 333 0112.) While viewing the water-meter, the giant paper boat – another art project – might just cruise by on the Danube to puzzle you with a Swiftian play on proportions.

Budapest's most monumental piece of street art is the giant hourglass set up behind the Műcsarnok to mark the Millennium. No Y2K problems here – the thing is wholly mechanical. No last-minute celebratory crap, this 60-ton, 8-metre-tall granite and steel device was planned well in advance and after the turn of the Millenium is to be turned at each turn of the year.

Knoll Galéria Budapest – *conceptual work by east European artists. See page 100.*

with artists and critics, performances, film screenings and the like. (*See also chapters* **Music: Rock, Roots & Jazz, Nightlife** and **Theatre & Dance**.)
Website: www.c3.hu/trafo

U.F.F. Galéria

IX. Közraktár utca 10 (215 3093). Tram 2, 47, 49. **Open** 10am-6pm Tue-Fri. Openings on Fri. Closed July, Aug. **Admission** free. Some English spoken. **Map D5**
Behind the **Great Market Hall** (*see chapter* **Sightseeing**), a new gallery showing young, progressive Hungarian and international artists. First shows and emphasis on multimedia work. Openings lure a flashy crowd.

Vigadó Galéria

V. Vigadó tér 2 (318 7932). M1 Vörösmarty tér/tram 2. **Open** 10am-6pm Tue-Sun. **Admission** free. Some English spoken. **Map C4**
Next to the concert hall of the same name, a prominent and roomy exhibition space for members of the Hungarian Creative Artists Assembly. The link with a state organisation lends an establishment feel to the place. Rarely challenging.

Vizivárosi Galéria

II. Kapás utca 55 (201 6925). Tram 4, 6. **Open** 1-6pm Tue-Fri; 10am-2pm Sat. Closed in Aug. Openings first Thur of the month. **Admission** free. Some English spoken. **Map A2**

Shows Hungarian and foreign artists in traditional and new media. Struggles to please both the general public and professionals.

Zenit Galéria

VII. Rumbach Sebestyén utca 15/b (352 1985). M1, M2, M3 Deák tér/tram 47, 49. **Open** noon-6pm Mon-Fri. Openings on Thur. **Admission** free. Some English spoken. **Map D4**
Tongue-in-cheek shows often playing with the themes of fame, money, materialism and Hungarians' new free-market identities.

Commercial galleries

Bolt Galéria

VIII. Leonardo da Vinci utca 40 (312 1603). M3 Klinikák. **Open** only by appointment. **No credit cards. Map E5**
Deals in experimental photography and mixed media, blurring the boundaries between painting and traditional photography, and organises quirky exhibitions in established spaces.
Website: www.c3.hu/~bolt

Deák Erika Galéria

VI. Jókai tér 1 (353 1068). M1 Oktogon/tram 4, 6. **Open** noon-6pm Wed-Sat. **No credit cards.** Some English spoken. **Map D3**
New gallery promoting mainly Hungarian and central and eastern European post-media art.

Dovin Galéria

V. Galamb utca 6 (318 3673/fax 318 3659). M1 Vörösmarty tér/tram 2. **Open** noon-6pm Tue-Fri; 11am-2pm Sat. **Admission** free. **No credit cards.** Some English spoken. **Map C4**
Established in 1993, the spacious Dovin deals in younger contemporary artists, many of international repute, such as Márton Barabás, El Kazovszkij, Kelemen Ketten Brücke, Baranyai Levente and László Révész, and hosts one international guest per year.

Galéria 56

V. Falk Miksa utca 7 (269 2529). M3 Nyugati/tram 4, 6. **Open** noon-6pm Tue-Sat. **Admission** free. **No credit cards.** English spoken. **Map C2**
Leading commercial space for household-name American artists. Pop art and derivatives figure strongly – Lichtenstein, Mapplethorpe, Rauschenberg and the like. Owner Samuel Havadtőy (Mr Yoko Ono) also promotes up-and-coming Hungarian artists that catch his eye.

Illárium Művészeti Galéria

VIII. Köztársaság tér 15 (210 4883). M2 Keleti or Blaha Lujza tér/bus 7. **Open** 10am-4pm Mon-Fri; 10am-2pm Sat. **Admission** free. **No credit cards.** Some English spoken. **Map E4**
On sale are figurative paintings by Art Academy graduates from the late 1980s in a Bauhaus building from 1933. Might change its present ice-cream shop façade into constructivist design to look like a 'proper' gallery.

Goethe Institut – *increasingly active profile. See page 101.*

Knoll Galéria Budapest
VI Liszt Ferenc tér 10 (267 3842). M1 Oktogon/tram 4, 6. **Open** 2-6.30pm Tue-Fri; 11am-2pm Sat. Closed August. **Admission** free. Some English spoken.
Map D3
Established in 1989 and one of Budapest's first commercial galleries, this branch of a Viennese gallery shows conceptual art, installations and multimedia works by central and eastern European artists.
Website: www.artist-info.com/gallery/galeria-knoll/

Mai Manó Fotógaléria
Magyar Fotográfusok Háza, VI. Nagymező utca 20 (302 4398). M1 Opera. **Open** 2-6pm Mon-Fri. **No credit cards.** Some English spoken. **Map D3**
Cosy exhibition space at the House of Hungarian Photographers displays contemporary as well as retrospective photography and art as well as commercial work. Well-stocked general art bookshop.

Qualitás Galéria
V. Haris köz 1 IV.2 (318 4438/fax 266 3508). M3 Ferenciek tere/bus 7. **Open** 11am-5pm Mon-Fri; 11am-1pm Sat. **Admission** free. **Credit** AmEx, DC, JCB, MC, V. Some English spoken. **Map C4**
Loaded with cash and want to buy dead Hungarian painters? This is the place to come. Qualitás deals in classics and modern artists that fill the National Gallery – such as József Rippl-Rónai, László Mednyánszky, Béla Czóbel. Do Hungary a favour: take these paintings out of the country.

Rácz Stúdió Galéria
VII. Madách Imre utca 3 (342 2342/ ratzg@matavnet.hu). M1, M2, M3 Deák tér/tram 47, 49. **Open** 10am-6pm Mon-Fri. **No credit cards.** Some English spoken. **Map C4**

Rácz Stúdió Galéria Specialises in minimalist, constructivist and conceptual art, promoting established names such as Imre Bak, László Fehér, Gyula Gulyás and Tamás Hencze. Conveniently located next to three other small galleries dealing in contemporary Hungarian and international artists and objects made of glass.

Várfok 14 Galéria
I. Várfok utca 14 (213 5155). M2 Moszkva tér/ tram 4, 6, 18. **Open** 11am-6pm Tue-Sat. **Admission** free. **Credit** AmEx, MC, JCB, V. Free guided tours on Tue. English spoken.
Map A3
One of Budapest's first commercial galleries, deals with six established artists – El Kazovszkij, Imre Bukta, László Fehér, Nádler István, Szirtes András and András Böröcz. The newer, more spacious Spiritusz galéria upstairs hosts a permanent show of the gallery's artists. The same owners run Gallery XO across the street at Várfok utca 11 (214 0373), hosting individual shows.

Vintage Galéria
V. Magyar utca 26 (337 0584). M2 Astoria/ tram 47, 49/bus 7. **Open** 2-7pm Tue-Fri. Openings on Tue. Closed July, Aug. **Admission** free. **No credit cards.** Some English spoken. **Map D4**
Vintage Galéria is a Pleasant airy gallery next to Károlyi kert devoted exclusively to fine-art photography. The gallery specialises in Hungarian Modernists (1919-48) and quality works by less famous contemporary artists whose work transcends the boundaries between photography and fine art.
Website: www.c3.hu/~vintage

Artpool Art Research Centre

VI. Liszt Ferenc tér 10 (268 0114). M1
Oktogon/tram 4, 6. **Open** 2pm-6pm Wed, Fri. Closed
July, Aug. English spoken. **Map D3**
The Artpool Archive was founded in 1979 by sculptor and mail artist Gyorgy Galántai, a pivotal figure
in the Kádár-era opposition, and his partner Júlia
Klaniczay. Illegal but tolerated, the archive was
housed in their apartment until finally moving here
and opening to the public in 1992. Artpool holds
extensive archives of underground art, music, literature and videos from the 1960s to 1989 and probably the most extensive mail-art collection in the
world. There's an annual topic, such as Erdély or
Year Of Contexts, and lectures and online publications are built around them. Since 1997 they've also
had a space, P60, round the corner at Paulay Ede
utca 60, used for occasional shows of Fluxus, performance art and new media.
Website: www.artpool.hu

c3

Center for Culture and Communication
I. Országház utca 9 (214 6856/fax 214 6872/
info@c3.hu). Várbusz from M2 Moszkva tér/bus 16.
Open *library* 10am-6pm Mon-Fri; *labs* (by
appointment) 9am-9pm Mon-Thur; 9am-6pm Fri;
10am-6pm Sat, Sun. **Admission** free. English
spoken. **Map B3**
Probably the most eastward-looking front of media
art experimentation, production and delivery –
bristling with bright young things and flash computer gadgetry. Catch the screening of experimental videos and occasional lectures by passing digirati
such as Victor Burgin, Stelarc or Ars Electronica
prize-winner Etoy.
Website: www.c3.hu

Centrális Galéria

V. Nádor utca 11 (327 3250). M2 Kossuth tér/M3
Arany János utca/tram 2. **Open** 2pm-6pm Tue-Fri;
10am-6pm Sat. **Admission** free. Some English
spoken. **Map C5**
Although not an art gallery as such Centrális Galéria
analyses the representation of the Communist past
from the extensive archives of Radio Free
Europe/Radio Liberty. Via video, CD-rom, sound
and artefacts, it summons up often suppressed mem-
ories. Recent exhibitions included 'The Commissar
Disappears', about the air-brushing of history, and
'The Gulags'. Cathartic for locals and illuminating
for foreigners.
Website: www.osa.ceu.hu/events/galeria

Institut Français

I. Fő utca 17 (202 1133/fax 202 1323). Tram 19,
M2 Batthyány tér. **Open** 1am-7pm Mon-Fri.
Admission *exhibitions* free. Some English spoken.
Map B3
Housed in George Morriose's pastel pink and green
cube on the Buda Danube promenade (*see chapter*
Architecture), this is the liveliest of the foreign cul-
tural centres. A vibrant programme of theatre, music
and excellent film is complemented by exhibitions

of modern art and photography (French and
Hungarian) plus annual Bastille Day celebrations.
Website: www.inst-france.hu

Goethe Institut

VI. Andrássy út 64 (374 4070/fax 374 4080/
goethe@goethe.hu.). M1 Opera. **Open** noon-7pm
Tue-Fri; noon-4pm Sat. **Admission** *exhibitions* free.
English spoken. **Map D3**
Increasingly active with a regular programme of
exhibits and performances by both German and
Hungarian artists. It also sponsors retropectives of
German filmmakers at the **Örökmozgó** (*see chap-*
ter **Film**), writers' readings, exhibitions and the
occasional concert on Margaret Island. Dive into its
Eckermann café next door for a pretzel. *See chapter*
Cafés & Coffeehouses.
Website: www.goethe.de/ms/bud

Magyar Fotográfusok Háza

House of Hungarian Photographers
VI. Nagymező utca 20 (302 4496). M1 Opera. **Open**
2-6pm. **Admission** Ft200; Ft100 concs. Openings on
Mon. English spoken. **Map D3**
This building, with camera-toting cherubs on its
gaudy Zsolnay façade, once housed the Manó Mai
Imperial and Royal Court Photographer's Studio.
Currently an archeological site with exhibitions still
taking place while the building is being renovated.
Established as a long-awaited centre for Hungarian
photography. A potentially significant new institution. The big banner drooping from the building
advertises three simultaneous shows.

Instytut Polski

Polish Institute
VI. Nagymező utca 15 (331 1168). M1 Opera. **Open**
8am-8pm Mon-Thur; 8am-5pm Fri. **Admission**
exhibitions free. **No credit cards. Map D3**
Brings the lively Polish arts scene to Budapest, hosting more unconventional and adventurous exhibitions than the other state-funded institutions, but not
necessarily at this venue – at press time they were
planning to move the gallery to Andrássy út around
the corner. Recent exhibitions included photography
by Artur Zmijewski and 'Black Money' by young
Hungarian artists.

Collections

Imre Varga Exhibit

Varga Imre Állandó Kiállítás
III. Laktanya utca 7 (250 0274). HÉV Árpád híd.
Open 10am-5pm Tue-Sun. **Admission** Ft200; Ft100
concs. **No credit cards.** No English spoken.
Varga was the favoured sculptor of the Kádár
regime, but his talent is unquestionable. Political
themes dominate the official works – nuclear apocalypse, Jewish resistance – as well as a crop of ema-
ciated poets and approved national heroes. Yet his
figures are distinguished by their evident humani-
ty and emotion. The garden houses some of his most
touching portraits – those of Franz Liszt, martyred
poet Miklós Radnóti and sculptor Alajos Stróbl.

Kassák Múzeum

Zichy Mansion, III. Fő tér 1 (368 7021). HÉV Árpád hid. **Open** 10am-6pm Tue-Sun. **Admission** Ft100; Ft50 children. **No credit cards**. No English spoken.

Lajos Kassák (1887-1967), a poet and Constructivist painter, was the leading advocate in Hungary of all strands of the early European and Russian avant garde through his journals *A tett* (*Action*) and *Ma* (*Today*), on display in this tiny exhibit of his book design, publishing, poetry, painting and sculpture. The Kassák circle (including Surrealist poet Tibor Déry and László Moholy-Nagy) was held together not by a style but by a belief that 'art transforms us and we become capable of transforming the world'. This disdain of propaganda inevitably brought him into sharp conflict with left-ist governments as well as the Horthy régime who forced him briefly into exile. The gallery also hosts exhibits of twentieth-century Hungarian artists and forgotten works from private collections.

Molnár C. Pál Magángyűjtemény

XI. Ménesi út 65 (385 3637). Tram 61. **Open** *May-June* 3-6pm Tue-Thur; *Oct-Apr* 3-6pm Tue-Thur; 10am-1pm Sun. **Admission** Ft 90; Ft50 children. **No credit cards**. Some English spoken. **Map B6**

Graphic artist, painter and illustrator Pál C. Molnár (1894-1981) was preoccupied with Christian themes and created many altar pieces. This private collection is curated by his daughter, Éva Csillag, and includes many of his better-known graphic works. M-C P, as he signed his paintings, is regarded as a forerunner of Hungarian Surrealism. His altar paintings can be seen in situ at the **Church of St Anne** and the **Inner City Parish Church**, *for both see chapter* **Sightseeing**.

Vasarely Múzeum

Zichy Mansion, III. Szentélek tér 6 (388 7551/250 1523). HÉV Árpád híd. **Open** 10am-5.30pm Tue-Sun. **Admission** Ft200; Ft100 concs. **No credit cards**. No English spoken.

This historically complete exhibit (360 works donated by the artist) takes you through Vasarely's development as an artist – from commercial graphic design as a student of Sándor Bortnyik to fame in Paris as one of the founders of the Op Art movement in the late 1960s. Described by André Breton as 'the true Surrealist painter', Vasarely's play with spatial disorientation and illusory perspective is clear in the many monumental canvases. His smaller kinetic sculptures use the distortion of geometry through parallel glass and the shifting forms of the moiré effect. The tapestries were made by Vasarely's wife.

Szentendre

Don't be fooled by the picturesque ambience of this town 20km north of Budapest. There is a quiet tension between the iconoclastic artistic community, the 'official' aesthetics of the state-funded exhibition spaces and the hordes that descend to coo over the naive ceramics of Margit Kovács. While you might still catch the spirit of the spontaneity of the 1970s experimental art scene at a performance by István ef Zámbó's Happy Dead Band, it's easy enough simply to beat the crowds by visiting the galleries themselves, which include two run by the artists.

The original artists' colony was founded in the early 1920s as a summer retreat. It became more established in the 1930s and 1940s, when Surrealist and Constructivist painters took up base here – trends that are still strong. After World War II, the town briefly became the centre of the 'European School' – artists who saw links with major European art trends as the key to a healthy local artistic culture, 'controversial' in the Rákosi era. The permanent colony was established in 1968, and the all-male Vajda Lajos Stúdió (VLS) was established in 1972 as a centre of 'Edwinism' – a psychedelic version of Dada. The core of this group is still active and some of them have reached international recognition. These days about 150 artists make up the colony.

The smaller museums are open only at the weekend and often only until 4pm. Weekday appointments for visiting groups can be arranged by calling 06 26 310 244. Tentative spaces such as Téli Galéria (above the Szentendrei képtár on Fő tér) and the ambitious Malom Múzeum és Művészeti Központ (Bogdány utca 32) struggle to create an alternative to the ubiquitous arts and crafts, VLS painters and commercial galleries.

Anna Margit – Ámos Imre Múzeum

2000 Szentendre, Bogdányi utca 10 (no phone). HÉV Szentendre. **Open** 10am-4pm Fri-Sun **Admission** Ft150; Ft100 children. **No credit cards**. Some English spoken.

Two very different personalities, lyric painter Imre Ámos and his partner, Surrealist Anna Margit, lived together at this address before the Holocaust swallowed up Ámos in 1944. Premonitions of death and apocalypse overshadow Ámos' work upstairs, mingling with Chagallesque symbolism of rural Jewish life. This incredibly moving exhibit also has documents from Ámos' forced labour in the Ukraine. Downstairs, Anna's naive Surrealist portraits combine peasant characters with allusions to totalitarian insanity as she dealt with her grief at the loss of her husband. Anna Margit died in 1991 and is buried in the courtyard. The paintings in the museum were selected by herself before her death.

Art.éria

2000 Szentendre, Városház tér 1 (06 26 310 111). HÉV Szentendre. **Open** 10am-1pm, 2-5pm Wed-Sun. **Admission** free. **Credit** AmEx, DC, MC, JCB, V. Some English spoken.

The first private gallery in Szentendre, owned by 20 artists. This tiny space crammed with paintings tends to exhibit VLS artists (István ef Zámbó, László

fe Lugossy, Imre Bukta, András Wahorn) and more institutional artists such as István Nádler, Pál Deim, Ilona Keserü and Imre Bak.

Barcsay Múzeum

2000 Szentendre, Dumtsa Jenő utca 10 (no phone). *HÉV Szentendre.* **Open** 10am-4pm Fri-Sun. **Admission** Ft150, Ft100 children. **No credit cards.** Some English spoken.

One of the larger Szentendre museums, containing the works of Constructivist Jenő Barcsay. Much of his inspiration was evidently drawn from the town and its buildings, such as the Klee-derivative works from around 1945 and the minimalist geometry of pieces from the late 1960s, 1970s and 1980s, which have the precision of architectural plans. His use of colour is particularly striking – sombre rather than vivid, some with the richness of Orthodox icons. The gallery also contains his mosaics and tapestries.

Czóbel Béla Múzeum

2000 Szentendre, Templom tér 1 (06 26 312 721). *HÉV Szentendre.* **Open** 10am-4pm Fri-Sun. **Admission** Ft150; Ft100 children. **No credit cards.** Some English spoken.

One of Hungary's most prominent twentieth-century painters, Béla Czóbel (1883-1976) joined the Fauvist movement in Paris and hung out with Matisse before retreating to Szentendre. Here he created his best work, such as the bikini-clad *Venus of Szentendre* (1968), displayed here amid romanticised scenes of markets and the rather passionless portraits of his pre-war years.

Erdész Galéria

2000 Szentendre, Fő tér 20 (06 26 310 139) *& Bercsényi utca 4 (26 317 925).* *HÉV Szentendre.* **Open** 10am-6pm Tue-Sun. **Admission** free. **Credit** AmEx, DC, MC, JCB, V. English spoken.

Deals in classical and contemporary art mainly from Szentendre and Hungary, but Dali and Vasarely prints are on sale, too. The Bercsenyi location has a permanent collection of Sándor Bortnyik, Lajos Kassák, József Rippl-Rónai, László Moholy-Nagy and Lajos Vajda and also sells wallets, jewellery and glass items by local craftspeople. Many different styles are represented, although Constructivist and Surrealist painters are the strongest. The place on the main square deals in contemporary art, with occasional individual shows.

Ferenczy Múzeum

2000 Szentendre, Fő tér 6 (06 26 310 790). HÉV *Szentendre.* **Open** 10am-4pm Wed-Sun. **Admission** Ft150; Ft100 children. **No credit cards.** Some English spoken.

The works of the Ferenczy family are spread over four floors of one of the first museums to be opened in Szentendre. Károly Ferenczy was a founder of the Nagybánya colony of Impressionists. His wife Olga Fialka was an established Wiener Biedermeier painter. His eldest son Valér was only a mediocre talent, but the twins Béni (a sculptor) and Noémi Ferenczy (who created symbolist gobelin works) both earned a reputation as exalted as their father's.

Kmetty János Múzeum

2000 Szentendre, Fő tér 21 (06 26 310 790). HÉV *Szentendre.* **Open** 10am-4pm Tue-Sun. **Admission** Ft150; Ft100 children. **No credit cards.** Some English spoken.

Cubist János Kmetty (1889-1975), a member of the Kassák circle, studied in Paris and worked in Szentendre from 1930. Among the many Cezanne-inspired still lifes are frequent self-portraits revealing a suspicious weasel-like man glaring out of the canvases. Experimentation with stained glass led to angularity in his painting. A disturbing collection.

Kovács Margit Múzeum

2000 Szentendre, Vastagh György utca 1 (06 26 310 *790). HÉV Szentendre.* **Open** 10am-6pm daily. **Admission** Ft250; Ft150 children. **No credit cards.** Some English spoken.

Margit Kovács (1902-77) was probably the most popular Hungarian 'sculptor' (she was really a ceramicist) ever. In the lowest-common-denominator aesthetics that dominated Kadár-era officially approved art, Kovács was queen. To be fair, it's not all kitsch. There are certain votive aspects to her ceramics, more reminiscent of Etruscan or Persian religious mythology than Hungarian folktales. Her later work reveals her fear of death as she battled with cancer. Overpriced and not worth the effort if you're pushed for time.

Vajda Lajos Múzeum

2000 Szentendre, Hunyadi utca 1 (no phone). HÉV *Szentendre.* **Open** 10am-4pm Fri-Sun. **Admission** Ft150; Ft100 children. **No credit cards.** Some English spoken.

The montages and Surrealist paintings of Lajos Vajda (1908-41), a member of the Kassák circle, while not as apocalyptic as those of Imre Ámos, are a powerful commentary on looming disaster as World War II approached. While his montages comment on current political events in much the same way as those of John Heartfield did, his paintings are the most disturbing: vegetation twisted with violent energy into a war dynamic. Gentler are his city scenes with their disorientating multiple perspectives. Downstairs is another gallery with other Szentendre-based Surrealist painters. Look out for Endre Bálint's ghostly village scenes, such as the *Shop Window of an Undertaker* (1970) and geometric dancing insects of the *wedding of the cricket* by Dezső Korniss (1948).

Vajda Lajos Pincegaléria

2000 Szentendre, Péter Pál utca 6 (06 26 310 593). *HÉV Szentendre.* **Open** 10am-6pm Tue-Sat. **Admission** free. **No credit cards.** English spoken.

This deep cellar has been hosting exhibitions by the VLS artists for 17 years now. Young followers and international artists creating along the same aesthetics of spontaneity are also occasionally invited.

Consumer

Accommodation

Five-star riverside luxury, garden hotels in the Buda hills, hostel beds all over town – but remember to book in advance.

Finding a place to stay in Budapest involves two basic questions: Pest or Buda? And is the place you'd like to stay already booked up? The first is mere preference. Accommodation in Pest put you within minutes of the major sights, shopping, museums and nightlife. The ideal *panzió* (pension) in Buda places you farther from the centre, but can reward with a pleasant, cool garden and a view out over the city.

As for the second question, it's not that there aren't plenty of rooms. Rather, finding a room in the right location and in the right price range can be difficult, especially in the Moderate and Budget categories. Thus we'd advise booking in advance whenever possible. A fax in English at least two weeks (one month in the summer) before you plan to arrive with a follow-up call should suffice. (Receptionists in nearly all hotels and *panziók* listed here speak enough English to read a fax or handle a basic telephone conversation.) One helpful innovation is the Hungary Info Website (*www.hotelinfo.hu* or *www.hotels.hu*), which offers up-to-date information on almost all hotels in Hungary.

If you arrive without a booking, **IBUSZ** (open 24 hours daily; *see below*) is reliable for local accommodation and will book free of charge. Though staff here do have their favourites, don't be afraid to ask them for help in contacting a specific place. **American Express** (*see below*) books hotels, but requires a $20 service fee for non-cardholders. To book yourself, **Tourinform** (*see below*) provides a free brochure with current listings for most hotels and panziók in Hungary.

High season runs from late spring to early autumn with prices increased accordingly. During the spring festival (11 March-3 April in 2000) and the Hungarian Grand Prix (first or second week of August) it is best to book at least a month in advance to ensure something in your price range.

WHAT'S ON OFFER?

With the exception of the **Hilton** in the Castle District and the **Kempinski** on Erzsébet tér, Budapest's major hotels line the Pest bank of the Danube, just south of the Chain Bridge. All were either built after 1990 or have been renovated since then. While they all claim to be five-star hotels and

Hotel Gellért – *where Budapest's Silver Age still shines. See page 113.*

Hotel Victoria – *comfort and location at half the price. See page 116.*

services are extensive, there's little feeling of luxury except, perhaps, at the Kempinski. Less expensive hotels are scattered around the city; those built after 1990 or under private ownership tend to have better rooms, more facilities and friendlier staff.

Most of the Communist-era hotels – despite, in some cases, renovations that have traded 1970s kitsch for the 1990s version – still have average restaurants and a cavalier attitude towards service. On the bright side, alternatives in the moderate price range are increasing every year and panziók offer many of the same services found in hotels, but with a more personal touch.

Spa hotels are an interesting alternative. The **Danubius Thermal Hotel Helia**, **Hotel Gellért**, **Corinthia Hotel Aquincum**, **Thermal Hotel Margitsziget** and **Danubius Grand** (*all below*) have on-site spa facilities. Stay a few nights or book a one- or two-week 'cure' and you can use not only swimming pools, saunas, and thermal pools of varying temperatures, but medical and beauty services, including massage, mud baths and hydrotherapy. *See also chapter* **Baths**.

Non-smoking rooms used to be a rarity in Hungary but many hotels are now offering these. Still, if getting one is a must, make sure you specify this in your reservation.

RENTING ROOMS

Private rooms (*fizetővendég szolgálat*) are the least expensive choice in the city outside of the youth hostel scene (singles range from Ft1,000 to Ft2,000, doubles Ft3,000 to Ft5,000). IBUSZ (*see below*) books private rooms and Keleti station is the hunting ground for Hungarians with rooms to let. Ask to see where you'll be staying before accepting a room or agreeing a price – breakfast of some kind should be included. Though many are very comfortable, rooms and their owners receive only cursory inspection by the tourist board. Beware of ending up stranded out in District XVI with a landlady from hell looking through your dirty socks and expecting you to be home before ten.

Finding a more permanent residence in Budapest is, if anything, even harder than finding a hotel. Word of mouth is best for inexpensive digs, followed by the *Expressz* daily classified ad paper (*see chapter* **Media**). Watch out, though; most apartments are listed by agencies that will charge Ft2,500 for a list of addresses that may be out of date. If you have a bit more money to spend, try one of the real estate agents advertised in *Budapest Sun*. Expect to pay up to Ft35,000-Ft50,000 for a one-room flat, or Ft50,000-Ft70,000 for a two-room flat per month plus utilities, in the centre.

PRICES

Prices in the Hungarian tourist industry are usually pegged to the Deutschmark and hotels list prices in this currency, although payments can be made in forints and both US dollars and pounds sterling are increasingly accepted. We have therefore listed hotel prices in this guide in Deutschmarks. At the time of going to press, DM1 was buying around Ft150, though this will undoubtedly change.

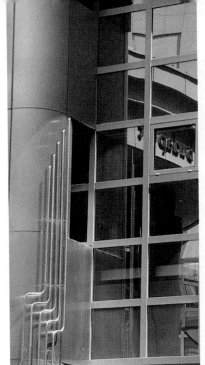

Grand Hotel Korvinus Kempinski. *Page 112.*

Unless otherwise noted, breakfast is included. Usually this is a cold buffet of bread, cheeses and cold cuts. Some hotels offer an 'American' breakfast, which includes a hot and cold buffet. If two prices are listed they indicate the high- and low-season rates. Price categories are as follows: a double room in a deluxe hotel costs DM330 or more; an expensive hotel DM230 or more; a moderate hotel DM130 or more. The rest are budget.

Booking

American Express

V. Deák Ferenc utca 10 (235 4330/fax 267 2028/2029). M1, M2, M3 Deák tér/tram 47, 49. **Open** *Sept-May* 9am-5.30pm Mon-Fri; 9am-2pm Sat. *June-Aug* 9am-6.30pm Mon-Fri; 9am-2pm Sat. **Credit** AmEx. **Map C4**
Hotel reservations free for AmEx cardholders, $20 for anyone else.

IBUSZ

V. Apáczai Csere János utca 1 (318 4848/fax 317 9099). M1 Vörösmarty tér/tram 2. **Open** 24 hours daily. **Map C4**
Books for around 80 per cent of Budapest's hotels and panziók free of charge, and will often get a better rate than you would by going directly to the hotel. Courteous though harried staff will also find private rooms or short-stay apartments (up to 2-3 weeks).

Tourinform

V. Sütő utca 2 (317 9800/fax 317 9656/ tourinfo@tourinform.hu). M1, M2, M3, Deák tér/tram 47, 49. **Open** 9am-7pm Mon-Fri; 9am-4pm Sat, Sun. **No credit cards. Map C4**
No room booking, but stop by anytime to pick up a comprehensive list of hotels in Hungary, or collect brochures, entertaiment programmes, train schedules and all sorts of other information. *Website: www.hungary.com/tourinform/*

Deluxe

Buda

Budapest Hilton Hotel

I. Hess András tér 1-3 (488 6600/fax 488 6644/ hiltonhu@hungary.net). M2 Moszkva tér, then Várbusz/bus 16. **Rates** *single* DM270-DM530; *double* DM300-DM580; *suite* DM900; *extra bed* DM85.
Credit AmEx, DC, EC, JCB, MC, TC, V. **Map A3**
Spectacular views over the Danube are the trade-off for a location away from central Pest (rooms without views make up for the lack with extra spaciousness). Right in the heart of the Castle District, it's designed around a seventeenth-century façade (once part of a Jesuit cloister) and the remains of a thirteenth-century Gothic church, with a small, open-air concert hall between the two wings, used for summer opera performances. Service lives up to its reputation and can count among the best in town. Reserve several weeks in advance.
Hotel services *Air-conditioning. Babysitting. Bars (2). Beauty salon. Business centre. Car park (DM32). Casino. Coffee shop. Conference facilities (17 rooms). Currency exchange. Disabled: access (plus three specially equipped rooms). Fax. Laundry. Lift. Non-smoking rooms (68). Restaurants (2). Safe. Fitness & sauna centre. Solarium. Swimming pool.*
Room services *Hairdryer. Internet. Minibar. Radio. Room service (24-hour). Safe. Telephone. TV.*

Corinthia Hotel Aquincum

III. Árpád fejedelem útja 94 (436 4100/fax 436 4156/cor.hot@aqu.hu). HÉV Árpád híd/bus 26. **Rates** *single* DM298; *double* DM369; *suite* DM480.
Credit AmEx, DC, EC, JCB, MC, V.
A pleasant hotel that ranks near the five-star downtown hotels in overall services, the Aquincum just misses the mark because of both décor (cheesy and brash) and service (obsequious and smug). Though a bit of a haul from the centre, it is still good value and the extensive spa facilities make up for a few more minutes in a taxi. You can also hire a bike and pedal into the city. *See chapters* **Baths** *and* **Sport & Fitness.**
Hotel services *Air-conditioning. Babysitting. Bars (3). Beauty salon. Bicycle rental. Car park (DM18). Conference facilities. Currency exchange. Disabled: access. Fax. Laundry. Lift. Non-smoking rooms (80). Restaurants (2). Safe. Sauna. Solarium. Swimming pool.*
Room services *Hairdryer. Minibar. Radio. Room service (24-hour). Telephone. TV.*

*Backpacking with delusions of grandeur – **Caterina Hostel**, see page 123.*

Pest

Danubius Thermal Hotel Helia

*XIII. Kárpát utca 62-64 (452 5800/fax 452
5801/hhelia@mail.matav.hu). Trolleybus 79 Dráva
utca.* **Rates** *single* DM200-DM280; *double* DM240-
DM340; *suite* DM470-DM660. **Credit** AmEx, DC, EC,
JCB, MC, V.
Budapest's most modern spa hotel is decked out in
warm, pleasant colours, with pine furniture and
open spaces, and its spa facilities are the cleanest in
town (*see chapters* **Baths** *and* **Sport & Fitness**).
Along with a fitness centre, there's also a medical
clinic catering to English-speaking clients. Rooms
are comfortable and light and all suites have their
own sauna. Good breakfast and lunch buffet. Five
rooms with exceptional facilities for wheelchairs.
Hotel services *Air-conditioning. Babysitting. Bar.
Beauty salon. Business centre. Car park. Conference
facilities. Currency exchange (24-hour). Non-smoking
rooms (20). Disabled: access (5 rooms). Gym.
Laundry. Lift. Massage. Medical clinic. Restaurants
(2). Safe. Sauna. Solarium. Swimming pool.*
Room services *Minibar. Radio. Room service.
Telephone. TV.*

Hyatt Regency Budapest

*V. Roosevelt tér 2 (266 1234/fax 266 9101/
atriumhyatt@pannoniahotels.hu). M1 Vörösmarty
tér/tram 2.* **Rates** *single* DM300-DM440; *double*
DM250-DM490; *suite* DM590; *extra bed* DM60-DM86.
Credit AmEx, DC, EC, JCB, MC, V. **Map C4**
Formerly the Atrium and still featuring one as its centrepiece, the Hyatt is decorated in faintly cheesy 1970s
American style (fountains, potted palms, terrace bar
with cane furniture). Otherwise, service is polite and
the Balloon Bar remains an excellent spot with an
unequalled view of the river, Chain Bridge and Castle
Hill. Frequently used by business travellers. For those
wanting to entertain on a grand scale, the Hyatt will
cater the nearby **Museum of Ethnography** and
provide catering. *See chapter* **Museums**.
Hotel services *Air-conditioning. Bar. Beauty salon.
Business centre. Café. Car park (Ft3,000). Casino.
Conference facilities (10). Currency exchange. Fitness
centre. Laundry. Lift. Massage. Non-smoking rooms
(110). Disabled access (2 rooms). Restaurants (2).
Safe. Sauna. Solarium. Swimming pool.*
Room services *Hairdryer. Minibar. Radio. Room
service (24-hour). Safe. Telephone. TV.*

Hotel Inter-Continental Budapest

*V. Apáczai Csere János utca 12-14 (327 6333/fax
327 6357/budapest@interconti.com). M1
Vörösmarty tér/tram 2.* **Rates** *single* or *double*
DM380-DM510; *triple* DM700; *suite* DM850; *breakfast*
DM31. **Credit** AmEx, DC, EC, JCB, MC, V. **Map C4**
Formerly the Forum but taken over by Inter-
Continental in 1997. Renovations have brightened
up the lobby and seven of the nine floors, with the
rest to be finished in 2001. Rooms have a newish feel
and are nothing special, but each has a Danube view.
The staff are also trying to live up to the new
changes, with professional and courteous service.
The lobby hums with business deals in the making.

Top tips

Best place to pretend to have conquered
Europe over a cappuccino and scones
Hotel Astoria

Best Communist-era light fittings
Hotel Agro

Best place to imagine you're a rock star or
plot your next leveraged buy-out
Grand Hotel Korvinus Kempinski

Cheapest rooms with a view
Budai Sport Centrum

The hostel that most wants to be a hotel
Hotel Ernitus

Finest breakfast terrace
Molnár Panzió

Best deal on well-located, nondescript rooms
in the city centre
City Panzió Mátyás

Best place to pacify your gout in an old-
fashioned spa atmosphere
Hotel Gellért

Most genteel atmosphere for the seasoned
traveller
Ábel Panzió

Grandest reception for backpackers
Caterina Hostel

Finest paddling facilities
Alfa Hotel

Strangest collection of services
Hotel Benczúr

Only five-star hotel with riverside view
whose view isn't spoilt by the Budapest
Hilton
Budapest Hilton Hotel

Hotel services *Air-conditioning. Babysitting. Bar.
Beauty salon. Business centre. Car parking (DM27).
Casino. Coffee and cake shop. Conference facilities.
Currency exchange. Disabled: access. Fax machine.
Laundry facilities. Lift. Massage. Non-smoking rooms
(50). Restaurants (2). Sauna. Solarium. Swimming
pool.*
Room services *Hairdryer. Minibar. Radio. Room
service. Safe. Telephone. TV.*

Grand Hotel Korvinus Kempinski

V. Erzsébet tér 7-8 (429 3777/fax 429 4777/
hotel@kempinski.hu). M1, M2, M3 Deák tér/tram
47, 49. **Rates** *single DM480-DM520; double DM560-*
DM600; *suite DM800-DM4,000; extra bed DM80;*
breakfast DM33. **Credit** AmEx, DC, EC, JCB, MC, V.
Map C4

Built in 1992, the Kempinski offers true luxury in
both service and facilities right in the centre of
downtown Budapest. Designed specifically for the
hotel, the art deco furnishings in the rooms are worthy of particular note as well as the big bathrooms
and extras such as down duvets and slippers.
Suites are bigger than most Budapest apartments
and there are extensive fitness and leisure facilities. Staff are courteous and attentive without being
overbearing, though the Kempinski Grill isn't spectacular. Where Madonna or Michael Jackson stay
when in town.

Hotel services *Air-conditioning. Airport shuttle.*
Babysitting. Bars (3). Beauty salon. Business centre.
Car park (Ft3,500). Coffee shop. Conference
facilities. Currency exchange. Disabled: access. Fitness
centre. Laundry. Lift. Non-smoking rooms (120).
Restaurants (2). Sauna. Solarium. Swimming pool.
Room services *Hairdryer. Minibar. Radio. Room*
service. Safe. Telephone. TV.

Budapest Marriott Hotel

Apáczai Csere János utca 4 (266 7000/fax 266
5000/marriott.budapest@pronet.hu). M1
Vörösmarty tér/tram 2. **Rates** *single DM300-DM400;*
double DM400-DM500; suite DM700-DM2,450
breakfast DM30. **Credit** AmEx, DC, EC, JCB, MC, V.
Map C4

A favourite with the local business community for
hosting conferences, the Marriott has a reputation
for looking after its guests, and every room has a
Danube view. Rooms are well furnished and the
hotel offers extras such as theme brunches and a
fitness room looking over the river. The business
lounge on the top floor has one of the best views in
the city, though it's restricted to guests in the
'Concierge'-level rooms. The lobby also has a pleasing view of the Castle and a nice selection of pastries. Madonna may have stayed at the Kempinski
while filming *Evita*, but all of her staff stayed at the
Marriott.

Hotel services *Air-conditioning. Babysitting. Bar.*
Business centre. Car park. Coffee shop. Conference
facilities. Currency exchange. Disabled: access.
Laundry. Lift. Non-smoking rooms (180).
Restaurants (3). Sauna. Solarium. Swimming pool.
Room services *Hairdryer. Minibar. Radio. Safe.*
service. Safe. Telephone. TV.

Marriott Executive Apartments

V. Pesti Barnabás utca 4 (235 1800/fax 235 1900).
M3 Ferenciek tere/tram 2/bus 7. **Rates** *(for 1-3*
months) DM184-DM235; one-bedroom DM150-
DM250; *two-bedroom DM268-DM350.* **Credit** AmEx,
DC, EC, JCB, MC, V. **Map C4**

The concept is five-star luxury services for travellers
spending more than a few weeks in Budapest. The
historic Vasudvar was redesigned to become the

Corinthia Hotel Aquincum – *page 109.*

first short-term residential apartment/hotel service
in the city, with a high-end shopping centre. The
hotel is clean and bright, matched with comfortable,
friendly yet top-quality facilities. There is a house-
keeping and shopping service and guests have
access to all facilities at the nearby Marriott and
receive a 20 per cent discount in the restaurant.

Hotel services *Air-conditioning. Babysitting. Bar.*
Beauty salon. Business centre. Car park. Conference
room. Fitness centre. Kitchen with dishwasher.
Offices to rent. Shopping centre. TV/VCR.
Website: www.executiveresidences.com

Radisson SAS Béke Hotel

VI. Teréz körút 43 (301 1600/fax 301 1615/
sales@budzh.rdsas.com). M3 Nyugati/tram 4, 6.
Rates *single or double DM195-DM310; suite DM600;*
extra bed DM60; breakfast DM25. **Credit** AmEx, DC,
EC, JCB, MC, V. **Map D2**

Cordial service, from well-turned-out doormen to
helpful desk staff, and an excellent location near
Nyugati station on the glitziest stretch of the körút.
The city lights and the casino inside create a swank
city high-life feel. The rooms are comfortable with
handsome, tasteful furnishings. The full buffet
breakfast in the skylit Shakespeare room is pleasant and brunch is recommended in the pink
Zsolnay Coffee Shop, with a bust of the famous
ceramicist. This isn't considered a five-star hotel
by the tourist office, but it is by this book.

Hotel services *Air-conditioning. Babysitting. Bars (2). Business centre. Car park (DM25). Casino. Coffee shop. Conference facilities. Currency exchange. Disabled: access. Pharmacy. Fax machine. Laundry facilities. Lift. Massage. Non-smoking rooms (38). Restaurant. Safe. Sauna. Solarium. Swimming pool. Travel agency.*
Room services *Hairdryer. Minibar. Radio. Room service. Safe. Telephone. TV.*

Expensive

Danubius Grand Hotel

XIII. Margitsziget (329 2300/fax 329 3923/ margotel@hungary.net). Bus 26. **Rates** *single* DM170-DM270; *double* DM220-DM320; *suite* DM370-DM420; *apartment* DM520, *extra bed* DM50. **Credit** AmEx, DC, JCB, MC, V.

Recently bought up by Danubius, this establishment shares spa facilities with its sister hotel the **Thermal Hotel Margitsziget** (*see below*). They are connected by an underground tunnel. The Grand has a slightly more pleasant atmosphere and bigger, cleaner rooms. Though not air-conditioned, most rooms do have a balcony and all contain period furnishings which reflect the Grand's proud century-old history. The charming lobby and outside terraces serving the restaurant, ice-cream shop and pizzeria also help generate a certain turn-of-the-century feel.

Hotel services *Babysitting. Bars (2). Beauty salon. Business centre. Car park (free outside). Coffee shop. Conference facilities. Currency exchange. Disabled: access. Fax. Fitness centre. Laundry. Lift. Non-smoking rooms (20). Restaurant. Safe. Sauna. Solarium. Swimming pool.*
Room services *Hairdryer. Minibar. Radio. Room service. Telephone. TV.*

Thermal Hotel Margitsziget

XIII. Margitsziget (329 2300/fax 329 3923/ margotel@hungary.net). Bus 26. **Rates** *single* DM170-DM270; *double* DM220-DM320; *suite* DM370-DM420; *extra bed* DM50. **Credit** AmEx, DC, MC, V.

This place is absolutely bustling in the summer months so book well in advance. Nevertheless the rooms are rather small with outdated furnishings reflecting the somewhat 1970s feel of the entire hotel (unfortunately service included). Air-conditioning is also often not up to the mark and in summer open windows invite copious mosquito bites. To make up for it, the hotel's spa facilities are extensive. The recent merge with the Grand Hotel promises renovations hopefully bringing this hotel up to par with its counterpart. *See chapters* **Baths** *and* **Sport & Fitness**.

Hotel services *Air-conditioning. Babysitting. Bars (2). Beauty salon. Business centre. Car park (DM20; free outside). Conference facilities. Currency exchange. Disabled: access. Hairdryers. Laundry. Lift. Non-smoking rooms (45). Restaurant. Safe. Sauna. Solarium. Swimming pool.*
Room services *Minibar. Radio. Room service. Telephone. TV.*

Buda

Hotel Flamenco Budapest

XI. Tas vezér utca 7 (372 2000/fax 365 8007/ budfla@hungary.net). Tram 61 Tas vezér utca. **Rates** *single* DM170-DM220; *double* DM210-DM270; *suite* DM350; *extra bed* DM50-DM60. **Credit** AmEx, DC, EC, JCB, MC, V. **Map B6**

The Flamenco's monstrous Communist-era concrete and glass exterior makes its tasteful and elegant interior that much more surprising. The staff are perfectly friendly and professional with it – another pleasant surprise. The atrium coffee shop is especially nice, as is the terrace restaurant with its view of the neighbouring park and supposedly bottomless lake. Conference facilities have been added but renovations to the downstairs area and the basement swimming pool were not finished at the time of going to press and no one seemed to know when they would be. Enormous suites and a handy location not too far from the central business district.

Hotel services *Air-conditioning. Babysitting. Beauty salon. Business centre. Car park (DM15 underground, DM5 on the roof). Casino. Coffee shop. Conference facilities. Currency exchange. Disabled: access. Fax. Laundry. Lift. Nightclub. Non-smoking rooms (68). Restaurants (2). Safe. Sauna. Solarium. Swimming pool. Wine cellar.*

Hotel Gellért

XI. Szent Gellért tér 1 (385 2200/fax 466 6631/ resoff@gellert.hu). Tram 18, 19, 47, 49/bus 7. **Rates** *single* DM105-DM220; *double* DM280-DM410; *suite* DM480-DM560; *extra bed* DM100. **Credit** AmEx, DC, EC, JCB, MC, V. **Map C5**

Once Budapest's most spectacular spa hotel, and still its most famous, the art nouveau Gellért (built 1912-18) earned its reputation in the period between the wars – Budapest's 'silver age', when a stay at the Gellért was all part of the Grand Tour. Restaurateur Károly Gundel, who also then ran the Városliget restaurant that still bears his name, entertained visiting dignitaries with Hungarian delicacies. In 1927, when Gundel took over the restaurant here, a swimming pool with artificial waves and garden terraces were created out back. Built on the site of an old Turkish bath house, the spa facilities also date from the interwar period and radiate period charm (*see chapters* **Baths** *and* **Sport & Fitness**). The lobby, which looks out onto the Danube, was finally rebuilt at the beginning of the 1960s after suffering serious damage in the war. Danubius began major renovations in the autumn of 1997 and many of the rooms as well as the outdoor swimming facilities have been redone. The rooms are fresh and clean but each has its own atmosphere, while still holding to the original style of the building.

Hotel services *Air-conditioning (32). Babysitting. Bar. Beauty salon. Business centre. Car park. Casino. Coffee shop. Conference facilities. Currency exchange. Laundry. Lift. Massage. Non-smoking rooms (24). Restaurant. Safe. Sauna. Solarium. Swimming pool.*
Room services *Hairdryer. Minibar. Radio. Room service. Telephone. TV (most rooms).*

Novotel Budapest Centrum

XII. Alkotás utca 63-67 (209 1990/fax 466 5636/
novotel.reservation@pannoniahotels.hu). Tram 61
from M2 Moszkva tér. **Rates** *single & double*
DM180-DM200; *suite* DM220; *extra bed* DM33-DM43;
breakfast DM20. **Credit** AmEx, DC, EC, JCB, MC, V.
Map A5
The Budapest Conference Centre next door and a convenient location for motorists are the only outstanding features. Catering mostly to business people, it has
average rooms that go with the 1982 tower construction. Facilities in the complex include bars and restaurants and a ten-pin bowling alley. Just as well, really,
as there's little else going on in this drab part of town.
Hotel services *Air-conditioning. Babysitting. Bars*
(2). Beauty Salon. Business centre. Car park.
Conference facilities. Currency exchange. Hairdryers.
Laundry. Lift. Massage. Non-smoking rooms (68).
Restaurant.
Room services *Minibar. Radio. Room service. Safe.*
Telephone. TV.

Pest

Hotel Astoria

V. Kossuth Lajos utca 19-21 (317 3411/fax 318
6798/astoria@hungary.net). M2 Astoria/tram 47,
49/bus 7. **Rates** *single* DM140-DM180; *double*
DM180-DM250; *suite* DM280-DM320. **Credit** AmEx,
DC, EC, JCB, MC, V. **Map D4**
Built between 1912 and 1914 and lending its name to
the busy intersection on which it stands, the Astoria

Hotel Mercure Korona. *See page 116.*

is reasonable, central and reeks of old *Mitteleuropa.*
The first Hungarian government was formed here in
1918. The Astoria went on to become the favourite
hangout of Nazi officials during World War II (the
hotel is located near the Jewish Ghetto), and the headquarters for Soviet forces during the 1956 revolution.
The elegant chandeliered art nouveau coffee lounge
on the ground floor recalls the atmosphere of pre-war
Budapest (*see chapter* **Cafés & Coffeehouses**).
Managed by the state-owned HungarHotel chain, it
does not offer superb service but is still the only place
that advertises a room for people with allergies. The
spacious rooms at the front are noisy, the smaller
rooms at the back more peaceful. The baroque dining room is one of the most spectacular places to
breakfast in Budapest.
Hotel services *Café. Car park. Casino. Conference*
facilities. Currency exchange. Disabled: access. Fax.
Hypo-allergenic room (1). Laundry. Lift. Non-
smoking room. Restaurant. Safe.
Room services *Hairdryers. Minibar. Telephone.*
TV.

Hotel Erzsébet

V. Károlyi Mihály utca 11-15 (328 5700/fax 328
5763/buderz@euroweb.hu). M3 Ferenciek tere/tram
2/bus 7. **Rates** *single* DM135-DM210; *double* DM150-
DM250; *triple* DM280-DM340. **Credit** AmEx, DC,
JCB, MC, V. **Map C4**
A dark wood and beige interior betrays Communist-
era origins, but the staff are friendly enough and the
rooms are air-conditioned. The restaurant/bar downstairs is rather naff, with a rustic illustration of
Hungarian folk-tale hero János Vitéz, and the
upstairs restaurant has the look and feel of a cafeteria. But conference facilities and good discounts
for groups ensure its popularity with business travellers who are looking for a downtown location without downtown prices.
Hotel services *Air-conditioning. Bar. Car park.*
Casino. Conference facilities. Currency exchange. Fax.
Gift shop. Hairdryers. Laundry. Lift. Non-smoking
rooms (16). Pharmacy. Restaurant. Safe.
Room services *Minibar. Radio. Telephone. TV.*

K+K Hotel Opera

VI. Révay utca 24 (269 0222/fax 269 0230/
kk.hotel.opera@kk.hotel.hu). M1 Opera. **Rates** *single*
DM200-DM240; *double* DM260-DM280; *suite* DM410-
DM550; *extra bed* DM62-DM85. **Credit** AmEx, DC,
EC, MC, V. **Map C3**
The ultra-modern interior radiates Austrian efficiency and the quiet location around the corner from
the Opera House can't be beat. Ninety rooms have
recently been added, almost doubling the size of the
hotel, and further changes continue. Service remains
attentive and friendly and there's a big buffet breakfast. No restaurant, but there are plenty of eateries
in the vicinity.
Hotel services *Air-conditioning. Babysitting. Bar.*
Car park (DM13). Conference facilities. Currency
exchange. Fax. Laundry. Lift. Snack bar.
Room services *Hairdryer. Minibar. Radio. Room*
service. Safe. Telephone. TV.

Hotel Mercure Korona

V. Kecskeméti utca 14 (317 4111/fax 318 3867/mercurekorona@pannoniahotels.hu). M3 Kálvin tér/tram 47, 49. **Rates** *single* DM200-DM230; *double* DM220-DM270; *suite* DM395; *extra bed* DM40. **Credit** AmEx, DC, JCB, MC, V. **Map D5**
Built in 1990 and dominating one side of Kálvin tér. Black columns and green marble make the reception feel like a fish tank. Service curt but rooms nice, fitness facilities extensive, breakfast buffet ample. Café in the glass bridge connecting the two buildings.
Hotel services *Air-conditioning. Babysitting. Bar. Beauty salon. Business centre. Car park (DM22). Coffee shop. Conference facilities. Currency exchange. Disabled: access. Fax. Laundry. Lift. Massage. Restaurants (2). Safe. Sauna. Solarium. Swimming pool.*
Room services *Minibar. Radio. Room service. Safe. Telephone. TV.*

Hotel Taverna

V. Váci utca 20 (338 4999/fax 485 3111/ hotel@hoteltaverna.hu). M3 Ferenciek tere/tram 2/bus 7. **Rates** *single* DM210-DM215; *double* DM275-DM285; *suite* DM590. **Credit** AmEx, DC, EC, JCB, MC, V. **Map C4**
Standard business hotel in the middle of Váci's pedestrianised zone. Some rooms are rather cramped, but it's well located and the management will give significant discounts for longer stays.
Hotel services *Air-conditioning (98 rooms). Babysitting. Bar. Beauty salon. Café. Car park (DM22). Conference facilities. Currency exchange. Fax. Gift shop. Laundry. Lift. Non-smoking rooms (45). Restaurant. Sauna.*
Room services *Hairdryer. Minibar. Radio. Room service. Safe. Telephone. TV.*

Moderate

Buda

Alba Hotel Budapest

I. Apor Péter utca 3 (375 9244/fax 375 9899). Bus 16 Clark Ádám tér. **Rates** *single* DM170; *double* DM200. **Credit** AmEx, DC, JCB, MC, V. **Map B3**
At the foot of Castle Hill, with an excellent view of the Vizíváros from the top floors. Rooms are spartan but spacious with large, well-lit bathrooms, and the three-bedded room is almost big enough to be a suite. The lobby is rather stark, but there's a large breakfast buffet and a Greek restaurant next door.
Hotel services *Air-conditioning. Babysitting. Bar. Car park (DM22). Non-smoking rooms (10). Conference facilities. Currency exchange. Fax. Laundry. Lift. Safe.*
Room services *Hairdryer. Minibar. Room service. Telephone. TV.*
Website: www.justweb.com

Petneházy Country Club Hotel

II. Feketefej utca 2-4 (376 5992/376 5738/ petnehaz@mail.matav.hu). Bus 56 (red) Adyliget. **Rates** *small bungalow (2-4 people)* DM220; *large bungalow (4-6 people)* DM280; *extra bed* DM30. **Credit** AmEx, DC, EC, JCB, MC, V.
Doubling as a country club, this hotel is actually 45 private bungalows – four with disabled access – with a central building housing the reception, pool and restaurant. Remote location but a peaceful setting and loads of sports and leisure facilities – horseback riding next door, organised bus and boat excursions. Plans are underway for 45 additional bungalows, a sauna cabin and a covered outdoor theatre.
Hotel services *Babysitting. Bar. Bicycles. Car park. Conference facilities. Currency exchange. Disabled: access. Fax. Laundry. Restaurant. Safe. Sauna. Solarium. Swimming pool.*
Room services *Kitchen. Minibar. Radio. Room service. Safe. Sauna. Telephone. TV.*

Hotel Victoria

I. Bem rakpart 11 (457 8080/fax 457 8088/ victoria@victoria.hu). Bus 16 Clark Ádám tér. **Rates** *single* DM144-DM189; *double* DM154-DM199; *extra bed* DM60-DM80. **Credit** AmEx, DC, EC, JCB, MC, TC, V. **Map B3**
One of Budapest's first private panziók occupies a townhouse below the castle, facing the Danube and within easy reach of the main sights. Rooms are comfortable, commanding a view of the river, and their garden rooms offer nice patios at no extra charge. Excellent value, especially for Buda. American breakfast but no restaurant.
Hotel services *Air-conditioning. Babysitting. Bar. Car park (security). Casino. Coffee shop. Conference facilities. Currency exchange. Fax. Internet. Laundry. Lift. Sauna.*
Room services *Hairdryer. Minibar. Radio. Room service. Safe. Telephone. TV.*

Pest

Hotel Art

V. Királyi Pál utca 12 (266 2166/fax 266 2170/ hotelart@mail.matav.hu). M3 Kálvin tér/tram 47, 49. **Rates** *single* DM150-DM170; *double* DM180-DM200; *triple* DM245-DM285; *suite* DM285; *extra bed* DM60. **Credit** AmEx, DC, EC, JCB, MC, V. **Map D5**
Near the quiet end of Váci utca, this hotel is conveniently central and there are several good bars in the neighbourhood. The attempt at art deco style fittings – marble detailing, frosted lampshades – leave something to be desired, but it's friendly, comfortable and the rooms are at a good price. American breakfast.
Hotel services *Air-conditioning. Bar. Car park (Ft2,800). Currency exchange. Disabled: access. Fax. Fitness centre. Hairdryer. Laundry. Lift. Safe. Sauna.*
Room services *Minibar. Room service. Telephone. TV.*

Hotel Central

VI. Munkácsy Mihály utca 5-7 (321 2000/fax 322 9445). M1 Bajza utca. **Rates** *single* DM150; *double* DM157; *suite* DM284-DM300. **Credit** AmEx, EC, JCB, MC, V. **Map E2**
Once owned by the Communist Party, in its current incarnation the Central is a pleasant place in its own sort of way. Dark furnishings complement the 1930s building and the quiet setting of the embassy district,

Clean and spacious but starkly modern – **Hotel Liget**. *See page 118.*

resulting in an intriguing time-warp feel. Staff and services are acceptable but dine elsewhere.
Hotel services *Bar. Car park. Currency exchange. Fax. Laundry. Lift. Restaurant. Safe.*
Room services *Hairdryer. Minibar. Radio. Telephone. TV.*

City Panzió Mátyás

V. Március 15 tér (338 4711/fax 317 9086/ matyas@taverna.hu). M3 Ferenciek tere/tram 2/bus 7. **Rates** *single* DM54-DM125; *double* DM74-DM160; *triple* DM199; *apartment* DM129-DM230; *extra bed* DM17-DM39. **Credit** AmEx, DC, EC, JCB, MC, V. **Map C4**
Excellent value in a great location near the river. Friendly staff and well-appointed rooms with no frills, and Pest's attractions are just steps away.
Hotel services *Car park (nearby). Currency exchange. Laundry. Safe.*

City Panzió Pilvax

V. Pilvax köz 1-3. (266 7648/fax 317 6396/ 100324.235@compuserve.com). M3 Ferenciek tere. **Rates** *single* DM80-DM125; *double* DM100-DM160; *extra bed* DM39. **Credit** AmEx, EC, MC, V. **Map C4**
The breakfast room and outside terrace were one of the haunts of Hungarian heroes Sándor Petőfi and Mór Jókai, and in later days, dissidents of the Communist era. It's still a lovely place to sit and watch the world go by. Inside you'll find a modern hotel right in the heart of the city. Efficient and friendly service. Long-term guests should negotiate a discount.
Hotel services *Bar. Conference facilities. Currency exchange. Fax. Laundry. Restaurant. Safe.*
Room services *Minibar. Radio. Telephone. TV.*

City Panzió Ring

XIII. Szent István körút 22 (340 5450/fax 340 4884/ring@taverna.hu). M3 Nyugati/tram 4, 6. **Rates** *single* DM80-DM125; *double* DM120-DM160; *extra bed* DM17-DM36. **Credit** AmEx, DC, EC, MC, V. **Map C2**
Young downtown hotel. Rooms are decorated in blue and cream with light pine accents. The breakfast room is bright and airy, and the hotel is good value, with generous discounts for long-term stays. Services are minimal (don't ask to use the lift unless you physically can't get up the stairs), but there are lots of shops and restaurants nearby and good public transport links.
Hotel services *Car park (Ft2,000). Currency exchange. Laundry. Non-smoking rooms (8). Safe.*
Room services *Minibar. Radio. Telephone. TV.*

Grand Hotel Hungaria

VII. Rákóczi út 90 (322 9050/fax 352 1858/
grandhun@hungary.net). M2 Keleti/bus 7. **Rates**
single DM150-DM220; *double* DM180-DM270; *triple*
DM320-DM370; *extra bed* DM100. **Credit** AmEx,
DC, EC, JCB, MC, V. **Map E4**
A jovial atmosphere pervades a lobby buzzing with
coachloads of tour groups. Budapest's largest hotel
has extensive, though not exceptional, restaurant
and conference facilities. Rooms are generally comfortable and tidy and a dozen of them have been
knocked out to make them all much the same generous size. If you need to stretch your legs, take a
stroll on the rooftop. Conveniently located across
from Keleti station.
Hotel services *Air-conditioning. Bars (2). Beauty
salon. Business centre. Car park (DM25). Conference
facilities. Currency exchange. Fax. Fitness centre.
Laundry. Lift. Restaurants (2). Safe. Sauna. Solarium.*
Room services *Minibar. Radio. Room service.
Telephone. TV.*

Hotel Liget

*VI. Dózsa György út 106 (269 5300/fax 269
5329/hotel@liget.hu). M1 Hősök tere.* **Rates** *single*
DM145-DM180; *double* DM190-DM230; *extra bed*
DM50. **Credit** AmEx, DC, JCB, MC, V. **Map E1**
Pleasantly situated next to the Városliget but with
a rather stark modern feel, this place targets people
on the move. Common areas are minimal and the

entrance and outside terrace are dominated by the
ramp to the car park. However, the 139 rooms are
clean and spacious and the first five floors are air-
conditioned.
Hotel services *Air-conditioning. Bar. Business
centre. Car park (DM15). Coffee shop. Conference
facilities. Currency exchange. Fax. Lift. Massage.
Non-smoking rooms (24). Safe. Sauna. Solarium.*
Room services *Minibar. Radio. Room service. Safe.
Telephone. TV.*

Pannonia Hotel Nemzeti

*VIII. József körút 4 (477 2000/fax 477 2001/
nemzeti@pannoniahotels.hu). M2 Blaha Lujza/tram
4, 6/bus 7, 7A, 78.* **Rates** *single* DM100-DM160;
double DM110-DM200; *extra bed* DM50. **Credit**
AmEx, DC, EC, JCB, MC, V. **Map E1**
Watching Budapest walk by from the red velvet
chairs in the time-worn lobby that looks out over
bustling Blaha Lujza tér is one of the finest ways to
see the city. This plus the grand stairway and dining room and friendly staff are the 100-year-old
Nemzeti's best features. Renovations continue, all
street-facing windows are sound-proofed, and the
newest rooms are the best ones. Near the city's red-
light district, so be wary walking back late at night.
Hotel services *Air-conditioning. Bar. Currency
exchange. Fax. Hairdryers. Laundry. Non-smoking
rooms (5). Restaurant. Safe.*
Room services *Minibar. Radio. Telephone. TV.*

The ivy-covered **Ábel Panzió** *– Buda's most beautiful budget option. See page 119.*

Budget

Buda

Ábel Panzió

XI. Ábel Jenő utca 9 (tel/fax 209 2537). Tram 61.
Rates *single DM80-DM90; double DM90-DM100.*
No credit cards. Map A6
The most beautiful panzió in Budapest. An ivy-covered turn-of-the-century house on a quiet side-street and fitted with period furniture in common areas. The area is quiet and safe, a couple of tram stops from Móricz Zsigmond körtér. Though some are smaller than others, the ten rooms are sunny and clean with simple modern furniture. Breakfast around a common dining table overlooking a terrace and well-kept garden recalls a mode of travelling long since past. Book well in advance.
Hotel services *Bar. Car park. Casino. Coffee shop. Conference facilities. Fax. Hairdryer. TV.*
Room services *Safe. Telephone.*

Hotel Agro

XII. Normafa út 54 (375 4011/fax 375 6164/ h.agro.budapest@mail.matav.hu). Bus 21 Normafa.
Rates *single DM75-DM115; double DM90-DM145; suite DM110-DM175; extra bed DM20.* **Credit** AmEx, DC, EC, MC, V.
High in the Buda hills, the former guesthouse for Hungary's agricultural élites has gone public but still radiates its best Socialist-era charm. Rooms aren't exceptional, but the views from the rooms and the fifth-floor restaurant are great. A drink or two in the boozer (and a quick round on the bowling alley) offer a taste of Hungary's not-so-distant past.
Hotel services *Bars (2). Car park. Coffee shop. Conference facilities. Currency exchange. Fax. Laundry. Lift. Restaurant. Sauna. Swimming pool. Tennis courts.*
Room services *Hairdryer. Minibar. Radio. Safe. Telephone. TV.*

Alfa Hotel

III. Kossuth Lajos Üdülőpart 102 (260 2971/fax 260 7824). HÉV Árpád hid/bus 34. **Rates** *single DM55; double DM70; triple DM90; 2-person dormitories DM30.* **Credit** AmEx, DC, EC, JCB, MC, V.
Beautiful view over the river and perfect for some serious water-sporting. Rent a canoe for the day and paddle right back up to your hotel door that night. The rooms are nice and spacious, if nothing too special. The second-floor restaurant doesn't offer much.
Hotel services *Bar. Canoes. Car park. Conference facilities. Fax. Laundry. Lift. Restaurant. Safe. Tennis courts.*
Room services *Minibar. Radio. Telephone. TV.*

Beatrix Panzió

II Széher út 3 (275 0550/fax 394 3730/ beatrix@pronet.hu). Tram 59 Farkasréti tér. **Rates** *single DM70-DM90; double DM80-DM100; triple DM90-DM120; apartment DM150.* **No credit cards.**
Seventeen small but comfortable rooms on a quiet residential street offer a peaceful getaway. Moszkva tér isn't too far away, and the hotel offers special tours

into the Hungarian countryside. Summer barbecues in the pretty garden at the rear. American breakfast.
Hotel services *Bar. Car park. Currency exchange. Disabled: access. Fax. Safe. Sauna.*
Room services *Telephone. TV.*

Buda Centre Hotel

II. Csalogány utca 23 (201 6333/fax 201 7843). Bus 39 Fazekas utca. **Rates** *single DM65-DM100; double DM80-DM120; triple DM100-DM140; extra bed DM20.*
Credit AmEx, EC, MC, V. **Map A2**
Conference facilities are in the office space that takes up half of the building. Services are minimal and rooms are small but clean with new furniture. Pay a little extra and get air-conditioning. The downstairs bar has an impressive selection of beers and there's a sleepy Chinese restaurant in the foyer.
Hotel services *Air-conditioning. Babysitting. Bar. Car park (DM15). Conference facilities. Currency exchange. Fax. Hairdryers. Laundry. Lift. Non-smoking rooms (4). Restaurant. Safe.*
Room services *Minibar. Telephone. TV.*

Budai Sport Centrum

XII. Jánoshegyi út (275 4029/fax 395 6491). Bus 21 (red) Jánoshegy. **Rates** *single DM60; double DM80; apartment DM100; extra bed no charge.* **Credit** MC, EC, V.
High above the city on János Hill, this is about 20 minutes from Moszkva tér by bus and has Budapest's most inexpensive rooms with a view. Friendly staff and lots of sport and relaxation possibilities in the acres and acres of parkland nearby.
Hotel services *Bar. Car park. Fax. Laundry. Lift. Massage. Restaurant. Safe. Sauna. Solarium. Swimming pool. Tennis courts.*
Room services *Hairdryer. Minibar. Radio. Room service. Safe. Telephone. TV.*

Charles Apartment House

I. Hegyalja út 23 (201 1796/fax 202 2984/ charles@mail.matav.hu). Bus 8, 112 Mészáros utca. **Rates** *single DM80-DM89; double DM96-DM104; triple DM120-DM129; extra bed DM19.* **Credit** EC, MC, V. **Map B5**
Spacious studio flats in a converted apartment block are fully self-catering, though young and enthusiastic staff remain at reception 24 hours. The flats consist of kitchen, generous bathroom and very large bedroom/sitting-room, all with magnificent views over Buda – decent value for longer stays.
Hotel services *Car park (Ft11,000). Currency exchange. Disabled: access. Fax. Hairdryer. Internet. Laundry. Lift. Photocopying. Safe.*
Room services *Internet. Minibar. Telephone. TV.*

Hotel Dunapart

I. Szilágyi Dezső tér (355 9244/fax 355 3770). M2 Batthyány tér/tram 19. **Rates** *single DM100-DM140; double DM130-DM170; triple DM150-DM180; extra bed DM15.* **Credit** AmEx, DC, EC, JCB, MC, V. **Map B3**
Thirty-two tiny air-conditioned cabins offer an unusual water-level view of Parliament from this floating hotel, moored near Batthyány tér on the Alsó rakpart. The restaurant is expensive, but the fine

view toward the Chain Bridge from the terrace on the back deck can be worth it on summer evenings.
Hotel services *Air-conditioning. Bar. Car park. Currency exchange. Fax. Laundry. Restaurant. Safe.*
Room services *Radio. Room service. Telephone. TV.*

Hotel Express

XII. Beethoven utca 7-9 (tel/fax 375 3082/ hostels@elender.hu). Tram 59 Királyhágó tér. **Rates** *single* DM33; *double* DM55; *triple* DM74. **No credit cards.**
One of the few remaining cheap hostel-style hotels in Buda is frequented by people with backpacks. Rooms are clean, if a bit worn, and bathroom and showers are in the hall. Breakfast included, served in an open dining area. Quiet, secluded location not far from Moszkva tér offers both restaurant and supermarket options.
Hotel services *Car park. Conference facilities. Currency exchange. Fax. Safe. TV.*

Kulturinov Hotel

I. Szentháromság tér 6 (355 0122/fax 375 1886). M2 Moszkva tér then Várbusz/bus 16. **Rates** *single* DM100; *double* DM130; *extra bed* DM40. **Credit** AmEx, DC, JCB, MC, V. **Map A3**
Location and price are the attractions in a building that also houses the Hungarian Cultural Foundation. Upstairs and to the right from the huge vaulted

Kulturinov Hotel – *in the Castle District.*

entry, the cell-like rooms have few luxuries, but the Castle District sights are just outside the door.
Hotel services *Babysitting. Bar. Car park (DM16). Conference facilities. Currency exchange. Laundry. Fax. Gift shop. Safe. Telephone. TV.*
Room service *Telephone.*

Molnár Panzió

XII. Fodor utca 143 (395 1875/tel/fax 395 1872). Bus 53 Rácz Aladár utca. **Rates** *single* DM70-DM90; *double* DM90-DM110; *triple* DM100-DM130. **Credit** AmEx, DC, EC, MC, V.
High on a Buda hill and boasting three-star services, the Molnár has a range of older and newer rooms with unique features and tasteful décor. Some nestle under wood-panelled eaves; others have sunken bathtubs and windows looking out over Pest. There's even an A-frame cabin in the beautiful back garden. Service is meticulous and the terrace restaurant an excellent spot for summertime meals.
Hotel services *Bar. Beauty salon. Car park. Conference facilities. Currency exchange. Fax. Fitness room. Laundry. Restaurant. Safe. Sauna.*
Room services *Minibar. Telephone. TV.*

Queen Mary Hotel

XII. Béla Király út 47 (274 4000/fax 395 8377). Bus 28 Béla Király út. **Rates** *single* DM80-DM100; *double* DM95-DM130; *extra bed* DM40. **Credit** AmEx, DC, JCB, MC, V.
Popular with families bringing their children to the nearby Pető Institute, this quiet panzió in the Buda Hills gladly arranges discounts for extended stays.
Hotel services *Bar. Car park. Currency exchange. Fax. Laundry. Restaurant. Safe. Sauna. Solarium.*
Room services *Minibar. Telephone. TV.*

UhU Villa

II. Keselyű út 1/A (275 1002/fax 394 3876/ uhuvilla@elender.hu). Tram 56 Vadaskerti utca. **Rates** *single* DM100-DM170; *double* DM140-DM180; *apartment* DM160-DM2,100; *extra bed* DM20. **No credit cards.**
Ideal for those with children and a car, or who don't mind a bit of hiking, this is a lovely panzió nestled among fir trees around 15 minutes from Moszkva tér. The turn-of-the-century villa has small but cosy rooms and a quaint charm pervades the common areas. American breakfast overlooking the flower garden is the perfect prelude to a short walk down the hill to the tram and the heart of Budapest.
Hotel services *Air-conditioning (1 apt). Fax. Safe. Solarium.*
Room services *Minibar. Telephone. TV.*

Walzer Hotel

XII. Németvölgyi út 110 (319 1212/fax 319 2964) Tram 59 Liptó utca. **Rates** *single* DM130-DM153; *double* DM174-DM205; *triple* DM217-DM255; *extra bed* DM35. **Credit** AmEx, DC, EC, JCB, MC, V.
In a quiet hillside garden neighbourhood, the Walzer is a recently built mansion in which rooms with reproduction Biedermeier furniture look over **Farkasréti cemetery** (*see chapter*

Hotel Benczúr – *all this and their own in-house dentist too.*

Sightseeing) across the street. Immaculate, spacious bathrooms, pleasant common areas and a well-appointed dining room and restaurant with adjoining lawn.

Hotel services *Babysitting. Car park. Currency exchange. Fax. Laundry. Lift. Restaurant. Safe.*
Room services *Minibar. Radio. Telephone. TV.*

Pest

Hotel Benczúr

VI. Benczúr utca 35 (342 7970/fax 342 1558/ hotel@hotelbenczur.hu). M1 Hősök tere. **Rates** *single* DM109-DM145; *double* DM129-DM175; *triple* DM163-DM205. **Credit** MC, V. **Map E2**

This rather stuffy hotel offers three things: reasonable prices, a central location and adequate services. Tacky décor has survived earlier renovations, as have rather dark, cramped rooms. Although communicating with the staff on anything more than a basic level of English is like pulling teeth, an added advantage is that they have a dentist who can do that for you. Thai massage and casino too.

Hotel services *Bars (2). Car park. Casino. Conference facilities. Currency exchange. Dentist. Fax. Laundry. Lift. Massage. Restaurant. Souvenir shop.*
Room services *Minibar. Telephone. TV.*

Hotel EMKE

VII. Akácfa utca 1-3 (322 9230/fax 322 9233/ emke@pannoniahotels.hu). M2 Blaha Lujza tér/tram 4, 6/bus 7. **Rates** *single* DM130; *double* DM160; *apartment* DM210; *extra bed* DM40. **Credit** AmEx, DC, EC, MC, V. **Map E4**

Behind the exterior of an unrelieved Socialist monstrosity is the pleasing relief of an interior where rooms have been remodelled and common areas refurbished. Few services and no restaurant, but good location. Friendly staff. Group rates.

Hotel services *Currency exchange. Fax. Laundry. Lift. Non-smoking rooms (30). Safe.*
Room services *Minibar. Radio. Telephone. TV.*

Hotel Ernitus

VII. Nyár utca 6 (342 9586/fax 342 9589/ ernitus@elender.hu). M2 Blaha Lujza tér/tram 4, 6/bus 7. **Rates** *single* DM98; *double* DM120; *triple* DM148; *dormitory (6-12 beds)* DM35. **Credit** Maestro, EC, MC, V. **Map D4**

Opened in 1997 as a youth hostel, the Ernitus has changed its name and upgraded to offer what it claims are three-star services, but the place still feels somewhat like a hostel. The colourful rooms have a detergent ultra-cleanliness and there are dorms, which are a bit expensive, but have two showers en suite. A nice terrace, laundry and e-mail lifeline are the biggest pluses, along with a central location.

Hotel services *Car park (Ft900). Currency exchange. Fax. Internet. Laundry. Lift. Restaurant. Safe.*
Room services *Telephone. TV (Ft500).*

Expo Hotel

X. Albertirsai út 10 (263 7600/fax 263 7616/ hhtours1@hungary.net). M2 Pillangó utca. **Rates** *single* DM66-DM105; *double* DM88-DM125; *triple* DM156. **Credit** AmEx, DC, EC, JCB, MC, V.

If you're attending or planning one of the many conferences at the Budapest Expo grounds nearby, this hotel has 33 bedrooms, but should be booked as far

*'We all live in the **Yellow Submarine-Lotus Youth Hostel.**' See page 123.*

in advance as possible. Rooms are spacious, each with a bathtub, and there's a cosy bar area in the lobby, but it's far from the city centre and there's nothing else out here apart from the racecourse. Airport 20 minutes away by cab.

Hotel services *Car park (Ft1,000). Conference facilities. Expo grounds. Currency exchange. Laundry. Lift. Fax. Restaurant. Safe. Restaurant.*
Room services *Minibar. Radio. Telephone. TV.*

King's Hotel

VII. Nagy Diófa utca 25-27 (352 7621). M2 Blaha Lujza/tram 4, 6/bus 7. **Rates** *single $60; double $80; triple $120.* **Credit** AmEx, DC, MC, V. **Map D4**
Family-run hotel in the heart of the Jewish quarter with a variety of room-types to suit particular needs. The location and price are a good package and it has the prize attraction of a Mehadrin kosher restaurant (many of the guests are Orthodox Jews). Your visit may coincide with one of the many Hasidic weddings the hotel hosts. The main currency accepted for payment of rooms is US dollars.

Hotel services *Air-conditioning. Currency exchange. Fax. Laundry. Lift. Restaurant. Safe.*
Room services *Air-conditioning. Safe. Telephone. TV.*

Medosz Hotel

VI. Jókai tér (374 3000/fax 332 4316). M1 Oktogon/tram 4, 6. **Rates** *single* DM67; *double* DM80; *triple* DM95; *apartment* DM120. **No credit cards. Map D3**
Not the most luxurious hotel in the city centre, but one of the least expensive. Rooms are simple though a bit stuffy and spartan, and beds can be lumpy. But right next to fashionable Liszt Ferenc tér, Oktogon and steps away from the Opera House, it's an alternative that will allow you to meet with a variety of mid-budget tourists and sample lots of cafés.

Hotel services *Car park. Conference facilities. Fax. Lift. Restaurant. Safe.*
Room services *Telephone. TV.*

Omnibusz Hotel

X. Üllői út 108 (263 0794/fax 263 1163). M3 Nagyvárad tér. **Rates** *single* DM63-DM75; *double* DM79-DM100; *triple* DM95-DM120. **Credit** AmEx, DC, EC, JCB, MC, V. **Map F6**
In brick mock country-house style, with a faux medieval church and a McDonald's across the road – you really need a sense of irony to enjoy the surroundings. The interior provides a friendly environment and the petrol station down the street makes it convenient for those with cars.

Hotel services *Babysitting. Car park. Currency exchange. Fax. Laundry. Lift. Restaurant. Safe.*
Room services *Minibar. Radio. Telephone. TV.*

Richter Panzió

XIV. Thököly út 111 (363 5761/fax 363 3956). Bus 7 Amerikai út. **Rates** *single* DM90-DM100; *double* DM100-DM110; *quad* DM120-DM140; *extra bed* DM20. **No credit cards. Map F3**
On the inner edge of a Pest garden suburb, the Richter is in a pleasant neighbourhood less than ten minutes from the city centre by bus. Staff are helpful, though rooms are basic and services are minimal. The sauna helps to ensure a relaxing visit and conveniently located for the Népstadion.

Hotel services *Bar. Car park. Currency exchange. Fax. Laundry. Safe. Sauna.*
Room services *Telephone. TV.*

Youth hostels

These days e-mail is the easiest way to contact youth hostels – one day's notice is usually sufficient – but if you prefer the personal touch, Keleti station is full of energetic hostel-hustlers willing to take you back to their place. Paid on a commission basis, they represent Budapest's hostels with brochures and a multi-lingual smile. At press time, however, the government was planning to end the melée at Keleti, which many find offputting.

Keleti station also has three Travellers Youth Hostel Information desks (343 0748; open 7am-10pm daily) where you can find a place in one of their ten hostels. Rates are about Ft1,000-Ft2,000 per night for dormitories and Ft2,000-Ft5,000 for singles and doubles. An ASIC or International Youth Hostel card can usually conjure up a ten per cent discount.

Backpack Guest House

XIII. Takács Menyhért utca 33 (209 8406/fax 385 8946/backpackguest@hotmail.com). Bus 7 Tétényi út. **Rates** *dorm* Ft1,200-Ft1,500; *double* Ft1,800. **No credit cards. Map A6**
Popular for its jovial atmosphere; many former guests come back to have a drink, shoot some pool or just relax. Sign up for caving, water skiing or rock climbing or take your book to the back garden and enjoy a bit of peace. Traveller/owner Atilla is rarely home, but Alex the Irish Setter seems to run the place well enough without him.
Bar. Internet. Kitchen. Laundry. Nine rooms. Safe. TV/VCR.

Caterina Hostel

VI. Andrássy út 47 III/18 (291 9538/fax 352 6147). M1 Oktogon/tram 4, 6. **Rates** *dorm* Ft1,500-Ft2,000. **No credit cards. Map D3**
Inside a nineteenth-century apartment block on the corner of Oktogon; the columned balconies and marble pillars in the entrance grant a glimpse into this place's grand past. No one has a bad thing to say about Caterina herself, who keeps things clean and comfortable and will wash your clothes for you if you ask nicely.
Front door keys. Kitchen. Laundry. Lift. Private houses available. TV. Tours.

Citadella Hotel

XI. Citadella sétány (466-5794/fax 386 0505). Bus 27 from Móricz Zsigmond körtér. **Rates** *dorm* DM85-DM100. **Credit TC. Map D5**
View sunrise from the top of Gellért Hill overlooking the Danube. This bird's-eye location comes highly recommended by those who do not mind a hike if the reward is a spectacular vista over the city. If you do not fancy the long walk downhill, check out the **Citadella** club nearby (*see chapter* **Nightlife**).
Currency exchange. Fax. Safe.

Diák Sport-Travellers Youth Hostel

XIII. Dózsa György út 152 (340 8585/fax 320 8425/travellers@mail.matav.hu). M3 to Dózsa György út. **Rates** *dorm* Ft2,000; *single* Ft3,300; *double* Ft6,800. **Credit** AmEx, MC, V. **Map F3**
Recently renovated – you would hardly imagine you're staying in a converted dormitory anymore. The dormitories have been redone and the dining area has been turned into a fully-fledged bar complete with live music. The HQ for all other Traveller Youth Hostels; you can always count on Diák to find you a place at one of their ten locations in town.
Bar (24-hour). Internet. Kitchen. Laundry. Security. Parking. Safe. TV.

Yellow Submarine-Lotus Youth Hostel

VI. Teréz körút 56, 3rd floor (tel/fax 331 9896/yellowsubmarine@mail.interware.hu). M3 Nyugati/tram 4, 6. **Rates** *dorm* Ft1,700-Ft1,800; *single* Ft4,600; *double* Ft3,000; *room (four beds)* Ft2,000. **Credit** MC, V. **Map D2**
The eastern theme is more in attitude than in décor. Staff are friendly and laid-back, going out of their way to help guests with the difficulties that arise when travelling. They have a range of international travel books and can even give you with a good price on train tickets.
Internet. Kitchen. Laundry. Reception (24-hour). Telephone. Safe.

Camping

There are eight campsites in Budapest, some situated right by the river and four open all year round. Others are run from May to September. Prices can vary from around Ft1,000 to pitch a tent, to Ft1,500 for caravans and Ft2,000 for bungalows. Tourinform (*see above*) can provide you with a location and service map covering all the sites in Hungary. All the following listed below have hot and cold water, electrical outlets, restaurants and money-changing facilities, and all except one are pet-friendly.

Csillebérci Autóscamping

XII. Konkoly-Thege utca 21 (275 4033/fax 395 7327/csill@mail.datanet.hu). Bus 21 (red) to Normafa. **Open** year round.
Bungalows. Sports equipment available. Swimming pool. Safe. Tennis courts. Tent sites.

Metro Tenisz Camping

XVI. Csömöri út 158 (406 5584/fax 405 1050). Bus 130 Metro. **Open** May-Sept. No pets.
Bungalows. Tennis courts. Tent sites.

Mini Camping

III. Királyok útja 307 (06 30 210 178). Bus 34 Hadrianus utca. **Open** May-Sept.
Bungalows. Fishing. Petrol, auto repair and car wash at Királyok útja 178. River access. Tent sites (river).

Római Camping

III. Szentendrei út 189 (368 6260/fax 250 0426/ibusz@mail.matav.hu). HÉV to Rómaifürdő. **Open** year round.
Bungalows. Laundry. Safe. Tent sites.

Római-Parti Camping

III. Királyok útja 19-21/Kossuth Lajos Üdülőpart 1-3. (368 4008). Bus 34. **Open** May-Sept.
Connected to the other Római, this is the site with all the summer sports facilities.
Bungalows. Post office. River access. Sports equipment.

Zugligeti 'Niche' Camping

XII. Zugligeti út 101 (200 8346). Bus 158 from Moszkva tér. **Open** year round.
Bungalows. Disabled: access. Safe. Tent sites (green).

Cafés & Coffeehouses

Caffeine cravings can be satisfied all over town, while Budapesters set about reinventing the coffeehouse.

Szalai Cukrászda – *dangerously affordable confections. See page 128.*

Budapest caters well for the coffee drinker. The post-communist acceleration in the pace of daily life hasn't quite eradicated the luxury of sitting down for a quiet cappuccino and watching the world hurry by. Indeed, the fact that many Hungarians now need at least two jobs to survive has sharpened the necessity for the caffeine fix. From the humble eszpresszó or the classy cukrászda to the grand remnants of Habsburg coffeehouse culture and modern cafés in a variety of idioms, the city teems with opportunities to satisfy that caffeine craving and binge on a dangerously affordable variety of accompanying confections.

The traditional coffeehouse just about survives, catering these days mainly to tourists, but new coffeehouses have begun to open up in a postmodern updating of the phenomenon. See page 126 **Reinventing the coffeehouse**. The new places tend to be a better bet for breakfast, not a great Magyar tradition. Eszpresszós – smaller, seedier and markedly less inspiring – had grown in popularity during the 1930s Depression. These were encouraged in the coffeehouse's place and flourished in the 1960s. The city is full of them, and here and in *chapter* **Pubs & Bars** (in this town there's often an alcoholically blurred line between what consititutes a café and what makes a bar) we've listed some examples of the genre.

The cukrászda is a confectioner's or pastry shop which also serves coffee. You can buy cakes to take away or consume on the premises. Some are self-service, stand-up joints best suited to the urgent

caffeine fix. Others are essentially sit-down cafés. The smaller cukrászdák are often family businesses, and some have flourished for generations.

Hungarian coffee protocols are a hybrid of Italian and Austrian. Ask for a *kávé*, and you'll get a simple espresso with sugar and milk on the side. A *dupla* is a double measure. For a large, milky coffee resembling a French *café au lait*, order a *tejeskávé*. Certain more cosmopolitan cafés offer a Viennese *mélange* (like a cappuccino without chocolate or cinnamon) or the Italian *macchiato*, an espresso 'stained' with a dash of milk. Decaffeinated is *koffeinmentes*.

Buda

Castle District

Café Miró
I. Úri utca 30 (375 5458). Várbusz from M2 Moszkva tér/bus 16. **Open** 9am-midnight daily. **No credit cards.** Some English spoken. **Map A3**
Although, like everywhere in the Castle District, frequented mostly by tourists, this place has resisted the temptation towards the phonily historical. Décor and furniture has been designed in the shapes and colours of Joan Miró. The green metal chairs look crazy but are surprisingly comfortable; extraordinary sofas and hatstands impel you to pause and admire. Service ranges from cute to competent but there's a fine selection of cakes and snacks.

Litea
I. Hess András tér 4 (375 6987). Várbusz from M2 Moszkva tér/bus 16. **Open** 10am-6pm daily. **Credit** AmEx, DC, EC, MC, V. English spoken. **Map A3**
Inside the Fortuna Passage, an attractively glass-roofed bookshop/café with tables scattered among the shelves. Teas are the speciality here, but they also serve coffees, cakes and ices. Courtyard tables.

Pierrot
I. Fortuna utca 14 (375 6971). Várbusz from M2 Moszkva tér/bus 16. **Open** 11am-1am daily. **Credit** AmEx, DC, EC, MC, V. English spoken. **Map A3**
Essentially a café but with a long Hungarian-international menu if you feel like a meal (and eating it off rather low café-style tables). Otherwise, crepes are the speciality, served in a quiet, comfortable room with a piano, cane chairs, discreet lighting and paintings of Pierrots. It's far from cheap, even for this area, but service is fine, the wares are nicely presented and it does offer some respite from the tourist hordes.

Ruszwurm Cukrászda
I. Szentháromság utca 7 (375 5284). Várbusz from M2 Moszkva tér/bus 16. Open 10am-7pm daily. No credit cards. English spoken. **Map A3**
Budapest's oldest cukrászda has been going since 1827 and still retains some 1840s Empire-style cherrywood fittings. These days it's tourist hell, though, and you're unlikely to be able to sit down for coffee, cakes or ices without a long wait.

Tabán, Gellért Hill & Surrounds

Café Déryné
I. Krisztina tér 3 (212 3804). Tram 18/bus 78, 105. **Open** 8am-10pm Mon-Sat; 9am-9pm Sun. **No credit cards.** Some English spoken. **Map A4**
A modern café where down-at-heel locals pop in to read through the daily papers while flaky entrepreneurs do their deals over mobile phones. The Déryné has a large interior in fake 'old' style, dominated by a grand piano. The cake counter is impressive and there's a decent variety of pastries, salads, sandwiches and ices. The service is generally brisk and flexible. Summer tables outside.

Erzsébet Híd Eszpresszó
I. Döbrentei tér 2 (212 2127). Bus 5, 7/tram 18. **Open** 9am-10.30pm daily. **No credit cards.** English spoken. **Map B5**
Refurbished but rather cramped inside, the attraction here is the terrace by the tramlines, looking out over the Danube and the busy flyover above. The clientèle is mixed, the décor in the narrow bar area kitsch, cake selection minimal, service sluggish, but the Buda bank of the river is so underused as a drinking venue that even the most modest of presszós will do on a baking hot afternoon.

Gellért Eszpresszó
Hotel Gellért, XI. Szent Gellért tér 1 (385 2200). Tram 18, 19, 47, 49. **Open** 7.30am-8.30pm daily. **Credit** AmEx, DC, EC, JCB, MC, V. English spoken. **Map C5**
Elegant but conservative café attached to the Gellért Hotel (its slightly chintzy décor is essentially a Communist idea of what German tourists find congenial) offers coffees, teas, cakes and strudels and a terrace marred by too much traffic noise. Stiff but efficient service. Excellent spot for a coffee after a soporific stint in the Gellért baths.

Víziváros

Angelika
I. Batthyány tér 7 (212 3784). M2 Batthyány tér. **Open** 10am-10pm daily. **No credit cards.** Some English spoken. **Map B3**
Located in the former crypt of St Anne's Church on the south side of Batthyány tér, this refined café is where the middle-class ladies of Buda come to gossip. When the sun is streaming through the stained-glass windows on a late September afternoon, it's a most atmospheric venue for coffee and cakes. The terrace is open in summer.

Moszkva tér & Rózsadomb

Bambi Presszó
II. Frankel Leó utca 2-4. (212 3171). Bus 60, 86. **Open** 7am-9pm Mon-Fri; 9am-8pm Sat, Sun. **No credit cards.** No English spoken. **Map B2**
Somewhere in Budapest it is forever 1965, and this is that somewhere. A classic example of the presszó genre, with the rattle of dominoes echoing off mosa-

Reinventing the coffeehouse

The coffeehouse – *kávéház* – has long been an essential part of Budapest's urban fabric. Some traditional establishments have survived, but these days while tourists gulp down coffee and cakes at the **Művész** or **Gerbeaud**, young Hungarians are more likely to be found sipping cocktails or munching salads at one of various new places that are updating the tradition.

Coffee arrived in Hungary with the Ottomans and coffeehouses were a feature of Budapest long before they appeared in Paris or Vienna. But it was along Viennese lines that the Budapest coffeehouse developed and the institution reached its heyday in the final decades of the Habsburg Empire. At the turn of the century Budapest had some 600 coffeehouses.

In the nineteenth century these both embodied a Habsburg ideal – that people of all classes, races and nations could mingle under one roof – and were a breeding-ground for burgeoning Magyar culture. A list of regulars at the Café Japan (now the **Írók Boltya** – *see chapter* **Shopping & Services**) reads like a who's who of Hungarian painting. Writers gathered at the New York Kávéház. Even the 1848 revolution against Habsburg rule started in a coffeehouse.

Combining the neighbourliness of a local pub, the facilities of a gentleman's club and the intellectual activity of a free university, coffeehouses were places to feel at ease. You could wolf down a full meal or linger for hours over one cup of coffee. Writers were provided with pens and paper. Playwrights and sculptors, painters and musicians, would gather at particular tables. A journalist didn't even need to leave his spot to catch the latest stories and scandals, write an article and dispatch it to the paper – coffeehouse regulars could send and receive messages.

The cream of the crop was the **New York Kávéház**, whose century-long demise epitomises the fate of kávéház culture. On its opening in 1894, the New York's marble and bronze interior was decorated with frescoes from leading painters and literary figures used to hob-nob at its tables. It thrived on between the wars, when visiting Hollywood moguls were as vital to the atmosphere as the literary set. Then fascism, war and communism came along, destroying not just the actual coffeehouses, but the social classes and independent artistic scene which had brought them life. The New York was turned into a sports shop, later to reopen as the Café Hungaria. Now re-renamed New York, it just about still functions – a shoddy state-run trap for tourists who are charged entry to gawp at an Art Nouveau interior defaced with communist-era light-fittings.

But the growth of a burgeoning social class of young *nouveau riche* types has meanwhile sparked a coffeehouse revival around Budapest, with heavy investment going into spacious new designer cafés such as the **Odeon** or **Café Vian**. Mostly they are to be found in up-and-coming areas of downtown Pest, such as VI. Liszt Ferenc tér (Café Vian) or IX. Ráday utca (**El Greco**) and while by Budapest standards they're hardly cheap, they do mostly offer decent service, good light meals, and an imaginative selection of coffees and teas for a young, cosmopolitan and well-heeled clientèle. These new café regulars certainly spend more time chattering on their mobiles than discussing painting, sculpture or literature, but that's the difference a century makes. The postmodern reinvention of the coffeehouse is a welcome addition to the cityscape.

---

ic tiles and tacky light fittings, this is an oasis of calm set in from the traffic fumes of Fő utca. A Ft300 omelette on the terrace by the corner of Bem tér is a fine start to the day. Classic old neon sign.

Café Gusto

II. Frankel Leó utca 12 (316 3970). Tram 4, 6.
Open 10am-10pm Mon-Sat. **No credit cards.** Some English spoken. **Map B2**
Classy joint a short walk from Margaret Bridge, with a terrace overlooking a quiet sidestreet. Inside, the kind of place you wouldn't be embarrassed taking an Italian friend to, with coffee to match, possibly the best in town. Excellent selection on the menu, including fish and other seafood, fresh orange juice and decent salads.

Pest

Belváros

Anna Café

V. Váci utca 7 (266 9080). M1 Vörösmarty utca/tram 2. **Open** 8.30am-2am daily. **Credit** AmEx. English spoken. **Map C4**
Touristy and a bit characterless but a good spot for gawping at Váci. Decent pastries and coffee. Nighttime sees an influx of hustlers and operators.

Astoria Café

V. Kossuth Lajos utca 19-21 (317 3411). M2 Astoria. **Open** 7am-11pm daily. **Credit** AmEx, DC, JCB, MC, V. Some English spoken. **Map D4**

Elegant but not overbearing or overpriced, the high-ceilinged café of the Astoria Hotel (*see chapter* **Accommodation**) has big windows, comfortable leather chairs, and offers basic coffee, cakes and snacks. The haunt of both Nazi (1944-45) and Soviet (1956) officialdom, and despite being part of a state hotel chain for decades, the Astoria has managed to retain its turn-of-the-century feel. Cafés don't come more grandly *mitteleuropäisch* than this.

Auguszt Cukrászda

V. Kossuth Lajos utca 14-16 (337 6379). M2 Astoria/tram 47, 49/bus 7. **Open** 10am-6pm Tue-Fri; 10am-2pm Sat. **No credit cards.** English spoken. **Map C4**

A venerable institution, run by the Auguszt family since 1870. Strictly speaking, this one is the branch, but their flagship premises near Moszkva tér offer only a stand-up shelf for consuming their excellent coffees, pastries and cakes. Here there are tables both within the cosy shop, and out in the expansive Neo-Renaissance courtyard. A speciality is the E-80 cake (chocolate with a marzipan filling, coffee icing and almonds), created for the 80th birthday of Elemér Auguszt, father of current owner József. **Branch:** II. Fény utca 8 (316 8931).

Bon Café

V. Károly körút 10 (266 4230). M2 Astoria/tram 47, 49/bus 7. **Open** 8am-8pm Mon-Fri; 9am-2pm Sat. **No credit cards.** Some English spoken. **Map D4.**

Small, young, friendly pitstop in the fashion courtyard that contains **Impresszió** and **Artz Modell** (*see chapter* **Shopping & Services**). Breakfasts until noon, a good selection of croissants and sandwiches, home-made lemonade to pacify your hangover, and usually some decent music.

Gerbeaud

V. Vörösmarty tér 7 (429 9000). M1 Vörösmarty tér/tram 2. **Open** 9am-10pm daily. **Credit** AmEx, DC, JCB, MC, V. Some English spoken. **Map C4**

On this imposing site since 1870, and with turn-of-the-century fittings, these days Gerbeaud's elegance is mostly reserved for tourists, who stop off after a stroll up Váci. It was here that Émil Gerbeaud invented the cognac cherry and there is still a huge choice of patisserie items, both Hungarian and Viennese. Service runs from rude to efficient in dealing with the scores of outdoor tables set against the slipstream of Budapest's busiest square in high season.

Ibolya

V. Ferenciek tere 5 (267 0239). M3 Ferenciek tere/tram 2/bus 7. **Open** *summer* 8am-11pm Mon-Sat; noon-10pm Sun; *winter* 7am-10pm Mon-Sat; noon-8pm Sun. **No credit cards.** Some English spoken. **Map C4**

Opposite the ELTE University Library, Ibolya is among the best and most central of the surviving communist-era *eszpresszós*: staff are slow, but you can have fine salads, sandwiches and drinks. Avoid the microwaved meat. Take a seat on the terrace if you prefer traffic fumes to cigarette smoke.

Bon Café – *let them eat croissants.*

Odeon

V. Semmelweis utca 2 (317 5162). M2 Astoria//tram 47, 49/bus 7. **Open** 9am-midnight daily. **No credit cards.** Some English spoken. **Map D4**

One of the better of Budapest's new coffeehouses, although the arty decor isn't a patch on the elegant **Puskin** cinema foyer (*see chapter* **Film**) accessible through a side door. Spacious interior, with a summer terrace overlooking leafy Semmelweis utca, the Odeon is pleasant and understated. Occasional exhibitions upstairs, decent selection of fruit teas downstairs, but not much in the way of food.

Talk Talk

V. Magyar utca 12-14 (266 2145). M2 Astoria/tram 47, 49/bus 7. **Open** 10am-midnight daily. **No credit cards.** English spoken. **Map D4**

Just around the corner from the Astoria, this was one of the city's first modern cafés. Though fashionable Budapest has now largely moved on, and the Talk Talk has shortened its round-the-clock opening hours, this is still one of the best options in the area if it's more of a snack or light meal you're after rather than just a coffee or tea. The music's a mite unimaginative, though – usually just the Rádió Danubius blaring inanely – and some menu items frustratingly never seem to be available.

Lipótváros

István Cukrászda

V. Október 6 utca 17 (331 3274). M3 Arany János utca. **Open** 10am-6pm daily. **No credit cards.** No English spoken. **Map C3**

The nicest feature of this small downtown cake shop is the dumb-waiter that ushers your gooey purchase upstairs. Order at the counter, then proceed to the

Café Vian – *summer in Liszt Ferenc tér.*

small upper room. The arrival of your coffee and cake will be heralded by an emphatic buzz. It can get somewhat airless in the summer but a useful spot to read whatever you have just purchased at **Bestsellers** bookshop down the street. *See chapter* **Shopping & Services**.

Markó Könyvszalon

V. Balassi Bálint utca 6 (302 5008). Tram 2, 4, 6. **Open** 8am-10pm Mon-Sat. **Credit** AmEx, MC, V. No English spoken. **Map B2**
Well-intentioned but cheesily executed bookshop café surrounded by small galleries and antique shops. You wouldn't come here for the décor (extremely tacky upholstery with bookshelf motif, tangerine walls) , and certainly not for the music (Tubular Bells, Dark Side of the Moon) or the books themselves (mostly Hungarian, plus assorted English-language guide books), but it's a relaxing place to consume a wide and well-priced choice of juices, coffees, salads, snacks and light meals that include good vegetarian and breakfast options. Bumbling service, though.

Szalai Cukrászda

V. Balassi Bálint utca 7 (269 3210). Tram 2, 4, 6. **Open** 9am-7pm Mon, Wed-Sun. **No credit cards**. Some English spoken. **Map B2**
Just north of **Parliament** (*see chapter* **Sightseeing**), an excellent old-fashioned family-run cukrászda with a city-wide reputation for its cakes and pastries. These can be consumed sitting on stools at any one of half a dozen low tables, or carried away in handsomely crafted boxes. A handful of large, gilt-framed mirrors challenge the tawdriness of the modern brand-names festooned on walls also hung with ancient and modern certificates testifying to the quality of the wares on offer.

Andrássy út & District VI

Eckermann

VI. Andrássy út 24 (374 4076). M1 *Opera.* **Open** 8am-10pm Mon-Fri; 9am-10pm Sat. **No credit cards.** Some English spoken. **Map D3**
The **Goethe Insitut** café seems to have attracted the literary locals who used the now tourist-dominated Művész opposite. Excellent coffee including huge bowls of German-style *Milchkaffee*, Hungarian and German newspapers, some pastries and sandwiches, and three computers for net-surfing.

Fashion Café

VI. Andrássy út 36 (311 8060). M1 *Opera.* **Open** 11am-1am daily. **No credit cards.** Some English spoken. **Map D3**
Attempt at sophistication which trips over its nouveau-riche aspirations and lands face-first somewhere in the 1980s. A lot of money's been wasted on dull décor and fashion photos fill the walls, but it has no obvious crowd and the long drinks menu demonstrates a naive faith in the cachet of brand-name booze. Small selection of decent sandwiches for around Ft550, dated disco music, and ten per cent service slapped on the bill.

Komédias Kávéház

VI. Nagymező utca 26 (302 0901). M1 *Oktogon/tram 4, 6.* **Open** 8am-midnight Mon-Fri; 4pm-midnight Sat, Sun. **No credit cards.** Some English spoken. **Map D3**
New and friendly little café in faux Nouveau style on Budapest's Broadway adjoining the refurbished **Thália színház** (*see chapter* **Theatre & Dance**). Sandwiches, salads and cakes, a selection of egg dishes for breakfast, and piano music in the evenings from Thursday to Sunday. Cheaper than it looks. Tables outside in summer.

Lukács

VI. Andrássy út 70 (302 8747). M1 *Vörösmarty utca.* **Open** 9am-8pm, Mon-Fri; 10am-8pm Sat, Sun. **No credit cards.** Some English spoken. **Map D2**
This historically infamous kávéház is now part of the main office for CIB Bank, but for a dark decade was the cafeteria for the secret police, whose headquarters were at No.60. Lukács' present-day pretence at elegance is spoiled by the correct impression that you are walking into a bank. Not even the gooey cake display by the main entrance can persuade you otherwise, nor the tea-time piano player, nor the waitresses' frilly uniforms.

Művész

VI. Andrássy út 29 (352 1337). M1 *Opera.* **Open** 9am-midnight daily. **No credit cards.** Some English spoken. **Map D3**
Although its unpretentious period décor still has a turn-of-the-century feel, new management at the Művész have cashed in on its reputation, upping prices and replacing friendly staff with sullen ones, forcing out regulars to the nearby **Eckermann** (*above*) and beyond. Limited selection of cakes, savouries and ice creams – try the *alma torta* (apple cake). The summer terrace is still a grand spot.

Operett Söröző-Kávéház

VI. Nagymező utca 19 (269 5001). M1 Oktogon.
Open 9am-midnight daily. **Credit** AmEx, MC, V.
Some English spoken. **Map D3**
Pleasant annexe to the Operett Theatre on
Budapest's quickly reviving Broadway, with a tree-
lined terrace and wooden interior. Great spot for
breakfast, served until noon, lunches and main
meals thereafter. Mainly used as a meeting place for
actors making drinks stretch between jobs.

Café Vian

*VI. Liszt Ferenc tér 9 (268 1154). M1 Oktogon/tram
4, 6.* **Open** 10am-1am daily. **Credit** AmEx, MC, V.
Some English spoken. **Map D3**
A pinkly postmodern reinvention of the coffeehouse,
catering to a well-heeled crowd on the ever up-and-
coming Liszt tér. The décor's a bit over the top and
it's hardly the cheapest place in town, but it does
offer an imaginative selection of salads, quiches and
sandwiches, plus milk shakes, fresh juices and a
decent cocktail menu, in an ambience suitable for
relaxed supping, chatting and people-watching.
Decent service; summer tables on the square outside.

District VII

Fröhlich Cukrászda

*VII. Dob utca 22 (321 6741). M2 Astoria/tram 47,
49.* **Open** *summer* 10am-6pm Mon-Thur; 10am-2pm
Fri; 11am-4pm Sun; *winter* 10am-5pm Mon-Thur;
7am-2pm Fri; 8am-8pm Sun. **No credit cards**.
English spoken. **Map D4**
Community baker's serving kosher pastries in the
Jewish quarter. Old Mr Fröhlich still stumbles out of
the bakery covered in flour, only to be shooed back
in by his wife at the counter. The traditional *flodni* –
apple, poppy seeds and hazelnuts – is the star of the
pastry counter. Various teas complement coffee dis-
pensed from a beautiful old Casino espresso machine.

Café Mozart

VII. Erzsébet körút 36 (352 0664). Tram 4, 6.
Open 9am-11pm Mon-Fri, Sun; 9am-midnight Sat.
No credit cards. English spoken. **Map D3**
Laughable simulation of coffeehouse culture: waitresses in Baroque costume, phony period furniture,
crap *mitteleuropäisch* murals, inept portraits of
Mozart and 62 different kinds of coffee, all with
straight-faced descriptions so absurd it's almost
worth going in just to deride the menu. ('Espresso:
strong, black coffee made out of carefully selected
coffee beans, served in a small cup'). Overlit, sterile
and naff as ninepence, this is the unacceptable face
of capitalist Budapest. Avoid also its sister establishment, the equally asinine Café Verdi at Astoria.

New York Kávéház

*VII. Erzsébet körút 9-11 (322 3849). M2 Blaha Lujza
tér/tram 4, 6.* **Open** 9am-midnight daily. **Credit**
AmEx, DC, MC, V. Some English spoken. **Map E4**
Budapest's most famous coffeehouse is a sad ruin of
its former self. Opened in 1894 to a design by Alajos
Hauszmann and once the main haunt of Pest's artis-

tic life, it's been run down by decades of communism
and is now too expensive for the locals. Tourists who
can afford what is more of a museum than a living
coffeehouse (and can find their way in through the
wooden scaffolding that's been propping up the
façade since 1956 when a Soviet tank slammed into
it) are greeted with some of the most indifferent service in town. A tragedy, though the sumptuous interior is still worth a look. (*See also chapter*
Sightseeing.)

District VIII

Budapest Blue

*VIII. Somogyi Béla utca 8 (266 0084). M2 Blaha
Lujza tér/tram 4, 6.* **Open** *café* 9am-midnight daily.
No credit cards. Some English spoken. **Map E4**
Round the side of the **Corvin** department store (*see
chapter* **Shopping & Services**), a subdued diner-
style establishment offering various breakfast
options (Ft300-500), a huge selection of warm and
cold open sandwiches (basically half a baguette with
a generous topping), 'Pacific' (actually pan-Asian)
dishes, set lunch menus at Ft500, and friendly
English-speaking waiters to help you through it all.
Tables outside in summer.

District IX

El Greco

IX. Ráday utca 11-13 (217 6986). M3 Kálvin tér.
Open 10am-1am Mon-Fri; noon-1am Sat, Sun. **No**
credit cards. Some English spoken. **Map D5**
Part of the Ráday utca renaissance. The name indicates a vaguely Greek theme – it's nothing to do with
the painter. A big space with friendly wooden tables
and simple décor for the black-clad studenty clientele to play backgammon, eat tzatziki (Ft390) or a
Greek salad (Ft520) and pose with a beer or coffee.
Menu of daily Italo-Greek specials (average Ft1,000)
and occasionally Greek music to go with them. But
also non-Greek features such as *pogácsa* on the
tables and Sacher Torte on the menu.

Eckermann – *haunt of literary locals.*

Pubs & Bars

Sup with the yuppies, drink a pálinka or wind down on cheap wine – Budapest has bars and booze for all occasions.

Budapest's savage drinking culture has traditionally been fuelled by cheap wine, but Hungary's position at the crossroads between spirit-swilling Slav countries and the beery expanses of Germanic Europe has also affected local customs. Add nearly a decade of cosmopolitan western influences and you get a mixed bag of drinking habits and places in which to indulge them.

Many aren't too sophisticated, with dreary décor, terrible toilets and the radio tuned to some top-40 station. Hungarians aren't that bothered as long as they've got a drink in front of them. Standing at counters is rare, but table service, though the norm, varies from slow to practically stationary. Bar snacks are starchy and simple: the *pogácsa*, a salty scone, the *meleg szendvics*, a grilled slice of bread topped with cheese and either mushrooms or a mystery meat, or *zsíros kenyér* – bread and dripping with raw onions.

Apart from all the theme pubs, there are three traditional mainstays: the *borozó*, a cheap and unpretentious wine cellar; the *söröző*, a beer bar inferior to those of Germany or the Czech Republic; and the *presszó*, a sort of 1960s-style Communist coffee bar straddling the alcoholically blurred line between pub and café. The söröző is beginning to decline in importance, overwhelmed by a wave of dodgy new theme pubs. Borozós are dank, dark and start filling before dawn. Here, wine is priced by the decilitre and ladled from tureens; white is often mixed with soda water to create *fröccs* – spritzers – and red is often mixed with cola.

Hungarian beer is acceptable if it's cold. Borsodi is your best option on draught, otherwise Austrian and German brews are widely available. The younger generation have taken to drinking pints (*korsó*; a smaller glass is a *pohár*) instead of the wine their dads drank. No one clinks their beer glasses, though. *See page 135* **To clink or not to clink**.

Beers are chased with shots of Unicum, a robust herb liqueur – *see page 132* **The national Accelerator** – or *pálinka*, fruit brandy. The latter comes in several fiery varieties. Stick to either *szilva* (plum) or *vilmos* (pear) pálinka, and consider cancelling tomorrow's sightseeing plans if anyone offers you lethal, home-brewed *házi pálinka*.

Prices vary wildly. The borozó clientele can get shitfaced for a handful of coins. Beer drinkers will be paying around Ft200-Ft300 for their pint. Pubs

appealing to Budapest's expatriate community will happily charge double that.

The area around the south end of Váci utca is decent for pub crawling, with an assortment of bars in its waterfront backstreets. The patch around Oktogon and the Opera offers a more refined crawl, with Liszt tér as teeming summer drinking central. The backstreets of Districts VI and VII feature some of the city's more intriguing bars. Most borozós and many presszós close at around 8pm. Most pubs and bars stay open until midnight to 2am, though there are plenty still going if you want to continue until dawn. *See also chapters* **Nightlife** *and* **Cafés & Coffeehouses**.

Buda

Tabán, Gellért Hill & surrounds

Libella

XI. Budafoki út 7 (209 4761). Tram 18, 47, 49. **Open** 8am-1.30am Mon-Sat. **No credit cards**. Some English spoken. **Map C6**

Relaxed and unpretentious café/bar attracting an arty clientele. Dark and light beers on draught, chess games in the corner, and possibly Budapest's best meleg szendvics – though it usually takes a while to arrive. Good spot for a laid-back late afternoon beer.

Rác kert

I. Hadnagy utca 8-10 (no phone). Tram 18, 19/bus 7/night bus É78. **Open** *May-Sept* 2pm-5am daily. **No credit cards**. Some English spoken. **Map B5**

The garden next door to the baths of the same name (*see chapter* **Baths**) becomes the hippest watering hole in town on warm summer nights. Surrounded by trees and old stone walls and with a refreshing lack of neighbours to annoy, it heaves at weekends and even on Tuesdays will buzz until dawn with a sexy, relaxed but only slightly showy crowd. Action spreads across big tables between two bars and spills out into the leafy Tabán beyond, and a big screen goes up in the middle for football World Cups and European championships. Basic snacks and a decent selection of bottled Czech beers at around Ft400.

Café Zacc

XI. Bocskai utca 12 (209 1593). Tram 18, 47/bus 7. **Open** noon-2am Mon-Fri; 10am-2am Sat; 3pm-midnight Sun. **No credit cards**. Some English spoken. **Map B6**

Modest but fun-loving bar a short hop from Móricz Zsigmond körtér. The décor wavers between pop-

art and a local youth club, with customers to match. Decent sounds, much football talk, and a grimly imaginative range of cheap and lethal cocktails. Tables outside in summer.

Víziváros

Belgian Brasserie
I. Bem rakpart 12 (201 5082). M2 Batthyány tér/tram 19/bus 86. **Open** noon-midnight daily. **No credit cards.** Some English spoken. **Map B3**
Although a reasonable restaurant in its own right, the raison d'être for this fine if pricey establishment is its extensive beer menu. The best Belgium has to offer – Kriek, Chimay, Hoegaarden – can be enjoyed on the riverside terrace, a rarity in Buda. *See also chapter* **Restaurants**.

Moszkva tér & Rózsadomb

Móri Borozó
I. Fiáth János utca 16 (no phone). M2 Moszkva tér. **Open** 2-11pm Mon-Fri; 2-9pm Sat, Sun. **No credit cards.** No English spoken. **Map A2**
Comfortable wine bar singled out by its younger clientele. In the 1970s Moszkva tér was a meeting place for young rockers with nowhere else to go. The Móri still attracts the leather waistcoat brigade, one generation down from the messy mac merchants who usually frequent these joints. Friendly atmosphere, Innstadt beer on draught, cheap wine.

Oscar Café
II. Ostrom utca 14 (212 8017). M2 Moszkva tér/tram 4, 6. **Open** 5pm-2am Sun; noon-3pm, 5pm-2am, Mon-Thur; noon-3pm, 5pm-4am, Fri; 5pm-4am Sat. **No credit cards.** No English spoken. **Map A3**

Dark, cinematically-themed pub a short hop from Moszkva tér, whose main feature is its irresistibly long bar counter. Silly 'Nam corner with camouflage nets, but otherwise classic shots, stills and stars from the world of Hollywood and Magyar movies make for a pleasant backdrop. Mixed, well-heeled young crowd.

Rózsadomb
II. Margit körút 7 (212 5145). Tram 4, 6. **Open** 9am-10pm daily. **No credit cards.** Some English spoken. **Map B2**
An inaccurate reflection of its namesake, the posh and barless residential area in the hills beyond, this humble eszpresszó is an oasis of low-priced entertainment. This is presszó life at its best, a celebration of the tacky and the tasteless. As cheap a draught Borsodi as anywhere in town.

Vox
II. Marczibányi tér 5A (315 0592). M2 Moszkva tér/tram 4, 6, 18. **Open** 1pm-2am daily. **No credit cards.** Some English spoken. **Map A2**
Handy if you're visiting the concrete and brick **Művelődési Központ** culture centre, scene of many dance houses (*see chapter* **Folklore**), but otherwise rather out of the way. Vox occupies the culture centre's basement and has its own separate entrance. The bar is pleasant if unremarkable, occasionally hosting bands and DJs. Airy terracing outside is the best feature.

Pest

Belváros

Club Verne
V. Váci utca 60 (318 6274). M3 Ferenciek tere. **Open** noon-2am daily. **Credit** AmEx, MC, V. Some English spoken. **Map 5C**
Huge and heavily themed cellar not quite 20,000 leagues under street level but offering sanctuary from the blazing heat, tourists and sponsored umbrellas of the terrace bars along this pedestrianised stretch of Váci. Long and shaped like one of Jules' underwater contraptions, the Verne has bar areas at either end – one with a stage for live acts ranging from folk to jazz to Chippendales – but its most pleasant spot is the row of tables facing the main bar. Interesting cocktail menu.

Fregatt
V. Molnár utca 26 (318 9997). Tram 2, 47, 49. **Open** 3pm-1am daily. **Credit** AmEx. Some English spoken. **Map C5**
Once the main hangout for anglophone expats and those who wished to meet them, these days just an enjoyably quiet British-style pub. Air-conditioning and rudimentary food.

Rózsadomb Eszpresszó – *a celebration of tack, tastelessness and classy old neon.*

The national Accelerator

Unicum baffles the first-time imbiber. In a bottle that looks like an old-style anarchist's bomb, Hungary's national herb liqueur is a dark-brown liquid that smells like a hospital corridor and packs a punch like Koko Kovács. 'Uch!' is a normal first reaction, followed by the feeling that it must be good for you since it tastes so foul. Cough medicine that tasted this way went out with the bubble car.

But, made from a secret recipe that was smuggled out of the country during the Communist era and has since been brought back, Unicum has a taste that is easy to acquire: vaguely sweet and mint, but bitter as a midwinter night. A good rule of thumb is not to drink more than three in one evening, but of course everyone does and the hangovers can be spectacular. No problem, as Hungarians consider Unicum (along with sour cabbage juice) to be the premier hangover cure.

Italians may favour Fernet Branca, Germans might hymn Jägermeister, but the taste and effect of these digestifs is belittled by the mighty Unicum. Unicum settles the stomach. Unicum keeps out the cold. But above all else Unicum is The Accelerator. Drink five beers and feel bloated. Drink five beers and whack back one Unicum and feel like five more beers – and several more Unicums. After that, forget the holes in the feet and walk across the Danube.

Galéria

V. Vitkovics Mihály utca 6 (337 6180). M1 M2, M3 Deák tér/tram 47, 49. **Open** 10am-midnight Mon-Fri; 3pm-midnight Sat, Sun. **No credit cards**. No English spoken. **Map C4**
Serene and pretty bar that has been here forever, tucked away in a quiet Belváros backwater. Cosy bar area and back room, embellished with vases of dried flowers and dinky stools. Summer terrace.

Irish Cat

V. Múzeum körút 41 (266 4085). M3 Kálvin tér/tram 47, 49. **Open** 11am-2am Mon-Sat; 5pm-2am Sun. **No credit cards**. Some English spoken. **Map D5**
Every major European city seems to have an Irish pub that functions as a meat market. This is Budapest's. Crowded bar area with intimate wooden booths and back section for overspill and smooching. Packed after midnight.

Rác kert *– smokers' garden of delights.*

Janis Pub

V. Királyi Pál utca 8 (266 2619). M3 Kálvin tér/tram 47, 49. **Open** 4pm-2am Mon-Thur; 4pm-3am Fri, Sat. **No credit cards**. Some English spoken. **Map D5**
Quiet pub tucked away in the narrow backstreets between Kálvin tér and Ferenciek tere. Ms Joplin would have been pretty disappointed if someone had dragged her here, although Southern Comfort can be had to chase the Guinness. Attracts an expatriate and native crowd.

Lipótváros

Beckett's

V. Bajcsy-Zsilinszky út 72 (311 1033). M3 Nyugati/tram 4, 6. **Open** *bar* noon-1am Mon-Thur; noon-2am Fri-Sun. **Credit** *over* Ft3,000: AmEx, DC, JCB, MC, V. Some English spoken. **Map C2**
Enormous Irish pub and principal watering hole for Budapest's anglophone expat business community. Although it's pricey for Budapest, some Hungarians do wander in too. Friday night is the liveliest, as consultants and chancers quaff away the cares of the week, and the place can also heave for major sports events on Sky. The live music, which usually starts around 11pm, is loud and mostly dreadful – trad jazz or Beatles impersonators.

No. 1 Presszó

V. Sas utca 9 (267 0235). M3 Arany János utca. **Open** 9am-midnight Mon-Fri; 6pm-midnight Sat. **No credit cards**. No English spoken. **Map C3**
Fine presszó slap-bang in Budapest's business quarter. The prominent bar counter is offset by a spacious room of brown furniture, set against incongruous paintings and signed photos of theatre stars. Draught Zipfer and cocktails of questionable parentage share the menu with toasted sandwiches and cappuccinos. As far away from the city beat as it is possible to get in the same postal district.

Andrássy út & District VI

Aloe Kávézó

VI. Zichy Jenő utca 34 (269 4536). M1 Opera/M3 Arany János utca. **Open** 5pm-2am daily. **No credit cards.** No English spoken. **Map D3**

Comfortably warrenous cellar bar with sofas and armchairs for a young, vaguely literary and occasionally rowdy crowd. Old radios, period posters and tatty rugs make up the décor. Toasted sandwiches and instant soups complement a drinks menu with various coffees and cocktails, plus draught Stella at Ft190 a korsó. Friendly place.

Crazy Café

VI. Jókai utca 30 (302 4003). M3 Nyugati/tram 4, 6. **Open** 11am-1am Mon-Sat; 11am-midnight Sun. **No credit cards.** Some English spoken. **Map C2**

The name and long row of beer signs outside refer to the ridiculous choice of drinks: up to 18 types of draught beer, nearly 100 bottled beers and some 50 cocktails. Two restaurant areas serving pizzas and Hungarian standards, two bars and an area for live music and karaoke.

Incognito

VI. Liszt Ferenc tér 3 (351 9428). M1 Oktogon. **Open** 10am-midnight Mon-Fri; noon-midnight Sat, Sun. **No credit cards.** Some English spoken. **Map D3**

Large bar area with walls covered in classic jazz album sleeves. Although it has an adventurous drinks menu – 20 types of coffee, ten teas, two dozen cocktails – the Incognito isn't as cool as it thinks it is. It could be the loud jazz, it could be the dim lighting, it could be the extortionate prices. At its best in the summer, when the many outside tables fill up night and day.

Média Club Étterem

VI. Andrássy út 101 (322 1639). M1 Bajza utca. **Open** 10am-midnight Mon-Sat; 10am-4pm Sun. **No credit cards.** Some English spoken. **Map E2**

Hungary's journalists' club has the finest bar terrace along Andrássy út, open to the general public amid trees in the grounds of a grand old building that also houses a restaurant.

Café Mediterran

VI. Liszt Ferenc tér 10 (342 1959). M1 Oktogon/ tram 4, 6. **Open** 10am-2am daily. **No credit cards.** No English spoken. **Map D3**

Another bar on the popular, pedestrianised Liszt Ferenc tér, opposite Incognito (*see above*) and a marginally preferable option. Smaller, less pretentious and certainly redder than its rival, the Mediterran is a smart, friendly bar for an Amstel or three with a popular summer terrace just along from the recently opened **Café Vian** (*see chapter* **Cafés & Coffeehouses**) and above the **Undergrass** cellar disco (*see chapter* **Nightlife**).

Underground

VI. Teréz körút 30 (311 1481). M3 Nyugati/tram 4, 6. **Open** 6pm-2am Mon-Wed; 6pm-4am Thur-Sun. **No credit cards.** Some English spoken. **Map C2**

Aloe Kávézó *– your bar stool awaits.*

Underneath the Művész cinema (*see chapter* **Film**), a popular subterranean space with décor intended to evoke Emir Kusturica's film of the same name. There's an attractive, long bar, a young and fashionable crowd, a reasonably priced menu and DJs spinning a mix of mainstream funk and garage. *See also chapter* **Nightlife**.

District VII

Amigo Bar

VII. Hársfa utca 1 (352 1424). M2 Blaha Lujza tér/tram 4, 6/bus 7. **Open** 3pm-3am Mon-Fri; 6pm-3am Sat, Sun. **No credit cards.** No English spoken. **Map E4**

Late-opening 1950s revival bar; downstairs there's billiard and jukebox rooms, upstairs three bar areas overseen by dozens of pictures of Elvis Presley, whose legs also dangle like a metronome from the bar clock. Music shuffles original rockabilly with tacky Hungarian imitations. Hardcore Elvis fans will find little to detain them, but it's not a bad late bar.

Jazz and Blues Kocsma

VII. Dob utca 83 (322 3536). Trolleybus 73, 76. **Open** 4pm-1am Mon-Thur; 4pm-2am, Fri, Sat. **No credit cards.** Some English spoken. **Map E3**

Despite the awful name – regulars call it simply 'The Club' – an excellent meeting place, with a lively and congenial atmosphere and rock-bottom prices: Ft150 for a Borsodi, Ft200 a Tuborg, seven draught options in all. The Club's narrow main bar area is bookended by a darts board and table football, with booth seating out back. Ring the bell for a piece of the smoky action.

Portside

VII. Dohány utca 7 (351 8405). M2 Astoria/tram 47, 49/bus 7. **Open** 11am-2am Mon-Sat; 4pm-2am Sun. **Credit** AmEx, V. English spoken. **Map D4**

Huge British-run cellar pub with nautical theme. Early evenings it's patronised by a smart, youngish and largely anglophone crowd – guys in suits and ties, and women who like guys in suits and ties. Later on it's even younger and even more of a meat market. Efficient staff, big menu, pool tables and disco standards, played rather too loud for comfort. Packed at weekends. *See also chapter* **Restaurants**.

Sixtus Kápolna

VII. Nagy Diófa utca 26-28 (352 1479). M2 Blaha Lujza tér/tram 4, 6/bus 7. **Open** 5.30pm-1am Mon-Sat. **No credit cards.** English spoken. **Map D4**

Key hangout for alternative types and cosmopolitan bohemia, with a crowd about half Hungarian, half tourist. Just a small bar in front and a few tables at the back – both rooms decorated with theatre posters – which can get uncomfortably crowded. The insider atmosphere – everyone knows everyone else – may also prove off-putting. But drinks are cheap, staff are sweethearts, and music veers from Jane's Addiction to Archie Shepp, calling at all points in between.

Wichmann

VII. Kazinczy utca 55 (342 6074). M1, M2, M3 Deák tér/tram 47, 49. **Open** 6pm-2am daily. **No credit cards.** Some English spoken. **Map D4**

Owned by former world champion canoeist Tamás Wichmann, this rough and smoky bar with no sign outside (it's just south of the corner with Király utca) seems largely untouched by recent history. Wine is appallingly cheap, young customers cluster around big and sociable wooden tables, and the staff have a daft sense of humour. A fine establishment.

District VIII

Ball 'n' Bull

VIII. Rákóczi út 29 (267 0286). M2 Blaha Lujza tér/tram 4, 6/bus 7. **Open** noon-1am daily. **Credit** AmEx, JCB, MC, V. English spoken. **Map D4**

'American sports bar', currently the city's least objectionable option for live Premiership football and assorted US sports. Four TVs, one big screen, sometimes tuned to different events – occasionally causing tension between British and American crowds. American bar food menu includes decent burgers. Invariably understaffed on big match nights.

Darshan Café

VIII. Krúdy Gyula utca 8 (266 7797). M3 Kálvin tér/tram 47, 49. **Open** 11am-midnight Mon-Sat; 3pm-midnight Sun. **No credit cards.** Some English spoken. **Map D5**

Imaginatively designed, laid back and with reasonable music (ambient and acid jazz), the Darshan could do with a better drinks selection – only one beer and a few desultory spirits. The Gaudí-ish mosaic entrance and gallery space are cool, though, and it's a better daytime option than **Darshan Udvar** opposite (*see below*). Slow counter service only.

Darshan Udvar

VIII. Krúdy Gyula utca 7 (266 5541). M3 Kálvin tér. **Open** 11am-1am Mon-Thur; 11am-3am Fri; 6pm-3am Sat; 6pm-1am Sun. **No credit cards.** Some English spoken. **Map D5**

Another mock Mongolian night out at the **Darshan Udvar**.

The beating heart of up-and-coming Krúdy Gyula utca – a huge and popular pub that's a centrepiece for the mock Mongolian courtyard of the same name, which also includes a couple of other bars, a Buddhist bookshop and the **Indigo** music shop (*see chapter* **Shopping & Services**). Lots of roomy tables but no area for mingling. Menu of daily specials, soundtrack of world music, reggae, jazz, dub, ambient and 'alternative'.

District IX

Paris, Texas

IX. Ráday utca 22 (217 7737). M3 Kálvin tér/tram 47, 49. **Open** 10am-3am Mon-Fri; 4pm-3am Sat, Sun. **No credit cards.** Some English spoken. **Map D5**
Decent bar on a lively street, decorated with dozens of period portrait photos – the atmosphere is reminiscent of an Amsterdam brown café. Upstairs is a relaxed bar area, downstairs there's a pool table and the occasional gig. Tables outside in summer. Pizza can be ordered from the restaurant next door.

District XIII

Akali Borozó

XIII. Szent István körút 2 (340 4354). Tram 2, 4, 6. **Open** 5.30am-11.30pm Mon-Fri; 8am-10.30pm Sat; 7am-9.30pm Sun. **No credit cards.** No English spoken. **Map C2**
Friendly borozó on the Pest side of Margaret Bridge. Wine tureens, bread and dripping, devoured by a morning clientele with faces let-down balloons. The Akali's attractive late-opening hours (for a borozó) then draw a more refined crowd later in the day. Good views of Körút action outside.

Yes

XIII. Hegedűs Gyula utca 1 (329 3105). M3 Nyugati/tram 4, 6. **Open** 10am-4am daily. **No credit cards.** No English spoken. **Map C2**
Recently smartened-up late-night haunt of Újlipótváros oddments. 'Yes' answers all questions. 'Do I really want one last beer with an Unicum chaser?' Yes. 'Will Ft120 buy me a toasted sandwich?' Yes. 'Is it always this full at five on a Sunday morning?' 'Have I really spent Ft5,000 tonight?' 'Is it dawn already?' Yes.

Óbuda

Rolling Rock

III. Bécsi út 53-55 (368 2298). Bus 6, 60. 86/tram 17. **Open** 9am-5am Mon-Fri; 10am-5pm Sat, Sun. **Credit** AmEx, JCB, MC, V. English spoken.
The place where many of the indigenous business crowd bleat and bleep, a US-style diner with predictable Monroe and motorbike motifs, steaks and cocktails. Apart from the house beer there are classic brews from Belgium chilling in the fridge. Packed to the gills by 9pm, when modest live acts take to the small stage. Part of the urban renewal of Óbuda, the Kolosy tér shopping development.

To clink or not to clink?

There you are with some new Hungarian friends, and someone's just bought a round of beers. You lift your glass to clink in a virtually international gesture of camaraderie – and suddenly you're greeted not by smiles and toasts but nasty looks and a drunken historical lecture. The Austrians clinked beers, you will be told, to celebrate the execution of 13 Magyar generals in 1849. Ever since then, Hungarians will never, repeat never, clink beer glasses.

Until now, that is. The 150-year-old interdiction on clinking beer glasses officially ended in October 1999. Historians and folklorists insist that the clinking ban was only supposed to last for 150 years and, well... here we are. Who it actually was that decided to curse clinking, or set the 150-year limit, is of course unknown. Folklore is like that, and Hungarian folklore even more so. Some even argue that the Austrians couldn't have clinked beers in the first place – at that time there was no brewery in Arad, where the executions took place.

Nevertheless, ever since 1849, clink-avoidance has grown as a reminder of the great dream of Magyar independence. After the Russians came along in 1945 and outlawed just about everything that Hungarians hold dear, small and modest actions such as not clinking glasses acquired an almost mystical significance. Even, perhaps especially, when travelling abroad, Magyars decline to clink beers, leaping at the opportunity to deliver a short speech on the sorrows of their homeland. The custom is part of Hungarian self-definition. They put their surnames before their given names, they stand silently when the National Anthem is played, and they do not clink beers.

So news of the ban's end has been greeted with shock and incredulity. Many have responded with a disgusted look and a hearty assurance that 'I'll never clink beers. Not me!' Some have begun the awkward process of learning to clink in public. Others see a cynical anti-Hungarian plot to undermine national pride. Will the populace suddenly go with the Euro-flow and start toasting with their beers, glass to glass? Off on their own corner table in the common European bar, Hungarians are not happy about the idea.

Restaurants

Mammoth portions might still be the yardstick of excellence, but Budapest is undergoing a restaurant renaissance.

When dining out in Budapest you are, whether conscious of it or not, witness to and participant in a remarkable transformation. The restaurant scene – drab beyond belief under Communism and pretty shaky during several years of 'transition' – is now in better shape than it has been for the best part of a century.

Although Budapest's restaurant world at the beginning of the twentieth century was famous, it was the preserve of the wealthy élite. For all its sins, Communist rule made eating out accessible to the common person, but didn't, unfortunately, teach them what to look for. Large portions were (and generally still are) the yardstick of excellence, and cost was everything. Also, because Hungary maintained an isolated stance from trends in the rest of world, the 1960s' wave of lighter European cuisine never broke here. The food was a grisly and heavy anachronism, served by waiters with no motivation and eaten in surroundings built and decorated by huge catering combines. The experience was, bluntly, dire.

Top tips

The *Time Out Budapest Guide*'s favourite establishments for the...

Best high-end Hungarian dining
Gundel

Best international dining
Lou Lou

Best medium-priced Hungarian food
Kéhli

Largest Dessert Ever To Have Existed Anywhere
Túrós gombóc at Náncsi Néni

Meatiest home delivery
Bécsi Szelet

Off-the-scale cholesterol count
Haxen Király

Cheapest substantial snack
Lángos

Nowadays, the growth of disposable income and competition, plus greater openness to outside influences, means anyone can eat well in the city if they try. Sure, you will still encounter places where standards aren't high and service is poor, but with the help of this chapter you should also find many memorable venues. You'll also find that eating out in Budapest is far more affordable than in most European capitals.

We've broken down the listings in this chapter by both price and cuisine type. The price categories are Top-range (average over Ft4,000), Mid-range (over Ft2,000) and Budget (anything under that), and under these we have included restaurants serving both Hungarian and international cuisine. We've added a *Étkezdék* category for the cost-conscious and those in a hurry, and have listed some fast food that you aren't likely to find in your high street back home. The latter part of the chapter is devoted to restaurants offering non-Hungarian cuisine, broken down into sub-categories from the Americas to Vegetarian.

Prices given are the average for a starter and a main course for one person. These should be treated as guidelines rather than gospel. It's often possible to eat cheaply even in quite pricey Hungarian restaurants. Although it's easy to find something to eat in the small hours (*see also chapter* **Nightlife**), most places wind down before midnight.

THE MAGYAR MENU

By far the most numerous and most affordable type of restaurant in town is the standard *étterem* or *vendéglő*, serving traditional Hungarian restaurant fare, which is worth a brief examination.

Whatever you may have heard, Hungarian food is not fiery hot or spicy. On the contrary, most westerners are surprised at the conservative use of seasonings other than salt and pepper, and the resultant blandness of the cooking. Paprika is ubiquitous, it is true, but with exceptions tends to be sweet and fragrant rather than hot, and in fried foods is added more for decoration than flavour.

Paprika only comes into its own in dishes such as *töltött káposzta* (stuffed cabbage) or *pörkölt* (what you know as Hungarian goulash), when meat and onions are stewed together in a fat flavoured with paprika. Like all cuisines with roots in peasant culture, Hungarian food tends to be very fatty – don't be surprised if you find a slab of

Fin de Siécle ambience at the ever-popular **Múzeum**. *See page 142.*

lightly cooked pork fat on your plate next to the meat, and yes, you really are supposed to eat it. Another source of fat is sour cream, which also provides the smooth piquancy in that other paprika-flavoured local classic, *paprikás* – pörkölt thickened with a sour cream and flour mixture.

If goulash is really pörkölt, what, many might ask, is *gulyás*? Hungary's national meat soup, named after the people (gulyás means 'cow-herd') who lived off it. Soup is an important component of the Magyar meal. Most tend to be a thin consommé with some form of dumpling or pasta to

What's on the menu

I'd like a table for two. *Két fő részére kérek egy asztalt.*
Are these seats taken? *Ezek a helyek foglaltak?*
I'd like the menu, please. *Kérem az étlapot.*
I didn't order this. *Nem ezt rendeltem.*
I am a vegetarian. *Vegetáriánus vagyok.*
I am diabetic. *Diabetikus vagyok.*
Do you have...? *Van...?*
Bon appétit! *Jó étvágyat!*
Thank you. *Köszönöm.*
The bill, please. *Számlát kérek!*

Basics (Alapok)
Ashtray *Hamutartó*
Bill *Számla*
Bread *Kenyér*
Cup *Csésze*
Fork *Villa*
Glass *Pohár*
Knife *Kés*
Milk *Tej*
Napkin *Szalvéta*
Oil *Olaj*
Pepper *Bors*
Plate *Tanyér*
Salt *Só*
Spoon *Kanál*
Sugar *Cukor*
Teaspoon *Kiskanál*
Vinegar *Ecet*
Water *Víz*

Meats (Húsok)
Lamb *Bárány*
Thick goulash soup *Bográcsgulyás*
Veal *Borjú*
Leg *Comb*
Bean soup with pork knuckle *Jókai bableves*
Duck *Kacsa*
Butter or cheese-filled turkey in breadcrumbs *Kijevi pulykamell*
Goose *Liba*
Beef *Marha*
Liver *Máj*
Breast *Mell*
Rabbit *Nyúl*
Turkey *Pulyka*
Ham *Sonka*
Venison *Szarvas*

Fish/Seafood (Hal/tengeri gyülmölcs)
Grilled fillet of fish *Halfilé roston*
Lobster *Homár*
Shellfish, mussels *Kagyló*
Salmon *Lazac*
Trout *Pisztráng*
Carp *Ponty*
Crab, prawn *Rák*
Tuna *Tonhal*

Salads (Savanyúság)
Beetroot *Cékla*
Lettuce salad *Fejes saláta*
Tomato *Paradicsom*
Cucumber *Uborka*
Mixed salad with mayonnaise *Vitamin saláta*

Vegetables (Zöldség)
Cauliflower *Karfiol*
Sweetcorn *Kukorica*
Lentils *Lencse*
Pepper *Paprika*
Carrot *Sárgarépa*
Green beans *Zöldbab*
Green peas *Zöldborsó*

Fruit (Gyümölcs)
Apple *Alma*
Melon *Dinnye*
Nut, walnut *Dió*
Strawberry *Eper*
Chestnut *Gesztenye*
Sour cherry *Meggy*
Orange *Narancs*
Peach *Őszibarack*
Apricot *Sárgabarack*
Plum *Szilva*

Drinks (Italok)
Mineral Water *Ásványvíz*
Wine *Bor*
Sweet wine *Édes bor*
White wine *Fehér bor*
Coffee *Kávé*
Orange juice *Narancslé*
Fruit brandy *Pálinka*
Sparkling wine *Pezsgő*
Beer *Sör*
Dry wine *Száraz bor*
Red wine *Vörös bor*

give it some ballast, but Hungarians do make richer, heavier soups that are perhaps best kept for bleak winter evenings.

In all likelihood, most of the main courses on offer in a restaurant will be pan- or deep-fried (after being breaded). Restaurateurs like this style of cooking because it is quick and can employ that Hungarian favourite, pork. Deep-frying the meat means there is the opportunity to fry chips alongside it. If you're guessing at this point that fried meat and potatoes is a common offering, you're right. This has its upside, though: deep-fried food is often hot, rather than merely lukewarm, as the Hungarians prefer it.

Fish-lovers won't need to be told twice to sample *fogas*, the delicate pike-perch that is unique to Lake Balaton. Other popular fish include *harcsa* (catfish), often stewed *paprikás* style; *pisztráng* (trout), usually farmed but a revelation when fresh from a stream, and *ponty* (carp), too often the generic species when the menu just says 'fish'. Diners should examine a map before ordering sea fish in this land-locked country. Hungarian has just one word – *rák* – for all crustacea, from shrimp to lobsters.

'Salad' is a usual accompaniment to a main course, but not salad as we know it. It could either be made out of a single vegetable in a light, oil-free dressing – such as tomato or sliced cucumber with sour cream – or consist of pickled gherkins, pickled peppers and pickled cabbage. A mixed salad with vinaigrette is a rare occurence, rarer still without grated cheese or pieces of ham. This is a particularly harsh blow for vegetarians, who will find little of interest in most Hungarian eateries – fried cheese and breaded mushrooms, served with tartar sauce, are the hardy perennials, though a better variety is slowly beginning to creep on to Magyar menus. Budapest's few dedicated vegetarian restaurants tend to be either dour (**Govinda**) or blissed-out (**Gandhi**), though international cuisine offers some other herbivorous options.

If you have room for dessert (given that portions are probably larger than you're used to), the traditional favourites are pancakes and bready, dumpling-like creations with cream or jam. A local oddity is that desserts and pasta dishes usually share the same section of the menu, so you have no guarantee that your dessert will be sweet. (Other oddities include serving ketchup with pizza, and calling anything with corn in it 'Mexican'.)

BEYOND BULL'S BLOOD

Hungary is a wine-producer. At one end of the spectrum, this means cheap spritzers in the corner *borozó* (*see chapter* **Pubs & Bars**). At the other it means some wines which, after a post-communist influx of western investment and expertise, are a fine accompaniment to a good meal. Hungarians, however, aren't fussy about what to drink with

which kind of food and won't comment on, say, white wine with beef stew: order whatever you think suits you best. Here are some suggestions about what to look for, but understand that you're unlikely to find many bargains on a restaurant wine list.

At the lighter end of the white wine list will be Szürkebarát (Pinot Gris) and Leányka, the latter usually from Eger. Powerfully fragrant and blossomy dry Muskotály (Muscat Ottonel) is also worth a try. The Lake Balaton region produces medium-bodied Olasz Rízling (Italian Riesling) plus all the major white wines (look for Figula, Szeremley and Legli). The worldwide Chardonnay craze cannot be escaped in Hungary, either.

Kékfrankos (Blaufrankisch) and Kékoportó (Blauportugieser) are Hungary's most widely grown young reds. Both are natural pairings with traditional Hungarian dishes. Standard reds such as Merlot and Cabernet Sauvignon will also appear on the menu. Gorgeous, hefty blends (Le Sommelier, Bock, Gere & Weninger) are usually Cabernet-based and go well with hearty dishes and red meat, as does Bull's Blood (known in Hungary as Egri Bikavér) which is primarily Kékfrankos blended with several other varieties.

Hungary also has an excellent range of dessert wines: Tokaji Aszu, from the Tokaj region. The higher the *puttony* number, which ranges from three to six, the sweeter the wine. It simply indicates the number of baskets – puttony – of nobly-rotted grapes used to make it.

After the meal espresso coffee of variable quality is almost compulsory; if you want to accompany it with a digestive, the local clear brandies (*pálinka*) or the local bitter Unicum should be a cheap and cheerful choice.

Tipping is expected (often irrespective of quality of service); 10-15 per cent is the norm, though if the attention you received didn't please you, by all means give the exact sum only. Many restaurants have begun adding a service charge to the bill on the quiet, hoping to collect an extra tip on top. Examine the bill closely for this trickery.

Once the dining room staff notice a foreigner, they will probably do what they can to help negotiate the menu. Don't be afraid to experiment – you never know what discoveries await you.

Top-range

Dominican Restaurant Hilton

I. Hilton Hotel, Hess András ter 1-3 (488 6757). Várbusz from M2 Moszkva tér/bus 16. **Open** *summer* 7pm-midnight daily; *winter* noon-3pm, 7pm-midnight daily. **Average** Ft4,000. **Credit** AmEx, DC, JCB, MC, V. English spoken. **Map A3**
Solid and reliable hotel restaurant cooking, with stiff service compensated by the view and surroundings. This place is dear but predictably so, and therefore

less of a risk than other Castle District possibilities. Good venue for business lunch: the set menu is served swiftly but without rushing you.

Gundel

XIV. Állatkerti út 2 (321 3550/fax 342 2917). M1 Hősök tere/trolleybus 72, 75, 79. **Open** noon-4pm, 6.30pm-midnight, daily. **Average** Ft7,000. **Credit** AmEx, DC, MC, V. English spoken. **Map E1**
Still the city's most famous and elegant restaurant. Originally opened in 1894 as the Wampetics, it was

Let's have a butcher's

Hungarians often eat lunch at the *hentesáru* or butcher's shop. For one thing, it's cheap. Very cheap. And all Hungarians eat *kolbász* (smoked sausage) and there is only one place to eat kolbász besides your own kitchen: the butcher's shop.

Disregard the menu listing and look around for the steaming trays and vats containing the day's offerings. You will usually find kolbász, which looks a lot like, well, a sausage. It is best boiled (*főtt*) or roasted (*sült*). You may also find shorter links of *debreceni kolbász*, a spicier version native to the eastern plains. Often there are virsli (hot dogs), *szafaládé* and *krinolin* (*knockwursts*). There may be *főtt tarja* (steamed smoked ham) or maybe *főtt fej* (boiled pig's head). A grease-filled tray may contain shrivelled *hurka*, either the black *véres* or grey *májas* (blood filled or liver filled, mixed with spiced rice.) Blood hurka resembles the black puddings of northern England while liver hurka is none other than the pricey Louisiana boudin in Magyar guise.

Order by specifying the amount you wish. '*Tiz deka kolbászt, kérek*' and you get a snack portion of 100 grams of sausage. Twenty dekas (*húsz deka*) is a lunch-sized serving. Bread (*kenyér*), rolls (*zsemle*) and mustard (*mustár*) are classic accompaniments, but there are also bowls of pickled cucumbers (*uborka*) and vinegared peppers (*ecetes paprika*). The butcher will tally up your order on a sheet of paper, which you then take to the cashier, pay, and return it to the person at the counter.

It takes skill to stack and carry your messy purchase to the nearby counter. Most Hungarians carry a pocket knife for alfresco butcher's shop dining. Sausages, particularly debreceni kolbász, have a tendency to splatter indelible paprika grease, so take care.

taken over in 1910 by chef Károly Gundel. He proceeded to Frenchify Hungarian cuisine, inventing many now standard dishes, such as the ubiquitous Gundel pancakes. A tourist trap under Communism, in 1991 it was acquired by Hungarian-American restaurateur George Lang and given a multimillion-dollar makeover with the aim of recreating the glory days. It's a huge place, in an Art Nouveau mansion by the Zoo, with a ballroom, garden and terrace, and several private dining rooms as well as the large main room hung with paintings by Hungarian masters. Tables are laid with Zsolnay porcelain and sterling silver and the gypsy band is slick.

The menu is, not surprisingly, a little old-fashioned, and starters and desserts tend to outshine the main courses, but award-winning chef Kálmán Kalla has created fine versions of Hungarian standards, and Hungarianised versions of international dishes, such as the Tournedos Franz Liszt, made with local goose liver. A long and authoritative list of Hungarian wines is rounded off with excellent sweet Tokaj from the restaurant's own vineyard. Service is smooth and formal (tending towards self-satisfied when the owner is out of town), and dining at Gundel is always a memorable experience.

Irene Légrádi Antique

V. Bárczy István utca 3-5 (266 4993). M1, M2, M3 Deák tér/tram 47, 49. **Open** noon-3pm, 7pm-midnight Mon-Fri. **Average** Ft 4,000. **Credit** AmEx, DC, MC, V. English spoken. **Map C4**
Difficult to find (it's hidden in an antique shop – take the staircase opposite the door), this special restaurant is elegant and comfortable, with heavy antique furniture and waiters wearing tails. The hors d'oeuvres trolley selection is limited but represents a nice taster of the best of Hungarian cooking, including fish terrine, foie gras, steak tartare and quails' eggs. The main courses include pork stuffed with goose liver, excellent steaks and a wide selection of game and local fish. Gypsy music in the evenings.

Légrádi Testvérek

V. Magyar utca 23 (318 6804). M3 Kálvin tér/tram 47, 49. **Open** 6pm-midnight Mon-Sat. **Average** Ft4,000. **Credit** AmEx. English spoken. **Map D5**
Owned by Hungary's answer to the Roux brothers and one of the oldest upscale restaurants in town. The basement is a comfortable drawing room that serves very similar Franco-Hungarian food to its sister restaurant, **Irene Légrádi Antique** (*above*), though with a more formal setting and style.

Robinson

XIV. Városliget, tósziget (343 0955). M1 Hősök tere. **Open** noon-4pm, 6pm-midnight, daily. **Average** Ft5,000. Credit AmEx, DC, JCB, MC, V. English spoken. **Map E1**
So-called because it's situated on an 'island' (about a yard from the shore) in the Városliget duckpond, Robinson is a living reproach to the 'location, location, location' theory of restaurant management. In spite of its wonderful waterside terrace and its occasionally inspired kitchen, this place just doesn't get

it together enough to constitute what makes a good restaurant. The menu veers wildly from cheap and plain to expensive and incomprehensible, the service is bumbling at very best, the wines are exorbitant, and on any occasion the customer can expect to find mysterious and uncalled-for charges on the bill. At one time it was considered Budapest's best restaurant by many knowledgeable critics. It has an enormous distance to cover if it is to win that title again.

Szindbád
V. Markó utca 33 (332 2966/132 2749/fax 112 3836). M3 Nyugati/tram 4, 6. **Open** noon-3.30pm, 6.30pm-midnight, Mon-Fri; 6pm-midnight Sat, Sun. **Average** Ft4,000. **Credit** AmEx, DC, MC, V. English spoken. **Map C2**
In Budapest's business district and very much a business venue. The bar area (which they refer to as 'the club') is full of heavy Chesterfields and the dining room is comfortable in a formal sort of way. The menu contains a few surprises but emphasises Hungarian international cuisine, and this the chefs do very well. Perhaps a little formal to relax *à deux*, but very good for an important business dinner. Attentive and clever service.

Vadrózsa
II. Pentelei Molnár utca 15 (326 5817). Bus 11, 91. **Open** noon-3pm, 7pm-midnight, daily. **Average** Ft4,000. **Credit** AmEx, DC, MC, V. English spoken.
In a beautiful small villa halfway up the Rózsadomb, this was once one of the few top-flight restaurants in Budapest, but is these days past its best. The custom of eschewing a written menu, instead inviting guests to choose from a plateful of raw ingredients such as goose liver, fogas, wild boar, venison, filet mignon and Russian caviar, harks back to black market days when so much fine produce was something pretty special. The resulting meals are well-prepared but a mite plain. Elegant garden for summer dining.

Mid-range

Adria Grill
II. Zilah utca 9 (356 2291). Bus 49. **Open** noon-midnight daily. **Average** Ft3,500. **Credit** AmEx, EC, MC, V. English spoken.
A modern villa in a smart residential area, Adria's main attraction is its nicely maintained garden. All the more peculiar is the fact that Adria's interior is decorated with plastic flowers. As for the food on offer, vast Balkan-style grills are the specialities, and the potato soup is a meal in itself.

Articsóka
VI Zichy Jenő utca 17 (302 7757). M1 Opera/M3 Arany János utca. **Open** noon-midnight daily. **Average** Ft3,500. **Credit** DC, MC, V. English spoken. **Map D3**
Music, theatre, fashion shows and Budapest's poseurs all compete for attention in this yuppie hangout. Food is Mediterranean-influenced Modern European cuisine, and although vegetarians get a

Feszek – *cloistered dining. See page 147.*

look in, it is biased towards expensive seafood and ranges from the elegantly understated to the pretentious. So, with its straight-backed, painted wooden chairs, ceramic wine coolers and tropical palms, do the surroundings. Occasionally a fun place, and probably better for lunch than dinner, but not to be taken too seriously.

Avant Garde
V. Sas utca 4. 266 1332. M1, M2, M3 Deák tér/tram 47, 49. **Open** 11am-midnight Mon-Fri; 11am-3am Sat. **Average** Ft2,000. **No credit cards**. English spoken. **Map C3**
The latest attempt at a French bistro in Budapest looks better than it really is, but it's large, vaguely trendy, reasonably priced and open late, and to expect haute cuisine in these circumstances seems foolishly optimistic. The French onion soup resembles no other we've ever eaten and rather sets the tone of the place, but if you order carefully you can get an acceptable dinner with acceptable service – expect bistro classics such as Parma ham and melon and steak with pepper sauce. Extensive cocktail list, which might well be what it is all about.

Bagolyvár
XIV. Állatkerti út 2 (321 3550). M1 Hősök tere. **Open** noon-11pm daily. **Average** Ft2,000. **Credit** AmEx, DC, V. English spoken. **Map E1**
In a mock Transylvanian castle attached to the Gundel and owned by the same people – locals refer to it as 'Junior Gundel'. It's run by women because proprietor George Lang reckons they're the best home cooks, and this place is all about home cooking. The menu varies daily and features some very good soups and other basic offerings such as roulade of fresh breads, served with various spreads, that is part of the starter.

Biarritz

V. Kossuth Lajos tér 18 (311 4413). Tram 2. **Open**
noon-midnight daily. **Average** Ft2,300. **Credit**
AmEx, DC, JCB, MC, V. English spoken. **Map C2**
Fashionable and centrally located restaurant with
innovative Hungarian and Modern European menu.
The presentation of the food is attractive yet unpretentious. Biarritz's location near the White House, the
riverside office building that houses MPs, ensures a
steady stream of custom, attracted as much by the
pleasant terrace as the high-quality food.

Café Kör

V. Sas utca 17 (311 0053). M3 Arany Janos utca.
Open 10am-10pm Mon-Sat. **Average** Ft2,000. **No
credit cards.** English spoken. **Map C3**
With a comfortable, bistro-like atmosphere more
reminiscent of Vienna or Berlin than Budapest, Café
Kör has a great bar and some small café tables as
well as more a formal dining space. Furnishings
have been chosen with care and a simple Hungarian
international menu is complemented by daily specials. Service can be slow but is generally friendly
and knowledgeable. One of the few places in Hungary
to offer a truly top-notch steak. Excellent grilled goat's
cheese is one of the few vegetarian options. Good spot
for breakfast, served until 11.30am.

Carmel Pince

*VII. Dob utca 31; entrance from Kazinczy utca (322
1834/342 4585). M2 Astoria.* **Open** noon-11pm
daily. **Average** Ft2,000. **Credit** AmEx, DC, JCB,
MC, V. English spoken. **Map D4**
The sign announces that this is not a Kosher restaurant but, right next door to the Orthodox synagogue,
it is defiantly Jewish – and maybe plays up the fact
just a little too much. The vaulted cellar is comfortable and shows the maturity of age, with an easy
ambience afforded by stained glass and interesting
knick-knacks. The food is traditional Hungarian
Jewish, with goose as the speciality. Cooking is dull
but satisfactory and the service normally helpful.

Cosmo

*V. Kristóf tér 7-8 (266 4747). M1 Vörösmarty
tér/tram 2.* **Open** noon-4pm, 4.30pm-midnight, daily.
Average Ft3,000. **Credit** Amex, DC, JCB, MC, V.
English spoken. **Map C4**
Above the **Cyrano** (*see below*) and owned by the
same people, this new addition to the restaurant
scene aims at a more businessy crowd than its sister establishment. Its elegant surroundings and creative new European menu show promise, and
though you don't need to book at the time of writing, you probably will have to soon. Nice terrace.

Cyrano

V. Kristóf tér 7-8 (266 3096). M1 Vörösmarty tér.
Open noon-3pm, 5pm-midnight, daily. **Average**
Ft2,800. **Credit** AmEx, DC, MC. Some English
spoken. **Map C4**
Just off the brash end of Váci and one of the few
places to dine in that neighbourhood that doesn't
constitute a bad mistake. The menu is long – most-

ly French-accented Hungarian and international
dishes with some vegetarian options – and a little
pretentious. But if you like 'imaginative' food such
as peach stuffed with Roquefort or duck breast in
soy and honey you shouldn't be disappointed. The
main room is beautiful, crowned with the chandelier
used in Depardieu's movie of the same name. In summer the terrace offers a vantage as passers-by pause
to splash in the small fountain outside. Booking recommended. Service poor enough to justify some
resentment at the swingeing 15 per cent service
charge slapped on the bill.

Haxen Király

VII. Király utca 100 (351 6793). Trolleybus 70, 78.
Open noon-midnight daily. **Average** Ft2,100.
Credit EC, MC, V. English spoken. **Map E3**
Authentic and entertaining Bavarian restaurant that
serves delicious pig hocks spit-roasted in full view
of the assembled carnivores. Both the limited starter
selection and the main courses are all about meat
and lots of it. The hocks are the speciality; one
between two is a massive portion of high-fat food.
At least nobody around you will be muttering about
cholesterol – they will just be tucking in and enjoying themselves.

Kéhli

*III. Mókus utca 22 (250 4241). HÉV Árpád híd/tram
1.* **Open** 6pm-midnight Mon-Fri; 10am-midnight Sat,
Sun. **Average** Ft2,000. **Credit** AmEx, DC, EC, MC,
V. Some English spoken.
Set in ghastly Socialist-realist surroundings, this is
rated by many as Budapest's best Hungarian restaurant. The main area with its gypsy band is difficult
to get into without booking, but there are several
other rooms in which to perch (though do try to
avoid the awful cellar with red plastic candles and
armchair-style seating). One of the specialities is a
rich bone marrow soup: first drink the soup, then
scrape out the marrow and spread it on toast with
garlic. Portions are mountainous. Raucous but competent band, and generally excellent value.

Kisbuda Gyöngye

III. Kenyeres utca 34 (368 6402). Tram 17. **Open**
noon-midnight Mon-Sat. **Average** Ft3,000. **Credit**
AmEx, DC, EC, MC, V. Some English spoken.
A sidestreet favourite with Óbuda locals, the 'Pearl
of Kisbuda' is part of the standard restaurant circuit
for visitors to town. Walls are panelled with parts
of old wardrobes and the seating is an assortment
of old and not always terribly comfortable kitchen
chairs. A pretty run-of-the-mill Hungarian menu
with some interesting daily specials. The venison fillet with wild mushrooms and brandy sauce is a real
plateful and demonstrates the best of the perhaps
rather overrated kitchen.

Múzeum

*VIII. Múzeum körút 12 (267 0375). M3 Kálvin
tér/tram 47, 49.* **Open** 10.30am-1.30am Mon-Sat.
Average Ft3,000. **Credit** AmEx. English spoken.
Map D4

Cosmo – *elegant surroundings and creative new European menu.*

High ceilings, tiled walls, tall windows providing plenty of light and well-spaced tables embellish the fin-de-siècle ambience at the ever-popular Múzeum, next to the National Museum and founded in 1885. The menu is impressive, with an enormous difference in price from one dish to another – you can easily spend a fortune in here or you can dine quite cheaply. The Hungarian and international food is carefully prepared, but presentation (artfully done to make vast portions resemble nouvelle cuisine) just occasionally wins out over culinary good taste. Smooth service and the pleasant surroundings keep this old place buzzing. Good spot for late dining.

Portside

VII. Dohány utca 7 (351 8405, 351 8406). M2 Astoria/tram 47, 49/bus 7. **Open** noon-2am Mon-Thur, Sun; noon-4am Fri, Sat; food served until midnight daily. **Average** Ft2,000. **Credit** AmEx, V. English spoken. **Map D4**

One of Budapest's best British-style pubs also offers some of the best food in the Modern European vein in its price bracket. Portions are large, carefully prepared, beautifully presented and served by friendly, efficient staff. If you think that they can't serve a decent steak in Hungary (an accusation by and large true), try one here. Loud music and heaving crowds by the middle of the evening means that the Portside is a better lunch venue.

Remiz

II. Budakeszi út 5 (275 1396). Bus 22. **Open** 9am-midnight daily. **Average** Ft3,000. **Credit** AmEx, DC, MC, V. English spoken.

Smugly aware of its enviable reputation for the wonderful sheltered garden and separate grill kitchen, which churns out summer barbie-type food. There are a few vegetarian dishes, the salads aren't bad by Hungarian standards, and the Russian caviar is the cheapest in town. The grills, proudly served from wooden platters, tend to be cremated rather than cooked. Patchy service.

Budget

Bohémtanya

VI. Paulay Ede utca 6 (267 3504). M1, M2, M3 Deák tér/tram 47, 49. **Open** noon-11pm daily. **Average** Ft1,500. **No credit cards**. Some English spoken. **Map D3**

The owners accidentally killed off the eponymous Bohemian atmosphere during a recent renovation, and this venerable student hangout now resembles something dire and Austrian, with attendance down accordingly. A shame, but at least you can now get in without problems and enjoy the cooking, which is as good, plentiful and inexpensive as it has always been. In case you need reminding that breaded deep-fried food can actually taste and smell good, this is the place for you. The Wiener schnitzel (*Bécsi szelet* on the menu) is a triumph of the genre and gets a plate to itself: the accompanying potatoes and optional salad travel separately.

La Bodega. *See page 150.*

Claudia Restaurant

V. Bástya utca 27-29 (267 0329). M3 Kalvin tér/tram 47, 49. **Open** noon-11pm Mon-Fri; noon-midnight Sat, Sun. **Average** Ft1,300. **Credit** AmEx, DC, MC, JCB, V. English spoken. **Map D5**

Average-to-good traditional Hungarian food in a distended sub-basement in the backstreets of District V. Portions large and soups especially good. The steak tartare is also worth trying even if you let the waiter mix it: ketchup and salt get no more than a cursory look-in. A well-kept secret, given its extremely central location.

Fatál

V. Váci utca 67; entrance in Pintér utca (266 2607). Tram 2. **Open** 11.30am-2am daily. **Average** Ft1,500. **No credit cards.** Some English spoken. **Map C5**

The name means 'wooden platter', and Fatál is a country-style restaurant with mock stained-glass windows serving dauntingly large portions of well-prepared traditional food in a variety of fearsome-looking receptacles. There are even a few vegetarian choices, though these involve lots of batter. Great value but indifferent service. Popular with locals; booking essential.

Fészek

VII. Kertész utca 36; corner of Dob utca (322 6043). Tram 4, 6. **Open** noon-1am daily. **Average** Ft1,500. **Credit** AmEx, EC, MC, V. Some English spoken. **Map D3**

An artists' club since the turn of the century but in practice open to anyone (with a Ft200 entrance fee in the evening), Fészek offers stylish dining at bargain prices. The ornate high-ceilinged main room is attractive enough, but the real bonus is the appealingly dilapidated Venetian-style courtyard, formerly a monks' cloister and one of the most beautiful places in central Pest to while away a long summer lunchtime. Service can be slow and inaccurate and the menu is simply too extensive to excel at anything, but the price is right and the atmosphere is relaxing and unique.

Marquis de Salade

VI. Hajós utca 43 (302 4086). M3 Nyugati. **Open** 11am-midnight daily. **Average** Ft1,800. **No credit cards.** English spoken. **Map C3**

Big selection of salads, augmented by assorted dishes from Italy, China, north Africa, Bangladesh and the former Soviet Union. A better spot for lunch than a sit-down dinner, especially considering the Ft750 special day-time deals, but vegetarians will sigh with relief at any time. The steaks push up the average price; it's possible to eat here very cheaply.

Márkus Vendéglő

II Lövőház utca 17 (212 3153). M2 Moszkva tér/tram 18, 59. **Open** 11am-1am Mon-Sat; noon-midnight Sun. **Average** Ft1,300. **Credit** MC, V. Some English spoken. **Map A2**

Offers the standard rich soups, pickled salads, *főzelék* (vegetable porridge), breaded deep-fried meat dishes with chips, and invariable pancakes for

Tüköry Söröző – see page 149.

dessert that are the antithesis of modern healthy cooking, but that, on a cold winter's day, are just what you are crying out for. The food court of the neighbouring **Mamut Center** (*see chapter* **Shopping & Services**) may yet sound the death knell to this venerable old establishment. Try and go while you still can.

Művész Bohém Kávéház

XIII. Vigszínház utca 3 (339 8008). M3 Nyugati/tram 2, 4, 6. **Open** 11am-11pm Mon-Sat. **Average** Ft1,800. **No credit cards.** Some English spoken. **Map C2**

Romantic venue behind the **Vigszínház** (*see chapter* **Theatre & Dance**), decked out with old posters and photos of former stars, plus an assortment of knick-knacks and antique furnishings that fall just the right side of twee. The food is Hungarian with a Bohemian accent – hearty soups, meat, poultry and fish dishes, plus the odd vegetarian dish. Not earth-shaking cuisine, but a lovely place and good value.

Náncsi Néni

II. Ördögárok út 80 (376 5809). Tram 56 then bus 157. **Open** noon-11pm daily. **Average** Ft1,800. **Credit** AmEx, MC, V. English spoken.

City-dwellers flock here at weekends, pretending it is in the country, although actually it is now well into suburbia. Both location and food retain a rustic charm, with a leafy garden, extravagant portions and reasonable prices. The food is Hungarian home cooking. Excellent soups and the *túrós gombóc* dessert – a cannonball-sized dumpling stuffed with cottage cheese – are the specialities, along with a few out-of-place seafood options. Notably child-friendly.

Szilvakék Paradicsom

XIII. Pannónia utca 5-7 (349 2599). Tram 2, 4, 6.
Open noon-midnight daily. **Average** Ft1,800.
Credit AmEx, MC, V. Some English spoken. **Map**
C2
Extraordinarily eclectic menu – Hungarian, Italian,
Greek, American and even Mexican dishes, including some decent vegetarian options – served up in a
pub-style setting, with summer tables outside.

Tüköry Söröző

V. Hold utca 15 (269 5027). M3 Arany János utca.
Open 11am-11pm Mon-Fri. **Average** Ft700. **No**
credit cards. Some English spoken. A cheap restaurant rather than the beer hall its name
suggests. Tables fill from around noon. Grab one by
the window and watch shoppers come and go at the
indoor market next door. Menu changes weekly.

Étkezdék

The *Étkezde* is a small, cheap and often family-run
places that provides simple home cooking. It will
have few vegetarian options but offers a hearty
lunch for between Ft450-700 for two courses.

Bécsi Szelet

VIII. Üllői út 16A (267 4937). M3 Kálvin tér. **Open**
noon-11pm daily. **Average** Ft1,000. **No credit**
cards. Some English spoken. **Map D5**
One of a brace of cheap eateries which exist to serve
those addicted to Wiener schnitzel, priding itself on
the '23cm slice' to the exclusion of everything else.
Garnish is boiled spuds in parsley, a chunk of lemon
and a smile. You'll either love it or hate it. Home
deliveries (0630 933 9951) arrive in large pizza-style
boxes and are a pleasing carnivorous alternative.
Branch: VII. Király utca 69 (351 6043).

Green's Söröző & Főzelékbár

VII. Dob utca 3 (352 8515). M1, M2, M3 Deák
tér/tram 47, 49. **Open** 11am-midnight daily.
Average Ft900. **Credit** DC. Some English spoken.
Map D4
This compact cellar eatery is in the crossover area
between *étkezde* and restaurant, and offers the
opportunity to sample that curiously Hungarian
phenomenon, *főzelék*, a vegetable stew thickened
with flour and usually sour cream, served either by
itself or with a (usually fried) accompaniment –
sausage, eggs or mushrooms, say. (Be aware that
though vegetable based, főzelék often uses animal
fat.) Green's also serves Hungarian standards and
seamlessly turns into a pub at night.

Happy Bank

V. Bank utca 4 (no phone). M3 Arany János utca.
Open 11am-9pm Mon-Fri. **Average** Ft1,100. **No**
credit cards. Some English spoken. **Map C3**
Fast downtown lunch venue (fast, that is, unless you
are in a hurry) popular with local office workers.
Silly high stools and long tables provide an uncomfortable perch to eat your pasta. Good value, acceptable quality, served piping hot – rare in Hungary.

Házias Étkezde

I. Várfok utca 8 (315 2931). Várbusz from M2
Moszkva tér/bus 16. **Open** noon-5pm Mon-Fri; noon-4pm Sat. **Average** Ft600. **No credit cards**. Some
English spoken. **Map A3**
Five minutes' walk from the Castle District, Házias
is a tiny eatery with a limited menu and no alcohol.
The food is standard, but you will welcome the lack
of tourist kitsch.

Kádár Étkezde

VII. Klauzál utca 10 (no phone). Trolleybus 74. **Open**
11.30am-3.30pm Tue-Fri. **Average** Ft600. **No**
credit cards. Some English spoken. **Map D3**
Signed celebrity photos plastering the walls testify
to Kádár's former glory. Menu changes daily to keep
the regulars' interest, with a fair selection of puddings. Pay at the cash desk by the door.

Kisharang Étkezde

VI. Október 6 utca 17 (269 3861). M3 Arany János
utca. **Open** 11am-9pm Mon-Fri; 11am-4.30pm Sat,
Sun. **Average** Ft700. **No credit cards**. Some
English spoken. **Map D3**
'The Little Bell' bustles near Budapest's business
quarter: quick, clean and efficient. Main dishes are
not for the meek and are served with rice, parsley
potatoes and salad. They can be ordered in half-portions or the staff will lovingly wrap leftovers for a
small extra charge.

Fast food

Eating on the hoof is a daily necessity for many
Hungarians, a fact not lost on American fast-food
chains which dominate downtown Budapest.
Small bakery kiosks sell cheap snacks at main
metro stations. The gyros (also known as shawarma and döner) gains popularity daily, as does its
vegetarian sibling, the falafel. Look for the familiar revolving vertical spit. Indigenous Hungarian
fast food outlets have all but disappeared in
Budapest, but you should still find *lángos* (fried
dough) and *kolbász* (boiled or fried sausage). *See*
page 140 **Let's have a butcher's.**

Duran Szendvics

V. Bajcsy-Zsilinszky út 7 (267 9624). M3 Arany
János utca. **Open** 8am-6pm Mon-Fri; 9am-1pm Sat.
No credit cards. Some English spoken. **Map C3**
Viennese *Imbiß* (snack) chain offering more than 20
kinds of small, delicately-made, canapé-style open
sandwiches at around Ft75 per piece. Excellent
capuccino. Takeaway boxes for up to 25 items.
Branch: VI. Október 6 utca 15 (332 9348).

Házi Rétes

VII. Király utca 70 (no phone). Tram 4, 6 Király
utca. **Open** 9am-7pm Mon-Fri; 9am-3pm Sat. **No**
credit cards. Some English spoken. **Map D3**
As the sign says, 'Ahogy Nagymama Sütött' – just
how grandma used to make. The best takeaway
strudel in Budapest: apple, cherry, plum and cabbage at around Ft70 a throw.

LÁNGOS, BÜFÉ

ALAPÍTVA: „1987"

Lángos – dyspepsia to go.

Lángos
V. Hold utca market. M3 Arany Janos utca. **Open** 8am-2.30pm daily. **No credit cards**. Some English spoken. **Map C3**
Serves that characteristically Hungarian fried-dough snack, *lángos*. Choose your topping from the extraordinary photo-menu on the wall. Even the fanciest won't set you back more than Ft150 and will keep you happily dyspeptic for hours. Definitely worth sampling at least once.

Marie Kristensen Sandwich Bar
IX. Ráday utca 7 (218 1673). M3 Kálvin tér/tram 47, 49. **Open** 8am-9pm Mon-Fri; 11am-8pm Sat. **No credit cards**. English spoken. **Map D5**
Budapest's first sandwich bar, and a little pricey at that, but worth the occasional indulgence given the general lack of breakfast options elsewhere.

Pizza Kuckó
VII. Károly körút 6 (no phone). M2 Astoria/tram 47, 49/bus 7, 9. **Open** 9am-9pm Mon-Fri; 9am-2pm Sat. **No credit cards**. Some English spoken. **Map D4**
Popular Hungarian pizza slice takeaway. Assorted varieties, often served painfully slowly.

Pizza Mix
V. Mérleg utca 10 (317 3579). Tram 2. **Open** 11am-10pm daily. **No credit cards**. Some English spoken. **Map C3**
Order by filling in a form at the counter specifying the (single or double) toppings of your choice. A large pizza is Ft520 plus Ft30 per topping and is a lot better that you have any right to expect at the price. Eat-in, delivery and takeaway all possible.

Szultán Büfé
VII. Király utca 80 (351 8987). Tram 4, 6 Király utca. **Open** 11am-10pm Mon-Sat. **No credit cards**. Some English spoken. **Map D3**
Cheap Turkish fast-food fare, with an excellent *çorba* soup well worth Ft200, and bread and tea for free. Can get cramped and humid.

Szendvics Bár Center
VI. Teréz körút 46 (302 5242). M3 Nyugati/tram 4, 6. **Open** 9am-3am daily. **Average** Ft600. **No credit cards**. Some English spoken. **Map D2**
These Thai sandwich bars must rank as the oddest additions to the lunch scene, but try them: you won't be disappointed by the excellent made-to-order sandwiches combining familiar and unfamiliar ingredients, both to take away and eat in. Stir-fried fast food also available. Crowded at lunchtime, but the turnover's very fast.
Branch: VI. Rákóczi út 8A (302 5242).

The world on your plate
The Americas

Iguana
V. Zoltán utca 16 (331 4352). M3 Arany Janos utca/tram 2. **Open** 11.30am-1am daily. **Average** Ft2,400. **Credit** AmEx, EC, MC, V. English spoken. **Map C3**
This American-owned Tex-Mex joint is expat central and you'll hear more English than Hungarian spoken by those who come to sample the flexible menu of margaritas and Mexican standards. It's a big place in a good location: a quiet street off Szabadság tér. The food is merely average, and when the owners aren't present the service can be dreadful. Nonetheless, a fun and popular place that seems to do its best.

La Bodega
VII. Wesselényi utca 35 (267 5056). Tram 4, 6. **Open** noon-1am Mon-Sat; 6pm-1am Sun. **Average** Ft2,000. **Credit** DC, MC, V. English spoken. **Map D4**
A Spanish/South American haunt boasting good but meaty dishes (including meat in the salads), live Latin music and 22 kinds of tequila. Friendly management and plenty of atmosphere. South American wines and genuine *maté* available.

Leroy's Country Pub
XIII. Visegrádi utca 50 (340 3316). M3 Lehel tér. **Open** noon-2am daily. **Average** Ft2,300. **Credit** AmEx, EC, MC, V. Some English spoken. **Map C1**
American theme bar decked with old enamel signs, wire netting and ramshackle furniture. The clientele tend to be local 'entrepreneurs' who double-park as near to the door as possible and spend their time on mobile phones. A gangland bomb carved a crater outside Leroy's in 1997. Despite all this, the food is wholesome, the steaks are among the best in Budapest, there are vegetarian options, the service is good and there is normally a buzz in the air.

Asian

Chan-Chan
V. Só utca 3 (318 4266). Tram 47, 49. **Open** noon-11pm daily. **Average** Ft3,200. **Credit** AmEx, MC, V. English spoken. **Map D5**

Run by Laotians, this Thai restaurant occupies a generous cellar space decked with fishtanks, Buddhist tat and signed photographs of celebrity diners. The menu is extensive and meat-heavy, but includes a large assortment of prawn, squid and fish dishes and a modest vegetarian selection. The overall quality has perhaps begun to sag somewhat, though the soups are good and the spring rolls are said to be the finest in Hungary.

Hong Kong Pearl Garden
II. Margit körút 2 (212 3131). Tram 4, 6. **Open** noon–11pm daily. **Average** Ft2,500. **Credit** AmEx, EC, DC, V. Some English spoken. **Map B2**
The huge mural of the Hong Kong skyline is a mite tacky and the huge room authentically recreates the slightly intimidating feel of a Kowloon restaurant, but this place offers some of the best Chinese food in town. The extensive menu spans many regional styles, with a big selection of seafood, excellent duck, lobster fresh from the tank by the door and a couple of interesting vegetarian items.

Mekong
VII. Rózsa utca 39 (351 5649). M1 Vörösmarty utca. **Open** noon–11pm daily. **Average** Ft 1,600. **Credit** AmEx, MC, V. English spoken. **Map E3**
This Thai/Vietnamese eatery is, like **Chan-Chan** (*above*) run by Laotians (why Laotians choose not to cook their own cuisine abroad is a mystery) and but for inept and frustrating service provided by the Hungarian waiting staff would actually rate as fair in both styles. Thai spring rolls and Vietnamese lettuce rolls are good, as are the Thai curries and the Vietnamese *phò* (though the bowl is rather small). Rather gloomy at times, but not bad.

Paradise Chinese Restaurant
V. Szabadsajtó út 6 (266 4541). M3 Ferenciek tere/bus 7. **Open** 11.30am–11.30pm daily. **Average** Ft2,500. **Credit** AmEx, JCB, MC, V. English spoken. **Map C4**
Reassuringly full of portly Chinese families sitting at the large round tables most early evenings. The waiters, who know their way around the menu, all speak English and are genuinely helpful, even in matters such as having the kitchen cut back MSG levels. The food – cheaper than at most downtown Chinese restaurants – is average, although a few of the 'special' dishes are inspired and the Peking duck is close enough to the real thing to merit ordering. Stunningly tasteless waterfall mural.

Seoul House
I. Fő utca 8 (201 7452). Tram 19/bus 86, 105. **Open** noon–11pm Mon-Sat. **Average** Ft2,500. **Credit** AmEx, DC, MC, V. English spoken. **Map B3**
The only place in town for Korean food. Ghastly Seoul Olympics décor and poor lighting can't detract from the excellence of the food, or the table-top barbecues, which allow those in the know to order strange and wonderful dishes to cook themselves. Like Korean places the world over, not really suitable for vegetarians and too pricey for every day.

Shiki Japanese Restaurant
II. Zsigmond tér 8 (335 4249). Tram 17. **Open** noon–3pm, 6pm–11pm, daily. **Average** Ft3,000. **No credit cards**. Some English spoken.
Managed by Hungarians and comparing well to the places under Japanese management – a fact attested by the number of Japanese businessmen who always seem to be tucking in. They are here for the sushi and sashimi prepared in the open-plan kitchen, but equally good (and cheaper) are the tempura, yakitori or steaks. Drinks are pretty expensive, but you can always have a pre-prandial bevvy in one of the many bars nearby.

Sushi An
V. Harmincad utca 4 (317 4239). M1 Vörösmarty tér. **Open** noon–3.30pm, 5pm–10pm, daily. **Average** Ft2,200. **Credit** AmEx, DC, JCB, MC, V. English spoken. **Map C4**
Surprisingly good sushi and sashimi (Ft 350-Ft600 per piece) in this simple, clean, traditionally styled sushi bar right next to the British Embassy. Vegetarian seaweed rolls are also on the short menu, along with one excellent tofu dish. Attracts a cosmopolitan crowd including many Japanese. The food is good value but the alcohol is overpriced. The branch at the Hilton is done out to look like a Japanese garden.
Branch: Hilton Hotel, I.Hess Andras tér 1-3 (488 6861).

Simple, clean, traditional: **Sushi An.**

Tian Tan Chinese Restaurant

V. Duna utca 1 (318 6444). M3 Ferenciek tere.
Open noon-midnight daily. **Average** Ft2,500.
Credit AmEx, DC, JCB, MC, V. English spoken.
Map C4
With its labyrinthine interior of dark lacquer and
back-lit multicoloured panels, dotted with fountains,
fishtanks and jade sculptures, entering this place is
like stepping into some kind of fiendish Chinese
computer game. The menu is huge, with 14 categories of main course, including good duck and
shrimp and some tasty tofu variations, but by international standards the food is just competent rather
than outstanding. Possible to eat reasonably cheaply if you lay off the seafood.

Xi-Hu

V. Nádor utca 5 (267 0337). Tram 2. **Open** noon-
11pm daily. **Average** Ft2,500. **Credit** AmEx, DC,
MC, V. Some English spoken. **Map C3**
Probably Hungary's best Chinese restaurant, though
its charm has faded since the karaoke room was
closed. Vaguely Cantonese dishes (including a couple of dim sum favourites hidden at the end of the
menu) and good (but expensive) fish served by
Hungarian staff who know what they're doing. The
larger room with the round tables and lazy susans
is at the back. If you are sensitive to MSG, tell the
waiter in advance, because otherwise a lot is used.

Balkan/Middle Eastern

Al-Amir

*VII. Király utca 17 (352 1422). M1, M2, M3 Deák
tér/tram 47, 49.* **Open** 11am-11pm Mon-Sat; 1.30pm-
11pm Sun. **Average** Ft1,400. **No credit cards**,
cash only. English spoken. **Map D3**
Satisfactory Syrian offering fragrant Arab specialities and wonderful bread made on the premises. A
wide range of starters available, with grilled meats
and a limited number of vegetarian dishes to follow.
Salads a tad fatigued, good baklava and first-rate
cardamom-scented coffee, but no alcohol served.
Takeaway hatch on the street.

Falafel

*VI. Paulay Ede utca 53 (no phone). M1
Oktogon/tram 4, 6.* **Open** 10am-8pm Mon-Fri; 10am-
6pm Sat. **Average** Ft500. **No credit cards.** Some
English spoken. **Map D3**
Build your own falafel or fill your own salad bowl
from the excellent salad bar. Takeaway cartons
available if you feel like eating on a bench in nearby Liszt tér; otherwise tables upstairs. Excellent
value for money and healthy too.

Semiramis

*V. Alkotmány utca 20 (311 7627). M3 Nyugati/tram
4, 6.* **Open** noon-9pm Mon-Sat. **Average** Ft950. **No
credit cards.** Some English spoken. **Map C2**
Small, friendly Syrian joint offering the usual spread
of Middle Eastern stuff: lentil soup, lamb and chick-
en dishes, salads, kebabs. Cheap and cheerful without frills, pretensions or alcohol.

Shiraz Persian Sandwich Club

*IX. Ráday utca 21 (217 4547). M3 Kálvin tér/tram
47, 49.* **Open** 9am-midnight daily. **Average** Ft500.
No credit cards. Some English spoken. **Map D5**
Offers a selection of kebabs, falafel and gyros. The
more spacious sit-down sister restaurant round the
corner is decked out with Persian rugs and has a
more complex menu, many vegetarian options, and
water pipes with flavoured tobacco for Ft800.
Summer tables on Ráday utca serve both venues.
Branch: IX. Mátyás utca 22 (218 0881).

Taverna Dionysos

V. Belgrád rakpart 16 (318 1222). Tram 2, 47, 49.
Open noon-midnight daily. **Average** Ft2,000.
Credit AmEx, EC, MC, V. English spoken. **Map C5**
The whitewashed and blue interior is more Greek
than Greece; the riverside terrace, overlooking
Gellért Hill, can be noisy but boasts a unique view.
Service can be offhand, but it's a well-run place offer-
ing acceptable versions of Aegean standards. Non-
carnivores will enjoy picking among the starters.

French

Belgian Brasserie

*I. Bem rakpart 12 (201 5082). M2 Batthyány
tér/tram 19.* **Open** noon-midnight daily. **Average**
Ft1,200. **No credit cards.** English spoken. **Map B3**
Artfully placed to tempt the Francophiles that frequent the Institut Français, this looks the part and
serves Walloon classics such as carbonnade (a little
thin, perhaps) and brasserie food such as bavette
steak with Béarnaise and pommes pailles. Good, filling stuff with no ideas above its station. Stella Artois
and Hoegaarden on tap plus bottled Chimay, Leffe
and Duvel. *See chapter* **Pubs & Bars.**

Chez Daniel

VI. Szív utca 32 (302 4039). M1 Kodály körönd.
Open 11am-3pm, 6.30pm-11pm, daily **Average**
Ft3,000. **Credit** AmEx, DC, JCB, MC, V. English
spoken. **Map D2**
Once Budapest's best French restaurant, now sur-
passed but still worth a visit for its friendly atmosphere. The restaurant is in a six-table cellar space,
complemented in summer by a peaceful back courtyard (separate entrance to the left) that manages a
remarkably Mediterranean atmosphere despite an
assortment of *Brazil*-like ducts. The food – Gallic
standards with nouvelle leanings – is mostly seasonal stuff, so ignore the menu and go for the specials. Service is knowledgeable but shambolic.

La Bisquine

VII. Kertész utca 48 (no phone). Tram 4, 6. **Open**
noon-10pm Mon-Thur, Sun; noon-midnight Fri, Sat.
Average Ft500. **No credit cards.** Some English
spoken. **Map D3**
Small, agreeable creperie that imports buckwheat
flour to make a traditional Breton *galette*. There are
35 savoury options, plus another 30 or so sweet varieties, plus French cider to wash them down. Tables
upstairs, or you can eat around the bar.

Shiraz Persian Sandwich Club – *can you stomach it?*

La Fontaine

V. Mérleg utca 10 (317 3715). Tram 2. **Open** 10am-11pm daily. **Average** Ft2,000. **Credit** AmEx, MC, V. English spoken. **Map C3**
Beautiful spacious bistro with mirrors and long windows, but sadly a small and somewhat dreary French menu. With the exception of a couple of well-dressed salads, vegetarians may as well not bother turning up. The bar, shipped over especially from Paris along with most of the furniture, is La Fontaine's best feature. You're probably better off with a coffee and the dessert of the day than any full-blown meal, unless you're prepared to throw money at the problem.

Le Cardinal

V. Hercegprimás utca 18 (269 0220). M3 Arany Janos utca. **Open** noon-3pm, 6pm-11pm Mon-Sat. **Average** Ft3,000. **Credit** Amex, DC, MC, V. English spoken. **Map C3**
An unprepossessing entrance leads down to an elegantly outfitted cellar space with immaculately laid tables. Service is understated but authoritative and the food – traditional Île-de-France restaurant cooking with its carefully prepared sauces – doesn't usually disappoint, but the logistics, in particular the wine and apéritif supplies, need some working on. A decent but relatively pricey recreation of an elegant French restaurant.

Lou Lou

V. Vigyázó Ferenc utca 4 (312 4505). Tram 2. **Average** Ft 2,900. **Open** noon-3pm, 7pm-midnight, Mon-Fri; 7pm-midnight Sat-Sun. **Credit** AmEx. English spoken. **Map C3**

Maybe the cleverest current choice for dinner in Budapest. Dark green woodwork and pale ochre walls hung with old prints complement nouvelle-cuisine Franco-Hungarian food served in Hungarian-sized portions. Typical dishes are salmon steak with lemongrass sauce or rack of lamb in a parmesan jacket with tomato vinaigrette. Superb food, thoughtful wine list, charming place, agreeable service, and just seven tables. Booking essential.

Indian

Bombay Palace

VI. Andrássy út 44 (332 8363/331 3787). M1 Oktogon/tram 4, 6. **Open** noon-3pm, 6pm-11.30pm, daily. **Average** Ft3,500. **Credit** AmEx, DC, JCB, MC, V. English spoken. **Map D3**
Hungary's best Indian, but also its most formal and expensive. A branch of the international chain in suitably palatial premises with marble floors, chandeliers and almost too many service staff. The fare is usually good, displaying no particular regional bias. Fair tandoori selection but vegetarian options are the wiser choice for both quality and price and there's a fine basket of assorted naan breads.

Govinda

V. Belgrád rakpart 18 (318 1144). Tram 2, 2A. **Open** noon-9pm Tue-Sun. **Average** Ft 800. **No credit cards.** Some English spoken. **Map C5**
A Hare Krishna restaurant, offering an edible but drab Indian vegetarian set meal and little else of note except a decent home-made gingery lemonade. Nice location by the Danube, but no tables outside.

Shalimar

VII. Dob utca 50 (352 0297). Tram 4, 6. **Open**
noon-4pm, 6pm-midnight, daily. **Average** Ft2,000.
Credit AmEx, MC, V. English spoken. **Map D3**
In a cellar made to look Indian with assorted statues
and trinkets. The cooks are Indian and the waiting
staff Hungarian – meaning the service is useless
while the food is excellent, including tandoori dishes, eight types of bread and a host of vegetarian
options. Butter chicken and palak paneer are perhaps the stars of the show, but on busy nights be
prepared to wait up to an hour for them to arrive.

Italian

Al Piccolo Mondo

*V. Arany Janos utca 17 (311 0816). M3 Arany
Janos utca/tram 2.* **Open** 11.30am-11pm daily.
Average Ft2,300. **Credit** DC, MC, V. English
spoken. **Map C3**
Elegant Italian and Mediterranean restaurant whose
friendly management and mould-breaking menu is
marred by the bad selection of wines and occasional indifference of the waitresses. The ravioli with
sage and butter is a revelation and at least three sub-
species of tomato sauce for pasta and meat are made
nightly. With work this could be a superb place.

Fausto's

*VII. Dohány utca 5 (269 6806). M2 Astoria/tram 47,
49.* **Open** noon-3pm, 7pm-11pm, Mon-Sat. **Average**
Ft3,600. **Credit** AmEx, EC, JCB, MC, V. English
spoken. **Map E3**
Possibly the best restaurant in town, though it's in
danger of resting on its laurels, Fausto's is small,
slick, elegant and unpretentious and offers inventive
Italian dishes that make good use of local ingredients. Excellent wine list, too. Booking essential, as
is sitting with your back to the Venetian canal mural
and its disconcerting perspectives.

Okay Italia

*XIII. Szent István körút 20 (349 2991). M3
Nyugati/tram 4, 6.* **Open** noon-midnight daily.
Average Ft1,600. **No credit cards.** English
spoken. **Map C2**
These days there's plenty of competition, but when
it opened in 1993 Okay Italia was a revelation for
Budapest: genuine Italian food at reasonable prices
in an unpretentious atmosphere. Staffing the place
with fit waitresses in very short skirts and a chain-
smoking Neapolitan chef was also part of a strategy that proved so popular they opened up a second
branch round the corner, universally known as
'Okay 2'. The branches have slightly different
menus, each offering a good general selection of
dishes which change according to season.
Branch: V. Nyugati tér 6 (332 6960).

Pizza Bella

*VI. Teréz körút 32 (332 4462). M1 Oktogon/tram 4,
6.* **Open** 10am-midnight Mon-Sat; 3pm-midnight
Sun. **Average** Ft 1,400. **No credit cards.** Some
English spoken. **Map D3**

A tiny, no-frills Italian joint serving some of the best
mid-price pasta and pizza in town, though very little else. Simple, unfussy touches (even the busty
wall-to-ceiling murals somehow manage to be unobtrusive), friendly service and a fine house grappa.

Ristorante Via Luna

*V. Nagysándor Jozsef utca 1 (312 8058). M3 Arany
János utca.* **Open** 11am-11pm daily. **Average**
Ft1,900. **Credit** AmEx, DC, MC, V. English spoken.
Map C3
Attractive and spacious with a long though somewhat old-fashioned menu of traditional fare, including 25 pasta dishes and generous appetisers. Roomy,
well-spaced tables encourage relaxed conversation
but the food arrives almost too quickly. The short
wine list is a mite overpriced but good value and possibly the best profiteroles in town.

Theme

Barokk

VI. Mozsár utca 12 (331 8942). M1 Oktogon. **Open**
noon-midnight daily. **Average** Ft3,500. AmEx, DC,
MC, V. English spoken. **Map D3**
A theme restaurant that offers a luxurious baroque
feel, complete with staff in period costume, taped
baroque music, gilt-framed paintings and Louis-XV
style chairs, while astonishingly managing to avoid
tackines. The menu labours the point with largely
incomprehensible language, and the dishes can be
authentic to the point of weirdness. Despite the gim-
micks, though, this is a genuinely good and well-
managed restaurant, and an excellent venue for a
more formal dinner. Booking advisable.

Belcanto

*VI. Dalszinház utca 8 (269 3101/311 9547). M1
Opera.* **Open** 6pm-2am daily. **Average** Ft4,000.
Credit AmEx, DC, MC, V. Some English spoken.
Map D3
In a splendid baroque room, with unique entertainment: stars from the Opera next door wander around
delivering hits of the 1890s and standards of the
1980s. Just when you think the coast is clear, the
entire waiting staff appears as a chorus line. The
menu tries hard, but lacks the freshness and spontaneity required to be really first class. The various
steak options are probably the best bet. Service is
pretty good, considering the waiters have to remain
aware their cue might be coming up at any moment.
Best time is just before the Opera tips out.
Wonderful spot for a party. Booking essential.

Lancelot Lovági Étterem

*VI. Podmaniczky utca 14 (302 4456). M3
Nyugati/tram 4, 6.* **Open** noon-1am daily. **Average**
Ft1,800. **Credit** AmEx, DC, MC, V. English spoken.
Map C2
Bizarre medieval theme restaurant where you sit at
long wooden benches in front of vast portions of
meat and garnish served on wooden platters. As at
its sister restaurant, King Arthur's, diners are waited upon by fair maidens wrapped in skimpy, mock-

medieval costumes. The food is the sort that people ate several hundred years ago when the plague usually got to them before heart disease did – mountains of meat eaten with a knife and by hand. The salt content means you are in need of the good beer and wine on offer. A fun venue for a group night out but doesn't merit repeat visits.
Branch: King Arthur's, III. Bécsi út 38-44 (437 8243).

Marxim
II. Kis Rókus utca 23 (316 0231). Tram 4, 6. **Open** noon-1am Mon-Thur; noon-2am Fri, Sat; 6pm-1am Sun. **Average** Ft500. **No credit cards**. Some English spoken. **Map A2**
In an appropriately industrial setting behind a Buda tram factory, this pizzeria has a Communist kitsch theme. There's a small showcase of Stalinist trinkets by the door, red flags and trade union banners festoon the interior, chicken-wire separates the tables and the pizzas have names such as Anarchismo and Gulag. Alas, it isn't only the décor that harks back to Communist days: the pizzas are so tough they can bend the cheap cutlery.

Restaurant Tchaikovsky
V. Október 6 utca 5 (317 2987). Tram 2. **Open** noon-1am Mon-Fri; 6pm-1am Sat, Sun. **Average** Ft6,500. **Credit** AmEx, DC JCB, MC, V. English spoken. **Map C3**
Extravagant, expensive and beautifully executed, but ultimately a limp experience. The Tchaikovsky aims to offer the haute cuisine of the Imperial Russian court, and has page after bewildering page of expensive items to tempt you with. The problem is that the food is neither good nor ample and certainly not worth the sum you will be billed. The distressingly empty dining room and the dispirited Russian singers don't help.

Vegetarian

Gandhi
V. Vigyázó Ferenc utca 4 (269 1625). Tram 2. **Open** noon-10.30pm daily. **Average** Ft750. **Credit** DC, MC, V. English spoken. **Map C3**
Cellar vegetarian place decked in warm colours; a small fountain and a photo gallery of gurus (Gandhi, the Dalai Lama, Baghwan) set the somewhat blissed-out tone. Two daily set menus (one 'lunar', the other 'solar'), plus soups and an interesting salad bar. Lots of juices and teas. No smoking.

Rhythm & Food Music Club
V. Cukor utca 3 (267 0322). M3 Ferenciek tere/tram 2. **Open** noon-10pm daily. **Average** Ft1,000. **Credit** AmEx, MC, V. English spoken. **Map C4**
Once the city's only vegetarian restaurant, this now has poultry and fish on the menu. There is beer and wine, a few vegan and macrobiotic dishes among more standard vegetarian fare, and it's strictly no smoking. The atmosphere is austere, the food plain and solid. Usually a queue in the evenings when a classical guitarist entertains diners at booth tables.

How to speak vegetables

Hungarians discuss eating the way other people discuss football or the weather, and it is perfectly normal to discuss a previous meal while you are sitting down eating an entirely different one. Little wonder, then, that Hungarian is littered with food idioms and eating expressions.

Someone young and inexperienced, for example, may be called 'sour-cream-mouthed' (*tejfölös szájú*), though exactly why is a mystery. Less obtusely, a tense atmosphere might be said, in a nod to the king of Hungarian spice, to be 'peppery' or 'paprika-flavoured' (*paprikás*).

'Together, fried or boiled' (*sülve főve együtt vannak*), you might hear of a couple: it means they're inseparable. When warning someone to avoid cheap imitations, Hungarians say 'cheap meat has a thin broth' (*olcsó húsnak híg a leve*). Still on the matter of soup, when complaining that someone spoiled something for you, you could cry that he 'spat in my soup' (*beleköpött a levesembe*), for some stomach-churning Hungarian authenticity.

The old adage involving silk purses and sow's ears gets a pragmatic and down-to-earth reworking in Magyar: 'you don't get bacon from a dog' (*kutyából nem lesz szalonna*) – a good one because it links two favourite linguistic workhorses: the poor old dog also does overtime in Hungarian, and is in scores of expressions in its own right.

Vegetarians who suspect they are treated with wary loathing in this carnivorous country can relax: Of course they are. If told that you 'speak vegetables' (*zöldségeket beszél*), it means you're talking bollocks.

'Don't wait for the roast chicken to fly into your mouth' (*ne várd, hogy a sült csirke szádba repüljön*), someone tells you. Sound advice in any circumstances, you might think. But in fact they will be commenting on your passiveness or indolence, and advising you to get active and take the initiative.

But our all-time favourite foodie expression is the envious comment to the effect that elsewhere the streets are paved with gold. Over there, Hungarians will say with a smacking of the lips and jealous rolling of the eyes, *a kerítés is kolbászbol van* – 'even the fence is made of sausage'.

Shopping & Services

The malls may move in, but traditional businesses survive and even thrive – shopping in Budapest offers something for every taste.

Finding the unexpected is always one of the pleasures of shopping, and while Budapest has expanded its retail horizons to include all of Europe's best-known brands, patience and persistence will also be rewarded with unusual goodies to take home. Though megastores sprout, small retailers also seem to be holding their own in a kaleidoscope of ever-changing shops throughout the city. Antiques and antiquarian books are found in abundance at moderate prices. Handmade porcelain, folk art and local wines are unique and relatively cheap purchases. Hand-tailored clothes, handmade shoes and the work of local designers are where the city's true bargains are to be found, and a trip to the market – for produce, antiques or just junk – is a must on any itinerary. For children's clothing and toys *see chapter* **Children**.

Buda has trees and pleasant vistas, but is a dud for shopping. In Pest, the main shopping district centres around Váci utca. The bustling north side flaunts souvenir stalls, trendy clothing shops and expensive folk-art stores, while the quieter part south of Kossuth utca tends toward antique shops, exclusive boutiques and pavement cafes. The small streets leading off the main pedestrian areas are filled with hundreds of little shops. Other areas of interest include Kossuth utca/Rákóczi út from the Erzsébet bridge to Blaha Lujza tér and both the Kiskörút and Nagykörút. Király utca is good for anything second-hand. The Castle District has a smattering of everything, though prices do reflect that it's the city's main tourist attraction.

Services are of generally good quality and surprisingly cost little compared with the rest of Europe. This is the place to treat yourself to a facial or massage, have a suit made or repair your watch for a fraction of what it would cost at home. That said, Hungarians have been slow to pick up on Western customer service standards and are notoriously reluctant to learn foreign languages. Outside the malls and central shopping districts, it's handy to have a Hungarian speaker along for more than a simple transaction. Another source of frustration is that it's usually the customer who's expected to have the change.

The Phone Book, now in its sixth edition, is a useful guide for finding products or services. It can be found at most English-language bookshops or ordered (free of charge) from CoMo Media (V. Kossuth Lajos utca 17/266 4916/fax 317 9695/como@mail.datanet.hu).

Opening hours

Standard opening hours are 10am to 5pm or 6pm on weekdays and 10am-1pm on Saturdays. Many shops now keep extended hours on Thursday evenings, and are open till later on Saturday afternoons. On Sunday, stick to Váci utca and the Castle District, or head to the malls – most will be open until 6pm at the weekend. For basic necessities at all hours, there's a non-stop in every neighbourhood. *See chapter* **Nightlife**.

The *rögtön jövök* (back in ten) sign you might find hanging on a locked door during normal business hours actually means 'I'll be back at some vague and probably distant point in the future'. If no one shows up in a few minutes, try the next day (or the day after that). Most places are closed around major holidays, including 15 March, 20 August, and 23 October. Absolutely everything shuts up shop at Christmas – even non-stops stop on 24 and 25 December.

Antiques

The traditional antiques district centres around V. Falk Miksa utca, while less expensive shops can be found in District IX – particularly on Vámház körút and Lónyay utca. The south end of Váci utca also contains some interesting shops, with prices more reasonable than on the north side. Shops in the Castle District are also interesting, but more expensive. For genuine junk, go to the **Városligeti Bolhapiac** (*see below*, **Flea markets**), or discover the joys of the *Lomtalánítás – see page 176* **De-junking the districts**.

Antique Art

V. Váci utca 53 (337 5082/06 309 311 233). M3 Ferenciek tere/tram 2/bus 7. **Open** 9am-7pm Mon-

The Great Market Hall on Fővám tér – everything (and everyone) under one roof.

Fri; 9am-6pm Sat, Sun. **Credit** AmEx, MC, JCB, V. Some English spoken. **Map C5**

One of few antique shops to carry genuine bric-à-brac. Tin toys are jumbled in a steamer trunk and every available surface is covered with interesting odds and ends – coffee grinders, wooden boxes, old adverts, opera glasses, jewellery and figurines.

BÁV

V. Bécsi utca 1-3 (317 2548). M3 Ferenciek tere/tram 2/bus 7. **Open** 10am-6pm Mon-Fri; 9am-1pm Sat. **Credit** AmEx, DC, EC, JCB, MC, V. Some English spoken. **Map C4**

BÁV stores are state-run pawn shops. Outlets all over the city buy and sell everything from high-quality antiques to used refrigerators and can be recognised by a maroon-and-white Venus de Milo sign. Each branch has a different speciality, and they're a good bet for reasonably priced antiques or inexpensive furnishings. Auctions are held several times a year, and schedules can be picked up at main branches. For further information contact the main auction house at IX. Lónyay utca 31-32 (342 7953). **Branches**: V. Szent István körút 3 (331 4534/fax 331 0106); VII. Dohány utca 16-18 (342 7935).

Judaica Gallery

VII. Wesselényi utca 13 (267 8502/fax 331 4208). M2 Astoria/tram 47, 49/bus 7. **Open** 10am-6pm Mon-Thur; 10am-2pm Fri. **Credit** AmEx, EC, MC, V. English spoken. **Map D4**

Articles related to Hungarian Jewish culture: old

prayer books, work by local artists and village pottery with Hebrew sayings. Also Israeli Dead Sea mud products and books in English on Jewish themes.

Múlt Idő

VI. Ó utca 19 (269 2746). M1 Opera. **Open** 10am-6pm Mon-Fri; 10am-1pm Sat. **No credit cards**. No English spoken. **Map C3**

A treasure trove of knick-knacks from a Hungarian grandmother's house. Tins, tablecloths, hat pins, embroideries, pictures and postcards.

Pintér Antik Diszkont

V. Falk Miksa utca 10 (311 3030). Tram 2, 4, 6 Jászai Mari tér. **Open** 10am-6pm Mon-Fri; 10am-2pm Sat. **Credit** AmEx, DC, EC, JCB, MC, V. English spoken. **Map C2**

Over 1,000 sq m of floor space in a former World War II bomb shelter. Features new chandeliers by Bohemia Crystal and antiques and furniture in all price ranges. The teashop is a welcome relief after winding through the maze of rooms.

Relikvia

I. Fortuna utca 14 (376 9973). Várbusz from M2 Moszkva tér/bus 16. **Open** 10am-6pm daily. **Credit** AmEx, DC, EC, JCB, MC, V. English spoken. **Map A3**

Specialises in fine furniture, paintings and porcelain. Don't expect bargains, but this is certainly the best antique shop in the Castle District. **Branches**: I. Fortuna utca 21 (355 9973); Hilton Hotel, I. Hess András tér 1-3 (488 6886).

Auctions

Első Budai Árverező Ház – Bedő Papírrégiség Bolt

II. Kapás utca 5-9 (214 7952). M2 Batthyány tér/tram 19. **Open** 10am-6pm Mon-Wed, Fri; 10am-3pm Thur, Sat. **No credit cards**. No English spoken. **Map A2**

Furniture, jewellery, porcelain, games and paintings hit the auction block every Thursday. Ephemera can be picked up at auctions on every last Wednesday of the month (5pm). You can browse in a small shop with porcelain figurines and other odds and ends, or deal with one of the specialists for postcards, banknotes and stamps.

Nagyházi Galéria

V. Balaton utca 8 (312 5631/fax 331 7133). Tram 2, 4, 6 Jászai Mari tér. **Open** 10am-6pm Mon-Fri; 10am-1pm Sat. **Credit** DC, EB, EC, MC, V. English spoken. **Map C2**

One of the city's biggest auction houses holds catalogue auctions each spring and autumn. Stop by for a programme and look around their gallery for Hungarian paintings and furniture from all periods.

Art supplies & stationery

Ápisz

VI. Andrássy út 3 (268 0534). M1 Bajcsy-Zsilinszky. **Open** 9am-6pm Mon-Fri; 9am-1pm Sat. **Credit** EC, MC, V. No English spoken. **Map C3**

One remnant of the old regime is the designation of certain categories of goods to particular shops. Ápisz is where to go for paper – toilet paper, writing paper, wrapping paper. Non-paper items include pens and markers, school and office supplies, aluminium baking tins, diskettes, string and plastic cups; all Hungarian made, all cheap.

Branches: V. Szent István körút 21 (312 0425); IX. Kálvin tér 9 (217 6295); XI. Bartók Béla út 1 (466-6880); V. Kossuth Lajos utca 2A (318 3492).

Interieur Studio

V. Vitkovics Mihály utca 6 (337 7005). M2 Astoria/tram 47, 49. **Open** 10am-6pm Mon-Fri; 10am-2pm Sat. **No credit cards**. Some English spoken. **Map C4**

Handmade paper goods, fancy gift trimmings, dried flowers and local handicrafts – a good place to pick up an unusual gift. Bath oils, hand-dipped candles, paper boxes and baskets fill the rest of the space.

Branch: Pólus Center (419 4166).

Művészellátó Szaküzlet

VI. Nagymező utca 45 (332 6163/311 7040). M3 Arany János utca. **Open** 9am-6pm Mon-Fri; 10am-1pm Sat. **Credit** AmEx, DC, MC, V. No English spoken. **Map C3**

The best selection of art supplies in Budapest. Western brands available for paints, pencils, brushes and drafting tools along with their local (and generally less expensive) counterparts. Frames and glass cut to order.

Pirex

VI. Paulay Ede utca 17 (322-7067/fax 341 4360). M1 Opera. **Open** 8.30am-5pm Mon-Fri. **Credit** AmEx, EC, MC, V. Some English spoken. **Map D3**

A step up from Ápisz (*see above*), Pirex stocks a wide selection of stationery and office supplies as well as basic graphics and art materials, and computer stuff too.

Branch: II. Margit körút 13 (335 2002).

Books, maps & newsagents

For international newspapers, the newsagents (*hírlapbolt*) in the underpasses at Nyugati and Keleti stations are open from 4am until 9pm or 10pm.

A Világsajtó Háza

V. Városház utca 3-5 (317 1311/fax 318 1928). M3 Ferenciek tere/tram 2/bus 7. **Open** 7am-7pm Mon-Fri; 7am-6pm Sat; 8am-4pm Sun. **No credit cards**. Some English spoken. **Map C4**

Choose from Budapest's largest selection of international magazines and newspapers.

Branch: V. Kálvin tér 3 (266 9730).

Atlantisz Könyvsziget

V. Piarista köz 1 (266 9100 ext 5326). M3 Ferenciek tere/tram 2/bus 7. **Open** 10am-6pm Mon-Fri; 10am-3pm Sat. **Credit** AmEx, EC, MC, V. Some English spoken. **Map C4**

About a quarter of their books are in English, mostly on academic subjects. Check the sale shelf for discounts and peruse postcards of Budapest – much better than the tourist crap in Váci utca outside.

Bestsellers

V. Október 6 utca 11 (312 1295). M3 Arany János utca. **Open** 9am-6.30pm Mon-Fri; 10am-6pm Sat; 10am-4pm Sun. **Credit** AmEx, DC, MC, V. English spoken. **Map C3**

Best place in the city for current novels, children's and travel books in English as well as magazines and newspapers. Steepish prices. Ordering service.

CEU Academic Bookshop

V. Nádor utca 9 (327 3096). M3 Arany János utca. **Open** 9am-6pm Mon-Fri; 9am-6.30pm Wed; 10am-4pm Sat. **Credit** AmEx, DC, MC, V. English Spoken. **Map C3**

The studious cousin of Bestsellers (*see above*) attached to the Central European University stocks an excellent collection of literature on central and eastern Europe and the former Soviet Union. Ten per cent discount during 'happy hour' every Wednesday 4.30-6.30pm.

Helikon

VI. Bajcsy-Zsilinszky út 37 (302 4406). M3 Arany János utca. **Open** 10am-7pm Mon-Fri; 10am-2pm Sat. **Credit** AmEx, EC, MC, V. Some English spoken. **Map C3**

Modest selection of Hungarian literature in translation, local travel guides and cookbooks plus an assortment of English lit popular in Hungary – all at reasonable prices.

Írók Boltja

VI. Andrássy út 45 (322 1645). M1 Oktogon/tram 4, 6. **Open** 10am-6pm Mon-Fri; 10am-1pm Sat (Sept-June). **Credit** AmEx, EC, JCB, MC, V. Some English spoken. **Map D3**
The 'Writers' Bookshop' offers only the basics in English, but interesting art books and calendars and a coffee corner for looking over potential purchases.

Rhythm 'N' Books

V. Szerb utca 21-23 (266 9833 ext 2226). M3 Kálvin tér/tram 47, 49. **No credit cards.** English spoken. **Map D5**
Big selection of new and second-hand books, and will trade old books for cash or credit. Small selection of second-hand CDs and cassettes.

Térképkirály

V. Sas utca 1 (266 0552). M1, M2, M3, Deák tér/tram 47, 49. **Open** 9am-7pm Mon-Fri. **Credit** AmEx, DC, EC, MC, V. No English spoken. **Map C3**
Stop here for assorted maps of Budapest, Hungary and just about everywhere else.

Antiquarian bookshops

The free leaflet with map, *Second-hand Bookshops in Budapest* (available at most shops) lists 35 second-hand and rare bookshops. For rare editions, phone Ferenc Kollin at his District IX home (217 9189/217 3910). His son András speaks English. *See also* **Judaica Gallery** under **Antiques**.

Bibliotéka Antikvárium

VI. Andrássy út 2 (331 5132). M1 Bajcsy-Zsilinszky. **Open** 10am-6pm Mon-Fri; 9am-1pm Sat. **Credit** AmEx, DC, EC, JCB, MC, V. English spoken. **Map C3**
Large but still comfortable for browsing. Rare editions upstairs and knowledgeable staff. Biggish selection of second-hand books in English.

Ferenczy Galéria

V. Ferenczy István utca 28 (318 1007). M2 Astoria/tram 47, 49. **Open** 1-7pm Mon-Fri; 10am-2pm Sat. **Credit** AmEx, DC, EC, JCB, MC, V. English spoken. **Map D4**
Shelves of art books in many languages, and an interesting selection of twentieth-century posters with some prints, maps and drawings.

Központi Antikvárium

V. Múzeum körút 13-15 (317 3781/317 3514). M2 Astoria. **Open** 10am-6pm Mon-Fri; 10am-2pm Sat. **Credit** AmEx, EC, MC, V. English spoken. **Map D4**
Spacious shop of interest for collectors. Otherwise a decent selection of second-hand books in English.

Philon Antikvárium

VII. Dob utca 32 (352 2970). M1 Opera. **Open** noon-7pm Mon-Thur; noon-6pm Fri. **No credit cards.** No English spoken. **Map D3**
Eclectic but interesting mix of English books at modest prices, plus large selection on Jewish subjects in various languages. Across the street from **Concerto** record shop (*see below*).

Stúdió Antikvárium

VI. Jókai tér 7 (312 6294). M1 Oktogon/tram 4, 6. **Open** 9am-7pm Mon-Fri; 9am-2pm Sat. **No credit cards.** No English spoken. **Map D3**
A cosy shop with books piled on all surfaces. Not a huge turnover of English books. Some children's books and a good selection of postcards.

Ulysses

VIII. Rákóczi út 7 (338 0247). M2 Astoria/tram 47, 49/bus 7. **Open** 10am-6pm Mon-Fri. **Credit** AmEx, EC, DC, MC, V. Some English spoken. **Map D4**
Tidy shop in the back of a courtyard. Good selection of art and graphics books, plus a well-organised collection of postcards, maps and prints.

Department stores & malls

See also page 161 **Mall mania**.

Corvin Áruház

VIII. Blaha Lujza tér 1-2 (338 4160). M2 Blaha Lujza tér/tram 4, 6/bus 7. **Open** 9am-7pm Mon-Fri; 10am-3pm Sat. **Credit** AmEx, DC, EC, MC, V. **Map E4**
One stop for inexpensive appliances (western), linens, underwear and tacky but serviceable home furnishings (Hungarian). Don't come if you're in a hurry though. To buy something, you must take a docket, pay at the *pénztár*, and return to collect your purchase. Payment by credit card will mean an extra 20 minutes' wait.

Duna Plaza

XIII. Váci út 178 (465 1220). M3 Gyöngyösi utca. **Open** 10am-9pm Mon-Fri; 10am-7pm Sat, Sun.
Not particularly close to the centre, but easily accessible by the blue metro line. Always packed but there's little to drag the casual shopper up here apart from the Virgin Megastore, the multiplex cinema and a bowling alley.

Flavius Center

VII. Rákóczi út 36 (322 1047). M2 Blaha Lujza. **Open** 10am-7pm Mon-Fri; 10am-2pm Sat. **Map E4**
One of the better of several shopping arcades along Rákóczi út. Trendy clothing shops come and go on a regular basis, but there's usually a good selection of inexpensive, but hip duds and shoes.

Fontana Department Store

V. Váci utca 16 (266 6400). M1 Vörösmarty tér/tram 2. **Open** 10am-7pm Mon-Fri; 10am-3pm Sat. **Credit** AmEx, DC, EC, JCB, MC, V. Some English spoken. **Map C4**
Not exactly Harrods, but a reasonable selection of clothing, cosmetics, kiddie things and luggage, and a sunny rooftop café.

Lurdy Ház

IX. Könyves Kálmán körút 12-14 (456 1100). Tram 23, 30. **Open** 10am-8pm daily. **Map F6**
Another massive new mall on the outskirts of Pest. Everything you'd expect – chrome and glass everywhere, a cinema and bazillions of boutiques.

Mamut Center – *for a wild and woolly retail experience.*

Mall mania

If the success of Hungary's economic transition were measured in the number of shopping malls, the 1990s will be remembered as the boom years. The same people who embraced 'goulash Communism' have seamlessly upgraded to the commercial mecca of the mall. No matter that there just seems to be a bigger selection of the same brands and styles found elsewhere in the city, the fairy-ring of malls sprouting around the city attract customers with hundreds of shops, late and weekend opening hours, child depositories (that is, video arcades) and cinemas.

If you believe some local retailers, they're an alien life-form come to quash home-grown culture with the worst of western capitalism. But paradoxically, retail space in the centre is full, and despite grumbling concessions toward longer opening hours at the weekend, local businesses seem to be puttering along just fine. At the same time, Sunday at the mall seems to have become a national pastime. The advantages are clear to anyone who works normal office hours and can't bear to get up before noon on Saturday.

Nevertheless, there's a distinctly silly side to the local variant. Pólus wins hands down for its Wild West theme food-park complete with Chinese buffet and miniature ice rink (worth a look if only to later stroll down Sunset Boulevard to Tesco). A close second is the Mamut Center with its Smurf-blue Marilyn Monroe/Statue of Liberty effigy in the corner of the video arcade – leading to the faux 1950s diner that doesn't serve burgers.

And there's more to come. As we go to press the West End Center is due to open on a gargantuan five-hectare site next to Nyugati station. With 83,500 square metres of floor space, this will be the biggest mall in Hungary and one of the largest in Europe. A 14-screen multiplex and a Hilton are just two of the planned attractions.

Love 'em or leave 'em, the malls are here to stay. From city hall to local pub, Hungarians debate whether they're the harbinger of death to cultural independence or the mark of a firm grip on the future. Hungary's definitely addicted.

For addresses of malls, *see* **Department stores & malls**.

Mamut Center

II. Lövőház utca 2-6 (345 8020). M2 Moszkva tér/tram 4, 6 Széna tér. **Open** 10am-9pm Mon-Sat; 10am-6pm Sun. **Map A2**
Hundreds of little boutiques and many European labels are interspersed with shoe-repair and key-cutting shops, and there's an enormous Julius Meinl in the basement. Nothing special about the food court other than a fantastic view over the rooftops around Moszkva tér.

Pólus Center

XV. Szentmihályi út (410 2405/419 4028). Special buses from Nyugati & Keleti stations. **Open** 10am-8pm daily.
Pass the ridiculous Wild West food court and stroll down Rodeo Drive or Sunset Boulevard to the real destination – Tesco. Here's everything Brits miss from home, including Marmite, HP Sauce, Branston Pickle, PG Tips (sometimes), Patak curry pastes and cheap underwear. Excellent cheese counter too. City transport tickets valid on the regular bus service.

Design & household goods

Hephaistos Háza

V. Molnár utca 27 (tel/fax 266 1550). M3 Ferenciek tere/tram 2/bus 7. **Open** 11am-6pm Mon-Fri; 10am-2pm Sat. **Credit** EC, JCB, MC, V. English spoken. **Map D3**

Old-style blacksmiths might be pleasantly surprised to see the way Eszter Gál carries on the tradition. Eccentric wrought-iron furniture and accessories to take away or made to order.

Holló Folkart Gallery

V. Vitkovics Mihály utca 12 (317 8103). M2 Astoria/tram 47, 49/bus 7, 9. **Open** 10am-6pm Mon-Fri; 10am-1pm Sat. **Credit** AmEx, DC, MC, V. No English spoken. **Map C4**
Subdued, folksy hardwood furniture by László Holló using traditional decorative motifs.

Impresszió

V. Károly körút 10 (337 2772). M2 Astoria/tram 47, 49/bus 7, 9. **Open** 10am-7pm Mon-Fri; 10am-2pm Sat. **No credit cards.** Some English spoken. **Map D4**
Tiny shop sharing a courtyard with a number of interesting fashion shops and the **Bon Café** (*see* chapter **Cafés & Coffeehouses**). Owner Sándor supports local artists by peddling candles, baskets, beads, bath oils and assorted gifts.

Style Antique

VII. Király utca 25 (321 3473). M1 Opera. **Open** 10am-7pm Mon-Fri; 10am-5pm Sat. **No credit cards.** English spoken. **Map D3**
Beautiful new and restored folk-inspired pine and hardwood furniture. Not cheap by any means, but the workmanship is first-class and they will happily do custom restoration.

Household goods

Transformers to convert American appliances to European 220v current are nearly impossible to find in Budapest. If coming from North America and planning a long stay, pack appropriate transformers. If you're setting up house, bits and pieces can be found in three types of shops: *bárkacs* for locks, wood and brass fittings, *vásedény* for kitchen tools and *műanyag* for plastics.

1,000 Aprócikk

V. Bajcsy-Zsilinszky út 3 (269 6620/322 6420). M1, M2, M3, Deák tér/tram 47, 49. **Open** 9am-6pm Mon-Fri; 9am-1pm Sat. **No credit cards.** No English spoken. **Map C4**

If you melt the rubber gasket in your *eszpresszo*maker, this is the place to get a new one, plus 999 other household gadgets and spare parts.

Boszorkánykonyha

VI. Teréz körút 58 (312 3089). M3 Nyugati/tram 4, 6. **Open** 10am-6pm Mon-Fri; 10am-1pm Sat. **No credit cards.** Some English spoken. **Map C4**

Bold-coloured, country-style crockery and tasteful kitchen accessories in the 'witch's kitchen'. Somewhat cute, but a step up from most stores and better than what is likely to be found in a rented flat. **Branches:** V. Petőfi Sándor utca 16 (318 3223). Pólus Center, Duna Plaza.

IKEA

XIV. Örs vezér tere (460 3100). M2 Örs vezér tere. **Open** 10am-8pm Mon-Fri; 10am-5pm Sat; 10am-3pm Sun. **No credit cards.** English spoken.

Bigger pieces of furniture can be delivered. Other conveniences include underground parking, cafés, a supervised playroom for kids and a smoking lounge.

Kátay

VI. Teréz körút 28 (311 0116). M1 Oktogon/tram 4, 6. **Open** 9am-6pm Mon-Fri; 9am-7pm Thur; 9am-2pm Sat. **Credit** AmEx, DC, EC, MC, V. No English spoken. **Map D3**

Excellent stop for things to put in the kitchen, fix up the bathroom, tidy the garden and set the table.

Keravill

V. Kossuth Lajos utca 2 (317 6422). M3 Ferenciek tere/tram 2/bus 7. **Open** 10am-7pm Mon-Fri; 9am-2pm Sat. **Credit** DC, EC, MC, V. Some English spoken. **Map C4**

National chain for electronics and appliances. No great bargains, but quality local and European brands. Larger outlets in most malls.
Branches: VI. Teréz körút 36 (331 6912) (household goods); Erzsébet körút 41 (322 6094) (lighting); VII. Rákóczi út 30 (342 0100) (electronics).

Fashion

While impossibly short minis do have an undeniable appeal in the right circumstances, finding shop after dull shop full of the same club duds can be frustrating. If that's what you're looking for,

though, try Teréz körút between Oktogon and Nyugati for boutiques, or Rákóczi út between Blaha Lujza tér and Astoria for a number of shops and arcades. Major brands such as Marks & Spencer and Adidas are found on Váci utca or in the malls.

Local designers are where it's at if you're looking for a fashion find in Budapest. A handful of young designers are making a name for themselves walking a fine line between hip and classic. Folk influences have also made a mark, and many shops feature simple dresses and skirts in natural fibres. Although Budapest is abysmal for men's clothing, a hand-tailored suit is a good buy.

Accessories & jewellery

Bijoux

V. Károly körút 3 (317 6450). M2 Astoria/tram 47, 49/bus 7. **Open** 10am-6pm Mon-Wed, Fri; 10am-7pm Thur; 10am-2pm Sat. **No credit cards.** Some English spoken. **Map D4**

Wacky and tacky selection of fake, fluorescent, fluffy and flamboyant jewellery and hair accessories.

Craft Design

VI. Klauzál tér 1 (322 4006/322 7480). Tram 4, 6. **Open** 10am-5pm Mon-Fri. **Credit** EC, MC, V. Some English spoken. **Map D3**

Quiet corner shop with locally made wallets, handbags, silk scarves and other tasteful accessories.

Marácz Kalap

VII. Wesselényi utca 41 (no phone). Tram 4, 6. **Open** 10am-6pm Mon-Fri. **No credit cards.** No English spoken. **Map D3**

The best bet for authentic Magyar headgear is a trip to Transylvania. Barring that, Marácz has fedoras and women's hats for all occasions.

Ómama Bizsuja

V. Szent István körút 1 (312 6812). Tram 2, 4, 6. **Open** 10am-6pm Mon-Fri; 10am-2pm Sat. **No credit cards.** Some English spoken. **Map C2**

A trove of nifty bijoux – display cases of rhinestones, beads of all sorts, semi-precious stones and silverwork, all at extremely reasonable prices. **Branch:** II. Frankel Leó utca 7 (315 0807).

ProMix Manager Shop

V. Szent István tér 3 (317 3569). M3 Arany János. **Open** 9am-5pm Mon, Wed, Fri; 10am-6pm Tue, Thur. **Credit** AmEx, MC, V. Some English spoken. **Map C3**

A Magyar *menedzser* apparently needs a Parker pen, a digital travel clock, Samsonite luggage, a classy umbrella, a sharp leather belt, a silk tie and a good selection of imported whiskies.

Rácz Mária Szűcsmester

V. Bárczi István utca 3 (337 7139). M1, 2, 3 Deák tér/tram 47, 49. **Open** 10am-2pm, 3pm-6pm, Mon-Fri. **No credit cards.** Some English spoken. **Map C4**

Hephaistos Háza – *eccentric wrought-iron ornaments to go. See page 161.*

Un-PC Magyars still love to strut their stuff in fox and mink. Pick up a cossack hat from Ft19,000.

Satöbbi Sajátos Tárgyak Boltja

VI. Hajós utca 7 (312 0343). M1 Opera. **Open** 10am-6pm Mon-Wed, Fri; 10am-6.30pm Thur; 10am-1pm Sat. **No credit cards.** No English spoken. **Map C3**

Accessories with an Indian flavour, plus Hungarian crafts, jewellery, journals and leather goods.

Clothing

Artz Modell

V. Károly körút 10 (337 5566). M2 Astoria/tram 47, 49/bus 7. **Open** 10am-6pm Mon-Fri; 10am-1.30pm Sat. **Credit** AmEx, DC, MC, V. Some English spoken. **Map D4**

Brace yourself for Fashion Don'ts that seem to work anyway. Part of the fashion courtyard at this address, the designers spice their collections with flashy colours and unexpected angles. Good for party suits and evening dresses. They'll alter any item or custom make to your specs for an extra ten per cent.

Christina Designer Shop

V. Semmelweis utca 8 (266 8009). M2 Astoria/tram 47, 49/bus 7. **Open** 10am-6pm Mon-Fri; 10am-2pm Sat. **Credit** AmEx, DC, EC, MC, V. No English spoken. **Map D4**

On one side, embroidered sheets, lace and table-cloths. On the other, things made from luxurious 100 per cent cotton terry, such as bath robes and beach wraps. Also beach bags, slippers and swimsuits, all in bright summer colours and made in-house.

Gréti Szalon

V. Bárczy István utca 3 (317 8500). M1, M2, M3 Deák tér. **Open** 10am-6pm Mon-Fri. **No credit cards.** English spoken. **Map C4**

The *grande dame* of Hungarian fashion, Greti's creations reflect years of experience in classic, elegant suits and eveningwear for women. Sexy lingerie and a small selection of Italian shoes too.

Grisby

VI. Paulay Ede utca 67 (318 0102). M1 Oktogon/tram 4, 6. **Open** 10am-6pm Mon-Fri; 10am-2pm Sat. **Credit** MC, V. English spoken. **Map D3**

Owner Péter travels monthly to Barcelona to replenish a small but exquisite collection of men's clothing by Grisby. Prices lower than you might expect.

Home Boy

V. Irányi utca 5 and 9 (266 4641). M3 Ferenciek tere/tram 2/bus 7. **Open** 10am-6pm Mon-Fri; 10am-1pm Sat. **Credit** EC, MC, V. Some English spoken. **Map C5**

Baggies for boys, with club/skate gear from Stüssy, Fresh Jive, Dready and adidas imported by this German chain. Tattooing and piercing performed in the basement.

Jackpot & Cottonfield

V. Váci utca 9 (266 0221). M1 Oktogon/tram 4, 6. **Open** 10am-7pm Mon, Tue; 10am-7pm Wed-Sat; 11am-6pm Sun. **Credit** AmEx, DC, EC, JCB, MC, V. Some English spoken. **Map C4**

Danish casualwear for men and women. With natural fabrics, naive colours and simple cuts, this is the closest thing you'll find to the Gap. **Branch**: VI. Teréz körút 24 (311 0483).

Sixville Collection – *elegant and wearable.*

Manu Art

V. Múzeum körút 7 (266 3080). M2 Astoria/tram 47, 49/bus 7, 9. **Open** 10am-6pm Mon-Fri; 10am-1pm Sat. **Credit** EC, MC, V. Some English spoken. **Map D4**
A longtime favourite with the folk set, Manu Art has a decent selection of simple cotton dresses, skirts and blouses at excellent prices. A new line of canvas jackets, T-shirts and clothes for men can also be found in the Károly körút location.
Branch: V. Károly körút 10 (266 8136).

Monarchia

V. Szabadsajtó út 6 (318 3146). M3 Ferenciek tere/tram 2/bus 7. **Open** 10am-6.30pm Mon-Wed, Fri; 10am-7pm Thur; 10am-1.30pm Sat. **Credit** AmEx, DC, EC, MC, V. Some English spoken. **Map C5**
Five domestic designers devoted to women's looks whose work walks a thin line between classic chic and daring hip. Their window displays of suits and eveningwear change daily. Custom orders taken for 26 per cent extra.

Ria Divat

I. Bem József utca 22 (202 1421). M2 Batthyány tér/tram 4, 6, bus 11. **Open** 10am-6pm Mon-Fri; 10am-1pm Sat. **No credit cards.** Some English spoken. **Map B2**
The first private boutique in Budapest holds an amazing range of tastefully chosen women's clothing to suit three generations of dedicated customers.

Sixville Collection

V. Kecskeméti utca 8 (317 4834/06 309 422 098). M3 Kálvin tér/tram 47, 49. **Open** 11am-7pm Mon-Fri; 10am-3pm Sat. English spoken. **Map D5**
Meticulously tailored men's suits by Vilmos Lostis. Italian and local fabrics used to advantage in simple, elegant, wearable clothing.

V-50 Design Art Studio

V. Váci utca 50, entrance on Nyáry Pál utca (337 5320). M3 Ferenciek tere/tram 2/bus 7. **Open** 1-6pm Mon-Fri. **No credit cards.** Some English spoken. **Map C5**
Hats with a whimsical twist by Valéria Fazekas complement her line of minimalist dresses, suits and jackets for women. The Belgrád rakpart branch features a bigger selection of clothing.
Branch: V. Belgrád rakpart 16 (337 0327).

Shoes & leather goods

Hungarian women have a fascination with platform shoes that defies explanation. Even worse, Hungary is afflicted with a shoe curse that ten years of 'transition' hasn't solved. There are probably more shoe shops per capita than in any other European capital, but 99 per cent of them sell expensive, ugly, badly made footwear. And if you have big feet, don't even bother looking. Still, there are some bright spots and a few local cobblers produce quality products.

La Boutique

VI. Andrássy út 16 (302 5646). M1 Opera. **Open** 10am-8pm Mon-Fri; 10am-4pm Sat. **Credit** AmEx, DC, EC, V. English spoken. **Map D3**
Budapest's best selection of fine shoes with prices to match. Owner Irena Dragolevic has an eye for Italy's best, and is one step ahead of the rest in catching the latest trends. Fine accessories, late hours.

Junia

V. Váci utca 41A (318 1799). M3 Ferenciek tere/tram 2/bus 7. **Open** 10am-6pm Mon-Fri; 10am-2pm Sat. **Credit** EC, MC, V. Some English spoken. **Map C4**
Lovely selection of reasonably priced Italian leather accessories for men and women. Silk scarves, hats and some shoes too.

Kaláka Studio

V. Haris köz 2 (318 3313). M3 Ferenciek tere/tram 2/bus 7. **Open** 10am-6pm Mon-Wed, Fri; 10am-7pm Thur; 10am-2pm Sat (*summer* 10am-7pm Mon-Sat). **No credit cards.** Some English spoken. **Map C4**
Simple shoes in soft, pastel suede are Ágnes Bodor's trademark. Match an outfit you already have, or pick something new from the small but solid selection of local designer frocks on the other side of the shop. Branches in most major shopping malls.

Krokodil

VI. Teréz körút 20 (332 0540). M1 Oktogon/tram 4, 6. **Open** 10am-7pm Mon-Fri; 10am-2pm Sat. **No credit cards.** No English spoken. **Map C4**

Krokodil is a cut above the Humanic and Salamander chains with reasonably priced European imports of better quality. Styles are a bit more hip too, and there are four shops on Rákóczi út and four more between Oktogon and Nyugati tér, each with a slightly different selection.
Branches: VII. Rákóczi út 38 (342 0954); VI. Teréz körút 40 (323 3176).

V.I.P.

V. Károly körút 10 (no phone). M2 Astoria/tram 47, 49/bus 7, 7A, 9, 78. **Open** 10am-6pm Mon-Fri; 10am-2pm Sat. **No credit cards.** Some English spoken. **Map D4**
A modest but well-chosen collection of Italian handbags, belts, gloves and wallets.

Shoemakers & handmade shoes

Cipőkészítő GMK

IX. Vámház körút 7 (218 7893). M3 Kálvin tér/tram 47, 49. **Open** 10am-6pm Mon-Fri; 10am-2pm Sat. **No credit cards.** No English spoken. **Map D5**
Simple walking shoes and sandals all handmade by this local cobbler from Ft5,000, but take along a Hungarian-speaker to get exactly what you want.

Vass

V. Haris köz 2 (318 2375). M3 Ferenciek tere/tram 2/bus 7. **Open** 10am-6pm Mon-Fri; 9.30am-2pm Sat. **Credit** AmEx, DC, EC, JCB, MC, V. Some English spoken. **Map C4**
Fine men's shoes custom-made to order in about a month, starting from Ft85,000. Decent selection of shoes off the rack for Ft65,000 and discounts negotiable for cash purchases.

Zabrak Shoes

Kempinski Hotel, V. Erzsébet tér 7-8 (266 8175). M1, M2, M3 Deák tér/tram 47, 49. **Open** 9am-6pm Mon-Fri; 9am-2pm Sat. **Credit** AmEx, DC, EC, JCB, MC, V. English spoken. **Map C4**
Men's shoes off the rack or made to order for between Ft55,000-Ft100,000, plus a one-time Ft22,500 supplement for the latter. Allow up to three months for delivery.

Tailors

Merino-Szivárvány

V. Petőfi Sándor utca 18 (318 7332). M1, M2, M3 Deák tér/tram 47, 49. **Open** 10am-6pm Mon-Fri; 9am-1pm Sat. **Credit** AmEx, EC, MC, V. Some English spoken. **Map C4**
Founded at the turn of the century and preserving the feel of an old-fashioned dry goods store, Merino-Szivárvany have fine lace, velvet silks and woollens stacked on wide shelves lining wood-panelled walls. Pick out something to be specially made up by a local designer, or visit the in-house tailor next door (suits start from around Ft60,000).

Taylor & Schneider

VI. Nagymező utca 31 (312 0842/06 20 419 721). M1 Opera. **Open** 7am-5pm Mon-Thur; 7am-4pm Fri. **No credit cards.** No English spoken. **Map D3**
Have a complete suit made up for Ft27,000 and up, plus the cost of the fabric – bring your own or choose from their selection of sober woollens. British or American, single- or double-breasted, made to order, and there's a handy collection of fashion mags to help you decide. Bring a friend to translate, though.

Ciánkáli – *Budapest's finest selection of vintage clothing. See page 167.*

Manier for all seasons

Anikó Németh began her career as an interior designer but switched to fashion in the 1980s and opened her **Manier** studio in 1993. Her atelier in Váci utca is now the birthplace of some of the most luxuriously exotic in Hungarian fashion design. Németh's first major splash came in the early 1990s, with a line of Renaissance-inspired costumes and frocks that made the pages of *Vogue* and *Harper's Bazaar*. Since then, her yearly collections reflect her passion for history and an instinctive feel for form and line, texture and colour. In one season, knotted raffia and African beads dominated; in another, severe Chinese-influenced cuts in radiant blues and pink.

Németh shares her Váci utca shop with three other local designers. Timea Balak weaves copper wire into eccentric jewellery and handbags, while Zita Attalai's fine leather shoes are wearable art. Together they represent some of the most unique work in contemporary Hungarian fashion. The studio across the street is packed with pictures, one-of-a-kind pieces and bolts of fabric. And as much as Németh indulges her trend-setting creativity, she's equally happy to work closely with her customers to create unique, personal pieces. And prices are extremely reasonable – a steal, actually, by European standards.

While Manier has been successful, the slew of local designers that burst out in the early years of transition have had to adapt to Hungary's rapidly changing fashion sense. With the influx of western labels, locals are less trustful of home-grown talent, and some have closed their doors. Others, such as **Artz Modell**, have standardised their collections and expanded their retail outlets to the malls.

Manier prefers to stay small and retain its independence – relying on a loyal base of international customers to fill the gaps in the local market.

Manier

V. Váci utca 48 (318 1292). M3 Ferenciek tere/tram 2/bus 7. **Open** 10am-6pm Mon-Fri; 10am-2pm Sat. **Credit** AmEx, EC, MC, V. English spoken. **Map C4**

Anikó Németh – passion for history.

Vintage & second-hand clothes

Not many shops carry truly antique clothing, so for anything made before the 1950s, head to **Ecseri piac** (*see below*, **Flea markets**), where there are several stalls with vintage clothes. *Kilós ruha* shops all over the city sell imported used clothes from western Europe for around Ft1,000 per kilo; simply pile your cheap goodies into the basket and a kind old lady will weigh and wrap with loving care .

Ciánkáli

VII. Dohány utca 94 (215 9714). M2 Blaha Lujza. **Open** 10am-7pm Mon-Fri; 9am-1pm Sat. **No credit cards.** Some English spoken. **Map D4**
Best collection of vintage clothes in the city. All kinds of polyester, lots of shoes, jewellery, and leather jackets from Ft3,500.

Egyedi Ruha Galéria

VIII. Baross utca 4 (318 2056). M3 Kálvin tér/tram 47, 49. **Open** 10am-6pm Mon-Fri. **No credit cards.** No English spoken. **Map D5**
The Egyedi window display might draw you in, but their best pieces are not usually for sale. Still, rare gems can be sniffed out from the overcrowded racks and under heaped baskets, but you'll have to beat off the swarms of ferocious grannies first.

Iguana

VIII. Krúdy Gyula utca 9 (317 1627). Tram 4, 6. **Open** 10am-7pm Mon-Fri; 10am-2pm Sat. **No credit cards.** Some English spoken. **Map D5**
Scores of funky duds from the 1960s and 1970s and even some new accessories: sunglasses, Indian jewellery, belts, bags and the like. Plus you'll be shopping to old hip hop tunes under a flashy turquoise and orange ceiling mural – let tack be your guide.

Costume rental

MAFILM Jelmez és Mértékutáni Ruhaszalon

XIV. Róna utca 174 (251 9778). Bus 7. **Open** 8am-4pm Mon-Thur; 8am-1pm Fri. **No credit cards.** Some English spoken.

Costumes from the film company's studio collection for Ft3,000 and Ft5,000. If they don't have a polar bear suit in your size, they'll happily make one up.

Flea markets

Ecseri piac

XIX. Nagykőrösi út 156. Bus 52 from Boráros tér. **Open** 7am-early afternoon Mon-Sat. **Admission** free. **No credit cards.**

You know to get off the bus when everyone else around you starts shuffling and the second-hand car market comes into view on the left – allow about half-an-hour from Boráros tér. Early Saturday morning generally offers the best pickings, but watch out for prices specially inflated for foreigners and be prepared for tough haggling. The outside stalls are still the best bet in town for good deals on folk costumes and textiles, Communist artefacts and other interesting junk from around the region.

Józsefvárosi piac

VII. Kőbányai út 21-23. Tram 28, 37. **Open** 6am-6pm daily. **No credit cards.**

Note the 'Beware of pickpockets' sign in seven languages (but not English, French or German) and be warned. The shoppers here are Hungarian, Polish and Romanian, the stallholders Chinese, their assistants gypsy and the moneychangers Turkish. Don't expect any antiques, but be aware that much of the clothing sold in trendy no-name shops downtown comes from here and avoid the mark-up. Good place for absurd brand names.

Varosligeti Bolhapiac

Petőfi Csarnok, XIV. Zichy Mihály út (251 2485). M1 Széchenyi fürdő. **Open** 7am-2pm Sat-Sun. **Admission** Ft20. **No credit cards.**

Little cousin to Esceri (*see above*) and a weekly pilgrimage for some. Old shoes, icons, tatty paintings, second-hand toys, musical instruments, communist relics – a paradise of affordable junk. Lapel-busting collections of tacky socialist badges.

Flowers

The flower stand on the Pest side of Margaret Bridge is open 24 hours daily.

Fleur de Lis

XIII. Szent István körút 24 (340 4391). M3 Nyugati/tram 4, 6. **Open** 8am-8pm Mon-Fri; 8am-5pm Sat; 9am-4pm Sun. **No credit cards.** No English spoken. **Map** C2

Unusual fresh and dried flowers for all occasions and a decent selection of house plants. Delivery service (Interflora) and custom orders of any size.

Yucca

V. Váci utca 54 (337 3307). M3 Ferenciek tere/tram 2/bus 7. **Open** 9am-6pm Mon-Fri; 9am-2pm Sat. **No credit cards.** Some English spoken. **Map** C4

Delightful speciality flowers from orchids to iris, and dried flowers and house plants too.

Folklore

Authentic folk costumes and linens can be found on the first floor of the **Great Market Hall** on Fővám tér for significantly less than on Váci utca.

Anna Antikvitás

V. Falk Miksa utca 18-20 (302 5461). Tram 2, 4, 6. **Open** 10am-6pm Mon-Fri; 10am-2.30pm Sat. **Credit** EC, MC, V. No English spoken. **Map** C2

A beautiful collection of Transylvanian and Hungarian embroidered linens at reasonable prices.

Folkart Centrum

V. Váci utca 14 (318 5840). M1 Vörösmarty tér. **Open** *shop* 9.30am-7pm daily; *souvenir shop* 9.30am-4pm daily. **Credit** AmEx, DC, EC, JCB, MC, V. English spoken. **Map** C4

The best bet for folk items on Váci utca; hundreds of local artists sell their wares through this state-owned shop. Wooden knick-knacks, embroidery and clothing, plus a selection of rugs and pottery.

Tangó Romantic

V. Váci utca 8 (318 9741). M1 Vörösmarty tér/tram 2. **Open** 10am-6pm Mon-Fri; 10am-1pm Sat. **Credit** AmEx, EC, MC, V. Some English spoken. **Map** C4

Unusual and wearable adaptations of traditional Hungarian linens. Simple blouses, dresses and jackets re-cut from handwoven peasant clothes with crocheted lace detailing. Sister shop across the courtyard has the real thing, with fine antique hemp and linen tablecloths, pillowcases and bed covers. **Branch**: **Tangó Classic** V. Apáczai Csere János utca 3 (318 4394).

Ceramics & pottery

Haas & Czjek

VI. Bajcsy-Zsilinszky út 23 (311 4094). M3 Arany János utca. **Open** 10am-6pm Mon-Fri; 9am-1pm Sat. **Credit** AmEx, DC, EC, MC, V. Some English spoken. **Map** C3

Large selection of Czech crystal and Hungarian porcelain. Somewhat weak in Zsolnay and Herend, so look instead to Hollóháza and Alföldi for reasonably priced dinner and tea services.

Herend Porcelain

V. József Nádor tér 11 (317 2622). M1 Vörösmarty tér. **Open** 10am-6pm Mon-Fri; 10am-1pm Sat. **Credit** AmEx, DC, EC, MC, V. English spoken. **Map** C4

Herend is Hungary's finest porcelain since 1826; Queen Victoria picked out its delicate birds and butterfly pattern at the 1896 Paris exhibition to put on her own table. For antique pieces, head to Falk Miksa utca or Esceri piac. **Branch**: V. Kigyó utca 5 (318 3439).

Zsolnay Porcelain – *free-flowing designs in traditional weatherproof glaze.*

Zsolnay Porcelain

V. Kígyó utca 4 (318 3712). M3 Ferenciek tere/tram 2/bus 7. **Open** 10am-6pm Mon-Fri; 10am-1pm Sat. **Credit** AmEx, MC, V. English spoken. **Map C4**
Not as refined as big sister Herend, Zsolnay's designs are more free-flowing and better suited to the art nouveau patterns it commonly uses. Most famous for a patented weatherproof glaze developed in the late-nineteenth century that resulted in the beautiful mosaic roof tiles still found on the Mátyás church, the Central Market and the Applied Arts Museum, the firm spent much of the Communist era producing insulators for power lines. It's happily returned to fine porcelain, though, and has recently come out with some bold new patterns.

The best places for basics are the various district market halls, or the **Nagy Vasárcsarnok** at IX. Fővám tér. *See chapter* **Sightseeing**.

1000 Teas

V. Váci utca 65 (337 8217). M3 Ferenciek tere/tram 2/bus 7. **Open** noon-9pm Mon-Fri; 11am-9pm Sat. **No credit cards**. English spoken. **Map C4**
The world's finest teas selected, imported and sold for from Ft600 to Ft2,800 per 100 grams. Quiet tearoom and summer terrace for a break from busy Váci utca.

Ázsia

IX. Vámház körút 1 (217 6067). M3 Kálvin tér/tram 47, 49. **Open** 10am-5pm Mon; 7am-6pm Tue-Fri;

7am-1pm Sat. **No credit cards**. Some English spoken. **Map D5**
This is expat home-cooking central, and the prices show the owners know it. All the basics for Asian, Indian and Italian cuisine, including fancy sauces, black beans, taco shells, frozen squid and a glorious selection of spices.

Coquan's Kávé

IX. Ráday utca 15 (215 2444 ext 252). M3 Kálvin tér. **Open** 8am-6pm Mon-Fri; 7am-2pm Sat; 11am-5pm Sun. **No credit cards**. Some English spoken. **Map D5**
Coffee beans roasted daily on the premises. Usually about ten varieties to choose from, or just take a minute for an espresso and excellent lemon cake. **Branch**: V. Nádor utca 5 (266 9936).

Rana Center ABC

VII. Nefelejcs utca 27-29 (352 2348). M2 Keleti/bus 7/trolleybus 78, 79. **Open** 8am-11pm Mon-Sat; 10am-11pm Sun. **No credit cards**. Some English spoken. **Map F3**
Loads of Middle Eastern ingredients and spices, including fresh lamb, feta cheese, pitta, Turkish delight and vats of olives. Excellent selection of nuts. Late hours a bonus.

Rothschild Kóser Élelmiszer

VII. Dob utca 12 (267 5691). M1, M2, M3 Deák tér/tram 47, 49. **Open** 8.30am-6pm Mon-Thur; 8.30am-2.30pm Fri. **No credit cards**. No English spoken. **Map D4**
Israeli import shop filling the food needs of the orthodox. Worth a visit for nifty tins of odd things, ramen noodles, sweets and exotic nuts.

T. Nagy Tamás Sajtüzlete

V. Gerlóczy utca 3 (317 4268). M1, M2, M3 Deák tér/tram 47, 49. **Open** 9am-6pm Mon-Fri; 9am-1pm Sat. **No credit cards.** Some English spoken. **Map C4**
Some of the bigger supermarkets have begun to stock better-quality cheese, but 'Big Tom' remains the best in town with around 150 types to choose from. A sure-fire bet for good Brie, fresh Parmesan and assorted English cheeses.

Supermarkets

Csemege Julius Meinl

VIII. Rákóczi út 59 (313 7232). M2 Blaha Lujza/tram 4, 6/bus 7. **Open** 7am-7.30pm Mon-Fri; 7am-2pm Sat. **Credit** AmEx, EC, MC, V. No English spoken. **Map E4**
With branches all over the city, Meinl is a good place to stop for culinary basics plus moderately priced wines and spirits. This location was the first shop in Budapest to open late and still keeps later hours than most – and accepts credit cards.

Kaiser's Metro

VI. Nyugati tér (332 2531). M3 Nyugati/tram 4, 6. **Open** 7am-8pm Mon-Fri; 7am-1pm Sat. **Credit** AmEx, MC, V. No English spoken. **Map C2**
Supermarket entrance right ahead of you at underground level as you come out of Nyugati metro. German chain that stocks just about everything you'd want in a supermarket, even peanut butter and Heinz baked beans. Quality fresh meats, a good selection of cheeses. Late hours another bonus.
Branches: XI. Október 23 utca 6-10 (385 0189); VIII. Blaha Lujza tér 1-2 (338 3791).

Rothschild

VII. Károly körút 9 (342 9733). M1, M2, M3 Deák tér/tram 47, 49. **Open** 7am-10pm Mon-Fri; 8am-6pm Sat; 9am-5pm Sun. **Credit** DC, EC, JCB, MC, V. No English spoken. **Map C4**
Open evenings and Sundays and selling imported 'western' food. Free next-day delivery for purchases over Ft5,000.
Branch: XIII. Szent István körút 4 (329 3566).

Vegetarian & health food

Vegetarianism still hasn't caught on in Hungary and there are few specialist stores. Basics like soy sauce, rolled grains and crackers can be found at larger supermarkets like Kaiser's (*see above* **Supermarkets**), and many shops carry a variety of dry soy products. Vitamins are sold in drug stores, but a better bet are body-building shops such as branches of **Mini-Mix Gyógynövény**.

Béres Egészségtár

VI. Bajcsy köz 1 (311 0009). M3 Arany János utca. **Open** 9am-7pm Mon-Fri; 9am-1pm Sat. **Credit** DC, EC, MC, V. No English spoken. **Map C3**
Speciality foods, a wide range of natural beauty products, vitamins, essential oils, teas and incense.

Bio-ABC

Múzeum körút 19 (317 3043). M2 Astoria/tram 47, 49/bus 7. **Open** 10am-7pm Mon-Fri; 10am-2pm Sat. **No credit cards.** Some English spoken. **Map D5**
Soy milk and sausages, carrot juice, organic produce, wholegrains, natural cosmetics, herbal teas, essential oils, medicinal herbs and jars of Marmite.

Kaiser's Metro *– just about everything you'd want in a* szupermarket.

Drogéria Testkultúra

VI. Oktogon 4 (302 1324). M1 Oktogon/tram 4,6.
Open 8.30am-7pm Mon-Fri; 8.30am-2pm Sat. **No
credit cards**. No English spoken. **Map D3**
This is a mix of a body-building shop and a miniature health food shop all in one, concentrating on
cosmetics, basic foods and assorted vitamins
imported from the USA.

Egészségbolt

*XII. Csaba utca 3 (212 2542). M2 Moszkva tér/tram
4, 6.* **Open** 8.30am-8pm Mon-Fri; 8.30am-3pm Sat.
No credit cards. No English spoken.
Longer opening hours and its convenient location
near Moszkva tér make the Egészségbolt one of the
better speciality stores in town. Plentiful supply of
health food basics, vitamins, cosmetics and various
fresh breads.

Galgafarm

*VII. Eötvös utca 8 (351 2441). M1 Oktogon/tram 4,
6.* **Open** 10am-6pm Mon-Fri; 10am-1pm Sat. **No
credit cards**. No English spoken. **Map D3**
One of Budapest's lesser-known speciality stores
stocks a range of organic produce, including whole-
grain breads and lots of natural and organic
Hungarian food and cosmetics.

Wine

Budapest Wine Society

I. Batthyány utca 59 (212 2569). M2 Batthyány tér.
Open 10am-8pm Mon-Fri; 10am-6pm Sat. **Credit**
AmEx, EC, MC, V. English spoken. **Map B2**
The best wines from all over Hungary and knowledgeable staff to help you pick out something in
your price range. Free wine tastings between 2pm
and 5pm Saturday afternoons.

La Boutique des Vins

*V. József Attila utca 12 (317 5909). M1 Vörösmarty
tér/tram 2.* **Open** 10am-6pm Mon-Fri; 10am-3pm Sat.
Credit AmEx. English spoken. **Map C3**
The former sommelier of the Gundel restaurant (*see*
chapter **Restaurants**) presides over an excellent
collection of Hungarian and select imported wines.

Food delivery

Maharaja Indian Restaurant

*III. Bécsi út 89-91 (250 7544/fax 388 6863). Tram
17.* **Open** noon-11pm Tue-Sun. **No credit cards**.
English spoken.
Fast and friendly delivery of Indian eats during
business hours. At other times, large orders only.

Bringing it all back home

If you are stopped at customs on the way into
Hungary (a definite possibility if you arrive with
lots of luggage), make sure to save all the bits of
paper you are given and call a customs expediter.
Fines can be outrageous, waits interminable, and
it is not unknown for swarms of customs officers
to descend on the homes of unsuspecting foreigners who somehow forgot to declare the dirty
socks they used to pack their stereo in.

On the way home, Murphy's law of baggage
states that 'stuff' will expand to exceed the capacity of whatever size bag you brought. Shipping it
home is an easy solution, but be aware that
antiques over 70 years old require a special export
stamp – ask your antiques dealer for details.

For smaller packages, the post office is the
cheapest solution, though be prepared for a head-
on collision with Magyar bureaucracy. Packages
of up to Ft10,000 in value can be sent surface to
any destination for Ft2,800. Bring your packed
box (not sealed), or purchase one at the *cso-
magfelvétel* window upon arrival (Ft80-Ft140). At
the same window, pick up a blue *vámáru-nyilatkozat* (customs form conveniently in Hungarian
and French). Itemise the contents of your package, estimate the value of each item and fill in
sender/receiver details. You have, of course,
remembered to bring your own packing tape and

string, which you will use to seal the box at the
levélfelvétel window as you hand in the blue slip.

One last tip: post from Hungary is notoriously slow (allow one month to the USA and two
weeks to the UK), and has a nasty habit of disappearing completely – especially nice sweaters
and CDs. To track a package and its contents,
fill out the white *ajánlott* form also found at the
levélfelvétel window. This gives you a serial
number that can be traced from both the sending and receiving end, and adds Ft120 to the
price of your parcel.

Business Umbrella

*V. Aranykéz utca 2 (tel/fax 318 4126/318 7244).
M1 Vörösmarty tér/tram 2.* **Open** 9am-5pm Mon-
Thur; 9am-4pm Fri. **No credit cards**. English
spoken.
Although they won't actually ship your things, if
you get caught in a customs mess, call them. They
handle customs clearance, residence permits
(Ft40,000), work permits (Ft25,000) and car and
business registration.

First European Shipping

*II. Rózsahegy utca 8 (tel/fax 216 7587/
1steuros@elender.hu). Tram 4, 6/bus 11.* **Open**
10am-6pm Mon-Fri.
They'll get your things home and also offer an
antiques-finding and customs clearance service.

Pink Cadillac

IX. Ráday utca 22 (216 1412/218 9382). M3 Kálvin tér/tram 47, 49. **Open** 11.30am-midnight Mon-Thur, Sun; 11.30am-1am Fri, Sat. **No credit cards.** Some English spoken. **Map D5**
Reasonable selection of pasta and salads, decent pizza. Free but not very speedy delivery in neighbouring central districts.

Sushi An

V. Harmicad utca 4 (317 4239). M1 Vörösmarty tér. **Open** noon-3.15pm, 5-9.45pm, daily. **No credit cards** for delivery. Some English spoken. **Map C4**
Sushi delivered for the taxi fare to get it to you.

Seefisch

Mamut Center, II. Lövőház utca 2-6 (345 8040). M2 Moszkva tér/tram, 4, 6 Széna tér. **Open** 11am-10pm daily. **No credit cards.** Some English spoken.
Seafood sandwiches plus fish and chips with a modest selection of pasta dishes and other entrées delivered to central districts.

Health & beauty

Most major brand names can be found on Váci utca or nearby: Clinique, Estée Lauder and Christian Dior between numbers 8 and 12. Guerlain on Haris köz 6 and Yves St Laurent in the Kempinski Hotel. Various branches of Nature Blue offer an unsatisfying Body Shop substitute.

Azúr

V. Petőfi Sándor utca 11 (318 5394). M3 Ferenciek tere/tram 2/bus 7. **Open** 8am-8pm Mon-Fri; 9am-2pm Sat. **Credit** AmEx, EC, MC, V. No English spoken. **Map C4**
Nothing too special, but essential cosmetics, perfumes, shampoo, toothbrushes, creams, plasters, and bunion pads. Look for Hungarian-made, natural cosmetics by Helia-D, Ilcsi and Anaconda.

Kállos Illatszer és Fodrászcikk

VII. Nagydiófa utca 1 (268 0930). M2 Blaha Lujza tér. **Open** 10am-6pm Mon-Fri; 9am-1pm Sat. **No credit cards.** No English spoken. **Map D4**
Catering primarily to beauty salons, Kállos carries well-known names such as Nivea, L'Oréal, Helia D, Anaconda and Freeman at the best prices in town.

Beauty salons

Beauty treatments in Budapest are a bargain by western European standards, and generally of reasonable quality.

Exclusive Szépségszalon

V. Veres Pálné utca 22 (266 7228/266 7229). M3 Ferenciek tere/tram 2/bus 7. **Open** 8am-8pm Mon-Fri; 8am-2pm Sat. **No credit cards.** Some English spoken. **Map C4**
A busy salon with a huge range of treatments. Facials are between Ft4,000 and Ft5,000; other exotic treatments include 'hand and foot care with paraffin' and 'body shaping with acupuncture'.

Picurka Salon

VII. Lövölde tér 2 (341 2339). Tram 4, 6. **Open** 7am-7pm Mon-Fri. **No credit cards.** No English spoken. **Map E3**
Reputedly the best facial in town, so it's worth negotiations in sign language before you sit back and enjoy. Prices a fraction of downtown salons.

Vivien Talpai

II. Fillér utca 10/b (213 1445). M2 Moszkva tér/tram 4, 6. **Open** 8am-6pm Mon-Fri; 8am-noon Sat. **No credit cards.** Some English spoken.
Good things for your feet including pedicures, acupuncture (Ft1,400-Ft2,200), foot massage (Ft620) and computer-assisted examinations for custom-fit insoles (Ft3,400 and ready within a week).

Hair salons

Jacques Dessange

V. Deák Ferenc utca 10 (266 8167/429 3883). M1, M2, M3 Deák tér/tram 47, 49. **Open** 9am-8pm Mon-Wed, Fri; 9am-7pm Thur; 9am-4pm Sat. **Credit** AmEx. English spoken. **Map C4**
The safest bet for a cut, but it's in the Kempinski Hotel and the prices at Jacques Dessange match the quality of the service. All the receptionists are multilingual, as are most of the staff. Fashionable cuts, Dessange hair-care products, facials, body treatments, manicures and make-overs.

Perino Péter

VI. Izabella utca 45 (352 1404). M1 Vörösmarty utca. **Open** 10am-6pm Mon-Fri; 9am-2pm Sat. **No credit cards.** English spoken. **Map D3**
Hungarians swear by Roland and Péter for fashionable, inexpensive hairstyles, so make sure to call a few days in advance for an appointment. They also stock Tigri, Paul Mitchell and other quality hair-care products, and there'll be a cosmetician on hand for facials, waxing and other fancies. Their most expensive haircut costs Ft2,500.

Zsidró

VI. Andrássy út 17 (342 7366). M1 Opera. **Open** 8am-9pm Mon-Fri; 9am-2pm Sat. **No credit cards.** Some English spoken. **Map D3**
Hip central for hair fashion and cosmetic treats from facials to waxing. Make an appointment or just walk in – there's magazines and overpriced coffee while you watch Budapest's finest under the scissors.

Barbers

Traditional Hungarian barbers – *férfi fodrász* – can also give you an alcohol scalp massage as a refreshing conclusion to a reasonably-priced wash and trim.

Férfi Fodrász

XI. Karinthy Frigyes út (209 1655). Tram 16, 19, 47, 49. **Open** 7am-8pm Mon-Fri; 7am-1pm Sat. **No credit cards.** No English spoken. **Map C6**
Friendly barber shop offers a wash and trim costs Ft900, including alcohol scalp massage.

Férfi Fodrász – *cheap cuts, bargain rinses and rock-bottom alcohol rubs.*

Férfi Fodrász

XIII. Nyugati tér 4 (329 2103). M3 Nyugati/tram 4, 6. **Open** 6.30am-7pm Mon-Fri; 6.30am-2pm Sat. **No credit cards**. No English spoken. **Map C2**

Handily located barbers with rock-bottom prices: Ft500 for a basic cut; trim, wash and styling for Ft750. Alcohol scalp massage is an extra Ft150.

Laundry & dry-cleaning

Patyolat is the Hungarian for laundry but there aren't many around these days. Prices go by the kilo and ironing and folding are usually included.

Crystal

V. Arany János utca 34 (331 8307). M3 Arany János utca. **Open** 7am-7pm Mon-Fri; 8am-1pm Sat. **No credit cards**. No English spoken. **Map C3**

Next-day dry-cleaning, as well as leather clothing and winter jackets within a week.

Harmat Textil Tisztitó

II. Margit körút 62 (201 4764). Tram 4, 6. **Open** 7am-7pm Mon-Fri. **No credit cards**. No English spoken. **Map A2**

Old-fashioned Hungarian laundry with dry-cleaning too. Prices by the kilo, shirts from Ft280.

The Home Laundry

II. Máriaremetei út 70B (397 4591). Bus 5. **Open** 8am-7.30pm Mon-Fri; 9am-1pm Sat. **No credit cards**. English spoken.

A number of branches – mostly in Buda – but with delivery all over town. Your clothes are cleaned with TLC, and dry-cleaning is reliable. Regular laundry by the kilo for sheets, underwear and towels (Ft649). Other clothing charged by the piece (Ft399 for shirts, Ft849 for dresses) with extras such as folding, ironing and starching. Pick-up and delivery costs Ft800. Choose from regular or express services. Friendly, English-speaking staff.

Music

CD Bar

VIII. Krúdy Gyula utca 6 (338 4281). M3 Kálvin tér/tram 4, 6. **Open** 10am-8pm Mon-Fri; 10am-4pm Sat. **No credit cards**. Some English spoken. **Map D5**

Take your time browsing around a wide-ranging selection of contemporary and classical jazz in a relaxed atmosphere with staff who know their stock and comfy chairs in which to listen to whatever strikes your fancy. Classical, pop, world and folk music also available.

Concerto Records

VII. Dob utca 33 (268 9631). M1 Opera/tram 4, 6/trolleybus 74. **Open** noon-7pm Mon-Fri; noon-4pm Sun. **Credit** AmEx, DC, EC, MC, V. Some English spoken. **Map D3**

Crowded but charming shop near the Orthodox Synagogue offering an impressive collection of new and second-hand vinyl and CDs. Stock is mostly classical and opera with a little bit of jazz and folk.

Fonó Budai Zeneház

XI. Sztregova utca 3 (206 5300). Tram 47. **Open** 10am-midnight Tue-Sat. **No credit cards**. Some English spoken.

Far from the centre, but an excellent selection of local folk and world music. *See page 32* **Buda's acoustic oasis.**

Fotex

V. Szervita tér 2 (318 3395). M1 Vörösmarty tér. **Open** 10am-9pm daily. **Credit** AmEx, DC, EC, JCB, MC, V. Some English spoken. **Map C4**

Large amounts of depressingly mainstream pop, and Fotex can't even claim to be the biggest music store in Budapest anymore (that's the Virgin Megastore at Duna Plaza), but it's central and convenient if you want to find all genres in one shop.

MCD

V. Vörösmarty tér 1 (no phone). M1 Vörösmarty tér/tram 2 . **Open** 9.30am-9.30pm daily. **No credit cards.** No English spoken. **Map C4**
A central place to pick out some Hungarian classics. Divided between pop and classical, there's always something good in the sales racks.
Branch: VI. Jókai utca 40.

Neuma

VII. Dohány utca 57 (322 0626). M2 Blaha Lujza. **Open** 10am-6pm Mon-Fri; 9am-1pm Sat. **No credit cards.** Some English spoken. **Map D4**
Lots of local stuff for a serious collectors of nostalgia music – LPs and 78s from the 1920s to the 1960s.

Rózsavölgyi Zeneműbolt

V. Szervita tér 5 (318 3500). M1, M2, M3 Deák tér/ tram 47, 49. **Open** 10am-7pm Mon-Fri; 10am-5pm Sat; 10am-6pm Sun. **Credit** AmEx, DC, EC, JCB, MC, V. English spoken. **Map C4**
In the back you'll find an excellent selection of classical, ballet and opera, with special attention paid to central European composers and orchestras. Big collection of sheet music as well and folk and popular music downstairs. Lots of cheap old vinyl.

Wave/Trance

VI. Révay köz 2 (269 3135). M3 Arany János utca. **Open** 11am-7pm Mon-Fri; 11am-2pm Sat. **No credit cards.** Some English spoken. **Map C3**
The first alternative music shop in Budapest consists of two neighbouring branches. Wave provides a solid choice of alternative guitar-oriented music while Trance focuses on underground dance. Good place for flyers and concert information.

Opticians

Ofotért-Optinoa Magyar-Amerikai Optikai Kft

V. Múzeum körút 13 (317 3559/266 2137). M2 Astoria/tram 47, 49/bus 7. **Open** 10am-6pm Mon-Fri; 10am-1pm Sat. **Credit** AmEx, DC, EC, JCB, MC, V. English spoken. **Map D4**
English-speaking opticians to conduct eye exams or fill in a prescription for new contact lenses. Head here to replenish stocks of contact lens cleaning supplies. A large selection of international (expensive) and Hungarian (cheaper) frames.

Photocopying & printing

Copy General

V. Semmelweis utca 4 (266 6564). M2 Astoria/tram 47, 49/bus 7. **Open** 7am-10pm daily. **No credit cards.** English spoken. **Map D4**
Six branches serve day-and-night printing and photocopy needs in Budapest. Pick up and delivery for a nominal fee (Ft800 each way). The Lónyay utca branch is open 24 hours and also offers desktop publishing and computer rental.
Branches: I. Krisztina körút 83 (212 0906/356 8772); IX. Lónyay utca 13 (216 8880/217 1592).

Photography

Ofotért

V. Károly körút 14 (317 6313). M2 Astoria/tram 47, 49/bus 7. **Open** 9am-7pm Mon-Fri; 9am-2pm Sat. **Credit** AmEx, DC, EC, MC, V. Some English spoken. **Map D4**
Hungarian film-processing is not that much cheaper than in the west, and certainly not as good unless done at a professional studio. Nevertheless, Ofotért is considered to maintain more consistent quality than its nearest competitor, Fotex.

Fotolux

V. Károly körút 14 (342 1538). M2 Astoria/tram 47, 49/bus 7. **Open** 8am-9pm Mon-Fri; 9am-7pm Sat. **No credit cards.** Some English spoken. **Map C4**
Budapest's certified Nikon dealer has camera supplies, colour and slide processing and will help you find camera repair services.

Antique & second-hand cameras

Soós Kereskedés

V. József Attila utca 84 (317 2341). M1, M2, M3 Deák tér/tram 47, 49. **Open** 9am-5pm Mon-Fri; 10am-1pm Sat. **No credit cards.** Some English spoken. **Map C3**
One set of display windows holds tacky gifts, the other rows of old cameras. The same schizophrenia reigns inside, so walk past the bins of cheap junk to the back counter and side room, which houses more cameras, used enlargers, a film-processing service and miscellaneous parts.

Repairs

Bicycle repair

Túra Mobil Discount Store

VI. Nagymező utca 43 (312 5073). M1 Opera. **Open** 9am-6pm Mon-Fri; 9am-2pm Sat. **No credit cards.** No English spoken. **Map D3**
Túra's reliable and professional staff repair mountain and touring bikes. They also provide a selection of accessories, parts for DIY repairs and a small stock of new bikes.

Computer repair

Macropolis Notebook Computer

VI. Teréz körút 11 (343 2949/fax 352 1434). M1 Oktogon/tram 4, 6. **Open** 10am-6pm Mon-Fri. **Credit** MC, V. Some English spoken. **Map D3**
Diagnosis of laptop problems for Ft5,000 plus sales and service of most major notebook brands. PC sales and service at the Thököly út branch.
Branches: XII. Márvány utca 24B (212 9780/fax 212 4894); VII. Thököly út 23 (tel/fax 351 3531).

Re-Mac Computer Kft.

V. Bajcsy-Zsilinszky út 62 (312 5870). M3 Arany János utca. **Open** 8am-6pm Mon-Thur; 8am-5pm Fri. **No credit cards.** English spoken. **Map C3**
Authorised sale and service of Apple computers.

De-junking the districts

One day a year, sometime between May and September, each Budapest district undergoes a ritual purification – the *Lomtálánítás*, or 'de-junking'. Piles of worn-out furniture, old clothes, ancient appliances, unloved ornaments and yellowing periodicals are dumped out on the pavement and spill into the street. Pedestrians pause to rummage around, pocketing an item here, tossing back another there. The unwary visitor, negotiating this mess, might be forgiven for thinking they've touched down in some mad Third World country.

Actually, *Lomtálánítás* is a primitive but effective form of recycling. Each postal district has its day, listed in local newspapers. As the hour approaches, locals start eyeing the oddments stacked at the back of the pantry, consider whether they really need the old footstool now they've bought that nice new beanbag at IKEA, leap at the chance to dispose of that malfunctioning communist-era fridge, too heavy to lug further than the doorstep.

Stuff starts appearing the evening before. By morning the pavements brim over. All day long, passers-by cluster and peruse. Gangs of specialists cruise in trucks, instantly sizing up and hauling off whatever scrap metal, old porcelain or discarded TV set might be worth a few forints. Gypsies root around for serviceable clothes. Pensioners drag home oddments of furniture. Expats unearth amusing ornaments. People move from one pile to another, nervous that the garbage might be greener on the other side.

Pickings may seem slim, but some people furnish entire flats this way. It's certainly a lot cheaper than going to the flea markets, is usually more fun, and often happens right outside your own doorstep. By the evening, absolutely anything usable will have found some kind of a home. First thing the next morning, city trucks come and cart away whatever's left. And inside people's apartments, new junk starts accumulating for next year's *Lomtálánítás*.

Appliance repairs

Time rather than price is the problem in getting appliances repaired in Budapest, and much energy can be wasted trudging around town looking for someone that can handle your particular job. The city is still full of obscure repair shops (umbrellas, cigarette lighters) but finding them in a hurry is another matter. **Telinformix** (269 3333; open 8am-8pm daily) will direct you to the nearest and most suitable repair shop for your appliance. Make sure to have a Hungarian on hand to explain your predicament.

Luggage repair

Flekk GMK

VI. Podmaniczky utca 19 (311 0316). M3 Nyugati/tram 4, 6. **Open** 9am-6pm Mon-Fri; 9am-1pm Sat. **No credit cards**. No English spoken. **Map D3**
There's a shop like this in nearly every neighbourhood where you can copy keys, fix your shoes or pick up an assortment of DIY supplies. Luggage and zip repair within a few days.

Mountex

IX. Üllői út 7 (217 2426). M3 Kálvin tér/tram 47, 49. **Open** 10am-6pm Mon-Fri; 10am-1pm Sat. **Credit** EC, MC, V. English spoken. **Map D5**
All-round camping, caving and climbing outfitter that will also fix backpack blowouts and handle general equipment repair.
Branch: II. Margit körút 61 (212 4086).

Shoe repair

Mister Minit

Skála Metro, VI. Nyugati tér (353 2222). M3 Nyugati/tram 4, 6. **Open** 9am-6.30pm Mon-Fri; 9am-2pm Sat. **No credit cards**. Some English spoken. **Map C2**
This American chain has 20 locations all over Budapest, dealing in shoe repair, key cutting and knife sharpening, many also with photocopying services.

Watch & jewellery repairs

Orex Óraszalon

V. Petőfi Sándor utca 6 (337 4915). M3 Ferenciek tere/tram 2/bus 7. **Open** 10am-6pm Mon-Fri; 10am-1pm Sat. **Credit** AmEx, DC, EC, MC, V. English spoken. **Map C4**
Many little family-run shops will be happy to change a battery or make a repair, but the reliable staff at this location speak English.

Sporting goods

Mallory Sport

VII. Király utca 59A (342 0744). Tram 4, 6. **Open** 10am-6pm Mon-Wed, Fri; 10am-7pm Thur; 10am-1.30pm Sat. **Credit** EC, MC, V. Some English spoken. **Map D3**
Named after the famous mountaineer, Mallory carries indoor and outdoor sporting supplies covering everything from aerobics to racquet sports.

Arts & Entertainment

Baths

Whether in an Ottoman original or an art nouveau extravaganza, a long, slow soak is one of Budapest's hedonistic highlights.

Rudas Gyógyfürdő – *authentic Ottoman soaking experience. See page 180.*

Budapest is Europe's largest spa town and the 120 or so thermal springs that gush up from Buda's limestone bedrock have long inspired a culture of bathing. Indeed, the mineral-rich waters seem to have been one of the reasons why there was ever a settlement here in the first place. There is evidence that Neolithic peoples were drawn to Buda's warm springs, and later the Romans brought their bathing customs and built aqueducts and bathhouses. From the ninth century, the Magyars continued this watery tradition, but it was under the Ottomans in the sixteenth and seventeenth centuries that bathing in Buda achieved its golden age.

The natural and abundant supply, combined with the demands of Islam that its followers adhere to a strict set of rules for ablutions in running water before praying five times a day, inspired an aquatic and hedonistic culture that still thrives today. The Ottoman mosques, monasteries and schools that once filled the streets of Buda are all long gone, but centuries later it is still possible to bathe under an original Ottoman dome in

the **Király**, **Rudas** or **Rác** – the only significant remains of the period.

The original Turkish baths have mostly been added to – their magnificent domes and pools are intact but now they're surrounded by more recent structures – and newer thermal facilities have been built in a similar tradition, such as the **Gellért** or the **Széchenyi** complex. Along the way, the bathing habit has become part of Budapest life and all of the city take to the waters. Tattooed mafiosi wallow next to ailing old codgers at the Rudas, chess-players make queen swaps and families cavort at the Széchenyi, old matrons paddle a determined breast stroke at the **Lukács** while the gay community gets together at the Rác.

Many of these places – still state-run and subsidised to keep the prices down – are quite dilapidated. In some measure this can add to their charm, but concerns about the quality of the water were among the reasons for recent renovations at the Széchenyi and the city is slowly having to fix the circulation systems at all the major baths. But this is only a drop in the pool. Some have not been

renovated for more than half a century and city officials maintain that something around Ft100 billion (£264 million) would be the figure required for a complete facelift of all the spa facilities in Budapest.

Despite rising ticket prices the baths barely break even and the city is unlikely to be able to raise this kind of money without eventually having to privatise some of the spa facilities. This is a thorny subject. The baths are part of Budapest's identity and their egalitarian tradition is a local point of pride. But it's not unlikely that, say, Danubius – which owns the Gellért Hotel and the **Danubius Thermal Hotel Helia** – may end up buying into control of the spas adjacent to the hotels and limiting admission to the public.

But for now it's still a case of anyone and everyone goes, and often the very tattiness of the facilities abets the sensation, not just of lolling peacefully in the waters, but also of floating gently back in time.

BARE ESSENTIALS

For anyone without much command of Hungarian, entering the baths for the first time can be a baffling experience. Lengthy menus offer such treats as ultra-sound or a pedicure as well as massage. Instructions in Hungarian, German and Russian explain that customers can stay for an hour and a half, although this rule is rarely enforced.

The routine is similar in all the Turkish baths, though it varies at the mixed facilities. After buying a ticket you enter a warren of passageways, the entrance to which is guarded by a white-clothed attendant. Hand over your ticket and you will be given a white (well, it was white once) flap of cloth that is to be tied around your waist for the modesty's sake. The ones for women have an apron-like addition that supposedly covers the breasts, but few women bother to wear them at all. Men tend to keep theirs on, though, sometimes swivelling them round to cover their behinds, to prevent scorched buttocks on the wooden sauna seats. For the mixed facilities you'll need to take a swimming costume.

Once in the changing rooms, either the attendant will show you a cubicle, or else you find one yourself, but each is locked twice and reliably secure. In some places the attendant has one key and you keep the other: tie it to the spare string on your once-white cloth flap thing.

The baths generally have one or two main pools and a series of smaller ones around the perimeter, all of different temperatures, ranging from dauntingly hot to icily cold. The precise drill depends on individual preference, but involves moving between different pools, taking in the dry heat of the sauna and the extreme humidity of the steam rooms, alternating temperatures and finally relaxing in gentle warm water.

An hour or two is usually sufficient and is extremely relaxing. The waters also ease stiff joints and rheumatic complaints. Afterwards you shower (take soap) and, in the Király and Rudas, are provided with a towel – take your own to the others. Most baths have a restroom, where you can take a short nap before changing back into street clothes. On the way out, tip the attendant Ft50-100.

Apart from pools, saunas and steam rooms, most sites also offer massages. These come in two types: *vizi* (water) massage and *orvosi* (medical) massage – the latter is the gentler experience. Masseurs are professional but inattentive, chatting away to their colleagues as they work. Tip them Ft100 or so.

A full visit to one of the baths demands a whole morning or afternoon. There's usually somewhere in the foyer to get a cold drink, coffee or snack, plus a stall selling soap and other toiletries. Don't expect to have the energy to do very much afterwards except settle down for a long lunch or stretch out for a nap, but do remember to drink lots of water to rehydrate.

Apart from the baths listed here, there are also limited thermal facilities at the **Palatinus** and **Dagály** strands. (*See also chapters* **Sport & Fitness** *and* **Gay & Lesbian**.)

Note that ticket offices shut up shop an hour before listed closing times.

The baths

Gellért Gyógyfürdő

XI. Kelenhegyi út 4 (466 6166). Trams 18, 19, 47, 49/bus 7 to Gellért tér. **Open** 6am-7pm daily. **Admission** Ft1,500; Ft750 concs. Mixed. Some English spoken. **Map C5**

The most expensive of all the baths, but you do get an art nouveau swimming pool chucked in for your money. In the summer your Ft1,200 also allows access to the several outside pools (the wave machine is popular with children) and sunbathing areas, complete with terrace restaurant. There was a hospital on this site as early as the thirteenth century, and the Turks also had a spa here. Now the beauty of this art nouveau extravaganza, built in the inter-war years, is matched only by the surliness of most of its staff, who all seem to be graduates of the Josef Stalin charm school, class of 1950. The separate thermal pools – one for men, one for women – lead off from the main 33-metre swimming pool, which also has its own small warm water pool. The secessionist theme continues in the maze of steam rooms and saunas that gives the Gellért a different atmosphere to the Turkish Rudas or Király. The clientele are also quite entertaining, composed mainly of startled tourists and, in the male half, gay men on the prowl. The restroom is sometimes extremely active. Crowded during tourist season. The thermal water here contains a lot of carbonic gases and is recommended for people with blood pressure problems and coronary heart disease.

Király Gyógyfürdő

II. Fő utca 84 (201 4392). M2 Batthyány tér. **Open** *men* 6.30am-7pm Mon, Wed, Fri; *women* 6.30am-7pm Tue, Thur, Sat. **Admission** Ft500. No English spoken. **Map B2**

Along with the Rudas, the Király is one of the city's most significant Ottoman monuments, particularly the sixteenth-century pool. Originally called the Bath of the Cock Tower, it takes its present name from the nineteenth-century owners, the König (King) family, who changed their name to its Hungarian equivalent – Király. Construction of the Turkish part began in 1566 and was completed by Pasha Sokoli Mustapha in 1570. Located within the Viziváros town walls, it meant the Ottoman garrison could enjoy a good soak even during a siege. The classical bits were added in the early eighteenth century. The Király follows the traditional pattern of a main pool surrounded by smaller ones of different temperatures, plus saunas and steam rooms, but is not as beautiful as the Rudas. The bath's environs are lighter and airier though, and three Turkish-style reliefs mark the entrance corridor. There is a big gay scene on men's days, particularly in the late afternoon.

Lukács Gyógyfürdő és Strandfürdő

II. Frankel Leó út 25-29 (326 1695). Tram 4, 6. **Open** 6am-7pm Mon-Sat; 6am-5pm Sun. **Admission** Ft500; Ft400 concs. No English spoken. **Map B1**

A complex of two outdoor swimming pools set in attractive grounds and thermal baths, in this case the Turkish-period Császár Baths, although there aren't that many original features left and the layout is quite different from the other Turkish places. The baths are mixed, which also lends a different atmosphere to that at the Rudas or Király. There's something of an institutional feel to this warren-like facility, but the setting is verdant and restful. On the wall outside the entrance to the changing rooms, you'll find a selection of old stone plaques, testaments from satisfied customers – the waters are said to be efficacious for orthopaedic diseases. Bring towel and swimming costume.

Rác Gyógyfürdő

I. Hadnagy utca 8-10 (356 1322). Tram 18, 19, 47, 49. **Open** 6am-6pm *women* Mon, Wed, Fri; *men* Tue, Thur, Sat. **Admission** Ft500. No English spoken. **Map B5**

Tucked under Gellért Hill, with a pleasant outdoor café overlooking the leafy Tabán, the Rác baths are named after the Hungarian word for the Serb community that once lived by the river. Though the exterior is nineteenth century (designed by Miklós Ybl), the octagonal pool and dome inside date back to Turkish times, although they're drabber than those at the Király or Rudas. The Rác offers the same menu of pools, steam and sauna as the other two Turkish-built facilities and on men's days has the most active gay scene of all the baths, especially on a Saturday afternoon. Its thermal waters are suitable for treating chronic arthritis, muscle and nerve pain.

Rudas Gyógyfürdő

I. Döbrentei tér 9 (356 1322). Tram 18, 19/bus 7 to Döbrentei tér. **Open** 6am-7pm Mon-Fri; 6am-1pm Sat, Sun. Closed Sun during summer (15 June-31 Aug). **Admission** Ft500; Ft400 concs. No English spoken. **Map C5**

This is the finest and most atmospheric of Budapest's original Turkish baths (men only, mixed swimming pool), especially when rays of sunlight stab through the hexagonal windows in the domed roof and fan out through the steam above the central pool. The intensity of the aesthetic experience is further enhanced by an extraordinary liquid ambience, as the sound of running water and the chatter of bathers echo from the shadowy corners and up into the dome. The first baths on this site date from the late fourteenth century. The new site was constructed by the Pasha of Buda in the sixteenth century and his plaque still stands in the main chamber. The original cupola, vaulted corridor and main octagonal pool remain, although heavily restored. The Rudas has three saunas and two steam rooms as well as six pools of differing temperatures. Women can get a look inside on Vizimozi nights when the complex hosts a watery rave and throngs with undressed party-goers. *See chapter* **Nightlife**.

Széchenyi Gyógyfürdő és Strandfürdő

XIV. Állatkerti körút 11 (321 0310). M1 Széchenyi fürdő. **Open strand** 6am-7pm daily. *Mixed thermal baths* Apr-Sept 6am-7pm daily; Oct-Mar 6am-5pm Mon-Sat, 6am-4pm Sun. **Admission** Ft500; Ft400 concs. No English spoken. **Map F1**

In the middle of the City Park, an attractive complex of swimming pools and thermal baths, complete with restaurant, the Széchenyi is Europe's largest health spa, with an annual two million visitors. Its waters are used for treating arthritis, gout, gynaecological and respiratory diseases and, if you drink them, gall bladder disease. Outside is a statue of Zsigmond Vilmos, who discovered the thermal spring that fills the outdoor pool. The Széchenyi is probably the best choice for a day of relaxation as it offers outdoor thermal and swimming pools plus the usual indoor assortment of thermal baths and steam rooms, so customers can exercise, laze and sunbathe all on one site. At weekends it throngs with crowds of all ages, lending an endearing holiday atmosphere. Outside pools are beautifully laid out, with a swimming pool as well as a thermal one, open all year round. Here bathers play chess with steam rising around them – a popular guidebook image. Recent renovations have sadly removed the ivy cladding from the façade.

Spa hotels

The facilities at these hotels can also be used by non-residents. *See also chapter* **Accommodation**.

Thermal Hotel Margitsziget

XIII. Margaret Island (329 2300). Bus 26. **Open** 7am-8pm daily. **Admission** *day ticket* Ft1,600; *after 6pm* Ft1,000; Ft700 concs. English spoken.

Have a whale of a time at the **Széchenyi Gyógyfürdő és Strandfürdő.** *See page 180.*

A modern luxury hotel in the middle of Margaret Island, the Thermal offers a squeaky clean complex of three mixed thermal pools, swimming pool, sauna and steam room. It provides a different experience to one of the Turkish baths, more orientated towards sport and fitness than hedonism. The Thermal Hotel also offers a solarium, a pedicure and two sorts of massage – sport and Swedish – which sounds intriguing. Carlos the Jackal apparently used to stay here, though whether or not he used to take the waters is open to conjecture.

Thermal Hotel Aquincum

III. Árpád fejedelem útja 94 (250 3360). Tram 1 from M3 Árpád híd. **Open** *7am-9pm daily.* **Admission** *weekday tickets purchased before 10am* Ft900; *otherwise* Ft1,750; *weekend day ticket* Ft2,150. English spoken.
A not-quite-luxury hotel named after the ancient Roman town that once stood here. The Romans had baths around here and now the Aquincum offers a modern complex of thermal baths, steam room, sauna, whirlpool, swimming pool and gym.

Danubius Thermal Hotel Helia

XIII. Kárpát utca 62-64 (270 3277). M3 Dózsa György út/trolleybus 79 to Kárpát utca. **Open** *7am-10pm daily.* **Admission** *weekday morning ticket to 3pm* Ft1,000; *3-10pm* Ft1,900; *weekend or full day ticket* Ft2,500. English spoken.

Perched by the Danube, on the edge of a working-class suburb, this luxury hotel features a modern complex of swimming pool, thermal pools, sauna, steam room and exercise machines. Massages (Ft950) have to be booked in advance. Popular with 'businessmen' from the former Soviet Union discussing 'contracts' as they soak. There is also a roof terrace.

Farther-flung facilities

Dandár utcai Gyógyfürdő

IX. Dandár utca 5-7 (215 7084). Bus 33. **Open** 6am-6pm Mon-Fri; 6am-noon Sat. **Admission** Ft300. No English spoken. **Map E6**
Way off the tourist trail, these mixed baths are small and crowded with locals rather than expatriates or visitors. Make sure to bring a swimming costume and towel and watch a working-class suburb take the waters.

Pestszenterzsébet jódos Sósfürdő

XX. Vizisport utca 2 (283 1097). Bus 23 from Boráros tér. **Open** men 7am-3pm Tue, Thur, Sat; women 7am-3pm Mon, Wed, Fri. **Admission** Ft300. No English spoken.
Cheapest and most distant of the thermal baths. This spa offers salty water and the usual assortment of steam room, sauna and thermal pools.

Children

Shows, rides, parks, slides – Budapest brims over with enough child-orientated entertainment to keep everyone amused.

Splash away the whole day at the Palatinus Strand on **Margaret Island**. See page 184.

Budapest can be a fun city to visit with kids. But it can be a difficult one, too. Very often it's both. You might enjoy finding an ancient tram or a great toy exhibit and then discover the pushchair doesn't fit through the door or that the exhibit closed an hour early. But there are still a lot of appealingly old-fashioned entertainments for children: puppet theatres, folk dance clubs, eccentric conveyances and prehistoric fairground rides. If kids don't find these interesting, then there are all the usual hamburgers, playgrounds and video arcades.

Though Hungarians love children, families are getting smaller. Since the fairly parent-friendly childcare allowance system was abolished, it's even harder to make ends meet if you have two or three kids. Moreover, the divorce rate is so high and the housing problem so serious that young parents often live at the grandparents' for years.

The Hungarian family is still fairly traditional in its approach to child-rearing. You don't see too many parents with small children in restaurants, or other 'grown-up' places, because children are supposed to stay at home with their mothers until

they learn how to behave like little adults. But don't be surprised if people, especially old ladies, stop to stroke and praise your children. Or to criticise their behaviour.

PRACTICALITIES & DIFFICULTIES

Under-12s may not travel in the front seats of cars, but seat belts and baby-seats are not compulsory in the back. Children under six travel free of charge on all public transport vehicles. If eating out, don't take high chairs and child-size meals for granted. On the other hand, disposable nappies, baby food and other essential baby and child equipment are available all over the city.

Heavy traffic and air pollution mean that long weekday walks along busy downtown streets are not advisable. Instead try the Danube Korzó, the pedestrian streets around Váci utca, or one of the parks and playgrounds listed below. Only the narrowest pushchairs can get through the doors of buses and trams. Access can also be a problem when shopping, except in a few new, spacious Western-style shops in the downtown area or the various new malls.

Information

Check the listings in the English-language weekly *Budapest Sun*, try the Hungarian *MaNcs* or *Pesti Műsor* under *Gyerekeknek ajánlott műsorok* (shows recommended for children), or call **Tourinform** (317 9800).

Children's activity centres

Activity centres offer a variety of programmes for kids during the school year and organise day-camps and special events in school holidays. Check programmes and prices with the venues.

Almássy tér Recreation Centre

Almássy téri Szabadidő Központ
VII. Almássy tér 6 (352 1572). M2 Blaha Lujza tér/tram 4, 6. **Admission** varies. English spoken. **Map E3**
Open every Sunday morning from September to June. Activities include craft workshops, singing, dancing and puppet shows. Special events on other days range from giant hands-on toy exhibits to performances by popular children's entertainers. Also crafts, karate and swimming courses for children.

Marczibányi tér Culture House

Marczibányi téri Művelődési Ház
II. Marczibányi tér 5/a (212 4885). M2 Moszkva tér/tram 4, 6. **Admission** varies. Some English spoken. **Map A2**
Craft workshops, a folk dance club, a yoga course for 10-14 year-olds and an excellent playground for younger kids. Special events include puppet shows, pet fairs and concerts by performers such as Vilmos Gryllus and Péter Levente.

Children's theatres

Budapest Puppet Theatre

Budapest Bábszínház
VI. Andrássy út 69 (321 5200). M1 Vörösmarty utca. **Shows** 3pm Mon-Thur; 10.30am, 4pm, Fri-Sun. Closed in summer. **Admission** Ft300. **No credit cards. Map D2**
Both international fairy tales and Hungarian folk stories in the repertoire. Language is usually not a problem and the shows are highly original.

Kolibri Theatre

VI. Jókai tér 10 (353 4633). M1 Oktogon/tram 4, 6. **Shows** 10am daily; 3pm Fri-Sun. **Open** box office 2-6pm daily. Closed in summer. **Admission** Ft300-Ft400. **No credit cards. Map D3**
Small theatre that presents fairy tales.

Circus

XIV. Állatkerti körút 7 (343 9630). M1 Széchenyi fürdő. **Open** 3pm, 7pm, Mon-Sat; 10am, 3pm, 7pm, Sun. **Admission** Ft400-Ft700. **No credit cards. Map F1**
A permanent building with shows year-round, although inside it looks just like an old-fashioned travelling circus. International and Hungarian performances with acrobats, magicians, jugglers, clowns and animals. Book in advance to avoid sitting next to the deafening orchestra.

Planetarium

Népliget, south-west corner (265 0725). M3 Népliget. **Open** 9.30am-3.30pm Mon-Fri; 9am-4pm Sat, Sun. Laser shows 7pm. **Admission** Ft390. Laser shows Ft1190; Ft790 children. **No credit cards.**
Temporary exhibits as well as educational children's shows. Popular with older kids.

Eating out

Although the number of restaurants that carry high-chairs and have children's menus has been growing, it's a good idea to call and enquire and maybe even reserve a high chair. A lot of Hungarian restaurants aren't very child-friendly, but **Náncsi Néni**, **Bagolyvár**, **Gundel** and **Fészek** are exceptions. You can also be sure of enjoying your meal at **Shalimar**, **Café Kör**, **Lou Lou**, **Gandhi**, **Via Luna** and **Dionysos**. *See chapter* **Restaurants**.

Films & TV

Several Budapest cinemas show cartoons and children's films. Most, however, are dubbed into Hungarian. Check film listings or look in the local English-language papers. Most hotels and flats for rent have satellite and/or cable TV, including Cartoon Network. *See chapter* **Media**.

Music

Classical

In the country of Bartók and Kodály, you're bound to find classical-music performances for children. Their nickname is *Kakaó koncert*, because children get hot chocolate at the end of the concert. The most popular is the one given by the Budapest Fesztivál Zenekar in Óbuda, introduced by conductor Iván Fischer in a funny and child-centred way.

Budapest Fesztivál Zenekar

V. Vörösmarty tér 1 (266 2312). M1 Vörösmarty tér/tram 2. **Tickets** Ft600. **Open** *Sept-Apr* 9.30am-4pm Mon-Fri. **No credit cards.** English spoken. **Map C4**
Information and tickets for the Kakaó koncert series, as well as the rest of the Orchestra's activities.

Folk music

The folk music movement (*see chapter* **Folk & Folklore**) does not leave kids out of the fun. Venues may be closed in July and August, but if you are ready for a week of intensive boot-slapping and craft workshops, you should call any of

the Dance Houses (*táncházak*) and enquire about summer camps.

Muzsikás, the best-known Hungarian folk band, offer a weekly *táncház* for youngsters at Fővárosi Művelődési Központ (XI. Fehérvári út 47; 203 3868) with live folk music and the teaching of traditional dances, including folk tales and games in a playful atmosphere. **Kalamajka Dance House**, which turns into a wild grown-up *táncház* at night, is right in the city centre and songs, dances and folk tales are also taught by talented folk singer Éva Fábián. For details *see chapter* **Folk & Folklore**.

Museums

Budapest has some excellent museums for children, but here more than anywhere kids are expected to behave. Museum attendants often scold visiting children for being too rambunctious. Nonetheless, the **Transport Museum** can be fun with its life-size and model trains, cars and ships. You can climb the steps of an old train engine and peek into the wagons, you can also turn a ship's wheel, but that's pretty much it for hands-on stuff. The aviation section next door has a nice collection of old aeroplanes. The **Natural History Museum** and the **Palace of Wonders** are the most interactive museums in Budapest, with buttons to push, levers to pull levers and computers to learn about the environment or the laws of physics. The **Open Air Village Museum** in Szentendre can also be worth a visit in good weather. Others that can be interesting for children include the **Underground Railway Museum**, the **Museum of Military History**, the **Telephone Museum** and the **Stamp Museum**. *See chapter* **Museums**.

Outdoor activities

Zoo

Állatkert
XIV. Városligeti körút 6-12 (343 6075). M1 Széchenyi fürdő. **Open** *summer* 9am-7pm, *winter* 9am-4pm, daily. **Admission** Ft500 adults; Ft400 children; free for under-2s; Ft1,500 family of four. **No credit cards. Map E1**
The Zoo has begun to change from the sad facility of old. There are new green areas, more animal-friendly cages and a great new playground. Animal names are written in both English and Hungarian, and an English-language booklet with map is available for Ft300. You need three or four hours to see everything. Apart from the usual animals there are stunning Art Nouveau buildings, pony-carts, a beautiful exotic bird house, a small petting corner and one of the few public nappy-changing rooms in town. Check out the recently renovated Elephant House and the Africa House.

Amusement Park

Vidám Park
XIV. Városligeti körút 14-16 (343 0996). M1 Széchenyi fürdő. **Open** *summer* 9.45am-8pm; *winter* 9.45am-sunset. **Admission** Ft100 adults; Ft50 children; Ft100-500 a ride. **No credit cards. Map F1**
A big tacky old place with a rickety wooden roller coaster, big wheel, ancient merry-go-round and unfrightening ghost trains next to a few newer, scarier rides. Next door is the renovated fun fair (Kis Vidám Park) for toddlers and pre-schoolers.

Parks & playgrounds

Margaret Island

Margitsziget
Tram 4, 6 to Margaret Bridge or bus 26 from Nyugati station. **Map B1**
A huge recreational area with grassy spaces, old trees, swimming pools, playgrounds and a small zoo with domestic animals. You can rent bicycles, four-wheel pedalos and tiny electric cars for children. Horse-drawn carts and open-topped minibuses leave on round trips every half hour. The best playground is near the Alfréd Hajós swimming pool on the south-west side and the best swimming at the Palatinus Strand, which also has an open-air thermal pool. *See also chapters* **Sightseeing** *and* **Sport & Fitness**.

City Park

Városliget
M1 Hősök tere. **Map E1**
Lots here apart from the Zoo, Amusement Park and Circus listed above. Behind Heroes' Square and the boating pond is Vajdahunyad Castle, which houses the **Agriculture Museum** with stuffed animals and tools. Safety standards are low on the slides and wooden castles in the south corner, but there is a new fenced-around playground with a treehouse, safe slides and monkey-bars. The playground between the Zoo and the pond is also in good shape and has a trampoline area where children can bounce up and down for Ft120 five minutes. There are also ping-pong tables. For ball games check out the football fields, basketball and tennis courts behind **Petőfi Csarnok** on the east side of the park. *See also chapters* **Sightseeing** *and* **Museums**.

Óbuda Island

Óbudai/Hajógyári sziget
HÉV to Filatorigát, bus 142 or boat from Vigadó tér. An island full of green areas and long slides just north of Árpád bridge. Ideal for picnics, kite flyers and not-so-professional skaters and bikers.

Károlyi Garden

Károlyi kert
M2 Astoria, M3 Kálvin tér/tram 47, 49. **Open** 8am-sunset daily. **Admission** free. Dogs not allowed. **Map D4**
One of the new clean fenced-around playgrounds downtown. Sand box, slide, ride-on toys, two ball areas and no dogs.

József Nádor tér

M1, M2, M3 Deák tér/tram 47, 49. **Open** 7am-sunset daily. **Admission** free. Dogs not allowed.
Map C4
A great new playground with wooden castles, a ship with slides, swings, ride-on toys, a sandpit and a stream with tiny dams for watery experiments. Heavy traffic in the neighbourhood, though.

Klauzál tér

M2 Blaha Lujza tér/tram 4, 6. **Open** 8am-sunset daily. **Admission** free. **Map D3**
It's fantastic to find such a nice new playground in the heart of busy and sometimes smelly District VII. Dogs have their own park (that is, toilet) next door.

Roller-skating & skateboarding

Although Heroes' Square (Hősök tere) is teen Budapest's favourite roller-skating and skateboarding area, more fanatic skaters can go to **Görzenál Skatepark** (*see chapter* **Sport & Fitness**) for hours of well-paved fun. In-line skates and skateboards can be rented on the spot.

If you and/or your children are into ice-skating, the boating pond in the **City Park** turns into an ice-skating rink in winter. In summer you can go to the ice-skating rinks operated in **Pólus Center** or **Duna Plaza Shopping Mall** (*see chapter* **Shopping**.) For teenagers who like to dance to disco music on ice, the **Budapest Sportcsarnok** has a 'Super Ice Disco' every Friday and Saturday evening. *See chapter* **Sport & Fitness**.

Train & boat rides

You can go up to the Buda hills on the cogwheel train that departs across the street from the **Budapest Hotel** (M2 Moszkva tér then two stops on trams 18 or 56). If you take it all the way up to Széchenyi-hegy, which takes about 25 minutes, you can walk across the park to the Children's Railway – operated by children, except for the engine drivers. This does not run very often, so it's best to check the schedule when you get there and spend waiting time in the neighbouring playground (*see chapter* **Getting Around**).

Nostalgia Train

Nosztalgia vonat
Information & tickets: *Nyugati station. VI. Nyugati tér (269 5242). M3 Nyugati/tram 4, 6.* **Tickets** Ft548-Ft624; Ft243-Ft268 concs.
The Hungarian Railway Company (MÁV) operates a steam engine and old-fashioned carriages, which leaves Nyugati at 9.45am and takes an hour and a half to puff its way up to Szob on the Danube every Saturday from May to September. After time for lunch and a walk along the river, the train returns at 4.35pm, arriving back at Nyugati at 6pm. Tickets are priced as regular trains, but for an extra charge you can buy a ticket that will allow you to visit the engine driver and get an 'official' steam engine driver's licence.

The **Zoo** *– animals and Art Nouveau.*

Chairlift

Libegő
(394 3764). M2 Moszkva tér then bus 158. **Open** summer 9am-5pm, winter 9.30am-4pm, Tue-Sun. **Fare** Ft250; Ft 150 children. **Map B4**
This slow and gentle ski-lift-style ride sweeps right up to the top of Jánoshegy, highest hill within Budapest city limits and equipped with a look-out tower. The view looks best on the way down.

Funicular

Sikló
I. Clark Ádám tér. Tram 19. Open 7.30am-10pm Tue-Sun. **Fare** Ft200; Ft100 children. **Map B4**
The funicular (Sikló) goes from Clark Ádám tér up to the Castle District. It's a short ride, but both the view and the carriages are cool. (*See also chapter* **Sightseeing**.)

Boat trips

There are several possibilities for taking a boat ride down the Danube. The cheapest is the ferry which runs between the Pest end of Petőfi Bridge and Pünkösdfürdő in the north of Budapest, on the way stopping at each of the bridges and at Vigadó tér. This is free for under-4s and about Ft250 for everyone else (*see chapter* **Getting Around**). A sightseeing cruise costs about Ft600-Ft800 (half price for under-14s) and offers a bigger boat, usually equipped with some kind of bar, and a tour guide. Call **IBUSZ** or **Tourinform** for details (*see chapter* **Essential Information**).

Baby-sitters

Young Hungarian parents tend to use their grandparents as baby-sitters (always enthusiastic and free). If you didn't happen to bring any with you, the following agencies listed below provide the most reliable and best qualified child-minding services in Budapest. You might also be able to arrange baby-sitting facilities through your workplace or hotel, although bear in mind that English-speaking minders could work out more expensive.

Minerva Family Helping Service
Minerva Családsegítő Szolgálat
VIII. Szerdahelyi utca 10 (313 6365). Tram 28, 29. **Open** 24-hour answering machine. **No credit cards.** English spoken. **Map F4**
English-, German-, French- and Spanish-speaking baby-sitters and full- or part-time nannies. Sitting is Ft400 and up per hour.

Ficuka Kid Center
Baby Hotel & Baby-sitter Service
V. Váci utca 11/B, First Floor (338 2836). M1, 2, 3 Deák tér/tram 47, 49. **Open** 9am-5pm daily. **Prices** average Ft400 and up per hour. **No credit cards.** English spoken. **Map C4**
Leave your kids here while you shop on Váci utca or call them for night-time baby-sitting.

Health

In an emergency call 104 or 311 1666 and ask for someone who speaks English. With sick children you can also go to Heim Pál Children's Hospital 24 hours a day.

Heim Pál Gyermekkórház
VIII. Üllői út 86 (264 3314/210 0720). M3 Nagyvárad tér. **Map F6**

International schools

Magyar-British International Elementary School *XI. Kamaraerdei út 12-14 (209 1218). Bus 87.*
American International School of Budapest *XI. Kakukk utca 1/3 (275 4519). Bus 21.*
International Kindergarten & School *XII. Konkoly Thege utca 19B. (395 9310). Bus 21, 90.*
Magyar-English Bilingual Elementary School *XIV. Hermina út 9-15 (343 8125). Bus 7.*
Magyar-English Bilingual Secondary School *XVIII. Thököly út 7 (290 4316). Bus 36, 93, 136.*

Shopping

Budapest has plenty of clothing and toy stores and children's sections in the bigger department stores. If you need your children to be watched while you shop, **IKEA**, **Duna Plaza** and **Europark** all have supervised playrooms for 3-12 year-olds. *See chapter* **Shopping & Services.**

Burattino
IX. Ráday utca 47 (215 5621). M3 Kálvin tér/tram 47, 49. **Open** 10am-6pm Mon-Fri; 10am-1pm Sat. **No credit cards.** Some English spoken. **Map D5**
Great selection of wooden blocks, trains and puzzles.

Fakopáncs Fajátékbolt
VIII. Baross utca 46 (337 0992). Tram 4, 6. **Open** 10am-6pm Mon-Fri; 9am-1pm Sat. **No credit cards.** Some English spoken. **Map E5**
Great wooden trains, garden tools and looms.

Gondolkodó Toy Store
VI. Király utca 25 (322 8884). M1 Opera. **Open** 10am-6pm Mon-Fri; 9am-1pm Sat. **No credit cards.** Some English spoken. **Map D3**
Games from chess software to beautiful wooden puzzles and local hero Rubik's latest inventions.

Götz Bababolt
V. Váci utca 11A (318 3115). M3 Ferenciek tere/tram 2/bus 7. **Open** 10am-6pm Mon-Fri; 10am-4pm Sat. **Credit** AmEx, DC, JCB, MC, V. English spoken. **Map C4**
Central location for all baby and toddler supplies.

Puppet Show
V. Párizsi utca 3 (318 8453). M3 Ferenciek tere/bus 7. **Open** 10am-6pm Mon-Fri; 10am-1.30pm Sat. **No credit cards.** English spoken. **Map C4**
A little shop in a courtyard with lots of cute animal puppets. Friendly staff demonstrate how to make them move.

Totyi & Tini
V. Bárczy István utca 1-3 (317 9429). M1, M2, M3 Deák tér/tram 47, 49. **Open** 10am-6pm Mon-Fri; 10am-1pm Sat. **Credit** AmEx, DC, JCB, MC, V. Some English spoken. **Map C4**
Hungarian-designed dress-up and play clothes at fair prices.

Budapest Puppet Theatre. *See page 183.*

Film

Cheap tickets, gracious old theatres, state-of-the-art multiplexes and cutting-edge festivals – Budapest is a film-lover's paradise.

The grand foyer of the **Puskin** – elegance recently renovated. See page 188.

Whether they consider film as culture or escapism, English-speaking movie-lovers find Budapest an excellent town for cinema-going. Any night will feature classics, independent films and the ubiquitous Hollywood blockbusters at some 30 regular venues. Add movie festivals worthy of a major film centre and the city will not leave you wanting for cinematic entertainment.

As in any other major media market, the spectre of America's motion picture industry hangs over the proceedings; a new multiplex seemingly sprouts every week and local theatres import around 50 Hollywood releases a year, usually after at least a three-month lag from the North American release date. If you're desperate for an evening of viewing, odds are you'll be checking out a mega-studio offering; US and UK releases account for about 85 per cent of showings in Budapest.

Most English-language movies are subtitled in Hungarian. Dubbing is reserved for cartoons, some action films, family-orientated movies and dumb comedy (sorry, Jim Carrey and Eddie Murphy fans). Only the biggest and/or award-winning

European films play here, such as Iran's Cannes-winner *A Taste of Cherry*, Roberto Benigni's *Life is Beautiful* and the French box-office bonanza *Les Visiteurs*.

While more than three dozen smaller venues have closed in the past 15 years, Budapest's old single-screeners and arthouse standbys survive, and even thrive. Movie houses such as the Puskin and Átrium have interiors grand enough to remind some popcorn-munchers that there's more to life than THX Quadrophonic sound, while cinemas such as the Toldi, Művész and Hunnia show stuff from the medium's weirder side.

Movie-going is also cheap and convenient. Nine theatres sport a location on the Körút, with most others a few steps away from a metro stop. Tickets run from about Ft260 to Ft600. For popular and first-week releases, reservations are recommended. Many theatres have matinee prices before around 5pm. Seating is usually assigned by seat and row number. Note that *szék* is seat; *sor* is row; *bal oldal* designates the left side, *jobb oldal* the right side, *közép* the middle; and *erkély* is the balcony.

Cirko-gejzír – *an eclectic programme of obscure independent movies. See page 189.*

Programme information

The major English-language movie guide is featured in the weekly *Budapest Sun*, although it often misses out the more esoteric cinemas, their listings are frequently unreliable, and the film reviews often make little sense. Also useful are the Hungarian magazines *Pesti Műsor, Open* and *Pesti Est*. These last two can be picked up free at many cinemas, and *Pesti Est* includes a film guide in English (see chapter **Media)**. The entries state if the movie is subtitled *(feliratos)* or dubbed *(szinkronizált)*. In some Hungarian programmes, E refers to the show times: n9 is 8.15pm, f9 is 8.30pm, h9 is 8.45pm. *De* means morning, *Du* is afternoon, *este* is evening and *éjjel* refers to late screenings.

Cinemas

Átrium

II. Margit körút 55 (212 5398). Tram 4, 6. **Box office** *from* 10.30am, **last show** 8.30pm; 10pm Fri, Sat. **Tickets** Ft350-Ft500. **No credit cards.** One screen. Some English spoken. **Map A2**
One of the few large houses to be found on the Buda side and a major venue for more mainstream Hollywood movies. The magnificent 1936 building by Lajos Kozma (see chapter **Architecture**) underwent a complete renovation inside and out in the 1980s.

Duna

XIII. Hollán Ernő utca 7 (320 4947). Tram 4, 6. **Box office** *from* 10.30am, **last show** 9pm. **Tickets** Ft280-Ft500. **No credit cards.** One screen. Some English spoken. **Map C2**
On the Pest side of Margaret Bridge, this 1937 movie house features children's shows earlier in the day and new releases at night. The Duna can also boast its own excellent in-house video rental shop (see *below* **Odeon**).

Kossuth

XIII. Váci út 14 (349 3771). M3 Nyugati/tram 4, 6. **Box office** *from* 9.30am, **last show** 10.30pm. **Tickets** Ft350-Ft550. **No credit cards.** Four screens. Some English spoken. **Map D2**
Decent seats and a first-rate sound system are the important elements here, as is the Kossuth's policy of featuring English-language first-runs that other cinemas around town will only exhibit in synchronised versions.

Puskin

V. Kossuth Lajos utca 18 (429 6080). M2 Astoria/tram 47, 49/bus 7. **Box office** *from* 10.30am, **last show** 10.30pm. **Tickets** Ft390-Ft550. **No credit cards.** Two screens. Some English spoken. **Map D4**
This 420-seat house features major Hollywood releases. Its second screen plays previously released movies, art films and Hungarian releases. Originally constructed in 1926, the elegant interior was recently renovated and is connected to the **Odeon** café around the corner. *See chapter* **Cafés & Coffeehouses.**

Vörösmarty

VIII. Üllői út 4 (317 4542). M3 Kálvin tér/tram 47, 49. **Box office** *from* 3.30pm daily, **last show** 9pm. **Tickets** Ft150-Ft400. **No credit cards.** One screen. English spoken. **Map D5**
The standard single screening room isn't that noteworthy, but the cinema makes for interesting pre-movie distraction with its clothing shop, café corner and mini-bookstore with a few titles in English.

Multiplexes

In the last couple of years, multiplexes have sprouted all over Budapest – the most recent a 14-screen cinema at the West End City Center mall behind Nyugati station – and are usually all showing the same half-dozen blockbuster movies.

Corvin Budapest Filmpalota

*VIII. Corvin köz 1 (459 5050). M3 Ferenc
körút/tram 4, 6.* **Box office** *from* 10am, **last show**
11pm. **Tickets** Ft390-Ft590. **No credit cards.**
Eight screens. Some English spoken. **Map E5**

The best multiplex in Budapest. The eyecatching
building at Corvin köz, one of the key resistance
strongholds during the 1956 uprising (*see chapter*
History), now proudly displays all the newest techniques in cinematic projection and sound, a branch
of the **Odeon** video rental service (*see below*) and a
more than adequate café. This extremely comfortable cinema also serves as the main venue for the
Magyar Filmszemle (*see below*). If you get lost,
though, it's not your fault – the Corvin's layout is
absolutely labyrinthine and its signage leaves a lot
to be desired.

Art cinemas & second-run houses

Blue Box

*IX. Kinizsi utca 28 (218 0983). M3 Ferenc
körút/tram 4, 6.* **Box office** *from* 3pm, **last show**
8pm. **Tickets** Ft200-Ft300. **No credit cards.**
One screen, two in summer. Some English spoken.
Map D5

A former nightclub that now screens everything
from *Tom & Jerry* to *Tarkovsky*. Seating is removed
for occasional events such as jazz concerts and raves
and the cinema was used as the location for Elemér
Káldor's 1993 film *Blue Box*. In the summer months,
movies are regularly shown in the garden, convivially equipped with a bar, with drinks served as
the film is playing.

Cirko-gejzír

VIII. Balassi Bálint utca 15-17 (269 1915). Tram 2.
Box office *from* 3.30pm, **last show** 9pm. **Tickets**
Ft280-Ft350. **No credit cards.** One screen. Some
English spoken. **Map D5**

A badly-needed relocation for this cinema that
showcases obscure independent movies from all
over the world. New photo exhibitions weekly.

Hunnia

*VII. Erzsébet körút 26 (322 3471). M2 Blaha Lujza
tér/tram 4, 6.* **Box office** *from* 4.30pm, **last show**
9pm; 10pm Fri, Sat. **Tickets** Ft200-Ft350. **No credit
cards.** One screen. No English spoken. **Map E3**

Kevin Smith fans search no further! The Hunnia specialises in cult classics such as *Clerks* and *Pulp
Fiction* peppered with the occasional money-maker.
The café, open from 3pm to midnight, is a popular
meeting place whatever movie is playing.

Metro

*VI. Teréz körút 62 (353 4266). M3 Nyugati/tram
4, 6.* **Box office** *from* 9.30am, **last show** 10.30pm.
Tickets Ft380-Ft500. **No credit cards.**
Two screens. English spoken. **Map D2**

Originally opened in 1925 as the UFA, owned by the
German film company, the Metro was bought out by
Metro-Goldwyn-Mayer in 1925 – hence the current
name. Reconstructed in the 1970s, Budapest's most
eclectic cinema features popular commercial releases on the main screen while the 42-seat
Kamaraterem often plays Hungarian-made movies
and international art films. The retractable ceiling
of the main room is sometimes opened on swelter-
ing summer nights.

Művész – *Central Europe's most successful art-house cinema. See page 190.*

Tabán – *dodgy sound but friendly café.*

Művész

VI. Teréz körút 30 (332 6726). M1 Oktogon/tram 4, 6. **Box office** *from* 4.30pm, **last show** 10pm. **Tickets** Ft280-Ft550. **No credit cards.** Five screens. Some English spoken. **Map D3**
One of the most stylish art cinemas in Budapest and certainly the most successful in the region. The Művész is usually playing one or two brand-new independent releases, with the remainder of its five halls featuring nightly-changing programmes of the world's art films from any time within the last ten years or so. There is a restaurant in the basement, the Federico, after Fellini, and the screening rooms have also been given names after legendary figures in cinema. This place is popular, so get here early and check out the soundtrack CDs and art books for sale. After a late performance, there is food and music on offer at the **Underground** club below. *See* chapter **Nightlife**.

Örökmozgó Filmmúzeum

VII. Erzsébet körút 39 (342 2167). Tram 4, 6 to Wesselényi utca. **Box office** *from* 4pm, **last show** 8.30pm. **Tickets** Ft220-Ft300. **No credit cards.** One screen, video upstairs. Some English spoken. **Map D3**
Best known for its proudly eclectic weekly schedule of everything from silent classics to documentaries. Foreign-language films in this small house subsidised by the Hungarian Film Archive are often played in their original sound with simultaneous Hungarian translation via headsets. Get a monthly programme guide at the cinema, as English-language coverage of this movie-lover's paradise is usually non-existent. There is a small coffeeshop in the lobby, and an adjoining book shop with a handful of English titles.

Szindbád

XIII. Szent István körút 16 (349 2773). M3 Nyugati/tram 4, 6. **Box office** *from* 3pm, **last show** 8.30pm. **Tickets** Ft300-Ft450. **No credit cards.** Two screens. No English spoken. **Map C2**
A decent two-screen art-movie house with surly staff. Often the only place to see contemporary Hungarian releases with English subtitles. There's also a small video rental outlet and temporary art exhibitions.

Tabán

I. Krisztina körút 87-89 (356 8162). Tram 18 to Krisztina tér/bus 5, 78, 105 and red 4. **Box office** *from* 3pm, **last show** 9pm. **Tickets** Ft200-Ft350. **No credit cards.** One screen. Some English spoken. **Map A3**
Nestled in the old Serbian quarter of the city, this tiny theatre usually plays several English-language gems a week. German and French films also feature. Sound and picture quality are sometimes dodgy. There's also a video rental library, including a handful of English-language movies. Friendly café.

Toldi Stúdió Mozi

V. Bajcsy-Zsilinszky út 36-38 (311 2809). M3 Arany János. **Box office** 3.30pm-4.30pm, **last show** 9pm. **Tickets** Ft150-Ft400. **No credit cards.** Two screens. Some English spoken. **Map C3**
Large venue for contemporary independent releases from Mike Leigh to Tarantino and Hungarian features both old and new. There is a small bar and a gift shop (posters, books, postcards, CDs). Venue for the **Titanic International Filmpresence Festival** (*see below*).

Video rental

Budapest has many video rental shops. Most English-language videos are dubbed into Hungarian but older releases are often subtitled. Video boxes indicate if a film is dubbed (*szinkronizált*) or subtitled (*feliratos*) from English (*angol*). Any video shop will have titles in English.

British Council Library

VII. Benczúr utca 26 (321 4039/7/8). M1 Bajza utca. **Open** 11am-6pm Mon-Thur; 11am-5pm Fri. English spoken. **Map E2**
Membership (Ft1,000 per year) essential for access to this extensive video library. Superb selection of British TV shows, with everything from documentaries to sitcoms.

English Language Video Club and Shop

VI. Zichy Jenő utca 44 (302 0291). Tram 4, 6 to Oktogon. **Open** 10am-10pm daily. **Membership** Ft2,000. **Rental** Ft300-Ft500 per video per night. English spoken. **Map D3**
Wide range of Hollywood fare, independent and European arthouse movies. Over 1,000 films in English, or with English subtitles, so the best place to rent movies not yet shown in Hungary.
Branch: XII. Hajnóczy József utca 11 (214 9499).

Odeon

XIII. Hollán Ernő utca 7 (320 4947). Tram 4, 6 to Jászai Mari tér. **Open** 2-9pm daily. **Rental** Ft300-Ft600 per tape per day (plus refundable Ft1,500 deposit). Some English spoken. **Map C2**
Original-soundtrack videos of US and UK features. Renowned for its large collection of Magyar classics subtitled in English. Viewing room on the premises.
Branch: Corvin Multiplex, VIII. Corvin köz 1 (333 5707).

The reel Hungary

Cinematically speaking, the 1990s will be known as the decade Hungarians discovered the business side of film-making. Though it's always been home to a thriving film culture, this country's major talents have mostly fled abroad. Adolph Zucker, for example, was an emigré whose *Queen Elizabeth* in 1912 is cited as the first feature-length film ever made.

By the 1930s, Hungarians represented some of the finest directorial talent in Hollywood, with names such as Michael Curtiz (*Casablanca, Gone with the Wind*) and George Cukor (*The Philadelphia Story, Adam's Rib*) habitually appearing on silver screens. In front of the camera, Béla Lugosi, Tony Curtis and the Gábor sisters lent Hungary a mysterious and sexy image.

The 1960s marked a golden era in Hungarian film-making, with films such as Miklós Jancsó's *Szegénylegények* (*The Round-Up*, 1965), István Szabó's *Apa* (*Father*, 1966), Péter Bacsó's *A Tanú* (*The Witness*, 1968) and Károly Makk's *Szerelem* (*Love*, 1970) earning Hungary a reputation as an important European film centre. The irony was that such witty and darkly satirical films as *A Tanú* and the Cannes-acclaimed *A Rongyos Élet* (*Oh Bloody Life*, 1983) were better-known in the west than in a Hungary burdened with heavy censorship.

In 1990 and 1991 the industry was still cranking out 50 movies a year, but in 1992 government funding slowed to a trickle (ending completely in 1996). Production collapsed, so that by 1997 only 23 features were released. The decade was spent learning how to solicit private investment. In the end Hungarian-born Hollywood producer Andrew Vajna showed everyone how to do it. After shooting *Evita* in Budapest, he put together *A Miniszter Félrelép* (*Out of Order*) – a film distinctly Hungarian yet uncharacteristically high-budget, an object lesson in techniques of budget-building and promotion.

The lesson seems to have taken. The 1999 Filmszemle exhibited some four dozen feature films, nearly all privately funded. Rising star directors such as Péter Timár (*6-3, Csinibaba, Zimmer Feri*) and Tamás Sas (*Presszó, Kalózok*) have created slick productions packed full of local references and in-jokes. Side matters taken for granted in the western world of movie hype, such as soundtracks and advance clips on nightly talk shows, are becoming commonplace.

For the curious anglophone, outside of the Filmszemle, the Szindbád and sometimes the Művész screen Hungarian productions with English subtitles. Odeon, meanwhile, hires out subtitled Hungarian classics.

Video Mania

VI. Andrássy út 33 (269 6812). M1 Oktogon/tram 4, 6. **Open** 10am-10pm Mon-Thur, Sun; 10am-midnight Fri, Sat. **Rental** Ft320-Ft600 per video per night, plus one-off Ft2,000 deposit. English spoken. **Map D3**

The newest video outlet in Budapest, offering a selection of movies in several European languages as well as in English.

Film festivals

Magyar Filmszemle

c/o Filmúnió Hungary, VI. Városligeti fasor 38 (351 7760/7761/fax 351 7766). **Date** Feb. English spoken.

The major event in the Hungarian cinema calendar. Each February at the **Corvin** (*see above*), the Magyar Filmszemle (Hungarian Film Festival) shows all domestic features, documentaries and shorts produced within the previous calendar year. There's a competition with one main prize for the best movie, plus several smaller awards. Simultaneous translation via headphones (and the occasional subtitled film) is often available — but not always.

Mediawave

Festival office H-9028 Győr, Soproni út 45 (06 96 449 444/06 96 328 888/fax 06 96 449 445). **Date** Apr. English spoken.

Otherwise known as the International Festival of Visual Arts in Győr, 125km west of Budapest, and characterised by productions from around the Central and Eastern European region. Mediawave runs every year for five days at the end of April, showing independent films and videos, with an international jury awarding a main prize. Independent of categories, special prizes are also presented. There are exhibitions, lectures, concerts and an 'à la carte' room, where any productions entered in the festival can be screened on request.

Titanic International Filmpresence Festival

Information *Toldi, V. Bajcsy-Zsilinszky út 36-38 (311 2809).* **Date** Oct. Some English spoken.

A priceless showing of new arthouse and cult movies. Anything goes at this festival, with works from Asia, Europe and North America, plus an excellent dual-language catalogue. This is *the* festival to check out, come October, though its future was in doubt at the time of going to press.

Gay & Lesbian

Whether chilling in bars, steaming in baths or cruising the Danube – the scene may be small but does size always matter?

Gábor and Laci, editors of **Mások**, *compare notes outside* **Capella**.

Just by sitting for a while at sunset on the Korzó – the promenade on the Pest embankment between Erzsébet bridge and Március 15 tér – you can get a good first impression of gay society in Budapest. You'll find yourself in a very public (and very beautiful) gay cruising area, visited by locals, foreigners and hustlers.

In Budapest all gay bars and clubs attract gays of every age and preference – you won't find anywhere that targets a particular audience, such as leather bars. Neither will you find a gay place that is open in the day time. The commercial infrastructure hasn't much to offer lesbians – one gay/lesbian bar and Friday nights in a dance club is all there is. That said, Budapest's gay and lesbian nightspots are typically crowded and here, as well as in the city's famous bathhouses, you will find a gay community that is able to enjoy itself.

This is despite the fact that most Hungarian gays and lesbians still live entirely without any personal experience of the gay liberation movement. Indeed many have difficulty acknowledging their gay identity. Maybe this is in part the heritage of the period before 1989, when Hungarian

society was infused by mistrust between 'intellectuals' and non-intellectuals: Hungary's gay and lesbian organisations still attract only a certain type of person and make little effort to be present at lesbian and gay nightspots or get people involved in other ways.

This is probably one reason why the number of participants at the annual Lesbian and Gay Pride event has never risen beyond the 250-300 who attended the first one in 1997. There is only one gay magazine, *Mások* – a monthly published since 1992 and reaching a nationwide audience of 15,000 – plus *Labrisz*, an irregularly published magazine for lesbians. There are two gay radio programmes: one on former pirate station Tilos Radio (FM98.0; every second Thursday 11pm-midnight), the other on state-run Petőfi Radio (FM94.8; every fourth Monday 10-11pm). Both are presented by Balázs Pálfi, who interviews people and takes calls from listeners.

Balázs was one of the founders of Szivárvány ('Rainbow'), a group intending to offer legal assistance and support for gay rights. But Hungary's courts refused to recognise it, declaring that

Szivárvány could neither allow under-age youth to become members nor use the word *meleg* (Hungarian for gay, literally 'warm') in their sub-title. Szivárvány's case is due to be heard in the European Court for Human Rights some time before the end of 2001.

The age of consent for gay sex is 18 (for hetero-sexuals it's 14). Gay marriage is not possible, but gay couples can register themselves as 'partners living together' just like heterosexuals.

Media & information

Gay Switchboard Budapest
(06 30 932 3334/budapest@gayguide.net). **Open** 4-8pm daily.
Founded by a group of gay expatriates. Their web page provides an up-to-date gay guide with accom-modation, gay tour and general city information. They also operate an Info-Hotline 365 days a year, replying to every e-mail within 48 hours. You can contact them before, during and after your trip, sub-scribe to their mailing list or insert a classified ad into their web page in order to make contacts before going to Budapest.
Website: gayguide.net/europe/hungary/budapest/

Labrisz
1554 Budapest, PO Box 50 (350 96 50/ Hatter@c3.hu).
Hungary's first lesbian magazine. Every fourth Friday the three editors host a gathering of writers and read-ers. For location and date ask **Háttér** (*see below*).
Website: www.c3.hu/~hatter/labrisz/

Mások
1461 Budapest, PO Box 388 (266 9959/ masok@masok.hu).
Hungary's only gay magazine, available in gay venues and at central newsstands.
Website: www.masok.hu

Para Radio
para@c3.hu
The gay show of Para Radio is available only via the Internet. Every Wednesday, 6pm.
Website: http://www.c3.hu/para

#Gay.hu
webmaster@fules.c3.hu
The website of the IRC channel #Gay.hu is a kind of online magazine with articles, discussions and links to the homepages of many regular visitors.
Website: fules.c3.hu/gay.hu/

Bars & clubs

Action Bar
V. Magyar utca 42 (266 9148). M3 Kálvin tér/tram 47, 49/night bus 50E, 14E. **Open** 3pm-4am daily. **Admission** Ft700 minimum consumption.
No credit cards. Some English spoken. **Map D4**
Popular cellar bar with videos and the busiest dark-room in town.

Angyal Club
VII. Szövetség utca 33 (351 64 90). M2 Blaha Lujza tér/tram 4, 6/night bus 6E, 78E. **Open** 10pm-midnight Thur; 10pm-dawn Fri, Sat. **Admission** Ft400-Ft600. **No credit cards.** No English spoken.
Map E3
Budapest's most popular club since 1989, now in its fourth incarnation. Downstairs is a well-lit basement bar, a crowded cave-like disco and dark-room. Upstairs there's a restaurant and a stage for drag shows (midnight every Friday, and Sunday and the last Saturday of the month). Friday is favoured by dykes, Saturday is men only, Sunday is a mixed crowd.

Capella
V. Belgrád rakpart 23 (318 6231). M3 Ferenciek tere/tram 2/night bus 78E. **Open** 9pm-5am Tue-Sun. **Admission** Ft500 plus minimum consumption of Ft500. **No credit cards.** English spoken. **Map C5**
A cellar labyrinth of bars and dancefloors. Wednesdays and Saturdays are the gay nights. Otherwise it's a mixed crowd, and there are drag shows every Wednesday, Friday, Saturday and Sunday, the last featuring the excellent Marlon Extravaganza. Rarely gets going before midnight. The owners don't allow the distribution of gay or AIDS-related material, as they worry about scaring away the straights.

Darling Bar
V. Szép utca 1 (267 33 15). M2 Astoria/tram 47, 49/night bus 14E, 50E, 78E. **Open** 7pm-2am daily. **Admission** free. **No credit cards.** Some English spoken. **Map D4**
A small cosy bar that seats a few people downstairs. Upstairs are bench-lined walls for intimate video viewing, with a larger video room behind the bar.

Mystery Bar-Klub
V. Nagysándor József utca 3 (312 1436). M3 Arany János utca/night bus 50E, 14E. **Open** 9pm-4am Mon-Sat. **No credit cards.** Some English spoken. **Map C3**
The second oldest lesbian and gay bar in Budapest offers a quiet, friendly sit-down environment to meet your friends and chat. Snacks available.

Eating out

Amstel River Café
V. Párizsi utca 6 (266 4334). M1 Vörösmarty tér. **Open** 9am-11pm Mon-Sat; 11am-11pm Sun. **Average** Ft1500. **No credit cards. Map C4**
A café-restaurant frequented by gays, in the tourist area near the Danube. Outside tables.

Club 93 Pizzeria
VIII. Vas utca 2 (338 1119). M2 Blaha Lujza tér/tram 4, 6/bus 7, 78/night bus 78E. **Open** noon-1am daily. **Average** Ft1,000. **No credit cards. Map D4**
A popular pizza place that's gay-owned and gay-staffed, and frequented by local lesbians and gay men. Popular place to meet before going out.

Balázs Pálfi – rainbow warrior and radio ham.

Baths & beaches

Budapest has several baths, and some of them have been attracting a gay clientele for decades. Go to the **Gellért** between 4 and 6.30pm; to the **Király** late afternoon on Monday, Wednesday or Friday; to the **Rác** on Saturday from 3pm to meet gay locals or to **Palatinus Strand** any time at all. *See chapters* **Baths** *and* **Sport & Fitness**.

To the north of town is Omszki Lake, where the nudist area is recommended for swimming and cruising. Take the HÉV from Batthyány tér to Budakalász. The lake is about 30 minutes' walk.

Cruising areas

The Danube Cruise, running along the Pest embankment between Vigadó tér and the statue of Petőfi near Erzsébet Bridge, is active day and night, but busiest around sunset with locals, foreigners and hustler traffic. Not everyone looking for action will be a hustler. Also known for nighttime activity are the Germanus Gyula Park just north of the Buda foot of Margaret Bridge, and the Népliget in the area around the Planetarium.

Gay & lesbian organisations

Habeas Corpus Jogsegély

1360 Budapest, PO Box 1 (06 309 334 601/ hc@www.netstudio.hu).
A group addressing the legal issues of sexuality in Hungary.

Háttér Baráti Társaság a Melegekért

Háttér Support Society for Gays and Lesbians
1554 Budapest, PO Box 50 (office 350 9650/helpline 329 3380/Hatter@c3.hu). **Open** 6-11pm daily.
Formed in 1995, Háttér ('background') is the largest gay and lesbian organisation in Hungary with 70 members. It runs several projects, including a hotline offering information and counselling, an HIV/AIDS prevention project and a self-help group. They also operate a gay and lesbian archive and are the main organisers of the Gay and Lesbian Film and Cultural Festival, the Budapest Pride March and the Positive Festival.
Website: www.c3.hu/~hatter

Késergay

1554 Budapest, PO Box 50.
Hungarian Jewish lesbian and gay social group.

Öt Kenyér

1461 Budapest, PO Box 25.

Catholic gay group meets Thursdays at 7pm. For details call **Háttér** (*see above*).

Vándor Mások

1360 Budapest, PO Box 2 (466 0156/ vandorm@freemail.c3.hu).
Gay and lesbian hiking group. Dates of excursions are published monthly in *Mások*.

Condoms & lubricant

Strong condoms for anal intercourse such as Durex Extra, Hot Rubber and HT are available in pharmacy chains such as Azur or Rossmann. Lubricants can only be purchased in sex shops.

HIV & AIDS

Since 1 January 1998, the government has insisted that HIV-positive people must be centrally registered. As a result, only a first HIV test can be done without showing a passport. If the result is positive and a second verification test is required, you can go to Vienna for an anonymous free test.

AIDS-segélyszolgálat

XI. Karolina út 35/b (466 9283). Tram 14, 49. **Open** 5-8pm Mon, Wed, Thur; 9am-noon Tue, Fri.
HIV testing. Talk to them about anonymity first.

Aids-Hilfe Wien

Mariahilfer Gurtel 4, Vienna 6 (00 41 1 599 37/wien@aidshilfe.or.at). **Open** 4-7pm Mon, Wed; 9am-noon Thur; 2-5pm Fri.
Test results one week later, but must be collected in person. English and German spoken.

META Foundation

1387 Budapest, PO Box 44 (247 01 88/06 20 936 5224).
Foundation supporting people with HIV and AIDS.

PLUSS

1450 Budapest, PO Box 29 (06 60 343 773).
Support group for people with HIV and AIDS.

Events

For info on the annual Gay Pride Day and Gay and Lesbian Cultural Festival (June or July) and World Aids Day (1 December) contact Háttér (*see above*) or e-mail Gay Pride at gayinfo@gaypride.hu or visit their website at www.gaypride.hu/

Sex shop

Apolló Video Shop

VI. Teréz körút 3 (342 1911). M1 Oktogon. **Open** 10am-6pm Mon-Fri. **No credit cards.** Some English spoken. **Map D2**
Air-conditioned video screening room and shop with a principally gay clientele. Large video selection.

Media

Over-opinionated press, oodles of government interference, farcical cable TV, and an alternative that's just clinging on.

If there is anything a Hungarian loves more than their own language, it's the means of spreading it. Hungarians publish an incredible amount of newspapers, magazines and books for a language spoken by just 15 million people. Eighty-seven per cent of Hungarians watch at least three hours of television per day, and the blare of radio fills every last flower shop, taxi and restaurant. Hungarians are media obsessed – as long as the media is in Hungarian.

Hungarian discourse loves opinion, and the press is full of just that. Newspapers and magazines are either pro or anti, left or right – nobody cares much for the middle. Journalistic standards vary from excellent (*Magyar Hírlap*) to Cro-Magnon (*Magyar Fórum*). High-brow literary journals fill news kiosk racks alongside trashy romance magazines and aquarium fanciers' newsletters. Whatever is lacking in quality is more than made up for in quantity.

Hungarian journalism has developed a few unique features. Although no longer the tool of the Communists, it still seems to pine to be somebody's tool. With stiff competition for readers and advertisers, Hungary's 12 national dailies, and countless magazines and regional newspapers, often feature paid-for editorial and indulge in blatant self-censorship in sympathy with political figures. Stories tend to be centred around 'scandals', and background is invariably lacking. Many journalists treat their job as translators of foreign news stories – direct plagiarism from western news sources is more the rule than the exception. Almost all writers double as journalists, and the line between journalist and novelist is often blurry.

Government interference didn't end with Communism either. The control of information is seen as a government prerogative, and when the present FIDESZ-led coalition came to power, it managed to silence critical media – such as the tabloid *Kurír* or the anarcho-cultural weekly *Magyar Narancs* (*see page 196* **The orange alternative**) – simply by taking over the banks that owned them and shutting them down.

Hungarian television is a treat not to be missed. Since 1990 the state-run Magyar Televízió has been a *causus belli* for the various governments and the control of state TV and manipulation of public TV is still usually at the centre of any current political debate. Since 1997 privately owned cable stations have given state TV a run for its money, offering Brazilian soaps, live broadcasts from suburban discos and Malaysian commando films dubbed into Magyar. One cable show features old ladies talking about shoes seated next to what appears to be a potted marijuana plant. Don't miss this.

Hungarian press

Népszabadság

The most widely read national daily, once the mouthpiece of the Communists, remains aligned with the centre-left Socialist Party. Dry and thorough and Hungary's closest thing to a paper of record.

Magyar Hírlap

Bright and colourful, *Hírlap* has been one of the most influential dailies since 1968. Aligned with dissident intellectuals and the SZDSZ, it has a liberal attitude and a sharp focus on economy and finance.

Népszava

Old organ of the Communist trade unions, *Népszava* remains the filling stodge of newspapers, sustained by an ageing but loyal readership. Close to the Socialists but more critical than *Népszabadság*.

Magyar Nemzet

The oldest established daily still offers excellent local reportage and poetry on its editorial pages, but government co-option has blunted its critical edge.

MaNcs

Hungary's only alternative newspaper has survived numerous attempts to close it down. Fresh and liberal, with extensive coverage of minority issues, in-depth news features and extensive listings. *See page 196* **The orange alternative**.

Magyar Fórum

A nationalist rag edited by right-wing fruitcake and MIÉP party chief István Csurka, the *Fórum* is Hungary's answer to *Der Sturmer*. It is ull of anti-semitic rants, racist cartoons and text in capital letters so that you know the writer is screaming at you. A unique souvenir.

Mai Nap, Blikk

The tabloids. *Mai Nap* is the bible of afternoon commuters, *Blikk* is more colourful and quirky.

Nemzeti Sport

The national sports daily, and Hungary's third most widely read paper. Heavy on football coverage, with a bias towards Ferencváros.

Expressz

Daily classifieds paper. People queue outside the offices to get first crack at its listings of flats for rent.

Weeklies

Heti Világgazdaság (HVG)

Hungary's version of *The Economist*, covering politics, economy, finance and corporate news. The most influential weekly for over two decades.

168 Óra

Weekly, consisting mostly of interviews. Maintains a respectable old dissident/liberal slant, and has managed to enrage every government since its 1980s founding.

Listings magazines

Pesti Est, Open

These two useful pocket-sized weekly freebies are available from venues around Budapest every Thursday. *Pesti Est* offers the more comprehensive service, including separate listings for English-language films — although the reviews will be in Hungarian. *Open* is sharper about nightlife (*Könnyű*) and includes a guide in hilariously inaccurate English.

Pesti Műsor

What's-on weekly (Ft59) with comprehensive listings, also featuring events outside Budapest. A little light on low-brow culture.

The orange alternative

To paraphrase the Zen koan, if an alternative movement raves in the woods, does it make a sound? Only if there is a media voice for it. In Hungary the best, and only, alternative press is *MaNcs*.

Launched in 1989 by young journalists associated with then ascendant youth party FIDESZ, the plucky paper was originally called *Magyar Narancs* ('Hungarian Orange'), a reference to the film *A Tanú*, in which Communist scientists attempt to grow a Hungarian orange. The Hungarian orange became the symbol of innovative renaissance for both FIDESZ and its press voice. Backed with money from George Soros, *Magyar Narancs* was the birthing ground for a whole generation of new Hungarian writers and journalists. Marked from its beginnings with an anarcho-liberal stamp and famous for using colloquial language, *Narancs* soon severed its ties with FIDESZ and merrily went on its own antic way.

Narancs played a key role in forming the idea of alternative taste in music, style and writing for the post-1990 generation. Strongly supportive of liberal issues such as minority and gay rights, drug issues, jazz, rave and world music, and blessed with a group of excellent writers, it was little surprise that *Narancs* came under heavy fire from successive post-Communist governments. Their style is such that they refused to refer to right-wing leader István Csurka by name, preferring 'that fat fascist'. The best read may well

be the first page, in which the editors excerpt some of the stupidest, most bizarre and most provocative comments made in the press each week.

As is often the case with alternative independent press, *Narancs* has always teetered on the verge of going broke. They have been housed in everything from spacious offices to apartments to factories. The staff often works without pay. When things get really bad, they sponsor a rave, the loyal supporters come out in droves, and yet again they pay the rent and meet the next deadline.

This proved too much for FIDESZ to bear. Resurrected as a conservative party, the former allies of *Magyar Narancs* attempted to close the paper in 1998. Having inherited the Postabank, which owned several newspapers, FIDESZ pulled funding from both the liberal tabloid *Kurír* (which then folded) and *Narancs*. When *Narancs* persisted, the government forbade the postal office from delivering its papers. *Narancs* developed a new distribution system. FIDESZ then sued to prevent it from using the FIDESZ symbol of a Hungarian orange as its name. Reluctantly, *Narancs* changed its name to the abbreviation *MaNcs*, which means 'paw' in Hungarian.

And the amazing thing is that it is still here – full of odd reviews of fish soup, old men's bars, Communist-era cars and the latest restaurants. Truly innovative. Truly a Hungarian Orange.

Foreign press

International newspapers are widely available downtown, from vendors on Váci utca and around the Castle District, in hotels and at stations, and from some kiosks. Foreign dailies often don't arrive at all or run out by the early afternoon.

Local English-language press

Budapest Business Journal

Ably covering business and finance issues, the *BBJ* is the only profitable English-language publication in town. Part of a chain of business papers including editions in Prague and Warsaw.

Budapest Sun

Owned by Britain's Associated Newspapers, the *Sun* transplants provincial British tabloid style to Budapest. Fawning and naive coverage of the insular expat community, crap film listings, pompous editorialising and lots of 'escort service' ads.

The Hungarian Quarterly

quarterly@mail.datanet.hu
Academic journal in English with essays on Hungarian history, politics, literature, art and current affairs, plus book, film and music reviews. Usually available in downtown bookstores.
Website: www.hungary.com/hungq/

E-mail & fax services

Hungary Around the Clock

Subscription rates 351 7142/fax 351 7141/ info@kingfish.hu.
An English digest compiled from the Hungarian press and faxed or e-mailed to subscribers by 9am each business day.

Television

The Hungarian appetite for the boob tube is bottomless, and, predictably, everything foreign is dubbed into Magyar – the *Flintstones* speak in rhyme and Bart Simpson never makes fart jokes.

MTV1

The official state TV station is fine for sports, feature films, documentaries, and news the way the government wants you to hear it.

MTV2

The now privatised former state TV station offers sports, films, documentaries and news the way the government does not necessarily want you to hear it.

Duna TV

Premier public service station angled to the needs of Hungarian-speaking minorities in neighbouring countries. Excellent selection of classic Magyar films plus documentaries and interviews with peasants from Slovakia about sheep-breeding.

*Piles of **Pesti Est** – mag about town.*

Cable TV

Each Budapest district has one or two cable TV sources. Relatively little is available in English, although CNN, Eurosport or TNT/Cartoon Network are carried by some outlets. Quality varies from good (TV3, MSAT/Nickelodeon) to laughable – one station actually broadcasts Tetris games during the afternoon.

Radio

There are three state-run stations. **Kossuth Radio** (540 MW) is the national station, offering a gabby yet informative mix of talk and music with doggedly poor sound quality. **Petőfi Radio** (98.4 FM) provides Hungaropop music, sport and political discussion. **Bartók Radio** (105.3 FM) plays the highbrow card, with classical music, poetry and dramas.

The FM band is crammed with commercial pop and rock, plus occasional phone-in shows and news snippets. Alternative radio is confined to 98.00 FM, shared by three stations. The formerly pirate **Tilos Radio** broadcasts from 10pm to 10am. The first few hours include excellent programmes produced by Roma, local French and German, folk and experimental music fanatics, and then goes into reggae and techno mixes until morning, when there are wonderfully quirky talk shows. From 10am to 4pm **Civil Radio** takes over, dedicated to non-profit civil organisations, and from 4pm to 10pm it's **Fix Radio**, dedicated amateurs who occasionally turn the station off while trying to switch records.

BBC World Service

BBC frequencies change every six months. For up to date frequencies call 020 7557 1165. At presstime the following were the best frequencies for reception.
Morning
6,195 kHz SW; 7,325 kHz SW; 9,410 kHz SW.
Daytime
12,095 kHz SW; 15,575 kHz SW; 17,640 kHz SW.
Evening
6,195 kHz SW; 9,410kHz SW; 12,095 kHz SW.

Music: Classical & Opera

Though top talent may flee abroad, the land of Bartók and Kodály continues to revel in a rich concert culture and musical life.

Ivories are still regularly tinkled at the **Bartók Memorial House**. *See page 200.*

In no other country east of Germany will you find a musical identity as potent as that of Hungary. In the nineteenth century, Hungarian musicians imitated the Viennese, producing good habits in teaching and playing, but bad ones in composition. At the turn of the century, young composers began seeking an alternative, and Bartók and Kodály finally provided one by setting out to document the living folk traditions of Greater Hungary. What began as ethnography unexpectedly led to contemporary Hungarian music finally losing its German accent. Bartók is now recognised as one of the giants of twentieth-century music. Kodály's music is more overtly Magyar and he is the more popular composer with Hungarian audiences – his international renown is as the inventor of a system of musical education based on folk melodies that has shaped musical appreciation in Hungary and elsewhere.

STRONG FOUNDATIONS

The Communists lavishly sponsored musical culture. Cynics say it was a way of keeping the masses happy. Others argue that it shows Communism had its good points. Either way, audiences could enjoy a musical life comparable with any in Europe, and such great names as Richter, Stravinsky and Bernstein were welcomed as guests. The authorities also made laudable attempts to bring musical culture to the masses. Young musicians such as pianist András Schiff were allowed to build reputations abroad. In return, they were contracted to give 20 concerts a year in community halls to audiences very different from those found at the Zeneakadémia. All this ended when Communism collapsed and local musicians found themselves fighting over dwindling subsidies.

But despite catastrophic disorganisation, Hungary's musical life remains rich. Programmes still tend to the conservative and staid, but this is changing. There is a thriving 'ancient music' scene and the experimental percussion group Amadinda has a cult following.

You can count on two or three concerts every night of the week during the concert season, which runs from late September to early June. In summer, the major orchestras pack up for either holidays or foreign tours, leaving smaller ensembles and ad-hoc groups to entertain the tourists.

A free monthly listing of classical and opera events, *Koncert Kalandárium* (only in Hungarian), is available at all ticket agencies and some record shops. Listings in English can be found in the *Budapest Sun*.

Orchestras & choirs

There are more professional orchestras in Budapest than in New York State, but this does mean that talent is spread too thin. Wages are often dismal (the average take-home pay for a member of the Nemzeti Filharmonikusok is $150 a month) and Budapest's orchestras are inconsistent and slightly below the highest standards.

The exception is the **Budapesti Fesztivál Zenekar** which, with its principal conductor Iván Fischer, won the prestigious Gramophone Award for best orchestra in 1998. Starting out as an ad-hoc group of the country's best musicians, it only became a full-time orchestra in 1993. With more corporate funding than any other orchestra, the BFZ is able not only to offer the highest salaries to its excellent musicians, but is also in a position to invite renowned international soloists and conductors. Their programming is imaginative and most concerts sell out.

The former Hungarian state orchestra finally became independent in 1998, and renamed itself the **Nemzeti Filharmonikusok**. Its general music director, Zoltán Kocsis, promised exciting new programmes with an emphasis on new music. He installed the promising 30-year-old Zsolt Hamar as resident conductor, and the new regime began serving up Schoenberg to an audience who were inclined to equate him with the devil. Kocsis' charisma triumphed and audiences lapped it all up. Unhappily, the orchestra's finances remain in a wretched state and this is having a detrimental effect on morale.

Conducted by Tamás Vásáry, the **MRT Szimfonikus Zenekara** (Hungarian Radio and Television Orchestra) is the most capricious Budapest ensemble. Often, it can sound like an indifferent school orchestra, but then something clicks, and they give a performance you feel you've waited half your life to hear. The repertoire of their subscription series rarely ventures beyond established warhorses, but tickets are snapped up months in advance.

Hungary has a thriving choir culture – part of the Kodály legacy – and professional choirs, such as the **Nemzeti Énekkar** (National Choir) and **MRT Énekkara** (Hungarian Radio Choir), offer a higher level of performance than the orchestras. The most distinguished has the youngest singers – the **MRT Gyermek Kórusa** (Hungarian Radio Children's Choir), four decades old and with few equals anywhere. Conducted by the charismatic Gabriella Thész, their concerts are joyous, informal affairs, with the children, ranging from 8 to 18, clearly singing for the love of it.

Instrumentalists

For real value for money, forget orchestras and seek out soloists and chamber groups. The legendary **Bartók Vonósnégyes** (Bartók String Quartet) still perform regularly – a bit shakier than they used to be but they remain a force to be reckoned with. You won't find a better cellist than Miklós Perényi and if you are seeking future world stars, then look no further than young violinists Kristóf Baráti and József Lendvay. The latter's flamboyant encores cause even jaded critics to shake their heads in disbelief.

Concert venues

Despite the large number of musicians and performing ensembles, there is a severe shortage of appropriate concert venues in Budapest. Only one orchestra (the MATÁV) has its own concert hall, the rest have to fight over the ones listed below. Competition gets fiercer in the summer when the larger venues close, making just about any courtyard or garden a good place for a concert.

Principal concert halls

Zeneakadémia

VI. Liszt Ferenc tér 8 (342 0179). M1 Oktogon/tram 4, 6 Király u. **Open** box office 10am-1pm, 2-8pm, Mon-Fri; 2-8pm Sat, Sun. Can close earlier if there is no concert that day. **No credit cards.** English spoken. **Map D3**

Really a music school, the legendary Franz Liszt Music Academy, which moved to this building in 1907. Nearly all of Hungary's musicians learned their craft here from some of the most respected names in music – who did the same a generation earlier. Concerts are held most nights in the 1,200-seat Nagyterem (Large Concert Hall), the country's primary classical music venue. The ornate wood-panelled interior provides the best acoustics this side of the Danube for both chamber recitals and orchestral concerts. There is also a smaller hall, the Kisterem, with less flattering acoustics. The academy is closed in late July and August, but amateur groups touring

Europe in these months sometimes provide an excuse to light the stage for a night.

Pesti Vigadó
V. Vigadó utca 5 (338 4721). M1 Vörösmarty tér. **Open** *box office* 10am-6pm Mon-Fri; 10am-2pm Sat; 5-7pm Sun when there is a concert. Closed July, Aug. **No credit cards.** Some English spoken. **Map C4**

Nicely situated by the Danube but toilet-bowl acoustics coupled with an interior that might be similarly described make this one of the worst concert halls in town – something definitely went wrong when it was rebuilt after bombing in World War II. Nevertheless, the Vigadó has a colourful guest register, including Brahms, who visited at the end of the nineteenth century. Mainly used during festivals and by ensembles who couldn't get the Zeneakadémia that evening.

Other venues

Budapest Congress Centre
Budapest Kongresszusi Központ
XII. Jagelló út 1-3 (209 1990). M2 Déli, tram 61. **Open** *box office* 4-7pm Wed, Fri or on day of concert. **No credit cards.** Some English spoken. **Map A5**
Modern convention centre with poor acoustics, but a larger seating capacity than the Zeneakadémia. Used mainly during festivals.

Óbuda Social Circle
Óbudai Társaskör
III. Kiskorona utca 7 (250 0288). M3 Árpád híd/tram 1. **Open** *box office* 10am-6pm daily. **No credit cards.** No English spoken.
A charming little building in the middle of a Legoland housing estate, hosting recitals and some chamber orchestras. Intimate, and often the site of some of the best concerts around.

Bartók Memorial House
Bartók Emlékház
II. Csalán utca 29 (394 2100). Bus 5, 29. **Open** *no box office*; *museum* 10am-5pm Tue-Sun; *tickets* on sale one hour before performance and during museum hours. Closed Aug. **No credit cards.** No English spoken.
Bartók's last Budapest residence, now a museum, hosts a series of Friday evening chamber concerts by the best of Hungary's musicians. Sometimes also used on other days of the week. The low ceiling can be a little claustrophobic, but the chairs are the most luxurious and comfortable of any venue in Budapest. *See also chapter* **Museums**.

MATÁV Zeneház
IX. Páva utca 10-12 (215 7901). 4/6 tram Boráros tér. **Open** *box office* Sept-May 9am-6pm Mon-Fri. June 9am-2pm Mon-Fri. Closed July, Aug. **No credit cards.** No English spoken. **Map E6**

Can play, won't play

The patron saint of pianists and Hungarian musicians alike is Franz Liszt. He inspired a tradition that has produced a staggering array of Hungarian piano players. Sadly for Hungarian audiences, they seem increasingly unwilling to show what they do best. Zoltán Kocsis, who as a teenager scandalised the nation by playing John Cage on a TV talent show, has been bitten by the conducting bug, and no longer gives solo recitals in Hungary. The same applies to the hugely respected Tamás Vásáry. Both are as conspicuous in a *Who's Who* of great pianists as they are by their absence from books on conductors. And with emigrés such as András Schiff, György Sebők and Peter Frankl making only sporadic appearances, your best bet for hearing Hungary's piano greats is in a CD shop. Kocsis records for Phillips and his Bartók and Debussy series are the best available. Schiff has recorded most of Bach and Mozart to universal acclaim, and is currently rediscovering forgotten works by Czech composers such as Dvořák and Smetana.

While you're there look out for the Beethoven recordings of Annie Fischer, perhaps the finest – and most reluctant – pianist of all. This eccentric woman had no problems performing. Instead, she refused to make records. In the 1970s, a frustrated culture minister ordered her into the recording studio, virtually at gunpoint, where she was commanded to record Beethoven's 32 sonatas. Twice she recorded them, only to demand they be wiped. On the third occasion, the tapes were spirited away, and she spent the rest of her life scheming to have them incinerated. After her death in 1995, Hungaroton controversially released them on nine CDs, but the recordings turned out to be artistically superb so arguments over the morality of the release have been forgotten. Snap them up – you'll be paying double for them abroad.

Amadeus CD Shop
V. Szende Pál utca 1 (318 6691). Tram 2 Vigadó tér. **Open** *1 Apr-31 Dec* 9.30am-9.30pm; *1 Jan-31 Mar* 9.30am-7pm daily. **No credit cards.** English spoken. **Map C4**
Widest selection of classical and jazz CDs in the city, including the biggest stock of Hungaroton Classics, and Budapest's lowest prices for non-Hungarian CDs. The staff are young, helpful, and happy to let you listen to what takes your fancy.

The recently renovated 200-seat home of the MATÁV Symphony Orchestra. What it lacks in seating capacity it makes up for in great acoustics and it is likely to be used more and more in the coming years.

Mátyás Templom

I. Szentháromság tér 2 (no phone). M2 Moszkva tér then Várbusz/bus 16. **Tickets** on sale at the venue one hour before performance. **No credit cards.** Some English spoken. **Map A3**
A top venue for organ recitals and choir concerts all the year round. Despite the typically drowning acoustics, works for choir and orchestra are also sometimes given here, particularly during festivals.

Opera

Although the Hungarian State Opera is the only opera company in Budapest, it divides its repertoire of nearly 60 opera and ballet productions a year between three houses. Higher profile productions are held in the historic **Opera House** on Andrássy út, a gem of a theatre that has everything an opera house should have except top-notch performers. The other main house, a stark monument to Socialism so enormous it almost seems empty even when it's full, is the **Erkel Színház**. **Thália Színház** in Nagymező utca is also occasionally pressed into service.

Despite the rich history of the Opera House (Gustav Mahler and Otto Klemperer both had regimes here) the 1990s have proved trying. Threats of bankruptcy hang in the air while old-style mismanagement has successfully squandered most of the company's best talent. The brightest young singers stay around only long enough to be spotted by some international agent, leaving singing duties to well-intentioned veterans. Even worse off are the musicians in the pit – overstaffed, underpaid and usually under-rehearsed.

But, depending on the director, State Opera productions are not always without a sense of invention: sometimes what is lacking in musical or dramatic talent is balanced by creative set design and original staging. With at least four opera and three ballet premières a year, the State Opera is trying to cultivate an image of resourceful innovation in the face of impending financial ruin.

The State Opera publishes a monthly schedule, available at the Opera House and ticket agencies.

Opera House

Magyar Állami Operaház
VI. Andrássy út 22 (353 0170). M1 Opera. **Open** *box office* 10am-7pm Tue-Sat when there is a performance; 10am-1pm, 4-7pm, Sun when there is a performance. **Credit** AmEx. Some English spoken. **Map D3**
See also chapter **Sightseeing**.

Erkel Színház

VIII. Köztársaság tér 30 (333 0540). M2 Blaha Lujza tér. **Open** *box office* 10am-7pm Tue-Sat performance days; 10am-1pm, 4-7pm, Sun performance days. **Credit** AmEx. Some English spoken. **Map E4**

Thália Színház

VI Nagymező utca 22-24 (331 0500). M1 Oktogon. **Open** *box office* 10am-6pm Mon-Fri; 2-6pm Sat. **Credit** AmEx. Some English spoken. **Map D3**
See also chapter **Theatre & Dance**.

Ticket agencies

Few classical concerts in Budapest sell out. With the exception of the BFZ and MRT Szimfonikus's subscription series, tickets are usually available and affordable unless a major international artist is involved. Tickets for most concerts can be bought at the Vigadó Ticket Service or the Zeneakadémia. What isn't available there is best bought at the venue an hour or so before the performance. Tickets for the State Opera and Erkel Színház are only available at the respective box offices and at the State Opera Ticket Office a few doors down Andrássy út. Most places only accept cash, but prices are not extortionate. *Koncert Kalandárium* notes where tickets are available for each event.

Vigadó Ticket Service

V. Vörösmarty tér 1 (327 4322). M1 Vörösmarty tér. **Open** 9am-7pm Mon-Fri; 10am-3pm Sat, Sun. **No credit cards.** English spoken. **Map C4**
Centrally located office that has almost everything.

Music Academy Ticket Office

VI. Liszt Ferenc tér 8 (342 0179). M1 Oktogon/tram 4, 6 Király u. **Open** *box office* 10am-1pm, 2-8pm, Mon-Fri; 2-8pm Sat, Sun. Can close earlier if no concert that day. **No credit cards.** English spoken. **Map D3**
Supplies tickets for events all over the city.

State Opera Ticket Office

VI. Andrássy út 20 (353 0170). M1 Opera. **Open** 10am-5.30pm Mon-Thur; 10am-4.30pm Fri. **Credit** AmEx. Some English spoken. **Map D3**

Festivals

The Hungarian media has an obsession with festivals, which are proclaimed with metronomic regularity. Few are of much significance except to give journalists press conferences to attend. The exception is the Budapest Spring Festival – a huge cultural extravaganza over two and a half weeks in March (*see also chapter* **Budapest by Season**). Lack of funds prevent it being the truly international festival it once was, but distinguished artists and orchestras are still regularly persuaded to perform. Tickets are available at the regular outlets.

Budapest Festival Office

VIII. Rákóczi út 66 (210 2795/133 2337). M2 Blaha Lujza tér/tram 4, 6.

Music: Rock, Roots & Jazz

Local acts in all idioms, central Europe's largest rock festival and, although it's no rapper's delight, a heaving Hungarian hip hop scene.

The music scene in Hungary is like that of any western country but reflected in a funhouse mirror. Global fashions have always had a strong, if slightly delayed, influence and most Magyar acts ape foreign artists. Sometimes they add an interesting Hungarian twist, but more often than not they're just cut-rate knock-offs for the local market. Most genres boast at least one local example. Reggae? Try skanking to Ladánybene 27. Heavy metal? Tankcsapda, Hungary's answer to Motörhead, will bludgeon your ears nicely.

But the development of local artists is limited. Homegrown talent has to compete with international acts in a small, cash-poor pond where a gold record means just 25,000 sales. The market is dominated by commercial stars such as soppy Jimmy Zámbó, sensitive balladeer Zorán and no less than four local versions of the Spice Girls.

Abroad, Hungarians are saddled with a language that doesn't lend itself to pop structures or travel well, but singing in English can backfire by alienating the core home audience. No groups have met real success by taking this route. The Bowie-esque Ákos, the only young local rocker who can fill stadiums, has a ghost of a chance and determinedly releases English versions of his recordings. Old rockers, meanwhile, obstinately refuse to fade away. Communist Hungary had plenty of long-haired bands such as Omega and Illés who still attract huge audiences to their revival shows.

Punk and new wave had an impact here and helped foster a 1980s underground scene. Their subculture, with its edge of anger and bittersweet resignation, remains an important influence on alternative bands. Survivors from the 1980s include Balaton, led by Mihály Víg, a romantic loser in the Pete Shelley mould; ef Zámbó, who occasionally ventures forth from his artist's studio in Szentendre to play in Budapest with his Happy Dead Band; and Vágtázó Halottkémek – the Galloping Coroners, or VHK – shamanistic punks namechecked by the likes of Henry Rollins. For trad punk noise, catch a show by Auróra, stalwarts from Győr famous for bidding the Soviets goodbye with their call to arms, *Viszlát Iván*.

Contemporary chart artists are a dismaying bunch, and Eurocheese of all flavours sells by the bucketload. Republic do tolerable stadium pop, and rap duo Animal Cannibals (*see page 204* **Goulash gangstas**) can amuse. Kispál és a Borz from Pécs are the country's best-loved indie rock outfit. Budapest's club circuit has some promisingly individual acts, such as the goofily alternative Publo Hunny or the darkly cheerful Quimby. The cheeky art-school element is represented by the female and foul-mouthed Tereskova. Tudósok (The Scientists) are less melodic but even more demented. For competent indie pop/rock in the early REM and Blur vein, lend an ear to Heaven Street Seven.

Korai Öröm, with their fluctuating horde of drummers and DJs, bridge world music, techno and psychedelia to unique effect. Másfél crank up a tremendous jazz-rock-fusion racket. Avant-gardists Kampec Dolores also succeed by genre-hopping – in their case between folk and rock – as do Anima Sound System, a collective of sample and scratch wizards who combine a compelling female singer with folk, dub and trance.

The best crash course in these and about 200 other bands is August's Sziget Festival on Óbuda Island (*see chapter* **By Season**). Seven days of cheap drinks, dust and mayhem, it's a prime annual get-together for Hungarians and travellers. Attendance was 250,000 in 1998, and with corporate sponsorship the festival lures the likes of Iggy Pop, Therapy? and Asian Dub Foundation. Tickets are cheap, and visitors can camp on the island for the full festival experience.

Tickets & information

Concert details and previews can be found in *Pesti Est* and *Open* and erratically in the *Budapest Sun*. See chapter **Media**. Concerts rarely sell out but advance tickets can be bought at:

Music Mix

V. Váci utca 33 (338 2237). M3 Ferenciek tere/bus 7. **Open** 10am-6pm Mon-Fri; 10am-2pm Sat. **No credit cards. Map C4**

Korai Öröm – drums and DJs, collectively.

Large events hall in City Park. The indoor arena – a soulless barn with poor sound – is too large for most Hungarian bands but many mid-range Western acts will stop off here. The outdoor concert area in summer has the better atmosphere. Both spaces hold around 2,500 people.

Live music clubs

Certain smaller venues in *chapters* **Nightlife, Cafés & Coffeehouses** *and* **Pubs & Bars** also host live music. Of these, **Miró** has jazz and Latin, **Crazy Café** has pop and funk, **E-Klub** has rock concerts, **Fat Mo's** offers jazz and blues and **Darshan Udvar** occasionally hosts visiting performers.

Banán Klub
III. Mátyás király út 13-15 (240 0491). HÉV to Csillaghegy. **Open** *Sept-June* from 7pm on concert nights. **Admission** Ft300-Ft1,000. Some English spoken.
A fair way from the centre but one of the few clubs left offering affordable non-mainstream music for a friendly circle of musicians and their fans. Decent bar away from the numbers. Worth the trek for the right band. Concerts begin at 9.30-10.30pm.

Benczúr Klub
VI. Benczúr utca 27 (321 7334). M1 Bajza utca. **Open** 7-11pm Wed; 7pm-midnight Thur; 7pm-1am Fri, Sat. **Admission** Ft300-Ft500. Some English spoken. **Map E2**
Charmless room in the basement of a cultural centre with utterly un-clubby atmosphere. Nonetheless, the Benczúr is devoted to local music and has a pleasant crowd. Wednesdays are jazz; other nights feature Scots-Irish folk by locals MÉZ, plus assorted rock, blues and underground concerts. Pleasant outdoor venue in summer.

Fél 10
VIII. Baross utca 30 (06 20 988 2318). M3 Kálvin tér/tram 4, 6 to Baross utca. **Open** 6pm-4am Wed-Sun, concerts from 9.30pm. **Admission** Ft400 (higher for major acts). English spoken. **Map D5**
The name means 'half ten' (as in 9.30 – pronounce it 'fail tease' for the taxi driver). An acoustically perfect but logistically flawed venue (bottlenecks, poor ventilation) where you can catch local or international blues, funk and pop acts. An absolute meat market on weekends, with plenty of poseurs gyrating to techno-free dance music.

Jailhouse Rock
IX. Tűzoltó utca 22 (218 1368). M3 Ferenc körút/tram 4, 6 to Üllői út. **Open** 6pm-4am Fri, Sat; 6pm-midnight Sun. **Admission** Ft300-Ft500. Some English spoken. **Map E5**
Looks convincingly like a small dungeon, with appropriate comfort level. Scruffy student crowd drawn by cheap drinks and underground music – usually hardcore punk, metal or indie. Completely crap sound system suits shouty bands best.

Ticket Express
MCD, VI. Jókai utca 40 (353 0692). M3 Nyugati pu. **Open** 9.30am-9.30pm daily. **No credit cards. Map C2**
Tickets for rock concerts and some other cultural events, in the back of a big music store.
Branch: MCD, VIII. József körút 50 (334 0369).
Website: www.ticketexpress.hu.

Venues

Large venues include **Népstadion, MTK**'s stadium and the **Budapest Sportcsarnok** (*see chapter* **Sport & Fitness**).

Almássy tér Recreation Centre
Almássy téri Szabadidőközpont
VII. Almássy tér 6 (352 1572). M2, tram 4/6 to Blaha Lujza tér. **Open** 7pm-dawn on concert nights. **Admission** varies. Some English spoken. **Map E3**
Of all the cultural centres in town, the one most willing and suitable for live music of non-folk genres. With bars upstairs and down, a mid-size concert hall and central location, it's a popular spot for mid-level bands, eclectic parties and smaller music festivals.

Budai Parkszínpad
XI. Kosztolányi Dezső tér (466 9849). Tram 49/bus 7. **Open** from 7pm. **Admission** varies. Some English spoken. **Map B6**
The main summer outdoor venue, comprising a few hundred chairs and a huge stage in the small park near Kosztolányi Dezső tér. Concerts tend to be mainstream pop, although the venue hosts various folk events and the annual World Music Festival in June. *See chapter* **By Season**.

Petőfi Csarnok
XIV. Városliget, Zichy Mihály út 14 (343 4327). M1 Széchenyi fürdő/trolleybus 70. **Open** from 8pm for concerts. **Admission** varies. Some English spoken. **Map F2**

Kalóztanya

VII. Huszár utca 7 (06 20 962 9267). M2 Keleti/bus 7. **Open** noon-1am Mon-Fri; 2pm-2am Sat, Sun. **Concerts** start 9pm. **Admission** free. No English spoken. **Map E3**

A great place to get bombed – literally. An explosive was tossed in here during a 1997 mafia row. Patched up since, it now has a mild crowd and live blues, pub rock or funk nightly. Pirate theme.

Lyuk

VIII. Golgota utca 3 (210 0491). Tram 23, 24/bus 99. **Open** 9pm-5am Fri, Sat; 5-11pm Sun. **Admission** Ft300-Ft800 (more for foreign acts). Some English spoken.

Risen again from the grave, the 'Hole' has had many incarnations in its long history as one of Budapest's few real underground clubs. A Stygian pit where misfits of all stripes can gather undis-

Goulash gangstas

Ganxsta Zolee – from the ghetto... not!

He's a big man, usually pictured with shades and knives and tattoos – the whole cartoon bad-boy kit. But this homeboy is home grown. He's Ganxsta Zolee, baddest Magyar rapper on the block, leader of his very own 'kartel' and point man for the latest pop craze in Hungary.

Hip hop might seem an improbable transplant and there's a strong whiff of absurdity to most Magyar rap. Thus Zolee, the Unoriginal Gangster. He might aspire to ghetto menace, but everyone knows he grew up in the well-heeled Buda suburb of Rózsadomb, the son of popular actor József Zana. Zolee got his start as the drummer in naughty rock band Sex Action then reinvented himself along the lines of Tupac, Snoop and company. He's built up a posse of beefy semi-toughs and released pose-heavy albums such as *Egyenesen a gettóból* (*Straight from the Ghetto*) and

the western-themed *Helldorádo*. Zolee even put out a Christmas CD, *Fehér hó*, featuring himself as a machine-gun toting Santa Claus holding the reins for two pneumatic women. Kids and junior mafiosi lapped it up, and a new genre was born.

But rap actually has older roots in Hungary, starting with early 1990s supergroup Rapülők, led by multi-talented svengali Péter Geszti. Rapülők specialised in commercial disco-pop, and pioneered a surprisingly successful pairing of hip hop beats and witty Magyar lyrics. With its rigid stress and intonation, Hungarian has always been a tough fit for melodic rock, but rap's street poet wordplay suits it to a T.

Following Zolee's foul-mouthed lead is László 'Dopeman' Pityinger, another player purporting to be the only real gangsta. Dopeman can at least claim to walk the walk – he's from Józsefváros, the notorious District VIII of real-life pimps, whores, crumbling estates and petty crime. Playing straight to the mafia types, Dopeman's raps bear titles like *Babycunthunter* and *A Dead Slut Doesn't Bark*.

Also from Józsefváros, but less ridiculous, are Animal Cannibals, a pair of Fila-sponsored youths (MC Qka and Ritchie P) who deliver witty raps about everyday concerns (*Cleaning Lady* was their first single; they've since had a platinum album). The Hip Hop Boyz, a dayglo techno dance act, also go down well with the teen set.

But hip hop should be the music of oppressed minorities. Or so argue Fekete Vonat, a trio of young Roma rappers named after the 'black train' that many gypsies ride, commuting into Budapest from outlying villages. Former protegés of Dopeman but considerably more serious, their raps mix Roma and Hungarian and comment on social issues. On their first single *Forró a vérem* (*My Blood is Hot*) the interplay between Fatima's singing and Beat's raps almost suggests the Fugees. Claiming they want to bring down walls between Hungarians and Romas, they're the only local hip hop product with an original identity.

turbed, it's under a community centre at the gloomy arse-end of District VIII. Concerts span the gamut of alternative options. You've got to really, really want to see a thrash band to come here, having run the gauntlet of change-beggars all the way down the bleak expanses of Golgota utca, but visiting name acts are sometimes worth it. If you find grit in your cup of cheap wine, don't worry – it's just the ceiling plaster turning to powder under the decibel assault.
Website: www.lyuk.hu.

Old Man's Music Pub

VII. Akácfa utca 13 (322 7645). M2 Blaha Lujza tér/tram 4, 6 Wesselényi utca. **Open** 3pm-3am daily. **Concerts** start 9pm. **Admission** free. Some English spoken. **Map A5**
Large and comfortably furnished, this is the place to catch local blues acts such as Muddy Shoes (acoustic Delta), György Ferenczi (mean harmonica), Mama Killed A Chicken (powerful female singer) and Dr Valter & The Lawbreakers (1930s blues). There are also appearances by Magyar elder bluesmen such as Ádám Török, Tamás Takáts and the towering, Yeti-like Hobo. Occasional jazz events plus a downstairs dancefloor with mainstream rock, funk and disco. Good acoustics, but book a table if you want a view of the small stage. Surprisingly courteous service and vast multilingual menu stretching from fried cheese to roast ostrich.

Wigwam

XI. Fehérvári út 202 (208 5569) Tram 47/bus 3. **Open** 8pm-5am Thur-Sun. **Admission** Ft500. Some English spoken.
Barn-sized venue with overdone Wild West theme but one of Budapest's few large stages for rock bands. An older crowd twists again at weekly 1950s rock 'n' roll parties; other nights feature rock and heavy metal acts and attract a younger, hairier audience. Three bars, dancefloor and games room. Far from the centre but very near the tram stop.

Jazz venues

In the Socialist era, older Hungarians listened to jazz on Radio Free Europe, and the music retains a certain western cachet. But sadly the best homegrown jazzmen often leave for greener pastures abroad. Two top talents who make frequent return appearances are saxophonist Tony Lakatos and guitarist Ferenc Snétberger. Guitarist Gyula Babos, former leader of Saturnus and jazz chair at the **Zeneakadémia**, is one Hungarian artist who has earned such recognition but stayed home.

Mihály Dresch is a world-class saxophonist who creates his own distinctive folk-jazz, spinning ancient Hungarian tones into avant-garde experiments. Other ethno-jazzers worth seeking out include Tin Tin Trio, Makám, Dél-Alföldi Szaxofonegyüttes and violin prodigy Félix Lajkó. Closer to straight jazz is sax player István Grencsó. Trio Midnight play tight mainstream and Aladár Pege is Hungary's double bassist of distinction. Pianist-dentist György Vukán plays when he's not pulling teeth, and is also a respected composer.

Jazz Garden

V. Veres Pálné utca 44/a (266 7364). M3 Kálvin tér. **Open** 6pm-1am daily. **Concerts** 9pm-midnight daily. Some English spoken. **Map D5**
Cellar club decorated with plants and patio finishings for a virtual outdoor effect. The ceiling is carpeted in black and studded with LEDs patterned as constellations, while air-conditioning creates a breeze. Beyond the bar/garden space is a rose-hued restaurant area where the live jazz is audible but unobtrusive. A Ft500 cover must be paid on entry but it's deducted from the final bill. Awful pizza, good acoustics, well-heeled clientele, and fine local groups with an emphasis on vocal jazz. Perverse in warmer months, a welcome illusion in winter.

Long Jazz Club

VII. Dohány utca 22-24 (322 0006). M2 Astoria/bus 7/tram 47, 49. **Open** 8pm-2am Tue-Sun. **Admission** free. English spoken. **Map D4**
Relaxed place with live jazz nightly and decent Hungarian fare. More L-shaped than long, it has a small, intimate stage in the corner, visible but not overbearing for those seated at either of the two bar areas. Good place to catch up-and-coming local acts.

Specialist shops

See also chapter **Shopping & Services**. To see what's hot and what's not in Hungary, visit the website of MAHASZ, the country's authority on record sales, at www.externet.hu/mahasz.

Tangó

VI. Klauzál utca 9 (352 1146). M2 Blaha Lujza tér/tram 4, 6. **Open** 11am-6pm Mon-Fri; 10am-1pm Sat. **No credit cards**. Some English spoken. **Map D4**
Buys, sells and exchanges used CDs. Idiosyncratic and ever-changing selection. Perfect for bargain-hunting.

Violin 2000 Zenestúdió

IX. Ferenc körút 19-21 (215 4551). M3 Ferenc körút/tram 4, 6 Mester utca. **Open** 9am-11.30pm daily. Some English spoken. **Map E5**
General music shop with long opening hours and a counter where you can listen before buying.

Z Hanglemez

VIII. Rákóczi út 47 (333 0143). M2 Blaha Lujza tér/tram 4, 6. **Open** noon-6pm Mon-Fri. **No credit cards**. Some English spoken. **Map E4**
Tiny courtyard shop devoted entirely to the works of Frank Zappa. The friendly proprietor bears more than a passing resemblance to FZ himself.

Nightlife

A relaxed scene, cheap drinks and a thriving rave network more than make up for a certain distance from the cutting edge.

Budapest is a liberating place for anyone used to the constraints of a pathetically over-regulated country such as Britain. Cheap taxis, cheap drinks and lots of cheap laughs more than make up for a certain distance from the cutting-edge. It might not be London or Berlin in standards of either DJing or décor, but the scene is relaxed and friendly and nights are both long and unpredictable.

Despite recent price rises, you can still order a round of shots for everyone in the vicinity without having to empty your wallet. Admission fees tend to be reasonable, taxis are mostly likewise (if you phone one, or flag down a Fő, you won't be ripped off – *see chapter* **Getting Around**), and the night bus network is efficient, so running around town and checking out several places in one night (the best bars and clubs are not all concentrated in any particular area) presents no obstacles beyond your own stamina. Getting past the door is also usually no problem; there are rarely queues, even at the most popular places, and the bouncers don't care how you dress or what state you're in.

Drugs are relatively few and far between – especially since insanely draconian new drug laws were introduced in early 1999 (*see page 255* **Old habits, new laws**). Good DJs are also hard to find. New clubs open all the time but the same dozen or so DJs play at every event – leaving little space for any rising young talent – and few of them seem to have either much money for new records or much sense of what's going to get the dancefloor going. But where Budapest really shines is in the one-off party scene. Raves abound in a variety of venues – not just warehouses and cultural centres, but also quarries, Buda hilltops, Danube islands and Turkish baths. The summer scene is particularly refreshingly, with loose-limbed outdoor events practically every weekend. *See* **One-off venues** *below and page 214* **Party in the place to be**.

Along with places to drink and dance, there are plenty of late-night restaurants and snack bars. For the impromptu *házibuli* – party at home – call in at a non-stop and stock up on beer and other essentials at any time of the night or day. Or you can wind down after a long night by sipping a last beer on the terrace of a late bar and watching the solid citizens begin their daily scurry to work.

Most of the people you'll meet in the bars and clubs of Budapest will be amiable and easy-going, although some of them will be very drunk indeed. You might see some dangerous-looking characters, but in practice there's less casual violence than in most European cities. Bouncers, though, can get really nasty if they think you're taking the piss; avoid doing anything to provoke them.

As in any city, it's also a fluid scene. Places come and go. Ownership changes and music policy mutates. To find out what's new, look out in venues and shops for flyers advertising events, and also for the freebie weeklies *Open* and *Pesti Est*.

Or just go to a few of the places listed here and start asking around. Before you know it, you'll be part of the crowd strap-hanging it on the midnight bus across Margaret Bridge, the lights of the Castle District floating in the darkness beyond, on your way from some crazy bar to some even crazier event in a factory or swimming pool. At the turn of the millennium, there are few cities that can still offer raves in such an affordable variety of cool and curious locations.

Dance bars

Places listed in this section are hybrid café-bar-restaurants with dancefloors. The majority are in cellars and in central Pest. Most are easygoing, fun places to have a drink, perhaps a bite to eat, and get down on the dancefloor. During the week they tend to be either packed or deserted, depending on the mysteriously shifting loyalties of the party crowd. At weekends they're mostly heaving.

Bamboo Music Club

VI. Dessewffy utca 44 (312 3619). M1 Oktogon/ tram 4, 6/night bus 6E. **Open** 7pm-4am Tue-Sat. **Admission** free to Ft500. **No credit cards.** Some English spoken. **Map D2**
Tropical-style theme bar in a small cellar. Usually packed with a young crowd who make the most of the tiny dancefloor to the rhythm of ancient pop hits from Thursday to Saturday. There's a more credible music policy midweek when it's soul and funk, and it's almost fashionable on Tuesdays, when Szörp (a band) and DJ Deky play acid jazz for the regulars.
Website: www.extra.hu/bamboo

*Stock up for an impromptu házibuli any time of day or night – **Makulet** non-stop. P 217.*

Boulevard Café

VI. Hajós utca 2 (342 6700). M1 Opera.
Open 10pm-2am daily. **Admission** Ft500. **No credit cards**. Some English spoken. **Map D3**
Smart restaurant/café. Clientele are mostly nondescript rich young things and curious tourists. Thursday, which traditionally a quiet night for Budapest, is busy here as the partying crowd follow their favourite DJs and entrance is free with a flyer.

The Club Café and Restaurant

V. Apáczai Csere János utca 13 (266 6223). M1 Vörösmarty tér/tram 2, 2A. **Open** noon-5am daily. **Admission** free to FT500. **No credit cards**. Some English spoken. **Map C4**
Spacious, vaulted dancefloor and an adjacent, relatively restful chill-out café with windows at street level. Their ridiculously eclectic music policy means you could find yourself having a Latin, Greek, soul,

rock, lesbian, karaoke or Chippendale night out, depending on the day of the week. Also a favourite venue for house/techno after-hours parties that generally kick off around 8am on Sundays to the bewilderment of local church-goers and dog-walkers.

Circus Music Club
VII. Dohány utca 20 (344 4107). M2 Astoria/tram 47, 49/night bus 182É. **Open** 7pm-3am Tue-Sun. **Admission** free to Ft500. **No credit cards**. Some English spoken. **Map D4**
Unpretentious place at the **Central Synagogue** end of Dohány utca. An L-shaped cellar bar with a DJ booth and dancefloor in the middle, and several long benches at the end. Friday funk nights were struggling to take off as we went to press.

Garage Café
V. Arany János utca 9 (302 6473). M3 Arany János utca/tram 2, 2A/night bus 182É. **Open** *bar* 11am-2am, *food served* 11am-2am daily. **Admission** free to FT500. Some English spoken. **Map C3**
Fairly plush, medium-sized restaurant/bar on three levels with pricey drinks to match its trendy aspirations and bank district location. Garage only really comes to life on Wednesdays for Future Sound of Budapest nights, when DJ Tommyboy and colleagues lay on the funky/house beats and their beautiful friends turn out for a midweek mingle on the packed but fast-moving dancefloor.

Made Inn
VI. Andrássy út 112 (311 3437). M1 Bajza utca. **Open** 10pm-4am Wed-Sun. **Admission** Ft500. English spoken. **Map E2**
A Greek restaurant on street level (open until 3am, average Ft1,200) with two dancefloors below. Has been attracting the young, rich and carefree for at least a decade with funky hits and atmosphere that tries hard to be posh and sexy.

Nincs Pardon
VII. Almássy tér 11 (351 4351). M2 Blaha Lujza tér/ tram 4, 6 Wesselényi utca/night bus 6É. **Open** 8pm-4am daily. **Admission** free to Ft200. **No credit cards**. Some English spoken. **Map E3**
A small cellar bar in the front, decorated with Gaudi-like shapes and tile mosaics. Dull and dated

Nincs Pardon – *no excuse not to party.*

disco animates the modest dancefloor in the back. A Budapest institution that caters for a mature and loyal crowd of media/showbiz cocktail-drinking regulars. Watch out for the steep, treacherous steps late at night. The name means 'no excuse'.

Piaf
VI. Nagymező utca 25 (312 3823). M1 Oktogon/tram 4, 6/night bus 6É. **Open** 10pm-6am daily. **Admission** Ft500 incl drink. **No credit cards**. Some English spoken. **Map D3**
Don't go before 1am and expect an initial chill from the woman at the door. Exchange your admission ticket for a drink at the bar. Upstairs, in a red-velvet room that resembles a bordello, showbiz types take refuge from 'Budapest's Broadway' outside. The atmosphere is sophisticated and decadent, and the music, whether from a piano player or the stereo, is jazzy. Down the nerve-wracking staircase there's an L-shaped cellar space with another bar and a tiny dancefloor enlivened by good old disco hits.

Roktogon Rock Local
VI. Nagymező utca 9 (353 0443). M1 Oktogon/tram 4, 6/night bus 6É. **Open** 9pm-4am Wed-Sat. **Admission** *after 10pm* Ft200. **No credit cards**. Some English spoken. **Map D3**
Not a rock disco but a medium-sized cellar dance bar where DJs play upbeat MTV hits to an excitable crowd of teenagers and students. Décor involves marble slabs, wooden benches and faded graffiti murals. The cover's cheap, so's the beer, and this is an unpretentious and friendly place to chat, drink and jump around to ultra-familiar tunes until late.

Trafó Pince
IX. Liliom utca 41 (456 2049). M3 Ferenc körút/tram 4, 6/night bus 182É, 6É. **Open** 4.30pm-5am daily. **Admission** free to Ft250. **No credit cards**. English spoken.
Large basement bar at Budapest's alternative theatre and cultural centre (*see chapter* **Theatre & Dance** *and* **Art Galleries**). On Wednesdays a third of the bar becomes a makeshift dancefloor packed with enthusiastic followers of Korai's Banditos, who keep the show lively with video projections, MCs and lashings of trip hop. The question is, why does a nice liberal institution like Trafó employ such horrible bouncers? Don't let them spoil your night.

The Vibe Dinner and Music Club
VII. Kertész utca 33 (267 8616). Tram 4, 6 Király utca/night bus 6É. **Open** 4pm-3am daily. **Admission** free. **No credit cards**. Some English spoken. **Map D3**
Go down the stairs, turn left and you're in a labyrinthine pizzeria that takes orders till 1am; turn right and you reach a bunker-like cavern with what looks like pasta glued to the walls. The dancefloor can get really steamy as the boys and girls get down to the Vibe's successful recipe of acid jazz, r&b, hip hop and soul, except Wednesday, which is drum 'n' bass night. Fun and easygoing.

*Pumping it up to the beat of pumping techno at **Supersonic Technicum**. See page 210.*

Undergrass Dance Klub

*VI. Liszt Ferenc tér 10 (322 0830). M1 Oktogon/
tram 4, 6/night bus 6É.* **Open** *7pm-4am Mon-Sat.*
Admission *free to Ft500.* **No credit cards.**
English spoken. **Map D3**
The Undergrass Dance Klub is under the **Café
Mediterran** (*see chapter* **Pubs & Bars**) in the popular and pedestrianised Liszt Ferenc tér. Shiny
metallic-themed cellar bar, with a small dancefloor
cut off by obtrusive sound-proof double doors,
where DJs play a mixture of unpretentious 1980s
and MTV hits for a happy crowd of drinkers and
dancers. Serves probably the stingiest *korsó* of
Amstel in Budapest (0.35l).

Underground

*VI. Teréz körút 30 (311 1481). M1 Oktogon/tram 4,
6/night bus 6É.* **Open** *3pm-3am daily.* **Admission**
free to Ft500. **No credit cards.** English spoken.
Map D3
Under the **Művész** cinema (*see chapter* **Film**). The
convenient location on the körút near Oktogon and
the dark metallic looks attract a lot of late-night custom to this long cellar space, which is two-thirds bar
with tables, one-third dancefloor. Music at the
Underground tends to be mainstream funk and
garage, but watch out for the occasional Goa party.
Food available.

Clubs & discos

Budapest is home to a growing number of commercial clubs playing mainstream house and techno, as well as a number of older discos that play
1980s pop hits and Magyar evergreens. Both offer
louder, longer and more intense nights out than the
smaller dance bars listed above.

Capella

*V. Belgrád Rakpart 23 (318 6231). M2 Ferenciek
tere/tram 2.* **Open** *9pm-2am Mon-Tue; 9pm-5.30am
Wed-Sun.* **Admission** *Ft400.* **No credit cards.**
English spoken. **Map C5**
Basically a gay club (*see chapter* **Gay & Lesbian**),
though straights are also welcome most nights to
take in the midnight drag show and get down to
disco and house beats until dawn. A mixed and
ageless crowd makes this cellar warren of bars and
dancefloors one of the best clubs in town.

Citadella Dance Club

XI. Citadella sétány 2 (06 30 407 066). Bus 27.
Open *10pm-5am Wed, Fri, Sat.* **Admission** *Ft1,000.*
No credit cards. *Some English spoken.* **Map B5**
An unbeatable view of the city from the top of
Gellért Hill can be had through the large windows
alongside the main dancefloor. There are go-go
dancers in cages, pricey drinks and mainstream
commercial dance music, which on Fridays goes out
live from here on Juventus Radio. Be warned, you
might get ripped off by unscrupulous taxi drivers
on the way home, as it's a long downhill traipse back
to civilisation.

E-Klub

*X. Népliget, next to Planetarium (263 1614). M3
Népliget/night bus 1É, 14É and 50É.* **Open** *9pm-5am
Fri, Sat.* **Admission** *Ft500.* **No credit cards.** *No
English spoken.*
Declining Communist-era rock disco recently reborn
as a mainstream house nightclub, now offering three
dancefloors with an improved sound system, laser
strobes and hot snacks to millennium-era teenagers.
Six metro stops from Deák tér and a bit of a trek
through spooky People's Park to get here.
Website: www.e-klub.hu

E-Play

VI. Teréz körút 55 (302 2849). M3 Nyugati/tram 4, 6/night bus 6É and 182É. **Open** 10pm-6am Thur, Sat; 10pm-4am Fri. **Admission** Ft800. **No credit cards.** No English spoken. **Map D2**

The name doesn't necessarily mean that the young crowd here is chemically altered – though a few of them certainly seem full of energy. Even if you're on nothing stronger than orange juice, you're likely to catch a buzz from the pumping beat of the high-street house music, the lurid neon décor, the deadly-serious go-go dancer, the smoke machine and the can't-stop-grinning, can't-stop-moving mob on the mirrored dancefloor upstairs.

Hotel Royal Club & Café

VII. Erzsébet körút 43-49 (no phone). M2 Blaha Lujza tér/tram 4, 6/night bus 6É. **Open** *café* 10am- 2am daily; *club* 10pm-6am Fri, Sat. **Admission** varies. **No credit cards.** No English spoken. **Map E3**

Huge, dilapidated former hotel colonised as a café and party venue, with a lease that's due to run out sometime in 2001. The café has house DJs every day from 5pm; the club area in the former hotel restaurant opens at weekends. House predominates but music and clientele vary a lot, depending on the profile of the DJ and the organisers of any given event. Décor is dated 1960s stuff and clocks on the wall behind the bar (converted reception desk) show the time in New York, Amsterdam, Kingston, Bangkok and Goa. At the same address as **Royal 2000 Funky Club** (*see below*).

Közgáz Pince Klub

IX. Fővám tér 8 (215 4359). M3 Kálvin tér/tram 2, 47, 49. **Open** 8pm-5am Mon-Sat. **Admission** Ft400. **No credit cards.** No English spoken. **Map C5**

Large and popular student disco under the Economics University by the Danube. Slightly more cosmopolitan than SOTE, but still a good place to sample such traditional Budapest nightlife staples as *boros kola* (cola with sweet red wine), *zsíros kenyér* (bread and dripping) and *vilmos körte* (pear brandy) and to watch or join tipsy teenagers dancing to timeless Magyar hits. Don't do anything to provoke the merciless thugs on the door. Busy every night.

Medúza

XI. Fehérvári út 87 (203 9400). Tram 18, 41, 47. **Open** 10pm-5am Wed, Fri, Sat. **Admission** Ft1,000. **No credit cards.** Some English spoken.

Commercial house for plastic people in a large, new, expensive club where you need to take a lift to get to the dancefloor.

Royal 2000 Funky Club

VII. Erzsébet körút 43-49 (no phone). M2 Blaha Lujza tér/tram 4, 6/night bus 6É. **Open** 10pm-6am on event nights. **Admission** varies. **No credit cards.** No English spoken. **Map E3**

Run by different people but at the same address as the **Hotel Royal Club & Café**, occupying a former cinema complex. Ascend a grand marble staircase to find a foyer bar and a generous dancefloor

space in the auditorium beyond. The crowd here tends to be a bit heavier, for some reason, than those who frequent the establishment next door, but a good venue for the right party – check what's on. Lease due to expire sometime in 2001.

SOTE Klub

VIII. Nagyvárad tér 4 (459 0351). M3 Nagyvárad tér. **Open** 9pm-4.30am Sat. **Admission** Ft700. **No credit cards.** No English spoken. **Map F6**

Once a week Budapest's medical university is transformed into a seemingly endless complex of dancefloors, stages and bars. Bring your passport to get in and watch young men in tight-fitting suits and with greased-back hair and girls in tiny dresses and platform shoes showing off, eyeing up and getting off. There's even a gallery to scan the strobe-lit disco in comfort for the partner of your dreams. Arrive in good time and you could get to hear one of the more popular Hungarian bands, such as Animal Cannibals, Pa-Dö-Dö or Ganxsta Zolee. There's also a cinema showing the latest Hollywood blockbuster, a pop techno room and ruinously cheap drinks. *Website: www.divat.net/sote*

Supersonic Technicum

III. Pacsirtamező utca 41 (334 6450). Bus 6, 86. **Open** 10pm-7am Sat; closed in summer. **Admission** Ft1,500. **No credit cards.** No English spoken.

Inconvenient location in Óbuda, but many make the trek to this former factory cellar that is trying very hard to be the headquarters of Budapest's underground dance scene. Three dancefloors, decked with ducts and pistons and fountains, two reasonably priced bars, and a relaxed attitude towards other intoxicants. Music veers from Goa to drum 'n' bass via reggae and good old-fashioned pumping techno.

Tölgyfa Klubgaléria

II. Henger utca 2 (212 3996). Tram 4, 6/night bus 6É. **Open** 9pm-5am Fri. **Admission** Ft200. **No credit cards.** Some English spoken. **Map B2**

Basement club under an art gallery on the Buda side of Margaret Bridge. A good dancefloor with adjacent chill-out room is just what the friendly crowd of alternative-minded people need to let their hair down, bump into old friends and make new ones. Especially good when there's a live act or a DJ from Tilos Radio, but it can get a little hot and smoky, the bar only stocks cheap Hungarian spirits or strange-tasting beer and the cloakroom is always full.

Trocadero

V. Szent István körút 15 (311 4691). M3 Nyugati/ tram 4, 6/night bus 6É, 182É. **Open** 9pm-3am Mon-Thur; 9pm-5am Fri-Sun. **Admission** free to Ft400. **No credit cards.** Some English spoken. **Map C2**

Go through the gate that says 'Nirvana Bar' in pink neon, but head past that establishment to find the understated entrance to the only Latin disco in town. Live salsa and merengue acts show up sporadically and the joint is packed when there's a show (week nights it can be a thin crowd). Refreshingly multinational crowd but irritatingly erratic DJing.

Royal 2000 Funky Club – *bright white clubbing until at least 2001.*

One-off venues

Chances are, especially during summer, that on any given weekend there'll be something worthwhile going on at at least one of the venues listed here. Prices and opening hours vary. *See also page 214* **Hills, thrills and bellyaches.**

Frankhegy

Budaörs, Gyöngyvirág utca (no phone). Bus 8 from Március 15 tér to Irhás árok then follow signs.
The king of Budapest raves. Walk for half an hour through a dark forest and if you choose the right fork in the road you'll find a large field on a hill looking down on the lights of Budaörs. Usually several sound systems and lots of happy, dancing people. *Website: www.integrity.hu/quartet/styles/ ambient/frankuk.htm*

Hajógyár 322

Hajógyári sziget 322 (no phone). HÉV Árpád híd.
Cross the concrete bridge to 'Shipyard Island', keep going past the crap disco on your right, turn left and walk until you reach a small booth, pay the friendly bouncers, cross the footbridge and follow the beat. You'll end up in a ramshackle complex of cheap bars and potholed dancefloors.

Kiscelli Crypt

III. Kiscelli utca 108 (no phone). Tram 17 from Buda end of Margit Híd.
Unusual venue under the **Kiscelli Museum** (*see chapter* **Museums**), home of forgotten baroque stat-
ues and the occasional Goa party. Large, booming Gothic cellar filled with frescoes and an in-the-know crowd who shake the foundations till dawn.

Patex

XI. Bocskai út 90 (no phone). Tram 19, 49 to Kosztolányi Dezső tér then 15 minutes walk.
Patex is a huge warehouse in an industrial pocket of Buda. Pass through the factory gates to find a labyrinth of pounding hardcore techno, dope smoke and speed freaks in tight, bulging T-shirts. Not a great place for striking up conversations with strangers but sometimes features 'name' DJs from the UK or US.

Törökbálint

Törökbálint (no phone). Usually an hourly party bus from Gellért tér or some other stop listed on flyers.
A disused quarry with several caves and tunnels hiding underground dancefloors and always a big bonfire in the middle of everything. At dawn, clamber up on to the grassy cliffs to watch the sun rise as the party beats on below. Lately there's been a deplorable tendency to host theme parties, so check posters and flyers to see who's DJing. *See p214* **Party at the place to be.**

Vizimozi

Rudas fürdő, I. Döbrentei tér 9 (356 1322). Tram 18,19/bus 7/night bus 78É. **Open** 9pm-3am every other Sat. **Admission** Ft2,000. **No credit cards.** Some English spoken. **Map C5**

*The Budapest wave scene – creating a splash at the **Vizimozi**.*

In the Rudas, the most beautiful of Budapest's Ottoman baths (*see chapter* **Baths**). Bring swimming gear and arrive early to enjoy splashing in the water of the main swimming pool while watching silent movies to the accompaniment of big beat and trip hop. Or chill out in the Turkish bath (closes 1am) to ethno/trance sounds and let the belly dancer put you in the mood. There are bars, a gallery, and another dancefloor in the hallway for a good-natured crowd of undressed partygoers. Flip-flops recommended.
Website: www.c3.hu/cinetrip

Late-night bars

Those who still aren't ready to call it a night can head for one (or more) of the establishments below.

Alagút
I. Alagút utca (212 3754). Tram 18. **Open** 24 hours daily. **No credit cards**. Some English spoken. **Map A4**
Alagút is a classic all-night bar clouded by traffic fumes from the nearby alagút, or tunnel, patronised by alcoholics from all walks of life and all parts of Buda. Chess and card games are popular and breakfast is available.

B-City Pub
VI. Zichy Jenő utca 32 (269 2962). M3 Arany János utca/night bus 182É. **Open** 10am-midnight daily. **No credit cards**. Some English spoken. **Map D3**
All-night bar with Pilsner Urquell on draught in the happening end of District VI.

Gong Presszó
VII. Erzsébet körút 13 (no phone). M2 Blaha Lujza tér/tram 4, 6/night bus 6É. **Open** 10am-late daily. **No credit cards**. No English spoken. **Map E3**
Small, seedy bar in red velvet with a television and pinball machine. Often has impromptu live synthesiser music in the small hours to entertain the local underworld. Good terrace on the körút in summer.

Museum Cukrászda
VIII. Múzeum körút 12 (267 0375). M2 Astoria/tram 47, 19/night bus 78É, 182É. **Open** 24 hours daily. **No credit cards**. Some English spoken. **Map D4**
Though this does offer coffee and cakes around the clock, most of the after-hours patrons are in search of something stronger. Centrally located between Astoria and Kálvin tér, it has an impressive selection of imported beers, and the outdoor tables in warm weather are a fine place to kick back and watch the rush hour begin. Packed at dawn in summer.

Night and Day
VI. Andrássy út 46 (no phone). M1 Oktogon/tram 4, 6/night bus 6É. **Open** 24 hours daily. **No credit cards**. Some English spoken. **Map D3**
Convenient location opposite Liszt Ferenc tér and tables outside make this a popular summer spot to watch the world go by when everywhere else is closed. The drinks are expensive by Budapest standards, and it's gloomy and seedy inside.

Noiret
VI. Dessewffy utca 8-10 (331 9103). M3 Arany János utca/night bus 182É. **Open** 2pm-4am daily. **No credit cards**. Some English spoken. **Map C3**

Billed as a pool and darts club, and renting big Brunswick tables for a few hundred forints an hour. There are also quiet tables for post-pool patter, pinball machines, an air-hockey table and a jukebox.

Roulette Café and Dance Club

V. Szent István körút 11 (374 3315). M3 Nyugati/ tram 4, 6/night bus 6É, 182É. **Open** *club* 6pm-5am; *bar* 24 hours daily. **No credit cards.** No English spoken. **Map C2**

Drink and gamble in the non-stop street-level bar, and if you arrive early enough (before 5am), there's a dancefloor in the cellar with an anti-techno policy.

Tulipán Presszó

V. Nádor utca 34 (269 5043). M2 Kossuth tér/ tram 2. **Open** 24 hours daily. **No credit cards.** No English spoken. **Map C3**

Friendly 24-hour bar that's a favourite of taxi drivers. The 1970s posters, card games in the big backroom and the feeling that everyone knows each other add to the charm. Outdoor tables in summer are ideal at night, when this neighbourhood is relatively traffic-free. Toasted sandwiches available.

Late-night restaurants

Many dance bars also double as restaurants, but if they're too noisy and crowded to dine in comfort, or if the kitchen's already closed, then try one of the following late-night eateries.

Berliner

IX. Ráday utca 5 (217 6757). M3 Kálvin tér/tram 47, 49/night bus 182É. **Open** 9am-3.30am Mon-Sat; 10am-midnight Sun. **Average** Ft1,000. **No credit cards.** Some English spoken. **Map D5**

Small bar upstairs. Spacious beer cellar with big wooden booths for late dining. Hearty helpings of basic Hungarian food served until at least 1am Monday to Saturday.

Dixie Csirke

VIII. József körút 46 (no phone). Tram 4, 6/night bus 6É. **Open** 24 hours daily. **Average** Ft600. **No credit cards.** No English spoken. **Map E5**

The charred-on-the-outside, pink-on-the-inside chicken pieces are sold by weight and aren't spectacularly good value, but this is strategically located next to the night bus stop and a seedy atmosphere is provided by local pimps and exhausted prostitutes.

Grill 99

VII. Dohány utca 52 (no phone). Bus 7/night bus 6É. **Open** 24 hours daily. **Average** Ft500. **No credit cards.** No English spoken. **Map D4**

Rundown, lowlife goulash joint with plastic garden chairs and a small, gloomy gallery. Large menu of basic Hungarian food. Supposedly a non-stop but the owner sometimes gets in a huff and closes early.

Gül Baba II

VII. Erzsébet körút 17 (342 2377). M2 Blaha Lujza tér/tram 4, 6/night bus 6É. **Open** 10am-4am daily. **No credit cards.** Some English spoken. **Map E3**

Waiting to see in the rush hour – the terrace at **Museum Cukrászda***. See page 212.*

Hills, thrills and bellyaches

Törökbálint – *bonfire-lit paradise of thudding techno and cheap drinks. See page 211.*

After the first wave of western products flooded Hungary following the end of Communism, along came Acid House. The anti-consumerist and free-dom-loving ethos of early rave culture was cele-brated by a few hundred amazed followers at parties in secret locations on the outskirts of Budapest. Nowadays, although the scene is more commercial and has to some extent been taken over by the *bunkó* contingent (Hungarian yuppies with muscles), it has yet to be systematically repressed or regulated out of existence. Most weekends there's going to be a party somewhere in or around town, where you can find under-ground dance music, a lot of stoned and friendly people and something a little subversive in the air.

The best parties are one-off events in carefully chosen places that are often deliberately difficult to reach by public transport. The scene is most active during the summer, when ravers take to the hills or find a quiet Danube island to transform into a bonfire-lit paradise of thudding techno and ruinously cheap drinks. Look out for flyers in bars or in specialist shops such as **Underground Records**, **I&I Records** (*below*) or **Wave/Trance** (*see chapter* **Shopping & Services**), and watch the fast-changing walls of posters for events. Another useful guide to the major parties is the pocket-size weekly *Open*, free in many cinemas and bars. Word of mouth is best of all, though, because the most intimate and alter-native raves are often the least well publicised. Ask around.

In addition to looking for events at places list-ed in the **One-off venues** section, look out for the names of the better-known Hungarian DJs on the bill (*see below*). Parties organised by Tilos Radio (often at the **Almássy tér Recreation Centre** or **Petőfi Csarnok** – *see chapter* **Music: Rock, Roots & Jazz**) are usually good, though they've lately been getting a little too big for their boots.

Consistently high-quality kebab shop near Blaha. For extra chilli sauce, say you want it *csípős* (pro-nounced 'cheap-ursh'). Also worth trying is the suc-culent baklava. Summer terrace on the körút.

Három Testvér

VI. Szent István körút 22 (329 2951). M3 Nyugati/tram 4, 6/night bus 6É. **Open** 11am-3am daily. **No credit cards.** No English spoken. **Map C2**
The 'Three Brothers' is another excellent Turkish takeaway near Nyugati station.

Hepicentrum

II. Bem alsó rakpart near Margit híd (212 4479). Tram 4, 6/night bus 6É. **Open** 24 hours daily. **Average** Ft550. **No credit cards.** Some English spoken. **Map B1**
A roadside salad bar with a view of the Danube, Parliament and passing lorries. Open 24 hours a day, Hepicentrum also serves basic hot snacks and a wide range of fruit juices. In summer take your tray up to the roof terrace to enjoy the early morn-ing sunshine and traffic.

Korai Öröm and Korai's Banditos, related collectives of drummers and DJs, also put on excellent parties.

On the rare weekend that there's no rave happening, the best clubs in which to catch some decent dance music are **Supersonic Technicum**, **E-Play** and **Capella** (*see* **Clubs & discos**). During the week, when most larger venues are closed or deserted, the permanently partying crowd take refugee in one of Budapest's dance bars (*see* **Dance bars**). It's hard to predict which, as new places open up all the time and the scene is fickle, but as we go to press, **Trafó Pince** is still popular and **Underground** is due for a revival.

Hungarian DJs range from mediocre to not bad. Tommyboy plays happy house anthems, as do Budai and Jutasi. Ramses and Virág usually spin Goa. With DJ Ozon it'll be hardcore jungle. Dorka plays Detroit, as does Naga. Palotai is always a crowd-puller, thanks to his skillful combining of drum 'n' bass, Detroit and anything else he feels like putting on the deck. Titusz is trippy and eclectic, while Flash puts out big beat and drum 'n' bass. Unfortunately it must be said that you'll probably end up having a great time despite, rather than thanks to, the DJs' best efforts.

I&I Records

XIII. Kádár utca 12 (349 2916/yoda-trx@elender.hu). M3 Nyugati/tram 4, 6. **Open** 10am-8pm Mon-Fri; noon-6pm Sat. **No credit cards**. Some English spoken. **Map C2**
Decent multi-genre dance music shop with CDs, vinyl and lots of flyers. They also organise their own raves and parties.

Underground Records

VI. Király utca 54 (343 2640). Tram 4, 6. **Open** 10am-7pm Mon-Fri; 10am-5pm Sat. **No credit cards**. Some English spoken. **Map D3**
This DJ shop also stocks a few CDs and is a good place to pick up flyers and catch news of parties.

Montana Pizzeria

XII. Alkotás utca 2 (213 1768). M2 Déli/tram 61. **Average** Ft600. **Open** 24 hours daily. **No credit cards**. Some English spoken. **Map A3**
Pizzas cooked in a brick oven and friendly, efficient service make Montana Pizzeria the best of the 24-hour establishments in the strip of shops by Déli station. It also serves pasta, steak and turkey dishes. The terrace can be a good spot when the traffic's not too heavy.

Nagymama Palacsintázója

I. Hattyú utca 16 (201 8605). M2 Moszkva tér/tram 4, 6, 59, 61/night bus 6É. **Open** 24 hours daily. **No credit cards**. No English spoken. **Map A2**
Popular 24-hour self-service pancake place on two levels. Regular patrons at Nagymama Palacsintázója include small-fry mafiosi.

Stex Alfréd

VIII. József körút 55-57 (318 5716). Tram 4, 6/night bus 6É. **Open** 8am-6am daily. **Average** Ft1,000. **No credit cards**. No English spoken. **Map E5**
Idiosyncratic complex offering billiards, bingo, computer games and a bar and restaurant serving tasty Hungarian fare. If you decide it's time for breakfast rather than dinner, they have a good choice of omelettes, as well as ham and eggs. Tables outside during summer.

Szent Jupát

II. Retek utca 16 (212 2923). M2 Moszkva tér/tram 4, 6, 59, 61/night bus 6É. **Open** 24 hours daily. **Average** Ft800. **No credit cards**. Some English spoken. **Map A2**
Szent Jupát serves huge plates of Magyar cuisine at reasonable prices. So popular that you may find yourself waiting for a table at any time of the night or day. Serves the best steak tartar in town, if you're feeling up to it.

Casinos

Budapest has ten casinos, though new laws probably mean that some will soon close. The best is Várkert, housed in a neo-Renaissance former pumphouse for the Royal Palace designed by Miklós Ybl. Its chief rival, Las Vegas, offers glitz rather than glamour. Take your passport and lots of hard cash.

Las Vegas

Atrium Hyatt Hotel, V. Roosevelt tér 2 (317 6022). Tram 2/bus 16, 105. **Open** 2pm-5am daily.
Admission $10. **Games** American roulette, poker, blackjack, punto banco, dice. **Credit** MC, DC, JCB, V. English spoken. **Map C4**

Várkert

I. Ybl Miklós tér 9 (202 4244). Tram 19.
Open 2pm-5am daily. **Admission** free. **Games** American roulette, poker, blackjack, punto banco, dice. **Credit** AmEx, MC, V. English spoken. **Map B4**

Non-stop shopping

There are dozens of late-night shops – 'non-stops' – all selling cigarettes, beer, *pezsgő* (sparkling wine), chocolate, condoms and basic groceries. Below are some conveniently located non-stops.

Hús Hentesáru

I. Alagút utca 1 (no phone). Tram 18. **Open** 24 hours. **No credit cards**. No English spoken. **Map A4**
A butchers selling sandwiches and basic food items.

Grill 99 – *goulash any time of day or night, except when the owner's in a huff. P 215.*

Super Sarok

II. Fillér utca 1 (no phone). M2 Moszkva tér/tram 4, 6, 59, 61/night bus 6É. **Open** 24 hours daily. **No credit cards.** Some English spoken. **Map A2**
Standard items and an eclectic collection of gourmet treats to please the high-rent Rózsadomb crowd.

Dóm Market

V. Bajcsy-Zsilinsz út 24 (no phone). M3 Arany János utca/night bus 182É. **Open** 24 hours daily. **No credit cards.** No English spoken. **Map C3**
Basic non-stop that also sells blood sausage, *fasírt* (meat rissoles) and other Magyar hot snacks.

Florists

V. Jászai Mari tér (no phone). Tram 4, 6/night bus 6É. **Open** 24 hours daily. **No credit cards.** No English spoken. **Map C2**
Two stalls on the Pest side of Margaret Bridge offer flowers, cigarettes and soft drinks.

György Fleur

V. Erzsébet tér, next to bus station. **Open** 24 hours daily. **No credit cards.** No English spoken. **Map C4**
Tiny stall next to a fruit stand has coffee, cigarettes, snacks, soda and a nice selection of booze.

Nyugati ABC

VI. Nyugati station (no phone). M3 Nyugati/tram 4, 6/night bus 6É, 182É. **Open** 24 hours daily. **No credit cards.** No English spoken. **Map D2**

Zöldség Gyümölcs

VI. Nagymező utca 50 (no phone). M1 Oktogon/tram 4, 6/night bus 6É. **Open** 24 hours daily. **No credit cards.** No English spoken. **Map D3**

Makulet

VII. Nagy Diófa utca 5 (no phone). Bus 7/night bus 78É. **Open** 24 hours daily. **No credit cards.** No English spoken. **Map D4**

Mindig Friss Zöldség Gyümölcs

VII. Teréz körút 15 (no phone). M1 Oktogon/tram 4, 6/night bus 6É. **Open** 24 hours daily. **No credit cards.** No English spoken. **Map D3**
Drinks, cigs and a decent selection of fruit and veg.

Reál Delikát

VII. Almássy tér 18 (no phone). Tram 4, 6/night bus 6É. **Open** 24 hours daily. **No credit cards.** No English spoken. **Map E3**
Superior non-stop with fruit, vegetables and a larger than usual selection of cold meats.

Zugevő Non-stop ABC

IX. Üllöi út 119 (215 9655). M3 Ferenc körút/tram 4, 6/night bus 6É, 182É. **Open** 24 hours daily. **No credit cards.** No English spoken. **Map E5**

AVT ABC

XII. Nagyenyed utca 2 (no phone). M2 Déli pu/tram 61. **Open** 24 hours daily. **No credit cards.** No English spoken. **Map A3**
Large grocery just across from Déli station.

Other late shops & services

Copy General

IX. Lónyay utca 36 (216 8880/217 6184). Tram 4, 6/ night bus 6É. **Open** 24 hours daily.
No credit cards. English spoken. **Map D5**
Round-the-clock photocopying and related services.

Tribus Travel Agency

V. Apáczai Csere János utca 1 (318 5776). M3 Ferenciek tere/night bus 78É. **Open** 24 hours daily. **Credit** AmEx. English spoken. **Map C4**
Tribus Travel Agency can arrange any kind of accommodation at all hours – hotels, private rooms, hostels, you name it.

Sport & Fitness

Flashy fitness clubs and brand new golf courses face off floundering football or a day at the races.

Despite its proud sporting tradition, Hungary trails behind its neighbours in today's lucrative televised spectator sports. Well placed in the Olympic medal tables in kayak-canoe, fencing, water polo and modern pentathlon, Hungary has no tennis or basketball stars to speak of, and its football team has been floundering in the lower European ranks for more than a decade.

Hungary's biggest sporting event is the Grand Prix, attracting fans from all over Europe. Political interference and squabbling at the highest level may prove Hungary's downfall in its bid to co-host soccer's European Championships in 2004, thus losing another generation of fans who are more used to watching top-class action on TV than to heading out to the stadium.

Sport, actively encouraged under Communism, still remains a vital part of the school curriculum, although many of the facilities provided under the old system are in a state of disrepair. One of Budapest mayor Gábor Demszky's pledges is to renovate the courts and pitches in the city's major parks. The Városliget now boasts floodlit five-a-side football and streetball, with further improvements expected for badminton and table tennis. In town, flashy fitness clubs abound, offering aerobics and bronzed body-building for the *menedzser* and his many mistresses.

Major stadia

Népstadion
XIV. Istvánmezei út 1-3 (251 1222). M2 Népstadion.
The national stadium, built by and for the people (*nép*) in 1953, was falling to bits until the major renovation for the European Athletics Championships in 1998. Now the VIP and press areas are as classy as any in eastern Europe, and new fences make the venue easy to segregate, as seen at the Hungary-England friendly in 1999. At the centre of the Austro-Hungarian bid to host the European Football Championships in 2004, by which time the Stalinist statues outside will have posed for half a century.

Budapest Sportcsarnok
XIV. Stefánia út 2 (251 9759). M2 Népstadion.
In the same complex as the Népstadion, the major indoor sports venue that last saw big-event excitement when national hero István 'Koko' Kovács became world featherweight boxing champion in 1997, in front of a 10,000 capacity crowd.

Spectator sports

Basketball
With football's decline, basketball is becoming increasingly popular, not least because of local boy Dávid Kornél's appearances with the Chicago Bulls. More and more kids are shooting hoops, and a handful of American NBA rejects are attracting bigger crowds to the domestic game, whose season runs from September to May. For fixture details see the daily *Nemzeti Sport* or call the Hungarian Basketball Federation (251 0554).

Danone Honvéd
XIV. Dózsa György út 53 (340 8915). M3 Dózsa György út.
Once the army team, now sponsored by French dairy company Danone. The most successful of the men's teams.

Ferencváros
VIII. Ferencváros Népligeti Sportcsarnok, Kőbányai út (260 5859). M3 Népliget.
The most popular women's basketball team, who play their games in the city's finest small-scale sports hall. Rowdy supporters.

Football
Hungarian football is weak and corrupt. The national team have not qualified for the final stages of a major tournament since 1986 – a miserable record considering their pedigree as the Mighty Magyars, who thrashed England 6-3 at Wembley in 1953 and came close to winning the World Cup a year later. For hardcore loyalists, Hungarian football is a painful sufferance. For visitors, especially those from the commercialised, all-seater world of the English Premiership, a game here will be a cold, crumbling blast from the past, with facilities similar to those lower-league football in the early 1970s. Average gates are under 5,000, with admission prices at around Ft500. A seat is *ülőhely*, a spot on the terraces *állóhely*, the *tribün* is the stand, *lelátó* the best view. Segregation exists, especially for derbies between the Budapest clubs who compose half of the top flight, the current 18-team PNB. This will be reduced to 16 for the 2000-2001 season, although if the football-mad FIDESZ-led government gets its way it may be reduced still further. The season runs from August to November, then March to June. The biggest

*Excited crowds mass on the terraces at Fáy utca for a crucial **Vasas-Ferencváros** derby.*

match of the year is between deadly rivals Ferencváros and Újpest, which may take place behind closed doors from the 1999-2000 season due to serious crowd trouble in recent years.

Ferencváros

IX. Üllői út 129 (215 3856). M3 Népliget.

Hungary's biggest club, Ferencváros (FTC or 'Fradi') have the most notorious following – barely discouraged by the current directorship, led by right-wing minister József Torgyán. Hungary's most titled team were a successful pre-war outfit who suffered under Communism, and were seen as the team of the people. Many of these people are now bone-headed racist imbeciles, and 'Fradi' feature in the tabloids almost daily. The 1998-9 season finished with Torgyán sacking able Croatian coach Marijan Vlak and singing the club song to bemused journalists at the subsequent press conference.

MTK

VIII. Salgótarjáni út 2-4 (303 0590). Tram 1/ trolleybus 75 or bus 9.

Hungary's richest club, thanks to the support of millionaire Gábor Várszegi, can boast domestic stars and recent league titles, but can barely attract more than 3,000 spectators to their improved Hungária körút ground. This is partly because the club have Jewish roots, partly because they are simply unfashionable. For this reason, at the end of the 1998-9 season, Várszegi began wooing cash-strapped Újpest with a view to merging the two clubs – an idea that horrifies both sets of supporters.

Újpest

IV. Megyeri út 13 (390 6181). M3 Újpest központ, then bus 104, 104A, 96/red 96 to Megyeri út.

The former team of the Interior Ministry, still remembered in England for its Fairs' Cup final defeat against Newcastle in 1969, Újpest have had a hard time of it since state support dropped. The title win of 1998 was followed by an exodus of key players, due to a bonus dispute, and the team were dumped out of Europe at the first hurdle. Their ground is in desperate need of repair, but this hardly seems to bother their colourful, if rowdy, fans.

Vasas

XIII. Fáy utca 58 (329 6073). M3 Forgách utca.

Despite their status as also-rans, Vasas deserve inclusion in anyone's book due to their key element – the Santa Fé bar behind the goal. The tactic of standing under cover with a window on to the action and a beer in your hand is a difficult one for rival clubs to compete against, and often swings the neutral vote on a Saturday. On the pitch, Vasas often play good football to little effect. A friendly club.

Horse racing

Of all Széchenyi's steals from the Empire – flush toilets, navigable rivers, Danube bridges – horse racing is the one left in the worst state after Communism. Although not encouraged, the track offered the thrill of dodgy deals and easy riches. These days the main course, Kincsem Park, named after the country's most famous racehorse, is a

wreck. The French consortium that has bought up the old trotting track for development, a prime piece of real estate near Keleti station, has promised as part of the deal to do up Kincsem in time for the 2000 summer season.

Kincsem will then stage both the flat and trotting races, but gambling on either is small potatoes. A win is a *tét*, a place is a *hely*, but neither will return any kind of money for your Ft20 minimum bet. To buy your next beer, choose three runners from your form programme *Magyar Turf* (Ft96), go to any window and either ask for a *befutó box* (any order) or *befutó* (in order), specifying to the old woman behind the counter which race you're betting on. Don't try and work out the odds, although scores of punters stand gawping at the handful of television screens attempting to do so. Pick up your meagre winnings from the same window ten minutes after your nags have come in.

Kincsem Park

X. Albertirsai út 2 (263 7858). M2 Pillangó utca. **Open** *Apr-Sept* 2-7pm Wed, Sun. **Admission** free-Ft500. **No credit cards**. No English spoken.

Ice hockey

Although Hungary has never produced a top ice-hockey team, the sport is a popular winter pastime, allowing the public displays of inebriated partisanship while footballers take a three-month break. Two of the four Budapest professional clubs, Ferencváros and Újpest, are in the Extra Liga, playing at the Kisstadion (part of the **Népstadion** complex; *see above*) and the Megyeri út rink (adjacent to **Újpest** football stadium; *see above*) respectively. Play-offs take place in February at the **Budapest Sportcsarnok** (*see above*). Fixture details can be found in the appropriate day's *Nemzeti Sport*.

Motor racing

The Hungarian Grand Prix has struggled on since its re-introduction in 1986, with losses and threats of closure almost annually. Recently the government stepped in to ensure its continuation past the year 2000, encouraged by the extra trade it brings to hotels and restaurants, which are packed for the second weekend in August. Special buses are laid on for what is the biggest event in the domestic sporting calendar.

Hungaroring

20km east of Budapest off the M3 motorway at Mogyoród (06 28 330 040). **Information** *Forma 1 Kft, V. Apáczai Csere János utca 11 (318 7610/ticket hotline 266 2040). M1, M2, M3 Deák tér/tram 47, 49.* **Open** 8am-4pm daily one month before the event. **Date** second weekend in Aug. **Admission** from Ft18,000 for a standing place on race day to Ft90,000 for the best seats over a whole weekend. **No credit cards**. English spoken.

Swimming & water polo

Hungary continues to produce Olympic and World champions in swimming, and enjoys a solid tradition in water polo, the main summer sport. Club teams such as Újpest, BVSC, Vasas and Ferencváros regularly feature in the finals of European competitions and these games guarantee a full house and a noisy atmosphere as football fans head for the pools.

For details of match times and swimming galas, check with the day's *Nemzeti Sport*.

Császár-Komjádi Sportuszoda

III. Árpád fejedelem útja 8 (212 2750). Bus 6, 60, 86. Some English spoken. **Map B1**
Hungary's national swimming stadium, named after the coach who led Hungary to its first Olympic water polo gold in 1932, is packed for top matches and major swimming galas.

Cycling

Congested traffic, cobbled streets, tram lines and a serious lack of bike lanes mean that Budapest is hardly an ideal city to cycle round. The government have responded by imposing absurd fines for faulty brakes or minor traffic infringements. Although some 120km of cycle lanes have been created over the last eight years, many inner-city ones have simply been drawn on pavements. For a pleasant afternoon's ride away from it all, Margaret Island has bike hire stalls near the main roundabout, or take the gentle road alongside the Danube up to Szentendre. Bikes can be taken on certain trains, but not on trams or the metro.

The Friends of City Cycling Group

III. Miklós tér 1 (311 7855). Tram 1/bus 6, 86. Some English spoken.
Produces a *Map for Budapest Cyclists*, detailing bike lanes, riding conditions and service shops.

Hungarian Cycling Association

XIV. Szabó József utca 3 (252 0879). Bus 7. Some English spoken.
The Millenáris cycle track here is the only one in Hungary.

National Rail Office

VI. Andrássy út 35 (322 8275). M1 Opera. **Open** *Apr-Sept* 9am-6pm Mon-Fri; *Oct-Mar* 9am-5pm Mon-Fri. Some English spoken. **Map D3**
The National Rail Office (MÁV) can provide a list of cycle-friendly stations and the surcharges per km for cycling tickets (*kerékpárjegy*).

Schwinn-Csepel

VI. Hegedű utca 6 (342 4620). M1 Oktogon/tram 4, 6. **Open** 10am-6pm Mon, Wed, Fri; 10am-7pm Thur; 10am-1pm Sat. **No credit cards**. Some English spoken. **Map D3**
A bike shop with a service and repair department.

Extreme sports

Today's Magyar teenager is nobody without the prerequisite skateboard and/or in-line skates. Regular competitions are run and specialist shops are opening all the time. The major malls each have a skate shop, as well as the one listed below.

Rollsport

IX. Kálvin tér 7 (217 4397). M3 Kálvin tér/tram 47, 49. **Open** 10am-6pm Mon-Fri; 10am-1pm Sat. **No credit cards.** Some English spoken. **Map D5**
At the back of a shopping centre, this small shop caters to every skate rat's need. All the major brands of in-line skating equipment including skates, protectors, clothing and helmets. Good place to find out the latest on competitions and venues.

Görzenál Skatepark

III. Árpád fejedelem útja 125 (250 4800). HÉV from Battyhány tér to Timár utca. **Open** 9am-10pm daily. **Admission** Ft400; Ft50 non-skating parents. **Rental** Ft400 for three hours. **No credit cards.** Some English spoken.

A teenage paradise. Roller-skating track, skateboard park, BMX/cycle track and jumps, two basketball courts and several 'freestyle' areas with ramps and jumps for bike, skate or board.

Golf

Inevitably membership of the golf club has become a status symbol among the local business community – although the handful of courses nearest to Budapest are pretty naff. For half-decent fairways, head down to the Hencse, by Lake Balaton, or the Birdland by the Austrian border.

Birdland Golf Country Club

240km from Budapest. M1 toward Győr, route 85 to Csorna, route 86 to Hegyfalug, route 86 toward Sopron, through Tompaládony to Bükfürdő. Thermal körút 10 (03 94 358 060/fax 03 94 359 000). **Open** 9am-8pm Mon-Fri; 8am-8pm Sat-Sun. **Fee** *per round* AS350 Mon-Thur; AS480 Fri-Sun. **Club rental** AS170 Mon-Fri; AS230 Sat, Sun. **Credit** AmEx, DC, MC, V. English spoken.

Görzenal Skatepark – *upside-down in a teenage paradise.*

Hungary's best course; championship-rated and sited in beautiful hills close to the Austrian border – and for this reason all prices are quoted in Austrian schillings.

Budapest Golfpark and Country Club
40km north of Budapest. Route 11 past Szentendre to Kisoroszi (26 392 463). **Open** *Apr-Oct* 7am-8pm daily. **Fee** Ft6,000 per round daily. **Club rental** Ft3,500. **No credit cards.** No English spoken.
The closest course to Budapest, but experienced golfers will curse its cow-pasture quality.

Hencse National Golf and Country Club
175km south-west of Budapest at Hencse, Kossuth Lajos utca 3 (82 481 245/fax 82 481 248). **Open** *Feb-1 Dec* 7am-dusk. **Fee** Ft7,200 Mon-Fri, Ft8,500 Sat, Sun. **Credit** AmEx, DC, MC, V. English spoken.
Splendidly sited in a National Park. Rooms cost DM150 for a single, DM180 for a double, with negotiable group fees.

Hotel Wien
XI. Budaörsi út 88-90 (310 2999). Bus 40 from Móricz Zsigmond körtér. **Open** according to reservation the previous day. **Fee** *per hour* Ft1,800 to members of other golf clubs, Ft2,500 nonmembers. **Credit** AmEx, DC, MC, V. English spoken.
Indoor simulated golf. Whack the ball at the padded screen showing the course at Pebble Beach Country Club, California, and a computer calculates the distances and direction of your shot.

Pannónia Golf and Country Club
38km west of Budapest at Máriavölgy. From M1 west of Budapest take Bicske exit, Rt 100 toward Tatabánya, Rt 811 to Alcsútdoboz, turn left, course is 3km (22 353 000). **Open** daylight-dusk year round. **Fee** Ft6,500 Mon-Fri (Ft3,500 for nine holes), Ft12,000 Sat, Sun (Ft6,000 nine holes). **Club rental** Ft3,000. **No credit cards.** English spoken.
On the former estate of the Habsburg-Lothringens, with a driving range and horse riding facilities. Occasional summer competitions feature childcare facilities and evening barbecue.

The 19th Hole Driving Range
Petneházy Club Hotel, II. Feketefej utca 2-4 (06 30 9 441 185). Tram 56 from Moszkva tér then bus 63. **Open** 9am-9pm Mon-Fri; 9am-8pm Sat, Sun. **Fee** Ft800 for a basket of 36 balls, Ft1,500 for 72, Ft500 per club. **No credit cards.** Some English spoken.
On a quiet Buda hill, hone your swing from covered stalls. Golf lessons also available, Ft4,700 for individuals, Ft3,500 a head for two or three people.

Health & fitness
Young Hungary has gone fitness mad. Gyms and solariums have sprung up all over town, though many new ones are unregulated and unprofessional. Better clubs, such as the ones listed here, meet standard regulations. Most of Budapest's major hotels will also have fitness facilities. Aerobics is also booming, spurred on by success at national level.

Andi Studio
V. Hold utca 29 (311 0740). M2 Kossuth tér/M3 Arany János utca. **Open** 6.30am-9pm Mon-Fri; 7.30am-2pm Sat. **Rates** *aerobics & sauna* Ft500; *gym & sauna* Ft500; *aerobics, gym & sauna* Ft800. **No credit cards.** Some English spoken. **Map C3**
Budapest's first western-style fitness club, which recently celebrated its tenth birthday. On-site cosmetician, bar and café.

A and Tsa
I. Pálya utca 9 (356 9530). M2 Déli/tram 18/bus 2, 78, 105. **Open** 7am-11pm Mon-Fri; 9am-9pm Sat, Sun. **Credit** AmEx, DC, MC, V. English spoken.
Wide range of services including sauna, steam bath, solarium and restaurant. Still one of the most upmarket clubs in Budapest, even after a recent change of name and management.

Marriott World Class Fitness Centre
V. Apáczai Csere János utca 4 (266 7000). M1 Vörösmarty tér/tram 2. **Open** 6am-11pm daily. **Rates** *aerobics* $10; *day ticket (gym & sauna)* $10; *annual membership & open use of facilities* $75. **Credit** AmEx, DC, MC, V. English spoken. **Map C4**
Personal trainers; rowing, cycling and running machines; sauna, solarium, squash court; Thai and Swedish massage.

Kayak & canoe
Although near Budapest kayak and canoe hire places are few and far between, Hungary remains one of the top nations in the sport. *See also* **Alfa Hotel** *in chapter* **Accommodation**.

Béke üdülőtelep *– see page 222.*

Béke Üdülőtelep

III. Nánási út 97 (388 9303). Bus 34. **Open** *1 Apr-15 Oct* 7am-6pm daily. **Rates** Ft400-Ft1,000 according to size of kayak or canoe. **No credit cards.** No English spoken.
On the banks of the Danube close to the Hotel Lido. Kayaks and canoes of various sizes available to rent.

Riding

The Magyars are famed for their horsemanship, and have a well-developed tourist industry for riding holidays around the Puszta and Lake Balaton.

Hungarian Equestrian Tourism Association

V. Ferenciek tere 4 (317 1259/mltsz@mail.matav.hu). M3 Ferenciek tere/tram 2/bus 7. **Open** 9am-5pm Mon-Thur; 9am-4pm Fri. Some English spoken.
Provides information on all kinds of riding holidays in Hungary.

Pegazus Tours

V. Ferenciek tere 5 (317 1644/fax 267 0171/pegazus@mail.datanet.hu). M3 Ferenciek tere/tram 2/bus 7. **Open** 9am-5pm Mon-Thur; 9am-4pm Fri. English spoken.
Centrally located tour company that provides a wide range of riding holidays across the country.

Petneházy Riding School

II. Feketefej utca 2-4 (275 7276). Tram 56 from Moszkva tér then bus 63. **Open** 9am-noon, 2-4pm, Tue-Fri; 9am-4pm Sat, Sun. **Rates** Ft2,000-Ft2,500 per hour. **No credit cards.** Some English spoken.
Next door to the **Petneházy Country Club Hotel** (*see chapter* **Accommodation**), around 10km from the city centre. Ft2,000 for beginners; Ft2,500 for those with some riding experience.

Squash

City Squash Club

II. Marczibányi tér 1-3 (212 3110). Tram 4, 6. **Open** 7am-midnight daily. **Rates** *off peak* Ft1,100, *peak* Ft1,500 (per person per hour). **No credit cards.** Some English spoken. **Map A2**
Four courts. Rates divided into off peak (7am-5pm, 10pm-midnight Mon-Fri; all day Sat, Sun), Ft2,200 per court per hour, and peak (5-10pm Mon-Fri), Ft3,000 per court per hour. Racquet hire Ft400. Light-coloured soles must be worn.

A and Tsa

I. Pálya utca 9 (356 9530). M2 Déli/bus 2, 78, 105. **Open** 7am-11pm Mon-Fri; 9am-9pm Sat, Sun. **Credit** AmEx, DC, MC, V. English spoken.
Two courts, on hire for Ft1,200 per hour until 4pm, Ft2,400 after. Racquet hire: Ft200 per session.

Hotel Marriott

V. Apáczai Csere János utca 4 (266 7000). M1 Vörösmarty tér/tram 2. **Open** 6am-11pm daily. **Credit** AmEx, DC, MC, V. English spoken.
One court, costing Ft3,500 per hour, sauna included. Racquet hire Ft300.

Swimming

Hungary has enjoyed remarkable success in competitive swimming since Alfréd Hajós won gold medals swimming in the Aegean at the first modern Olympics in 1896. He later designed the pool on Margaret Island where generations of champions have trained. In summer, similar open-air pools are extremely popular. Almost all swimming pools require swimming hats to be worn by both sexes, so come prepared – the ones available for hire look like polythene bakers' hats and are guaranteed to embarrass. Day tickets, except at the Gellért, cost around Ft400-Ft500, with books of 25 tickets Ft10,000. *See also chapters* **Baths** *and* **Accommodation**.

Gellért Gyógyfürdő

XI. Kelenhegyi út (466 6166). Tram 18, 19, 47, 49/bus 7. **Open** 6am-7pm daily. **Rates** *day ticket* Ft1,500; Ft750 concs; *after 5pm Mon-Fri* Ft750. **No credit cards.** Some English spoken. **Map B5**
Grand, if expensive, setting for knocking out a few lengths. Warm indoor pool, relaxing outdoor pool, wave pool, children's pool, thermal pool and sauna.

Hajós Alfréd Nemzeti Sportuszoda

XIII. Margitsziget (311 4046).
Closed for renovation at the time of going to press but likely to have reopened by summer 2000. Two outdoor pools, one indoor pool, sunbathing terrace and restaurant.

Lukács Gyógyfürdő és Strandfürdő

II. Frankel Leó utca 25-29 (326 1695). Tram 4, 6. **Open** 6am-7pm Mon-Sat; 6am-5pm Sun. **Rates** *day ticket* Ft500; Ft400 concs; *after 5pm Mon-Fri* Ft400. **No credit cards.** No English spoken. **Map B1**
Nineteenth-century bath house with two swimming pools, four thermal pools, a spa, a sauna, a mud bath and physiotherapy. Caters for an older set.

Széchenyi Gyógyfürdő és Strandfürdő

XIV. Állatkerti körút 11 (321 0310). M1 Széchenyi fürdő. **Open** 6am-7pm daily. **Rates** *day ticket* Ft500; Ft400 concs; *after 5pm Mon-Fri* Ft400. **No credit cards.** No English spoken. **Map F1**
Hottest thermal pools in Budapest, with a recently renovated outdoor swimming pool area. Reconstruction has not altered the elegance of the Széchenyi's neo-baroque architecture, set in the green of the City Park opposite the zoo and circus. In winter, hardy folk trek over the ice to spend the afternoon playing chess in the outdoors under clouds of steam. A host of treatments also available.

Corinthia Hotel Aquincum

III. Árpád fejedelem útja 94 (250 3360). HÉV to Árpád híd or tram 1 from M3 Árpád híd. **Open** 7am-9pm daily. **Admission** *weekday tickets purchased before 10am* Ft900; *otherwise Mon-Fri,* Ft1,750, *Sat, Sun* Ft2,100. **Credit** AmEx, DC, EC, JCB, MC, V.
A boon for guests, a bit expensive otherwise. Three pools, sauna and solarium.

Danubius Thermal Hotel Helia
XIII. Kárpát utca (350 3277). M3 Dózsa György út/trolleybus 79 from Kárpát utca. **Open** 7am-10pm daily. **Admission** *weekday ticket to 3pm* Ft1,700; *after 3pm* Ft2,100; *Sat-Sun* Ft2,700. English spoken. **Credit** AmEx, DC, EC, JCB, MC, V.
A wide range of thermal treatments on offer, with waters piped in directly from Margaret Island. Four pools, two thermal pools, sauna and underwater massage services.

Thermal Hotel Margitsziget
XIII. Margitsziget (329 2300). Bus 26. **Open** 7am-8pm daily. **Admission** Ft1,600; Ft600 concs; *after 6pm* Ft1,000. **Credit** AmEx, DC, MC, V. English spoken.
Constructed on the thermal springs of a former spa, this Margaret Island hotel and leisure complex has three thermal pools – at varying temperatures of 33, 35 and 36 degrees – two swimming pools, two single-sex saunas, plus a 28-degree swimming pool and a sunbathing terrace.

Strands

Doing the strand is an essential part of the Budapest summer, which means posing by the open-air swimming pool and dipping into the occasional beer, swim and *lángos*. Some are also part of thermal pool complexes, so you have the options of sunbathing, swimming, soaking or taking a sauna. Of Budapest's dozen or so strands, some are topless, and others have certain sections where visitors go naked.

Csillaghegyi Strand
III. Pusztakúti utca 3 (250 1533). HÉV Csillaghegy/bus 42. **Open** *1 May-15 Sept* 6am-7pm daily; swimming pool open all year. **Admission** *day ticket* Ft400; Ft300 concs; *after 5pm* Ft300. **No credit cards.** No English spoken.
Four pools in a picturesque setting, with a combined capacity of 3,000. Not as packed in summer as other strands more accessible to the city centre. Nude sunbathing on the southern slope.

The myth of the Fischer king

Those two great Magyar traditions, bathing and going bonkers, are also essential elements to what it takes to become a chess legend. The world's first official champion, for example, was Austrian Wilhelm Steinitz, a turn-of-the-century Jew-hating fruitcake who underwent a medical treatment of regular cold baths until his lonely death. The world's unofficial champion before him, American Charles Paul Morphy, was found dead in his bath, surrounded by women's shoes.

Although it's never produced any world champions, Hungary's obsession with the game is evident all over Budapest. People play chess in any and every public space – in bars and cafés, at bathhouses, in public parks and squares and even, when it's raining, with boards balanced on rubbish bins in station underpasses.

Hungary's current leading contenders for chess glory are the Polgár sisters. Judit, Zsófi and Zsuzsa were raised, almost scientifically so, by their father László, whose grandparents died at Auschwitz. His mother later fled Hungary, fearing a plot. 'I didn't have a childhood,' admits László Polgár, apparently bent on inflicting the same fate on his own offspring: 'Every child has the potential for genius. Day after day we guided our girls' development.' His girls only went to school to take exams, being educated at home in English, Russian, Esperanto, chess and more chess. The most talented daughter, Judit, is forbidden by her father to play against women, and regularly takes on the world's best – men.

Welcome home, Bobby Fischer. The reclusive former world champion, whose Cold War win over Russia's Boris Spassky in Iceland in 1972 spawned the Rice-Webber musical *Chess*, is alive and bonkers and living in Budapest. Here he can be found – if not approached – at any one of a number of the city's baths, taken each afternoon, or at any of the scores of outdoor games that take place in the city's parks and squares. He is driven around by his driver and minder, János Rigó ('Johnny Nightingale'), who protects him from an uninterested outside world – that is when half-Jewish Fischer is not spouting off anti-Semitic conspiracy theories on local Radio Calypso. Fischer has also been seen in Bestsellers bookstore downtown.

He didn't just come here for the waters. After 20 years of post-championship self-imposed obscurity, some of it spent with a religious cult in California, he was attracted to a re-match with Spassky in 1992, organised by Hungarian publisher János Kubat and backed by Serbian banker Jezdemir Vasiljević. The only trouble was its location: Belgrade. Despite beating Spassky again and re-establishing his dented reputation in the chess world – although it was only Spassky who would then go on to play the promising Polgár sister amid much pomp in Budapest's Duna Intercontinental Hotel in 1993 – the sanction-breaking Fischer would face jail and a hefty fine if he ever returns to Brooklyn from his watery exile.

Dagály Strand – *'I'll graduate to the grown-ups' pool if it kills me.'*

Dagály Strand

XIII. Népfürdő utca 36 (320 2203). M3 Lehel tér then bus 133. **Open** 6am-7pm daily. **Rates** *day ticket* Ft500; Ft400 concs; *after 5pm* Ft400. **No credit cards.** No English spoken.
Twelve pools with a capacity of 12,000. Also a sauna and keep-fit rooms.

Palatinus Strand

XIII. Margitsziget (340 4505). Tram 4/6 then bus 26. **Open** *1 May-15 Sept* 8am-7pm daily. **Rates** *day ticket* Ft500; *after 5pm* Ft400. **No credit cards.** No English spoken.
Seven pools include a thermal pool, two children's pools and a teaching pool, plus slides and wave machines. Capacity of 10,000 and on a hot Saturday afternoon in July it can feel like standing-room only.

Római Strandfürdő

III. Rozgonyi Piroska utca 2 (388 9740). HÉV Rómaifürdő. **Open** *1 May-15 Sept* 8am-7pm daily. **Rates** *day ticket* Ft400; Ft300 concs; *after 5pm* Ft300. **No credit cards.** No English spoken.
Three pools and a water chute.

Tennis

There are around 30 tennis clubs in Budapest, most with clay courts, and most charging around Ft1,000 per hour. Some offer coaching lessons. Hotels also hire out courts to non-guests. The following is a brief selection of courts.

Hungarian Tennis Association

XIV. Dózsa György út 1-3 (252 6687). M2 Népstadion.
The Népstadion based association has produced a yearbook (Ft900) that gives a full list of the country's clubs and courts – but no prices.

Római Teniszakadémia

III. Királyok útja 105 (240 9123). Bus 34. **Open** 6am-11pm daily. **Rates** Ft800-Ft1,000 per hour. Ten outdoor courts, ten indoor. **No credit cards.** Some English spoken.

Szépvölgyi Teniszcentrum

III. Virág Benedek utca 39-41 (388 1591). Bus 65. **Open** 7am-10pm daily. **Rates** *off peak (7am-3pm)* Ft1,100; *peak (3-10pm)* Ft2,300 per hour. Three indoor courts, three outdoor. **No credit cards.** Some English spoken.
Excellent lighting and ventilation.

Városmajor Teniszakadémia

XII. Városmajor utca 63-69 (202 5337). Bus 21, 121. **Open** 7am-10pm Mon-Fri; 7am-7pm Sat; 8am-7pm Sun. **Rates** Ft700-Ft1,200. Five courts. **No credit cards.** Some English spoken.
Two clay courts and three green set courts. Also a tennis school with qualified instructors.

Vasas SC

II. Pasaréti út 11-13 (320 9457). Bus 6. **Open** 7am-10pm daily. **Rates** Ft1,000-Ft1,200 per hour. Nine outdoor courts, two indoor. **No credit cards.** Some English spoken.

Ten-pin bowling

MVA Bowling Centre

Duna Plaza, XIII. Váci út 178 (239 3829). M3 Gyöngyösi út. **Open** 10am-1am daily. **Rates** *off peak (10am-3pm)* Ft1,500 per hour; *peak (3pm-6pm)* Ft2,000 per hour; *peak (6pm-1am)* Ft2,500 per hour. **Credit** AmEx, DC, MC, V. Some English spoken.
The city's main ten-pin bowling centre in the Duna Plaza is now attached to one of the Il Treno chain of pizzerias, so you'll get soft wafts of garlic as you bowl down one of the ten alleys.

Theatre & Dance

The new National Theatre's just a hole in the ground but performing arts flourish and Budapest's Broadway is on the up.

Take a stroll along Budapest's Broadway, Nagymező utca in District VI, at around 6pm and browse the buildings. Although yet to re-establish the glory days of the 1920s and '30s, you'll still find three theatres as well as the Mikroszkóp cabaret, the Operetta (closed until 2001), the Moulin Rouge nightclub and two galleries – all packed into a bustling 400-metre strip. Plans are in the air to pedestrianise the area but nobody's holding their breath. Still, it's a good area in which to soak up the atmosphere and maybe sip something at the Operett kávéház or Komédiás opposite (*see chapter* **Cafés & Coffeehouses**) while viewing the Magyar middle classes all dressed up to the nines. Or you might even take in a play.

Budapest is stuffed with playhouses but there's quality as well as quantity to be seen. 'See' may be the operative word, as there is the annoying matter of the language barrier. But take a chance on a play or playwright you recognise, take in the spectacle, and let the weird rhythms of Hungarian wash over you. The experience will be easily affordable. A decent night out can be had for between Ft300 and Ft1,000.

NATIONALISM & NATURALISM

Until the late eighteenth century, theatre in Budapest was basically a German affair. Ironically, it was a Habsburg emperor, Josef II, who first encouraged Hungarian-language theatre and by doing so unwittingly set in motion a new art form that would contribute much to the national revival movement throughout the next century.

Hungary gradually built up a respectable tradition that looked west for inspiration. Naturalism was introduced in the early twentieth century and although it took the Hungarians 400 years to translate late Shakespeare, they were staging Wilde and Gorky within a few years of their appearance. Shakespeare remains the national passion. Sándor Petőfi wrote that Shakespeare was half of all creation and at times it seems his works make up half of all performances here. Stanislavsky also made a big impact on the Hungarian stage and his realist method continues to hold sway today.

In the late 1940s and 1950s dull and didactic dross was the norm, but when Edmund Wilson visited in 1964 he professed his amazement at the sheer variety of theatre on offer. The change was

*Tipping-out time at the **Vigszinház**. See page 227.*

Footprints of the Magyar famous on Budapest's Broadway.

down to Kádár, who came into power after the 1956 revolution and decided that more bread and (slightly censored) circuses were in order. Today, though funding has been cut over the last ten years, there is still everything from Aristophanes to Arthur Miller. And lots of Shakespeare.

NATIONAL FARCE

It was the 'Greatest Hungarian' – anglophile and reformer Count Széchenyi – who caused the first National Theatre to be built. In 1837 things kicked off with a performance of *Árpád's Awakening* by Mihály Vörösmarty but since 1908 the venue has been shunted from site to site and now resides in inconvenient and unattractive premises. Moreover, some of the shows would send Árpád straight back to sleep. To remedy this, the previous Socialist government began erecting a new theatre in the middle of the city's busiest transport junction. But after the 1998 elections – in an example of the petty bickering and obstructionist tactics endemic to Hungarian politics – the new FIDESZ government blocked the proposal. Their attempts to move it to the City Park have so far been vetoed by the Socialist district council. All that's left is a huge hole in the ground in the middle of Deák tér which might turn into a car park. Thus a noble ambition descends into farce. Or tragedy.

Some argue that Hungary does not need a National Theatre – such funding as there is could better be used to spice up the fringe. Otherwise, doommongers predict, *Cats* and comedies will soon dominate, a few tried and (t)rusty favourites will grind on, and difficult or alternative stuff will be banished to rat-infested basements. This would be fine, as there are literally thousands of rat-infested cellars in Budapest, but it hasn't happened yet. Still, interesting experimental theatre, some of it in English, does hold its own tiny fort.

The number of plays in English varies. Sometimes there are three a week, other times none for months. Amateur companies disappear quickly – the oldest is the English Theatre Company (ETC), which puts on one or two shows annually. Otherwise it's pot-luck, but look out for shows by Foxy Divils or Phoenix. A few professional companies also make their way here.

Curtains usually rise at 7pm or 7.30pm. If they're not open all day, box offices begin selling tickets an hour prior to curtain. Wheelchair access and hearing systems are not available.

Ticket agencies

Central Theatre Booking Office

VI. Andrássy út 18 (312 0000). M1 Opera. **Open** 9am-1pm, 1.45-5.45pm, Mon-Fri. **No credit cards.** Some English spoken. **Map D3**
Tickets for all performance arts.
Branch: II. Moszkva tér 3 (335 9136).

Music Mix-33 Ticket Service

V. Váci utca 33 (338 2237/317 7736). M3 Ferenciek tere. **Open** 10am-6pm Mon-Fri; 10am-2pm Sat. **No credit cards.** Some English spoken. **Map C4**
Tickets for theatre and dance, plus rock and classical concerts and events abroad.

Dance & theatre listings

Pesti Est and *Pesti Műsor* cover just about everything happening. *Pesti Súgó*, put together by *Pesti Est*, is a free monthly dedicated to theatre in the city. The *Budapest Sun* also runs incomplete listings. The monthly guide *Nézőpont* is available for Ft130 from most ticket bureaux, and the British Council (321 4039, www.britcoun.org/hungary) will have advance information about visiting British companies.

Theatres
English-language venues

The Kolibri Cellar Club
Kolibri Pince és Klub
*VI. Andrássy út 77 (351 3348). M1 Vörösmarty
utca.* **Open** *3pm-2am daily. Closed June-Sept. Some
English spoken.* **Map D2**
Small and somewhat stuffy little place showing a
fair bit of not-too-mainstream English-language the-
atre, almost always by amateur companies.

Merlin International Theatre
*V. Gerlóczy utca 4 (317 9338/318 9844). M1, M2,
M3 Deák tér/tram 47, 49.* **Open** *10am-6pm daily,
and one hour before curtain. Closed June-Sept.
English spoken.* **Map C4**
The most professional and the best of the English-
language theatre venues.

International Buda Stage (IBS)
*II. Tárogató út 2-4 (391 2500). M2 to Moszkva tér
then tram 56.* **Open** *box office 8am-7pm daily.
Closed mid June-Sept. English spoken.*
English and Hungarian theatre as well as movies,
dance, concerts and cultural symposia. The English
shows have slowed to about one a month but there
is simultaneous translation into English during
Hungarian language shows.

Nagymező utca

Budapest Kamaraszínház
*VI. Nagymező utca 8 (351 6812). M1 Oktogon/tram
4, 6.* **Open** *box office 2-7pm daily. Closed June-Sept.
Some English spoken.* **Map D3**
Also called the Tivoli. Attractively Art Nouveau.
Tends to show modern classics and comedies.

Radnóti
*VI. Nagymező utca 11 (321 0600). M1
Oktogon/tram 4, 6.* **Open** *box office 1-7pm daily.
Closed June-Sept. Some English spoken.* **Map D3**
A highly-thought-of company that performs a wide
selection of highbrow classics.

Thália
*VI. Nagymező utca 22-24 (331 0500). M1
Oktogon/tram 4, 6.* **Open** *box office 10am-6pm daily.
Closed June-Sept. Some English spoken.* **Map D3**
Elegant venue for established dance and theatre com-
panies as well as the odd mainstream musical. Also
features Hungarian provincial and some foreign com-
panies.

Establishment theatres

Katona József
*V. Petőfi Sándor utca 6 (318 6599). M3 Ferenciek
tere/bus 7.* **Open** *box office 2-7pm daily. Closed June-
Sept. Some English spoken.* **Map C4**
The company with Hungary's highest reputation
and also well received abroad. Their sister company performs more alternative work at a smaller
space around the corner.

Branch: Katona József Kamra, V. Ferenciek tere 4
(318 2487).

Vígszínház
Comedy Theatre
*XIII. Szent István körút 14 (329 2340). M3 Nyugati/
tram 2, 4, 6.* **Open** *box office 1-7pm Mon-Fri; one
hour before curtain Sat, Sun. Closed June-Sept. Some
English spoken.* **Map C2**
A splendid baroque venue for large-scale musicals.
The name betrays the focus but productions run the
whole gamut. The same company performs less
mainstream stuff at the Pesti Színház.
Branch: Pesti Színház, V. Váci utca 9 (266 5245).

Alternative theatres

Mu Színház
*XI. Kőrösy utca 17 (466 4627). Tram 4, 47, 49
Fehérvári út.* **Open** *box office 10am-7pm Mon-Fri;
one hour before curtain Sat, Sun. Closed June-Sept.
Some English spoken.*
Space for small alternative companies, musicians
and dancers but no resident company. Worth check-
ing out to see what Hungary's cutting edge is up to.

Szkéné
*XI. Műegyetem rakpart 3 (463 2451). Tram 18, 19,
47, 49.* **Open** *9am-4pm Mon-Thur; 9am-2.30pm Fri;
1 hour before performance Sat, Sun. Closed June-Sept.
Some English spoken.* **Map D6**
A theatre that also sponsors the International
Meeting of Moving Theatres every other October, at
which obscure dance groups gather to expose them-
selves in this small black box, and the 12-day
Alternative Theatre Festival each April.

Trafó
*IX, Liliom utca 41 (215 1600). M3 Ferenc
körút/tram 4, 6.* **Open** *box office 5-8pm daily. Closed
July-Aug. English spoken.*
Arts centre with an imaginative and colourful blend
of dance, theatre, music and exhibitions, both foreign and Hungarian. Particularly hot on multimedia
stuff. *See also chapters* **Music: Rock, Roots &
Jazz** *and* **Nightlife**.

Új Színház
VI. Paulay Ede utca 35 (269 6021). M1 Opera.
Open *1-6pm Mon-Fri; one hour before curtain Sat,
Sun. Closed June-Aug. Some English spoken.*
Map D3
The 'New Theatre', originally designed by Béla
Lajta as the Parisiana nightclub, stages small off-
beat productions. *See also chapter* **Architecture**.

Dance

The ballet scene consists mainly of competently
executed traditional pieces drawing on Russian
and Hungarian traditions. Bartók's *Miraculous
Mandarin* and László Seregi's choreography of
Romeo and Juliet (Prokofiev) and *The Taming of
the Shrew* (Goldmark) by the **Hungarian
National Ballet** all rise above the standard.

Trafó – *an imaginative blend of dance, theatre, music and exhibitions. See page 227.*

Budapest hosts many international companies but there is also innovative home-grown work. Two artistes who have built up talented troupes are Yvettte Bozsik and Iván Markó. At 52, Markó is a little past anything too athletic but compensates for this with experience, grace and good ideas. Bozsik is an in-your-face physical dancer, full of vitality and sensuous vigour.

Contemporary Dance Theatre Society

Kortárs Táncszínházi Egyesület
XI. Kőrösy József utca 17 (366 4776). Tram 4, 6, 18, 19, 47, 49. **Open** 4-7pm Tue-Thur. Contact Adrienn Szabó. English spoken. **Map C6**
Represents most of the modern Hungarian dance groups in the city. Closed June to September.

Hungarian National Ballet

Magyar Nemzeti Balett
The Hungarian National Ballet perform in the splendid **Opera House** and its ugly sister, the **Erkel**. *See chapter* **Music: Classical & Opera.**

Táncfórum

I. Corvin tér 8 (201 8779). M2 Batthyány tér. **Open** 9am-3pm Mon-Fri. Some English spoken. **Map B3**
Information on the main companies and arranges the dance shows in the seasonal Festivals.

Festivals

Further information from the **Central Theatre Booking Office** (*above*) or the **National Philharmonic Ticket Office** (*see chapter* **Music: Classical & Opera**).
The Contemporary Drama Festival in April hosts companies from the region. Csepürágó Festival in June is an all-dayer on Castle Hill, followed by a week of outdoor performances.
The **Budapest Spring & Autumn Festivals**, though primarily classical music events, also feature local and international dance companies. *See chapters* **Budapest by Season** *and* **Music: Classical & Opera.**

Trips Out of Town

Getting Started

There's more than one way to get out of town.

Budapest contains 20 per cent of Hungary's population. No other town is a tenth of its size. Away from the capital and the major tourist destinations of the Balaton, you'll find a different world: sleepy, backward, friendly. Trips out of town can be like stepping back in time.

Hungary is a small country. By bus, rail or car, two or three hours is the longest it'll take to get just about anywhere. At a more leisurely pace, boats serve destinations along the Danube and hop between Balaton resorts. Hitching is popular among young Hungarians, especially around the Balaton in summer, but unless you're suddenly stranded or on an absurdly tight budget, it's not worth the bother. Trains and buses are frequent, reliable and cheap.

Driving on Hungary's single-carriageway road system can be hazardous and hair-raising (*see* chapter **Getting Around**). New motorways are either being planned or under construction.

The better hotels will be able to help you with information and transport bookings. For more information about travel outside Budapest, try:

Ibusz

V. Petőfi tér 3 (318 5707). M3 Ferenciek tere. **Open** 24 hours daily. **Credit** V. English spoken. **Map C4**
The national tourist agency has branches all over Hungary and can book accommodation, organise tours and train travel and provide information.

Tourinform

V. Sütő utca 2 (317 9800). M1, M2, M3 Deák tér/tram 47, 49. **Open** 9am-7pm Mon-Fri; 9am-4pm Sat, Sun. English spoken. **Map C4**
The helpful, multilingual staff at Tourinform can dispense lots of information about destinations outside Budapest.

By bus

Buses are cheap and reasonably comfortable. Prices are per kilometre, with no discount for returns, except for Bratislava and Vienna. All other prices listed below are for one-way tickets, which can be bought in advance or on the coach. There are three main bus terminals:

Erzsébet tér

V. Erzsébet tér (317 2966/int 317 2562). M1, M2, M3 Deák tér/tram 47, 49. **Open** 6am-9pm daily. No English spoken. **Map C4**
International destinations, south and west Hungary.

Népstadion

XIV. Népstadion (252 4496). M2 Népstadion. **Open** 6am-8pm daily. No English spoken.
Serves the north and east

Árpád híd

XIII. Árpád híd (329 1450). M3 Árpád híd. **Open** 6am-8pm daily. No English spoken.
Destinations north along the Danube

To Balatonfüred (132km): *Erzsébet tér.* Journey time about two hours 30 minutes. Ft1,080. Three buses daily 6.30am-4.40pm. Last return 4.20pm.
To Eger (128km): *Népstadion.* Journey time about two hours. Price Ft1,108. 14 buses daily 6.15am-8.45pm. Last return 6.45pm.
To Esztergom (66km): *Árpád híd.* Journey time about one hour 15 minutes. Price Ft395. Frequent buses 6am-10.50pm. Last return 9.25pm.
To Keszthely (190km): *Erzsébet tér.* Journey time about three hours 40 minutes. Price Ft1,598. Two buses daily 6.30am-3.40pm, two extra Sat, Sun. Last return 4.30pm.
To Pécs (198km): *Erzsébet tér.* Journey time about four hours. Price Ft1,698. Five buses daily 6am-4.20pm. Last return 4.30pm.
To Siófok (106km): *Erzsébet tér.* Journey time about two hours 15 minutes. Price Ft1,024. Six buses daily 6.30am-4.40pm. Last return 6.15pm.
To Sopron (210km): *Erzsébet tér.* Journey time about four hours. Price Ft1,626. Four buses daily 6.30am-4pm, two extra Mon-Fri. Last return 2.15pm.
To Szentendre (20km): *Árpád híd.* Journey time about 30 minutes. Price Ft168. Frequent buses 7am-10pm. Last return 7.20pm.
To Visegrád (43km): *Árpád híd.* Journey time about one hour 10 minutes. Price Ft344. Frequent buses 7.30am-8.30pm. Last return 8.25pm.
To Bratislava (Pozsony) (300km): *Erzsébet tér.* Journey time about four hours. Price single Ft3,200, return Ft5,200. One bus daily 7.20am. Last return 4.45pm.
To Vienna (Bécs) (265km): *Erzsébet tér.* Journey time about 4 hours 45 minutes. Price single Ft4,900, return Ft6,900. Three buses daily 7am-5pm. Last return 7pm.

By train

Trains are cheap and relatively reliable and most Hungarian stations are convivially equipped with a bar. Avoid *személy* trains, which stop at all stations. *Gyors* are supposedly fast trains. InterCity trains are the speediest and most comfortable, equipped with buffet cars and air-conditioning that sometimes works.

Keleti station – insane queues, intriguing destinations.

Tickets are priced by the kilometre with no discount for returns. For InterCity trains you have to reserve a seat for Ft160. At rush hours arrive at least half an hour before the train is due to leave, as there will be insane queues at ticket offices. You can also buy tickets from the conductor on the train, though you may have to fork out a small fine.

No one speaks English at stations. Yellow departure timetables are posted at all of them. At ticket offices it's easiest just to write what you want on a piece of paper: destination, number of tickets, and the time of the train you want.

Oda-vissza means return. *R* means you must reserve a seat. International student cards are not valid but if you're registered with a Hungarian college discounts can be had on local trains.

The three main stations are Keleti, Nyugati and Déli, all of which have their own underground station. There is no discernible logic as to which train goes from which station so it's always best to check.

MÁV Information

VI. Andrássy út 35 (461 5400/international 461 5500). M1 Opera. **Open** *Apr-Sept* 9am-6pm Mon-Fri; *Oct-Mar* 9am-5pm Mon-Fri. **Credit** MC, V. Some English spoken. **Map D3**

Easiest place to avoid the queues and buy tickets or obtain national and international train information. Usually an English-speaker around. Phone line manned until 8pm.

To Balatonfüred: *Déli*. Journey time about two hours 20 minutes. Price Ft920. Six trains daily 6.25am-5.20pm. Last return 5.20pm.
To Eger: *Keleti*. Journey time about two hours. Price Ft920. Four trains daily 7.05am-7.20pm. Last return 8.36pm.
To Esztergom: *Nyugati*. Journey time about 90 minutes. Price Ft348. Ten trains daily 6.35am-10.20pm. Last return 6.55pm.
To Pécs: *Déli*. Journey time about two hours 30 minutes. Price Ft1,530 plus Ft160 reservation. Four InterCity trains daily 7.30am-7.30pm. Last InterCity return 6.10pm.
To Keszthely: *Déli*. Journey time about three hours 15 minutes. Price Ft1,310. Five trains daily 7.10am-5.10pm. Last return 6.20pm. Make sure you're sitting in the right carriage as the train sometimes splits.
To Siófok: *Déli*. Journey time about 90 minutes. Price Ft786. Six trains daily 7.10am-9.10pm. Last return 8.15pm.
To Sopron: *Keleti*. Journey time about three hours. Price Ft1,496 plus Ft160 reservation. Three InterCity trains daily 7.20am-5.25pm. Last InterCity return 6.36pm.
To Szentendre: *HÉV Batthyány tér*. Journey time 40 minutes. Price Ft240. Trains every 10-15 minutes 3.50am-11.40pm. Last return 11.30pm.
To Bratislava (Pozsony): *Keleti/Nyugati*. Journey time about three hours. Price one way Ft4,100, return Ft3,700 payable in hard currency or in forints. Intercity: extra charge Ft320. Seven trains daily 6.25am-9.30pm. Last return 8.43pm.
To Vienna (Bécs): *Keleti/Déli*. Journey time about two hours 30 minutes. Price one way or five-day return Ft7,000. Five-day return ticket includes free city transport use in both Budapest and Vienna. Ten trains daily 6am-9.25pm. Last return 7.05pm.
To Zagreb (Zagráb): *Keleti/Déli*. Journey time about seven hours. Price one way or return Ft7,500 payable in hard currency or in forints. Three trains daily 6.20am-5.30pm. Last return 4.10pm.

By car

Most roads in Hungary are single carriageway and everybody seems to be in a hurry. Recent renovation of the main motorways has also seen the introduction of toll gates on certain sections.

Getting out of Budapest is easy and routes are well signposted. From Buda follow M1 signs for Vienna and Sopron, M7 for destinations to the Balaton or then down to Zagreb, and the single carriageway E73 for Pécs. From Pest follow M3/E71 signs for Eger. From Árpád híd take the 10 for Esztergom and the 11 for Szentendre and Visegrád, following the west bank of the Danube.

There are often lengthy queues on the M1 at the Hungarian-Austrian border. At weekends and high season you might have to wait an hour or so.

By boat

In the summer months, leisurely boats and nippy jetfoils cruise up the Danube to Szentendre, Visegrád and Esztergom. Jetfoils will also whisk you onwards to Vienna via Bratislava. Although it's interesting to arrive in a new country by river, disappointingly, the jetfoil to Vienna has no real deck area to catch the view, and not much of a view anyway after you've passed the Danube Bend. There's an expensive bar on board, but only the most rudimentary selection of sandwiches and cold cuts if you get hungry on the six-hour journey. Take a picnic and a good book.

All boats to and from Esztergom stop at Visegrád. Most Szentendre boats continue to Visegrád, making a total of five boats to Visegrád every day. It's easy to visit Visegrád plus either Esztergom or Szentendre in a day-trip. Taking in all three by boat on one day is theoretically possible but pushing it. Some Japanese seem to manage it, though.

Boats run daily from 1 April to 23 September. Esztergom jetfoils run from 26 May to 3 September on Saturdays and holidays, and also on Fridays between 30 June and 3 September. Vienna jetfoils run daily from 8 April to 29 October and tickets are priced in Austrian schillings, though any hard currency should be acceptable. Get tickets for the jetfoils in advance. Tickets for other boats can be bought on board or in advance at major hotels or the MAHART Tours booking office on Belgrád rakpart.

Boat to Szentendre and Visegrád: *Vigadó tér terminal (318 1223)*. Journey time to Szentendre about one hour 40 minutes; to Visegrád about three hours 30 minutes. Price to Szentendre Ft600; to Visegrád Ft650. Three boats daily 7.30am-2pm (on the 2pm change at Szentendre for Visegrád). Last return from Szentendre 7.40pm; from Visegrád 6.30pm.
Boat to Esztergom: *Vigadó tér terminal (318 1223)*. Journey time about five hours 20 minutes. Esztergom Ft690. One boats daily 7.30pm. Last return 5pm.
Jetfoil to Bratislava: *International terminal, V. Belgrád rakpart (between Elizabeth and Szabadság híd) (318 1223)*. Journey time about four hours 30 minutes. Price AS700 one way, AS1,000 return. One boat daily at 9am; from Bratislava 9.20am Mon-Thur, 2.20pm Fri-Sun. Arrive one hour prior to departure for check-in and passport control.
Jetfoil to Vienna: *International terminal, V. Belgrád rakpart (between Elizabeth and Szabadság Bridges) (318 1953)*. Journey time about six hours. Price AS780 one way AS1,100 return. Discounts for students; children under 6 free, 6-15 half-fare. One boat daily at 9am *April-May, Sept-Oct*. Two boats daily at 8am and 1pm *Thur-Sun June-Aug*; from Vienna 8am Mon-Thur, 1pm Fri-Sun. Arrive one hour prior to departure for check-in and passport control.

The Danube Bend

Day-trip destinations on the river's most scenic stretch.

The Danube Bend, 40 kilometres north of Budapest, is spectacular and beautiful: certainly the most scenic stretch on the river's 3,000-km course from the Black Forest to the Black Sea. Here the Danube widens and turns sharply south into a narrow valley between the Börzsöny and Pilis Hills before flowing onwards to Budapest.

The two main settlements on the west bank, Visegrád and Esztergom, were respectively a Hungarian medieval capital and royal seat. Both are easily accessible as day-trips by train, bus or regular summer boats from Budapest (*see chapter* **Getting Started**). Visegrád's hilltop citadel, the ruins of a thirteenth-century palace, is breathtaking. Esztergom, centre of Hungarian Catholicism, is dominated by the nation's largest cathedral.

Although both places can be fitted into one day, most visitors also aim for Szentendre, a quaint former Serbian village and artists' colony. Taking in all three sites will be stretching a day to its limits, so a couple of hotels in Esztergom, terminus for the Danube Bend ferry service, have been included.

Szentendre

The most obvious quick escape from Budapest is Szentendre, a settlement of 20,000 people just 20 kilometres north of the city.

The HÉV suburban train from Batthyány tér (*see page 269* **Getting Around**) takes a pleasant 45 minutes to pass gentle suburbs and grazing horses. The summer boat service from Vigadó tér is only an extra hour and the evening journey back to Budapest can be equally delightful.

Szentendre, long an artists' colony, has also become a major tourist destination – and it shows. Any place with a Marzipan Museum is obviously expecting tourists. Crafts and overpriced folklore are sold in hundreds of shops and outdoor stalls along the cobblestone streets. Galleries stock everything from unique artworks to 'artistically designed' dresses and plates.

But don't let the tourist tack put you off. Serbian refugees reached Szentendre centuries before Hungarian artists did, leaving a handful of Orthodox churches, some still in operation. Follow the occasional wafts of incense on a Sunday morn-

Szentendre – picturesque exteriors, occasional wafts of incense.

ing and you'll get a better impression of the town and its history than most galleries will give you.

The first wave of Serbian refugees moved here after the Turks won the Battle of Kosovo in 1389, building small wooden churches. The Turks then invaded Hungary. Although Szentendre was liberated in 1686, the Turkish recapture of Belgrade four years later caused a second flood of Serbian refugees. They enjoyed religious freedom under Habsburg rule and traded in leather and wine. Szentendre prospered and the Serbs rebuilt their churches, this time from stone. Although the exteriors are western baroque, the interiors preserve Orthodox traditions. All places of sanctuary had to face east, irrespective of dimension or streetscape. The resulting disjointed lay-out gives Szentendre its distinct Balkan atmosphere.

The first church the visitor comes to is the Pozarevacka, in Vuk Karadzics tér. For a token admission fee, an old lady will put Slavonic church music on the cranky reel-to-reel. The candlelight and Szentendre's oldest icon screen do the rest. You can still smell the incense in the Balkan Adria café opposite. In the main square, Fő tér, Blagovestenska Church provides a heady mix of deep music, incense and a huge, glorious iconostasis. Szentendre's most stunning place of worship is the Belgrade Cathedral, seat of the Serbian Orthodox Bishop, with its entrance in Pátriáka utca. This is only open for Sunday services, but these offer a moving experience. On the same grounds is a museum of Serbian Church Art, containing bishop's garments and icons.

In 1774 a royal decree demanded the Serbs take an oath of allegiance to Hungary or be otherwise forbidden to trade. This killed Szentendre as a trading centre. A series of floods and epidemics did the rest. Most Serbs moved on.

When a group of artists discovered Szentendre in the 1920s, they were delighted to find a living museum of Serbian houses and churches. Encouraged to stay, they formed an artists' colony. The **Barcsay Múzeum** contains the abstract works of one of the colony's founders. Later generations set up dozens of galleries, with varying degrees of artistic success. The recently opened Malom Múzeum és Művészeti Központ, an expansive space exhibiting recent work by local talent at Bogdányi utca 32 (06 26 312 912), shows that the artistic spirit still thrives. *See also chapter* **Art Galleries**.

The alternative set who formed the underground music and art group Bizottság also remain; check out the weird statues in ef Zámbó's garden on Bartók Béla utca. Musical activity is otherwise focused on the Dalmát Pince (Malom utca 5) a cellar ideal for regular live jazz gigs, or the Barlang (Dunakorzó 11a) a riverside cultural centre with an eclectic musical programme. Bars are often trendy (the Art Café in Fő tér) or overpriced (almost anywhere). The Szent Endre Pub, also known as the Yellow Pub (Római Sánc utca near

the HÉV) is a lively spot that draws locals. The Red Lion English Pub (Szerb utca 2A) also attracts more locals than the name might suggest.

Along the river, the Görög Kancsó, where Görög utca meets the Dunakorzó, is a decent mid-priced restaurant. You'll find finer, dearer Hungarian and continental cuisine at Chez Nicolas (Kigyó utca 10) although you'll have to climb uphill from the river to reach it. The Café Cousin (Fő tér 20) has vegetarian options and an extensive cocktail menu.

If you have time, it's worth visiting the huge **Open-air Folklore Museum**, a short bus journey away, showing three centuries of village life in Hungary. *See also chapter* **Museums**.

Tourinform Szentendre

Dumtsa Jenő utca 22 (06 26 317 965). **Open** *May-Sept* 8am-5pm Mon-Fri; 10am-2pm Sat, Sun. *Oct-April* 8.30am-4.30pm Mon-Fri.
Helpful and English-speaking.

Visegrád

Despite the spectacular mountain-top Citadel overlooking the most beautiful stretch of the Danube, the village below is small and sleepy with only the ruins of the lower Palace to make it worth a visit.

The Citadel and Palace were built in the thirteenth and fourteenth centuries. The latter was the setting for the Visegrád Congress of 1335, when the kings of Hungary, Czechoslovakia and Poland quaffed 10,000 litres of wine while discussing trade strategy. In a similar but more sober event 656 years later, the Visegrád Group of Hungary, Poland, the Czech Republic and Slovakia planned gradually to remove trade restrictions by 2001.

King Mátyás Corvinus overhauled Visegrád Palace in splendid Renaissance style. All this fell into ruin after the Turkish invasion and mud slides buried the Palace. It wasn't until bits of it were discovered in 1934 excavations that people believed there had ever been anything there in the first place. What you'll see today is mostly ruins. There are modern replicas of the Lion Fountain and the Hercules Fountain, but otherwise your imagination will have to do the rest. Some original pieces uncovered during excavations can be found at the Mátyás Museum, in the Salamon Tower halfway up the hill to the Citadel.

There are three ways up to the Citadel: a strenuous walk up the stony Path of Calvary (25 literally breathtaking minutes); one of the thrice daily buses from the village (ten minutes); or a taxi (call 397 372/3) or car up Panoráma út. You won't be disappointed. The exhibitions are naff and boring, but the view from the Citadel walls is magnificent, and worth the journey alone.

Before taking the boat back, a beer with a view can be had at the terrace bar above the kitschy Renaissanz restaurant opposite the landing. For a

The Cathedral in Esztergom – Hungary's answer to Canterbury.

longer lunch, the Fekete Holló, Rév utca 12, with its open fire, can rustle up reasonably priced chicken or trout with all the trimmings.

Probably the best way to see Visegrád is from the bank opposite. Take the hourly ferry across to Nagymaros, and splash around at the only spot on the river where it's possible to swim.

Visegrád Tours

Rév utca 15 (06 26 398 160). **Open** 9am-6pm daily.
They're a bit sullen here, but it's the only information office in town.

Esztergom

Although Esztergom is Hungary's most sacred city, home of the Archbishop and the nation's biggest church, it has a real-life edge that makes it worth a night's stopover. Not all of its 30,000 inhabitants are pious; there's a huge Suzuki car factory on the outskirts and in town a string of run-down bars full of drunken fishermen.

But it's the past that brings visitors here. Esztergom was Hungary's first real capital. The nation's first Christian king, Szent István, was crowned here on Christmas Day 1000. He built a royal palace, unearthed in 1934, parts of which can be seen in the Castle Museum south of the Cathedral.

For nearly three centuries Esztergom was the royal seat until the Mongol invasion all but destroyed the city. It suffered more damage under the Turks, but most of what's worth seeing was rebuilt in Baroque style some 250 years ago: the Víziváros Parish Church on Mindszenty tere; the Christian Museum on Berényi Zsigmond utca and the Balassi Bálint Museum in Pázmány Péter utca.

It's the Cathedral that dominates, though. What strikes most is the size of the thing. When the Catholic Church moved its base back to Esztergom in 1820, Archbishop Sándor Rudnay wanted a vast monument on the ruins of a twelfth-century church destroyed by the Turks. It took 40-odd years and three architects and fairly bleak it is too. Main bright spot is the Bakócz Chapel, built in red marble by Florentine craftsmen, dismantled during the Turkish era and reassembled in 1823.

The Treasury holds a collection of golden treasures rescued from the medieval church. The crypt contains the tomb of Cardinal Mindszenty, who was tortured by the Communists in 1948 and then holed up in the American Embassy for 15 years.

In town you'll find a dozen or so reasonable restaurants; the Csülök Csárda, Batthyány utca 9, is as good as any. The Pension Ria nearby at No. 11-13 (06 33 313 115) is charming, inexpensive and has bright modern bathrooms. The Alabardos Panzió, Bajcsy-Zsilinszky utca 49 (06 33 312 640), can also provide a cheapish double room. The Hotel Esztergom, Nagy Duna sétány (06 33 312 883), is a more expensive modern job with a river terrace and sports centre.

For the best view of Castle Hill and the city, walk up St Thomas Hill to the east. Although all you'll see there now is a modest nineteenth-century chapel – the original was destroyed by the Turks – this was the site of a religious chapter named after Thomas Becket. It was founded by French princess Margaret Capet whose father-in-law, King Henry II of England, was implicated in Becket's murder – appropriate for a town that is essentially the Magyar Canterbury.

GranTours

Széchenyi tér 25 (06 33 417 052). **Open** 8am-6pm Mon-Fri; 9am-noon Sat.
Efficient and English-speaking.

The Balaton

It may not be the French Riviera, but it's the only place you'll ever catch a fogas.

Hungary is a land-locked country, which perhaps explains why locals get so hyperbolic about the Balaton, the largest lake in west and central Europe. Take these words from turn-of-the-century writer Károly Eötvös, often quoted in Hungarian guide books:

'Lake Balaton is fantasy and poetry, history and tradition, a volume of bitter-sweet tales, the age-old home of wild Hungarians; it is both the pride of our past and a brilliant hope for our future.'

But while Hungarians experience the Balaton from the comfort and seclusion of weekend cottages, for the foreign tourist it's a different story: high-rise hotels and concrete beaches, white plastic chairs and advertising umbrellas, a string of over-priced resorts, the breeding-ground of wild mosquitoes.

Though there are some beautiful spots on and around the lake, particularly along the north shore, a trip to the Balaton is first and foremost an excursion into deepest naff – which doesn't mean to say that it can't also be a lot of fun.

Wild Hungarians may still be found in the bars and discos of Balatonlelle or Siófok, but this area was also an age-old home for all sorts of other folk, even before the lake formed around 20-22,000 years ago. Between then and the arrival of the Magyars in the late ninth century, there were Celts, Romans, Huns, Lombards, Avars, Franks and Slavs, whose word for swamp, *blatna*, probably gave the shallow lake its name. The Magyars brought fishing, agriculture, livestock-breeding and built a lot of churches before the Mongols came and trashed the place in 1242. The Turks later occupied the south shore and scuffled with Austrians along the other side throughout the sixteenth and seventeenth centuries. Once they were driven out, the Habsburgs came along and blew up any remaining Hungarian castles.

Most of the interesting sights, therefore, date from the eighteenth century, when agriculture and viticulture began to flourish and Hungarian landowners brought in Slav, German and Croat peasants to work their estates. It was a time of Baroque building and decoration, the best remaining examples of which are the Abbey Church in Tihany and the huge Festetics Mansion in Keszthely. Wine is still produced in large quantities, particularly in the area around Badacsony – full of small cellars where you can taste the wares and buy by the five-litre plastic container.

Although Balatonfüred was declared a spa in 1785, it wasn't until the nineteenth century that bathing and the therapeutic properties of the area's thermal springs began to draw the wealthy in large numbers. In 1836 Baron Miklós Wesselényi, leading reformer of the period, was the first to swim from Tihany to Balatonfüred. Lajos Kossuth suggested steamships, and Count István Széchenyi rustled some up. Passenger boat services still link most of the major resorts and are an appealing way to get around the area, although the ferry from the southern tip of the Tihany peninsula to Szántód – a ten-minute journey spanning the lake's narrowest point – is the only one that takes cars.

The southern shore – these days one 80-kilometre stretch of tacky resort after tacky resort – was developed after the opening of the railway in 1861, which runs along the lake en route from Budapest to Zagreb. The line along the hillier and marginally more tasteful north shore wasn't completed until 1910. Even so, the Balaton didn't become a playground for anyone but the well-to-do until after World War II, when the Communists reconstructed the area with an eye to mass recreation. You'll still see a category of lodging called an *üdülő*. Once holiday homes for the workers of particular factories or trade unions, many *üdülők* are now privatised.

Before the fall of the Berlin Wall, Hungary was one of the few places where East Germans could travel and the Balaton became the place where West Germans would meet up with their poor relations. Tourism is still heavily geared towards the needs of Germans and Austrians – and a smattering of Deutsch will prove much more useful than English in these parts. Though a trip to the Balaton is hardly getting away from it all, you'll at least be going somewhere not often frequented by Brits or Americans.

The lake itself is weird. A 77-kilometre-long rectangle, 14 kilometres at its widest, it covers an area of about 600 square kilometres but is shallow throughout. Lake Geneva contains 20 times as much water. At its deepest (the so-called 'Tihany Well' off the tip of the peninsula that almost chops the lake in half), the Balaton reaches only 12-13 metres. At Siófok and other south shore resorts you can paddle out 500-1,000 metres before the water gets up to your waist, which does mean it's very safe for children.

The shallow Balaton – in places you can paddle out for miles.

But it's not ideal swimming water. It's silty and milkily opaque and feels oily on the skin. The shallowness also means it warms up quickly, and isn't the most refreshing splash on a brain-baking July afternoon. It does, however, freeze well in the winter and is apparently good for ice-skating, but if you visit before May or after October (high season is July and August), you won't find very much open even in the larger towns.

Motor boats are strictly forbidden here but you'll find sailing and windsurfing on the lake. Fishing's popular, too. The Balaton is home to around 40 varieties of fish – including fogas, the Hungarian pike-perch, which is unique to the lake and a suitable accompaniment for one of the many drinkable local wines. The lake is also teeming with eels.

At high season there are also too many mosquitoes. There are continual arguments between different local and national authorities concerning precisely whose job it is to spray the lake and curb the bug population. The result is so many mosquitoes that you often can't go out at night without lathering yourself with repellents.

Another downer is the pegging of prices to the Deutschmark, which means the Balaton is getting expensive for everyone except the Germans. Affordable hotels do exist, but you pay a lot for what you get. Fine dining is hard to find, as is anything cheap and cheerful apart from the occasional pizza. Moderately expensive Hungarian restaurants serving up standard central European meat and vegetable dishes are the order of the day. Vegetarians will find little.

Nevertheless, the Balaton can make for a interesting trip out of town. Most destinations can be reached by train in two or three hours. Siófok and other resorts at the western end of the lake are doable in a day. Perhaps the most agreeable method is to take a long weekend circumnavigating the lake, stopping here and there for a swim or a beer, and driving up into the hills behind the northern shore. Here you've got rolling countryside, quiet villages, the occasional ostrich farm and roadsides decked with wild flowers. From the oddly-shaped volcanic hills above Badacsony (the Kisfaludy Ház restaurant, although somewhat tackily folkloric in theme, has a beautiful terrace), the view across vineyards and the milky green waters of the lake, ploughed by a steamship or two and fading into a distant heat haze, is pretty enough to touch a chord in even the most cynical of travellers.

Balatonfüred

The north shore's major resort is also the Balaton's oldest and has long been famed for the curative properties of its waters. The State Hospital of Cardiology and the Sanitorium dominate the Baroque and these days somewhat dilapidated Gyógy tér at the old town centre. In the middle of the square the Kossuth Well dispenses warm mineral-rich water, which is the closest you'll get to the thermal springs without checking into the hospital.

There also used to be a theatre here, built in the mid-nineteenth century when Balatonfüred was a major hangout for nationalist writers, artists and politicians. 'Patriotism towards our nationality' read the banner outside, and the theatre was intended to encourage Hungarian writing and acting at a time when German was still more widely spoken. Ironic, then, that tourism has reinstated German as the region's lingua franca.

There is a busy harbour with a pier, a shipyard, promenade, six major beaches and an assortment of not terribly inspiring things to see. Popular romantic writer Mór Jókai cranked out many of his 200 novels here, and his summer villa (at the corner of Jókai Mór utca and Honvéd utca) is now a memorial museum that includes a coffeehouse, the Jokai Kávézó. Across the road is the neoclassical Kerék templom (Round Church), built in 1846. The Lóczy Cave (*barlang*), off Öreghegy utca on the northern outskirts of town, is the largest hole in the ground hereabouts.

The Hotel Flamingo at Széchenyi utca 16 (87 340 392) is par for the tacky course, but has a private beach and rooms with balconies more or less overlooking the lake. Modest but comfortable is Hotel Thetis on Vörösmarty utca 7 (87 341 606).

Tihany's Abbey Church – Hungary's most important baroque monument.

Perhaps because of the many oldsters coming to take the waters, Balatonfüred is a calm and almost genteel place, although there is some life after dark. The Fregatt Dublin Irish Pub on Blaha Lujza utca is of course nothing of the sort, but is a pleasant enough spot for an early evening beer and also stays open until the small hours. After dinner at one of the many restaurants all along Tagore sétány and up Jókai Mór utca – the ones by the end of the pier all specialise in fish dishes – the Wagner Club and Galéria offer pop techno, go-go dancers and lots of teenagers on the dance floor. The Füredi Feszek Kávézó on Kisfaludy utca offers both pizzas and house music, 24 hours a day.

From the end of the pier, with the lights of Siófok in the distance and the Tihany peninsula looming darkly to the west, the lake looks delightful by moonlight.

Balatontourist Balatonfüred

Blaha Lujza utca 5 (87 342 823). **Open** *June-Sept* 8.30am-6.30pm Mon-Sat; 8.30am-noon Sun. *Oct-May* 8.30am-4pm Mon-Fri; 8.30am-noon Sat.

Tihany

Declared a national park in 1952, the Tihany Peninsula is one of the quietest and most unspoilt places in the Balaton region – though even in this picturesque, historic spot, summer means the blooming of Coke and Lucky Strike umbrellas.

The 12 square kilometres of the peninsula jut 5 kilometres into the lake, almost cutting it in half. Tihany village lies by the Inner Lake, separate from the Balaton – and a steep hike up from the small harbour, if you happen to arrive here by boat. On the hill above stands the twin-spired Abbey Church, completed in 1754. This is one of Hungary's most important Baroque monuments, and not just because of its outstanding wood-carvings – though there are certainly plenty of those. King Andrew I's 1055 deed of foundation for the church originally on this site was the first written document to contain any Hungarian – a few score place names in a mainly Latin text. (It now resides at the Pannonhalma Abbey near Győr.)

The Abbey museum in the former monastery next door has exhibits about Lake Balaton and a small collection of Roman statues in an enjoyably cool cellar. If you get tired of the splendid views right across the lake, nearby there are also museums dedicated to folklore, fishing, puppetry and pottery. **Tourinform Tihany** can provide information about walks in the area, which has a bird sanctuary, two small lakes, some geyser cones and an Echo Hill.

There isn't much else to see or do in Tihany proper, however. The Kakas, in a rambling old house below the Erika hotel, is an agreeable spot

for lunch or dinner and, unusually, open all year round. Otherwise there is an assortment of bars and restaurants around the main square and along Kossuth utca. Places to stay are limited, although the Hotel Park by the lake on Fürdőtelepi utca (87 348 611), formerly a Habsburg summer mansion, offers a modicum of elegance and its own private beach. Go for rooms 15, 16 or 17 (the expensive ones with grand balconies), and just say no if they try to stick you in the ugly 1970s annex on the same grounds. Otherwise private rooms in Tihany village can be arranged through Balatontourist.

We'd recommend staying in Balatonfüred, just 11 kilometres distant, and doing Tihany as a side-trip or stopover on the way to the next town.

Tourinform Tihany

Kossuth utca 20 (06 87 448 804). **Open** 9am-6pm Mon-Sat. Some English spoken.

Keszthely

The only town on the Balaton that isn't totally dependent on tourism, Keszthely has a mellow feel quite different from other lakeside resorts. The two busy strands seem to swallow up all the tourists, while the agricultural university means a bit of life off-season as well as some variety at night.

Main tourist attraction is the Festetics Palace, a 100-room Baroque pile in pleasant grounds at the north end of the town centre. The Festetics family owned this whole area and Count György (1755-1819) was the epitome of an enlightened aristocrat. He not only constructed the palace but also built ships, hosted a salon of leading Hungarian literary lights, and founded both the Helikon library – now in the southern part of the mansion and containing more than 80,000 volumes – and the original agricultural college, these days the Georgikon Museum at Bercsényi utca 67. There is also a Wine Museum, a Marzipan Museum and the Balaton Museum, dedicated to the history of the region, with artifacts dating back to the first century AD.

The Gothic Parish Church on Fő tér has a longer history than most Balaton buildings. Originally built in the 1380s, it was fortified in 1550 in the face of the Ottoman advance. Though the rest of the town was sacked, it managed to hold out against the Turks. In 1747 the church was rebuilt in the Baroque style.

The Hotel Bacchus at Erzsébet királyné utca 18 (83 314 096) is a small and friendly modern hotel, ideally located between the town centre and the strand, with a terrace restaurant that's one of the best in town. If you'd prefer a place by the lake try the Hotel Hullám at Balatonpart 1 (83 312 644), a 1930s joint with airy, high-ceilinged rooms.

There are many bars and restaurants on and around Kossuth Lajos utca, the main street, mostly catering to the town's student population. The Easy

Siófok – by day people do the strand.

Rider is the one everyone seems to favour The Donatello Pizzéria at Balaton utca 1 (83 315 989) is an acceptable Italian restaurant (average Ft1,000). There's a beautiful garden out the back with fishpond, fountain and rockery, and one feature all too rare in this part of the world: staff who try hard. The friendly Oazis Reform Étterem at Rákoczi tér 3 (just down Szalástó utca from the Festetics Palace) has an excellent self-service vegetarian and salad bar.

Keszthely is a good base for venturing up the lake towards Badacsony with its wine cellars and volcanic hills or the cute little village of Szigliget with its fourteenth-century castle ruins. Hévíz, eight kilometres inland (it's a 15-minute ride on the bus from stop number 4 in Fő tér) has the largest thermal lake in Europe. Bathing is possible all year round (in winter the lake steams dramatically). The deep blue and slightly radioactive warm water is full of Indian water lilies and middle-aged east Germans floating around with rubber rings. A 20-minute dousing is said to be efficacious for locomotive disorders and nervous ailments.

Tourinform Keszthely

Kossuth Lajos utca 28 (83 314 144). **Open** *June-Sept* 9am-5pm Mon-Fri; 9am-1pm Sat, Sun. *Oct-May* 8am-4pm Mon-Fri; 9am-1pm Sat. Some English spoken. Right across the street there's also a branch of Ibusz and a similar concern called Keszthely Tourist.

Siófok

Siófok is Balaton's sin city: big, loud, brash and packed in high season. Although it's the lake's largest resort – Greater Siófok stretches for 15 kilometres along the shore – there really isn't much in the way of sightseeing. Here hedonism reigns. By day people do the strand. Nights are devoted to drinking, dining, dancing and sex.

The Petőfi sétány strip runs for about two kilometres between the harbour, where the Sió canal meets the lake, and the four big Communist-built hotels – the Pannonia, Balaton, Hungaria and Lido. Ugly concrete blocks, their classy old neon signs nevertheless look great at sunset. In between are bars with oom-pah bands, amusement arcades, western-style steakhouses, topless places, portrait painters, video game arcades, parked cars blasting pop techno, naff T-shirt stalls, a reptile house full of scary snakes and an endless procession of Hungarian, German and Austrian tourists.

The Roxy at Szabadság tér 4 is a decent brasserie where the drinks are well-made. Flört at Sió utca 4 is one of Hungary's best nightclubs: two dance floors (one techno, one tacky), some occasionally excellent DJs, a succession of bars on different levels of the barn-like main room, and a roof terrace overlooking the Sió Canal. In summer young Budapesters sometimes drive down for the night just to come and dance here. Its main rival is The Palace, just out of town. Both clubs occasionally host big-name house and techno DJs. Less fashionable is the Paradiso, near the harbour. Coca-Cola have sponsored the Beach House on the main strand, offering occasional live concerts, dancing on the beach, and aerobics in the daytime.

There are restaurants everywhere, but unfortunately rather too many of them cater to German tastes. The Pizza Bella at Szabadság tér 1 (84 310 826) serves up average Italian eats. On the strip there are all sorts of food stalls. The Diana Hotel at Szent László utca 41/43 (84 315 296), one of the best hotels in town, also has a restaurant that, if you're going to try it anywhere, is the place to eat fogas. The Janus at Fő utca 93-85 (84 312 546) is another good new hotel, though pricey – but you'll not find very many bargains in this town. On the strip, the Hotel Napfény is a little cheaper. Situated by the harbour at Mártirok utca 8 (84 311 408), it at least has a selection of comfortable big rooms with balconies.

Tourinform Siófok

Fő tér 41 (84 310 117). **Open** *June-Sept* 8am-8pm daily; *Oct-May* 9am-4pm Mon-Fri; 9am-1pm Sat. Some English spoken.
In the summer months there's a also a small Tourinform office that's open in the water tower on Szabadság tér. All the other tourist agencies have offices nearby.

Overnighters

Eger and Pécs, Sopron and Szeged – whatever direction you head in, Hungary has curious cities to explore.

Eger

A sweet little town, 128 kilometres east of Budapest at the foot of the Bükk Hills, Eger is famous for three things: its fine Baroque buildings; a siege at which locals repelled the Turkish army; and Bull's Blood, the heavy red wine known in Hungarian as Egri Bikavér.

Eger is a playful sort of place, often full of visiting schoolchildren. It takes its history seriously, though. The siege of Eger, in which a force of local defenders held the Castle against a much larger Ottoman army, is one of Hungary's few famous victories. The Turks came back and finished the job 44 years later, but the earlier siege of Eger has been fixed in the nation's imagination by Géza Gárdonyi's 1901 adventure novel *Egri csillagok* (published in English as *Eclipse of the Crescent Moon*), required reading for every Hungarian schoolkid. Indeed, Gárdonyi's version seems almost to have replaced the actual history. There's a statue of the author within the Castle walls, plus a Panoptikum featuring wax versions of his characters. Copies of the novel are on sale all over town, and on Gárdonyi utca, there's the Gárdonyi Géza Memorial Museum, where his house has been preserved.

The Castle was later dynamited by the Habsburgs in 1702. What remains is big but pretty dull, although a walk along what's left of the battlements affords a fine view over Eger's Baroque and remarkably flatblock-free skyscape (you can either buy a ticket just to walk around, or one that also affords you entrance to the castle's various exhibits, most of which are closed on Monday). The one remaining Turkish minaret (the corner of Knézich utca and Markó Ferenc utca) also has a great view, although it's a long and claustrophobic climb to get to it. On Fürdő utca Eger also has an original Ottoman bathhouse, but viewed from the outside this is fairly unimpressive, and entrance is restricted to those with a doctor's note. The pool in the adjoining strand is fed by the same spring.

Eger's Baroque buildings are splendid, most notably the 1771 Minorite church, centrepiece of Dobó tér. There are more listed buildings in this town than anywhere else in Hungary bar Budapest

Dobó tér in Eger – a playful sort of town.

Eger Castle – scene of one of Hungary's few famous victories.

and Sopron. The Bazilika on Eszterházy tér is an imposing neo-classical monolith crowned with crucifix-brandishing statues of Faith, Hope and Charity. The Lyceum opposite (used as a teacher training college) has a nineteenth-century camera obscura in the observatory at the top of the east wing tower that projects a view of the entire town.

Small and with a mostly pedestrianised centre, Eger is ideal for strolling. One could easily do the town in a day, but it's a relaxing and rewarding overnighter. The Senátorház hotel at Dobó tér 11 (06 36 320 466) is comfortable and ideally situated. The Minaret Hotel (right beside the actual Minaret) at Knezich Károly utca 4 (06 36 410 020) is cheaper.

Local wines are most entertainingly sampled just out of town at Szépasszony-völgy, the Valley of Beautiful Women, a horseshoe-shaped area of dozens of wine cellars, many with tables outside.

Wine is cheap enough to allow a level of consumption that would diminish anyone's standards of feminine pulchritude (hence the name), Gypsy fiddlers entertain drinkers, and parties come to eat, dance and make excessively merry. Afternoon is best, as places start closing by early evening. Out of high season, it's also pretty dead on Sundays and Mondays. The Valley bustles most during the two-week harvest festival in September. It's a 25-minute walk from Dobó tér or a short cab ride. (It can be difficult finding a cab to get back – try calling City Taxi on 422 222.)

For dinner we'd recommend the Effendi at Kossuth Lajos utca 19, a laid-back and inexpensive cellar restaurant. Otherwise there is an assortment of eating options on Széchenyi utca, including a Greek restaurant, a cukrászda, a salad bar and a brand-name burger joint. The Pepi Kávéház on Dobó tér is a reasonable spot for

breakfast and the Stella pizzeria on Eszperanto setany is open nightly until 2am. Note the plaque to Esperanto inventor Zamenhof on the corner of the building.

Tourinform

Dobó tér 2 (06 36 321 807). **Open** *May-Oct* 9am-5.30pm Mon-Fri; 10am-1pm Sat. Some English spoken.
Friendly and helpful, and usually an English-speaker around.

Pécs

Spread out on the southern slopes of the Mecsek Hills, down near the ex-Yugoslavian border, Hungary's fourth-largest city has a warm and sheltered climate, enough fig trees and Turkish monuments to lend it a vaguely eastern air, a curious collection of architecture and a clutch of interesting art museums. It's a peaceful place by day, especially in summer, when it acquires a distinctly lazy feel. At night there are plenty of bars, cafés and restaurants – a reflection of both the town's large student population and its lively trade in conferences and festivals. If you're only going to make one foray out of Budapest, Pécs must be the main contender.

Romans settled here and called their town Sopianae – a name that survives as a Hungarian cigarette brand. Assorted tribes asserted squatting rights before the Magyars set up shop at the end of the ninth century. The town prospered on the trade route between Byzantium and Regensburg, King Stephen established the Pécs diocese in 1009, and Hungary's first university was founded here in 1367.

And then came the Turks in 1543, pushing the locals outside the walls that still define the city centre, and flattening the rest of the place. Thus, as in the rest of Hungary, little pre-Turkish stuff survives. But after staying here 143 years, the Turks did leave a couple of mementoes – with the possible exception of Buda's baths, the most significant Turkish monuments remaining anywhere in the country.

Széchenyi tér is dominated by the former mosque of Pasha Gazi Kassim, built from the stones of an old gothic church. Jesuits converted it to back to its present state, the Belvárosi Plébániatemplom (Inner City Parish Church). Domed and angled towards Mecca at variance with the square's north-south orientation, it gives the city's main intersection its eastern feel. The minaret was demolished in 1753, but inside, on the back wall, are recently uncovered Arabic texts. As if to counter this influence, the main interior decor features a grand mural depicting Hungarian battles with the Turks. Outside stands the statue of Hungarian leader János Hunyadi, who successfully thwarted an earlier Turkish invasion.

The mosque of Pasha Hassan Jokovali, complete with minaret, is at Rákóczi utca 2. The most intact Turkish structure in Hungary, this was also converted into a church but was later reconstructed as a mosque, and now functions as a museum.

After the Turks, Pécs was slow to revive. Coal-mining spurred prosperity in the nineteenth century. Since World War II there has been uranium-mining and, during the Balkan Wars, a thriving black market trade with nearby Serbia. Waves of prosperity are clear in the architecture: the forms of the Baroque and Art Nouveau buildings in the old centre are echoed in the 1970s shopping centres and office blocks down the slope.

Pécs is built around two main squares: the aforementioned Széchenyi tér and Dóm tér, at which stands the four-towered, mostly neo-Romanesque Basilica of St Peter. Below this is Szent István tér, with Roman ruins and a small park with cafés and a weekend market.

Káptalan utca runs east off Dóm tér. Pécs teems with art museums and many are to be found up here. Those dedicated to Csontváry, Hungary's answer to Van Gogh (nearby in Janus Pannonius utca 11) and Magyar op-artist Victor Vasarely (Káptalan utca 3) are the most interesting. Zsolnay tile, that coloured stuff you see on top of Budapest's more extravagant Dual Monarchy buildings (and in Pécs on top of new buildings too), is made in this town, but the Zsolnay Ceramics Exhibit just over the street from the Vasarely museum isn't that interesting: mostly vases in glass cases.

The Santa Maria at Klimó György utca 12, with an inexplicably nautical interior built into the old city walls, is a good spot for dinner. Otherwise Király utca, the pedestrian street off Széchenyi tér, bustles at night with bars, cafés and restaurants. You'll probably want to look at the neo-Renaissance Pécs National Theatre, which is just down here. You might also inspect the interior of the István Pince wine cellar at Kazinczy utca 1 – a fine old example of the borozó genre.

Pécs' best hotel, the Art Nouveau and genuinely elegant Palatinus, is down here at Király utca 5 (06 72 233 022), with rooms at DM130 a double. The friendly Hotel Fönix at Hunyadi út 2 (72 311 680), just north of Széchenyi tér, is just as central and far cheaper at Ft6,600 for a double in high season.

At weekends, on the outskirts of town, Pécs has one of Hungary's largest flea markets. Catch bus 3 or 50 from the station, or else hail a cab and ask for the Nagyvásár. You'll find acres and acres of junk at the end of the ten-minute ride.

Tourinform

Széchenyi tér 9 (06 72 212 632). **Open** 8am-5.30pm Mon-Fri; 10am-3pm Sat. Some English spoken.
Tourinform can provide information and help with choosing accommodation.

Sopron

Sopron is way up in the north-west of Hungary, in a little Magyar nodule that extrudes into Austria. The location has had two effects on this fascinating small, old town. The first is that it escaped devastation by both Mongols and Turks and has managed to retain a medieval feel you won't find anywhere else in Hungary outside Budapest's Castle District. The second is that Austrians flood over the border to go shopping on the cheap.

The Várkerület, which encircles the Old Town, bustles with tiny shops selling bargain booze and cigarettes, budget salamis and household gadgets. Opticians proliferate. There are dentists, hairdressers and beauticians everywhere. Just about every business doubles as a money-changer.

Stepping from all this through one of the entrances into the Old Town is like cracking open a stone to find an extraordinary crystal formation within. Here cobbled, medieval-patterned streets are relaxed and traffic-free. Practically every building is listed: medieval dwellings rub gables with Gothic churches and Baroque monuments. Commerce continues, but quietly, in discreet boutiques and jewellery shops nestling by small museums.

The Firewatch Tower, symbol of Sopron, sums up the town's history and offers a view that takes it all in. It's built on Roman foundations, with a twelfth-century base, a sixteenth-century column and balcony, a seventeenth-century spire, and a 'Fidelity Gate' installed in 1922 to mark the town's decision (they voted on it) to remain part of Hungary after Trianon. From the top you can see the streets and walls of the Old Town, following the lines of the previous Roman settlement, and the vine-covered hills beyond the outskirts.

Though there's plenty to look at it in the daytime – the various old houses and museums around Fő tér and the Medieval Synagogue at Új utca 22 are particularly interesting – it's at night, after the day-trippers have all gone, when Sopron is at its most atmospheric. Wandering the medieval streets, quiet except for the chatter and clatter from restaurants and wine cellars, only a rare parked car intrudes between you and the illusion that you have stepped back several centuries.

For breakfast or coffee try the restored 1920s Várkapu coffeehouse at Hátsókapu utca 3. For lunch the restaurants Gambrinus (inexpensive Hungarian standards) and Corvinus (reasonable pizzas) both have tables outside on Fő tér, centrepiece of the town. The baroque Gangel restaurant at Várkerület 25 is probably the most handsome spot for dinner. Strangely, the John Bull pub at Széchenyi tér 12 isn't bad either – and despite a menu with shepherd's pie and trifle, none of the staff speak English. The Mekong at Deák tér 46 offers some Vietnamese variety.

The Palatinus Hotel at Új utca 23 (06 99 311 395) is ugly and has small, dark rooms but is right in the middle of the Old Town. The Pannonia-Med at Várkerület 75 (06 99 312 180) is roomier but more expensive. The Jégverem Panzió, Jégverem utca 1 (06 99 312 004), a short walk from the centre across the Ikva river, has cheaper rooms.

Although most of the sights are in the Old Town, even the determinedly profit-seeking Várkerület contains some curiosities. Inspect the 1623 pharmacy at number 29, or the ancient Goger opticians opposite.

Locomotiv Tourist

Új utca 1 (06 99 311 111). **Open** Sept-Apr 9am-5pm Mon-Fri; 9am-1pm Sat. June-Aug 8.30am-4.30pm Sat. Some English spoken.
Friendly and helpful, with some English speakers on staff. They will happily show you round the Roman ruins of the Forum Museum below.

Tourinform

Előkapu 11 (06 99 338 892). **Open** May-Sept 9am-6pm Mon-Sat. Oct-Apr 9am-4pm Mon-Fri, 9am-noon Sat. Some English spoken.
Situated near the Firewatch tower. Can assist in finding accommodation.

Szeged

The first-time visitor to Szeged is invariably struck by its space and grandeur. One's immediate impressions of Hungary's third largest provincial city are of greenery and plazas, of broad boulevards and proud municipal buildings. Yet they hide a multitude of sin and misfortune, tied to the history and geography of this strangely atmospheric southern outpost. Szeged is very much a river city, but its position at the confluence of the Tisza and Maros rivers have not always done it great favour.

Szeged was all but wiped away in the Great Flood of 1879. Thanks to foreign aid, architect Lajos Lechner could produce an adventurous blueprint for a new model city of the late nineteenth century, meticulously planned with a uniform skyline. What remained of the city's era as a Turkish stronghold was washed away; Communism arrived too soon for its architects to affect the lie of the land. Across the river, Újszeged is blighted with tower blocks, but this rarely concerns most visitors. They pour into central Dóm tér in August for the annual open-air music and theatre festival. Out of season, Dóm tér is bold and imposing, with the twin spires of the Votive Church, built as a symbol of the city's post-flood renaissance, its main feature. Széchenyi tér further north is firmly the heart of the city, however – 50,000 square metres of trees, fountains and statues, presided over by the Town Hall.

Szeged – broad boulevards and proud municipal buildings.

But it is the Tisza river which is the city's leit-motif. It has both attracted and repelled scores of invaders, it made Szeged an important trading centre in the Middle Ages, and it brought the city to the centre of political debate in the middle of the last century, dividing reformers like Széchenyi who wanted to regulate and engineer against flood, and those whose livelihood had depended on it for generations. It was Count Széchenyi himself who sailed the first steamship down the Tisza to Szeged in 1833, riding through the waves in triumph as if in some Rodgers and Hammerstein musical, while Serbian women watched aghast, crossing themselves in fear.

The Tisza-Maros junction became a convenient backdrop for the redrafting of national borders following the Treaty of Trianon in 1920, which left the city vulnerable to whichever military or economic misfortunes would later befall Serbia and Romania, too often too close for comfort. With the war in Yugoslavia and subsequent economic sanctions, many became involved in the lucrative trade in smuggling petrol down south, and Szeged became synonymous with corruption and gangland killings. Economic migration from Romania and draft dodging from Serbia is visible in the scores of dodgy shops, bars and businesses opened almost overnight.

On the surface, however, the river is a pleasant amenity, convenient for summer disco boats, ideal for the mosquitos that feed off their clientele. Szeged's status as a university town does mean that much of its nightlife is affordable and lively. The JATE Klub, Toldy utca 1, attached to the college, offers a regular selection of name Hungarian bands during term time. For something more upmarket, try the Laguna cocktail bar, Híd utca 6, with its unusual decor and large collection of tropical fish.

The local dish is fish soup, *halászlé*, spiced with paprika, introduced by the Turks and as an important source of revenue to Szeged as mustard to Dijon. The Tisza Halászcsárda, Roosevelt tér 12, can serve up a mean one and certain tables offer a view of the main bridge, if not of the river itself. The most prestigious joint in town, the Alabárdos, Oskola utca 13 (06 62 420 914), requires reservations – but not on Sunday when it's closed.

Although the Royal, Kölcsey utca 1 (06 62 475 275) is Szeged's most famous hotel – Romanian gymnast Nadia Comaneci took refuge here after defecting – but its facilites do not match its high prices. Try the cheaper Hotel Hungária, Maros utca 2 (06 62 480 580) or the budget Marika Panzió, Nyíl utca 45 (06 62 443 861), tucked away near the train station.

Szeged Tourist

Klauzál tér 7 (06 62 425 731). **Open** May-Aug 9am-5pm Mon-Fri; 9am-1pm Sat. Sept-Apr Mon-Fri 9am-5pm. Some English spoken.
Can also book accommodation in private rooms. For festival tickets and other cultural information, go to the Szabadteri Jegyiroda in the same office.

Bratislava

The quirky Slovak capital offers an entertaining few days.

With a population of 450,000, Bratislava, nestled between Budapest, Vienna and Prague, is the runt of the Habsburg urban litter; it's definitely a quieter town with less going on than its bigger sisters, but is a fascinating place to poke around for a couple of days – and escape the crowds at the height of the tourist season.

The people here seem to have a youthful feeling of possibility and post-Communist enthusiasm that is missing in the larger, more cynical capitals of Prague and Budapest – especially since the electorate's September 1998 rejection of Vladimir Meciar, who had ruled with a nostalgia for the Communist days and a penchant for strong-man tactics. More than anything, the youthful feeling comes because this really is a new capital. Slovakia gained independence on 1 January 1993, when Czechoslovakia became the Czech and Slovak republics, in one of the most amicable separations this region has seen. New Year's Day is therefore a double celebration.

Though settlements and fortifications at this site date back to the Iron Age, only in 1919, after independent Czechoslovakia was carved from the ruins of the Habsburg Empire, did Slovaks take over the city and name it Bratislava. Once it was the Roman town of Posonium, perched at the edge of empire. As Breszalauspurc in the ninth century it had been part of the Great Moravian Empire. For most of the rest of history it was an Austro-Hungarian city known as Pressburg to the Germans, who provided around half its inhabitants until 1945, and as Pozsony to the Hungarians, who used it as their capital for several centuries after the Turks occupied Buda in 1541. There are still around 700,000 ethnic Hungarians in Slovakia, and you'll often hear Hungarian spoken in Bratislava.

The Habsburg empire gave Bratislava a quaint old town and a castle that looks like a giant upturned bedstead. But the old town is not always the first thing a visitor will see. There's been a lot of more recent development and the result is a strange mixture of baroque and misguided Communist-era architecture, with some recent capitalist kitsch thrown in. Persevere, and you will be rewarded by getting to know a pleasant town.

There are two sights that can properly be described as unmissable – both in the sense of must-see and of can't-be-avoided. One is the castle, up on its hill, from where there's an excellent view of the Danube and the river plain to the south and the east. The other is the Most SNP – the Bridge of the Slovak National Uprising, also known as the Nový Most, or New Bridge. This splendid example of spacey, Communist design is a single-span suspension affair, sporting a café and restaurant resembling a flying saucer, high above the Danube on its one double pylon. Catch the lift up to the restaurant from mid-bridge – although the saucer no longer revolves – the view from most tables is fantastic, either north across the city centre to the vineyard-covered small Carpathian foothills, or south over the huddled high-rise housing of Petržalka, which looks almost pretty when lit up at night.

Petržalka was once a quiet, tree-lined suburb, but its oil facilities made it a target for American bombers in World War II. During the Stalinist era, planners decided to rebuild on a grand, Socialist scale. They put up endless rows of ugly blocks to create one of the largest housing estates in the world. These acres of concrete, home to 150,000 people – a third of the city's population – are so uniform that visitors sometimes get lost for hours, unable to distinguish one street from another.

Fortunately, all that is across the river from the worthwhile part of town, and easy enough to avoid. Other vestiges of Communism include hotel porters who offer to change money on the sly, the vast square called námestie Slobody with its Fountain of Friendship and the world's largest post office, and the extraordinary inverted pyramid, on the way out of town, that houses Slovak Radio.

Even downtown, the old and new vie for attention. Right at the centre of the city, in Kamenné námestie, there is a sprawling Tesco and adjacent modern towers that house the Hotel Kyjev and the Charlie's Pub disco. Eastwards and uphill past the námestie SNP, there's the Michalská veža (Michael Tower). Legend holds that you shouldn't speak while passing through the arch at the tower's base, because the city guards were once ambushed here while chattering away. On the other side is the old town, where it's possible to get lost for a while and forget that modern architecture exists. There are several small museums and exhibits as well as some nice quiet restaurants, cafés and bars.

Compared to Budapest, Bratislava is definitely a beer town, and some local brews are certainly worth trying. Zlatý Bažant (Golden Pheasant) is now brewed under licence in Hungary and elsewhere, but the domestic version is better. Smädny Mnich (Thirsty Monk) is another delicious local brew. And, of course, you can find most of the pop-

Bratislava – the old and new vie for attention.

ular Czech beers at a great price, plus Becherovka – the deceptively sweet and easy-to-swallow Czech herbal liqueur. Enjoy a glass or two, perhaps with a beer chaser, but before you have half a dozen, try to remember what your worst hangover was like.

Typical Slovak food is bog-standard central European – schnitzel and the like – and the Hungarian influence seems evident. In fact, many restaurants are staffed by members of the city's large ethnic Hungarian population. Some uniquely Slovak dishes include *strapatzka,* egg noodles and cheese; *parenica,* decoratively twisted smoked cheese; and *cesnakova polievka,* garlic soup, which can be truly delicious.

Most of the old town shuts down by midnight, but other places are open late and filled with a young, friendly, unpretentious crowd. One of the later spots inside the old town is Bar 17s on Hviezdoslavovo námestie, a small, congenial pub that sometimes tries to squeeze live music in the back. For a beer and bar food during the day, or a late nightcap when other places close, try KGB, a long cellar bar with a not-too-obvious entrance along Obchodná (look for the picture of a beer mug) that sometimes hosts rock bands. For underground (literally) techno there's the U-Club at NAG Ludvika Svobodu, an old air-raid shelter at the foot of the castle hill that draws a tattooed-and-pierced crew. For the full Bratislava nightlife experience, it has to be Charlie's Pub, at Špitálska 4, a large underground space with two big

side rooms and a main dance floor animated by ancient pop and disco hits. Open until 4am, this is Bratislava's most popular nightspot, packed with revellers any night of the week.

There are several good hotels around the centre of town, some of which offer discounted rooms at weekends. The Perugia at Zeletná 5 (421 7 5443 1818) is the best looking of the posh new old town hotels. Fans of tatty Communist modernism will enjoy the skyrise Kyjev at Rajská 2 (421 7 361 082), just behind Tesco, with its delightfully dodgy nightclub and excellent views across the city. Some of the most affordable rooms in the heart of town are at the Gremium Penzion (421 7 544 306 53) at Gorkého 11, but it's small and often full. Most cheaper options tend to be a little out of town. BIS (below) can help in finding accommodation.

A handy pocket-sized guide and street atlas is available in various languages. The dreary local English-language paper, the fortnightly *Slovak Spectator,* is good for listings of venues and events, if little else.

BIS

Klobučnícka 2 (421 7 5443 3715). **Open** 8am-7pm Mon-Fri; 9am-2pm Sat, Sun. Some English spoken. Bratislava Information Service can help with accommodation, as well as providing information. Small selection of guidebooks on sale.
Branch: Hlavná stanica (main station) (421 7 5443 4370).

Vienna

Budapest's big sister – city state and cosmopolitan melting-pot.

Vienna is still often thought of as Budapest's 'sister city'. A big sister, certainly – and for most of history an extremely bossy sister too (though once it got tired of having its pigtails pulled, Budapest did learn how to fuss and scratch and get its own way sometimes).

Close but competitive in the Dual Monarchy days, the Danubian siblings long ago went their separate ways. You can still see they're related, though. Budapest and Vienna share Habsburg-era similarities but are distinguished by some very stark postwar contrasts – a mix that makes a visit to the Austrian capital a particularly rewarding side-trip. Where Budapest was run-down by decades of Communism, Vienna benefited from being on the frontline of western capitalism. Where Budapest is poor, self-conscious and shabby, Vienna is prosperous, smug and almost disconcertingly clean.

Budapest is very much a national capital, its whole nineteenth-century shape designed around a monumental celebration of Hungarian identity. Vienna, on the other hand, seems less the capital of Austria than a combination of the dynastic city-state it once was, and the present-day world city that is headquarters for so many international institutions. Long a cosmopolitan melting-pot, today registered foreigners count for more than one in ten of its 1.5 million inhabitants.

In Budapest the Danube dictates the whole feel of the city; in Vienna you'd hardly notice it was there. Arriving by jetfoil (*see chapter* **Getting Started**) you're dumped at a modern ferry terminal on the Danube Relief Channel, with nothing to see but a few cranes, dredgers and United Nations buildings, so far out of town that it can be hard even to find a taxi. Arriving any other way, you might not see the Danube at all, unless from the top of the big wheel in the Prater – a landmark still much the same as it was in Harry Lime's day, except with safer doors.

But prices are the first thing that hit home. A Wiener melange in a famous Viennese coffeehouse such as Sacher or Demel costs four or five times as much as a similar cup in Budapest's Művész or Gerbeaud. But at least Vienna can still afford its

Vienna – the feeling of power and wealth is still palpable.

coffeehouses and a couple of dozen old places are still pretty much intact and alive. Sacher is crap, mind you. Demel, on the other hand, at Kohlmarkt 14, is a trip: dauntingly Baroque, with waitresses who speak an absurd formal German no one uses anywhere else, and just about the most chocolatey chocolate cake in the world. At Central, on Herrengasse, where Trotsky once sat sipping coffee and planning the Russian Revolution, sits a dummy of poet Peter Altenberg, who in life more or less lived in the place.

While Budapest's ancient centre is now perched out of the way up on Castle Hill, the medieval heart of Vienna is still the city centre today. You could spend a couple of days exploring without ever having to step beyond the Ringstrasse – the circular avenue which follows the line of the old city walls. From the pedestrianised Stephansplatz, where St Stephen's Cathedral provides Vienna with its centrepiece, history radiates in concentric circles. In the medieval streets around the square and off bustly Kartner Strasse, you'll find backstreet palaces, small churches, atmospheric old squares and alleys, and any number of houses where Mozart once lived.

The area between the Cathedral and the Danube, on and around Rotenturmstrasse, is known as the Bermuda Dreiecke (Bermuda Triangle). This is the main nightlife area, where the visitor can disappear into one of dozens of late-night bars.

The next band of history, over in the south-west corner of the Innere Stadt, is dominated by the 59-acre Hofburg complex: a sprawl of palaces and parks, statues and fountains, Baroque squares and still-functioning imperial stables. This was the seat of the Habsburgs (among all the treasures and monarchical glitz you can still view the spartan iron bed that nightly reinforced Emperor Franz Joseph's sense of imperial duty) and the feeling of power and wealth, concentrated here for centuries, is still quite palpable.

The Ringstrasse (serviced, like Budapest's Nagykörút, by trams) runs in a polygonal horseshoe shape, beginning and ending at the Danube Canal. This was the line of the old city walls. Vienna has always been a border town, and the defences were knocked about and reinforced time and again throughout history (it was here that the Ottoman advance into Europe was halted in 1683) before Franz Joseph began demolishing them for good in 1857. Along the Ring, punctuated by gardens, are all the monumental public buildings of late Imperial Vienna: the ugly Opera House, the Natural History and Art History Museums (on a rainy day, check out the Breughels), the Parliament, City Hall, University and Burg Theater. It's all pretty dry stuff, in weighty neo-Gothic and neo-Renaissance styles.

It was in reaction to the pretentiousness of this façade that architect Alfred Loos designed his 'house without eyebrows' – utterly without ornamentation or illusions of past grandeur – which stands cheekily on the Michaeler Platz, opposite the gate into the Hofburg. (Griensteidl, on the ground floor, is a reasonable spot for lunch.)

For more of a taste of turn-of-the-century Vienna, move beyond the Ring to the next concentric circle. At Friedrichstrasse 12 stands the gilt-domed Sezession – home for Gustav Klimt, Otto Wagner and the 17 others who 'seceded' from the Viennese art establishment to found the local version of art nouveau. Northwards on the same radius you can visit the Sigmund Freud Museum at Berggasse 19, where the psychoanalyst's working rooms are now a public exhibit.

Beyond this outer ring lie the suburbs and working-class estates, breeding-ground of unrest and revolution in the city that Karl Kraus, on the eve of World War I, dubbed the 'proving-ground for world destruction'. The bureaucratic towers of UNO City, headquarters for the International Atomic Energy Authority, the United Nations Industrial Development Organisation and an assortment of other UN organisations, are the principal monuments to Austria's post-war neutrality.

Contemporary Vienna, removed from the centre-stage of history, is a relaxed and sleepily prosperous place where nothing very much happens any more. You can find just about anything you want in the shops and also eat very well. (After heavy Hungarian food, Neue Wiener Kuche is a light and pleasant shock to the system.) You'll mostly have to pay well for the privilege, though the Naschmarkt (just south-west of the Sezession) offers a centrally located Saturday morning flea market and daily stalls serving every kind of food you can imagine, from Japanese seafood to 'Hussar Sausages'. Vienna is full of shops selling pricey executive toys, designer fountain pens and improbable furniture, but second-hand book and music stores are dotted all over too.

Accommodation is expensive. If you want to splash out and get a true taste of *mitteleuropäisch* elegance, try the Bristol at Kärtner Ring 1 (00 43 1 515 160) or the Sacher round the corner at Philharmonikerstrasse 4 (00 43 1 514 56). There's no particularly good area for finding cheap hotels, but the Vienna Tourist Office will be able to help.

It's possible to get to Vienna and back in a day, but scarcely worth the bother. An overnighter makes more sense, but we'd recommend two nights as the ideal short stay. Just expect to spend as much in 48 hours as you would in a week in Budapest.

Vienna Tourist Office

1025 Augardenstraße 40 (00 43 1 211 140). **Open** 9am-7pm daily. English spoken.
Helpful and with English-speaking staff. For last-minute room bookings go the office at 1010 Kärtner Straße 38.
Branch: West Station (00 43 1 892 3392).

Zagreb

Should the Balkans beckon, the Croat capital offers some curiously uncosmopolitan contrasts.

Around six hours by train from Budapest, with a café culture, sense of style and cuisine of fresh fish and vegetables that mark it as a city more Mediterranean than *mitteleuropäisch*, Zagreb is a curious contrast to the Hungarian capital. Provincial and quiet, its proximity to Balkan flashpoints throughout the 1990s also means that it's refreshingly far from normal tourist trails.

There are at least three Zagrebs: the medieval twin towns of Gradec and Kaptol, perched on the foothills of Medvednica mountain; the carefully planned nineteenth-century Lower Town, with its abundance of parks, tree-lined avenues and public buildings; and the unloved twentieth-century city of heavy industry and housing estates that extends south across the river Sava. In the last century alone the city has experienced five different forms of political authority: nominal Hungarian control as part of the Habsburg Empire till 1918; the troubled Kingdom of Serbs, Croats and Slovenes between the wars; pseudo-independence as headquarters of the Nazi-sponsored Ustaša puppet state; semi-independence in the Socialist Federal Republic of Yugoslavia till 1990; and now a decade as the proud capital of the first fully sovereign Croatian state of modern times.

Independence has meant having to face the usual problems of post-Communist transition, plus the consequences of the fratricidal wars that followed the break-up of Yugoslavia. Nowadays most Zagrebians are impatient to speed up the process of European integration, consolidate their democratic culture and move on from the nationalist provincialism of the Tudjman era. The casual visitor will find the city less cosmopolitan and open than Budapest (or the Zagreb of the 1980s for that matter), but more friendly and global than it was in the immediate aftermath of the war.

The oldest and most atmospheric part of Zagreb is the Upper Town (Gornji Grad or Gradec), which until 1850 was administratively separate from Kaptol (seat of the bishopric, including the cathedral). A fun and lazy way to reach it is to take the funicular from Tomićeva, a couple of blocks west along Ilica from Jelačić Square. The white tower at the top has been firing a cannon salvo at noon since the sixteenth century, originally to scare away the Turks encamped across the river Sava. There's an ice-cream stand and a good view of the city from the promenade. At the centre of this virtually car-free

warren of streets, lit by gas lamps at night, are the late-Gothic Saint Mark's Church and the Croatian parliament, the Sobor. The recently renovated City of Zagreb Museum (Opatička 20) is worth a look both for the imaginatively presented history of the city (captions in Croatian and English), and for a taste of Tudjmanite ideological excesses in its treatment of World War II, Communism and the 'War of Croatian Independence'.

There's more living history to be had in a visit to Zagreb Cathedral, just up from Trg bana Jelačića and centre of the Kaptol district. The building reflects the vicissitudes of Zagreb's history. It was begun in 1276 in early Gothic, with the nave and aisles constructed in High Gothic in the fourteenth and fifteenth centuries. Attention turned in the sixteenth century to fortifying the city against the Turks, so finishing the cathedral had to wait another couple of hundred years. The organic harmony of its Gothic, Renaissance and baroque styles was lost when the cathedral was brutally restored in late-nineteenth century neo-Gothic, with a new façade, two tall spires and a Viennese-style roof of glazed tiles. Inside there are memorials to Croat heroes, including Stjepan Radić, murdered in the Belgrade parliament in 1928 by Serb extremists, and Archbishop Stepinac, imprisoned by Tito after World War II.

The elegant squares and architecture of the Lower Town (Donji Grad) are a product of nineteenth-century planning. 'Lenuzzi's horseshoe' (named after the chief engineer of the project) is a connected series of seven squares and green areas, each the site of an important public building. Heading north from the main railway station (1892), you come first to the Art Pavilion, a pre-fab metal structure transported from Budapest's Millennium exhibition and erected in 1898, and then to the neo-Renaissance Academy of Arts and Sciences (1884). The whole of Zagreb's 'green-belt' is a display of bourgeois taste, with flower beds, public benches, fountains and sculptures.

Further north is the main square, named after controversial governor Jelačić. His equestrian statue was erected in 1866 facing east towards Budapest – a symbol of anti-Hungarian feeling and Croatian aspirations for independence. Jelačić had helped to defeat the Revolution of 1848-49 by sending Croatian troops in support of the Habsburgs. In 1947 the statue was removed at the request of fraternal

Zagreb – squares, green areas and important public buildings.

Hungarian Communists, only to be returned in 1990; but, in an act of crude symbolism, he was repositioned charging south towards Serbian separatists in the Krajina region. Just north of the square is the Dolac market, where the range and quality of fruit and vegetables on display brings home how much closer to the Mediterranean Zagreb is than Budapest.

The British-style Maksimir Park (six stops east by tram 11 or 12 from Jelačić Square) is a splendid example of the horticultural aspirations of Romanticism and the first public park in south-east Europe. For a contrasting taste of the twentieth-century city, take tram 6 south from Jelačić Square; once beyond the railway lines you'll pass the vaguely constructivist main bus station, cross socialist-realist Vukovar Avenue, go under a motorway with stadium lighting, and rattle over the Sava on the Bridge of Youth into the high-rise Socialist-era suburbia of New Zagreb.

Accommodation is more expensive than in Budapest. At the budget end, there's the youth hostel at Petrinjska 77 (434 964), not far from the station. The 'B' category Astoria nearby at number 71 (430 444) is comfortable and serves a decent breakfast. The Dubrovnik is also mid-range and centrally located near Trg bana Jelačića at Gajeva 1 (455 5155). For locally flavoured luxury try the Esplanade at Mihanovićeva 1 (456 6666).

In the centre of town, it seems that every other building houses a café. Zagrebians love to put on their best clothes and stroll around, bump into friends, and find a table on their favourite terrace to enjoy a *kava s šlagom*. Always busy is the excellent Boban's on Gajeva, owned by Croatia's star footballer (get your souvenir key ring from the football shop on Trg bana Jelačića).

Nightlife usually begins in a café, especially on and around Tkalčićeva, a narrow street full of bars that runs off Jelačića and weaves up the gully between Kaptol and Gornji Grad. After chucking-out time (technically 11pm, but often later), there are nightclubs. Gjuro II (Medveščak 2) and Lapidarije (Habdelićeva 1) are popular alternative clubs, while house and rave can be found at Aquarius (in a tent by the Sava) and at the stupidly named but happening The Best, in the Mladost Sports Centre.

Zagreb restaurants tend to be overpriced and uninspiring, but the snack options are interesting. Around the Dolac market there are places specialising in *burek* (greasy pastry filled with white cheese or mince) and *cevapčiči* (spicy pork fingers in moist bread). Or seek out a Croatian fish shop – such as the Mali Phoenix at Jurišićeva 19, a couple of blocks east of Trg bana Jelačića – where you can get deep-fried sardines or squid (with chips if you want) fresh from the Adriatic. Pizzerias are ubiquitous; the Nocturno off Tkalčićeva at Skalinska 4 (276 428) is popular and well located.

For general what's-on information pick up the free monthly guide *Zagreb Events and Performances* from **Tourist Information** on Trg bana Jelačića. For more alternative happenings, a good source of flyers and rumours is Sublink, an Internet café at Klekovačka 30 (www.sublink.cr). Zagreb is something of an insiders' city, so your best bet is to find a decent café, get chatting to the locals and join the grapevine.

Tourist Information

Trg bana Jelečića 11 (00 385 1 481 4051). **Open** 8.30am-8pm Mon-Fri; 10am-6pm Sat; 10am-2pm Sun. On the main square. Lots of useful free information and maps. English spoken.
Branch: Trg Nicole Subića Zrinskog 14 (455 2867).

Further Abroad

Beyond Hungary, dodgy destinations and eastern delights.

Budapest is an excellent staging post for an assortment of uncommon destinations. UK citizens require visas for Romania, Serbia and the Ukraine, but not for Slovakia or Slovenia. Citizens of other countries should check with their embassies.

Romania

In Transylvanian Romania, you still see horses and carts sharing roadspace with oil tankers, and in parts some folk customs have remained largely unchanged for centuries.

In the cities, hotel prices are pegged five times higher for foreigners than for locals. Food and service are appalling and outside hotel bars and discos there is a lack of anything resembling decent nightlife. The people, though poor, are friendly enough. A visit to Romania, even nine years after Ceauşescu, is still a shock to the system. Visiting some rural areas is like travelling back in time to fourteenth-century Switzerland. Don't expect modern creature comforts, and if intending to stay in the country, remember to pack some flea powder.

Most Romanian cities are easily accessible from Budapest by rail, but expect some crowded and uncomfortable train journeys.

Slovakia

Beyond Bratislava, the Tatras, up on the border with Poland, are like a mini-Alps with possibly the cheapest skiing in Europe. Tatranska Lomnica is the most distinguished resort. Košice in East Slovakia is the country's second-largest city with substantial Gypsy and Hungarian populations. Referred to as Kassa by Hungarians, who ruled here until 1920, Košice is a short and worthwhile hop over the border from Miskolc. Much has been spent on renovating the lively, impressive town centre, but little on its drab and dodgy outskirts.

Slovenia

This small former Yugoslav state, with Alps and a short Adriatic coastline within 40 minutes of each other, is like a Slavic version of Austria. Lake Bled, surrounded by woodland and mountains, is a popular destination, but the capital, Ljubljana, is the main attraction (seven hours from Budapest by rail). A long-established radical art scene – this

The Ukraine – poor and in places irradiated.

is the home of NSK (Neue Slowenische Kunst) a multi-headed arts organisation centred on the group Laibach – is reflected in some interesting nightlife options.

The Ukraine

Poor and in places irradiated, with highwaymen who rob buses (and even give you a receipt you can show the next band of highwaymen to prove you've already been ripped off), a trip to the Ukraine really is a journey into the Wild East. Visas are issued only to people who have a letter of invitation from an official organisation. Kiev is beautiful, though.

Yugoslavia

The Kosovo conflict of 1999 means that a visit to Serbia is a daunting if not dangerous prospect. Apart from the tricky problem of obtaining a visa (even before the recent war UK citizens needed a prior letter of invitation), westerners are not likely to be welcomed in Serbia. Much of the country suffered serious damage by Nato forces and at press time the potentially explosive internal political situation was changing almost every day. No one can be sure what lies ahead.

Before the war, there was a regular train service from Budapest to Belgrade, taking seven hours plus an occasional long wait at the border. The Serbian capital, whose only real tourist attraction has always been the Kalemegdan fortress, once had a nightlife second to none in the former Yugoslavia. It is not yet clear how much the city's bars and clubs have been affected by the bombing, postwar economic woes and political instability.

Directory

Directory

Essential information

Crime

Although crime – particularly organised crime – has risen considerably in the 1990s, Budapest remains a relatively safe city. But as anywhere, a little common sense goes a long way. Watch out for pickpockets and purse-snatchers around Váci utca, the Castle District, Heroes' Square and at stations. Don't exchange money on the street. Be careful on trams 2, 4 and 6, where gangs sometimes operate. Be careful if walking alone at night around outlying areas of town or District VIII around Rákóczi tér.

If you are black, Asian or Middle Eastern in appearance, be wary of the growing number of racist, skinhead gangs. They hang around in outlying areas and metro stations, so consider taking a taxi if alone or in a dodgy-looking neighbourhood. The police tend not to be of much assistance.

You are obliged by law to carry identification on you at all times and the police can make spot checks. In practice you are unlikely to be checked.

Customs

Coming into Hungary, any items of clothing or objects that could be deemed to be for personal use are exempt from duties. Individuals over 16 years old are also allowed to bring in 250 cigarettes, 50 cigars or 250 grams of tobacco, as well as two litres of wine, one litre of spirits and five litres of beer. Merchandise up to a value of Ft30,300 is allowed in duty-free, after which a 15 per cent duty

Useful numbers

Inland operator: **191**
Directory enquiries: **198**
International operator (English spoken): **190**
International directory enquiries (English spoken): **199**
Police: **107**
Fire/emergency: **105**
Ambulance: **104** or (in English): **311 1666**
Sending telegrams (charged to your phone bill/English spoken): **192**
Wake-up service: **193**
Exact time: **080**

and two per cent customs tax are payable in addition to 25 per cent ÁFA (VAT). In practice, foreigners are rarely checked. There is no limit to the amount of foreign currency that you can bring in.

It is forbidden to bring in drugs or arms.

On exit the following limits apply:
● wine – 2 litres
● spirits – 1 litre
● 250 cigarettes or 50 cigars or 250g of tobacco
● Ft303,000 worth of gifts.
It is also forbidden to take more than Ft100,000 out of the country.

Dentists

See **Health**.

Disabled travellers

Despite being home to the world famous Pető Institute, which treats children with cerebral palsy, Budapest does not have much access for the disabled. Public transport is basically

inaccessible, apart from the M1 metro line. The airport minibus is accessible. There is a special BKV bus, use of which can be arranged through MEOSZ, who also have their own minibus and can provide a helper. The **Museum of Fine Arts**, **Museum of Applied Arts** and **Foundry Museum** (*see chapter* **Museums**) are now accessible, as is the **National Foreign-Language Library** (*see below* **Libraries**).

Wherever new stretches of street are built, there are ramps for wheelchairs, and all new buildings, such as Budapest's shopping malls (*see chapter* **Shopping & Services**) and the numerous new office blocks, are now designed with the disabled in mind. There are also a limited number of trips available, such as Balaton by train once a week. For more details phone:

Hungarian Disabled Association
MEOSZ
III. San Marco utca 76 (368 1758).
Tram 1. **Open** 8am-4pm Mon-Fri.
English spoken.

Doctors

See **Health**.

Driving in Budapest

Budapest has all the traffic problems of most modern European cities with a few extra ones thrown in. Hungarian driving is not good. Hungarians have constant urges to overtake in the most impossible places, they lack concentration and jump traffic lights. There are a lot of accidents, mostly cars going into the backs of other cars. Many vehicles are of poor quality. Roads are even worse. Cobbled streets abound, designed to tax even the sturdiest suspension. There has been a huge influx of western cars in recent years, increasing traffic levels and daytime parking problems. Practically all central streets are jammed from 7am to 7pm on weekdays due to roadworks and detours. This is the beginning of the long process of replacing cobblestones and old tram tracks, and making pavements inaccessible for parking cars. Talk of restricting traffic in certain areas has not yet amounted to much.

Keep cars locked and fitted with an alarm if possible. Take the radio out and do not leave anything visible inside.

Old habits, new laws

Across much of Europe, law-makers and enforcers are becoming less enthusiastic about locking up drug users. While America's 'war on drugs' accomplishes little more than bloating its prison population, many European states have effectively decriminalised the possession of moderate amounts of so-called soft drugs. Hungary, however, has moved in the opposite direction.

In force since May 1999, a law substantially stiffens the potential penalties for the possession of drugs, from cannabis to heroin. The law allows up to two years' imprisonment for possessing the smallest amount of marijuana, ecstasy or other recreational drugs even when it is obvious the offender had no intent to distribute the substance. For possession of a 'significant' amount, the maximum is five years in jail. Finally, if the offender had the intent to sell or otherwise distribute the drug, the minimum sentence is five years in jail, and maximum is life imprisonment.

In practice, police claim to have no plans to imprison small-time users. The harshest penalties, they say, are for dealers. Then why the option to imprison a first-time offender for up to two years?

There appear to be two reasons. First, authorities appear to believe drug use is primarily a threat to law and order (as opposed to the western European view of it as a health issue). Second, officials see drug use as an important and growing source of income for organised criminal groups, including Russian and Ukrainian groups considered some of the most dangerous in the world.

At a recent international conference on corruption and crime held in Budapest, Hungary's police commander, General László Orban, detailed his understanding of the link between drug use and other crime, stating that many using marijuana and ecstasy were 'students or unemployed' on limited incomes. Once they have spent their meagre funds on drugs in the first fortnight of the month, he explained, they clearly then financed their habits by stealing cars and breaking into homes. Thus the prevailing attitude in the senior ranks of Hungary's finest clearly links recreational drug use with reckless criminal behaviour.

With a potentially harsh sentence hanging over any pot-smoker, police obviously feel they have a trump card to play against offenders they see as on the road toward committing greater crimes.

As for organised crime, police are clearly challenged in trying to penetrate the upper reaches of the most dangerous gangs. Often, the latter are led by members of the former Soviet elite, who are well educated, highly sophisticated and adept at concealing their own connections to the illegal activity they control. In response, police have declared they will be more effective at chasing away organised crime by strangling their sources of cash from the bottom than by attempting to convict gangsters at the top.

Other governments have attacked from the same direction not by threatening drug users but by easing laws against drug use, thereby loosening the supply, lowering prices and taking trade away from criminal organisations. But such an approach would not sit well when the prevailing attitude among Hungarian police and politicians holds that each and every drug user is a potentially dangerous criminal.

Information essential

When in doubt, do it backwards – that's the rule of thumb in these parts. Hungarians put their family names first and their first names last. Addresses begin with the postcode, are followed by the city, then the street name and finally the house, floor and flat numbers.

All the stuff that would go in the top right-hand corner of a British or American letter (address, date etc) is placed in the bottom left-hand corner in Hungary. And don't forget that dates are written year/month/day.

Perhaps this follows from the Magyar tongue, which sort of works backwards as well. It's what linguists call an agglutinative language, in which all the defining bits of a word – the work that in English is done by prepositions and prefixes – get stacked up at the end of it. This is so different from English that it makes the process of learning Hungarian a little like having to rewire your brain. (*See chapter* **Language**.)

Also, remember that when going into a restaurant or bar, Hungarian men always enter before women. The final, surreal, touch is that Hungarians say 'Szia!' (pronounced 'seeya') where we would say 'hello' and say 'helló' where we might say 'see you'. *Helló!*

If you cannot find your car where you left it, it does not necessarily mean it has been stolen. It may have been towed away for illegal parking. If so, go to the nearest police station. In the centre this is at V. Szalay utca 11-13 near the Parliament.

● Seatbelts must be worn at all times.

● Always carry your passport, driving licence (not necessarily an international one – UK and US ones are generally accepted), vehicle registration document, evidence of motor insurance (green card insurance is not compulsory for those insured in the UK), and *zöldkártya* (exhaust emissions certificate for cars registered in Hungary. Do not leave anything of value in the car, especially car documents.

● Headlights are compulsory by day when driving outside town, although not on motorways.

● Priority is from the right unless you are on a priority road, signified by a yellow diamond on a white background. Whatever the case, drive with caution on one-way roads.

● Watch out for trams, particularly in places where the passengers alight in the middle of the road. Watch out for other drivers – they may not be watching you.

● The speed limit on motorways is 120 kph, on highways (signified by a white car on a blue background) 90 kph, on all other roads 80 kph unless otherwise indicated, and 50 kph in built-up areas. Speed traps abound, with spot fines that vary greatly, especially for foreigners.

● The alcohol limit is 0.08 per cent and there are many spot checks, especially at night, with severe penalties for the guilty. Take a taxi if drinking (*see* **Getting Around**).

Breakdowns

A 24-hour breakdown service is provided by the Magyar Autóklub, who have reciprocal agreements with many European associations. English and German are usually spoken, but if not they will ask you for the model (*típus*), colour (*szín*) and the number plate (*rendszám*) of the vehicle and also the location. Assistance is fairly rapid.

Magyar Autóklub

(212 3952/emergency 188). **Open** 24 hours daily. **No credit cards** but will accept a credit letter from affiliated organisations. English spoken.

There are also these private breakdown services:

City Segély

(334 2977). **Open** 24 hours daily. **No credit cards**. No English spoken.

Start

(276 8302). **Open** 24 hours daily. **No credit cards**. Some English spoken.

Túra Team Club Breakdown Service

(262 0189). **Open** 24 hours daily. **Credit** AmEx, MC, V. English spoken.

Parking

Parking is not easy any more and towing and wheel clamping are in force. Most parking is on the pavements – just copy everybody else. Certain areas have parking meters that, in working hours, cost Ft150-Ft200 an hour in the centre for a maximum of two hours, and Ft100-Ft150 in other districts. Parking attendants control certain central areas such as V. Március 15 tér or under the Nyugati station flyover where prices are Ft60-Ft80 an hour. Multi-storey car parks are on V. Bárczy István utca 2 just off Petőfi Sándor utca and another at V. Türr István utca 5. Both cost Ft300 an hour or Ft3,000 per day.

Petrol

Most filling stations are open 24 hours and sell all types of fuel. Unleaded is *ólommentes*. Stay away from any fuel marked with a K as this is for lawnmowers and Trabants.

Most stations are self-service but some still have attendants, to whom people generally give a modest tip. Nearly all petrol stations accept credit cards and sell tobacco and basic groceries.

Drugs

Drugs are illegal in Hungary and the police regularly raid certain bars in Budapest to enforce this. Strict new laws underline the FIDESZ government's commitment to solving the problem in the American way (*see page 255* **Old habits, new laws**).

If caught with a small amount of drugs, you can be sentenced to two years' imprisonment. If it is a first-time offence and you are not addicted and are not dealing, especially not to minors, at or near a school, dormitory or cultural centre, you might get away with a fine, compulsory social work or a warning.

Someone caught with more than a small amount of drugs can receive up to five years in prison. For someone arrested with a large amount of drugs, the punishment can be anything from a five-year imprisonment to a life sentence, depending on whether the drugs were for personal use or for peddling.

Small amounts of drugs are defined as follows:

Amphetamines 1-10 grams
Ecstasy 10-20 tablets
Heroin 1-6 grams
Cocaine 3-8 grams
LSD 5-15 pieces
Methadone 200 pieces
Grass 12-100 grams
Hashish 30-100 grams

Large amounts are defined as 20 times the small amounts.

If the police consider you suspicious, they have the right to stop and search, and if you were driving, they can give you a compulsory urine and blood test. In all these cases you have the right to ask for a lawyer or to call your own. In a drug-related medical emergency call 104. Doctors have to observe the strict laws of confidentiality.

Hungarian Civil Liberties Union

I. Jégverem utca 8. Third floor, door 12 (214 7102/fax 201 7375/ hclu@mail.c3.hu). Bus 16, 86, 105. **Open** 10am-4pm Mon-Fri. English spoken. **Map B3.**
Website: www.c3.hu/~hclu

Drog Stop Hotline

(06 80 50 56 78). **Open** 24 hours daily. Some English spoken.

Kék Pont Drug Consultation Center

(215 4922). **Open** *telephone enquiries* 10am-6pm Mon-Fri. Some English spoken.

Education

See also chapter **Children**.

Universities

Central European University (CEU)

V. Nádor utca 9 (327 3000/fax 327 3001). M2 Kossuth Lajos tér. **Open** 9am-5pm Mon-Thur; 9am-3pm Fri. **Map C3**
Founded in 1991 by George Soros, CEU offers postgraduate courses for students from central and eastern Europe and the former USSR. Departments include History, Legal Studies, Gender Studies and Political and Environmental Sciences.

Eötvös Loránd University

Eötvös Loránd Tudományos Egyetem (ELTE)
International Secretariat – V. Piarista köz 1 (postal address 1364 Budapest, PO Box 107) (267 0966 ext 5171/fax 266 3521). M3 Ferenciek tere. **Open** 10am-2pm Mon-Thur; 10am-noon Fri. **Map C4**
The largest and oldest Hungarian university, this was founded in 1635 in Nagyszombat (now Trnava, Slovakia), moved to Buda in 1777, and to Pest in 1784. Today there are 12,000 students at the Faculty of Humanities, Sciences, Law and the Institute of Sociology.

Budapest University of Economic Sciences

Budapesti Közgazdaságtudományi Egyetem (BKE)
International Studies Centre – IX. Fővám tér 8 (217 0608). Tram 2, 47, 49. **Open** 8am-noon, 1-4.30pm, Mon-Thur; 8am-2pm Fri. **Map D5**
An independent institution since 1948, the BKE (known as the *Közgáz*, 'public gas', a pun on *gazdaság*, 'economics':) issues diplomas in International Economics and Business, and Political Studies.

Budapest Technical University

Budapesti Műszaki Egyetem (BME)
International Student Centre – XI. Műegyetem rakpart 3 (463 1408/fax 463 2520). Bus 86. **Open** 9am-4pm Mon-Thur; 9am-2pm Fri. **Map C6**
Established in 1782, the BME has over 9,000 students studying at seven faculties that include Architecture and Chemical, Electrical and Civil Engineering. The education is highly practical, and BME is among the few Hungarian institutions whose diplomas are accepted throughout the world.

Semmelweis University of Medicine

Semmelweis Orvostudományi Egyetem (SOTE)
English Secretariat – VIII. Üllői út 26 (266 0452). M3 Klinikák. **Open** 1-4pm Mon; 10am-3pm Tue, Thur; 9am-1pm Fri.
Over 200 years old, and in its current form since 1955, when the faculties of Pharmacy and Dentistry were incorporated. Ignác Semmelweis, who discovered the cause of puerperal fever, taught here in the 1800s.

Learning Hungarian

Arany János Nyelviskola

VI. Csengery utca 68 (311 8870). M1 Oktogon/tram 4, 6. **Open** 10am-5.30pm Mon-Thur; 10am-3.30pm Fri. **Map D2**
One of the largest language schools, offering courses in most European tongues. Five-, ten- or 15-week courses of 60 lessons are available for Ft29,400. International student ID nets a ten per cent discount.

Eötvös Loránd University, Faculty of Humanities

V. Piarista köz 1 (267 0966/ext 5171). M3 Ferenciek tere. **Open** 9am-4pm Mon-Thur; 9am-2pm Fri. **Map C4**
ELTE organises a summer university for foreigners with Hungarian-language classes. During the

academic year, a two-term Hungarian course is available. Participants are registered as regular students, and, if they study at a college in their home country, may use the credits they receive here. ELTE also offers 20-week intensive Hungarian courses and survival evening courses at Ft800 for 45 minutes.

Hungarian Language School

VI. Rippl-Rónai utca 4 (351 1191). M1 Hősök tere. **Open** *9am-4pm Mon, Tue, Thur, Fri; 9am-7pm Wed.* **Map D3**
Two-, three-, and four-week courses throughout the year at different levels. A four-week survival course costs $90, a three-week intensive summer course with cultural programmes is around $210.

Kodolányi János Institute

XI. Zsombolyai utca 3 (385 2646). Bus 7. **Open** *office 8am-4pm Mon-Fri.* **Map B6**
A four-week intensive Hungarian course (80 lessons) is available in the summer for $350 and a 12-week evening course (22 lessons) is $240.

Katedra Nyelviskola

V. Fővám tér 2 (118 2051). M3 Kálvin tér/tram 2. **Open** *office 8am-4pm Mon-Fri.* **Map C5**
Intensive and not-so-intensive Hungarian courses at different levels. For between Ft12,000 and Ft20,000 for five or 10 weeks.

Electricity

The current used in Hungary is 220v, which works fine with British 240v appliances. If you have US 110v gadgets it is best to bring the appropriate transformers with you. Plugs have two round pins, so bring an adaptor for any other plug.

The Hungarian way of death

'Sunday is gloomy/With shadows I spend it all/My heart and I have/Decided to end it all...'
Gloomy Sunday: Billie Holiday sang the best-known version, sighing her way through the story of a poor young soul whose reason to live has died with her lover. It's so laden with dejection and self-pity that it should be no surprise to learn the original was Hungarian – a people with an ingrained sense of self-pity and alarming suicide rate.

Gloomy Sunday's lyrics were penned in 1927 by László Jávor at the Kulacs restaurant on VII. Osváth utca 11, to music by Rezső Seress. An immediate smash hit in Budapest, it inspired a rash of suicides. Several young men climbed to the upper reaches of the Chain Bridge, where they left behind a red rose and copy of the song's lyrics before leaping to silty deaths in the Danube.

Hungary's romance with suicide is long and painful. Until 1994, Hungarians were killing themselves at a faster rate than anyone else. In 1980, they reached 45 per 100,000 – miles ahead of the competition. Today they rank second at 32 per 100,000. By comparison, the US rate is 12. Today's top one and three are Estonians (37) and Finns (31), the only Europeans remotely related to Magyars. Is there something locked deep in the Finno-Ugric mind that leads them down the dark road of despair?

Hungarians, apart from tenuous links to Finns and Estonians, are culturally and linguistically isolated. A small nation prone to foreign domination, they have no bridge to any greater people, community or identity. They are alone. They excel in solitary, inspired endeavours, as in the arts or sciences. They are dismal team-players.

Speaking more concretely, Hungarians drink a lot, too. While public drunkness is not taboo, seeking treatment for an alcohol problem is. As a result, wholly untreated alcoholism is rampant, and alcoholics, say pyschologists, are 55 times more likely to commit suicide than non-alcoholics. (Hungarians also lead in deaths by falling, deaths by drowning, and incidence of cirrhosis of the liver.) Yet it is unclear whether suicides can be blamed on alcoholism or whether some separate set of demons contributes both to suicide and alcoholism.

While Hungarians are more likely to commit suicide than most, these are more likely to have their deaths recorded as such. There is no great shame brought upon the family when Uncle Pisti decides to go out on his own terms. His death is not quietly announced as an accident. He might even be judged to have taken an honourable exit. After all, he'd be joining illustrious company. In addition to the *Gloomy Sunday* brigade, many a famous Hungarian has committed suicide, often in dramatic or romantic fashion. Count István Széchenyi, 'the greatest Hungarian', killed himself in 1860. The nation's greatest poet, Attila József, jumped in front of a train in 1937. In 1941, when Hungary's leadership cast its lot with Nazi Germany, Prime Minister Pál Teleki registered his disappointment by shooting himself in the head. Miss Hungary 1985 swallowed a lethal dose of lidocaine.

But the numbers have been dropping in recent years, perhaps even further as Hungary moves closer to the EU and Hungarians come to believe they are not, after all, alone in the world.

Embassies & consulates

For a full list or embassies and consulates look in the phone book or Yellow Pages under *Külképviseletek*.

American Embassy
V. Szabadság tér 12 (267 4400/267 4614). M3 Arany János utca. **Open** 8.30-11am Mon-Fri. **Map C3**

Australian Embassy
XII. Királyhágó tér 8/9 (201 8899). M2 Déli. **Open** 9am-noon Mon-Fri.

British Embassy
V. Harmincad utca 6 (266 2888). M1 Vörösmarty tér/M1, M2, M3 Deák tér/tram 47, 49. **Open** 9.30am-noon, 2.30pm-4pm, Mon-Fri. **Map C4**

Canadian Embassy
XII Budakeszi út 32 (275 1200). Bus 22. **Open** 8am-noon Mon-Fri.

Croat Consulate
XII. Arató utca 22/B (249 2215). Tram 59. **Open** 10am-noon Mon-Fri.

Irish Embassy
V. Szabadság tér 7/9 (302 9600). M2 Kossuth tér. **Open** 9.30am-12.30pm, 2.30pm-4.30pm, Mon-Fri. **Map C3**

New Zealand Consulate
I. Attila út 125 (331 4908). M2 Déli. **Open** by appointment only. **Map A3**

Romanian Embassy
XIV. Thököly út 72 (352 0251). Bus 7. **Open** 8.30am-noon Mon-Wed; 8.30-11.30am Fri.

Russian Embassy
VI. Bajza utca 35 (302 5230). M1 Bajza utca. **Open** 8am-noon Mon, Wed, Fri. **Map E2**

Slovak Embassy
XIV. Stefánia út 22 (251 1700). Bus 7. **Open** 8.30-11.30am, 2-3.30pm, Mon-Fri.

Slovenian Embassy
II. Cseppkő utca 68 (325 9202). Bus 11. **Open** 9am-noon Mon-Fri.

South African Embassy
VIII.Rákóczi út 1-3 (267 4566). M2 Astoria. **Open** 9am-12.30pm Mon-Fri. **Map D4.**

Ukrainian Embassy
XII. Nógrádi utca 8 (355 2443). Bus 21. **Open** 9am-noon Mon-Wed, Fri.

Yugoslav Embassy
VII. Dózsa György út 92A (322 9838). M1 Hősök tere. **Open** 10am-1pm Mon-Fri. **Map E2**

Health

Despite severe cutbacks and restrictions, the Hungarian health service is still considered to be one of the best in Eastern Europe. The service provided is adequate, although a lot of queuing may be involved. Most doctors will speak some kind of English. Emergency care is provided free to citizens of the UK, Finland, Norway, Sweden and former socialist countries, although it is probably wise to take out medical insurance. Those working here should get a TB (social security) card through their employer, to obtain free state health treatment, and register with a local GP. Private clinics now offer the opportunity to avoid the queues and discuss problems in English.

Emergencies/hospitals

In an emergency the best thing to do is to go to the casualty department of the nearest hospital. Take along a Hungarian speaker and always carry with you some form of identification.

Ambulances

The normal emergency number is 104 but this will generally be Hungarian-speaking only. If you call 311 1666 you should be able get hold of an English or German speaker.

Private clinics

IMS
XIII. Váci út 202 (329 8423/349 9349). M3 Újpest Városkapu. **Open** 8am-8pm Mon-Fri. **Credit** AmEx, MC. English spoken.

Professional Orvosi Kft
V. Múzeum körút 35, Third Floor, no 6 (317 0631). M3 Kálvin tér. **Open** 4-8pm Mon; 8am-noon Tue, Thur; 8am-noon, 4-8pm, Wed. **No credit cards. Map D4**

R Klinika
II. Felsőzöldmáli út 13 (325 9999). Bus 29. **Open** 8am-6pm daily, 24 hours in emergencies. **Credit** AmEx, JCB, MC, V.

Pharmacies

Pharmacies (*patika* or *gyógyszertár*) are marked by a green cross outside. Opening hours are generally 8am-6pm or 8am-8pm Mon-Fri, with some also open on Saturday mornings. Some English will be spoken in all of these pharmacies. The following are open 24 hours:
II. Frankel Leó utca 22 (212 4406).
VI. Teréz körút 41 (311 4439).
VIII. Rákóczi út 39 (314 3695).
IX. Boráros tér 3 (217 5997).
XII. Alkotás út 1/B (355 4691).

Dentists

Although there is state dental care, most people go private if they can. Prices are reasonable compared to the West, as evidenced by the number of Austrians flocking over to have their molars scrutinised. German and/or English are spoken in the clinics listed below.

Dental Co-op
XII. Zugligeti út 58/60 (275 1444). Bus 158. **Open** 9am-6pm Mon-Fri; 1-6pm Thur. **Credit** AmEx, MC, V. Some English spoken.

Super Dent
XIII. Dózsa György út 65 (239 0569). M3 Dózsa György út. **Open** 8.30am-2pm Mon, Wed, Fri; 2-7pm Tue, Thur. **Credit** AmEx. English spoken.

SOS Dental Clinic
VI. Király utca 14 (267 9602/269 6010). M1, M2, M3 Deák tér/tram 47, 49. **Open** 24 hours daily. **Credit** AmEx, DC, JCB, MC, V. **Map C4**

Chiropractor

Dr Jack Conway
XI. Györök utca 2 (385 2515). Tram 19. **Open** 8-11am, 2-5pm, Mon-Fri. **No credit cards.** English spoken.

Poison control centres

Erzsébet Kórház
VII. Alsó Erdősor utca 7 (322 3450). M2 Blaha Lujza tér. Some English spoken. **Map E3**

Heim Pál Kórház
XI. Üllői út 86 (210 0720/333 5079). M3 Nagyvárad tér. Some English spoken. **Map F6** For children only.

Budapest by numbers

Population of Budapest **1,8 million**
Population of Budapest plus Pest county
2,85 million
Area of Budapest in square km **525**
Population of Hungary **10,1 million**
Area of Hungary in square km **93,030**

Number of foreigners visiting Hungary in
1998 **33,624,000**

Number of university/college students in
1999 **163,000**

Ethnic divisions: Hungarian **94.5%**
Gypsy **4.5%**
German **0.4%**
Croatian **0.2%**
Romanian **0.1%**
Slovak **0.1%**

Religions: Roman Catholic **65%**
Protestant **25%**
Eastern Orthodox **4%**
Jewish **3%**

Natural growth of population in 1980: **0.3
per 1,000 inhabitants**
Natural growth of population in 1998: **-4.3
per one thousand inhabitants**

Life expectancy: men **66.4 years**; women
75 years

Global ranking of Hungary for:
heart diseases **1**
tobacco consumption **2**
suicide **2**
alcohol consumption **3**
Olympic medals **9**

State budget revenues: **Ft 4,693 billion**
State budget expenditures: **Ft 4,846
billion**
Budget deficit: **Ft153 billion**
GDP: **$4,504 per capita**
Growth rate: **5.1%**
Expected growth rate in 1999: **4%**
Estimated ratio of the black economy: **30%**
Ratio of the private sector in the economy in
1998: **80%**

Directory

AIDS & STDs

AIDS remains at a relatively
low level in Hungary, although
this may soon be on the
increase with the influx of
foreigners, lack of public
awareness and high
promiscuity. *See also chapter*
Gay & Lesbian.

AIDS hotline
(338 2419). **Open** 8am-4pm Mon-
Thur; 8am-1pm Fri. Some English
spoken.

Skin & Genital Clinic
Bőr és Nemikórtani Klinika
VIII. Mária utca 41 (266 0465). M3
Ferenc körút. **Open** 8am-4pm Mon-
Fri. Some English spoken. **Map D5**
The place to go if you have STD prob-
lems. An AIDS test here costs Ft4,000.

Anonymous AIDS Advisory Service
Anonim AIDS Tanácsadó Szolgálat
XI. Karolina út 35B (466 9283).
Tram 61. **Open** *hotline* 9am-8pm
Mon-Sat; *in person* 5-8pm Mon, Wed,
Thur; 9am-12.30pm Tue, Fri. English
spoken. **Map A6**
Free anonymous AIDS tests.

Alcoholism

Alcoholics Anonymous
VII. Kertész utca 28 (352 1947). M2
Blaha Lujza tér. **Map E4**
Tuesdays and Sundays at 6pm.

Domestic violence

NaNE – Women United Against Violence
IX. Vámház körút 7 (216 5900). M3
Kálvin tér. **Open** 9am-6pm Mon-Fri.
English spoken. **Map D5**
See below **Women**.

Veterinarians

Budapest Állatkórház
*XIII. Lehel út 43/47 (350 0361/350
1166)*. M3 *Árpád híd/tram 1*. **Open**
24 hours daily. Some English spoken.

Contraception & abortion

Condoms are available at
chemists and many
supermarkets. Abortion is legal
and widely used. Refer to a
local doctor or gynaecologist.

Alternative medicine

Alternative medicine in
Hungary is still very much in
its infancy, with much talk of
wonder cures but as yet little
organisation or substance.
  There are now several
Chinese doctors in Budapest
who offer acupunture and
massage therapies. Pick up a
copy of the magazine *Harmadik
Szem* for comprehensive
listings of homeopaths and
Oriental practitioners. Or try:

Dr Funian Yu
XII. Vérmező út 10-12 (212 7509).
M2 Moszkva tér. **Open** 1pm-6pm
Mon-Fri (by appointment). **Rates**
Ft2,200 per session. **No credit
cards**. Some English spoken. **Map
A3**
Chinese acupuncture at a fraction of
western prices.

Homeopathic Doctors' Association
XI. Ratkóc köz 4 (246 2132). *Bus
139*. **Open** 2-7pm Mon, Wed, Fri;
9am-1pm Tue, Thur. Some English
spoken.

Number of enterprises with majority foreign capital in 1997: **25,706**
Ranking of Hungary in region for foreign investment: **1**
Claimant unemployment in Hungary in June 1999: **9.4%**
Claimant unemployment in Budapest in June 1999: **3.7%**
Average net monthly earnings of full-time employees (first quarter of 1999): **Ft46,867**
Price of a modest two-room flat in the outskirts of Budapest (1999): **Ft3,5 million**

Number of national daily newspapers published in Budapest: **12**
Number of political parties sitting in Hungarian Parliament: **8**
Total number of political parties: **52**

Number of telephone lines in Hungary in 1980: **617,243**
Number of telephone lines in Hungary in 1998: **3,095,000**

Number of mobile phones in 1998: **706,000**
Number of American-style shopping malls built in Budapest in 1999: **11**
Number of American fast-food joints in Budapest: **over 100**

Litres of wine consumed a year by a Hungarian: **30**
Estimated percentage of wine sold in Hungary that is not made of grapes: **68%**

Annual expenditures of households (Ft/capita) on:
tobacco **3,683**
alcoholic beverages **2,937**
books **513**
fresh vegetables **447**
theatre and cinema **166**.

Estimated number of dogs in Budapest: **160,000**
Amount of dog turd on the streets every day: **40 tons**

Insurance

Britain, Norway, Finland, Sweden and the former Warsaw Pact countries all have reciprocal agreements for free emergency treatment to their citizens. Non-emergency treatment is not covered. Taking out travel insurance, covering this and lost or stolen valuables, is wise.

Internet

The best places for Internet access are the cyber cafés in the new shopping malls (*see* chapter **Shopping & Services**). You can also try **c3** (Center for Culture and Communication) (*see* chapter **Art Galleries**).

The local dial-in number for Compuserve is 291 9999. The number for America Online and Prodigy is 457 8888. Microsoft Network is on 267 4636.

Internet cafés

Budapest Net
V. Kecskeméti utca 5 (328 0292).
M3 Kálvin tér. **Open** 10am-10pm daily. **Rates** Ft700 per hour. **No credit cards.** English spoken. **Map D5**
Large, functional downtown spot with 32 computers. Tutorials and games available. Atmosphere is more workshop than café. Lower rates for longer time blocks.
Website: www.budapestnet.hu.

c3
I. Országház utca 9 (214 6856).
Várbusz. **Open** 9am-9pm Mon-Thur; 9am-6pm Fri; 10am-6pm Sun. **Rates** free. English spoken. **Map A3**
Supported by the Soros Foundation. Offers free access on seven aging computers with a four-hour time limit. Reserve well in advance to have any hope of getting online.

Eckermann
Goethe Institute, VI. Andrássy út 24 (374 4076). M1 Opera. **Open** 2-10pm Mon-Fri; 10am-10pm Sat. **Rates** free. **No credit cards.** Some English spoken. **Map D3**
The only place in Budapest that approaches the stated concept: a coffeehouse with public Internet access. The Goethe has two computers with a one-hour time limit. Reserve at least a week in advance though. Pleasant atmosphere, espressos and snacks. *See chapter* **Cafés & Coffeehouses.**

Matávnet Internet Café
Budai Skala, XI. Október 23 utca 6-10 (464 7080). Tram 4, 18, 47. **Open** 9am-8pm Mon-Fri; 9am-3pm Sat. **Rates** Ft500 per hour. **No credit cards.** Some English spoken.
Chain of shops run by Matáv, Hungary's telephone company. This one is in a department store. Eight computers and speedy access.
Branches: *Europark Mall, XIX. Üllői út 201 (06 80 281 781); Mammut Center, II. Lövöház utca 2-6 (345 7450).*

Teleport Netc@fé
VIII. Vas utca 7 (267 6361). M2 Astoria/bus 7. **Open** noon-10pm Mon-Sat. **Rates** Ft700 per hour. **No credit cards.** Some English spoken. **Map D4**
An adolescent underground, complete with role-playing games, pet scorpions, ice-creams and fantasy coffees. A dimly lit teen hacker's paradise devoted to networked games. One dedicated Net computer, with others available.

Websites

Hungary's Internet culture is developing rapidly and supports thousands of specialised web pages. Most are in Hungarian, but there are several excellent English-language resources also.

General information

www.timeout.com/budapest *Time Out*'s Budapest page, with background information and entertainment events for the week.
lazarus.elte.hu/gb/hunkarta/ke zdo.htm maps of the country, counties and cities.
www.budapest.com the official (and slightly wacky) homepage of Budapest. Includes virtual tours, city history and a hotel reservations centre. Still a bit shaky.
www.hungary.com the Hungary Network, an oddly-arranged hub of information with extensive links in the 'exhibition hall'.
www.hungary.org well-organised information centre divided into sections on geography, travel, weather, history, culture, cuisine, sports, an automatic search of Yahoo's news headlines on Hungary, plus loads of links, including travel agencies.
www.ksh.hu the Hungarian Central Statistical Office, billed as 'Hungary in Figures'.
www.users.zetnet.co.uk/spalffy /h_hist.htm#contents a readable summary history of Hungary, with archives and downloadable texts. Quite current.

Travel & transportation

elvira.mavinformatika.hu excellent site with MÁV's train schedules, rail maps and itinerary-planning engines. English version available.
www.intellicast.com/weather/b ud/ intellicast's four-day weather forecast for Budapest.

Indices & search engines

www.altavizsla.matav.hu the Hungarian Alta Vista, named after the popular pooch. In Hungarian.
hudir.hungary.com Hungary Directory, an index of a few thousand Hungary-related web pages.
www.fsz.bme.hu/hungary/hom epage.html Hungary home page with numerous links, sorted by field and region. Heavy emphasis on educational institutions.
www.kincs.hu bills itself as the Hungarian Yahoo. Magyar only.

News & current events

www.budapestsun.hu the *Budapest Sun*'s website, with weekly news and weak arts coverage.

www.centraleurope.com excellent Prague-based site with regional news stories selected from the major wire services. Usually at least one story from Hungary daily, and an archive of recent articles. Free daily headline service delivered by e-mail. Maintains pages of information on Hungary and some useful links.
www.hvg.hu the online version of *HVG*, Hungary's answer to *The Economist*. English summaries of its top weekly analytical articles, plus daily stories in English.
www.insidehungary.com easily the best online news from Hungary you can get in English without paying for it. The site is updated daily, and offers a free daily e-mail bulletin with wire stories from Reuters and translated highlights from local newspapers.
www.omri.cz transitions Online. News, analysis and more on eastern Europe. Good for the wider, more thoughtful view. Ample regional links.
www.rferl.org/newsline radio Free Europe/Radio Liberty NewsLine. Capsulised daily reports via the site, or e-mail, both free of charge.
www.wrn.org/ondemand the World Radio Network. Click on 'Hungary' here and listen to Radio Budapest's 'Hungary Today' programme, with daily news and culture in English as sound files. You'll need a RealAudio player to hear the 29-minute broadcast.

Business & economics

www.bcemag.com website of *The Economist*'s monthly magazine on the region, *Business Central Europe*. Solid general analysis.
www.businessweb.hu business information about Hungary available with a free subscription. Heavy on statistics.
www.ceebiz.com joint website for the *Budapest, Prague* and *Warsaw Business Journals*. Daily and weekly headlines and leads for business stories, complete stories for paying subscribers.
interactive.wsj.com/ceer the *Wall Street Journal*'s monthly *Central European Economic Review* supplement, online. Very good on the region; always something from Hungary.

Online phone books

www.matav.hu Hungary's telephone company, with an English-language mirror site. Includes white pages with a search engine. Beats phoning directory enquiries.
www.yellowpages.hu rather amateurish version of commerical index.

Dictionaries & language learning

www.sztaki.hu/services/engdict /index.jhtml English-Hungarian and Hungarian-English dictionary. Much easier to use than the average print dictionary. English introductory text.
www.sas.upenn.edu/%7Earubi n/hungarian.html#contents Hungarian language course, step-by-step online.
www.travlang.com/ languages/cgi-bin/ langchoice.cgi Hungarian for travellers, including sound bites.

Culture & entertainment

www.budapestweek.hu films, restaurants, music and events listings.
www.port.hu/kultura/index_a. htm the Hungarian Cultural Homepage. Includes long list of specialized cultural organisations' sites, from folk bands to sculptors.
www.ticketexpress.hu concert listings, dates, ticket information and prices. In Hungarian, but easily understood.
www.kfki.hu/keptar fine arts in Hungary, with history, biographies and thousands of paintings.
www.hungary.com/hungq website of the *Hungarian Quarterly*. Academic articles in English.

Gay & lesbian

gayguide.net/europe/ hungary/budapest/ comprehensive resource ideal for homosexual visitors and residents, with a guide you can download.

Diversions

www.auracom.com/ ~tournier/webworld.htm 'Webworld of Bela Lugosi', Hungary's original vampire culture minister. Detailed biography, links and much more. A labour of love.
www.team.net/www/ ktud/trabi.html the tale of the Trabant, automotive poster child for Communist Hungary and eastern Europe.

Language schools

See **Education.**

Left luggage

Twenty-four-hour left-luggage facilities are available at Nyugati and Keleti stations: Ft120, or Ft240 for large items. Prices run from midnight to midnight. Some lockers (Ft 150) are available at all three

main stations. There are also facilities at Erzsébet tér bus terminal, open 6am-7pm Mon-Thur; 6am-9pm Fri; 6am-6pm Sat, Sun. Price Ft150 per item.

Legal help

If in need of legal assistance contact your embassy, who will provide you with a list of English-speaking lawyers. (*See also chapter* **Business**.)

Libraries

British Council Library
VI. Benczúr utca 26 (321 4039). M1 Bajza utca. **Open** 11am-6pm Mon-Thur; 11am-5pm Fri. **Map E2**
Excellent magazine and periodicals section and English-teaching section, plus a huge video library. Membership open to anyone over 16 for a one-off fee of Ft500 (Ft1,000 for the video library.)

National Foreign Language Library
V. Molnár utca 11 (318 3188/318 3688). M3 Ferenciek tere. **Open** 10am-8pm Mon, Tue, Thur, Fri; noon-8pm Wed. Closes 4pm during summer. English spoken. **Map C5**
Only foreigners with residence permits and a passport may check out books here. Good periodicals section; helpful staff.

National Széchényi Library
I. Buda Palace Wing F (224 3848). Várbusz from M2 Moszkva tér. **Open** 9am-9pm Tue-Sat during academic year. English spoken. **Map B4**
Hungary's biggest public library, with foreign-language books, periodicals, microfilms and inter-library services. Useful for research but you can't check books out.

Lost property

If you lose something, enquire at the police station in the area where you lost it. Take along a Hungarian speaker, especially if you need a statement for insurance purposes.

At Ferihegy Airport 2A phone 296 8108 and at Ferihegy 2B call 296 7690. For anything left on trains, go to the station and be persistent but pleasant; it can get results. For taxis,

phone the company you rode with. Főtaxi claims to hold on to items left in their vehicles for five years.

BKV Lost Property Office
Talált Tárgyak Osztálya
VII. Akácfa utca 18 (322 6613). M2 Blaha Lujza tér. **Open** 7.30am-3pm Mon-Thur; 7.30am-7pm Wed; 7.30am-2pm Fri. No English spoken. **Map E4**

Maps

There is a wide selection of Budapest maps. *Time Out* favours DIMAP's *Budapest Atlasz* at Ft1,200. Spiral-bound, it contains all public transport lines, bus numbers, house numbers, a full street index and an efficiently enlarged central section, and is sturdy enough to stand some battering. Free maps of central Budapest can be picked up at **Tourinform** (*see below*) and should be enough to see you around central areas during a short stay.

A good specialist map shop is **Térképkirály** (*see chapter* **Shopping & Services**).

Money

The Hungarian unit of currency is the forint, usually abbreviated as HUF or Ft – the convention we have used in this guide. Forint coins come in denominations of Ft1, Ft2, Ft5, Ft10, Ft20, Ft50 and Ft100. Notes come in denominations of Ft200, Ft500, Ft1,000, Ft2,000, Ft5,000 and Ft10,000.

Banks

Banks give better rates than change kiosks, but shop around as rates vary. Travellers' cheques are exchangeable at banks and change kiosks, although sometimes at a worse rate than cash.

Black market exchange is no longer worth it so don't be tempted to change on the street – it can only be a con.

Forints can be changed back into hard currency at any bank

and at the bureaux de change in the airport. When changing large amounts, some places may still demand exchange receipts with your passport number stamped on them.

The usual opening times for banks are 8.15am-6pm Mon; 8.15am-4pm Tue-Thur; 8.15am-1pm Fri. Apart from cash and travellers' cheques, most banks advance money on a credit card, but Postabank and Ibusz accept only Visa.

Bureaux de change

Usually open from 9am to 10pm daily. English is spoken in the places listed below.

Exklusiv
V. Váci utca 12 (267 4368). M1, M2, M3 Deák tér/tram 47, 49. **Open** 9am-6pm Mon-Sat; 10am-6pm Sun. **No credit cards. Map C4**

IBB/Intergold
VI. Teréz körút 62 (331 8361). M3 Nyugati/tram 4, 6. **Open** 10am-6pm daily. **No credit cards. Map D2**

24-hour exchange facilities

There are cash machines all over town. Apart from those on the Cirrus and Plus systems, allowing you to draw on a foreign bank account or credit card, there are also exchange machines, forints for foreign banknotes. American Express has a 24-hour machine and both Nyugati and Keleti stations have round-the-clock exchange facilities.

Ibusz Bank
V. Apáczai Csere János utca 1 (318 5707). M3 Ferenciek tere. **Open** 24 hours daily. **Map C4**
Will change cash and traveller's cheques or advance money on Visa, Diner's and JCB cards.

American Express
V. Deák Ferenc utca 10 (235 4315/travellers' cheques 266 8679). M1, M2, M3 Deák tér/tram 47, 49. **Open** 9am-6.30pm Mon-Fri; 9am-2pm Sat. **Map C4**
Currency exchange and cash advances, moneygrams, mail and fax delivery for card and travellers' cheque holders, hotel and airline reservations, all various fees.

Directory

Credit cards

Credit cards are accepted in thousands of outlets. For cash advances see previous section.

There are two English-language weekly newspapers: *Budapest Sun* (with an entertainment listings section) and *Budapest Business Journal*. Most newspaper kiosks and hotel lobbies will have some same-day foreign newspapers. The international press shops in Nyugati and Keleti stations stay open until 9pm or 10pm. **Bestsellers** bookshop carries many newspapers and magazines as well as a large stock of books in English. (*See also chapters* **Media** *and* **Shopping & Services**.)

Opening times

Opening hours vary according to the type of shop. Most shops open from 9am to 5pm Monday-Friday, and 9am to 1pm on Saturday. Department stores usually open at 10am. Supermarkets, greengrocers and bakeries usually open at 6.30am or 7am and close around 8pm Monday-Friday, or 1pm-3pm on Saturdays. *Rögton jövök* means that the owner will be back in five minutes – maybe. Many larger shops now stay open later on Saturdays and on Thursday evenings. There are many non-stops – small 24-hour corner shops, where you can buy basics and booze. Most restaurants will close by 11pm or midnight.

Passports

Hungarian law requires you to to carry your passport with you at all times and, although in practice you will rarely be checked, it is not unknown.

If you lose your passport, report it immediately to the police station nearest you. Then report it stolen to your embassy or consulate, who will issue you with an emergency one. You will not be allowed to leave Hungary without it. *See also* **Visas**.

Pharmacies

See **Health**.

Police

Unless you commit a crime, you should have not have much contact with the police, but they can stop and ask for ID. If you're robbed or lose something, report it to the police station nearest the incident. Take a Hungarian speaker and bank on filling in forms with little chance of success. It's only worth the bother if the item was valuable, or your insurance company needs the forms.

Post

The Hungarian postal service is reasonably efficient. Letters from the UK take about four working days to arrive. Post boxes are square and red with post horn and envelope symbols. It's more usual to take your letters to the post office, where staff will affix the stamp and post it for you. Expect to queue, especially at Christmas. Most post offices are open from 8am to 7pm on weekdays. There are no late-night post offices, but the ones at Keleti and Nyugati are open 7am to 9pm daily.

Postal rates & post boxes

Letters weighing up to 30g cost Ft27 within Budapest and Ft32 to the rest of Hungary. A letter weighing up to 20g to neighbouring countries costs Ft32. A letter to anywhere else in the world costs Ft110 up to 20g, Ft215 up to 100g. To send them airmail (*légiposta*) is an extra Ft24. Postcards to bordering countries are Ft27, Ft65 to elsewhere in Europe and Ft80 overseas.

To send something registered (*ajánlott*) is an extra Ft260 and express is an extra Ft200.

PO Boxes are obtainable at most post offices for Ft1,000-Ft1,500 for three months. Poste Restante letters go to the office at Nyugati Station.

For courier services and express mail *see chapters* **Business** *and* **Shopping & Services**.

American Express

Card-holders or clients with American Express travellers' cheques can use their mail service. Letters should be addressed to American Express Travel Service, Client Mail, Deák Ferenc utca 10, 1052 Budapest.

Sending packages

The Hungarian post has a complicated system for sending packages, depending on what you are sending, when and how. Keeping the package under 2kg ensures the cheapest rate, Ft480 up to 500g, Ft1,200 up to 2kg. Tie packages with string and fill out a blue customs declaration form (*vámáru-nyilatkozat*) from the post office.

Sending anything worth over Ft10,000 is so complicated it's hardly worth the bother. Special boxes can be purchased at the post office. Most post offices can supply a booklet in English detailing charges. (*See also page 172* **Bringing it all back home**.)

Public holidays

New Year's Day; 15 March, national holiday; Easter Monday; 1 May, Labour Day; Whit Monday; 20 August, St Stephen's Day; 23 October, Remembrance Day; 25, 26 December.

There is usually something open on most holidays apart

from the evening of 24
December when even the non-
stops stop. New Year's Eve is
very lively, as is St Stephen's
Day on 20 August, with
fireworks launched from Gellért
Hill. *See also chapter* **Budapest
by Season**.

Public toilets

There are public toilets at
various locations for which you
will have to pay a small fee to
an attendant. It's easier to pop
into a bar, although you also
often pay a Ft20 fee.

Religious services

International Church of Budapest
*III. Kiskorona utca 7 (376 4518). M3
Árpád híd.*
Multi-denominational worship in
English and children's ministry on
Sundays at 10.30am.

International Baptist Church
*Móricz Zsigmond Gimnázium, II.
Törökvész út 48-54 (Pastor Bob
Zbinden 250 3932). Bus 11.*
Services on Sundays from 10.30am.

Jézus Szíve Templom
*VIII. Mária utca 25 (318 3479). M3
Ferenc körút.*
Catholic mass in English on
Saturdays at 5pm.

Anglican services

St Columba Church of Scotland, Presbyterian and St Margaret's Anglican/Episcopal Chaplaincy
*VI. Vörösmarty utca 51 (no phone).
M1 Vörösmarty utca.* **Map D2**
Anglican Eucharist on first and third
Sundays at 11am. Anglican Holy
Communion second, fourth and fifth
Sundays of the month at 9am.
Presbyterian services second and
fourth Sundays at 11am. Joint
Presbyterian/Anglican service fifth
Sundays at 11am. Sunday school at
11am Sept-May.

Jewish services

Central Synagogue
*VII. Dohány utca 2 (no phone). M2
Astoria/tram 47, 49.* **Map D4**
Services take place at 9am Saturday;
6pm Sunday-Friday.

Jewish Community Centre
*VII. Síp utca 12 (342 1335). M2
Astoria/tram 47, 49.* **Open** 8am-
noon Mon-Fri. English spoken. **Map
D4**
Summer services in Hebrew.

Renting accommodation

Although cheap, rented
accommodation is increasingly
scarce in Budapest. To find it,
try an agency, classifieds in the
local press (*see chapter* **Media**)
or word of mouth. Look for
albérlet (sub-let), *lakás kiadó*
(flat to let) or *lakás eladó* (flat
for sale).

Repairs

See also chapter **Shopping &
Services**.

Exoterm
XI. Bogdánfy utca 8/a (209 2494).
Open 8am-4pm Mon-Fri. Some
English spoken.
Plumbing, gas and heating repairs

Evitex
VI. Szinyei Merse utca 7 (312 4835).
Open 7.30am-4pm Mon-Fri. English
spoken. **Map D2**
Electricity repairs. Send a fax after
4pm and they will call you back.

Zárcentrum
II. Margit körút 54 (201 3928).
Open 9am-6pm Mon-Fri; 9am-1pm
Sat. Some English spoken. **Map A2**
Key copying and lock repairs, great
selection of the latest locks for sale.
Branch: XI Fehérvári út 24
(466 5654).

Residency

See **Work permits**.

Seasons

Although Budapest can be icy
cold in winter and infernally
hot in summer, the climate is
basically agreeable. *See also
chapter* **Budapest by Season**.

Spring

*Average temperature 2-10 °C in
March; 11-22 °C in May.*
May is probably the most
pleasant month, before the

influx of tourists. Winter attire
gets discarded, though rain can
sometimes dampen spirits.

Summer

Average temperature 16-32 °C.
Most Hungarians leave
Budapest for the Balaton or
their weekend house. It can get
very hot, especially in July. If
there's a breeze off the Danube
it's pleasant – if not, expect a
pall of pollution.

Autumn

Average temperature 7-23 °C.
The weather is lovely in
September but it starts to get
cold in October when
everything moves inside and
the heating gets turned on.

Winter

Average temperature -4 to 4 °C.
Winters are cold and quite
long but not unbearably so: the
air is very dry and the central
heating is good. Snow usually
falls a few times, giving
Budapest a different light.
Smog can descend if there is no
breeze to blow away the fumes
from the coal used for heating.

Smoking

Smoking is banned on public
transport, in theatres and in
cinemas but allowed
everywhere else. Hungarians are
among the heaviest smokers in
Europe. It is quite normal for
people to ask strangers for a cigarette or a light on the street and
cigarettes are still often sold
singly at kiosks and non-stops.

Street names

Hungarian street names can be
confusing. The most common is
utca, often abbreviated to *u*,
meaning simply 'street'. This
should not be mixed up with an
út (*útja* in the genitive), which
is (usually) a big, wide, straight
road or avenue – unless it's a
körút, which means ring road.

Tér (genitive *tere*) is a square, *körtér* is a roundabout. Other Hungarian thoroughfares include *köz* (lane), *fasor* (alley), *sétány* (parade), *udvar* (passage, arcade or courtyard) and *rakpart* (embankment).

Temperatures

See **Seasons**.

Telephones

The old phone system has been largely modernised, and phoning home is easy, but remember there are no cheap hours for international calls.

Public phones

Most are card phones, costing Ft750 for 50 units or Ft1,600 for 120, on sale at post offices and newsagents. Some coin phones still exist, taking Ft10, Ft20 and Ft50 coins; a cheap local call costs Ft20.

Making calls

For an international call dial 00, wait for the second purring dial tone, then dial the country code and number: Australia 61, Canada 1, Eire 353, New Zealand 64, UK 44, USA 1.

To call other places in Hungary from Budapest or to call Budapest from the rest of the country you have to dial 06 first, wait for the second tone, and then follow with code and number. You also have to dial 06 before calling mobile phones, which are common in Hungary.

To call Hungary from abroad dial 36 and then 1 for Budapest. For a provincial Hungarian town from abroad, dial 36 then the town code – you do not need 06 beforehand.

Faxes

Some post offices have a fax service but this involves a lot of waiting around. Major hotels also have fax services. Otherwise try the following phone, fax and telex centre.

MATÁV
V. Petőfi Sándor utca 17 (317 5500). M3 Ferenciek tere. **Open** 8am-8pm Mon-Fri; 9am-3pm Sat. **No credit cards.** Some English spoken. **Map C4**

Mobile phones & pagers

If you need a phone but your apartment doesn't have one – not an uncommon occurrence – mobile phones or pagers are the best bet. The digital GSM system is fully established here and reliable, but costly: a phone and connection card will set you back something around Ft175,000. To buy the connection card you either need a resident's permit (*see* **Work Permits**) or get it through the company you work for. Two GSM companies are currently operating in Hungary:

Westel
X1. Karinthy utca 21 (265 8000). M3 Ferenciek tere/tram 47, 49. **Open** 9am-8pm Mon-Fri; 9am-5pm Sat, Sun. **Credit** AmEx, JCB, MC, V. English spoken. **Map C4**

Pannon GSM
XI Budafoki út 64 (464 6020). M3 Dózsa György út/tram 47, 49. **Open** 9am-7pm Mon-Fri; 9am-2pm Sat. **No credit cards.** English spoken.

There are two pager companies, both of which have English-language services. A pager will cost in the region of Ft50,000.

Eurohívó
XIII. Váci út 37 (350 4160). M3 Dózsa György út. **Open** 8am-6.30pm Mon-Fri; 8.30am-1.30pm Sat. **No credit cards.** English spoken.

Operator Hungária
XIV. Dózsa György út 84-86 (351 9911). M1 Hősök tere. **Open** 9am-3.30pm Mon-Fri. **No credit cards.** English spoken. **Map E1**

Time

Hungary is on Central European Time, which means that it is one hour ahead of British time except for two brief periods at either end of the summer.

Tipping

There are no fixed rules about tipping in Hungary but it is usual to round up the bill or leave about ten per cent for waiters in restaurants or bars.

As you pay, tell the waiter either how much your rounded-up amount comes to or how much change you would like back. Saying *köszönöm* (thank you) as you hand over a note means you want him to keep all the change. The same rule also applies to taxi drivers. You usually have to offer toilet attendants a Ft20 tip.

It's also customary to tip hairdressers, cloakroom attendants, repairmen, changing room attendants at baths and swimming pools, and even doctors and dentists.

Tourist information

The best place is **Tourinform**. Other national tourist agencies can also help, though not necessarily with a smile. Services are often duplicated. **Ibusz** is the best agency for accommodation. **Express** is essentially a student travel agency.

In addition to their offices, Tourinform have set up 11 'info-touch' terminals at different points around town.

The easiest way to find out at least some of what's going on in Budapest is the weekly English-language newspaper *Budapest Sun*. Locals use the free weeklies *Pesti Est* (with film listings in English) and *Open* (best for nightlife), or *Pesti Műsor* from newsagents for Ft59. *See chapter* **Media**.

Tourinform
V. Sütő utca 2 (317 9800). M1, M2, M3 Deák tér/tram 47, 49. **Open** 9am-7pm Mon-Fri; 9am-4pm Sat, Sun. English spoken. **Map C4** Staff are friendly, helpful and multilingual and have information on travel, sightseeing and entertainment. **Branches:** Nyugati station, main hall (302 8580); VII. Király utca 93 (352 1433).

Directory

Ibusz

*V. Petőfi tér 3 (318 5707). M3
Ferenciek tere.* **Open** 24 hours daily.
Credit EC, JCB, MC, V. Some
English spoken. **Map C4**
Hungary's national tourist agency can
book rooms, organise tours and
provide information as well as all the
other normal travel agency services
(flights, trains, holidays). The Petőfi
tér branch will change money at all
hours. Branches across Hungary and
at all main railway stations.

Budapest Tourist

*VIII. Baross tér 3 (333 6587). M3
Nyugati.* **Open** 9am-6pm Mon-Fri.
No credit cards. Map F3
*Nyugati station (332 6565). M3
Nyugati.* **Open** 9am-5.30pm Mon-Fri;
9am-12.30pm Sat. **No credit cards.
Map D2**
Déli station (355 7167). M2 Déli.
Open 9am-5pm Mon-Fri. **No credit
cards. Map A3**
Money exchange, information, tours,
holidays, flights.

Cooptourist

*Nyugati station (312 3621). M3
Nyugati.* **Open** 9am-4.30pm Mon-Fri.
No credit cards. Map D2
Money exchange, information, tours,
holidays, flights.

Express

*V. Szabadság tér 16 (331 6393). M2
Kossuth tér.* **Open** 8am-4pm Mon-
Thur; 8am-3pm Fri. **Credit** AmEx.
Map C3
Friendly staff, currency exchange,
some information, flights, student
cards, youth hostel cards.

Universities

See **Education**.

Visas

Citizens of the United States,
Canada and all European
countries apart from Turkey
and Albania can stay in
Hungary for up to 90 days
without a visa; only a
passport is required. South
Africans can stay up to 30
days. Citizens of Australia
and New Zealand still need
visas, which are valid for up
to 30 days. Visas can be
obtained from Hungarian
consulates, on the border if
arriving by car, not by train,
and at the airport.

The simplest way to get a
new stamp in your passport or
renew a visa is to take a day
trip to Vienna (*see chapter*
Trips Out of Town) or take
the train to Komárom (from
Keleti or Déli stations), get out
and walk over the bridge to
Komarno in Slovakia. (To meet
Slovak currency requirements,
you supposedly need a credit
card or the hard currency equivalent of $15 in your pocket.) Do
this once too often, though, and
you might get into trouble with
vigilant border officials. Visas
can also be renewed in Budapest
at your local police station if you
can produce exchange receipts
or slips from credit-card
automatic telling machines to
prove that you have been
keeping yourself. In theory, all
foreigners are required to show
that they have access to the
equivalent of Ft1,000 per day. In
practice, such proof is rarely
requested. If you do get asked,
the production of a credit card
will usually suffice. It is always
a good idea to carry around
small denominations of dollars
or Deutschmarks just in case.
See also **Work Permits**.

Water

The water in Hungary is clean
and safe to drink. In some old
houses there are still lead pipes,
so run the tap for a few minutes
before drinking.

Weights & measurements

Hungary has its own unique
system for measuring out
solids and liquids. A *deka* is ten
grams; a *deci* is ten centilitres.
In a bar, for example, you
might be asked whether you
want *két deci* or *három deci* (0.2
or 0.3 litres) of whatever drink
you just ordered. Wine in bars
(but not in restaurants) is
priced by the *deci*. At a fruit
stall, if you want 300 grams of
tomatoes, you would ask for 30
dekas – *harminc (30) deka
paradiscomot.*

Women

Although men and women are
equal by law in Hungary, there
are countless problems from
wage differentials to sexual
harassment at work, and from
the unfair division of labour
to domestic violence. Women's
organisations (*see below*) have
been set up since 1989 to help
solve these problems, but the
'feminist' is still an ugly word
in Hungary. Feminists are
seen as a bunch of militant
man-hating masculine women
who fight for something that
most Hungarian women think
they already have: equality.

The 'new' values imposed
upon the traditional division
of labour by the communist
régime meant that women
kept their traditional roles,
but were suddenly expected
also to work eight hours a day
outside the home. Thus were
the problems of
'emancipation' solved in
Hungary in the 1950s.
Meanwhile, women were made
to believe that driving tractors
meant that they had achieved
equality with the stronger sex.
By 1967, when it had become
obvious that many women
were exhausted with the
double shift, the three-year
childcare allowance system
came in. As fathers were not
expected, and until 1982 not
allowed, to stay at home with
their children as primary
carers, women's careers
suffered. Women also did all
the housework, teaching
children traditional roles.

With the women's movement
this has started to change.
Abortion is legal and
accessible, women's wages are
rising, sexual harassment and
wife beating are more often
reported and punished by law,
and more men do the
housework. Old values still
surface, such as sexist jibes,
gentlemanly courtesy, odd
looks if you enter a bar alone,
and macho attitudes.

Ariadne Gaia Foundation

Ariadne Gaia Alapítvány
*V. Szép utca 3 III/1 (317 4779). M3
Ferenciek tere.* Contact Magda
Rohánszky or Ágota Ruzsa. English
spoken. **Map C4**
Offers courses on assertiveness,
counselling training, and counselling,
in English if required.

Feminist Network

A Feminista Hálózat
Budapest 1399, PO Box 701/1092.
Contact Judit Acsády. English
spoken.
The first real grass-roots campaign
group for women in Hungary, the
Network organises meetings, training
and campaigning sessions and publishes
a quarterly magazine, *Nőszemély*
(*The Female Person*), focusing on the
social and political situation of women
in contemporary Hungary.

NaNE – Women United Against Violence

NaNE – Nők a Nőkért Együtt az
Erőszak Ellen
*IX. Vámház körút 7. Postal address:
1462 Budapest, PO Box 660 (337
2865/helpline 216 1670/fax 267
4900/tigress@nane.zpok.hu). M3
Kálvin tér/tram 47, 49.* **Open** *office*
9am-5pm, *helpline* 6-10pm daily.
Contact Antonia Burrow. English
spoken. **Map D5**
Rape and domestic violence are low-
profile issues in Hungary. There is
no law against marital rape and little
sympathy for rape victims. NaNE
gives information and support to bat-
tered and raped women and children,
campaigns for changes in law, and
challenges social attitudes to
violence.

Association of Hungarian Women

Magyar Nők Szövetsége
*VI. Andrássy út 124 (331 9734). M1
Hősök tere.* **Open** 10am-3pm Mon-
Fri. President Judit Thorma. Some
English spoken. **Map E2**
Now independent, the original
Communist-era association, so not
particularly radical. It has 40 member
organisations and 500 members, striv-
ing for equal opportunity and
participation.

MONA Hungarian Women's Foundation

Magyarországi Női Alapítvány
*Postal address: 1357 Budapest, PO
Box 453/277; XIII. Tátra utca 30B
(350 1311/mona@mail.c3.hm/fax
120 1115). Tram 4, 6.* **Open** 9am-
5pm Mon-Fri. Contact Violetta
Zentai. English spoken. **Map C2**
Draws together women from other
campaign organisations with
meetings for mayors, journalists and
businesswomen.

Ombudswoman

Ombudsnő
*VIII. Múzeum körút 4C (266 9833
ext 2308/hotline 06 80 50 5303). M2
Astoria/tram 47, 49.* Contact Maria
Adarnik. **Open** 2-6pm Thur. English
spoken. **Map D4**
Helps put women in touch with
psychiatrists, lawyers and social
workers. Hotline and Gender Studies
Centre, including a library.

Work permits

Non-Hungarian citizens who
wish to live in Hungary must
apply for a residence permit.
But before you do that, you
have to have a work permit, a
steady job and a permanent
address. The process of
obtaining all the necessary
documents should be started
before your visa expires and
three months before you
actually start working for a
company.

First you have to sign a
contract with your future
employer, and take this
contract to the **Fővárosi
Munkaügyi Központ**
(Capital City Labour Centre),
where they will assess
whether there is no Hungarian
to fill your future position.
This will take them 30 to 60
days.

During this time you can
have your diplomas and
certificates officially translated,
obtain a compulsory medical
certificate and fill in a great
number of forms. Once you
have submitted your
application for a work permit
with all the attachments, you
will have to wait for another
month to receive an answer
from the Labour Centre. Your
company may offer to do some
of these duties on your behalf.

Once your work permit is in
your hands, you can apply for
a residence permit, which
means more weeks' wait.

Requirements for a
residence permit include a
work permit, a legal
permanent residence, an AIDS
test at Ft12,000, a chest X-ray,
numerous value stamps that

you buy at post offices (ca.
Ft5,000), countless application
forms and passport photos,
your passport, and official
translations (at around
Ft3,000 per page) of every
foreign-language document
with stamps on them. The
whole process is long and
annoying and you have to
renew all your papers within a
year – unless you marry a
Hungarian, in which case the
process will be different.

Fővárosi Munkaügyi Központ

Capital City Labour Centre
*VIII. Kisfaludy utca 11 (303 0720).
Tram 4, 6.* **Open** 8.30am-3pm Mon-
Thur, 8.30am-1pm Fri. Some English
spoken. **Map E5**

Orvosi Rendelő

*XI. Budafoki út 111-113 (203 0091).
Bus 3, 10, 10A, 83, 110.* **Open** 8am-
noon Mon-Fri. No English spoken.
Map E6

KEOKH

*VI. Városligeti fasor 46/48 (311
8668). M1 Hősök tere.* **Open** 8.30am-
6pm Tue; 8.30am-1pm Wed; 10am-
6pm Thur; 8.30am-noon Fri. Some
English spoken. **Map E2**

Állami Népegészségügyi és Tiszti Orvosi Szolgálat (ÁNTSZ)

*XIII. Váci út 174 (329 0490). M3
Újpest Városkapu.* **Open** 8am-noon
Mon-Fri; 1-3pm Mon-Thur. No
English spoken.

US Chamber of Commerce

*V. Deák Ferenc utca 10 (266
9880/fax 266 9888). M1, M2, M3
Deák Ferenc tér.* **Open** 9am-5pm
Mon-Fri. **Map C4**

Országos Fordító Iroda

*VI. Bajza utca 52 (269 5730). M1
Bajza utca.* **Open** 9am-4pm Mon-
Thur; 9am-12.30pm Fri. English
spoken. **Map E2**

Settlers Hungary

*XII. Sashegyi út 18 (212 5989/212
8146). Tram 59.* **Open** 8am-5pm
Mon-Fri. **No credit cards.** English
spoken.
Can arrange work permits for
Ft25,000 and organises resident's
permit for Ft40,000.

Business Umbrella

*V. Aranykéz utca 2 (318 4126/ fax
and phone). M1 Vörösmarty tér.*
Open 9am-5pm Mon-Thur; 9am-4pm
Fri. **Map C4**
Work and residence permits.

Getting Around

Budapest is easy to explore on foot. The centre is relatively small, the rest an urban sprawl, and transport is cheap and comprehensive, and will drop you right by your destination. Taxis are also cheap – if you stick to recommended companies.

Budapest is constructed around a series of concentric ring roads, with other main roads radiating from the centre. Although traffic congestion has not yet reached western levels, lack of parking means it's best not to use a car during the daytime.

Arrival in Budapest

By air

Ferihegy airport (296 9696) is 20km (15 miles) to the south-east of Budapest on the E60 road. There are two modern terminals next to each other.

Ferihegy 2A & 2B

(arrivals 296 8000/departures 296 7000). English spoken. Terminal 2A is mostly Malév flights; 2B is all other airlines.

Airport Minibus Shuttle

(296 8555). **Open** 5am-10pm or until the last flight. English spoken. The best way into town: for Ft1,200 (Ft2,000 return) it will take you to any address within the Budapest city limits. Buy a ticket at the counter in the arrivals hall, tell staff where you're going, then wait for a driver to call your destination after they have planned their route. This can take five minutes or 30. To be picked up from town and taken to either terminal, phone a day in advance. Accessible for wheelchair users.

Airport City-Centre Shuttle

A Mercedes minibus with Centrum-Airport on the side runs from outside Ferihegy to the city centre, currently terminating outside the Kempinski Hotel, V. Erzsébet tér 7-8, across the street from its usual stop outside Erzsébet tér bus station, under construction until 2000. Tickets, Ft600 (free for under-6s), are bought on the bus, which leaves every half-hour from 6am to 10pm.

Public transport

Take the 93 bus to Kőbánya-Kispest metro station and the blue M3 metro from there for the cost of one public transport (BKV) ticket for each (Ft90 from the airport newsagent). Last buses from the airport are at 11.30pm. Last metro leaves at 11.10pm, or there's the 182É night bus from the station.

Taxis from the airport

Fixed taxi prices from Ferihegy to each district in town are clearly indicated on a board in the arrivals area. A taxi to the centre should cost under Ft3,000. Avoid the rogue taxi drivers who will pester you around the arrivals hall – you will be fleeced. Call any of the firms recommended (*see below* **Taxis**) to arrange one for the journey back – most will be able to quote you a fixed price to the airport.

Car hire

All the major car hire firms have stands at the airport (*see below* **Car hire**).

Airlines

Air France

V. Kristóf tér 6 (318 0411/airport 296 8415). M1, M2, M3 Deák tér. **Open** 8am-4.30pm Mon-Fri. **Credit** AmEx, DC, MC, V. **Map C4**

Austrian Airlines

V. Régiposta utca 5 (327 9080/ airport 296 0660). M1, M2, M3 Deák tér. **Open** 8.30am-12.30pm, 1.30-4.30pm, Mon-Fri. **Credit** AmEx, DC, MC, V. **Map C4**

British Airways

VIII. Rákóczi út 1/3 (266 6696/ airport 296 0650). M2 Astoria. **Open** 8am-5pm Mon-Fri. **Credit** AmEx, DC, MC, V. **Map D4**

Delta Air Lines

V. Apáczai Csere János utca 4 (318 7266/airport 294 4400). M1, M2, M3 Deák tér. **Open** 8.30am-5pm Mon-Fri. **Credit** AmEx, DC, MC, V. **Map C4**

KLM

VIII. Rákóczi út 1/3 (373 7737/airport 296 5747). M2 Astoria. **Open** 8.30am-4.30pm Mon-Fri. **Credit** AmEx, DC, MC, V. **Map D4**

Lufthansa

V. Váci utca 19/21 (266 4511/airport 292 1970). M1, M2, M3 Deák tér/tram 47, 49. **Open** 8.30am-5pm Mon-Fri. **Credit** AmEx, DC, MC, V. **Map C4**

Malév

V. Dorottya utca 2 (235 3535). M1 Vörösmarty tér. **Open** 8.30am-4.30pm daily. **Map C4**
V. Ferenciek tere 2 (266 5913) M3 Ferenciek tere. **Open** 9am-5.30pm. *Both* **Credit** AmEx, DC, MC, V. **Map C4**
Malév's 24-hour information service for both terminals is on 296 7155. Ticket reservations can be made on 235 3888.

Swissair

V. Kristóf tér 7/8 (328 5000/ airport 157 4370). M1, M2, M3 Deák tér/tram 47, 49. **Open** 8.30am-5pm Mon-Fri. **Credit** AmEx, DC, MC, V. **Map C4**

By bus

If arriving by bus you will be dropped at the bus terminal on Erzsébet tér (317 2562; 6am-6pm Mon-Fri; 6.30am-4pm Sat, Sun. No English spoken). There are exchange and left luggage facilities here (*see chapter* **Essential Information**).

By train

Budapest has three main train stations: Déli (south), Keleti (east) and Nyugati (west), all with metro stops of the same name. The Hungarian for a main station is *pályaudvar*, often written as *pu*. Keleti station serves most trains to Vienna, Bucharest, Warsaw, Bulgaria, Turkey and north-western Hungary. Déli station also serves Vienna and Austria as well as Croatia, Slovenia and south-eastern Hungary. Nyugati station is the main point of departure for Transylvania and Bratislava. Services can get moved around.

The visitor will hear offers of taxis and accommodation. Avoid taxi touts and stick to the recommended companies – not always the first cabs in the ranks outside. All three stations have exchange facilities and tourist information but only Keleti and Nyugati have 24-hour left-luggage facilities.

MÁV Information

VI. Andrássy út 35 (322 9035/ national enquiries 461 5400/ international enquiries 461 5500). M1 Opera. **Open** *Apr-Sept* 9am-6pm Mon-Fri; *Oct-Mar* 9am-5pm Mon-Fri. **Credit** MC, V. Some English spoken. **Map D3**
Often the easiest place to buy tickets in advance. Phone lines are open 6am to 8pm daily. After that, call one of the stations listed below.

Keleti station

VIII. Baross tér (313 6835). M2 Keleti/bus 7. **Open** 8pm-6am daily. Some English spoken. **Map F3**

Nyugati station

VI. Nyugati tér (349 0115). M3 Nyugati/tram 4, 6. **Open** 8pm-6am daily. Some English spoken. **Map D2**

Déli station

I. Alkotás út (375 6293). M2 Déli/tram 18, 59, 61. **Open** 8pm-6am daily. No English spoken.

Public transport

The Budapest transport company (BKV) is cheap and efficient, and gets you to within about a hundred yards of any destination. The network consists of three metro lines, trams, buses, trolleybuses and local trains. In summer there are also BKV Danube ferries. Maps of the system can be bought at main metro stations for Ft190. Street atlases also mark the routes.

Public transport starts around 4.30am and finishes around 11pm, although there is a limited night bus network along major routes. Tickets can be bought at all metro stations, and at some tram stops and newsstands. A ticket is valid for one journey on one piece of transport (except the ferries, which have a separate system), so if you change from metro to tram, or even from metro line to metro line, you have to punch a new ticket.

On trams, buses and trolleybuses the contraption for validating your ticket is not intuitively designed. Punch your ticket by sliding the business end (the bit with the circled numbers) into the black slot at the top of the red box, then pull the slot-thing towards you hard until it clicks. Maybe it's best to observe how locals do it first.

Day, three-day, weekly, fortnightly and monthly tickets are also available from metro stations, although you will need a photograph to obtain anything but a one-day or three-day pass. Take your photo to Deák tér metro (or one of the other main stations) to be issued with a photopass. For a ticket longer than one day you have to ask for *egy napi bérlet* (one day), *egy heti bérlet* (one week), *két heti bérlet* (two weeks) or *egy havi bérlet* (one month). All these tickets run from the day of purchase, apart from the monthly, which is valid per calendar month. There is also a 30-day pass (*egy harminc napos bérlet*) valid from the day of purchase. It is possible to ride without a ticket, but plain-clothes inspectors (who put on a red armband before demanding your ticket) are common and can levy on-the-spot fines of Ft1,200. Playing the dumb foreigner doesn't usually work.

Prices

Single – Ft90
Metro ticket for up to 3 stops – Ft60
Metro ticket for up to 5 stops – Ft95
Metro transfer ticket – Ft135
10 tickets – Ft810
20 tickets – Ft1,500
Day – Ft700
three-day – Ft1,400
Week – Ft1,750
Passes (with photo)
Week – Ft1,650
two-week – Ft2,250
Month – Ft3,400
30 day – Ft3,400

BKV Information

317 5518.

Metro

The Budapest metro is safe, clean, regular and simple. There are three lines: yellow M1, red M2 and blue M3. These connect the main stations and intersect at Deák tér. The renovated M1 line, originally constructed for the 1896 exhibition, was the first underground railway in continental Europe. The other lines, constructed post-war with Soviet assistance, still have Russian trains.

Trains run every two to three minutes (the length of time since the last train is shown on a clock on the platform). Single tickets, three-stop, five-stop and metro transfer tickets can be purchased from either the ticket machines or ticket office in the stations. Validate tickets in the machines at the top of the escalators and in Deák tér passageways when changing lines. The first trains run from 4.30am and the last ones leave around 11pm.

There is currently much political wrangling over a projected fourth Metro line that would run via Deák tér to Kelenföld, essentially under the route of the current tram 49. The city is for this idea, the FIDESZ government against it, and studies are constantly published highlighting different versions of the pros and cons.

Buses & trolleybuses

There is a comprehensive bus and trolleybus network, the main lines being line 1 from Kelenföld station to the centre and then following the M1 metro line, and line 7 connecting Bosnyák tér, Keleti station, Blaha Lujza tér, Astoria, Ferenciek tere, Móricz Zsigmond körtér and Kelenföld. The castle bus (Várbusz) goes from Moszkva tér round the castle area and back. Buses with red numbers are expresses that miss certain stops. Most stops have routes and times listed.

Trams

Like many central European cities, Budapest has retained and expanded its tram network. The most important routes are lines 4 and 6, which follow the

In the way

It'll happen a dozen times a week. You'll be walking down the körút, in brisk western manner, with the express intention of getting somewhere or other, and a Hungarian will amble from a shop or sidestreet. Not hurrying. Far from it. But nevertheless, looking neither right nor left, they'll be moving just fast enough to intersect your trajectory and, occasioning a metaphoric screech of brakes, end up...

In the way.

Or you'll be trying to get through the doors of a public building, and there'll be a Hungarian sort of stalled there for no apparent reason, just staring into the middle distance, completely blocking the entrance for anyone else.

In the way.

Metro escalators are just one long people jam. Pavements are blocked by dawdling couples. Cars park all over backstreet pavements, in the way of pedestrians, who are forced out into the road – to be honked at by other cars for being in the way.

Hungarians have a remarkable talent for being in the way. They're not deliberate about it. They're just sort of gently oblivious to whatever is going on around them. Try this simple test. Walk into a shop two doors away from a shop selling, say, footwear. Then ask if they know anywhere you can buy a pair of shoes. Most will simply shrug their shoulders, even if, just ten metres away, there's a store purveying everything from hiking boots to platforms.

Or consider the intriguing statistic that Hungary has the world's highest rate of death by domestic accident. Can it be a result of the same skewed sense of spatial awareness, the fact that an alarming number of Magyars are tumbling to their doom from ordinary household stepladders?

Or watch a Magyar football match. In most soccer cultures, players call out to each other on the field, letting their teammates know where they are. But not in Hungary. Here players barge mutely about, relying on others to notice where they are, hoping that sooner or later the ball will chance in their direction and they'll be the lucky ones – in the way.

At root, all this probably comes from belonging to such an isolated language group. It's hardly surprising that Hungary has an inward-looking, self-absorbed culture. And sometimes it seems most Magyars wander around in a historical dream, lost in contemplation of ancient injustices. Communism is also offered as an explanation. People don't look around so much because for several decades they had a succession of big brothers to do the looking out for them. But one can sense a parallel here that goes much further back.

In the seventh century the Khazar empire employed the Magyars as border guards. From the eleventh century onwards, Hungary was useful to the rest of Europe as a buffer against any other tribes that might come sweeping in out of central Asia. When it came to marauding Turks or invading Russians, there was poor old Hungary: very much in the way.

Nagykörút from Moszkva tér to Fehérvári út and Móricz Zsigmond körtér respectively, line 2, which runs up the Pest side of the Danube, and lines 47 and 49, which run from Deák tér to Móricz Zsigmond körtér and beyond into wildest Buda.

Local trains (HÉV)

There are four HÉV lines. You will probably only need the one from Batthyány tér to Szentendre , price Ft240 (a normal BKV ticket valid up to Békásmegyer, an extra Ft60 thereafter). First and last trains from Batthyány tér are at 3.50am and 11.40pm, and from Szentendre, 3.30am and 10.30pm. Other lines run from Örs vezér tere to Gödöllő, Vágóhíd to Ráckeve, and Boráros tér to Csepel.

Night buses & trams

A reduced but reliable service works at night following the main routes and is usually full of drunks on week nights and teenagers at weekends. Handiest are the 6É following the Nagykörút, the 182É following the blue M3 metro line, and the 78É from Döbrentei tér on the Buda side of Erzsébet Bridge to Örs Vezér tere, following, from Astoria, more or less the M2 route. On these routes buses run every 15 minutes.

Danube ferries

Undoubtedly the most civilised method of travelling within Budapest, the BKV Danube ferries also offer a river ride that is exceedingly cheap when compared with the various organised tours. The local service runs from May to the end of September between Pünkösdfürdő north of the city and Boráros tér at the Pest foot of Petőfi Bridge,

stopping at most of the bridges, Vigadó tér and either end of Margaret Island. Fares vary between Ft150-Ft300. Boats, however, only run once every couple of hours, with extra services at weekends. Timetables are posted at all stops. Boats to Szentendre, Visegrád and Esztergom on the Danube bend leave from Vigadó tér. (*See also chapters* **Trips Out of Town** *and* **Getting Started**.)

Ferry Information
Jászai Mari tér terminal (Margaret Bridge, Pest side) (369 1359). Or try BKV information as listed above.

Eccentric conveyances

Budapest has a bizarre assortment of one-off public transports.

For the price of a normal BKV ticket the cog-wheel railway takes you up Széchenyi-hegy. It runs from opposite the Budapest Hotel, two stops from Moszkva tér on tram 56 or 18. Last train down is at 11.30pm.

Across the park from the cog-wheel railway is the terminal of the narrow-gauge Children's Railway (*gyermekvasút*; 395 5420), which wends its way through the wooded Buda hills to Hűvösvölgy. Formerly the Pioneer Railway, then run by the Communist youth organisation, many of the jobs are done by children. Trains leave hourly between 9am-5pm and tickets cost Ft120 (Ft40 children).

Another way up into the hills is the chair-lift (*libegő*; 394 3764) up to Jánoshegy – at 520 metres the highest point of Budapest. Take the 158 bus from Moszkva tér to the terminus at Zugligeti út. It costs Ft250 (Ft150 children) and runs between 9am-5pm from May-September, 9.30am-4pm October-April (closed every second Monday). There are cafés and bars at the top, and you can walk to Erszébet lookout tower or the Jánoshegy stop on the children's railway.

Tamer but more central, the funicular (*sikló*) takes a minute to run up from Clark Ádám tér to the Castle District. It's a short, vertiginous ride but the view is good. This runs from 7.30am-10pm (closed every second Monday morning) and a one-way ticket costs Ft200 adults, Ft100 children.

There is also the **Nostalgia Train** – a steam engine with old-fashioned carriages which puffs its way from Nyugati up to the Danube Bend every Saturday. *See chapter* **Children**.

Taxis

Rates in Budapest vary from the cheap to the outrageous. Stick to cabs displaying the logo of one of the companies mentioned below. Others often have tampered meters or will take you by the scenic route. Avoid expensive western-model cars hanging around outside hotels and tourist spots. They are usually crooks. Not that drivers of small cars are necessarily above ripping you off too. The cheap and reliable **Főtaxi** have red-and-white checkered patterns on their doors and can be spotted from a distance by their oval-shaped lights. Watch out for impostors, though. If you're calling for a cab, the dispatchers at **City Taxi** speak English. If you're always calling from the same address, City Taxi have a databank that records your address the first time, meaning you merely have to give your telephone number on subsequent calls.

A receipt should be available on request. Say '*számlát kérek*'. A small tip is usual but not compulsory. All legitimate taxis should have yellow number plates.

The most reliable companies are the following:

City Taxi *(211 1111)*.

Főtaxi *(222 2222)*.

Rádio Taxi *(377 7777)*.

Tele5 *(355 5555)*.

Volán Taxi *(466 6666)*.

Car hire

Cars vary from Ladas to limousines. A credit card is usually necessary for the deposit. Check that the price includes ÁFA (VAT). There's an insurance charge and varying rates of mileage. Longer-term rates are available. The main companies have desks at both airport terminals.

Americana Rent-a-car
Pannónia Hotel Volga, XIII. Dózsa György út 65 (350 2542). M3 Dózsa György út. **Open** 8am-7pm Mon-Fri; 8am-3pm Sat; 8am-1pm Sun. **Credit** AmEx, DC, MC, V. English spoken.

Avis
V. Szervita tér 8 (318 4158). M1, M2, M3 Deák tér. **Open** 8am-6pm Mon-Sat; 8am-noon Sun. **Credit** AmEx, DC, MC, V. English spoken. **Map C4**

Budget
I. Krisztina körút 41-43 (214 0420). M2 Déli pu. **Open** 8am-8pm Mon-Sat; 8am-6pm Sun. **Credit** AmEx, DC, MC, V. English spoken.

Europcar
VIII. Üllői út 62 (313 1492/Ferihegy 296 6610). M3 Ferenc körút. **Open** 8am-7pm Mon-Fri; 8am-noon Sun. Credit AmEx, DC, MC, V. English spoken. **Map E5**

Főtaxi
VII. Kertész utca 24-28 (455 7567). M2 Blaha Lujza tér. **Open** 7am-5.30pm Mon-Thur; 7am-2pm Fri. Credit AmEx, DC, MC, V. No English spoken. **Map E4**

Bicycles

Budapest is not bike-friendly. Pollution is high and drivers unwary. Bike use is on the increase and there are some bicycle lanes. Bikes can be hired on Margaret Island. *See chapter* **Sport & Fitness**.

Maps

City centre maps and metro maps are included at the back of this guide. Free maps are also available from Tourinform *see above* **Tourist information**. All metro stations have detailed street and transport maps placed near the entrance.

Business

Ask a Hungarian for assistance – directions, change, a little advice – and they will be delighted, even honoured, to help... unless it happens to be their job.

In shops, restaurants and ticket offices, visitors often confront the *sajnos* factor. Sajnos means 'unfortunately' and is usually announced either just before a non-negotiable 'I can't do that', or 'We're all out'. The sajnos factor, the basic inability to understand the idea of striving meet the customer or client's requirements in order to reap an economic benefit, becomes a different kind of problem for foreigners trying to do business in today's Hungary.

No, it's not as bad as in Russia. You shouldn't have to pay out protection money to short-haired thugs in every line of business (though nightclub and restaurant owners do) and rule-of-law is not an alien concept. But business practices in Hungary are still suffering from a Communist hangover.

In general terms, the older the local businessman you're dealing with (and it usually *is* a man), the more likely they are to be short-sighted, the less likely to feel bound by written contracts (which are difficult to enforce) and the more likely to wear purple shell suits.

Perhaps the most frustrating manifestation of this for foreign businesspeople is the penchant of Hungarians for changing the terms of an agreement well after everything was, ostensibly, settled. An old saying goes that real negotiations begin after the contract is signed. Anglo-Saxons, in particular, will also be dismayed at how corrupt local bosses can be. It's hard to break habits learned during the days when circumventing regulations was a noble pursuit. Oppressively high taxes don't

help matters, either. Value-added tax is 25 per cent on most items. To see that a worker takes home £200 a month, an employer must shell out about £450-£500 a month to the state. No wonder the size of Hungary's 'shadow' economy (that is, its untaxed business) is estimated at between one quarter and one-third the total real economy.

There are exceptions to the mess. Hungary's top private companies have managed to collect the balance of middle-aged Hungarians with any international business experience, and have begun learning the great market phrase 'transparency'. Companies such as OTP Bank, pharmaceuticals maker Richter Gedeon and telephone company Matáv have even gained reputations for possessing the best management teams in post-Communist Europe. Besides gobbling up Hungary's small allotment of well-dressed executives, this thin tier of companies, particularly export manufacturers, has also attracted enormous foreign investment and driven Hungary's economic growth. That growth was fairly impressive in 1998, at more than five per cent of GDP. As for the economic outlook, things will continue rosily if the Hungarian government manages not to spend much more than it collects each year and if western Europe doesn't sputter to a halt. Two big ifs.

But the greatest promise for Hungary's still faltering economy is the generation of ambitious and talented kids that has begun to shake up Hungary's business culture. The young could always rely on being educated, but now they are travelled, confident, and bold, taking decisions and getting things done. And they'll

be the ones who'll be running the country in the next decade.

Meanwhile, business travellers may appreciate older Hungarian habits. Although they have taken to mobile phones, Magyars still prefer face-to-face meetings for even minor conferences. Strong business relationships are much more dependent on strong personal ones. And bring plenty of business cards – Hungarians scatter them about like confetti. **Note:** Rt – similar to PLC; Kft – limited company.

Stock Exchange

In the Habsburg days Budapest was the financial capital of the Austro-Hungarian empire and the Budapest Stock Exchange (BSE) was Europe's second most active. After a 40-year interlude, the BSE re-opened in June 1990, the first *bourse* to recommence in the former Communist countries. By 1996 it was the second fastest growing bourse in the world (after Moscow's). Government securities still account for the overwhelming majority of transactions, and foreign institutional investors for over half the equity turnover.

Budapest Stock Exchange
Budapesti Értéktőzsde
V. Deák Ferenc utca 5 (429 6636/ fax 266 5677). M1 Vörösmarty tér/tram 2, 2A. **Open** 10am-4.30pm Mon-Fri. English spoken. **Map C4**
Visitors can watch trading through the glass walls. The best times to visit the Stock Exchange are 11am till noon, and 1pm till 3pm. To organise a personal tour contact Sándor Lévai (266 9566/fax 266 6203).

Budapest Commodity Exchange
Budapesti Árútőzsde
XIII. Róbert Károly körút 61-65 (465 6971/fax 269 8575). M3 Árpád híd. **Open** 9.30am-noon Mon-Fri. English spoken.
Visitors are welcome to see the Exchange in action. Officials recommend 9.30-11am as the best time. Contact Zsolt Szerémy.

Banks

Credit and debit cards connected to any of half-a-dozen international clearance systems can be used to receive forints at thousands of ATMs around Hungary – most of them located in Budapest. Wire transfers are very quickly and easily arranged (although expect a one-day delay). Unfortunately, cheques are still practically non-existent and cannot be cashed in less than three weeks, and only then at grievous personal expense.

The following are the head offices for the major banks in Budapest.

ABN Amro

XII. Nagy Jenő 12 (202 2722/fax 201 3685). Bus 105. **Open** 8am-3pm Mon-Fri. English spoken.

Budapest Bank

V. Alkotmány utca 3 (269 2333/fax 269 2400). M2 Kossuth Lajos tér/tram 2, 2A. **Open** 8am-5pm Mon-Thur; 8am-3pm Fri. Some English spoken. **Map C2**

Central-European International Bank (CIB)

Közép-Európai Nemzetközi Bank
V. Váci utca 16 (212 1330/fax 212 4200). M1 Vörösmarty tér, M3 Ferenciek tere. **Open** 8.30am-3pm Mon, Tue, Thur; 8.30am-6pm Wed; 8.30am-1.30pm Fri. English spoken. **Map C4**

Citibank Budapest

V. Váci utca 19-21 (374 5000). M1 Vörösmarty tér, M3 Ferenciek tere. **Open** 9am-5pm Mon-Thur; 9am-4pm Fri. English spoken. **Map C4**

Creditanstalt

V. Akadémia utca 17 (269 0812/fax 153 4959). M2 Kossuth Lajos tér/tram 2, 2A. **Open** 9am-3pm Mon-Thur; 9am-1pm Fri. Some English spoken. **Map C3**

Hungarian Foreign Trade Bank

Magyar Külkereskedelmi Bank Rt
V. Váci u 38 (269 0922/fax 268 8245). M1 Bajcsy-Zsilinszky, M3 Arany János utca. **Open** 8am-4.30pm Mon-Thur; 8am-3pm Fri. English spoken. **Map C3**

ING Bank

VI. Andrássy út 9 (268 0140/fax 268 0159). M1 Bajcsy-Zsilinszky. **Open** 9am-3.30pm Mon-Fri. English spoken. **Map C3**

Commercial & Credit Bank

Kereskedelmi & Hitel Bank (K&H)
V. Vigadó tér 1 (267 5000/fax 266 9696). M1 Vörösmarty tér. **Open** 9am-5pm Mon; 9am-4.30pm Tue-Thur; 9am-1pm Fri. English spoken. **Map C4**

OTP Bank

V. Nádor utca 16 (353 1444/fax 312 6858). Bus 15, 105. **Open** 8am-4pm Mon; 8am-3pm Tue-Fri. Some English spoken. **Map C3**

Postabank

V. József Nádor tér 1 (318 0855/fax 117 1369). M1 Vörösmarty tér. **Open** 8am-6pm Mon, Thur; 8am-1.30pm Tue, Wed, Fri. No English spoken. **Map C4**

Government organisations

Hungarian Investment & Trade Development Agency

Magyar Befektetés és Kereskedelem Fejlesztési Rt
V. Dorottya utca 4 (266 7034/fax 318 6064). M1 Vörösmarty tér/tram 2, 2A. **Open** 8am-4.30pm Mon-Thur; 8am-2pm Fri. English spoken. **Map C4**
ITD is a very good first point of contact for foreigners looking to do business in Hungary. They have a useful library and can provide plenty of information, some in English.

Hungarian National Bank

Magyar Nemzeti Bank
V. Szabadság tér 8-9 (269 4760/fax 332 3913). M2 Kossuth Lajos tér/bus 15. **Open** 8am-1pm Mon-Fri. Some English spoken. **Map C3**

Ministry of Industry, Trade & Tourism

Ipari, Kereskedelmi és Turisztikai Minisztérium
V. Honvéd utca 13-15 (302 2355/fax 302 2394). M2 Kossuth Lajos tér/bus 15. **Open** 8am-4.30pm Mon-Thur; 8am-2pm Fri. English spoken. **Map C3**
The information department at the ministry is very helpful and staff can speak good English.

State Privatisation & Holding Company

Állami Privatizációs És Vagyonkezelő Rt
XIII. Pozsonyi út 56 (359 7600/fax 349 5745). Trolleybus 76, 79. **Open** 8am-4pm Mon-Thur; 8am-3pm Fri. Some English spoken. **Map C1**
The organisation responsible for selling state-owned assets.

Embassies & agencies

American Embassy (Commercial Department)

V. Bank Center Building, Szabadság tér 7 (302 6200/fax 302 0089). M2 Kossuth tér. **Open** 9am-4.30pm Mon-Fri. **Map C3**
Hosts new electronic business library (11am-5pm Tues and Thur) including extensive business databases.

American Chamber of Commerce

V. Deák Ferenc utca 10 (266 9880/fax 266 9888). M1, M2, M3 Deák tér. **Open** 9am-5pm Mon-Fri. **Map C4**
Consultations by appointment only.

British Embassy (Commercial Section)

II. Hűvösvölgyi út 54 (202 2526/fax 202 2526). Bus 56. **Open** 8.30am-5pm Mon-Fri.

British Chamber of Commerce

V. Bank utca 6 II/7 (302 5200/fax 115 5496). M2 Batthyány tér. **Open** 9am-noon, 2pm-5pm, Mon-Fri. **Map B3**
Consultations by appointment only.

Business services

Accountants & consultants

All of the 'Big Six' are in Budapest and have been for a number of years. Office hours given are official ones, but you can usually reach someone much later.

Arthur Andersen/ Andersen Consulting

VIII. East-West Centre, Rákóczi út 1-3 (266 7707/fax 327 7199/ 266 7709). M2 Astoria/bus 7, 7A, 9, 78/tram 47, 49. **Open** 8.30am-5.30pm Mon-Fri. **Map D4**

Coopers & Lybrand

III. Lövőház utca 30 (212 4720/345 1100/fax 346 4895). M2 Moszkva tér/tram 4, 6. **Open** 8.30am-5.30pm Mon-Fri. **Map A2**

Deloitte & Touche

V. Vármegye utca 3-5 (328 6800/fax 267 4182). M3 Ferenciek tere. **Open** 8.30am-5.30pm mon-Fri. **Map C4**

Ernst & Young

XIV. Hermina út 17 (252 8333/fax 251 8778). Trolleybus 72, 74. **Open** 8.30am-5.30pm Mon-Fri. **Map F1**

Speculating for democracy

Hungarian-born George Soros' claim to fame rests both on his reputation as a ruthless financial speculator, terrorising central banks worldwide with aggressive gambling against local currencies, and on his Robin Hood side, as he races to give away his fortune to support fledgling civil societies in post-Communist countries. Soros became a household name in September 1992, when he single handedly forced Britain out of the Exchange Rate Mechanism by betting huge sums against the pound, netting $2 billion in a day. More recently he's been blamed for triggering devaluation in Russia and south-east Asia, and even destabilising the Euro.

But Soros has also played a pivotal role in reshaping eastern Europe since the fall of Communism, using his Open Society foundations to uphold the rule of law, protect minorities and improve education. Motivation for his efforts to encourage democracy in the region probably lies both in youthful experience of Nazi and Stalinist dictatorship in the 1940s, and the influence of his mentor Karl Popper at the London School of Economics in the 1950s. *The Open Society and its Enemies* was a seminal text for Soros. His first foundation was set up in Hungary in 1984 and there are now more than 30 in countries as far flung as Burma and Mongolia.

The flagship of the Soros philanthropic enterprise in Budapest, and the institution most likely to endure and prosper in the long term, is the **Central European University** (*see above* **Education**). The CEU provides postgraduate courses in the humanities to students drawn predominantly from eastern Europe and the former Soviet Union. As well as gaining a useful qualification, the future élites of the region come into contact with modern ideas and teaching methods in a multi-national environment. The campus itself is a bizarre maze of towers and converted courtyards – walk confidently past the guards and see how many languages you can recognise in the lift up to the tenth-floor restaurant.

Much of Budapest's cultural and social life revolves around the Soros network. Many productions enjoy Soros funding. In the world of new media, **c3** (Centre for Culture and Communication – *see chapter* **Art Galleries** *and* **Directory**) is a pioneering institution, with grassroots internet access.

Ridiculed by other academics, Soros' philosophy is one of a practical idealist who's given away millions but is still considered the UK's third richest man. His *Crisis of Global Capitalism* (1998) points at the potential collapse of the international financial system – if we don't spend money to support democracy.

KPMG Reviconsult

XIII. Váci út 99 (270 7100/fax 270 7101). M3 Forgách utca. **Open** 7am-7pm Mon-Fri.

Price Waterhouse

VII. Wesselényi utca 16/C (461 9100/ fax 461 9101). M2 Astoria. **Open** 7.30am-7.30pm Mon-Fri. **Map D4**

Conference facilities

Budapest Convention Centre

Budapest Kongresszusi Központ
XI. Jagelló út 1-3 (209 1990/fax 466 5636). Tram 61/bus 8, 12, 112. **Open** 8am-7pm Mon-Fri. English spoken. **Map A5**

European Serviced Offices (ESO)

VI. Révay utca 10 (269 1100/fax 269 1030). M1 Bajcsy-Zsilinszky út. **Open** 24 hours daily. English spoken. **Map C3**

As well as providing conference facilities, ESO lets out offices on a short-term basis and offers multilingual secretarial services.

Regus Business Centre

Emke Building, VII. Rákóczi út 42 (267 9111/fax 267 9100). M2 Blaha Lujza tér/tram 4, 6. **Open** 8.30am-5.30pm Mon-Fri. English spoken. **Map E4**

Offices can also be leased on short-term contracts with multilingual secretarial services.

Couriers

The following companies will pick up packages, for fees ranging from Ft3,000 to Ft8,000.

DHL Hungary

VIII. Rákóczi út 1-3 (382 3499). M2 Astoria/bus 7, 7A, 9, 78/tram 47, 49. **Open** 8am-6pm Mon-Fri; 8am-noon Sat. **Credit** AmEx, MC, V. **Map D4**

Royal Express

IX. Nádasdy utca 2-4 (216 3606/216 3707/fax 218 3808). Tram 23, 24, 30. **Open** 8am-6pm Mon-Fri; 9am-1pm Sat. **Credit** AmEx, V. Federal Express affiliate.

TNT Express Hungary

X. Fertő utca 5 (431 3000/fax 431 3096). Bus 99, 99A. **Open** 7.30am-6pm Mon-Fri. **No credit cards**.

UPS

X. Kozma utca 4 (432 2200/fax 432 2213). Bus 68. **Open** 8am-5pm Mon-Fri. **Credit** AmEx.

Commercial estate agencies

In mid-1999, top-quality office space cost DM35-DM45 per square metre per month. Rents are stated in Deutschmarks as a hedge against inflation, though

it is illegal to charge rent in foreign currency.

British firms pretty much dominate the commercial property scene and all the offices listed have English-speaking staff.

Colliers International

II. Horvát utca 14-24 (214 0601/fax 201 3041). M2 Batthyány tér/bus 11, tram 19. **Open** 8am-7pm Mon-Fri. **Map B2**

DTZ Hungary

VII. Rumbach Sebestyén utca 21 (269 6999/fax 269 6987). M1, M2, M3 Deák Ferenc tér/tram 47, 49. **Open** 8.30am-5pm Mon-Fri. **Map D4**

Healey & Baker

Emke Building, VII. Rákóczi út 42 (268 1288/fax 268 1289). M2 Blaha Lujza tér/tram 4, 6. **Open** 8.30am-6pm Mon-Fri. **Map E4**

Jones Lang Wootton

East-West Centre, VIII. Rákóczi út 1-3 (266 4981/fax 266 0142). M2 Astoria/tram 47, 49. **Open** 8am-6pm Mon-Fri. **Map D4**

Lawyers

The following firms have English-speaking lawyers.

Allen & Overy/Déry & Co.

Madách Trade Centre, VII. Madách Imre út 13-14, Floor 4 (268 1511/fax 268 1515). M1, M2, M3 Deák Ferenc tér/tram 47, 49. **Open** 9am-6pm Mon-Fri. **Map C4**

Baker & McKenzie

VI. Andrássy út 102 (302 3330/fax 302 3331). M1 Hősök tere. **Open** 8am-8pm Mon-Fri. **Map E2**

Clifford Chance/Köves és Társai

Madách Trade Centre, VII. Madách Imre út 13-14 (268 1600/fax 268 1610). M1, M2, M3 Deák Ferenc tér/tram 47, 49. **Open** 8am-8pm Mon-Fri. **Map C4**

McKenna & Co/Verőci, Őrmai és Társa

Bank Center building, V. Szabadság tér 7 (302 9302/fax 302 9300). M3 Arany János utca, bus 15. **Open** 8.30am-8pm Mon-Fri. **Map C3**

Relocation services

The following companies help deal with residence and work permits, to save you the time queuing – for various fees.

Business Umbrella

V. Aranykéz utca 2 (318 4126). M1 Vörösmarty tér. **Open** 9am-5pm Mon-Thur; 9am-4pm Fri. **Map C4**
Also arranges translation, interpreting and customs clearance.

Settlers Hungary

XII. Szánkó utca 3 (212 5989/fax 212 8146/100263.1233 @compuserve.com). Bus 8, 8A. **Open** 8.30am-4.30pm Mon-Thur; 8.30am-4pm Fri.
Also helps with finding schools, registering cars and customs clearance.

Staff hire agencies

Adecco

VI. Bajcsy-Zsilinszky út 27 (269 1164/fax 269 3774). M1 Bajcsy-Zsilinszky út. **Open** 10am-3pm Mon-Fri. **Map C3**

Further reading

Books from Corvina, City Hall and other Hungarian publishers are unlikely to be readily available in the UK or US. In Budapest you'll find them in good general bookshops as well specialist ones in British publications. At Bestsellers bookshop and its academic branch at the CEU, you should be able to find almost anything on Hungary in print. See chapter **Shopping & Services**.

History

Bender, Thomas & Schorske, Carl Budapest & New York: Studies in Metropolitan Transformation 1870-1930
Patchy compilation of academic essays comparing the two capitals.
Buza, Péter Bridges of the Danube (City Hall)
Everything you could ever want to know about Budapest's famous bridges, with occasional absurd asides.
Crankshaw, Edward The Fall of the House of Habsburg (Papermac)
Solid, and solidly anti-Hungarian, account of the end of the Habsburg dynasty.

Frigyesi, Judit Béla Bartók and Turn-of-the-Century Budapest (University of California Press)
Grounds Bartók's work in the milieu of Golden Age Budapest and the creativity of the Modernist movement.
Garton Ash, Timothy We the People: The Revolution of 1989 Witnessed in Warsaw, Budapest, Berlin and Prague (Granta, 1990)
Instant history by this on-the-spot Oxford academic.
Gerő, András The Hungarian Parliament (1867-1918): A Mirage of Power (Columbia University Press)
Academic analysis of Parliamentary representation during the Dual Monarchy period.
Gerő, András (ed.) Modern Hungarian Society in the Making (CEU Press)
Collection of essays on the last 150 years of Hungarian political, social and cultural history. Includes a particularly interesting piece on Széchenyi.
Hanak, Peter & Schorske, Carl E. The Garden and the Workshop: Essays on the cultural history of Vienna and Budapest (Princeton University Press)
Comparative cultural history of the Golden Age in the two capitals of the Austro-Hungarian empire.

Hoensch, Jörg K. A History of Modern Hungary 1867-1994 (Longman)
Updated from an original 1986 edition, a thorough account of Magyar mishaps from the beginnings of the Dual Monarchy to the present.
Kovács, Mária M. Liberal Professions and Illiberal Politics: Hungary from the Habsburgs to the Holocaust (Woodrow Wilson Center Press/Oxford University Press)
Detailed account of the struggle between liberal and anti-semitic politics during the Horthy years.
Lázár, István Hungary: A Brief History (Corvina)
This 'colourful essay presenting the story of the Hungarians as one person sees it' is mostly a load of bollocks – unfortunately the only single-volume history of Hungary available in English.
Litván, György (ed.) The Hungarian Revolution of 1956: Reform, Revolt and Repression 1953-1963 (Longman)
Five Hungarian members of the Institute for the History of the Hungarian Revolution offer a blow-by-blow account of the uprising.
Lukács, John Budapest 1900 (Weidenfeld)
Extremely readable and erudite literary and historical snapshot of

Budapest at its height. Probably the best book about the city's history and culture currently in print.

Swain, Nigel *Hungary: The Rise and Fall of Feasible Socialism* (Verso)
Authoritative explanation of the demise of goulash socialism.

Taylor, AJP *The Habsburg Monarchy 1809-1918* (Penguin)
Terse history of the twilight of the Habsburg era.

Biography, memoir & travel

Fermor, Patrick Leigh *Between the Woods and the Water/A Time of Gifts* (Penguin)
In the 1930s Fermor took a bike from Holland to Istanbul, stopping off in Budapest along the way. These picaresque and evocative memoirs were the result.

Magris, Claudio *Danube*
Excellent literary travelogue following the course of central Europe's main waterway. The chapter on Budapest is short, but gets the point.

Márai, Sándor *Memoir of Hungary 1944-48* (Corvina)
Detailed and insightful memoir by exiled Magyar author.

Pressburger, Giorgio & Nicola *Homage to the Eighth District* (Readers International)
Authentic and touching street-level recollections of the now-vanished Budapest Jewish society before and during World War II.

Rimmer, Dave *Once Upon a Time in the East* (Fourth Estate)
Communism seen stoned and from ground level – eccentric travelogue of lamentable behaviour in Berlin, Budapest, Romania and assorted east European revolutions. Both comic and touching.

Szep, Ernő *The Smell of Humans*
One survivor's short, stark memoir of the Hungarian Holocaust.

Literature & fiction

Ady, Endre *Neighbours of the Night: Selected Short Stories* (Corvina)
Prose pieces from the poet featured on the Ft500 note. Somewhat stiffly rendered in English, but at least they translate, unlike his gloomy but stirring poetry.

Alexander, Lynne *Safe Houses* (Penguin)
Brilliant, disturbing novel of Hungarian emigrés in New York.

Eszterházy, Péter *A Little Hungarian Pornography* (Corvina/Quartet)/*Helping Verbs of the Heart* (Corvina)/*The Glance of Countess Hahn-Hahn* (Weidenfeld & Nicholson)/*She Loves Me* (Corvina)

One of Hungary's most popular contemporary writers, Eszterházy's postmodern style represents a radical break with Hungarian literary tradition.

Fischer, Tibor *Under the Frog* (Penguin)
Seriously funny and impeccably researched Booker-nominated romp through Hungarian basketball, Stalinism and the 1956 revolution.

Göncz, Árpád *Homecoming & Other Stories* (Corvina)
Dry short stories from Hungary's popular president, playwright and translator of Hemingway.

Konrád, George *The Case Worker/The Loser* (Penguin)
Dark, depressing stuff by Communist Hungary's most prominent dissident.

Kosztolányi, Dezső *Skylark* (Chatto)/*Anna Édes* (Corvina)/*Darker Muses, The Poet Nero* (Corvina)
Kosztolányi, who wrote these novels in the 1920s, was probably the best Magyar prose writer this century. Hungarians claim his translations of Winnie-the-Pooh are even better than the original. But they would.

Örkény, István *One Minute Stories* (Corvina)
Vignettes of contemporary Budapest: absurd, ironic, often hilarious and all extremely short.

Anthologies

Hungarian Plays (Nick Hern Books)
Four modern Magyar playwrights in English translation: Péter Kárpáti, András Nagy, Ákos Németh and Andor Szillágyi.

In Quest of the Miracle Stag: An Anthology of Hungarian Poetry from the 13th Century to the Present (Atlantis-Centaur/Corvina/M. Szivárvány)
Huge and dauntingly comprehensive survey of Hungarian poetry in English translation.

The Kiss: Twentieth-century Hungarian Short Stories (Corvina)
From Ady to Eszterházy: 31 short stories add up to a good sampler of modern Magyar lit.

Children

Dent, Bob *Budapest for Children* (City Hall)
Slim volume full of suggestions for keeping the little ones entertained.

Gárdonyi, Géza *Eclipse of the Crescent Moon* (Corvina)
Boy's-own adventure about the 1552 Turkish siege of Eger.

Molnar, Ferenc *The Paul Street Boys* (Corvina)
Turn-of-the-century juvenile classic of boys' gang warfare over a derelict District VIII building site.

Hungary: A Fun Guide for Children (Szalontai)
Games, stories, pictures and puzzles relating to Magyar geography, history and culture.

Art & architecture

A Golden Age: Art & Society in Hungary 1896-1914 (Corvina)
Colourful coffee table compendium of turn-of-the-century art and architecture includes examples of work by all the Hungarian greats. Drab essays, though.

Art and Society in the Age of Stalin (Corvina)
Interesting collection of essays on Socialist realism.

Budapest Architectural Guide (6 BT)
Building-by-building guide to Budapest's twentieth-century architecture. A useful handbook, though the commentary (in both Hungarian and English) isn't terribly illuminating.

Language

Payne, Jerry *Colloquial Hungarian* (Routledge)
Much more entertaining than most language books, drawing on interesting and potentially romantic situations for its dialogues. Grammar introduced a little too rapidly in earlier chapters.

Hungarian-English English-Hungarian Tourist's Dictionary (Akadémiai Kiadó)
Cheap, serviceable and pocket-sized.

Miscellaneous

Bodor, Ferenc *Coffee Houses* (City Hall)
Utterly brilliant vignettes of Budapest coffee culture. Sadly many of the places included are now closed.

Gundel, Károly *Gundel's Hungarian Cookbook* (Corvina)
The best of Hungarian recipe books, by the man who more or less invented Hungarian cuisine.

Kocsis, Irma *A Tour of our Locals* (City Hall)
Idiosyncratic and personal crawl around dozens of old Budapest bars. Not as good as Bodor's similar *Coffee Houses* (*above*) but still interesting.

Lang, George *The Cuisine of Hungary* (Bonanza)
Detailed study of the development of Magyar cuisine.

Various, *Restaurants of Days Gone By* (Tegnap és Ma Alapítvány)
Only available at the Museum of Commerce and Catering: absorbing and beautiful collection of photos and memorabilia from the golden age of Magyar gastronomy.

Advertisers' Index

Please refer to the relevant sections for
addresses/telephone numbers

Index

Note: Page numbers in **bold** indicate the main reference to a topic. Page numbers in *italics* refer to illustrations.

Let the Tourism Office of Budapest
be your guide!

These brochures are available in your hotel and the information offices.

Budapest Information Offices

NYUGATI (WESTERN) STATION, Main Hall Tel/Fax: (36-1) 302-8580
BUDAÖRS, AGIP COMPLEX (M1 & M7 motorway junction)
  Tel: (36 23) 417 518, (from Hungary 06-23) 417-518
TOURINFORM Király utca 93, District VII. Tel.: (36-1) 352-1433
TOURINFORM Downtown, Sütő utca 2. Tel.: (36-1) 317-9800

Budapest Card

transportation **FREE**   museums **FREE**

cultural and folklore programmes **-15, -20%**

restaurants, shops **-10, -20%**

sightseeing **-24, -50%**

airport-minibus, rent a car **-15%**

for 2 days 2450 Ft ('99)
for 3 days 2950 Ft ('99)

On sale at more than 250 selling points in Budapest: main underground ticket offices, tourist information offices, travel agencies and hotels.

Tourism Office of Budapest

H-1364 Budapest, Pf.: 215 e-mail: info@budtour.hu
Tel.: (36-1) 266-0479 Fax: (36-1) 266-7477

Maps

Budapest

Districts - Kerületek

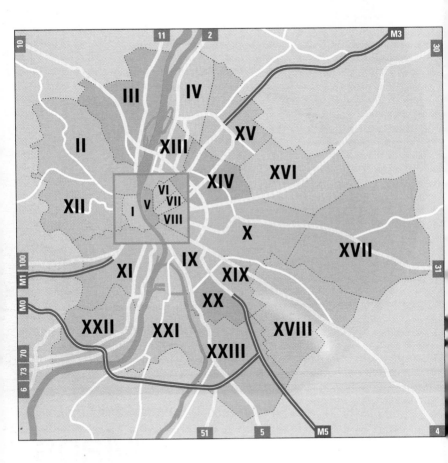

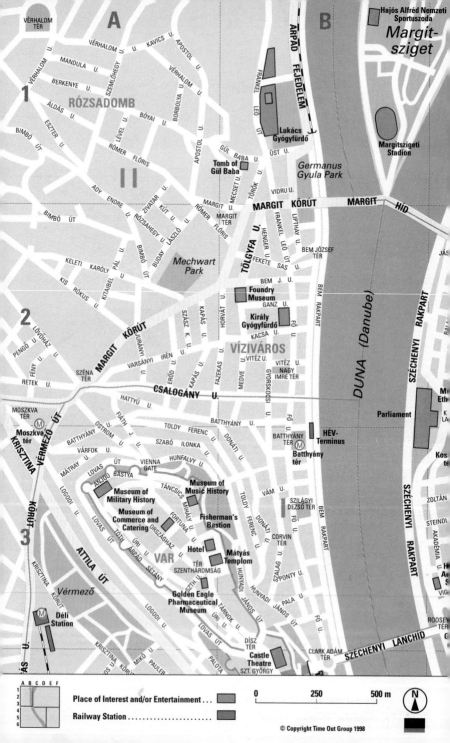

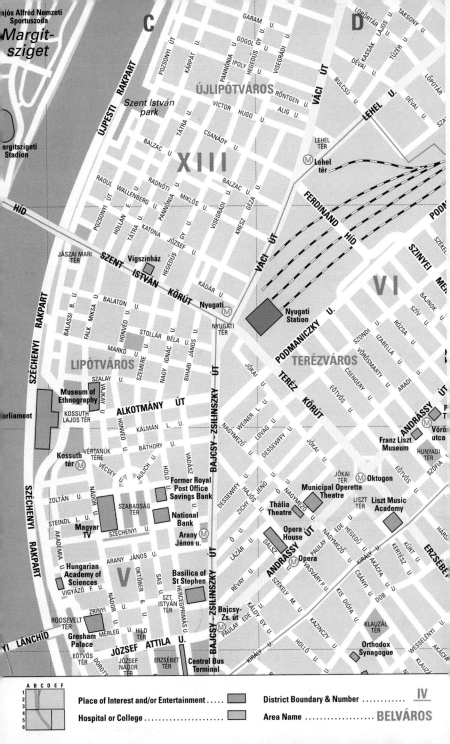

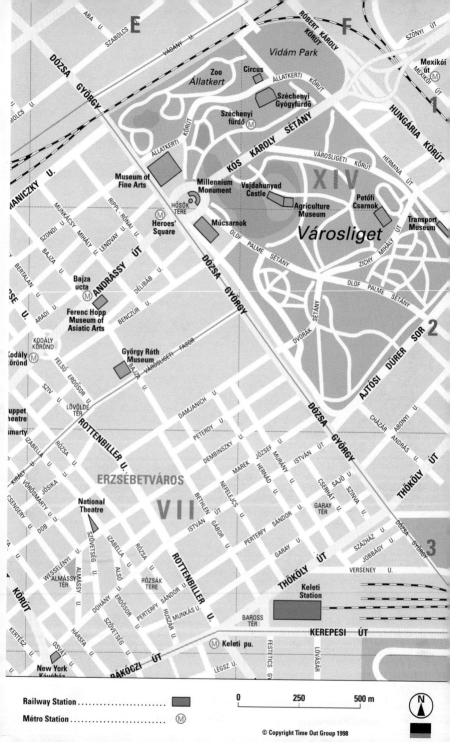

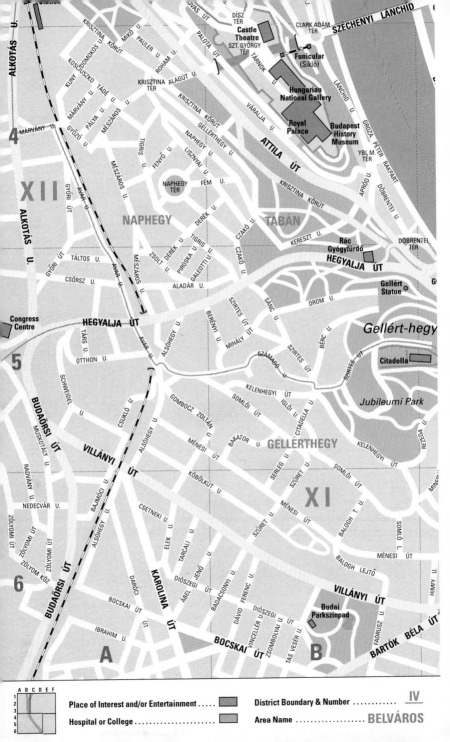

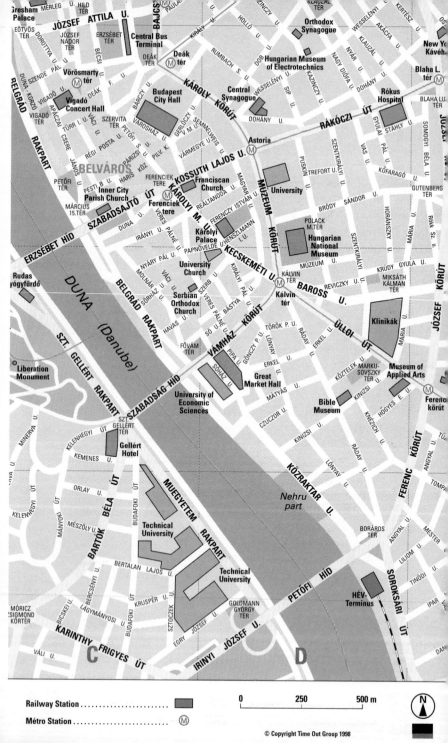

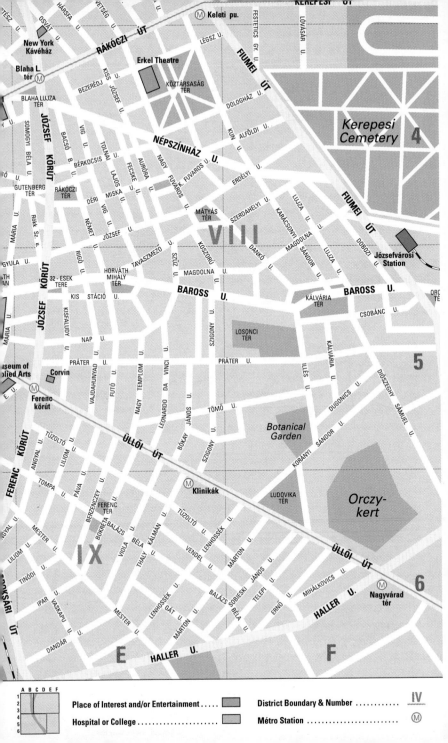

Street Index

Ajtósi Dürer sor - F2
Akadémia utca - C3
Alkotás utca - A4/A5
Alkotmány út - C2
Állatkerti körút - E1/E2
Andrássy út - D3/E2
Apáczai Csere János utca - C4
Árpád fejedelem - B2
Attila út - A3/B4
Aulich utca - C3
Bajcsy-Zsilinszky út - C2/C3
Bajza utca - E2
Bárczy utca - C4
Baross tér - F3
Baross utca - D5/F5
Bartók Béla út - B6/C6
Batthyány tér - B2
Belgrád rakpart - C4/C5
Bem József tér - B2
Bem József utca - B2
Blaha Lujza tér - E4
Bocskai út - B6
Boráros tér - D6
Bródy Sándor utca - D4
Budaörsi út - A5/A6
Clark Ádám tér - B4
Csalogány utca - A2
Csarnok tér - D5
Dalszínház utca - D3
Deák Ferenc utca - C4
Deák tér - C4
Dísz tér - B3
Döbrentei tér - B4
Dohány utca - D4
Dorottya utca - C4
Dózsa György - E1/F3
Duna-Korzó - C4
Eötvös tér - C4
Erzsébet híd - C5
Erzsébet körút - D3
Erzsébet tér - C4
Ferdinánd híd - D1
Ferenc körút - D6
Ferenciek tere - C4
Fiumei út - F4
Fő utca - B2/B3
Fortuna utca - A3
Frankel Leó út - B1/B2
Ganz utca - B2
Gerlóczy utca - C4
Goldmann György tér - D6
Gyulai Pál utca - D4
Hajós Alfréd sétány - B1
Hajós utca - C3
Haller utca - E6/F6
Haris köz - C4
Hegyalja út - A5/B5
Hermina út - F1
Hevesi Sándor tér - E3
Hild tér - C3

Hőgyes Endre utca - D5
Hold utca - C3
Honvéd utca - C2
Horváth Mihály tér - E5
Hősök tere - E1
Hungária körút - F1
Hunyadi tér - D3
Irinyi József utca - D6
Izabella utca - D2/E3
Jókai utca C2/D3
József Attila utca - C4
József körút - E4/E5
József nádor tér - C4
Kacsa utca - B2
Kálvin tér - D5
Karinthy Frigyes út - C6
Karolina út - A6
Károly körút - C4
Károlyi Mihály utca - C4
Kecskeméti utca - D5
Kelenhegyi út - C5
Kemenes utca - C5
Kinizsi utca - D5
Király utca - C4/D3
Klauzál tér - D3
Kodály körönd - E2
Kós Károly sétany - F1
Kossuth Lajos tér - C2
Kossuth Lajos utca - C4
Kozraktár utca - D5
Köztársaság tér - E4
Krisztina körút - A3
Krisztina körút - A3/A4
Kulturális központ - D4
Lázár utca - C3
Lehel tér - D1
Lehel utca - D1
Losonci tér - F5
Lövölde tér - E2
Ludovikai tér - F6
Luther utca - E4
Magyar Jakobinusok tere - A3
Március 15. tér - C4
Margit híd - B1
Margit körút - A2/B2
Margit tér - B2
Markusovszky tér - D5
Medve utca - B2
Móricz Zsigmond körtér - A6
Moszkva tér - A2
Műegyetem rakpart - C6
Múzeum körút - D4
Múzeum utca - D5
Nádor utca - C3
Nagy Korona utca - C3
Nagymező utca - C3/D3
Naphegy tér - A4
Népszínház utca - E4
Nyugati - C2
Országház utca - A3

Párizsi utca - C4
Pesti Barnabás utca - C4
Petőfi Sándor utca - C4
Petőfi híd - D6
Pilvax köz - C4
Pipa utca - D5
Podmaniczky utca - D2/E1
Ráday utca - D5
Rákóczi tér - E4
Rákóczi út - D4/E4
Régiposta utca - C4
Róbert Károly körút - F1
Roosevelt tér - C3
Rottenbiller utca - E2/E3
Rózsák tere - E3
Sóház utca - D5
Soroksári út - D6
Stáhly utca - D4
Szabadság híd - C5
Szabadság tér - C3
Szabadsajtó út - C4
Szarvas tér - B4
Széchenyi lánchíd - B4
Széchenyi rakpart - B2/B3
Széchenyi utca - C3
Széna tér - A2
Szende Pál utca - C4
Szent István körút - C2
Szentháromság tér - A3
Szervita tér - C4
Szilágyi Desző tér - B3
Szinyei M. utca- D2
Szirtes út - B5
Szt. Gellért rakpart - C5
Szt. Gellért tér - C5
Szt. György tér - B4
Szt. István tér - C3
Tárnok utca - B3/B4
Teréz körút - D2
Thököly út - F3
Tölgyfa utca - B2
Türr István utca - C4
Újpesti rakpart - C1
Üllői út - D5/F6
Úri utca - A3/B3
Váci utca - C4/C5
Váci út - D2/D1
Vámház körút - D5
Városház utca - C4
Városligeti fasor - E2
Városligeti körút - F1
Vécsey utca - C3
Vérhalom tér - A1
Vérmező út - A3
Vértanúk tere - C3
Vigadó tér - C4
Vigadó utca - C4
Villányi út - A5/B6
Vörösmarty utca - D2/E3
Wesselényi utca - D4

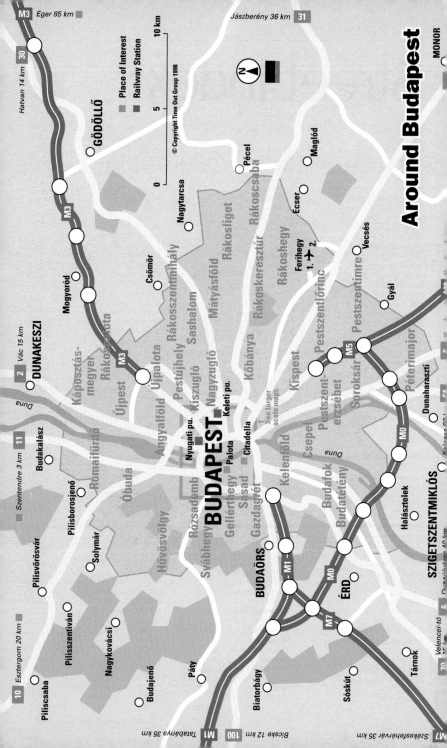

Around Budapest

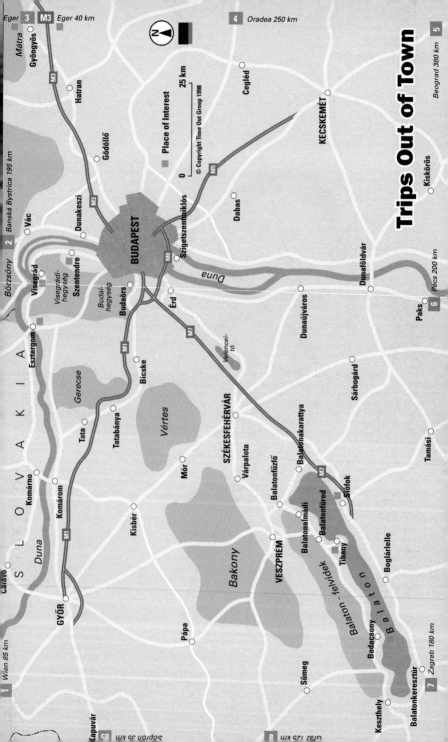

Trips Out of Town

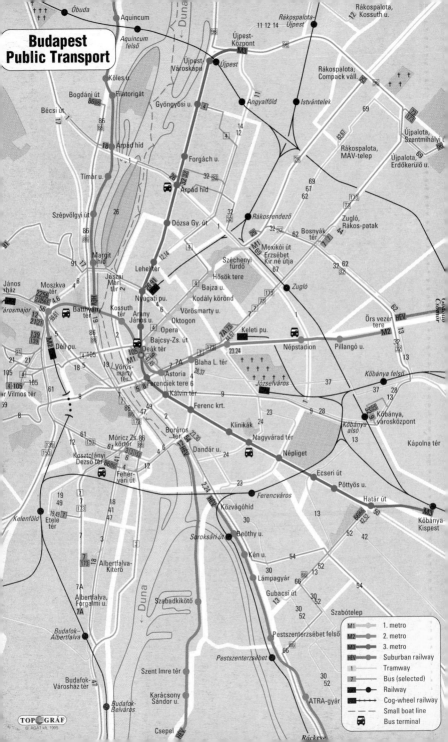